THE LIFE

OF

WILLIAM EWART GLADSTONE

Walker & Cockerell. ph. sc.

William Ewart Gladstone
from a photograph by The London Stereoscopic Company.

THE LIFE OF

WILLIAM EWART

GLADSTONE

BY

JOHN MORLEY

IN THREE VOLUMES — VOL. III
(1880-1898)

GREENWOOD PRESS, PUBLISHERS
NEW YORK

CONTENTS

BOOK VIII

(1880–1885)

CHAPTER   PAGE

    I.   OPENING DAYS OF THE NEW PARLIAMENT   .   .   1

   II.   AN EPISODE IN TOLERATION   11

  III.   MAJUBA   22

  IV.   NEW PHASES OF THE IRISH REVOLUTION .   .   47

   V.   EGYPT   72

  VI.   POLITICAL JUBILEE   87

 VII.   COLLEAGUES — NORTHERN CRUISE — EGYPT   .   .   110

VIII.   REFORM   123

  IX.   THE SOUDAN   144

   X.   INTERIOR OF THE CABINET   170

  XI.   DEFEAT OF MINISTERS   188

 XII.   ACCESSION OF LORD SALISBURY   .   .   .   202

BOOK IX

(1885–1886)

    I.   LEADERSHIP AND THE GENERAL ELECTION   .   .   219

   II.   THE POLLS IN 1885   246

  III.   A CRITICAL MONTH   256

  IV.   FALL OF THE FIRST SALISBURY GOVERNMENT .   .   277

   V.   THE NEW POLICY   290

  VI.   INTRODUCTION OF THE BILL   310

 VII.   THE POLITICAL ATMOSPHERE — DEFEAT OF THE BILL   321

BOOK X

(1886–1898)

CHAPTER		PAGE
I.	THE MORROW OF DEFEAT	350
II.	THE ALTERNATIVE POLICY IN ACT	362
III.	THE SPECIAL COMMISSION	390
IV.	AN INTERIM	413
V.	BREACH WITH MR. PARNELL	426
VI.	BIARRITZ	460
VII.	THE FOURTH ADMINISTRATION	490
VIII.	RETIREMENT FROM PUBLIC LIFE	506
IX.	THE CLOSE	517
X.	FINAL	534
	APPENDIX	553
	CHRONOLOGY	565
	INDEX	577

LIST OF ILLUSTRATIONS

WILLIAM EWART GLADSTONE, . . . *Frontispiece.*
From a photograph by The London Stereoscopic Company.

WILLIAM EWART GLADSTONE, . . . *to face page* 506
From a photograph by Mr. L. V. Harcourt.

ERRATA

CHAPTER I

OPENING DAYS OF THE NEW PARLIAMENT

(1880)

Il y a bien du factice dans le classement politique des hommes.

— GUIZOT.

There is plenty of what is purely artificial in the political classifica-
tion of men.

On May 20, after eight-and-forty years of strenuous public
life, Mr. Gladstone met his twelfth parliament, and the second
in which he had been chief minister of the crown. 'At 4.15,'
he records, ' I went down to the House with Herbert. There
was a great and fervent crowd in Palace Yard, and much
feeling in the House. It almost overpowered me, as I
thought by what deep and hidden agencies I have been
brought back into the midst of the vortex of political action
and contention. It has not been in my power during these
last six months to have made notes, as I would have wished,
of my own thoughts and observations from time to time ; of
the new access of strength which in some important respects
has been administered to me in my old age ; and of the
remarkable manner in which Holy Scripture has been
applied to me for admonition and for comfort. Looking
calmly on this course of experience, I do believe that the
Almighty has employed me for His purposes in a manner
larger or more special than before, and has strengthened me
and led me on accordingly, though I must not forget the

admirable saying of Hooker, that even ministers of good things are like torches, a light to others, waste and destruction to themselves.'

One who approached his task in such a spirit as this was at least impregnable to ordinary mortifications, and it was well; for before many days were over it became perceptible that the new parliament and the new majority would be no docile instrument of ministerial will. An acute chill followed the discovery that there was to be no recall of Frere or Layard. Very early in its history Speaker Brand, surveying his flock from the august altitude of the Chair with an acute, experienced, and friendly eye, made up his mind that the liberal party were ' not only strong, but determined to have their own way in spite of Mr. Gladstone. He has a difficult team to drive.' Two men of striking character on the benches opposite quickly became formidable. Lord Randolph Churchill headed a little group of four tories, and Mr. Parnell a resolute band of five and thirty Irishmen, with momentous results both for ministers and for the House of Commons.

No more capable set of ruling men were ever got together than the cabinet of 1880; no men who better represented the leading elements in the country, in all their variety and strength. The great possessors of land were there, and the heirs of long governing tradition were there; the industrious and the sedate of the middle classes found their men seated at the council board, by the side of others whose keen-sighted ambition sought sources of power in the ranks of manual toil; the church saw one of the most ardent of her sons upon the woolsack, and the most illustrious of them in the highest place of all; the people of the chapel beheld with complacency the rising man of the future in one who publicly boasted an unbroken line of nonconformist descent. They were all men well trained in the habits of business, of large affairs, and in experience of English life; they were all in spite of difference of shade genuinely liberal; and they all professed a devoted loyalty to their chief. The incident of the resolutions on the eastern question [1] was effaced from all

[1] Above, vol. ii. pp. 563-8.

memories, and men who in those days had assured themselves that there was no return from Elba, became faithful marshals of the conquering hero. Mediocrity in a long-lived cabinet in the earlier part of the century was the object of Disraeli's keenest mockery. Still a slight ballast of mediocrity in a government steadies the ship and makes for unity — a truth, by the way, that Mr. Disraeli himself, in forming governments, sometimes conspicuously put in practice.

In fact Mr. Gladstone found that the ministry of which he stood at the head was a coalition, and what was more, a coalition of that vexatious kind, where those who happened not to agree sometimes seemed to be almost as well pleased with contention as with harmony. The two sections were not always divided by differences of class or station, for some of the peers in the cabinet often showed as bold a liberalism as any of the commoners. This notwithstanding, it happened on more than one critical occasion, that all the peers *plus* Lord Hartington were on one side, and all the commoners on the other. Lord Hartington was in many respects the lineal successor of Palmerston in his coolness on parliamentary reform, in his inclination to stand in the old ways, in his extreme suspicion of what savoured of sentiment or idealism or high-flown profession. But he was a Palmerston who re-spected Mr. Gladstone, and desired to work faithfully under him, instead of being a Palmerston who always intended to keep the upper hand of him. Confronting Lord Hartington was Mr. Chamberlain, eager, intrepid, self-reliant, alert, dar-ing, with notions about property, taxation, land, schools, popular rights, that he expressed with a plainness and pun-gency of speech that had never been heard from a privy coun-cillor and cabinet minister before, that exasperated opponents, startled the whigs, and brought him hosts of adherents among radicals out of doors. It was at a very early stage in the existence of the government, that this important man said to an ally in the cabinet, 'I don't see how we are to get on, if Mr. Gladstone goes.' And here was the key to many lead-ing incidents, both during the life of this administration and for the eventful year in Mr. Gladstone's career that followed its demise.

The Duke of Argyll, who resigned very early, wrote to Mr. Gladstone after the government was overthrown (Dec. 18, 1885), urging him in effect to side definitely with the whigs against the radicals : —

From the moment our government was fairly under way, I saw and felt that speeches *outside* were allowed to affect opinion, and politically to commit the cabinet in a direction which was not determined by you deliberately, or by the government as a whole, but by the audacity · · · of our new associates. Month by month I became more and more uncomfortable, feeling that there was no paramount direction — nothing but *slip* and *slide*, what the Scotch call ' slithering.' The outside world, knowing your great gifts and powers, assume that you are dictator in your own cabinet. And in one sense you are so, that is to say, that when you choose to put your foot down, others will give way. But your amiability to colleagues, your even extreme gentleness towards them, whilst it has always endeared you to them personally, has enabled men playing their own game · · · to take out of your hands the *formation of* opinion.

On a connected aspect of the same thing, Mr. Gladstone wrote to Lord Rosebery (Sept. 16, 1880) : —

· · · All this is too long to bore people with — and yet it is not so long, nor so interesting, as one at least of the subjects which we just touched in conversation at Mentmore ; the future of politics, and the food they offer to the mind. What is outside parliament seems to me to be fast mounting, nay to have already mounted, to an importance much exceeding what is inside. Parliament deals with laws, and branches of the social tree, not with the root. I always admired Mrs. Grote's saying that politics and theology were the only two really great subjects ; it was wonderful considering the atmosphere in which she had lived. I do not doubt which of the two she would have put in the first place ; and to theology I have no doubt she would have given a wide sense, as including everything that touches the relation between the seen and the unseen.

What is curious to note is that, though Mr. Gladstone in making his cabinet had thrown the main weight against the radicals, yet when they got to work, it was with them he found himself more often than not in energetic agreement. In common talk and in partisan speeches, the prime minister was regarded as dictatorial and imperious. The complaint of some at least among his colleagues in the cabinet of 1880 was rather that he was not imperious enough. Almost from the first he too frequently allowed himself to be over-ruled; often in secondary matters, it is true, but sometimes also in matters on the uncertain frontier between secondary and primary. Then he adopted a practice of taking votes and counting numbers, of which more than one old hand complained as an innovation. Lord Granville said to him in 1886, 'I think you too often counted noses in your last cabinet.'

What Mr. Gladstone described as the severest fight that he had ever known in any cabinet occurred in 1883, upon the removal of the Duke of Wellington's statue from Hyde Park Corner. A vote took place, and three times over he took down the names. He was against removal, but was unable to have his own way over the majority. Members of the government thought themselves curiously free to walk out from divisions. On a Transvaal division two members of the cabinet abstained, and so did two other ministers out of the cabinet. In other cases, the same thing happened, not only breaking discipline, but breeding much trouble with the Queen. Then an unusual number of men of ability and of a degree of self-esteem not below their ability, had been left out of the inner circle; and they and their backers were sometimes apt to bring their pretensions rather fretfully forward. These were the things that to Mr. Gladstone's temperament proved more harassing than graver concerns.

II

All through the first two months of its business, the House showed signs of independence that almost broke the spirit of the ministerial whips. A bill about hares and rabbits produced lively excitement, ministerialists moved amendments upon the measure of their own leaders, and the minister in charge boldly taxed the mutineers with insincerity. A motion for local option was carried by 229 to 203, both Mr. Gladstone and Lord Hartington in the minority. On a motion about clerical restrictions, only a strong and conciliatory appeal from the prime minister averted defeat. A more remarkable demonstration soon followed. The Prince Imperial, unfortunate son of unfortunate sire, who had undergone his famous baptism of fire in the first reverses among the Vosges in the Franco-German war of 1870, was killed in our war in Zululand. Parliament was asked to sanction a vote of money for a memorial of him in the Abbey. A radical member brought forward a motion against it. Both Mr. Gladstone and Sir Stafford Northcote resisted him, yet by a considerable majority the radical carried his point. The feeling was so strong among the ministerialists, that notwithstanding Mr. Gladstone's earnest exhortation, they voted almost to a man against him, and he only carried into the lobby ten official votes on the treasury bench. The great case in which the government were taken to have missed the import of the election was the failure to recall Sir Bartle Frere from South Africa. Of this I shall have enough to say by and by. Meanwhile it gave an undoubted shock to the confidence of the party, and their energetic remonstrance on this head strained Mr. Gladstone's authority to the uttermost. The Queen complained of the tendency of the House of Commons to trench upon the business of the executive. Mr. Gladstone said in reply generally, that no doubt within the half century 'there had been considerable invasion by the House of Commons of the province assigned by the constitution to the executive,' but he perceived no increase in recent times or in the present House. Then he proceeded (June 8, 1880):—

. . . Your Majesty may possibly have in view the pressure which has been exercised on the present government in the case of Sir Bartle Frere. But apart from the fact that this pressure represents a feeling which extends far beyond the walls of parliament, your Majesty may probably remember that, in the early part of 1835, the House of Commons addressed the crown against the appointment of Lord Londonderry to be ambassador at St. Petersburg, on

account, if Mr. Gladstone remembers rightly, of a general ante-
cedent disapproval. This was an exercise of power going far
beyond what has happened now; nor does it seem easy in
principle to place the conduct of Sir B. Frere beyond that general
right of challenge and censure which is unquestionably within the
function of parliament and especially of the House of Commons.

In the field where mastery had never failed him, Mr. Gladstone achieved an early success, and he lost no time in justifying his assumption of the exchequer. The budget (June
10) was marked by the boldness of former days, and was
explained and defended in one of those statements of which
he alone possessed the secret. Even unfriendly witnesses
agreed that it was many years since the House of Commons
had the opportunity of enjoying so extraordinary an intellectual treat, where 'novelties assumed the air of indisputable
truths, and complicated figures were woven into the thread
of intelligible and animated narrative.' He converted the
malt tax into a beer duty, reduced the duties on light
foreign wines, added a penny to the income tax, and adjusted
the licence duties for the sale of alcoholic liquors. Everybody said that 'none but a *cordon bleu* could have made
such a sauce with so few materials.' The dish was excellently received, and the ministerial party were in high
spirits. The conservatives stood angry and amazed that
their own leaders had found no device for the repeal of
the malt duty. The farmer's friends, they cried, had been
in office for six years and had done nothing ; no sooner
is Gladstone at the exchequer than with magic wand he
effects a transformation, and the long-suffering agriculturist
has justice and relief.

In the course of an effort that seemed to show full vigour
of body and mind, Mr. Gladstone incidentally mentioned that
when a new member he recollected hearing a speech upon the
malt tax in the old House of Commons in the year 1833. Yet
the lapse of nearly half a century of life in that great arena
had not relaxed his stringent sense of parliamentary duty.
During most of the course of this first session, he was always
early in his place and always left late. In every discussion

he came to the front, and though an under-secretary made the official reply, it was the prime minister who wound up. One night he made no fewer than six speeches, touching all the questions raised in a miscellaneous night's sitting. In the middle of the summer Mr. Gladstone fell ill. Consternation reigned in London. It even exceeded the dismay caused by the defeat at Maiwand. A friend went to see him as he lay in bed. ' He talked most of the time, not on politics, but on Shakespeare's Henry VIII, and the decay of theological study at Oxford. He never intended his reform measure to produce this result.' After his recovery, he went for a cruise in the *Grantully Castle*, not returning to parliament until September 4, three days before the session ended, when he spoke with all his force on the eastern question.

III

In the electoral campaign Mr. Gladstone had used expressions about Austria that gave some offence at Vienna. On
coming into power he volunteered an assurance to the
Austrian ambassador that he would willingly withdraw his
language if he understood that he had misapprehended the
circumstances. The ambassador said that Austria meant
strictly to observe the treaty of Berlin. Mr. Gladstone then
expressed his regret for the words ' of a painful and wounding
character' that had fallen from him. At the time, he explained, he was ' in a position of greater freedom and less
responsibility.'

At the close of the session of 1880, ministers went to work
upon the unfulfilled portions of the Berlin treaty relating to
Greece and Montenegro. Those stipulations were positive in
the case of Montenegro; as to Greece they were less definite,
but they absolutely implied a cession of more or less territory
by Turkey. They formed the basis of Lord Salisbury's correspondence, but his arguments and representations were
without effect.

Mr. Gladstone and his colleagues went further. They proposed and obtained a demonstration off the Albanian coast
on behalf of Montenegro. Each great Power sent a man-
of-war, but the concert of Europe instantly became what

Mr. Gladstone called a farce, for Austria and Germany made known that under no circumstances would they fire a shot. France rather less prominently took the same course. This defection, which was almost boastful on the part of Austria and Germany, convinced the British cabinet that Turkish obduracy would only be overcome by force, and the question was how to apply force effectually with the least risk to peace. As it happened, the port of Smyrna received an amount of customs' duties too considerable for the Porte to spare it. The idea was that the united fleet at Cattaro should straightway sail to Smyrna and lay hold upon it. The cabinet, with experts from the two fighting departments, weighed carefully all the military responsibilities, and considered the sequestration of the customs' dues at Smyrna to be practicable. Russia and Italy were friendly. France had in a certain way assumed special cognisance of the Greek case, but did nothing particular. From Austria and Germany nothing was to be hoped. On October 4, the Sultan refused the joint European request for the fulfilment of the engagements entered into at Berlin. This refusal was despatched in ignorance of the intention to coerce. The British government had only resolved upon coercion in concert with Europe. Full concert was now out of the question. But on the morning of Sunday, the 10th, Mr. Gladstone and Lord Granville learned with as much surprise as delight from Mr. Goschen, then ambassador extraordinary at Constantinople, that the Sultan had heard of the British proposal of force, and apparently had not heard of the two refusals. On learning how far England had gone, he determined to give way on both the territorial questions. As Mr. Gladstone enters in his diary, 'a faint tinge of doubt remained.' That is to say, the Sultan might find out the rift in the concert and retract. Russia, however, had actually agreed to force. On Tuesday, the 12th, Mr. Gladstone, meeting Lord Granville and another colleague, was 'under the circumstances prepared to proceed en trois.' The other two 'rather differed.' Of course it would have been for the whole cabinet to decide. But between eleven and twelve Lord Granville came in with the news that the note had arrived and all was well.' 'The whole of this extraordinary

BOOK
VIII.

1880.

Volte-face,' as Mr. Gladstone said with some complacency,
' had been effected within six days ; and it was entirely due
not to a threat of coercion from Europe, but to the knowledge that Great Britain had asked Europe to coerce.'
Dulcigno was ceded by the Porte to Montenegro. On the
Greek side of the case, the minister for once was less
ardent than for the complete triumph of his heroic Monte-
negrins, but after tedious negotiations Mr. Gladstone had
the satisfaction of seeing an important rectification of the
Greek frontier, almost restoring his Homeric Greece. The
eastern question looked as if it might fall into one of
its fitful slumbers once more, but we shall soon see that
this was illusory. Mr. Goschen left Constantinople in May,
and the prime minister said to him (June 3, 1881) : —

I write principally for the purpose of offering you my hearty
congratulations on the place you have taken in diplomacy by force
of mind and character, and on the services which, in thus far serving the most honourable aims a man can have, you have rendered
to liberty and humanity.

Only in Afghanistan was there a direct reversal of the
policy of the fallen government. The new cabinet were not
long in deciding on a return to the older policy in respect
of the north-west frontier of India. All that had happened
since it had been abandoned, strengthened the case against
the new departure. The policy that had been pursued
amid so many lamentable and untoward circumstances,
including the destruction of a very gallant agent of England at Cabul, had involved the incorporation of Candahar
within the sphere of the Indian system. Mr. Gladstone
and his cabinet determined on the evacuation of Candahar.
The decision was made public in the royal speech of the
following January (1881). Lord Hartington stated the case
of the government with masterly and crushing force, in a
speech,[1] which is no less than a strong text-book of the
whole argument, if any reader should now desire to comprehend it. The evacuation was censured in the Lords by 165
against 79 ; in the Commons ministers carried the day by a
majority of 120.

<hr>

[1] March 25–6, 1881.

CHAPTER II

AN EPISODE IN TOLERATION

(1880-1883)

THE state, in choosing men to serve it, takes no notice of their opinions; if they be willing faithfully to serve it, that satisfies. · · · Take heed of being sharp, or too easily sharpened by others, against those to whom you can object little but that they square not with you in every opinion concerning matters of religion.

—OLIVER CROMWELL.

ONE discordant refrain rang hoarsely throughout the five years of this administration, and its first notes were heard even before Mr. Gladstone had taken his seat. It drew him into a controversy that was probably more distasteful to him than any other of the myriad contentions, small and great, with which his life was encumbered. Whether or not he threaded his way with his usual skill through a labyrinth of parliamentary tactics incomparably intricate, experts may dispute, but in an ordeal beyond the region of tactics he never swerved from the path alike of liberty and common-sense. It was a question of exacting the oath of allegiance before a member could take his seat.

Mr. Bradlaugh, the new member for Northampton, who now forced the question forward, as O'Connell had forced forward the civil equality of catholics, and Rothschild and others the civil equality of Jews, was a free-thinker of a daring and defiant type. Blank negation could go no further. He had abundant and genuine public spirit, and a strong love of truth according to his own lights, and he was both a brave and a disinterested man. This hard-grit secularism of his was not the worst of his offences in the view of the new majority and their constituents. He had published an impeachment of the House of Brunswick, which few members of parliament had ever heard of or looked at. But even abstract republicanism was not the worst. What placed him at extreme disadvantage in fighting the battle in which he was now engaged, was his republication of a pamphlet by an American doctor on that impracticable question of population, which though too rigorously excluded from public discussion, confessedly lies among the roots of most other social questions. For this he had some years before been indicted in the courts, and had only escaped conviction and punishment by a technicality. It was Mr. Bradlaugh's refusal to take the oath in a court of justice that led to the law of 1869, enabling a witness to affirm instead of swearing. He now carried the principle a step further.

When the time came, the Speaker (April 29) received a letter from the iconoclast, claiming to make an affirmation, instead of taking the oath of allegiance.[1] He consulted his legal advisers, and they gave an opinion strongly adverse to the claim. On this the Speaker wrote to Mr. Gladstone and to Sir Stafford Northcote, stating his concurrence in the opinion of the lawyers, and telling them that he should leave the question to the House. His practical suggestion was that on his statement being made, a motion should be proposed for a select committee. The committee was duly appointed, and it reported by a majority of one, against a minority that contained names so weighty as Sir Henry James, Herschell, Whitbread, and Bright, that the claim to affirm was not a good claim. So opened a series of incidents that went on as long as the parliament, clouded the radiance of the party triumph, threw the new government at once into a minority, dimmed the ascendency of the great minister, and what was more, showed human nature at its worst. The incidents themselves are in detail not worth recalling here, but they are a striking episode in the history of toleration, as well as a landmark in Mr. Gladstone's journey from the day five-and-forty years before when, in

---

[1] Bradlaugh, who was a little vain of his legal skill, founded this claim upon the Evidence Amendment Act, taken in connection with the Parliamentary Oaths and other Acts.

reference to Molesworth as candidate for Leeds, he had told his friends at Newark that men who had no belief in divine revelation were not the men to govern this nation whether they be whigs or radicals.[1]

His claim to affirm having been rejected, Bradlaugh next desired to swear. The ministerial whip reported that the feeling against him in the House was uncontrollable. The Speaker held a council in his library with Mr. Gladstone, the law officers, the whip, and two or three other persons of authority and sense. He told them that if Bradlaugh had in the first instance come to take the oath, he should have allowed no intervention, but that the case was altered by the claimant's open declaration that an oath was not binding on his conscience. A hostile motion was expected when Bradlaugh came to the table to be sworn, and the Speaker suggested that it should be met by the previous question, to be moved by Mr. Gladstone. Then the whip broke in with the assurance that the usual supporters of the government could not be relied upon. The Speaker went upstairs to dress, and on his return found that they had agreed on moving another select committee. He told them that he thought this a weak course, but if the previous question would be defeated, perhaps a committee could not be helped. Bradlaugh came to the table, and the hostile motion was made. Mr. Gladstone proposed his committee, and carried it by a good majority against the motion that Bradlaugh, being without religious belief, could not take an oath. The debate was warm, and the attacks on Bradlaugh were often gross. The Speaker honourably pointed out that such attacks on an elected member whose absence was enforced by their own order, were unfair and unbecoming, but the feelings of the House were too strong for him and too strong for chivalry. The opposition turned affairs to ignoble party account, and were not ashamed in their prints and elsewhere to level the charge of ' open patronage of unbelief and Malthusianism, Bradlaugh and Blasphemy,' against a government that contained Gladstone, Bright, and Selborne, three of the most conspicuously devout men to be found in all England. One

¹ See vol. i. p. 188.

expression of faith used by a leader in the attack on Brad-laugh lived in Mr. Gladstone's memory to the end of his days. 'You know, Mr. Speaker,' cried the champion of orthodox creeds, 'we all of us believe in a God of some sort or another.' That a man should consent to clothe the naked human soul in this truly singular and scanty remnant of spiritual apparel, was held to be the unalterable condition of fitness for a seat in parliament and the company of decent people. Well might Mr. Gladstone point out how vast a disparagement of Christianity, and of orthodox theism also, was here involved : —

They say this, that you may go any length you please in the denial of religion, provided only you do not reject the name of the Deity. They tear religion into shreds, so to speak, and say that there is one particular shred with which nothing will ever induce them to part. They divide religion into the dispensable and the indispensable, and among that kind which can be dispensed with — I am not now speaking of those who declare, or are admitted, under a special law, I am not speaking of Jews or those who make a declaration, I am speaking solely of those for whom no provision is made except the provision of oath — they divide, I say, religion into what can and what cannot be dispensed with. There is some-thing, however, that cannot be dispensed with. I am not willing, Sir, that Christianity, if the appeal is made to us as a Christian legislature, shall stand in any rank lower than that which is indis-pensable. I may illustrate what I mean. Suppose a commander has to despatch a small body of men on an expedition on which it is necessary for them to carry on their backs all that they can take with them ; the men will part with everything that is unnecessary, and take only that which is essential. That is the course you ask us to take in drawing us upon theological ground ; you require us to distinguish between superfluities and necessaries, and you tell us that Christianity is one of the superfluities, one of the excrescences, and has nothing to do with the vital substance, the name of the Deity, which is indispensable. I say that the adop-tion of such a proposition as that, which is in reality at the very root of your contention, is disparaging in the very highest degree to the Christian faith. . . .¹

¹ Speech on second reading of Affirmation bill, 1883.

Even viewed as a theistic test, he contended, this oath embraced no acknowledgment of Providence, of divine government, of responsibility, or retribution ; it involved nothing but a bare and abstract admission, a form void of all practical meaning and concern.

The House, however, speedily showed how inaccessible were most of its members to reason and argument of this kind or any kind. On June 21, Mr. Gladstone thus described the proceedings to the Queen. ' With the renewal of the discussion,' he wrote, ' the temper of the House does not improve, both excitement and suspicion appearing to prevail in different quarters.' A motion made by Mr. Bradlaugh's colleague that he should be permitted to affirm, was met by a motion that he should not be allowed either to affirm or to swear.

To the Queen.

Many warm speeches were made by the opposition in the name of religion ; to those Mr. Bright has warmly replied in the name of religious liberty. The contention on the other side really is that as to a certain ill-defined fragment of truth the House is still, under the Oaths Act, the guardian of religion. The primary question, whether the House has jurisdiction under the statute, is almost hopelessly mixed with the question whether an atheist, who has declared himself an atheist, ought to sit in parliament. Mr. Gladstone's own view is that the House has no jurisdiction for the purpose of excluding any one willing to qualify when he has been duly elected ; but he is very uncertain how the House will vote or what will be the end of the business, if the House undertakes the business of exclusion.

June 22. — The House of Commons has been occupied from the commencement of the evening until a late hour with the adjourned debate on the case of Mr. Bradlaugh. The divided state of opinion in the House made itself manifest throughout the evening. Mr. Newdegate made a speech which turned almost wholly upon the respective merits of theism and atheism. Mr. Gladstone thought it his duty to advise the House to beware of entangling itself in difficulties possibly of a serious character, by assuming a jurisdiction in cases of this class.

At one o'clock in the morning, the first great division was taken, and the House resolved by 275 votes against 230 that Mr. Bradlaugh should neither affirm nor swear. The excitement at this result was tremendous. Some minutes elapsed before the Speaker could declare the numbers. 'Indeed,' wrote Mr. Gladstone to the Queen, 'it was an ecstatic transport, and exceeded anything which Mr. Gladstone remembers to have witnesed. He read in it only a witness to the dangers of the course on which the House has entered, and to its unfitness for the office which it has rashly chosen to assume.' He might also have read in it, if he had liked, the exquisite delight of the first stroke of revenge for Midlothian.

The next day (June 23) the matter entered on a more violent phase.

To the Queen.

This day, when the Speaker took the chair at a quarter past twelve, Mr. Bradlaugh came to the table and claimed to take the oath. The Speaker read to him the resolution of the House which forbids it. Mr. Bradlaugh asked to be heard, and no objection was taken. He then addressed the House from the bar. His address was that of a consummate speaker. But it was an address which could not have any effect unless the House had undergone a complete revolution of mind. He challenged the legality of the act of the House, expressing hereby an opinion in which Mr. Gladstone himself, going beyond some other members of the minority, has the misfortune to lean towards agreeing with him. . . . The Speaker now again announced to Mr. Bradlaugh the resolution of the House. Only a small minority voted against enforcing it. Mr. Bradlaugh declining to withdraw, was removed by the serjeant-at-arms. Having suffered this removal, he again came beyond the bar, and entered into what was almost a corporal struggle with the serjeant. Hereupon Sir S. Northcote moved that Mr. Bradlaugh be committed for his offence. Mr. Gladstone said that while he thought it did not belong to him, under the circumstances of the case, to advise the House, he could take no objection to the advice thus given.

The Speaker, it may be said, thought this view of

Mr. Gladstone's a mistake, and that when Bradlaugh refused to withdraw, the leader of the House ought, as a matter of policy, to have been the person to move first the order to withdraw, next the committal to the custody of the serjeant-at-arms. ' I was placed in a false position,' says the Speaker, 'and so was the House, in having to follow the lead of the leader of the opposition, while the leader of the House and the great majority were passive spectators.'[1] As Mr. Gladstone and other members of the government voted for Bradlaugh's committal, on the ground that his resistance to the serjeant had nothing to do with the establishment of his rights before either a court or his constituency, it would seem that the Speaker's complaint is not unjust. To this position, however, Mr. Gladstone adhered, in entire conformity apparently to the wishes of the keenest members of his cabinet and the leading men of his party.

The Speaker wrote to Sir Stafford Northcote urging on him the propriety of allowing Bradlaugh to take the oath without question. But Northcote was forced on against his better judgment by his more ardent supporters. It was a strange and painful situation, and the party system assuredly did not work at its best — one leading man forced on to mischief by the least responsible of his sections, the other held back from providing a cure by the narrowest of the other sections. In the April of 1881 Mr. Gladstone gave notice of a bill providing for affirmation, but it was immediately apparent that the opposition would make the most of every obstacle to a settlement, and the proposal fell through. In August of this year the Speaker notes, 'The difficulties in the way of settling this question satisfactorily are great, and in the present temper of the House almost insuperable.'

II

It is not necessary to recount all the stages of this protracted struggle: what devices and expedients and motions, how many odious scenes of physical violence, how many hard-fought actions in the lawcourts, how many conflicts

[1] *Lord Hampden's Diaries.*

BOOK
VIII.
1883.

between the House of Commons and the constituency, what glee and rubbing of hands in the camp of the opposition at having thrust their rivals deep into a quagmire so unpleasant. The scandal was intolerable, but ministers were helpless, as a marked incident now demonstrated. It was not until 1883 that a serious attempt was made to change the law. The Affirmation bill of that year has a biographic place, because it marks in a definite way how far Mr. Gladstone's mind — perhaps not, as I have said before, by nature or by instinct peculiarly tolerant — had travelled along one of the grand highroads of human progress. The occasion was for many reasons one of great anxiety. Here are one or two short entries, the reader remembering that by this time the question was two years old : —

April 24, *Tuesday.* — On Sunday night a gap of three hours in my sleep was rather ominous; but it was not repeated. . . . Saw the Archbishop of Canterbury, with whom I had a very long conversation on the Affirmation bill and on *Church and State.* Policy generally as well as on special subjects. . . . Globe Theatre in the evening; excellent acting. . . . 25. . . . Worked on Oaths question. . . . 26. . . . Made a long and *begeistert*[1] speech on the Affirmation bill, taking the bull by the horns.

His speech upon this measure was a noble effort. It was delivered under circumstances of unsurpassed difficulty, for there was revolt in the party, the client was repugnant, the opinions brought into issue were to Mr. Gladstone hateful. Yet the speech proved one of his greatest. Imposing, lofty, persuasive, sage it would have been, from whatever lips it might have fallen; it was signal indeed as coming from one so fervid, so definite, so unfaltering in a faith of his own, one who had started from the opposite pole to that great civil principle of which he now displayed a grasp invincible. If it be true of a writer that the best style is that which most directly flows from living qualities in the writer's own mind and is a pattern of their actual working, so is the same thing to be said of oratory. These high themes of Faith, on the one hand, and Freedom on the

---

[1] Perhaps the best equivalent for *begeistert* here is ' *daemonic.* '

other, exactly fitted the range of the thoughts in which Mr.
Gladstone habitually lived. 'I have no fear of Atheism in
this House,' he said; 'Truth is the expression of the Divine
mind, and however little our feeble vision may be able to
discern the means by which God may provide for its preservation, we may leave the matter in His hands, and we may
be sure that a firm and courageous application of every
principle of equity and of justice is the best method we can
adopt for the preservation and influence of Truth.' This
was Mr. Gladstone at his sincerest and his highest. I
wonder, too, if there has been a leader in parliament
since the seventeenth century, who could venture to address it in the strain of the memorable passage now to be
transcribed : —

You draw your line at the point where the abstract denial of
God is severed from the abstract admission of the Deity. My proposition is that the line thus drawn is worthless, and that much on
your side of the line is as objectionable as the atheism on the other.
If you call upon us to make distinctions, let them at least be
rational; I do not say let them be Christian distinctions, but let
them be rational. I can understand one rational distinction, that
you should frame the oath in such a way as to recognise not only the
existence of the Deity, but the providence of the Deity, and man's
responsibility to the Deity ; and in such a way as to indicate the
knowledge in a man's own mind that he must answer to the Deity for
what he does, and is able to do. But is that your present rule ?
No, Sir, you know very well that from ancient times there have been
sects and schools that have admitted in the abstract as freely as
Christians the existence of a Deity, but have held that of practical
relations between Him and man there can be none. Many of the
members of this House will recollect the majestic and noble lines —

> Omnis enim per se divom natura necesse est
> Immortali ævo summa cum pace fruatur,
> Semota a nostris rebus sejunctaque longe.
> Nam privata dolore omni, privata periclis,
> Ipsa suis pollens opibus, nihil indiga nostri,
> Nec bene promeritis capitur, nec tangitur ira.[1]

---

[1] Lucretius, ii. 646. 'For the
nature of the gods must ever of itself
enjoy repose supreme through endless
time, far withdrawn from all concerns
of ours ; free from all our pains, free
from all our perils, strong in resources
of its own, needing nought from us,
no favours win it, no anger moves.'

'Divinity exists' — according to these, I must say, magnificent
lines — 'in remote and inaccessible recesses; but with us it has
no dealing, of us it has no need, with us it has no relation.'
I do not hesitate to say that the specific evil, the specific form of
irreligion, with which in the educated society of this country you
have to contend, and with respect to which you ought to be on
your guard, is not blank atheism. That is a rare opinion very
seldom met with; but what is frequently met with is that form
of opinion which would teach us that, whatever may be beyond
the visible things of this world, whatever there may be beyond
this short span of life, you know and you can know nothing of it,
and that it is a bootless undertaking to attempt to establish relations
with it. That is the mischief of the age, and that mischief you do
not attempt to touch.

The House, though but few perhaps recollected their Lucretius or had ever even read him, sat, as I well remember, with
reverential stillness, hearkening from this born master of
moving cadence and high sustained modulation to 'the rise
and long roll of the hexameter,' — to the plangent lines that
have come down across the night of time to us from great
Rome. But all these impressions of sublime feeling and
strong reasoning were soon effaced by honest bigotry, by
narrow and selfish calculation, by flat cowardice. The relieving bill was cast out by a majority of three. The catholics in the main voted against it, and many nonconformists,
hereditary champions of all the rights of private judgment,
either voted against it or did not vote at all. So soon in these
affairs, as the world has long ago found out, do bodies of men
forget in a day of power the maxims that they held sacred and
inviolable in days when they were weak.

The drama did not end here. In that parliament Bradlaugh was never allowed to discharge his duty as a member,
but when after the general election of 1885, being once more
chosen by Northampton, he went to the table to take the oath,
as in former days Mill and others of like non-theologic complexion had taken it, the Speaker would suffer no intervention
against him. Then in 1888, though the majority was conservative, Bradlaugh himself secured the passing of an affirmation

law.   Finally, in the beginning of 1891, upon the motion of
a Scotch member, supported by Mr. Gladstone, the House
formally struck out from its records the resolution of June
22, 1881, that had been passed, as we have seen, amid ' ecstatic
transports.'   Bradlaugh then lay upon his deathbed, and was
unconscious of what had been done.   Mr. Gladstone a few
days later, in moving a bill of his own to discard a lingering
case of civil disability attached to religious profession, made a
last reference to Mr. Bradlaugh : —

A distinguished man, he said, and admirable member of this
House, was laid yesterday in his mother-earth.   He was the subject
of a long controversy in this House — a controversy the beginning
of which we recollect, and the ending of which we recollect.   We
remember with what zeal it was prosecuted; we remember how
summarily it was dropped; we remember also what reparation
has been done within the last few days to the distinguished man
who was the immediate object of that controversy.   But does
anybody who hears me believe that that controversy, so prosecuted
and so abandoned, was beneficial to the Christian religion ? [1]

[1] Religious Disabilities Removal bill, Feb. 4, 1891.

CHAPTER III

MAJUBA

(1880–1881)

εἰς ἀπέραντον δίκτυον ἄτης
ἐμπλεχθήσεσθ' ὑπ' ἀνοίας.
— ÆSCH. *Prom.* 1078.

In a boundless coil of mischief pure senselessness will entangle you.

IT would almost need the pen of Tacitus or Dante to tell the story of European power in South Africa. For forty years, said Mr. Gladstone in 1881, 'I have always regarded the South African question as the one great unsolved and perhaps insoluble problem of our colonial system.' Among the other legacies of the forward policy that the constituencies had decisively condemned in 1880, this insoluble problem rapidly became acute and formidable.

One of the great heads of impeachment in Midlothian had been a war undertaken in 1878–9 against a fierce tribe on the borders of the colony of Natal. The author and instrument of the Zulu war was Sir Bartle Frere, a man of tenacious character and grave and lofty if ill-calculated aims. The conservative government, as I have already said,[1] without enthusiasm assented, and at one stage they even formally censured him. When Mr. Gladstone acceded to office, the expectation was universal that Sir Bartle would be at once recalled. At the first meeting of the new cabinet (May 3) it was decided to retain him. The prime minister at first was his marked protector. The substantial reason against recall was that his presence was needed to carry out the policy of confederation, and towards confederation it was hoped that the Cape parliament was immediately about to take

[1] Vol. ii. p. 583.

22

a long preliminary step. 'Confederation,' Mr. Gladstone said, 'is the pole-star of the present action of our government.' In a few weeks, for a reason that will be mentioned in treating the second episode of this chapter, confederation broke down. A less substantial but still not wholly inoperative reason was the strong feeling of the Queen for the high commissioner. The royal prepossessions notwithstanding, and in spite of the former leanings of Mr. Gladstone, the cabinet determined, at the end of July, that Sir Bartle should be recalled. The whole state of the case is made sufficiently clear in the two following communications from the prime minister to the Queen: —

To the Queen.

May 28, 1880. — Mr. Gladstone presents his humble duty, and has had the honour to receive your Majesty's telegram respecting Sir B. Frere. Mr. Gladstone used on Saturday his best efforts to avert a movement for his dismissal, which it was intended by a powerful body of members on the liberal side to promote by a memorial to Mr. Gladstone, and by a motion in the House. He hopes that he has in some degree succeeded, and he understands that it is to be decided on Monday whether they will at present desist or persevere. Of course no sign will be given by your Majesty's advisers which could tend to promote perseverance, at the same time Mr. Gladstone does not conceal from himself two things: the first, that the only chance of Sir B. Frere's remaining seems to depend upon his ability to make progress in the matter of confederation; the second, that if the agitation respecting him in the House, the press, and the country should continue, confidence in him may be so paralysed as to render his situation intolerable to a high-minded man and to weaken his hands fatally for any purpose of good.

July 29, 1880. — It was not without some differences of opinion among themselves that, upon their accession to office, the cabinet arrived at the conclusion that, if there was a prospect of progress in the great matter of confederation, this might afford a ground of co-operation between them and Sir B. Frere, notwithstanding the strong censures which many of them in opposition had pro-

nounced upon his policy. This conclusion gave the liveliest satisfaction to a large portion, perhaps to the majority, of the House
of Commons; but they embraced it with the more satisfaction
because of your Majesty's warm regard for Sir B. Frere, a
sentiment which some among them personally share.

It was evident, however, and it was perhaps in the nature of
the case, that a confidence thus restricted was far from agreeable
to Sir B. Frere, who, in the opinion of Mr. Gladstone, has only
been held back by a commendable self-restraint and sense of duty,
from declaring himself aggrieved. Thus, though the cabinet have
done the best they could, his standing ground was not firm, nor
could they make it so. But the total failure of the effort made to
induce the Cape parliament to move, has put confederation wholly
out of view, for a time quite indefinite, and almost certainly considerable. Mr. Gladstone has therefore the painful duty of sub-
mitting to your Majesty, on behalf of the Cabinet, the enclosed
copy of a ciphered telegram of recall.

II

The breaking of the military power of the Zulus was
destined to prove much less important than another proceeding closely related to it, though not drawing the same
attention at the moment. I advise the reader not to grudge
a rather strict regard to the main details of transactions that,
owing to unhappy events of later date, have to this day held
a conspicuous place in the general controversy as to the
great minister's statesmanship.

For some time past, powerful native tribes had been
slowly but steadily pushing the Boers of the Transvaal
back, and the inability to resist was now dangerously plain.
In 1876 the Boers had been worsted in one of their incessant struggles with the native races, and this time they had
barely been able to hold their own against an insignificant
tribe of one of the least warlike branches. It was thought
certain by English officials on the ground, that the example
would not be lost on fiercer warriors, and that a native conflagration might any day burst into blaze in other regions of
the immense territory. The British government despatched
an agent of great local experience; he found the Boer

government, which was loosely organised even at its best, now completely paralysed, without money, without internal authority, without defensive power against external foes. In alarm at the possible result of such a situation on the peace of the European domain in South Africa, he proclaimed the sovereignty of the Queen, and set up an administration. This he was empowered by secret instructions to do, if he should think fit. Here was the initial error. The secretary of state in Downing Street approved (June 21, 1877), on the express assumption that a sufficient number of the inhabitants desired to become the Queen's subjects. Some have thought that if he had waited the Boers would have sought annexation, but this seems to be highly improbable. In the annexation proclamation promises were made to the Boers of 'the fullest legislative privileges compatible with the circumstances of the country and the intelligence of the people.' An assembly was also promised.

The soundness of the assumption was immediately disputed. The Boer government protested against annexation. Two delegates — one of them Mr. Kruger — repaired to England, assured Lord Carnarvon that their fellow-Boers were vehemently opposed to annexation, and earnestly besought its reversal. The minister insisted that he was right and they were wrong. They went back, and in order to convince the government of the true strength of feeling for independence, petitions were prepared seeking the restoration of independence. The signatures were those of qualified electors of the old republic. The government were informed by Sir Garnet Wolseley that there were about 8000 persons of the age to be electors, of whom rather fewer than 7000 were Boers. To the petitions were appended almost exactly 7000 names. The colonial office recognised that the opposition of the Boers to annexation was practically unanimous. The comparatively insignificant addresses on the other side came from the town and digging population, which was as strong in favour of the suppression of the old republic, as the rural population was strong against it.

For many months the Boers persevered. They again sent Kruger and Joubert to England; they held huge mass meetings; they poured out prayers to the high commissioner to give back their independence; they sent memorial after memorial to the secretary of state. In the autumn of 1879 Sir Garnet Wolseley assumed the administration of the Transvaal, and issued a proclamation setting forth the will and determination of the government of the Queen that this Transvaal territory should be, and should continue to be for ever, an integral part of her dominions in South Africa. In the closing days of 1879 the secretary of state, Sir Michael Hicks Beach, who had succeeded Carnarvon (Jan. 1878), received from the same eminent soldier a comprehensive despatch, warning him that the meetings of protest against annexation, attended by thousands of armed men in angry mood, would be likely to end in a serious explosion. While putting all sides of the question before his government, Sir Garnet inserted one paragraph of momentous import. ' The Transvaal,' he said, ' is rich in minerals; gold has already been found in quantities, and there can be little doubt that larger and still more valuable goldfields will sooner or later be discovered. Any such discovery would soon bring a large British population here. The time must eventually arrive when the Boers will be in a small minority, as the country is very sparsely peopled, and would it not therefore be a very near-sighted policy to recede now from the position we have taken up here, simply because for some years to come, the retention of 2000 or 3000 troops may be necessary to reconsolidate our power?'[1] This pregnant and far-sighted warning seems to have been little considered by English statesmen of either party at this critical time or afterwards, though it proved a vital element in any far-sighted decision.

On March 9 — the day, as it happened, on which the intention to dissolve parliament was made public — Sir Garnet telegraphed for a renewed expression of the determination of the government to retain the country, and he received the assurance that he sought. The Vaal river, he told the Boers, would flow backwards through the Drakensberg sooner than the British would be withdrawn from the Transvaal. The picturesque figure did not soften the Boer heart.

[1] Sir Garnet Wolseley to Sir M. Hicks Beach, Nov. 13, 1879.

This was the final share of the conservative cabinet in the unfortunate enterprise on which they had allowed the country to be launched.

III

When the question of annexation had originally come before parliament, Mr. Gladstone was silent. He was averse to it; he believed that it would involve us in unmixed mischief; but he felt that to make this judgment known at that period would not have had any effect towards reversing what had been done, while it might impede the chances of a good issue, slender as these might be.[1] In the discussion at the opening of the final session of the old parliament, Lord Hartington as leader of the opposition, enforcing the general doctrine that it behoved us to concentrate our resources, and to limit instead of extending the empire, took the Transvaal for an illustration. It was now conclusively proved, he said, that a large majority of the Boers were bitterly against annexation. That being so, it ought not to be considered a settled question merely because annexation had taken place; and if we should find that the balance of advantage was in favour of the restoration of independence, no false sense of dignity should stand in the way. Mr. Gladstone in Midlothian had been more reserved. In that indictment, there are only two or three references, and those comparatively fugitive and secondary, to this article of charge. There is a sentence in one of the Midlothian speeches about bringing a territory inhabited by a free European Christian republic within the limits of a monarchy, though out of 8000 persons qualified to vote, 6500 voted against it. In another sentence he speaks of the Transvaal as a country 'where we have chosen most unwisely, I am tempted to say insanely, to place ourselves in the strange predicament of the free subjects of a monarchy going to coerce the free subjects of a republic, and to compel them to accept a citizenship which they decline and refuse; but if that is to be done, it must be done by force.'[2] A third sentence completes the tale: 'If Cyprus and the

[1] In H. of C., Jan. 21, 1881.   [2] Speeches in Scotland, i. pp. 48, 63.

Transvaal were as valuable as they are valueless, I would repudiate them because they are obtained by means dishonourable to the character of the country.' These utterances of the mighty unofficial chief and the responsible official leader of the opposition were all. The Boer republicans thought that they were enough.

On coming into power, the Gladstone government found the official evidence all to the effect that the political aspect of the Transvaal was decidedly improving. The commissioners, the administrators, the agents, were unanimous. Even those among them who insisted on the rooted dislike of the main body of the Boers to British authority, still thought that they were acquiescing, exactly as the Boers in the Cape Colony had acquiesced. Could ministers justify abandonment, without far stronger evidence than they then possessed that they could not govern the Transvaal peaceably? Among other things, they were assured that abandonment would be fatal to the prospects of confederation, and might besides entail a civil war. On May 7, Sir Bartle Frere pressed the new ministers for an early announcement of their policy, in order to prevent the mischiefs of agitation. The cabinet decided the question on May 12, and agreed upon the terms of a telegram [1] by which Lord Kimberley was to inform Frere that the sovereignty of the Queen over the Transvaal could not be relinquished, but that he hoped the speedy accomplishment of confederation would enable free institutions to be conferred with promptitude. In other words, in spite of all that had been defiantly said by Lord Hartington, and more cautiously implied by Mr. Gladstone, the new government at once placed themselves exactly in the position of the old one.[2]

The case was stated in his usual nervous language by Mr. Chamberlain a few months later.[3] 'When we came into

[1] C, 2586, No. 3.

[2] Mr. Grant Duff, then colonial under-secretary, said in the House of Commons, May 21, 1880, 'Under the very difficult circumstances of the case, the plan which seemed likely best to conciliate the interests at once of the Boers, the natives and the English population, was that the Trans-

vaal should receive, and receive with promptitude, as a portion of confederation, the largest possible measure of local liberties that could be granted, and that was the direction in which her Majesty's present advisers meant to move.'

[3] At Birmingham, June 1881.

office,' he said, 'we were all agreed that the original annexation was a mistake, that it ought never to have been made; and there arose the question could it then be undone? We were in possession of information to the effect that the great majority of the people of the Transvaal were reconciled to annexation; we were told that if we reversed the decision of the late government, there would be a great probability of civil war and anarchy; and acting upon these representations, we decided that we could not recommend the Queen to relinquish her sovereignty. But we assured the Boers that we would take the earliest opportunity of granting to them the freest and most complete local institutions compatible with the welfare of South Africa. It is easy to be wise after the event. It is easy to see now that we were wrong in so deciding. I frankly admit we made a mistake. Whatever the risk was, and I believe it was a great risk, of civil war and anarchy in the Transvaal, it was not so great a danger as that we actually incurred by maintaining the wrong of our predecessors.' Such was the language used by Mr. Chamberlain after special consultation with Lord Kimberley. With characteristic tenacity and that aversion ever to yield even the smallest point, which comes to a man saturated with the habit of a lifetime of debate, Mr. Gladstone wrote to Mr. Chamberlain (June 8, 1881): 'I have read with pleasure what you say of the Transvaal. Yet I am not prepared, for myself, to concede that we made a mistake in not advising a revocation of the annexation when we came in.'

At this instant a letter reached Mr. Gladstone from Kruger and Joubert (May 10, 1880), telling him that there was a firm belief among their people that truth prevailed. 'They were confident that one day or another, by the mercy of the Lord, the reins of the imperial government would be entrusted again to men who look out for the honour and glory of England, not by acts of injustice and crushing force, but by the way of justice and good faith. And, indeed, this belief has proven to be a good belief.' It would have been well for the Boers and well for us, if that had indeed been so. Unluckily the reply sent in Mr. Gladstone's name (June 15), informed them that obligations had now been contracted, especially towards the natives, that could not be set aside, but that consistently with the maintenance of the Queen's sovereignty over the Transvaal, ministers desired that the white inhabitants should enjoy the fullest liberty to manage their local affairs. 'We believe that this liberty may be most easily and promptly conceded to the Transvaal, as a member of a South African confederation.' Solemn and deliberate as this sounds, no step whatever was effectively taken towards conferring this full liberty, or any liberty at all.

It is worth while, on this material point, to look back. The original proclamation had promised the people the fullest legislative privileges compatible with the circumstances of the country and the intelligence of the people. Then, at a later date (April 1877), Sir Bartle Frere met a great assemblage of Boers, and told them that they should receive, as soon as circumstances rendered it practicable, as large a measure of self-government as was enjoyed by any colony in South Africa.[1] The secretary of state had also spoken to the same effect. During the short period in which Sir Bartle Frere was connected with the administration of the Transvaal, he earnestly pressed upon the government the necessity for redeeming the promises made at the time of annexation, 'of the same measure of perfect self-government now enjoyed by Cape Colony,' always, of course, under the authority of the crown.[2] As the months went on, no attempt was made to fulfil all these solemn pledges, and the Boers naturally began to look on them as so much mockery. Their anger in turn increased the timidity of government, and it was argued that the first use that the Boers would make of a free constitution would be to stop the supplies. So a thing called an Assembly was set up (November 9, 1879), composed partly of British officers and partly of nominated members. This was a complete falsification of a whole set of our national promises. Still annexation might conceivably have been

[1] C, 2367, p. 55.
[2] *Afghanistan and S. Africa :* A letter to Mr. Gladstone by Sir Bartle Frere. Murray, 1891, pp. 24–6. Frere, on his return to England, once more impressed on the colonial office the necessity of speedily granting the Boers a constitution, otherwise there would be serious trouble. (*Life,* ii. p. 408.)

accepted, even the sting might have been partially taken out of the delay of the promised free institutions, if only the administration had been considerate, judicious, and adapted to the ways and habits of the people. Instead of being all these things it was stiff, headstrong, and intensely stupid.[1]

The value of the official assurances from agents on the spot that restoration of independence would destroy the chances of confederation, and would give fuel to the fires of agitation, was speedily tested. It was precisely these results that flowed from the denial of independence. The incensed Boer leaders worked so successfully on the Cape parliament against confederation, that this favourite panacea was indefinitely hung up. Here, again, it is puzzling to know why ministers did not retrace their steps. Here, again, their blind guides in the Transvaal persisted that they knew the road; persisted that with the exception of a turbulent handful, the Boers of the Transvaal only sighed for the enjoyment of the *pax britannica*, or, if even that should happen to be not quite true, at any rate they were incapable of united action, were mortal cowards, and could never make a stand in the field. While folly of this kind was finding its way by every mail to Downing Street, violent disturbances broke out in the collection of taxes. Still Sir Owen Lanyon — who had been placed in control in the Transvaal in March 1879 — assured Lord Kimberley that no serious trouble would arise (November 14). At the end of the month he still denies that there is much or any cause for anxiety. In December several thousands of Boers assembled at Paardekraal, declared for the restoration of their republic, and a general rising followed. Colley, who had succeeded General Wolseley as governor of Natal and high commissioner for south-east Africa, had been so little prepared for this, that at the end of August he had recommended a reduction of the Transvaal garrisons,[2] and even now he

[1] Sir George Colley pressed Lord Kimberley in his correspondence with the reality of this grievance, and the urgency of trying to remove it. This was after the Boers had taken to arms at the end of 1880.

[2] Before the Gladstone government came into office, between August 1879 and April 1880, whilst General Wolseley was in command, the force in Natal and the Transvaal had been reduced by six batteries of artillery,

thought the case so little serious that he contented himself (December 4) with ordering four companies to march for the Transvaal. Then he and Lanyon began to get alarmed, and with good reason. The whole country, except three or four beleaguered British posts, fell into the hands of the Boers.

The pleas for failure to take measures to conciliate the Boers in the interval between Frere's recall and the outbreak, were that Sir Hercules Robinson had not arrived;[1] that confederation was not yet wholly given up; that resistance to annexation was said to be abating; that time was in our favour; that the one thing indispensable to conciliate the Boers was a railway to Delagoa Bay; that this needed a treaty, and we hoped soon to get Portugal to ratify a treaty, and then we might tell the Boers that we should soon make a survey, with a view at some early date to proceed with the project, and thus all would in the end come right. So a fresh page was turned in the story of loitering unwisdom.

IV

On December 6, Mr. Brand, the sagacious president of the Orange Free State, sent a message of anxious warning to the acting governor at Cape Town, urging that means should be devised to avert an imminent collision. That message, which might possibly have wakened up the colonial office to the real state of the case, did not reach London until December 30. Excuses for this fatal delay were abundant: a wire was broken; the governor did not think himself concerned with Transvaal affairs; he sent the message on to the general, supposing that the general would send it on home; and so forth. For a whole string of the very best reasons in the world the message that

three companies of engineers, one cavalry regiment, eleven battalions of infantry, and five companies of army service corps. The force at the time of the outbreak was: in Natal 1772, and in the Transvaal 1759 — a total of 3531. As soon as the news of the insurrection reached London, large reinforcements were at once despatched to Colley, the first of them leaving Gibraltar on Dec. 27, 1880.

[1] Sir B. Frere was recalled on August 1, 1880, and sailed for England September 15. Sir Hercules Robinson, his successor, did not reach the Cape until the end of January 1881. In the interval Sir George Strahan was acting governor.

might have prevented the outbreak, arrived through the slow post at Whitehall just eleven days after the outbreak had begun. Members of the legislature at the Cape urged the British government to send a special commissioner to inquire and report. The policy of giving consideration to the counsels of the Cape legislature had usually been pursued by the wiser heads concerned in South African affairs, and when the counsels of the chief of the Free State were urgent in the same direction, their weight should perhaps have been decisive. Lord Kimberley, however, did not think the moment opportune (Dec. 30).[1] Before many weeks, as it happened, a commission was indeed sent, but unfortunately not until after the mischief had been done. Meanwhile in the Queen's speech a week later an emphatic paragraph announced that the duty of vindicating her Majesty's authority had set aside for the time any plan for securing to European settlers in the Transvaal full control over their own local affairs. Seldom has the sovereign been made the mouthpiece of an utterance more shortsighted.

Again the curtain rose upon a new and memorable act. Four days after the Queen's speech, President Brand a second time appeared upon the scene (Jan. 10, 1881), with a message hoping that an effort would be made without the least delay to prevent further bloodshed. Lord Kimberley replied that provided the Boers would desist from their armed opposition, the government did not despair of making a satisfactory settlement. Two days later (Jan. 12) the president told the government that not a moment should be lost, and some one (say Chief Justice de Villiers) should be sent to the Transvaal burghers by the government, to stop further collision and with a clear and definite proposal

---

[1] Lord Kimberley justified this decision on the ground that it was impossible to send a commissioner to inquire and report, at a moment when our garrisons were besieged, and we had collected no troops to relieve them, and when we had just received the news that the detachment of the 94th had been cut off on the march from Lydenberg to Pretoria. 'Is it not practically certain,' he wrote, 'that the Boers would have refused at that time to listen to any reasonable terms, and would have simply insisted that we should withdraw our troops and quit the country?' Of course, the Boer overture, some six weeks after the rejection by Lord Kimberley of the Cape proposal, and after continued military success on the side of the Boers, showed that this supposed practical certainty was the exact reverse of certain.

for a settlement. 'Moments,' he said, 'are precious.' For twelve days these precious moments passed. On Jan. 26 the secretary of state informed the high commissioner at Cape Town, now Sir Hercules Robinson, that President Brand pressed for the offer of terms and conditions to the Boers through Robinson, 'provided they cease from armed opposition, making it clear to them how this is to be understood.' On this suggestion he instructed Robinson to inform Brand that if armed opposition should at once cease, the government 'would thereupon endeavour to frame such a scheme as in their belief would satisfy all friends of the Transvaal community.' Brand promptly advised that the Boers should be told of this forthwith, before the satisfactory arrangements proposed had been made more difficult by further collision. This was on Jan. 29. Unhappily on the very day before, the British force had been repulsed at Laing's Nek. Colley, on Jan. 23, had written to Joubert, calling on the Boer leaders to disperse, informing them that large forces were already arriving from England and India, and assuring them that if they would dismiss their followers, he would forward to London any statement of their grievances. It would have been a great deal more sensible to wait for an answer. Instead of waiting for an answer Colley attacked (Jan. 28) and was beaten back — the whole proceeding a rehearsal of a still more disastrous error a month later.

Brand was now more importunate than ever, earnestly urging on General Colley that the nature of the scheme should be made known to the Boers, and a guarantee undertaken that if they submitted they would not be treated as rebels. 'I have replied,' Colley tells Lord Kimberley, 'that I can give no such assurance, and can add nothing to your words.' In other correspondence he uses grim language about the deserts of some of the leaders. On this Mr. Gladstone, writing to Lord Kimberley (Feb. 5), says truly enough, 'Colley with a vengeance counts his chickens before they are hatched, and his curious letter throws some light backward on the proceedings in India. His line is singularly wide of ours.' The secretary of state, finding barrack-room rigidity out of place, directs Colley (Feb. 8) to inform Brand

that the government would be ready to give all reasonable guarantees as to treatment of Boers after submission,
if they ceased from armed opposition, and a scheme would
be framed for permanent friendly settlement. As it happened, on the day on which this was despatched from
Downing Street, Colley suffered a second check at the
Ingogo River (Feb. 8). Let us note that he was always eager
in his recognition of the readiness and promptitude of the
military support from the government at home.[1]

Then an important move took place from, the other
quarter. The Boers made their first overture. It came
in a letter from Kruger to Colley (Feb. 12). Its purport was fairly summarised by Colley in a telegram to
the colonial secretary, and the pith of it was that Kruger
and his Boers were so certain of the English government
being on their side if the truth only reached them, that they
would not fear the result of inquiry by a royal commission,
and were ready, if troops were ordered to withdraw from the
Transvaal, to retire from their position, and give such a
commission a free passage. This telegram reached London
on Feb. 13th, and on the 15th it was brought before the
cabinet.

Mr. Gladstone immediately informed the Queen (Feb. 15)
that viewing the likelihood of early and sanguinary actions,
Lord Kimberley thought that the receipt of such an overture
at such a juncture, although its terms were inadmissible,
made it a duty to examine whether it afforded any hope of
settlement. The cabinet were still more strongly inclined
towards coming to terms. Any other decision would have
broken up the government, for on at least one division in the
House on Transvaal affairs Mr. Bright and Mr. Chamberlain,
along with three other ministers not in the cabinet, had
abstained from voting. Colley was directed (Feb. 16)
to inform the Boers that on their desisting from armed
opposition, the government would be ready to send com-

---

[1] 'I do not know whether I am indebted to you or to Mr. Childers or to both, for the continuance of H.M.'s confidence, but I shall always feel more deeply grateful than I can express; and can never forget H.M.'s gracious message of encouragement at a time of great trouble.' — Colley to Kimberley, Jan. 31, 1881.

missioners to develop a scheme of settlement, and that meanwhile if this proposal were accepted, the English general
was authorised to agree to the suspension of hostilities.
This was in substance a conditional acceptance of the Boer
overture.[1] On the same day the general was told from the
war office that, as respected the interval before receiving a
reply from Mr. Kruger, the government did not bind his
discretion, but ' we are anxious for your making arrangements to avoid effusion of blood.' The spirit of these instructions was clear. A week later (Feb. 23) the general showed
that he understood this, for he wrote to Mr. Childers that
' he would not without strong reason undertake any operation likely to bring on another engagement, until Kruger's
reply was received.'[2] If he had only stood firm to this, a
tragedy would have been averted.

On receiving the telegram of Feb. 16, Colley was puzzled
to know what was the meaning of suspending hostilities if
armed opposition were abandoned by the Boers, and he asked
the plain question (Feb. 19) whether he was to leave Laing's
Nek (which was in Natal territory) in Boer occupation, and
our garrisons isolated and short of provisions, or was he
to occupy Laing's Nek and relieve the garrisons. Colley's in-
quiries were instantly considered by the cabinet, and the reply
settled. The garrisons were to be free to provision themselves and peaceful intercourse allowed; ' but,' Kimberley
tells Colley, ' we do not mean that you should march to
the relief of garrisons or occupy Laing's Nek, if the arrangement proceeds. *Fix reasonable time within which answer
must be sent by Boers.'*

On Feb. 21 Colley despatched a letter to Kruger, stating
that on the Boers ceasing from armed opposition, the Queen
would appoint a commission. He added that ' upon this
proposal being accepted *within forty-eight hours from the
receipt of this letter,*' he was authorised to agree to a suspension of hostilities on the part of the British.

---

[1] ' The directions to Colley,' says
Mr. Bright in a cabinet minute, ' intended to convey the offer of a suspension of hostilities on both sides,
with a proposal that a commissioner
should be appointed to enter into
negotiations and arrangements with
a view to peace.'
[2] *Life of Childers*, ii. p. 24.

V

In this interval a calamity, destined to be historic, occurred, trivial in a military sense, but formidable for many years to come in the issues moral and political that it raised, and in the passions for which it became a burning watchword. On the night of Feb. 26, Colley with a force of 359 men all told, made up of three different corps, marched out of his camp and occupied Majuba Hill. The general's motives for this precipitancy are obscure. The best explanation seems to be that he observed the Boers to be pushing gradually forward on to advanced ground, and thought it well, without waiting for Kruger's reply, to seize a height lying between the Nek and his own little camp, the possession of which would make Laing's Nek untenable. He probably did not expect that his move would necessarily lead to fighting, and in fact when they saw the height occupied, the Boers did at first for a little time actually begin to retire from the Nek, though they soon changed their minds.[1] The British operation is held by military experts to have been rash; proper steps were not taken by the general to protect himself upon Majuba, the men were not well handled, and the Boers showed determined intrepidity as they climbed steadily up the hill from platform to platform, taking from seven in the morning (Feb. 27) up to half-past eleven to advance some three thousand yards and not losing a man, until at last they scaled the crest and poured a deadly fire upon the small British force, driving them headlong from the summit, seasoned soldiers though most of them were. The general who was responsible for the disaster paid the penalty with his life. Some ninety others fell and sixty were taken prisoners.

At home the sensation was profound. The hysterical complaints about our men and officers, General Wood wrote to Childers, 'are more like French character than English used to be.' Mr. Gladstone and his colleagues had a political question to consider. Colley could not be technically accused of want of good faith in moving forward on the 26th, as the

[1] Colley's letter to Childers, Feb. 23, *Life of Childers*, ii. p. 24.

time that he had appointed had expired. But though Majuba is just inside Natal — some four miles over the border — his advance was, under the circumstances of the moment, essentially an aggressive movement. Could his defeat justify us in withdrawing our previous proposals to the Boers? Was a military miscarriage, of no magnitude in itself, to be turned into a plea for abandoning a policy deliberately adopted for what were thought powerful and decisive reasons? 'Suppose, for argument's sake,' Mr. Gladstone wrote to Lord Kimberley when the sinister news arrived (Mar. 2), 'that at the moment when Colley made the unhappy attack on Majuba Hill, there shall turn out to have been decided on, and possibly on its way, a satisfactory or friendly reply from the Boer government to your telegram? I fear the chances may be against this; but if it prove to be the case, we could not because we had failed on Sunday last, insist on shedding more blood.' As it happened, the Boer answer was decided on before the attack at Majuba, and was sent to Colley by Kruger at Heidelberg in ignorance of the event, the day after the ill-fated general's death. The members of the Transvaal government set out their gratitude for the declaration that under certain conditions the government of the Queen was inclined to cease hostilities; and expressed their opinion that a meeting of representatives from both sides would probably lead with all speed to a satisfactory result. This reply was despatched by Kruger on the day on which Colley's letter of the 21st came into his hands (Feb. 28), and it reached Colley's successor on March 7.

Sir Evelyn Wood, now after the death of Colley in chief command, throughout recommended military action. Considering the disasters we had sustained, he thought the happiest result would be that after a successful battle, which he hoped to fight in about a fortnight, the Boers would disperse without any guarantee, and many now in the field against their will would readily settle down. He explained that by happy result, he did not mean that a series of actions fought by any six companies could affect our military prestige, but that a British victory would enable the Boer leaders to quench a fire that had got beyond their control. The next day after this recommendation to fight (March 6), he, of his own motion, accepted a proposal telegraphed from Joubert at the instigation of the indefatigable Brand, for a suspension of hostilities for eight days, for the purpose of receiving Kruger's reply. There was a military reason behind. General Wood knew that the garrison in Potchefstrom must surrender unless the place were revictualled, and three other beleaguered garrisons were in almost equal danger. The government at once told him that his armistice was approved. This armistice, though Wood's reasons were military rather than diplomatic, virtually put a stop to suggestions for further fighting, for it implied, and could in truth mean nothing else, that if Kruger's reply were promising, the next step would not be a fight, but the continuance of negotiation. Sir Evelyn Wood had not advised a fight for the sake of restoring military prestige, but to make it easier for the Boer leaders to break up bands that were getting beyond their control. There was also present in his mind the intention, if the government would sanction it, of driving the Boers out of Natal, as soon as ever he had got his men up across the swollen river. So far from sanctioning it, the government expressly forbade him to take offensive action. On March 8, General Wood telegraphed home: 'Do not imagine I wish to fight. I know the attending misery too well. But now you have so many troops coming, I recommend decisive though lenient action; and I can, humanly speaking, promise victory. Sir G. Colley never engaged more than six companies. I shall use twenty and two regiments of cavalry in direction known to myself only, and undertake to enforce dispersion.' This then was General Wood's view. On the day before he sent this telegram, the general already had received Kruger's reply to the effect that they were anxious to negotiate, and it would be best for commissioners from the two sides to meet. It is important to add that the government were at the same time receiving urgent warnings from President Brand that Dutch sympathy, both in the Cape Colony and in the Orange Free State, with the Dutch in the Transvaal was growing dangerous, and that the prolongation of hostilities would end in a formidable extension of their area.[1] Even in January Lanyon had told Colley that men from the Free State were in the field against him. Three days before Majuba, Lord Kimberley had written to Colley (February 24), ' My great fear has been lest the Free State should take part against us, or even some movement take place in the Cape Colony. If our willingness to come to terms has avoided such a calamity, I shall consider it will have been a most important point gained.' [2]

Two memoranda for the Queen show the views of the cabinet on the new position of affairs : —

To the Queen.

March 8, 1881. — The cabinet considered with much care the terms of the reply to Sir Evelyn Wood's telegram reporting (not textually) the answer of the Boer leaders to the proposals which Sir George Colley had sent to them. They felt justified in construing the Boer answer as leaving the way open to the appointment of commissioners, according to the telegram previously seen and approved by your Majesty. They were anxious to keep the question moving in this direction, and under the extreme urgency of the circumstances as to time, they have despatched a telegram to Sir Evelyn Wood accordingly. Mr. Gladstone has always urged, and still feels, that the proposal of the Boers for the appointment of commissioners was fortunate on this among other grounds, that it involved a recognition of your Majesty's *de facto* authority in the Transvaal.

March 12. — The cabinet determined, in order to obviate misapprehension or suspicion, to desire Sir E. Wood to inform the government from what quarter the suggestion of an armistice

---

[1] See Selborne's *Memorials*, ii. p. 3, and also a speech by Lord Kimberley at Newcastle, Nov. 14, 1899.

[2] In a speech at Edinburgh (Sept. 1, 1884), Mr. Gladstone put the same argument — ' The people of the Transvaal, few in number, were in close and strong sympathy with their brethren in race, language, and religion. Throughout South Africa these men, partly British subjects and partly not, were as one man associated in feeling with the people of the Transvaal ; and had we persisted in that dishonourable attempt, against all our own interests, to coerce the Transvaal as we attempted to coerce Afghanistan, we should have had the whole mass of the Dutch population at the Cape and throughout South Africa rising in arms against us.'

actually proceeded. They agreed that the proper persons to be CHAP.
appointed as commissioners were Sir H. Robinson, Sir E. Wood, III.
and Mr. De Villiers, chief justice of the Cape; together with Mr. Æт. 72.
Brand of the Free State as *amicus curiæ*, should he be willing to
lend his good offices in the spirit in which he has hitherto acted.
The cabinet then considered fully the terms of the communication
to be made to the Boers by Sir E. Wood. In this, which is matter
of extreme urgency, they prescribe a time for the reply of the
Boers not later than the 18th; renew the promise of amnesty;
require the dispersion of the Boers to their own homes; and state
the general outlines of the permanent arrangement which they
would propose for the territory. . . . The cabinet believe that in
requiring the dispersion of the Boers to their homes, they will have
made the necessary provision for the vindication of your Majesty's
anthority, so as to open the way for considering terms of pacific
settlement.

On March 22, under instructions from home, the general
concluded an agreement for peace. The Boers made some
preliminary requests to which the government declined to
assent. Their proposal that the commission should be joint
was rejected; its members were named exclusively by the
crown. They agreed to withdraw from the Nek and disperse
to their homes; we agreed not to occupy the Nek, and not
to follow them up with troops, though General Roberts with
a large force had sailed for the Cape on March 6. Then the
political negotiation went forward. Would it have been wise,
as the question was well put by the Duke of Argyll (not then
a member of the government), 'to stop the negotiation for
the sake of defeating a body of farmers who had succeeded
under accidental circumstances and by great rashness on
the part of our commanders, in gaining a victory over us?'
This was the true point.

The parliamentary attack was severe. The galling
argument was that government had conceded to three
defeats what they had refused to ten times as many
petitions, memorials, remonstrances; and we had given to
men with arms in their hands what we refused to their
peaceful prayers. A great lawyer in the House of Lords made

the speech that is expected from a great lawyer who is
also a conspicuous party leader; and ministers undoubtedly
exposed an extent of surface that was not easy to defend,
not because they had made a peace, but because they had
failed to prevent the rising. High military authorities
found a curious plea for going on, in the fact that this was
our first contest with Europeans since the breech-loader
came in, and it was desirable to give our troops confidence
in the new-fashioned weapon. Reasons of a very different
sort from this were needed to overthrow the case for peace.
How could the miscarriage at Majuba, brought on by our
own action, warrant us in drawing back from an engagement already deliberately proffered? Would not such a
proceeding, asked Lord Kimberley, have been little short
of an act of bad faith? Or were we, in Mr. Gladstone's
language, to say to the Boers, 'Although we might have
treated with you before these military miscarriages, we
cannot do so now, until we offer up a certain number of
victims in expiation of the blood that has been shed. Until
that has been done, the very things which we believed
before to be reasonable, which we were ready to discuss
with you, we refuse to discuss now, and we must wait until
Moloch has been appeased'? We had opened a door for
negotiation; were we to close it again, because a handful
of our forces had rashly seized a post they could not hold?
The action of the Boers had been defensive of the *status quo*,
for if we had established ourselves on Majuba, their camp
at Laing's Nek would have been untenable. The minister
protested in the face of the House of Commons that 'it would
have been most unjust and cruel, it would have been cowardly
and mean, if on account of these defensive operations we
had refused to go forward with the negotiations which, before
the first of these miscarriages had occurred, we had already
declared that we were willing to promote and undertake.'[1]

The policy of the reversal of annexation is likely to remain
a topic of endless dispute.[2] As Sir Hercules Robinson put

[1] July 25, 1881.
[2] One of the most determined
enemies of the government in 1881,
ten years later, in a visit to South
Africa, changed his mind. 'The
Dutch sentiment in the Cape Colony,'
wrote Lord Randolph Churchill, 'had
been so exasperated by what it con-

it in a letter to Lord Kimberley, written a week before
Majuba (Feb. 21), no possible course was free from grave
objection. If you determine, he said, to hold by the annexation of the Transvaal, the country would have to be conquered and held in subjection for many years by a large
force. Free institutions and self-government under British
rule would be an impossibility. The only palliative would
be to dilute Dutch feeling by extensive English immigration, like that of 1820 to the Eastern Province. But that
would take time, and need careful watching; and in the
meantime the result of holding the Transvaal as a conquered colony would undoubtedly be to excite bitter hatred
between the English and Dutch throughout the Free State
and this colony, which would be a constant source of dis-
comfort and danger. On the other hand, he believed that
if they were, after a series of reverses and before any success,
to yield all the Boers asked for, they would be so overbearing
and quarrelsome that we should soon be at war with them
again. On the whole, Sir Hercules was disposed to think —
extraordinary as such a view must appear — that the best plan
would be to re-establish the supremacy of our arms, and
then let the malcontents go. He thought no middle course
any longer practicable. Yet surely this course was open to
all the objections. To hold on to annexation at any cost was
intelligible. But to face all the cost and all the risks of a
prolonged and a widely extended conflict, with the deliberate
intention of allowing the enemy to have his own way after
the conflict had been brought to an end, was not intelligible
and was not defensible.

Some have argued that we ought to have brought up an
overwhelming force, to demonstrate that we were able to
beat them, before we made peace. Unfortunately demonstrations of this species easily turn into provocations, and
talk of this kind mostly comes from those who believe, not

sidered the unjust, faithless, and
arbitrary policy pursued towards the
free Dutchmen of the Transvaal by
Frere, Shepstone, and Lanyon, that
the final triumph of the British arms,
mainly by brute force, would have
permanently and hopelessly alienated
it from Great Britain. . . . On the
whole, I find myself free to confess,
and without reluctance to admit,
that' the English escaped from a
wretched and discreditable muddle,
not without harm and damage, but
perhaps in the best possible manner.'

that peace was made in the wrong way, but that a peace giving their country back to the Boers ought never to have been made at all, on any terms or in any way. This was not the point from which either cabinet or parliament started. The government had decided that annexation had been an error. The Boers had proposed inquiry. The government assented on condition that the Boers dispersed. Without waiting a reasonable time for a reply, our general was worsted in a rash and trivial attack. Did this cancel our proffered bargain? The point was simple and unmistakable, though party heat at home, race passion in the colony, and our everlasting human proneness to mix up different questions, and to answer one point by arguments that belong to another, all combined to produce a confusion of mind that a certain school of partisans have traded upon ever since. Strange in mighty nations is moral cowardice, disguised as a Roman pride. All the more may we admire the moral courage of the minister. For moral courage may be needed even where aversion to bloodshed fortunately happens to coincide with high prudence and sound policy of state.

VI

The negotiations proceeded, if negotiation be the right word. The Boers disbanded, a powerful British force was encamped on the frontier, no Boer representative sat on the commission, and the terms of final agreement were in fact, as the Boers afterwards alleged, dictated and imposed. Mr. Gladstone watched with a closeness that, considering the tremendous load of Ireland, parliamentary procedure, and the incessant general business of a prime minister, is amazing. When the Boers were over-pressing, he warned them that it was only 'the unshorn strength' of the administration that enabled the English cabinet, rather to the surprise of the world, to spare them the sufferings of a war. 'We could not,' he said to Lord Kimberley, 'have carried our Transvaal policy, unless we had here a strong government, and we spent some, if not much, of our strength in carrying it.' A convention was concluded at Pretoria in

August, recognising the quasi-independence of the Trans- CHAP. III.
vaal, subject to the suzerainty of the Queen, and with
certain specified reservations. The Pretoria convention of Æt. 72.
1881 did not work smoothly. Transvaal affairs were discussed
from time to time in the cabinet, and Mr. Chamberlain became the spokesman of the government on a business where
he was destined many years after to make so conspicuous
and irreparable a mark. The Boers again sent Kruger
to London, and he made out a good enough case in the
opinion of Lord Derby, then secretary of state, to justify
a fresh arrangement. By the London convention of 1884,
the Transvaal state was restored to its old title of the South
African Republic; the assertion of suzerainty in the preamble
of the old convention did not appear in the new one;[1] and
various other modifications were introduced — the most
important of them, in the light of later events, being a
provision for white men to have full liberty to reside in any
part of the republic, to trade in it, and to be liable to the
same taxes only as those exacted from citizens of the
republic.

Whether we look at the Sand River Convention in 1852,
which conferred independence; or at Shepstone's proclamation in 1877, which took independence away; or at the convention of Pretoria in 1881, which in a qualified shape gave
it back; or at the convention of London in 1884, which qualified the qualification over again, till independence, subject to
two or three specified conditions, was restored, — we can but
recall the caustic apologue of sage Selden in his table-talk on

---

[1] 'I apprehend, whether you call it a Protectorate, or a Suzerainty, or the recognition of England as a Paramount Power, the fact is that a certain controlling power is retained when the state which exercises this suzerainty has a right to veto any negotiations into which the dependent state may enter with foreign powers. Whatever suzerainty meant in the Convention of Pretoria, the condition of things which it implied still remains; although the word is not actually employed, we have kept the substance. We have abstained from using the word because it was not capable of legal definition, and because it seemed to be a word which was likely to lead to misconception and misunderstanding.' — *Lord Derby in the House of Lords*, March 17, 1884. I do not desire to multiply points of controversy, but the ill-starred raising of the ghost of suzerainty in 1897–9 calls for the twofold remark that the preamble was struck out by Lord Derby's own hand, and that alike when Lord Knutsford and Lord Ripon were at the colonial office, answers were given in the House of Commons practically admitting that no claim of suzerainty could be put forward.

contracts. 'Lady Kent,' he says, 'articled with Sir Edward Herbert that he should come to her when she sent for him, and stay with her as long as she would have him; to which he set his hand. Then he articled with her that he should go away when he pleased, and stay away as long as he pleased; to which she set her hand. This is the epitome of all the contracts in the world, betwixt man and man, betwixt prince and subject.'

CHAPTER IV

NEW PHASES OF THE IRISH REVOLUTION

(*1880–1882*)

THE agitation of the Irish land league strikes at the roots of all contract, and therefore at the very foundations of modern society ; but if we would effectually withstand it, we must cease to insist on maintaining the forms of free contract where the reality is impossible. — T. H. GREEN.[1]

ON the day in 1880 when Lord Beaconsfield was finally quitting the official house in Downing Street, one who had been the ablest and most zealous supporter of his policy in the press, called to bid him good-bye. The visitor talked gloomily of the national prospect ; of difficulties with Austria, with Russia, with the Turk ; of the confusions to come upon Europe from the doctrines of Midlothian. The fallen minister listened. Then looking at his friend, he uttered in deep tones a single word. '*Ireland!*' he said.

In a speech made in 1882 Mr. Gladstone put the case to the House of Commons : —

The government had to deal with a state of things in Ireland entirely different from any that had been known there for fifty years. . . . With a political revolution we have ample strength to cope. There is no reason why our cheeks should grow pale, or why our hearts should sink, at the idea of grappling with a political revolution. The strength of this country is tenfold what is required for such a purpose. But a social revolution is a very different matter. . . . The seat and source of the movement was not to be found during the time the government was in power. It is to be looked for in the foundation of the land league.[2]

Two years later he said at Edinburgh : —

I frankly admit I had had much upon my hands connected with

---

[1] *Works of T. H. Green*, iii. 382.　　[2] House of Commons, April 4, 1882.

47

the doings of the Beaconsfield government in almost every quarter of the world, and I did not know, no one knew, the severity of the crisis that was already swelling upon the horizon, and that shortly after rushed upon us like a flood.[1]

So came upon them by degrees the predominance of Irish affairs and Irish activity in the parliament of 1880, which had been chosen without much reference to Ireland.

II

A social revolution with the land league for its organ in Ireland, and Mr. Parnell and his party for its organ in parliament, now, in Mr. Gladstone's words, rushed upon him and his government like a flood. The mind of the country was violently drawn from Dulcigno and Thessaly, from Batoum and Erzeroum, from the wild squalor of Macedonia and Armenia to squalor not less wild in Connaught and Munster, in Mayo, Galway, Sligo, Kerry. Agrarian agitation on the one hand, parliamentary violence on the other, were the two potent weapons by which the Irish revolutionary leader assailed the misrule of the British garrison as the agents of the British parliament in his country. This formidable movement slowly unmasked itself. The Irish government, represented by Mr. Forster in the cabinet, began by allowing the law conferring exceptional powers upon the executive to lapse. The main reason was want of time to pass a fresh Act. In view of the undoubted distress in some parts of Ireland, and of the harshness of certain evictions, the government further persuaded the House of Commons to pass a bill for compensating an evicted tenant on certain conditions, if the landlord turned him out of his holding. The bill was no easy dose either for the cabinet or its friends. Lord Lansdowne stirred much commotion by retiring from the government, and landowners and capitalists were full of consternation. At least one member of the cabinet was profoundly uneasy. It is impossible to read the letters of the Duke of Argyll to Mr. Gladstone on land, church establishment, the Zulu war, without wondering on what theory a cabinet was formed that included him, able and

[1] Edinburgh, Sept. 1, 1884.

upright as he was, along with radicals like Mr. Chamberlain. Before the cabinet was six months old the duke was plucking Mr. Gladstone's sleeve with some vivacity at the Birmingham language on Irish land. Mr. Parnell in the committee stage abstained from supporting the measure, sixteen liberals voted against the third reading, and the House of Lords, in which nationalist Ireland had not a single representative, threw out the bill by a majority of 282 against 51. It was said that if all the opposition peers had stayed away, still ministers would have been beaten by their own supporters.

Looking back upon these events, Mr. Gladstone set out in a memorandum of later years, that during the session of 1880 the details of the budget gave him a good deal to do, while the absorbing nature of foreign questions before and after his accession to office had withdrawn his attention from his own Land Act of 1870 : [1] —

Late in the session came the decisive and disastrous rejection by the House of Lords of the bill by means of which the government had hoped to arrest the progress of disorder, and avert the necessity for measures in the direction of coercion. The rapid and vast extension of agrarian disturbance followed, as was to be expected, this wild excess of landlordism, and the Irish government proceeded to warn the cabinet that coercive legislation would be necessary.

Forster allowed himself to be persuaded by the governmental agents in Ireland that the root of the evil lay within small compass; that there were in the several parishes a certain limited number of unreasonable and mischievous men, that these men were known to the police, and that if summary powers were confided to the Irish government, by the exercise of which these objectionable persons might be removed, the evil would die out of itself. I must say I never fell into this extraordinary illusion of Forster's about his 'village ruffian.' But he was a very impracticable man placed in a position of great responsibility. He was set upon a method of legislation adapted to the erroneous belief that the mischief lay only with a very limited number of well-known individuals, that is to say, the suspension of the Habeas Corpus

[1] See vol. ii. book vi. chap. ii.

Act. . . . Two points of difference arose: first, as to the nature of the coercion to be used; secondly, as to its time. I insisted that we were bound to try what we could do against Parnell under the existing law, before asking for extraordinary powers. Both Bright and Chamberlain, if I remember right, did very good service in protesting against haste, and resisting Forster's desire to anticipate the ordinary session for the purpose of obtaining coercive powers. When, however, the argument of time was exhausted by the Parnell trial[1] and otherwise, I obtained no support from them in regard to the kind of coercion we were to ask. I considered it should be done by giving stringency to the existing law, but not by abolishing the right to be tried before being imprisoned. I felt the pulse of various members of the cabinet, among whom I seem to recollect Kimberley and Carlingford, but I could obtain no sympathy, and to my dismay both Chamberlain and Bright arrived at the conclusion that if there was to be coercion at all, which they lamented, there was something simple 'and effective in the suspension of the Habeas Corpus Act which made such a method preferable to others.[2] I finally acquiesced. It may be asked why? My resistance would have broken up the government or involved my own retirement. My reason for acquiescence was that I bore in mind the special commission under which the government had taken office. It related to the foreign policy of the country, the whole spirit and effect of which we were to reconstruct. This work had not yet been fully accomplished, and it seemed to me that the effective prosecution of it was our first and highest duty. I therefore submitted.

By the end of November Mr. Gladstone explained to the Queen that the state of Ireland was menacing; its distinctive character was not so much that of general insecurity of life, as that of a widespread conspiracy against property. The worst of it was, he said, that the leaders, unlike O'Connell, failed to denounce crime. The outbreak was not comparable to that of 1832. In 1879 homicides were 64 against 242 for the earlier year of disturbance. But things were bad enough.

[1] Proceedings had been instituted in the Dublin courts against Parnell and others for seditious conspiracy. The jury were unable to agree on a verdict.

[2] Tried by Lord Spencer in Westmeath in 1871, it had been successful, but the area of disturbance was there comparatively insignificant.

In Galway they had a policeman for every forty-seven adult males, and a soldier for every ninety-seven. Yet dangerous terrorism was rampant. 'During more than thirty-seven years since I first entered a cabinet,' Mr. Gladstone told the Speaker (November 25), 'I have hardly known so difficult a question of administration, as that of the immediate duty of the government in the present state of Ireland. The multitude of circumstances to be taken into account must strike every observer. Among these stand the novelty of the suspension of Habeas Corpus in a case of agrarian crime stimulated by a public society, and the rather serious difficulty of obtaining it ; but more important than these is the grave doubt whether it would really reach the great characteristic evil of the time, namely, the paralysis of most important civil and proprietary rights, and whether the immediate proposal of a remedy, probably ineffective and even in a coercive sense partial, would not seriously damage the prospects of that arduous and comprehensive task which without doubt we must undertake when parliament is summoned.' In view of considerations of this kind, the awkwardness of directing an Act of parliament virtually against leaders who were at the moment the object of indictment in the Irish law courts ; difficulties of time ; doubts as to the case being really made out; doubts as to the efficacy of the proposed remedy, Mr. Forster did not carry the cabinet, but agreed to continue the experiment of the ordinary law. The experiment was no success, and coercion accompanied by land reform became the urgent policy.

III

The opening of the session of 1881 at once brought obstruction into full view. The Irish took up their position as a party of action. They spoke incessantly ; as Mr. Gladstone put it, 'sometimes rising to the level of mediocrity, and more often grovelling amidst mere trash in unbounded profusion.' Obstruction is obstruction all the world over. It was not quite new at Westminster, but it was new on this scale. Closure proposals sprang up like mushrooms. Liberal members with a historical bent ran privately to the Speaker with

ancient precedents of dictatorial powers asserted by his
official ancestors, and they exhorted him to revive them.

Mr. Forster brought in his bill. Its scope may be described in a sentence. It practically enabled the viceroy
to lock up anybody he pleased, and to detain him as long as
he pleased, while the Act remained in force.[1] The debate for
leave to introduce the bill lasted several days, without any
sign of coming to an end. Here is the Speaker's account
of his own memorable act in forcing a close : —

Monday, Jan. 31.—The House was boiling over with indignation
at the apparent triumph of obstruction, and Mr. G., yielding to
the pressure of his friends, committed himself unwisely, as I
thought, to a continuous sitting on this day in order to force the
bill through its first stage.

On Tuesday, after a sitting of twenty-four hours, I saw plainly
that this attempt to carry the bill by continuous sitting would
fail, the Parnell party being strong in numbers, discipline, and
organisation, and with great gifts of speech. I reflected on the
situation, and came to the conclusion that it was my duty to
extricate the House from the difficulty by closing the debate of my
own authority, and so asserting the undoubted will of the House
against a rebellious minority. I sent for Mr. G. on Tuesday
(Feb. 1), about noon, and told him that I should be prepared
to put the question in spite of obstruction on the following
conditions: 1. That the debate should be carried on until the
following morning, my object in this delay being to mark distinctly to the outside world the extreme gravity of the situation,
and the necessity of the step which I was about to take. 2. That
he should reconsider the regulation of business, either by giving
more authority to the House, or by conferring authority on the
Speaker.

He agreed to these conditions, and summoned a meeting of the
cabinet, which assembled in my library at four P.M. on Tuesday
while the House was sitting, and I was in the chair. At that
meeting the resolution as to business assumed the shape in which
it finally appeared on the following Thursday, it having been pre-

[1] For a plain and precise description of the Coercion Act of 1881, see
Dicey's *Law of the Constitution*, pp. 243–8.

viously considered at former meetings of the cabinet. I arranged
with Playfair to take the chair on Tuesday night about midnight,
engaging to resume it on Wednesday morning at nine. Accordingly at nine I took the chair, Biggar being in possession of the
House. I rose, and he resumed his seat. I proceeded with my
address as concerted with May, and when I had concluded I put
the question. The scene was most dramatic; but all passed off
without disturbance, the Irish party on the second division retiring
under protest.

I had communicated, with Mr. G.'s approval, my intention to
close the debate to Northcote, but to no one else, except May,
from whom I received much assistance. Northcote was startled,
but expressed no disapproval of the course proposed.

So ended the memorable sitting of January 31. At noon,
on February 2, the House assembled in much excitement.
The question was put challenging the Speaker's conduct.
'I answered,' he says, 'on the spur of the moment that I had
acted on my own responsibility, and from a sense of duty to
the House. I never heard such loud and protracted cheering, none cheering more loudly than Gladstone.' 'The
Speaker's firmness in mind,' Mr. Gladstone reported to the
Queen, 'his suavity in manner, his unwearied patience, his
incomparable temper, under a thousand provocations, have
rendered possible a really important result.'

IV

After coercion came a land bill, and here Mr. Gladstone
once more displayed his unequalled mastery of legislative
skill and power. He had to explain and be ready to
explain again and again, what he told Lord Selborne was
'the most difficult measure he had ever known to come
under the detailed consideration of a cabinet.' It was
no affair this time of speeches out of a railway carriage,
or addressed to excited multitudes in vast halls. That
might be, if you so pleased, 'the empty verbosity of exu-
berant rhetoric'; but nobody could say that of the contest
over the complexities of Irish tenure, against the clever and
indomitable Irish experts who fought under the banner of
Mr. Parnell. Northcote was not far wrong when he said

that though the bill was carried by two to one, there was hardly a man in the House beyond the Irish ranks who cared a straw about it.   Another critic said that if the prime minister had asked the House to pass the *Koran* or the *Nautical Almanac* as a land bill, he would have met no difficulty.

The history of the session was described as the carriage of a single measure by a single man.   Few British members understood it, none mastered it.   The whigs were disaffected about it, the radicals doubted it, the tories thought that property as a principle was ruined by it, the Irishmen, when the humour seized them, bade him send the bill to line trunks.   Mr. Gladstone, as one observer truly says, 'faced difficulties such as no other bill of this country has ever encountered, difficulties of politics and difficulties of law, difficulties of principle and difficulties of detail, difficulties of party and difficulties of personnel, difficulties of race and difficulties of class, and he has never once failed, or even seemed to fail, in his clear command of the question, in his dignity and authority of demeanour, in his impartiality in accepting amending suggestions, in his firmness in resisting destructive suggestions, in his clear perception of his aim, and his strong grasp of the fitting means.   And yet it is hardly possible to appreciate adequately the embarrassments of the situation.'

Enough has already been said of the legislation of 1870, and its establishment of the principle that Irish land is not the subject of an undivided ownership, but a partnership.[1] The act of 1870 failed because it had too many exceptions and limitations; because in administration the compensation to the tenant for disturbance was inadequate; and because it did not fix the cultivator in his holding.   Things had now ripened.   The Richmond Commission shortly before had pointed to a court for fixing rents; that is, for settling the terms of the partnership.   A commission nominated by Mr. Gladstone and presided over by Lord Bessborough had reported early in 1881 in favour not only of fair rents to be settled by a tribunal, but of fixity of tenure or the right of

1 See vol. ii. p. 284.

the tenant to remain in his holding if he paid his rent, and
of free sale ; that is, his right to part with his interest. These
' three F's ' were the substance of the legislation of 1881.

Rents could not be paid, and landlords either would not
or could not reduce them. In the deepest interests of social
order, and in confirmation of the tenant's equitable and
customary ownership, the only course open to the imperial
legislature was to erect machinery for fixing fair rents.
The alternative to what became matter of much objurgation
as dual ownership, was a single ownership that was only a
short name for allowing the landlord to deal as he liked
with the equitable interest of the tenant. Without the
machinery set up by Mr. Gladstone, there could be no
security for the protection of the cultivator's interest.
What is more, even in view of a wide and general extension
of the policy of buying out the landlord and turning the
tenant into single owner, still a process of valuation for
purposes of fair price would have been just as indispensable,
as under the existing system was the tiresome and costly
process of valuation for purposes of fair rent. It is true
that if the policy of purchase had been adopted, this process
would have been performed once for all. But opinion was
not nearly ready either in England or Ireland for general
purchase. And as Mr. Gladstone had put it to Bright in
1870, to turn a little handful of occupiers into owners would
not have touched the fringe of the case of the bulk of the
Irish cultivators, then undergoing acute mischief and urgently
crying for prompt relief. Mr. Bright's idea of purchase,
moreover, assumed that the buyer would come with at least
a quarter of the price in his hand, — an assumption not consistent with the practical possibilities of the case.

The legislation of 1881 no doubt encountered angry
criticism from the English conservative, and little more
than frigid approval from the Irish nationalist. It offended
the fundamental principle of the landlords ; its administration and the construction of some of its leading provisions
by the courts disappointed and irritated the tenant party.
Nevertheless any attempt in later times to impair the
authority of the Land Act of 1881 brought the fact instantly

to light, that the tenant knew it to be the fundamental charter of his redemption from worse than Egyptian bondage. In measuring this great agrarian law, not only by parliamentary force and legislative skill and power, but by the vast and abiding depth of its social results, both direct and still more indirect, many will be disposed to give it the highest place among Mr. Gladstone's achievements as lawmaker.

Fault has sometimes been found with Mr. Gladstone for not introducing his bill in the session of 1880. If this had been done, it is argued, Ireland would have been appeased, no coercion would have been necessary, and we should have been spared disastrous parliamentary exasperations and all the other mischiefs and perils of the quarrel between England and Ireland that followed. Criticism of this kind overlooks three facts. Neither Mr. Gladstone nor Forster nor the new House of Commons was at all ready in 1880 to accept the Three F's. Second, the Bessborough commission had not taken its evidence, and made its momentous report. Third, this argument assumes motives in Mr. Parnell, that probably do not at all cover the whole ground of his policy. As it happened, I called on Mr. Gladstone one morning early in 1881. 'You have heard,' I asked, 'that the Bessborough commission are to report for the Three F's ? ' ' I have not heard,' he said; ' it is incredible ! ' As so often comes to pass in politics, it was only a step from the incredible to the indispensable. But in 1880 the indispensable was also the impossible. It was the cruel winter of 1880–1 that made much difference.

In point of endurance the session was one of the most remarkable on record. The House of Commons sat 154 days and for 1400 hours; some 240 of these hours were after midnight. Only three times since the Reform bill had the House sat for more days; only once, in 1847, had the total number of hours been exceeded and that only by seven, and never before had the House sat so many hours after midnight. On the Coercion bill the House sat continuously once for 22 hours, and once for 41. The debates on the Land bill took up 58 sittings, and the Coercion bill 22. No such length of discussion, Mr. Gladstone told the Queen,

was recorded on any measure since the committee on the CHAP.
first Reform bill. The Reform bill of 1867 was the only IV.
measure since 1843 that took as many as 35 days of debate. Æt. 72.
The Irish Church bill took 21 days and the Land bill of
1870 took 25. Of the 14,836 speeches delivered, 6315 were
made by Irish members. The Speaker and chairman of
committees interposed on points of order nearly 2000 times
during the session. Mr. Parnell, the Speaker notes, 'with
his minority of 24 dominates the House. When will the
House take courage and reform its procedure?' After all,
the suspension of *habeas corpus* is a thing that men may well
think it worth while to fight about, and a revolution in a
country's land-system might be expected to take up a good
deal of time.

V

It soon appeared that no miracle had been wrought by
either Coercion Act or Land Act. Mr. Parnell drew up test
cases for submission to the new land court. His advice to
the army of tenants would depend, he said, on the fate of
these cases. In September Mr. Forster visited Hawarden,
and gave a bad account of the real meaning of Mr. Parnell's
plausible propositions for sending test cases to the newly
established land commission, as well as of other ugly circumstances. ' It is quite clear as you said,' wrote Mr. Gladstone
to Forster in Ireland, 'that Parnell means to present cases
which the commission must refuse, and then to treat their
refusal as showing that they cannot be trusted, and that the
bill has failed.' As he interpreted it afterwards, there was
no doubt that in one sense the Land Act tended to accelerate
a crisis in Ireland, for it brought to a head the affairs of the
party connected with the land league. It made it almost a
necessity for that party either to advance or to recede. They
chose the desperate course. At the same date, he wrote in a
letter to Lord Granville: —

With respect to Parnellism, I should not propose to do more
than a severe and strong denunciation of it by severing him
altogether from the Irish people and the mass of the Irish
members, and by saying that home rule has for one of its aims

local government — an excellent thing to which I would affix no limits except the supremacy of the imperial parliament, and the rights of all parts of the country to claim whatever might be accorded to Ireland. This is only a repetition of what I have often said before, and I have nothing to add or enlarge. But I have the fear that when the occasion for action comes, which will not be in my time, many liberals may perhaps hang back and may cause further trouble.

In view of what was to come four years later, one of his letters to Forster is interesting (April 12, 1882), among other reasons as illustrating the depth to which the essence of political liberalism had now penetrated Mr. Gladstone's mind : —

1. About local government for Ireland, the ideas which more and more establish themselves in my mind are such as these.

(1.) Until we have seriously responsible bodies to deal with us in Ireland, every plan we frame comes to Irishmen, say what we may, as an English plan. As such it is probably condemned. At best it is a one-sided bargain, which binds us, not them.

(2.) If your excellent plans for obtaining local aid towards the execution of the law break down, it will be on account of this miserable and almost total want of the sense of responsibility for the public good and public peace in Ireland; and this responsibility we cannot create except through local self-government.

(3.) If we say we must postpone the question till the state of the country is more fit for it, I should answer that the least danger is in going forward at once. It is liberty alone which fits men for liberty. This proposition, like every other in politics, has its bounds; but it is far safer than the counter doctrine, wait till they are fit.

(4.) In truth I should say (differing perhaps from many), that for the Ireland of to-day, the first question is the rectification of the relations between landlord and tenant, which happily is going on; the next is to relieve Great Britain from the enormous weight of the government of Ireland unaided by the people, and from the hopeless contradiction in which we stand while we give a parliamentary representation, hardly effective for anything but mischief

without the local institutions of self-government which it pre- CHAP.
supposes, and on which alone it can have a sound and healthy IV.
basis. Æt. 72.

We have before us in administration, he wrote to Forster
in September —

a problem not less delicate and arduous than the problem of
legislation with which we have lately had to deal in parliament.
Of the leaders, the officials, the skeleton of the land league I have
no hope whatever. The better the prospects of the Land Act
with their adherents outside the circle of wire-pullers, and with
the Irish people, the more bitter will be their hatred, and the
more sure they will be to go as far as fear of the people will allow
them in keeping up the agitation, which they cannot afford to part
with on account of their ulterior ends. All we can do is to turn
more and more the masses of their followers, to fine them down by
good laws and good government, and it is in this view that the
question of judicious releases from prison, should improving
statistics of crime encourage it, may become one of early
importance.

VI

It was in the autumn of 1881 that Mr. Gladstone visited
Leeds, in payment of the debt of gratitude due for his
triumphant return in the general election of the year before.
This progress extended over four days, and almost surpassed in
magnitude and fervour any of his experiences in other parts
of the kingdom. We have an interesting glimpse of the
physical effort of such experiences in a couple of his letters
written to Mr. Kitson, who with immense labour and spirit
had organized this severe if glorious enterprise : —

Hawarden Castle, Sept. 28, 1881. — I thank you for the very clear
and careful account of the proposed proceedings at Leeds. It lacks
as yet that *rough* statement of numbers at each meeting, which is
requisite to enable me to understand what I shall have to do. This
will be fixed by the scale of the meeting. I see no difficulty but
one — a procession through the principal thoroughfares is one of
the most exhausting processes I know as a *preliminary* to addressing a mass meeting. A mass meeting requires the physical powers

to be in their best and freshest state, as far as anything can be fresh in a man near seventy-two; and I have on one or more former occasions felt them wofully contracted. In Midlothian I never had anything of the kind before a great physical effort in speaking; and the lapse even of a couple of years is something. It would certainly be most desirable to have the mass meeting first, and then I have not any fear at all of the procession through whatever thoroughfares you think fit.

Oct. 2, 1881. — I should be very sorry to put aside any of the opportunities of vision at Leeds which the public may care to use; but what I had hoped was that these might come *after* any speeches of considerable effort and not *before* them. To understand what a physical drain, and what a reaction from tension of the senses is caused by a 'progress' before addressing a great audience, a person must probably have gone through it, and gone through it at my time of life. When I went to Midlothian, I begged that this might never happen; and it was avoided throughout. Since that time I have myself been sensible for the first time of a diminished power of voice in the House of Commons, and others also for the first time have remarked it.

Vast torchlight processions, addresses from the corporation, four score addresses from political bodies, a giant banquet in the Cloth Hall Yard covered in for the purpose, on one day; on another, more addresses, a public luncheon followed by a mass meeting of over five-and-twenty thousand persons, then a long journey through dense throngs vociferous with an exultation that knew no limits, a large dinner party, and at the end of all a night train. The only concessions that the veteran asked to weakness of the flesh, were that at the banquet he should not appear until the eating and drinking were over, and that at the mass meeting some preliminary speakers should intervene to give him time to take breath after his long and serious exercises of the morning. When the time came his voice was heard like the note of a clear and deeptoned bell. So much had vital energy, hardly less rare than his mental power, to do with the varied exploits of this spacious career.

The topics of his Leeds speeches I need not travel over.

What attracted most attention and perhaps drew most applause was his warning to Mr. Parnell. 'He desires,' said the minister, 'to arrest the operation of the Land Act; to stand as Moses stood between the living and the dead ; to stand there not as Moses stood, to arrest, but to spread the plague.' The menace that followed became a catchword of the day : ' If it shall appear that there is still to be fought a final conflict in Ireland between law on the one side and sheer lawlessness upon the other, if the law purged from defect and from any taint of injustice is still to be repelled and refused, and the first conditions of political society to remain unfulfilled, then I say, gentlemen, without hesitation, the resources of civilisation against its enemies are not yet exhausted.'[1]

Nor was the pageant all excitement. The long speech, which by way of prelusion to the great mass meeting he addressed to the chamber of commerce, was devoted to the destruction of the economic sophisters who tried to persuade us that ' the vampire of free-trade was insidiously sucking the life-blood of the country.' In large survey of broad social facts, exposition of diligently assorted figures, power of scientific analysis, sustained chain of reasoning, he was never better. The consummate mastery of this argumentative performance did not slay a heresy that has nine lives, but it drove the thing out of sight in Yorkshire for some time to come.[2]

VII

On Wednesday October 12, the cabinet met, and after five hours of deliberation decided that Mr. Parnell should be sent to prison under the Coercion Act. The Irish leader was arrested at his hotel the next morning, and carried off to Kilmainham, where he remained for some six months. The same day Mr. Gladstone was presented with an address from the Common Council of London, and in his speech at the Guildhall gave them the news : —

Our determination has been that to the best of our power, our words should be carried into acts [referring to what he had said

---

[1] At the Cloth Hall banquet, Leeds, Oct. 8, 1881.
[2] Speech to the Leeds Chamber of Commerce, Oct. 8, 1881.

at Leeds], and even within these few moments I have been informed that towards the vindication of law and order, of the rights of property, of the freedom of the land, of the first elements of political life and civilisation, the first step has been taken in the arrest of the man who unhappily from motives which I do not challenge, which I cannot examine and with which I have nothing to do, has made himself beyond all others prominent in the attempt to destroy the authority of the law, and to substitute what would end in being nothing more or less than anarchical oppression exercised upon the people of Ireland.

The arrest of Mr. Parnell was no doubt a pretty considerable strain upon powers conferred by parliament to put down village ruffians; but times were revolutionary, and though the Act of parliament was not a wise one, but altogether the reverse of wise, it was no wonder that having got the instrument, ministers thought they might as well use it. Still executive violence did not seem to work, and Mr. Gladstone looked in a natural direction for help in the milder way of persuasion. He wrote (December 17th) to Cardinal Newman: —

I will begin with defining strictly the limits of this appeal. I ask you to read the inclosed papers ; and to consider whether you will write anything to Rome upon them. I do not ask you to write, nor to tell me whether you write, nor to make any reply to this letter, beyond returning the inclosures in an envelope to me in Downing Street. I will state briefly the grounds of my request, thus limited. In 1844, when I was young as a cabinet minister, and the government of Sir R. Peel was troubled with the O'Connell manifestations, they made what I think was an appeal to Pope Gregory XVI. for his intervention to discourage agitation in Ireland. I should be very loath now to tender such a request at Rome. But now a different case arises. Some members of the Roman catholic priesthood in Ireland deliver certain sermons and otherwise express themselves in the way which my inclosures exhibit. I doubt whether if they were laymen we should not have settled their cases by putting them into gaol. I need not describe the sentiments uttered. Your eminence will feel them and judge them as strongly as I do. But now as to the Supreme

Pontiff. You will hardly be surprised when I say that I regard him, if apprised of the facts, as responsible for the conduct of these priests. For I know perfectly well that he has the means of silencing them; and that, if any one of them were in public to dispute the decrees of the council of 1870 as plainly as he has denounced law and order, he would be silenced.

Mr. Errington, who is at Rome, will I believe have seen these papers, and will I hope have brought the facts as far as he is able to the knowledge of his holiness. But I do not know how far he is able; nor how he may use his discretion. He is not our official servant, but an independent Roman catholic gentleman and a volunteer.

My wish is as regards Ireland, in this hour of her peril and her hope, to leave nothing undone by which to give heart and strength to the hope and to abate the peril. But my wish as regards the Pope is that he should have the means of bringing those for whom he is responsible to fulfil the elementary duties of citizenship. I say of citizenship; of Christianity, of priesthood, it is not for me to speak.

The cardinal replied that he would gladly find himself able to be of service, however slight it might be, in a political crisis which must be felt as of grave anxiety by all who understand the blessing of national unity and peace. He thought Mr. Gladstone overrated the pope's power in political and social matters. Absolute in questions of theology, it was not so in political matters. If the contest in Ireland were whether 'rebellion' or whether 'robbery' was a sin, we might expect him to anathematise its denial. But his action in concrete matters, as whether a political party is censurable or not, was not direct, and only in the long run effective. Local power and influence was often a match for Roman right. The pope's right keeps things together, it checks extravagances, and at length prevails, but not without a fight. Its exercise is a matter of great prudence, and depends upon times and circumstances. As for the intemperate dangerous words of priests and curates, surely such persons belonged to their respective bishops, and scarcely required the introduction of the Supreme Authority.

VIII

We have now arrived at April 1882. The reports brought to the cabinet by Mr. Forster were of the gloomiest. The Land Act had brought no improvement. In the south-west and many of the midland counties lawlessness and intimidation were worse than ever. Returns of agrarian crime were presented in every shape, and comparisons framed by weeks, by months, by quarters; do what the statisticians would, and in spite of fluctuations, murders and other serious outrages had increased. The policy of arbitrary arrest had completely failed, and the officials and crown lawyers at the Castle were at their wits' end.

While the cabinet was face to face with this ugly prospect, Mr. Gladstone received a communication volunteered by an Irish member, as to the new attitude of Mr. Parnell and the possibility of turning it to good account. Mr. Gladstone sent this letter on to Forster, replying meanwhile 'in the sense of not shutting the door.' When the thing came before the cabinet, Mr. Chamberlain—who had previously told Mr. Gladstone that he thought the time opportune for something like a reconciliation with the Irish party—with characteristic courage took his life in his hands, as he put it, and set to work to ascertain through the emissary what use for the public good could be made of Mr. Parnell's changed frame of mind. On April 25th, the cabinet heard what Mr. Chamberlain had to tell them, and it came to this, that Mr. Parnell was desirous to use his influence on behalf of peace, but his influence for good depended on the settlement of the question of arrears. Ministers decided that they could enter into no agreement and would give no pledge. They would act on their own responsibility in the light of the knowledge they had gained of Mr. Parnell's views. Mr. Gladstone was always impatient of any reference to 'reciprocal assurances' or 'tacit understanding' in respect of the dealings with the prisoner in Kilmainham. Still the nature of the proceedings was plain enough. The object of the communications to which the government were invited by Mr. Parnell through his emissary, was, supposing him to be anxious to do what

he could for law and order, to find out what action on the CHAP.
part of the government would enable him to adopt this line. IV.

Events then moved rapidly. Rumours that something Æt. 73.
was going on got abroad, and questions began to be put in
parliament. A stout tory gave notice of a motion aiming at
the release of the suspects. As Mr. Gladstone informed the
Queen, there was no doubt that the general opinion of the
public was moving in a direction adverse to arbitrary
imprisonment, though the question was a nice one for
consideration whether the recent surrender by the no-rent
party of its extreme and most subversive contentions,
amounted to anything like a guarantee for their future
conduct in respect of peace and order. The rising excitement was swelled by the retirement of Lord Cowper from
the viceroyalty, and the appointment as his successor of Lord
Spencer, who had filled that post in Mr. Gladstone's first
government. On May 2nd, Mr. Gladstone read a memorandum to the cabinet to which they agreed : —

The cabinet are of opinion that the time has now arrived when
with a view to the interests of law and order in Ireland, the three
members of parliament who have been imprisoned on suspicion
since last October, should be immediately released; and that the
list of suspects should be examined with a view to the release of
all persons not believed to be associated with crimes. They
propose at once to announce to parliament their intention to
propose, as soon as necessary business will permit, a bill to
strengthen the ordinary law in Ireland for the security of life
and property, while reserving their discretion with regard to the
Life and Property Protection Act [of 1881], which however they
do not at present think it will be possible to renew, if a favourable
state of affairs shall prevail in Ireland.

From this proceeding Mr. Forster dissented, and he
resigned his office. His point seems to have been that no
suspect should be released until the new Coercion Act had
been fashioned, whereas the rest of the cabinet held that there
was no excuse for the continued detention under arbitrary
warrant of men as to whom the ground for the ' reasonable
suspicion' required by the law had now disappeared. He

probably felt that the appointment of a viceroy of cabinet rank and with successful Irish experience was in fact his own supersession. ' I have received your letter,' Mr. Gladstone wrote to him (May 2), 'with much grief, but on this it would be selfish to expatiate. I have no choice ; followed or not followed I must go on. There are portions of the subject which touch you personally, and which seem to me to deserve *much* attention. But I have such an interest in the main issue, that I could not be deemed impartial ; so I had better not enter on them. One thing, however, I wish to say. You wish to minimise in any further statement the cause of your retreat. In my opinion — *and I speak from experience* — viewing the nature of that course, you will find this hardly possible. For a justification you, I fear, will have to found upon the doctrine of "a new departure." We must protest against it, and deny it with heart and soul.'

The way in which Mr. Gladstone chose to put things was stated in a letter to the Queen (May 3) : 'In his judgment there had been two, and only two, vital powers of commanding efficacy in Ireland, the Land Act, and the land league ; they had been locked in a combat of life and death ; and the cardinal question was which of the two would win. From the serious effort to amend the Land Act by the Arrears bill of the nationalists,[1] from the speeches made in support of it, and from information voluntarily tendered to the government as to the views of the leaders of the league, the cabinet believed that those who governed the land league were now conscious of having been defeated by the Land Act on the main question, that of paying rent.'

For the office of Irish secretary Mr. Gladstone selected Lord Frederick Cavendish, who was the husband of a niece of Mrs. Gladstone's, and one of the most devoted of his friends and adherents. The special reason for the choice of this capable and high-minded man, was that Lord Frederick had framed a plan of finance at the treasury for a new scheme of land purchase. The two freshly appointed Irish ministers at once crossed over to a country seething in disorder. The

[1] Introduced by Mr. Redmond.

afternoon of the fatal sixth of May was passed by the
new viceroy and Lord Frederick in that grim apartment in
Dublin Castle, where successive secretaries spend unshining
hours in saying No to impossible demands, and hunting
for plausible answers to insoluble riddles. Never did so
dreadful a shadow overhang it as on that day. The task
on which the two ministers were engaged was the consideration of the new provisions for coping with disorder, which
had been prepared in London. The under-secretary, Mr.
Burke, and one of the lawyers, were present. Lord Spencer
rode out to the park about five o'clock, and Lord Frederick
followed him an hour later. He was overtaken by the
under-secretary walking homewards, and as the two strolled
on together, they were both brutally murdered in front
of the vice-regal residence. The assassins did not know who
Lord Frederick was. Well has it been said that Ireland
seems the sport of a destiny that is aimless.[1]

The official world of London was on that Saturday night
in the full round of its pleasures. The Gladstones were
dining at the Austrian embassy. So, too, was Sir William
Harcourt, and to him as home secretary the black tidings
were sent from Dublin late in the evening. Mr. and Mrs.
Gladstone had already left, she for a party at the admiralty,
he walking home to Downing Street. At the admiralty
they told her of bad news from Ireland and hurried her
away. Mr. Gladstone arrived at home a few minutes after
her. When his secretary in the hall told him of the
horrible thing that had been done, it was as if he had
been felled to the ground. Then they hastened to bear
what solace they could, to the anguish-stricken home where
solace would be so sorely needed.

The effect of this blind and hideous crime was at once to
arrest the spirit and the policy of conciliation. While the
Irish leaders were locked up, a secret murder club had
taken matters in hand in their own way, and ripened plots

[1] It had been Mr. Burke's practice
to drive from the Castle to the Park
gate, then to descend and walk home,
followed by two detectives. On this
occasion he found at the gate that
the chief secretary had passed, and
drove forward to overtake him. The
detectives did not follow him as usual.
If they had followed, he would have
been saved.

within a stone's throw of the Castle. No worse blow could have been struck at Mr. Parnell's policy. It has been said that the nineteenth century had seen the course of its history twenty-five times diverted by actual or attempted crime. In that sinister list the murders in the Phœnix Park have a tragic place.

The voice of party was for the moment hushed. Sir Stafford Northcote wrote a letter of admirable feeling, saying that if there was any way in which Mr. Gladstone thought they could serve the government, he would of course let them know. The Prince of Wales wrote of his own horror and indignation at the crime, and of his sympathy with Mr. Gladstone in the loss of one who was not only a colleague of many merits, but a near connection and devoted friend. With one or two scandalous exceptions, the tone of the English press was sober, sensible, and self-possessed. ' If a nation,' said a leading journal in Paris, 'should be judged by the way in which it acts on grave occasions, the spectacle offered by England is calculated to produce a high opinion of the political character and spirit of the British people.' Things of the baser sort were not quite absent, but they did not matter. An appeal confronted the electors of the North-West Riding as they went to the poll at a bye-election a few days later, to ' Vote for ——, and avenge the death of Lord Frederick Cavendish ! ' They responded by placing ——'s opponent at the head of the poll by a majority of two thousand.

The scene in the House had all the air of tragedy, and Mr. Gladstone summoned courage enough to do his part with impressive composure. A colleague was doing some business with him in his room before the solemnity began. When it was over, they resumed it, Mr. Gladstone making no word of reference to the sombre interlude, before or after. ' Went reluctantly to the House,' he says in his diary, ' and by the help of God forced out what was needful on the question of the adjournment.' His words were not many, when after commemorating the marked qualities of Mr. Burke, he went on in laboured tones and slow speech and hardly repressed emotion : —

The hand of the assassin has come nearer home; and though I feel it difficult to say a word, yet I must say that one of the very noblest hearts in England has ceased to beat, and has ceased at the very moment when it was just devoted to the service of Ireland, full of love for that country, full of hope for her future, full of capacity to render her service.

Writing to Lady Frederick on a later day, he mentions a public reference to some pathetic words of hers (May 19) : —

Sexton just now returned to the subject, with much approval from the House. You will find it near the middle of a long speech. Nothing could be better either in feeling or in grace (the man is little short of a master), and I think it will warm your heart. You have made a mark deeper than any wound.

To Lord Ripon in India, he wrote (June 1) : —

The black act brought indeed a great personal grief to my wife and me; but we are bound to merge our own sorrow in the larger and deeper affliction of the widow and the father, in the sense of the public loss of a life so valuable to the nation, and in the consideration of the great and varied effects it may have on immediate and vital interests. Since the death of this dearly loved son, we have heard much good of the Duke, whom indeed we saw at Chatsworth after the funeral, and we have seen much of Lady Frederick, who has been good even beyond what we could have hoped. I have no doubt you have heard in India the echo of words spoken by Spencer from a letter of hers, in which she said she could give up even him if his death were to work good to his fellow-men, which indeed was the whole object of his life. These words have had a tender effect, as remarkable as the horror excited by the slaughter. Spencer wrote to me that a priest in Connemara read them from the altar; when the whole congregation spontaneously fell down upon their knees. In England, the national attitude has been admirable. The general strain of language has been, ' Do not let this terrible and flagitious crime deter you from persevering with the work of justice.

Well did Dean Church say that no Roman or Florentine lady ever uttered a more heroic thing than was said by this

English lady when on first seeing Mr. Gladstone that terrible midnight she said, 'You did right to send him to Ireland.'[1] 'The loss of F. Cavendish,' Mr. Gladstone wrote to his eldest son, 'will ever be to us all as an unhealed wound.'

On the day after the murders Mr. Gladstone received a note through the same channel by which Mr. Chamberlain had carried on his communications : 'I am authorised by Mr. Parnell to state that if Mr. Gladstone considers it necessary for the maintenance of his [Mr. G.'s] position and for carrying out his views, that Mr. Parnell should resign his seat, Mr. Parnell is prepared to do so immediately.' To this Mr. Gladstone replied (May 7) : —

My duty does not permit me for a moment to entertain Mr. Parnell's proposal, just conveyed to me by you, that he should if I think it needful resign his seat; but I am deeply sensible of the honourable motives by which it has been prompted.

'My opinion is,' said Mr. Gladstone to Lord Granville, 'that if Parnell goes, no restraining influence will remain ; the scale of outrages will be again enlarged ; and no repressive bill can avail to put it down.' Those of the cabinet who had the best chance of knowing, were convinced that Mr. Parnell was 'sincerely anxious for the pacification of Ireland.'

The reaction produced by the murders in the Park made perseverance in a milder policy impossible in face of English opinion, and parliament eagerly passed the Coercion Act of 1882. I once asked an Irishman of consummate experience and equitable mind, with no leanings that I know of to political nationalism, whether the task of any later ruler of Ireland was comparable to Lord Spencer's. 'Assuredly not,' he replied : 'in 1882 Ireland seemed to be literally a society on the eve of dissolution. The Invincibles still roved with knives about the streets of Dublin. Discontent had been stirred in the ranks of the Royal Irish Constabulary, and a dangerous mutiny broke out in the metropolitan force. Over half of the country the demoralisation of every class, the terror, the fierce hatred, the universal distrust, had grown to an incredible pitch. The moral cowardice of what ought

[1] *Life of Dean Church*, p. 299.

to have been the governing class was astounding. The landlords would hold meetings and agree not to go beyond a certain
abatement, and then they would go individually and privately
offer to the tenant a greater abatement. Even the agents
of the law and the courts were shaken in their duty. The
power of random arrest and detention under the Coercion
Act of 1881 had not improved the *moral* of magistrates and
police. The sheriff would let the word get out that he was
coming to make a seizure, and profess surprise that the
cattle had vanished. The whole country-side turned out in
thousands in half the counties in Ireland to attend flaming
meetings, and if a man did not attend, angry neighbours
trooped up to know the reason why. The clergy hardly
stirred a finger to restrain the wildness of the storm; some
did their best to raise it. All that was what Lord Spencer
had to deal with; the very foundations of the social fabric
rocking.'

The new viceroy attacked the formidable task before him
with resolution, minute assiduity, and an inexhaustible store
of that steady-eyed patience which is the sovereign requisite
of any man who, whether with coercion or without, takes in
hand the government of Ireland. He was seconded with high
ability and courage by Mr. Trevelyan, the new Irish secretary,
whose fortitude was subjected to a far severer trial than has
ever fallen to the lot of any Irish secretary before or since.
The coercion that Lord Spencer had to administer was at
least law. The coercion with which parliament entrusted
Mr. Forster the year before was the negation of the spirit of
law, and the substitution for it of naked and arbitrary
control over the liberty of the subject by executive power —
a system as unconstitutional in theory as it was infatuated
in policy and calamitous in result. Even before the end
of the parliament, Mr. Bright frankly told the House of
Commons of this Coercion Act: 'I think that the legislation of 1881 was unfortunately a great mistake, though I
was myself a member of the government concerned in it.'

CHAPTER V

(1881–1882)

I FIND many very ready to say what I ought to have done when
a battle is over; but I wish some of these persons would come
and tell me what to do before the battle. — WELLINGTON.

BOOK
VIII.

1881.

IN 1877 Mr. Gladstone penned words to which later events
gave an only too striking verification. 'Territorial questions,'
he said, 'are not to be disposed of by arbitrary limits; we
cannot enjoy the luxury of taking Egyptian soil by pinches.
We may seize an Aden and a Perim, where is no already
formed community of inhabitants, and circumscribe a tract
at will. But our first site in Egypt, be it by larceny or be it
by emption, will be the almost certain egg of a North African
empire, that will grow and grow until another Victoria and
another Albert, titles of the lake-sources of the White Nile,
come within our borders; and till we finally join hands
across the equator with Natal and Cape Town, to say nothing
of the Transvaal and the Orange River on the south, or of
Abyssinia or Zanzibar to be swallowed by way of viaticum on
our journey.'[1] It was one of the ironies in which every
active statesman's life abounds, that the author of that forecast should have been fated to take his country over its first
marches towards this uncoveted destination.

I

For many months after Mr. Gladstone formed his second
ministry, there was no reason to suppose that the Egyptian
branch of the eastern question, which for ever casts its

[1] *Nineteenth Century*, August, 1877; *Gleanings*, iv. p. 357.

perplexing shadow over Europe, was likely to give trouble. The new Khedive held a regularly defined position, alike towards his titular sovereign at Constantinople, towards reforming ministers at Cairo, towards the creditors of his state, and towards the two strong European Powers who for different reasons had the supervision of Egyptian affairs in charge. The oppression common to oriental governments seemed to be yielding before western standards. The load of interest on a profligate debt was heavy, but it was not unskilfully adjusted. The rate of village usury was falling, and the value of land was rising. Unluckily the Khedive and his ministers neglected the grievances of the army, and in January 1881 its leaders broke out in revolt. The Khedive, without an armed force on whose fidelity he could rely, gave way to the mutineers, and a situation was created, familiar enough in all oriental states, and not unlike that in our own country between Charles I., or in later days the parliament, and the roundhead troopers: anger and revenge in the breast of the affronted civil ruler, distrust and dread of punishment in the mind of the soldiery. During the autumn (1881) the crisis grew more alarming. The Khedive showed neither energy nor tact; he neither calmed the terror of the mutineers nor crushed them. Insubordination in the army began to affect the civil population, and a national party came into open existence in the chamber of notables. The soldiers found a head in Arabi, a native Egyptian, sprung of fellah origin. Want either of stern resolution or of politic vision in the Khedive and his minister had transferred the reality of power to the insurgents. The Sultan of Turkey here saw his chance; he made a series of diplomatic endeavours to reestablish a shattered sovereignty over his nominal feudatory on the Nile. This pretension, and ·the spreading tide of disorder, brought England and France actively upon the scene. We can see now, what expert observers on the spot saw then, that the two Powers mistook the nature of the Arabist movement. They perceived in it no more than a military rising. It was in truth national as well as military; it was anti-European, and above all, it was in its objects anti-Turk.

In 1879 the two governments had insisted on imposing over Egypt two controllers, with limited functions but irremovable. This, as Mr. Gladstone argued later, was to bring foreign intervention into the heart of the country, and to establish in the strictest sense a political control.[1] As a matter of fact, not then well known, in September 1879 Lord Salisbury had come to a definite understanding with the French ambassador in London, that the two governments would not tolerate the establishment in Egypt of political influence by any competing European Power ; and what was more important, that they were prepared to take action to any extent that might be found necessary to give effect to their views in this respect. The notable acquisition by Lord Beaconsfield of an interest in the Suez Canal, always regarded by Mr. Gladstone as a politically ill-advised and hazardous transaction, had tied the English knot in Egypt still tighter.

The policy of the Gladstone cabinet was defined in general words in a despatch from the foreign minister to the British agent at Cairo. Lord Granville (November 1881) disclaimed any self-aggrandising designs on the part of either England or France. He proclaimed the desire of the cabinet to uphold in Egypt the administrative independence secured to her by the decrees of the sovereign power on the Bosphorus. Finally he set forth that the only circumstances likely to force the government of the Queen to depart from this course of conduct, would be the occurrence in Egypt of a state of anarchy.[2]

Justly averse to a joint occupation of Egypt by England and France, as the most perilous of all possible courses, the London cabinet looked to the Sultan as the best instrument for restoring order. Here they were confronted by two insurmountable obstacles : first, the steadfast hostility of France to any form of Turkish intervention, and second, that strong current of antipathy to the Sultan which had been set flowing over British opinion in the days of Midlothian.[3]

[1] July 27, 1882.
[2] Granville and Malet, November 4, 1881.
[3] Before Midlothian, however, Mr.

Gladstone had in 1877 drawn an important distinction : ' If I find the Turk incapable of establishing a good, just, and well-proportioned govern-

In December (1881) the puissant genius of Gambetta acquired supremacy for a season, and he without delay pressed upon the British cabinet the necessity of preparing for joint and immediate action. Gambetta prevailed. The Turk was ruled out, and the two Powers of the west determined on action of their own. The particular mode of common action, however, in case action should become necessary, was left entirely open.

Meanwhile the British cabinet was induced to agree to Gambetta's proposal to send instructions to Cairo, assuring the Khedive that England and France were closely associated in the resolve to guard by their united efforts against all causes of complaint, internal or external, which might menace the existing order of things in Egypt. This was a memorable starting-point in what proved an amazing journey. This Joint Note (January 6, 1881) was the first link in a chain of proceedings that brought each of the two governments who were its authors, into the very position that they were most strenuously bent on averting; France eventually ousted herself from Egypt, and England was eventually landed in plenary and permanent occupation. So extraordinary a result only shows how impenetrable were the windings of the labyrinth. The foremost statesmen of England and France were in their conning towers, and England at any rate employed some of the ablest of her agents. Yet each was driven out of an appointed course to an unforeseen and an unwelcome termination. Circumstances like these might teach moderation both to the French partisans who curse the vacillations of M. de Freycinet, and to the English partisans who, while rejoicing in the ultimate result, curse the vacillations of the cabinet of Mr. Gladstone, in wisely striving to unravel a knot instead of at all risks cutting it.

II

The present writer described the effect of the Joint Note in the following words written at the time [1]: 'At Cairo the

ment over civilised and Christian races, it does not follow that he is under a similar incapacity when his task shall only be to hold empire over populations wholly or principally Orientals and Mahomedans.

On this head I do not know that any verdict of guilty has yet been found by a competent tribunal.' — *Gleanings*, iv. p. 364.

[1] *Fortnightly Review*, July 1882.

Note fell like a bombshell. Nobody there had expected any
such declaration, and nobody was aware of any reason why
it should have been launched. What was felt was that so
serious a step on such delicate ground could not have been
adopted without deliberate calculation, nor without some
grave intention. The Note was, therefore, taken to mean
that the Sultan was to be thrust still further in the background; that the Khedive was to become more plainly the
puppet of England and France; and that Egypt would sooner
or later in some shape or other be made to share the fate
of Tunis. The general effect was, therefore, mischievous in
the highest degree. The Khedive was encouraged in his
opposition to the sentiments of his Chamber. The military,
national, or popular party was alarmed. The Sultan was
irritated. The other European Powers were made uneasy.
Every element of disturbance was roused into activity.'

It is true that even if no Joint Note had ever been despatched, the prospects of order were unpromising. The
most careful analysis of the various elements of society in
Egypt by those best acquainted at first hand with all those
elements, whether internal or external, whether Egyptian or
European, and with all the roots of antagonism thriving
among them, exhibited no promise of stability. If Egypt
had been a simple case of an oriental government in revolutionary commotion, the ferment might have been left to
work itself out. Unfortunately Egypt, in spite of the maps,
lies in Europe. So far from being a simple case, it was
indescribably entangled, and even the desperate questions
that rise in our minds at the mention of the Balkan peninsula, of Armenia, of Constantinople, offer no such complex
of difficulties as the Egyptian riddle in 1881–2. The law of
liquidation [1] — whatever else we may think of it — at least
made the policy of Egypt for the Egyptians unworkable.
Yet the British cabinet were not wrong in thinking that
this was no reason for sliding into the competing policy of
Egypt for the English *and* the French, which would have
been more unworkable still.

England strove manfully to hold the ground that she

[1] Defining the claims of the European bondholder on revenue.

had taken in November. Lord Granville told the British ambassador in Paris that his government disliked intervention either by themselves or anybody else as much as ever; that they looked upon the experiment of the Chamber with favourable eyes; that they wished to keep the connection of the Porte with Egypt so far as it was compatible with Egyptian liberties; and that the object of the Joint Note was to strengthen the existing government of Egypt. Gambetta, on the other hand, was convinced that all explanations of this sort would only serve further to inflate the enemies of France and England in the Egyptian community, and would encourage their designs upon the law of liquidation. Lord Granville was honourably and consistently anxious to confine himself within the letter of international right, while Gambetta was equally anxious to intervene in Egyptian administration, within right or without it, and to force forward that Anglo-French occupation in which Lord Granville so justly saw nothing but danger and mischief. Once more Lord Granville, at the end of the month which had opened with the Joint Note, in a despatch to the ambassador at Paris (January 30), defined the position of the British cabinet. What measures should be taken to meet Egyptian disorders? The Queen's government had 'a strong objection to the occupation of Egypt by themselves.' Egypt and Turkey would oppose; it would arouse the jealousy of other Powers, who would, as there was even already good reason to believe, make counter demonstrations; and, finally, such an occupation would be as distasteful to the French nation as the sole occupation of Egypt by the French would be to ourselves. Joint occupation by England and France, in short, might lessen some difficulties, but it would seriously aggravate others. Turkish occupation would be a great evil, but it would not entail political dangers as great as those attending the other two courses. As for the French objections to the farther admission of the other European Powers to intervene in Egyptian affairs, the cabinet agreed that England and France had an exceptional position in Egypt, but might it not be desirable to enter into some communication with the other Powers, as to the best way of dealing with a state of

BOOK
VIII.

1882.

things that appeared likely to interfere both with the Sultan's firmans and with Egypt's international engagements?

At this critical moment Gambetta fell from power. The mark that he had set upon western policy in Egypt remained. Good observers on the spot, trained in the great school of India, thought that even if there were no more than a chance of working with the national party, the chance was well worth trying. As the case was put at the time, 'It is impossible to conceive a situation that more imperatively called for caution, circumspection, and deference to the knowledge of observers on the scene, or one that was actually handled with greater rashness and hurry. Gambetta had made up his mind that the military movement was leading to the abyss, and that it must be peremptorily arrested. It may be that he was right in supposing that the army, which had first found its power in the time of Ismail, would go from bad to worse. But everything turned upon the possibility of pulling up the army, without arousing other elements more dangerous still. M. Gambetta's impatient policy was worked out in his own head without reference to the conditions on the scene, and the result was what might have been expected.' [1]

III

The dual control, the system of carrying on the Egyptian government under the advice of an English and a French agent, came to an end. The rude administration in the provinces fell to pieces. The Khedive was helplessly involved in struggle after struggle with the military insurgents. The army became as undisputed masters of the government, as the Cromwellian army at some moments in our civil war. Meanwhile the British government, true to Mr. Gladstone's constant principle, endeavoured to turn the question from being purely Anglo-French, into an international question. The Powers were not unfavourable, but nothing came of it. Both from Paris and from London somewhat bewildered suggestions proceeded by way of evading the central enigma, whether the intervention should be Turkish

[1] *Fortnightly Review*, July 1882.

or Anglo-French. It was decided at any rate to send powerful Anglo-French fleets to Alexandria, and Mr. Gladstone
only regretted that the other Powers (including Turkey)
had not been invited to have their flags represented. To
this the French objected, with the evil result that the other
Powers were displeased, and the good effect that the appearance of the Sultan in the field might have had upon the
revolutionary parties in Egypt was lost. On May 21, 1882,
M. de Freycinet went so far as to say that, though he
was still opposed to Turkish intervention, he would not
regard as intervention a case in which Turkish forces were
summoned by England and France to operate under Anglo-
French control, upon conditions specified by the two
Powers. If it became advisable to land troops, recourse
should be had on these terms to Turkish troops and them
only. Lord Granville acceded. He proposed (May 24) to
address the Powers, to procure international sanction for the
possible despatch of Turkish troops to Egypt. M. Freycinet
insisted that no such step was necessary. At the same
time (June 1), M. de Freycinet told the Chamber that there
were various courses to which they might be led, but he
excluded one, and this was a French military intervention.
That declaration narrowed the case to a choice between
English intervention, or Turkish, or Anglo-Turkish, all of
them known to be profoundly unpalatable to French sentiment. Such was the end of Lord Granville's prudent and
loyal endeavour to move in step with France.

The next proposal from M. de Freycinet was a European
conference, as Prince Bismarck presumed, to cover the admis-
sibility of Turkish intervention. A conference was too much
in accord with the ideas of the British cabinet, not to be
welcomed by them. The Turk, however, who now might
have had the game in his own hands, after a curious exhibition of duplicity and folly, declined to join, and the conference at first met without him (June 23). Then, pursuing
tactics well known at all times at Constantinople, the Sultan
made one of his attempts to divide the Powers, by sending a
telegram to London (June 25), conferring upon England
rights of exclusive control in the administration of Egypt.

This Mr. Gladstone and Lord Granville declined without even consulting the cabinet, as too violent an infraction, I suppose, of the cardinal principle of European concert. The Queen, anxious for an undivided English control at any price, complained that the question was settled without reference to the cabinet, and here the Queen was clearly not wrong, on doctrines of cabinet authority and cabinet responsibility that were usually held by nobody more strongly than by the prime minister himself.

Mr. Gladstone and his cabinet fought as hard as they could, and for good reasons, against single-handed intervention by Great Britain. When they saw that order could not be re-established without the exercise of force from without, they insisted that this force should be applied by the Sultan as sovereign of Egypt. They proposed this solution to the conference, and Lord Dufferin urged it upon the Sultan. With curious infatuation (repeated a few years later) the Sultan stood aside. When it became necessary to make immediate provision for the safety of the Suez Canal, England proposed to undertake this duty conjointly with France, and solicited the co-operation of any other Power. Italy was specially invited to join. Then when the progress of the rebellion had broken the Khedive's authority and brought Egypt to anarchy, England invited France and Italy to act with her in putting the rebellion down. France and Italy declined. England still urged the Porte to send troops, insisting only on such conditions as were indispensable to secure united action. The Porte again held back, and before it carried out an agreement to sign a military convention, events had moved too fast.[1] Thus, by the Sultan's perversities and the fluctuations of purpose and temper in France, single-handed intervention was inexorably forced upon the one Power that had most consistently striven to avoid it. Bismarck, it is true, judged that Arabi was now a power to be reckoned with; the Austrian representatives used language of like purport; and Freycinet also inclined to coming to terms with Arabi. The British cabinet had persuaded themselves that the overthrow of the military

[1] Lord Granville to Lord Dufferin. Oct. 5, 1882.

party was an indispensable precedent to any return of decently stable order.

The situation in Egypt can hardly be adequately understood without a multiplicity of details for which this is no place, and in such cases details are everything. Diplomacy in which the Sultan of Turkey plays a part is always complicated, and at the Conference of Constantinople the cobwebs were spun and brushed away and spun again with diligence unexampled. The proceedings were without any effect upon the course of events. The Egyptian revolution ran its course. The moral support of Turkish commissioners sent by the Sultan to Cairo came to nothing, and the moral influence of the Anglo-French squadron at Alexandria came to nothing, and in truth it did more harm than good. The Khedive's throne and life were alike in danger. The Christians flocked down from the interior. The residents in Alexandria were trembling for their lives. At the end of May our agent at Cairo informed his government that a collision between Moslems and Christians might occur at any moment. On June 11 some fifty Europeans were massacred by a riotous mob at Alexandria. The British consul was severely wounded, and some sailors of the French fleet were among the killed. Greeks and Jews were murdered in other places. At last a decisive blow was struck. For several weeks the Egyptians had been at work upon the fortifications of Alexandria, and upon batteries commanding the British fleet. The British admiral was instructed (July 3) that if this operation were continued, he should immediately destroy the earthworks and silence the batteries. After due formalities he (July 11) opened fire at seven in the morning, and by half-past five in the evening the Alexandria guns were silenced. Incendiaries set the town on fire, the mob pillaged it, and some murders were committed. The French ships had sailed away, their government having previously informed the British ambassador in Paris that the proposed operation would be an act of war against Egypt, and such an act of war without the express consent of the Chamber would violate the constitution.

The new situation in which England now found herself
was quickly described by the prime minister to the House
of Commons. On July 22, he said: 'We should not fully
discharge our duty, if we did not endeavour to convert the
present interior state of Egypt from anarchy and conflict
to peace and order. We shall look during the time that
remains to us to the co-operation of the Powers of civilised
Europe, if it be in any case open to us. But if every chance
of obtaining co-operation is exhausted, the work will be
undertaken by the single power of England.' As for the
position of the Powers it may be described in this way.
Germany and Austria were cordial and respectful; France
anxious to retain a completely friendly understanding, but
wanting some equivalent for the inevitable decline of her
power in Egypt; Italy jealous of our renewing close relations with France; Russia still sore, and on the lookout
for some plausible excuse for getting the Berlin arrangement of 1878 revised in her favour, without getting into
difficulties with Berlin itself.

France was not unwilling to take joint action with
England for the defence of the canal, but would not join
England in intervention beyond that object. At the same
time Freycinet wished it to be understood that France had
no objection to our advance, if we decided to make an
advance. This was more than once repeated. Gambetta
in vehement wrath declared his dread lest the refusal to
co-operate with England should shake an alliance of price-
less value; and lest besides that immense catastrophe, it
should hand over to the possession of England for ever,
territories, rivers, and ports where the French right to
live and trade was as good as hers. The mighty orator
declaimed in vain. Suspicion of the craft of Bismarck was in
France more lively than suspicion of aggressive designs in
the cabinet of Mr. Gladstone, and the Chamber was reminded
how extremely well it would suit Germany that France
should lock up her military force in Tunis yesterday, in
Egypt to-day. Ingenious speakers, pointing to Europe
covered with camps of armed men; pointing to the artful
statesmanship that had pushed Austria into Bosnia and

Herzegovina, and encouraged France herself to occupy Tunis; pointing to the expectant nations reserving their liberty for future occasions — all urgently exhorted France now to reserve her own liberty of action too. Under the influence of such ideas as these, and by the working of rival personalities and parties, the Chamber by an immense majority turned the Freycinet government out of office (July 29) rather than sanction even such a degree of intervention as concerned the protection of the Suez Canal.

Nine days after the bombardment of Alexandria, the British cabinet decided on the despatch of what was mildly called an expeditionary force to the Mediterranean, under the command of Sir Garnet Wolseley. The general's alertness, energy, and prescient calculation brought him up to Arabi at Tel-el-Kebir (Sept. 13), and there at one rapid and decisive blow he crushed the military insurrection.[1]

IV

The bombardment of Alexandria cost Mr. Gladstone the British colleague who in fundamentals stood closest to him of them all. In the opening days of July, amid differences of opinion that revealed themselves in frequent and protracted meetings of the cabinet, it was thought probable that Mr. Gladstone and Bright would resign rather than be parties to despatching troops to the Mediterranean; and the two representative radicals were expected to join them. Then came the bombardment, but only Bright went — not until after earnest protestations from the prime minister. As Mr. Gladstone described things later to the Queen, Bright's letters and conversation consisted very much more of references to his past career and strong statements of feeling, than of attempts to reason on the existing facts of the case, with the obligations that they appeared to entail. Not satisfied with his own efforts, Mr. Gladstone turned to Lord Granville, who had been a stout friend in old days when Bright's was a name of reproach and obloquy : —

July 12. — Here is the apprehended letter from dear old John

[1] A share of the credit of success is due to the admirable efficiency of Mr. Childers at the War Office. See Sir Garnet's letter to him, *Life of Childers*, ii. p. 117.

Bright, which turns a white day into a black one. It would not be fair in me to beg an interview. His kindness would make him reluctant to decline ; but he would come laden with an apprehension, that I by impetuosity and tenacity should endeavour to overbear him. But pray consider whether you could do it. He would not have the same fear of your dealings with him. I do not think you could get a *reversal*, but perhaps he would give you another short delay, and at the end of this the sky might be further settled.

Two days later Mr. Gladstone and Bright had a long, and we may be sure that it was an earnest, conversation. The former of them the same day put his remarks into the shape of a letter, which the reader may care to have, as a statement of the case for the first act of armed intervention, which led up by a direct line to the English occupation of Egypt, Soudan wars, and to some other events from which the veil is not even yet lifted : —

The act of Tuesday [the bombardment of Alexandria] was a solemn and painful one, for which I feel myself to be highly responsible, and it is my earnest desire that we should all view it now, as we shall wish at the last that we had viewed it. Subject to this testing rule, I address you as one whom I suppose not to believe all use whatever of military force to be unlawful; as one who detests war in general and believes most wars to have been sad errors (in which I greatly agree with you), but who in regard to any particular use of force would look upon it for a justifying cause, and after it would endeavour to appreciate its actual effect.

The general situation in Egypt had latterly become one in which everything was governed by sheer military violence. Every legitimate authority — the Khedive, the Sultan, the notables, and the best men of the country, such as Cherif and Sultan pashas — had been put down, and a situation of *force* had been created, which could only be met by force. This being so, we had laboured to the uttermost, almost alone but not without success, to secure that if force were employed against the violence of Arabi, it should be force armed with the highest sanction of law ; that it should be the force of the sovereign, authorised and restrained by the united Powers of Europe, who in such a case represent the civilised world.

While this is going on, a by-question arises. The British fleet, lawfully present in the waters of Alexandria, had the right and duty of self-defence. It demanded the discontinuance of attempts made to strengthen the armament of the fortifications. . . . Met by fraud and falsehood in its demand, it required surrender with a view to immediate dismantling, and this being refused, it proceeded to destroy. . . . The conflagration which followed, the pillage and any other outrages effected by the released convicts, these are not due to us, but to the seemingly wanton wickedness of Arabi. . . .

Such being the amount of our act, what has been its reception and its effect? As to its reception, we have not received nor heard of a word of disapproval from any Power great or small, or from any source having the slightest authority. As to its effect, it has taught many lessons, struck a heavy, perhaps a deadly, blow at the reign of violence, brought again into light the beginnings of legitimate rule, shown the fanaticism of the East that massacre of Europeans is not likely to be perpetrated with impunity, and greatly advanced the Egyptian question towards a permanent and peaceable solution. I feel that in being party to this work I have been a labourer in the cause of peace. Your co-operation in that cause, with reference to preceding and collateral points, has been of the utmost value, and has enabled me to hold my ground, when without you it might have been difficult.

The correspondence closed with a wish from Mr. Gladstone: ' Believe in the sore sense of practical loss, and the (I trust) unalterable friendship and regard with which I remain, etc.' When Bright came to explain his resignation in parliament, he said something about the moral law, which led to a sharp retort from the prime minister, but still their friendship did appear to remain unalterable, as Mr. Gladstone trusted that it would.

When the question by and by arose whether Arabi should be put to death, Bright wrote to the .prime minister on behalf of clemency. Mr. Gladstone in replying took a severe line: 'I am sorry to say the inquiry is too likely to show that Arabi is very much more than a rebel. Crimes of the gravest kind have been committed; and with most of them he stands, I fear, in *presumptive* (that is, unproved) connection. In truth I must say that, having begun with no prejudice against him, and with the strong desire that he should be saved, I am almost driven to the conclusion that he is a bad man, and that it will not be an injustice if he goes the road which thousands of his innocent countrymen through him have trodden.' It is a great mistake to suppose that Mr. Gladstone was all leniency, or that when he thought ill of men, he stayed either at palliating words or at half-measures.

CHAPTER VI

POLITICAL JUBILEE

(1882–1883)

ἀγωνίζεται γὰρ ὥσπερ ἀθλητὴς κατὰ τὸν βίον, ὅταν δὲ διαγωνίσηται, τότε
τυγχάνει τῶν προσηκόντων. — PLUTARCH, *Moralia*, c. 18.

He strives like an athlete all his life long, and then when he comes
to the end of his striving, he has what is meet.

ἐπάμεροι· τί δέ τις; τί δ' οὔ τις; σκιᾶς ὄναρ
ἄνθρωπος. ἀλλ' ὅταν αἴγλα διόσδοτος ἔλθῃ,
λαμπρὸν φέγγος ἔπεστιν ἀνδρῶν καὶ μείλιχος αἰών.
— PINDAR, *Pyth.* viii. 135.

Things of a day! What is a man? What, when he is not? A
dream of shadow is mankind. Yet when there comes down glory imparted from God, radiant light shines among men and genial days.

θανεῖν δ' οἷσιν ἀνάγκα, τί κέ τις ἀνώνυμον
γῆρας ἐν σκότῳ καθήμενος ἕψοι μάταν; — *Ol.* i. 131.

Die since we must, wherefore should a man sit idle and nurse in
the gloom days of long life without aim, without name?

THE words from 'antique books' that I have just translated
and transcribed, were written out by Mr. Gladstone inside
the cover of the little diary for 1882–3. To what the old
world had to say, he added Dante's majestic commonplace:
'You were not to live like brutes, but to pursue virtue and
knowledge.'[1] These meditations on the human lot, on the
mingling of our great hopes with the implacable realities,
made the vital air in which all through his life he drew

[1] Considerate la vostra semenza :
Fatti non foste a viver come bruti,
Ma per seguir virtute e conoscenza.
— *Inferno*, xxvi. 118.

deep breath. Adjusted to his ever vivid religious creed, amid all the turbid business of the worldly elements, they were the sedative and the restorer. Yet here and always the last word was Effort. The moods that in less strenuous natures ended in melancholy, philosophic or poetic, to him were fresh incentives to redeem the time.

The middle of December 1882 marked his political jubilee. It was now half a century since he had entered public life, and the youthful graduate from Oxford had grown to be the foremost man in his country. Yet these fifty courses of the sun and all the pageant of the world had in some ways made but little difference in him. In some ways, it seemed as if time had rolled over him in vain. He had learned many lessons. He had changed his party, his horizons were far wider, new social truths had made their way into his impressionable mind, he recognised new social forces. His aims for the church, that he loved as ardently as he gloried in a powerful and beneficent state, had undergone a revolution. Since 1866 he had come into contact with democracy at close quarters; the Bulgarian campaign and Midlothian lighting up his early faith in liberty, had inflamed him with new feeling for the voice of the people. As much as in the early time when he had prayed to be allowed to go into orders, he was moved by a dominating sense of the common claims and interests of mankind. 'The contagion of the world's slow stain' had not infected him; the lustre and long continuity of his public performances still left all his innermost ideals constant and undimmed.

His fifty years of public life had wrought his early habits of severe toil, method, exactness, concentration, into cast-iron. Whether they had sharpened what is called knowledge of the world, or taught him insight into men and skill in discrimination among men, it is hard to say. He always talked as if he found the world pretty much what he had expected. Man, he used often to say, is the least comprehensible of creatures, and of men the most incomprehensible are the politicians. Yet nobody was less of the cynic. As for Weltschmerz, world-weariness, ennui, tedium vitæ — that enervating family were no acquaintances of his, now nor at any time. None of the vicissitudes of long experience ever tempted him either into the shallow satire on life that is so often the solace of the little and the weak; or on the other hand into the *saeva indignatio*, the sombre brooding reprobation, that has haunted some strong souls from Tacitus and Dante to Pascal, Butler, Swift, Turgot. We may, indeed, be sure that neither of these two moods can ever hold a place in the breast of a commanding orator.

II

I have spoken of his new feeling for democracy. At the point of time at which we have arrived, it was heartily reciprocated. The many difficulties in the course of public affairs that confronted parliament and the nation for two years or more after Mr. Gladstone's second accession to power, did little to weaken either his personal popularity or his hold upon the confidence of the constituencies. For many years he and Mr. Disraeli had stood out above the level of their adherents; they were the centre of every political storm. Disraeli was gone (April 19, 1881), commemorated by Mr. Gladstone in a parliamentary tribute that cost him much searching of heart beforehand, and was a masterpiece of grace and good feeling. Mr. Gladstone stood alone, concentrating upon himself by his personal ascendency and public history the bitter antagonism of his opponents, only matched by the enthusiasm and devotion of his followers. The rage of faction had seldom been more unbridled. The Irish and the young fourth party were rivals in malicious vituperation; of the two, the Irish on the whole observed the better manners. Once Mr. Gladstone was wounded to the quick, as letters show, when a member of the fourth party denounced as 'a government of infamy' the ministry with whose head he had long been on terms of more than friendship alike as host and guest. He could not fell his trees, he could not read the lessons in Hawarden church, without finding these innocent habits turned into material for platform mockery. 'In the eyes of the opposition, as indeed of the country,' said a great print that was never much his friend, 'he is the government and he is the liberal party,' and the writer went on to scold Lord Salisbury for wasting his time in the concoction of angry epigrams and pungent phrases that were neither new nor instructive.[1] They pierced no joint in the mail of the warrior at whom they were levelled. The nation at large knew nothing of difficulties at Windsor, nothing of awkward passages in the cabinet, nothing of the trying egotisms of gentlemen out of the cabinet who insisted that they ought to be in. Nor would such things have made any difference except in his favour, if the public had known all about them. The Duke of Argyll and Lord Lansdowne had left him; his Irish policy had cost him his Irish secretary, and his Egyptian policy had cost him Mr. Bright. They had got into a war, they had been baffled in legislation, they had to raise the most unpopular of taxes, there had been the frightful tragedy in Ireland. Yet all seemed to have been completely overcome in the public mind by the power of Mr. Gladstone in uniting his friends and frustrating his foes, and the more bitterly he was hated by society, the more warmly attached were the mass of the people. Anybody who had foreseen all this would have concluded that the government must be in extremity, but he went to the Guildhall on the 9th of November 1882, and had the best possible reception on that famous stage. One tory newspaper felt bound to admit that Mr. Gladstone and his colleagues had rehabilitated themselves in the public judgment with astounding rapidity, and were now almost as strong in popular and parliamentary support as when they first took office.[2] Another tory print declared Mr. Gladstone to be stronger, more popular, more despotic, than at any time since the policy to carry out which he was placed in office was disclosed.[3] The session of 1882 had only been exceeded in duration by two sessions for fifty years.

The reader has had pictures enough from friendly hands, so here is one from a persistent foe, one of the most brilliant journalists of that time, who listened to him from

---

[1] *Times*, Dec. 8, 1882.   [3] *Morning Post*, Oct. 20, 1882.
[2] *Standard*, Nov. 16, 1882.

the gallery for years. The words are from an imaginary dialogue, and are put into the mouth of a well-known whig in parliament: —

Sir, I can only tell you that, profoundly as I distrusted him, and lightly as on the whole I valued the external qualities of his eloquence, I have never listened to him even for a few minutes without ceasing to marvel at his influence over men. That white-hot face, stern as a Covenanter's yet mobile as a comedian's; those restless, flashing eyes; that wondrous voice, whose richness its northern burr enriched as the tang of the wood brings out the mellowness of a rare old wine; the masterly cadence of his elocution; the vivid energy of his attitudes; the fine animation of his gestures; — sir, when I am assailed through eye and ear by this compacted phalanx of assailants, what wonder that the stormed outposts of the senses should spread the contagion of their own surrender through the main encampment of the mind, and that against my judgment, in contempt of my conscience, nay, in defiance of my very will, I should exclaim, 'This is indeed the voice of truth and wisdom. This man is honest and sagacious beyond his fellows. He must be believed, he must be obeyed!'[1]

On the day of his political jubilee (Dec. 13), the event was celebrated in many parts of the country, and he received congratulatory telegrams from all parts of the world; for it was not only two hundred and forty liberal associations who sent him joyful addresses. The Roumelians poured out aloud their gratitude to him for the interest he constantly manifested in their cause, and for his powerful and persistent efforts for their emancipation. From Athens came the news that they had subscribed for the erection of his statue, and from the Greeks also came a splendid casket. In his letter of thanks,[2] after remonstrating against its too great material value, he said: —

I know not well how to accept it, yet I am still less able to decline it, when I read the touching lines of the accompanying address, in itself an ample token, in which you have so closely

[1] Traill's *New Lucian*, pp. 305–6, — in spite of politics, a book of admirable wit, scholarship, and ingenious play of mind.
[2] To Mr. Hazzopolo, Dec. 22, 1882.

associated my name with the history and destinies of your country.. I am not vain enough to think that I have deserved any of the numerous acknowledgments which I have received, especially from Greeks, on completing half a century of parliamentary life. Your over-estimate of my deeds ought rather to humble than to inflate me. But to have laboured within the measure of justice for the Greece of the future, is one of my happiest political recollections, and to have been trained in a partial knowledge of the Greece of the past has largely contributed to whatever slender faculties I possess for serving my own country or my kind. I earnestly thank you for your indulgent judgment and for your too costly gifts, and I have the honour to remain, etc.

What was deeper to him than statues or caskets was found in letters from comparative newcomers into the political arena thanking him not only for his long roll of public service, but much more for the example and encouragement that his life gave to younger men endeavouring to do something for the public good. To one of these he wrote (Dec. 15) : —

I thank you most sincerely for your kind and friendly letter. As regards the prospective part of it, I can assure you that I should be slow to plead the mere title to retirement which long labour is supposed to earn. But I have always watched, and worked according to what I felt to be the measure of my own mental force. A monitor from within tells me that though I may still be equal to some portions of my duties, or as little unequal as heretofore, there are others which I cannot face. I fear therefore I must keep in view an issue which cannot be evaded.

III

As it happened, this volume of testimony to the affection, gratitude, and admiration thus ready to go out to him from so many quarters coincided in point of time with one or two extreme vexations in the conduct of his daily business as head of the government. Some of them were aggravated by the loss of a man whom he regarded as one of his two or three most important friends. In September 1882 the Dean of Windsor died, and in his death Mr. Gladstone suffered a heavy blow. To the end he always spoke of Dr. Wellesley's friendship, and the value of his sagacity and honest service, with a warmth by this time given to few.

Death of the Dean of Windsor.

To Lord Granville, Sept. 18, 1882. — My belief is that he has been cognizant of every crown appointment in the church for nearly a quarter of a century, and that the whole of his influence has been exercised with a deep insight and a large heart for the best interests of the crown and the church. If their character during this period has been in the main more satisfactory to the general mind of the country than at some former periods, it has been in no small degree owing to him.

It has been my duty to recommend I think for fully forty of the higher appointments, including twelve which were episcopal. I rejoice to say that every one of them has had his approval. But I do not scruple to own that he has been in no small degree a help and guide to me; and as to the Queen, whose heart I am sure is at this moment bleeding, I do not believe she can possibly fill his place as a friendly adviser either in ecclesiastical or other matters.

To the Duchess of Wellington, Sept. 24. — He might, if he had chosen, have been on his way to the Archbishopric of Canterbury. Ten or eleven years ago, when the present primate was not expected to recover, the question of the succession was considered, and I had her Majesty's consent to the idea I have now mentioned. But, governed I think by his great modesty, he at once refused.

To Mrs. Wellesley, Nov. 19, 1882. — I have remained silent, at least to you, on a subject which for no day has been absent from my thoughts, because I felt that I could add nothing to your consolations and could take away nothing from your grief under your great calamity. But the time has perhaps come when I may record my sense of a loss of which even a small share is so large. The recollections of nearly sixty years are upon my mind, and through all that period I have felt more and more the force and value of your husband's simple and noble character. No less have I entertained an ever-growing sense of his great sagacity and the singularly true and just balance of his mind. We owe much

indeed to you both for your constantly renewed kindness, but
I have another debt to acknowledge in the invaluable assistance
which he afforded me in the discharge of one among the most
important and most delicate of my duties. This void never can be
filled, and it helps me in some degree to feel what must be the void
to you. Certainly he was happy in the enjoyment of love and
honour from all who knew him; yet these were few in comparison
with those whom he so wisely and so warmly served without their
knowing it; and the love and honour paid him, great as they were,
could not be as great as he deserved. His memory is blessed —
may his rest be deep and sweet, and may the memory and example
of him ever help you in your onward pilgrimage.

The same week Dr. Pusey died — a name that filled so
large a space in the religious history of England for some
thirty years of the century. Between Mr. Gladstone and
him the old relations of affectionate friendship subsisted
unbroken, notwithstanding the emancipation, as we may
call it, of the statesman from maxims and principles,
though not, so far as I know, from any of the leading
dogmatic beliefs cherished by the divine. 'I hope,' he
wrote to Phillimore (Sept. 20, 1882), 'to attend Dr. Pusey's
funeral to-morrow at Oxford. . . . I shall have another
mournful office to discharge in attending the funeral
of the Dean of Windsor, more mournful than the first.
Dr. Pusey's death is the ingathering of a ripe shock, and
I go to his obsequies in token of deep respect and in
memory of much kindness from him early in my life. But
the death of Dean Wellesley is to my wife and me an
unexpected and very heavy blow, also to me an irreparable
loss. I had honoured and loved him from Eton days.'
The loss of Dean Wellesley's counsels was especially felt
in ecclesiastical appointments, and the greatest of these was
made necessary by the death of the Archbishop of Canterbury at the beginning of December. That the prime
minister should regard so sage, conciliatory, and large-
minded a steersman as Dr. Tait with esteem was certain,
and their relations were easy and manly. Still, Tait had
been an active liberal when Mr. Gladstone was a tory, and

from the distant days of the *Tracts for the Times*, when Tait had stood amongst the foremost in open dislike of the new tenets, their paths in the region of theology lay wide apart. 'I well remember,' says Dean Lake, 'a conversation with Mr. Gladstone on Tait's appointment to London in 1856, when he was much annoyed at Tait's being preferred to Bishop Wilberforce, and of which he reminded me nearly thirty years afterwards, at the time of the archbishop's death, by saying, "Ah! I remember you maintaining to me at that time that his σεμνότης and his judgment would make him a great bishop." '[1] And so, from the point of ecclesiastical statesmanship, he unquestionably was.

The recommendation of a successor in the historic see of Canterbury, we may be very certain, was no common event to Mr. Gladstone. Tait on his deathbed had given his opinion that Dr. Harold Browne, the Bishop of Winchester, would do more than any other man to keep the peace of the church. The Queen was strong in the same sense, thinking that the bishop might resign in a year or two, if he could not do the work. He was now seventy-one years old, and Mr. Gladstone judged this to be too advanced an age for the metropolitan throne. He was himself now seventy-three, and though his sense of humour was not always of the protective kind, he felt the necessity of some explanatory reason, and with him to seek a plea was to find one. He wrote to the Bishop of Winchester : —

. . . It may seem strange that I, who in my own person exhibit so conspicuously the anomaly of a disparate conjunction between years and duties, should be thus forward in interpreting the circumstances of another case certainly more mitigated in many respects, yet differing from my own case in one vital point, the newness of the duties of the English, or rather anglican or British, primacy to a diocesan bishop, however able and experienced, and the newness of mental attitude and action, which they would require. Among the materials of judgment in such an instance, it seems right to reckon precedents for what they are worth; and I cannot find that from the time of Archbishop Sheldon any one has

[1] *Life of Tait*, i. p. 109.

assumed the primacy at so great an age as seventy. Juxon, the predecessor of Sheldon, was much older; but his case was altogether peculiar. I cannot say how pleasant it would have been to me personally, but for the barrier I have named, to mark my respect and affection for your lordship by making to you such a proposal. What is more important is, that I am directly authorised by her Majesty to state that this has been the single impediment to her conferring the honour, and imposing the burden, upon you of such an offer.[1]

The world made free with the honoured name of Church, the Dean of Saint Paul's, and it has constantly been said that he declined the august preferment to Canterbury on this occasion. In that story there is no truth. 'Formal offer,' the Dean himself wrote to a friend, 'there was none, and could not be, for I had already on another occasion told my mind to Gladstone, and said that reasons of health, apart from other reasons, made it impossible for me to think of anything, except a retirement altogether from office.'[2]

When it was rumoured that Mr. Gladstone intended to recommend Dr. Benson, then Bishop of Truro, to the archbishopric, a political supporter came to remonstrate with him. 'The Bishop of Truro is a strong tory,' he said, 'but that is not all. He has joined Mr. Raikes's election committee at Cambridge ; and it was only last week that Raikes made a violent personal attack on yourself.' 'Do you know,' replied Mr. Gladstone, 'you have just supplied me with a strong argument in Dr. Benson's favour ? For if he had been a worldly man or self-seeker, he would not have done anything so imprudent.' Perhaps we cannot wonder that whips and wirepullers deemed this to be somewhat over-ingenious, a Christianity out of season. Even liberals who took another point of view, still asked themselves how it was

---

[1] Bishop Browne writes to a friend (*Life*, p. 457) : 'Gladstone, I learned both from himself and others, searched into all precedents from the Commonwealth to the present day for a primate who began his work at seventy, and found none but Juxon. Curiously, I have been reading that he himself, prompted by Bishop Wilberforce, wanted Palmerston to appoint Sumner (of Winchester) when he was seventy-two. It was when they feared they could not get Longley (who was sixty-eight).'

[2] *Life and Letters of Dean Church*, p. 307.

that when church preferment came his way, the prime minister
so often found the best clergymen in the worst politicians.
They should have remembered that he was of those who
believed 'no more glorious church in Christendom to
exist than the church of England'; and its official ordering
was in his eyes not any less, even if it was not infinitely
more, important in the highest interests of the nation
than the construction of a cabinet or the appointment
of permanent heads of departments. The church was at
this moment, moreover, in one of those angry and perilous
crises that came of the Elizabethan settlement and the
Act of Uniformity, and the anglican revival forty years
ago, and all the other things that mark the arrested progress of the Reformation in England. The anti-ritualist
hunt was up. Civil courts were busy with the conscience
and conduct of the clergy. Harmless but contumacious
priests were under lock and key. It seemed as if more
might follow them, or else as if the shock of the great tractarian catastrophe of the forties might in some new shape
recur. To recommend an archbishop in times like these
could to a churchman be no light responsibility.

With such thoughts in his mind, however we may judge
them, it is not altogether surprising that in seeking an ecclesiastical governor for an institution to him the most sacred
and beloved of all forms of human association, Mr. Gladstone
should have cared very little whether the personage best
fitted in spirituals was quite of the right shade as to state
temporals. The labour that he now expended on finding the
best man is attested by voluminous correspondence. Dean
Church, who was perhaps the most freely consulted by the
prime minister, says, 'Of one thing I am quite certain, that
never for hundreds of years has so much honest disinterested
pains been taken to fill the primacy — such inquiry and
trouble resolutely followed out to find the really fittest man,
apart from every personal and political consideration, as in
this case.'[1]

Another ecclesiastical vacancy that led to volumes of
correspondence was the deanery of Westminster the year

[1] *Life and Letters of Dean Church*, p. 307.

before. In the summer of 1881 Dean Stanley died, and it is interesting to note how easy Mr. Gladstone found it to do full justice to one for whom as erastian and latitudinarian he could in opinion have such moderate approval. In offering to the Queen his 'cordial sympathy' for the friend whom she had lost, he told her how early in his own life and earlier still in the dean's he had opportunities of watching the development of his powers, for they had both been educated at a small school near the home of Mr. Gladstone's boyhood.[1] He went on to speak of Stanley's boundless generosity and brilliant gifts, his genial and attaching disposition. 'There may be,' he said, 'and must be much diversity as to parts of the opinions of Dean Stanley, but he will be long remembered as one who was capable of the deepest and widest love, and who received it in return.'

Far away from these regions of what he irreverently called the shovel hat, about this time Carlyle died (Feb. 4, 1881), a firm sympathiser with Mr. Gladstone in his views of the unspeakable Turk, but in all else the rather boisterous preacher of a gospel directly antipathetic. 'Carlyle is at least a great fact in the literature of his time; and has contributed largely, in some respects too largely, towards forming its characteristic habits of thought.' So Mr. Gladstone wrote in 1876, in a highly interesting parallel between Carlyle and Macaulay — both of them honest, he said, both notwithstanding their honesty partisans; both of them, though variously, poets using the vehicle of prose; both having the power of painting portraits extraordinary for vividness and strength; each of them vastly though diversely powerful in expression, each more powerful in expression than in thought; neither of them to be resorted to for comprehensive disquisition, nor for balanced and impartial judgments.[2] Perhaps it was too early in 1876 to speak of Carlyle as forming the characteristic habits of thought of his time, but undoubtedly now when he died, his influence was beginning to tell heavily against the speculative liberalism that had reigned in England for two generations, with enormous advantage to the peace, prosperity and power of

[1] See vol. i. p. 47.   [2] *Gleanings*, ii. p. 287.

the country and the two generations concerned. Half lights
and half truths are, as Mr. Gladstone implies, the utmost
that Carlyle's works were found to yield in philosophy and
history, but his half lights pointed in the direction in which
men for more material reasons thought that they desired
to go.

IV

A reconstruction of the ministry had become necessary by
his own abandonment of the exchequer. For one moment it
was thought that Lord Hartington might become chancellor,
leaving room for Lord Derby at the India office, but Lord
Derby was not yet ready to join. In inviting Mr. Childers to
take his place as chancellor of the exchequer, Mr. Gladstone
told him (Dec. 1, 1882): 'The basis of my action is not
so much a desire to be relieved from labour, as an anxiety
to give the country a much better finance minister than
myself, — one whose eyes will be always ranging freely and
vigilantly over the whole area of the great establishments,
the public service and the laws connected with his office,
for the purposes of improvement and of good husbandry.'

The claim of Sir Charles Dilke to a seat in the cabinet
had become irresistible alike by his good service as under-
secretary at the foreign office, and by his position out of
doors; and as the admission of a radical must be balanced
by a whig — so at least it was judged — Mr. Gladstone
succeeded in inducing Lord Derby to join, though he had
failed with him not long before.[1]

Apart from general objections at court, difficulties arose
about the distribution of office. Mr. Chamberlain, who has
always had his full share of the virtues of staunch friendship, agreed to give up to Sir C. Dilke his own office, which
he much liked, and take the duchy, which he did not like
at all. In acknowledging Mr. Chamberlain's letter (Dec. 14)
Mr. Gladstone wrote to him, 'I shall be glad, if I can, to
avoid acting upon it. But I cannot refrain from at once
writing a hearty line to acknowledge the self-sacrificing
spirit in which it is written; and which, I am sure, you
will never see cause to repent or change.' This, however,

[1] Lord Derby had refused office in the previous May.

BOOK
VIII.

1882.

was found to be no improvement, for Mr. Chamberlain's
language about ransoms to be paid by possessors of property, the offence of not toiling and spinning, and the
services rendered by courtiers to kings, was not much less
repugnant than rash assertions about the monarch evading the income-tax.   All contention on personal points
was a severe trial to Mr. Gladstone, and any conflict with
the wishes of the Queen tried him most of all.   One of his
audiences upon these affairs Mr. Gladstone mentions in his
diary: ' Dec. 11. — Off at 12.45 to Windsor in the frost and
fog.   Audience of her Majesty at 3.   Most difficult ground,
but aided by her beautiful manners, we got over it better
than might have been expected.'   The dispute was stubborn,
but like all else it came to an end; colleagues were obliging,
holes and pegs were accommodated, and Lord Derby went
to the colonial office, and Sir C. Dilke to the local government board.   An officer of the court, who was in all the
secrets and had foreseen all the difficulties, wrote that the
actual result was due ' to the judicious manner in which Mr.
Gladstone managed everything.   He argued in a friendly
way, urging his views with moderation, and appealed to the
Queen's sense of courtesy.'

In the course of his correspondence with the Queen, the
prime minister drew her attention (Dec. 18) to the fact that
when the cabinet was formed it included three ministers
reputed to belong to the radical section, Mr. Bright, Mr.
Forster, and Mr. Chamberlain, and of these only the last
remained.   The addition of Lord Derby was an addition
drawn from the other wing of the party.   Another point
presented itself.   The cabinet originally contained eight
commoners and six peers.   There were now seven peers
and six commoners.   This made it requisite to add a
commoner.   As for Mr. Chamberlain, the minister assured
the Queen that though he had not yet, like Mr. Bright,
undergone the mollifying influence of age and experience, his leanings on foreign policy would be far more
acceptable to her Majesty than those of Mr. Bright, while
his views were not known to be any more democratic in
principle.   He further expressed his firm opinion (Dec. 22)

that though Lord Derby might on questions of peace and war be some shades nearer to the views of Mr. Bright than the other members of the cabinet, yet he would never go anything like the length of Mr. Bright in such matters. In fact, said Mr. Gladstone, the cabinet must be deemed a little less pacific now than it was at its first formation. This at least was a consolatory reflection.

Ministerial reconstruction is a trying moment for the politician who thinks himself ' not a favourite with his stars,' and is in a hurry for a box seat before his time has come. Mr. Gladstone was now harassed with some importunities of this kind.[1] Personal collision with any who stood in the place of friends was always terrible to him. His gift of sleep deserted him. ' It is disagreeable to talk of oneself,' he wrote to Lord Granville (Jan. 2, 1883), 'when there is so much of more importance to think and speak about, but I am sorry to say that the incessant strain and pressure of work, and especially the multiplication of these personal questions, is overdoing me, and for the first time my power of sleep is seriously giving way. I dare say it would soon right itself if I could offer it any other medicine than the medicine in Hood's " Song of the Shirt." ' And the next day he wrote : ' Last night I improved, $3\frac{1}{2}$ hours to $4\frac{1}{2}$, but this is different from 7 and 8, my uniform standard through life.' And two days later : ' The matter of sleep is with me a very grave one. I am afraid I may have to go up and consult Clark. My habit has always been to reckon my hours rather exultingly, and say how little I am awake. It is not impossible that I may have to ask you to meet me in London, but I will not do this except in necessity. I think that, to convey a clear idea, I should say I attach no importance to the broken sleep itself ; it is the state of the brain, tested by my own sensations, when I begin my work in the morning, which may

[1] The matter itself has no importance, but a point of principle or etiquette at one time connected with it is perhaps worth mentioning. To a colleague earlier in the year Mr. Gladstone wrote : 'I can affirm with confidence that the notion of a title in the cabinet to be consulted on the succession to a cabinet office is absurd. It is a title which cabinet ministers do not possess. During thirty-eight years since I first entered the cabinet, I have never known more than a friendly announcement before publicity, and very partial consultation perhaps with one or two, especially the leaders in the second House.'

make me need higher assurance.' Sir Andrew Clark, 'overflowing with kindness, as always,' went down to Hawarden
(Jan. 7), examined, and listened to the tale of heavy wakeful
nights. While treating the case as one of temporary and
accidental derangement, he instantly forbade a projected
expedition to Midlothian, and urged change of air and scene.

This prohibition eased some of the difficulties at Windsor,
where Midlothian was a name of dubious association, and in
announcing to the Queen the abandonment by Dr. Clark's
orders of the intended journey to the north, Mr. Gladstone
wrote (Jan. 8, 1883): —

In your Majesty's very kind reference on the 5th to his former
visits to Midlothian, and to his own observations on the 24th
April 1880, your Majesty remarked that he had said he did not
then think himself a responsible person. He prays leave to fill up
the outline which these words convey by saying he at that time
(to the best of his recollection) humbly submitted to your Majesty
his admission that he must personally bear the consequences of all
that he had said, and that he thought some things suitable to be
said by a person out of office which could not suitably be said by a
person in office; also that, as is intimated by your Majesty's words,
the responsibilities of the two positions severally were different.
With respect to the political changes named by your Majesty, Mr.
Gladstone considers that the very safe measure of extending to the
counties the franchise enjoyed by the boroughs stands in all likelihood for early consideration; but he doubts whether there can be
any serious dealing of a general character with the land laws by
the present parliament, and so far as Scottish disestablishment
is concerned he does not conceive that that question has made
progress during recent years; and he may state that in making
arrangements recently for his expected visit to Midlothian, he had
received various overtures for deputations on this subject, which
he had been able to put aside.

V

On January 17, along with Mrs. Gladstone, at Charing
Cross he said good-bye to many friends, and at Dover to
Lord Granville, and the following afternoon he found himself
at Cannes, the guest of the Wolvertons at the Château

Scott, 'nobly situated, admirably planned, and the kindness exceeded even the beauty and the comfort.' 'Here,' he says, 'we fell in with the foreign hours, the snack early, déjeuner at noon, dinner at seven, break-up at ten. . . . I am stunned by this wonderful place, and so vast a change at a moment's notice in the conditions of life.' He read steadily through the *Odyssey*, Dixon's *History of the Church of England*, Scherer's *Miscellanies*, and *The Life of Clerk-Maxwell*, and every day he had long talks and walks with Lord Acton on themes personal, political and religious — and we may believe what a restorative he found in communion with that deep and well-filled mind — that 'most satisfactory mind,' as Mr. Gladstone here one day calls it. He took drives to gardens that struck him as fairyland. The Prince of Wales paid him kindly attentions as always. He had long conversations with the Comte de Paris, and with M. Clémenceau, and with the Duke of Argyll, the oldest of his surviving friends. In the evening he played whist. Home affairs he kept at bay pretty successfully, though a speech of Lord Hartington's about local government in Ireland drew from him a longish letter to Lord Granville that the reader, if he likes, will find elsewhere.[1] His conversation with M. Clémenceau (whom he found 'decidedly pleasing') was thought indiscreet, but though the most circumspect of men, the buckram of a spurious discretion was no favourite wear with Mr. Gladstone. As for the report of his conversation with the French radical, he wrote to Lord Granville, 'It includes much which Clémenceau did not say to me, and omits much which he did, for our principal conversation was on Egypt, about which he spoke in a most temperate and reasonable manner.' He read the 'harrowing details' of the terrible scene in the court-house at Kilmainham, where the murderous Invincibles were found out. 'About Carey,' he said to Lord Granville, 'the spectacle is indeed loathsome, but I cannot doubt that the Irish government are distinctly *right*. In accepting an approver you do not incite him to do what is in itself wrong; only his own bad mind can make it wrong to him. The government looks for the truth. Approvers are, I suppose,

CHAP.
VI.

Æt. 74.

[1] See Appendix.

for the most part base, but I do not see how you could act
on a distinction of degree between them. Still, one would
have heard the hiss from the dock with sympathy.'

Lord Granville wrote to him (Jan. 31, 1883) that the
Queen insisted much upon his diminishing the amount of
labour thrown upon him, and expressed her opinion that
his acceptance of a peerage would relieve him of the heavy
strain. Lord Granville told her that personally he should
be delighted to see him in the Lords, but that he had great
doubts whether Mr. Gladstone would be willing. From
Cannes Mr. Gladstone replied (Feb. 3): —

As to removal into the House of Lords, I think the reasons
against it of general application are conclusive. At least I cannot
see my way in regard to them. But at any rate it is obvious that
such a step is quite inapplicable to the circumstances created by
the present difficulty. It is really most kind of the Queen to
testify such an interest, and the question is how to answer her.
You would do this better and perhaps more easily than I.

Perhaps he remembered the case of Pulteney and of the
Great Commoner.

He was not without remorse at the thought of his colleagues in harness while he was lotus-eating. On the day
before the opening of the session he writes, 'I feel dual: I
am at Cannes, and in Downing Street eating my parliamentary dinner.' By February 21 he was able to write to
Lord Granville : —

As regards my health there is no excuse. It has got better and
better as I have stayed on, and is now, I think, on a higher level
than for a long time past. My sleep, for example, is now about as
good as it can be, and far better than it was during the autumn
sittings, *after* which it got so bad. The pleasure I have had in
staying does not make an argument at all; it is a mere expression
or anticipation of my desire to be turned out to grass for good. . . .

At last the end of the holiday came. 'I part from Cannes
with a heavy heart,' he records on Feb. 26 : —

Read the *Iliad*, copiously. Off by the 12.30 train. We
exchanged bright sun, splendid views, and a little dust at the

beginning of our journey, for frost and fog, which however hid no scenery, at the end. *27th, Tuesday.* — Reached Paris at 8, and drove to the Embassy, where we had a most kind reception [from Lord Lyons]. Wrote to Lord Granville, Lord Spencer, Sir W. Harcourt. Went with Lord L. to see M. Grévy ; also Challemel-Lacour in his most palatial abode. Looked about among the shops ; and at the sad face of the Tuileries. An embassy party to dinner; excellent company.

To Lord Granville.

Feb. 27th. — I have been with Lord Lyons to see Grévy and Challemel-Lacour. Grévy's conversation consisted of civilities and a mournful lecture on the political history of France, with many compliments to the superiority of England. Challemel thought the burdens of public life intolerable and greater here than in England, which is rather strong. Neither made the smallest allusion to present questions, and it was none of my business to introduce them. . . .

After three days of bookstalls, ivory-hunting, and conversation, by the evening of March 2 the travellers were once more after a bright day and rapid passage safe in Downing Street.

Shortly after their return from the south of France the Gladstones paid a visit to the Prince and Princess of Wales : —

March 30, 1883. — Off at 11.30 to Sandringham. Reception kinder if possible even than heretofore. Wrote. . . . Read and worked on London municipality. 31, *Saturday.* — Wrote. Root-cut a small tree in the forenoon ; then measured oaks in the park ; one of 30 feet. In the afternoon we drove to Houghton, a stately house and place, but woe-begone. Conversation with Archbishop of Canterbury, Prince of Wales and others. Read . . . *Life of Hatherley*, Law's account of Craig. *April* 1. — Sandringham church, morning. West Newton, evening. Good services and sermons from the archbishop. The Prince bade me read the lessons. Much conversation with the archbishop, also Duke of Cambridge. Read *Nineteenth Century* on Revised Version ; Manning on Education ; *Life of Hatherley;* Craig's *Catechism.* Wrote, etc. 2. — Off

at 11. D. Street 3.15. Wrote to the Queen. Long conversation
with the archbishop in the train.

Here a short letter or two may find a place : —

To Lady Jessel on her husband's death.

March 30. — Though I am reluctant to intrude upon your sorrow
still so fresh, and while I beg of you on no account to acknowledge
this note, I cannot refrain from writing to assure you not only of
my sympathy with your grief, but of my profound sense of the loss
which the country and its judiciary have sustained by the death of
your distinguished husband. From the time of his first entrance
into parliament I followed his legal expositions with an ignorant
but fervid admiration, and could not help placing him in the first
rank, a rank held by few, of the many able and powerful lawyers
whom during half a century I have known and heard in parliament. When I came to know him as a colleague, I found reason
to admire no less sincerely his superiority to considerations of
pecuniary interest, his strong and tenacious sense of the dignity of his office, and his thoroughly frank, resolute, and manly
character. These few words, if they be a feeble, yet I assure you
are also a genuine, tribute to a memory which I trust will long be
cherished. Earnestly anxious that you may have every consolation
in your heavy bereavement.

To Cardinal Manning.

April 19. — I thank you much for your kind note, though I am
sorry to have given you the trouble of writing it. Both of us have
much to be thankful for in the way of health, but I should have
hoped that your extremely spare living would have saved you
from the action of anything like gouty tendencies. As for myself,
I can in no way understand how it is that for a full half century
I have been permitted and enabled to resist a pressure of special
liabilities attaching to my path of life, to which so many have
given way. I am left as a solitary, surviving all his compeers.
But I trust it may not be long ere I escape into some position
better suited to declining years.

To Sir W. V. Harcourt.

April 27. — A separate line to thank you for your more than
kind words about my rather Alexandrine speech last night; as to

which I can only admit that it contained one fine passage — six
lines in length.[1] Your 'instincts' of kindliness in all personal
matters are known to all the world. I should be glad, on selfish
grounds, if I could feel sure that they had not a little warped your
judicial faculty for the moment. But this misgiving abates
nothing from my grateful acknowledgment.

An application was made to him on behalf of a member
of the opposite party for a political pension, and here is his
reply, to which it may be added that ten years later he had
come rather strongly to the view that political pensions
should be abolished, and he was only deterred from trying to carry out his view by the reminder from younger
ministers, not themselves applicants nor ever likely to be,
that it would hardly be a gracious thing to cut off benefac-
tions at a time when the bestowal of them was passing away
from him, though he had used them freely while that
bestowal was within his reach.

Political Pensions.

July 4, 1883. — You are probably aware that during the fifty
years which have passed since the system of political and civil
pensions was essentially remodelled, no political pension has been
granted by any minister except to one of those with whom he
stood on terms of general confidence and co-operation. It is
needless to refer to older practice.

This is not to be accounted for by the fact that after meeting
the just claims of political adherents, there has been nothing left
to bestow. For, although it has happened that the list of pensions
of the first class has usually been full, it has not been so with
political pensions of the other classes, which have, I think, rarely
if ever been granted to the fullest extent that the Acts have
allowed. At the present time, out of twelve pensions which may
legally be conferred, only seven have been actually given, if I
reckon rightly. I do not think that this state of facts can have
been due to the absence of cases entitled to consideration, and
I am quite certain that it is not to be accounted for by what
are commonly termed party motives. It was obvious to me that I

---

[1] The lines from Lucretius (in his speech on the Affirmation bill). See
above, p. 19.

BOOK
VIII.

1883.

could not create a precedent of deviation from a course undeviatingly pursued by my predecessors of all parties, without satisfying myself that a new form of proceeding would be reasonable and safe. The examination of private circumstances, such as I consider the Act to require, is from its own nature difficult and invidious: but the examination of competing cases in the ex-official corps is a function that could not, I think, be discharged with the necessary combination of free responsible action, and of exemption from offence and suspicion. Such cases plainly may occur.[1]

To H.R.H. the Prince of Wales.

August 14*th.* — I am much shocked at an omission which I made last night in failing to ask your royal Highness's leave to be the first to quit Lord Alcester's agreeable party, in order that I might attend to my duties in the House of Commons. In my early days not only did the whole company remain united, if a member of the royal family were present, until the exalted personage had departed; but I well recollect the application of the same rule in the case of the Archbishop (Howley) of Canterbury. I am sorry to say that I reached the House of Commons in time to hear some outrageous speeches from the ultra Irish members. I will not say that they were meant to encourage crime, but they tended directly to teach the Irish people to withhold their confidence from the law and its administrators; and they seemed to exhibit Lord Spencer as the enemy to the mass of the community — a sad and disgraceful fact, though I need not qualify what I told your royal Highness, that they had for some time past not been guilty of obstruction.

Even in pieces that were in their nature more or less official, he touched the occasions of life by a note that was not merely official, or was official in its best form. To Mrs. Garfield he wrote (July 21, 1881) : —

You will, I am sure, excuse me, though a personal stranger, for addressing you by letter, to convey to you the assurance of my

[1] In a party sense, as he told the cabinet, it might be wise enough to grant it, as it would please the public, displease the tories, and widen the breach between the fourth party and their front bench. Mr. Gladstone had suffered an unpleasant experience in another case, of the relations brought about by the refusal of a political pension after inquiry as to the accuracy of the necessary statement as to the applicant's need for it.

own feelings and those of my countrymen on the occasion of the late horrible attempt to murder the President of the United States, in a form more palpable at least than that of messages conveyed by telegraph. Those feelings have been feelings in the first instance of sympathy, and afterwards of joy and thankfulness, almost comparable, and I venture to say only second to the strong emotions of the great nation of which he is the appointed head. Individually I have, let me beg you to believe, had my full share in the sentiments which have possessed the British nation. They have been prompted and quickened largely by what I venture to think is the ever-growing sense of harmony and mutual respect and affection between the two countries, and of a relationship which from year to year becomes more and more a practical bond of union between us. But they have also drawn much of their strength from a cordial admiration of the simple heroism which has marked the personal conduct of the President, for we have not yet wholly lost the capacity of appreciating such an example of Christian faith and manly fortitude. This exemplary picture has been made complete by your own contribution to its noble and touching features, on which I only forbear to dwell because I am directly addressing you.

Under all the conventional solemnities in Mr. Gladstone on such occasions, we are conscious of a sincere feeling that they were in real relation to human life and all its chances and changes.

CHAPTER VII

COLLEAGUES — NORTHERN CRUISE — EGYPT

(1883)

Parran faville della sua virtute
In non curar d'argento nè d'affanni.
— *Paradiso*, xvii. 83.

Sparks of his worth shall show in the little heed he gives either to riches or to heavy toils.

THE session of 1883 was marked by one legislative performance of the first order, the bill devised against corrupt practices at elections. This invaluable measure was worked through the House of Commons mainly by Sir Henry James, the attorney general, whose skill and temper in a business that was made none the easier by the fact of every man in the House supposing himself to understand the subject, excited Mr. Gladstone's cordial admiration; it strengthened that peculiarly warm regard in which he held Sir Henry, not only now but even when the evil days of political severance came. The prime minister, though assiduous, as he always was, in the discharge of those routine and secondary duties which can never be neglected without damage to the House, had, for the first session in his career as head of a government, no burden in the shaping of a great bill. He insisted, in spite of some opposition in the cabinet, on accepting a motion pledging parliament to economy (April 3). In a debate on the Congo, he was taken by some to have gone near to giving up the treaty-making power of the crown. He had to face more than one of those emergencies that were naturally common for the leader of a party with a zealous radical wing represented in his cabinet, and in some measure these occasions beset Mr. Gladstone from 1869

110

onwards. His loyalty and kindness to colleagues who got themselves and him into scrapes by imprudent speeches, and his activity and resource in inventing ways out of scrapes, were always unfailing. Often the difficulty was with the Queen, sometimes with the House of Lords, occasionally with the Irish members. Birmingham, for instance, held a grand celebration (June 13) on the twenty-fifth anniversary of Mr. Bright's connection as its representative. Mr. Bright used strong language about 'Irish rebels,' and then learned that he would be called to account. He consulted Mr. Gladstone, and from him received a reply that exhibits the use of logic as applied to inconvenient displays of the sister art of rhetoric : —

To Mr. Bright.

June 15, 1883. — I have received your note, and I am extremely sorry either that you should have personal trouble after your great exertions, or that anything should occur to cloud the brilliancy or mar the satisfaction of your recent celebration in Birmingham. I have looked at the extract from your speech, which is to be alleged as the *corpus delicti*, with a jealous eye. It seems well to be prepared for the worst. The points are, I think, *three:* — 1. 'Not a few' tories are guilty of determined obstruction. I cannot conceive it possible that this can be deemed a breach of privilege. 2. These members are found 'in alliance' with the Irish party. Alliance is often predicated by those who disapprove, upon the ground that certain persons have been voting together. This I think can hardly be a breach of privilege even in cases where it may be disputable or untrue.

But then: 3. This Irish party are 'rebels' whose oath of allegiance is broken by association with the enemies of the country. Whether these allegations are true or not, the following questions arise : — (a) Can they be proved; (b) Are they allegations which would be allowed in debate ? I suppose you would agree with me that they cannot be proved; and I doubt whether they would be allowed in debate. The question whether they are a breach of privilege is for the House; but the Speaker would have to say, if called upon, whether they were allowable in debate. My impression is that he would say no; and I think you would not wish to use elsewhere expressions that you could not repeat in the House of Commons.

The Speaker has a jotting in his diary which may end this case of a great man's excess: —

June 18. — Exciting sitting. Bright's language about Irish rebels. Certainly his language was very strong and quite inadmissible if spoken within the House.   In conversation with Northcote I deprecated the taking notice of language outside the House, though I could not deny that the House, if it thought fit, might regard the words as a breach of privilege.   But Northcote was no doubt urged by his friends.

Mr. Chamberlain's was a heavier business, and led to much correspondence and difficult conversation in high places.   A little of it, containing general principles, will probably suffice here: —

To Sir Henry Ponsonby.

June 22. — *Re* Chamberlain's speech. I am sorry to say I had not read the report until I was warned by your letters to Granville and to Hamilton, for my sight does not allow me to read largely the small type of newspapers. I have now read it, and I must at once say with deep regret. We had done our best to keep the Bright celebration in harmony with the general tone of opinion by the mission which Granville kindly undertook. I am the more sorry about this speech, because Chamberlain has this year in parliament shown both tact and talent in the management of questions not polemical, such as the bankruptcy bill. The speech is open to exception from three points of view, as I think — first in relation to Bright, secondly in relation to the cabinet, thirdly and most especially in relation to the crown, to which the speech did not indicate the consciousness of his holding any special relation.

June 26. — It appeared to me in considering the case of Mr. Chamberlain's speech that by far the best correction would be found, if a natural opportunity should offer, in a speech differently coloured from himself. I found also that he was engaged to preside on Saturday next at the dinner of the Cobden Club. I addressed my-

self therefore to this point, and Mr. Chamberlain will revert, on CHAP.
that occasion, to the same line of thought. . . . But, like Gran- VII.
ville, I consider that the offence does not consist in holding cer- Æt. 74.
tain opinions, of which in my judgment the political force and
effect are greatly exaggerated, but in the attitude assumed, and
the tone and colour given to the speech.

To Lord Granville.

July 1, 1883. — I have read with care Chamberlain's speech of
last night [at the Cobden Club dinner]. . . . Am I right or
wrong in understanding the speech as follows? He admits without stint that in a cabinet concessions may be made as to action,
but he seems to claim an unlimited liberty of speech. Now I
should be as far as possible from asserting that under all circumstances speech must be confined within the exact limits to which
action is tied down. But I think the dignity and authority, not
to say the honour and integrity, of government require that the
liberty of speaking beyond those limits should be exercised
sparingly, reluctantly, and with much modesty and reserve.
Whereas Chamberlain's Birmingham speech exceeded it largely,
gratuitously, and with a total absence of recognition of the fact
that he was not an individual but a member of a body. And the
claim made last night to liberty of speech must be read with the
practical illustration afforded by the Birmingham discourse, which
evidently now stands as an instance, a sort of moral instance, of
the mode in which liberty of speech is to be reconciled with limi-
tation of action.[1]

In order to test the question, must we not bear in mind that the
liberty claimed in one wing of a cabinet may also be claimed in
another, and that while one minister says I support this measure,
though it does not go far enough, another may just as lawfully
say I support this measure, though it goes too far? For example,
Argyll agreed to the Disturbance Compensation bill in 1880

[1] By an odd coincidence, on the
day after my selection of this letter, I
read that the French prime minister,
M. Combes, laid down the doctrine
that the government is never committed by a minister's individual
declarations, but only by those of
the head of the government. He
alone has the power of making known
the direction given to policy, and
each minister individually has
authority only for the administration of his department (September
25, 1902). Of course this is wholly
incompatible with Mr. Gladstone's
ideas of parliamentary responsibility
and the cabinet system.

mainly out of regard to his colleagues and their authority. What if he had used in the House of Lords language like that I have just supposed ? Every extravagance of this kind puts weapons into the hands of opponents, and weakens the authority of government, which is hardly ever too strong, and is often too weak already.

In a letter written some years before when he was leader of the House, Mr. Gladstone on the subject of the internal discipline of a ministerial corps told one, who was at that time and now his colleague, a little story : —

As the subject is one of interest, perhaps you will let me mention the incident which first obliged me to reflect upon it. Nearly thirty years ago, my leader, Sir R. Peel, agreed in the Irish Tithes bills to give 25 per cent. of the tithe to the landlord in return for that ' Commutation.' Thinking this too much (you see that twist was then already in me), I happened to say so in a private letter to an Irish clergyman. Very shortly after I had a note from Peel, which inclosed one from Shaw, his head man in Ireland, complaining of my letter as making his work impossible if such things were allowed to go on. Sir R. Peel indorsed the remonstrance, and I had to sing small. The discipline was very tight in those days (and we were in opposition, not in government). But it worked well on the whole, and I must say it was accompanied on Sir R. Peel's part with a most rigid regard to rights of all kinds within the official or quasi-official corps, which has somewhat declined in more recent times.

A minister had made some reference in a public speech to what happened in the cabinet of which he was a member. ' I am sure it cannot have occurred to you,' Mr. Gladstone wrote, ' that the cabinet is the operative part of the privy council, that the privy councillor's oath is applicable to its proceedings, that this is a very high obligation, and that no one can dispense with it except the Queen. I may add that I believe no one is entitled even to make a note of the proceedings except the prime minister, who has to report its proceedings on every occasion of its meeting to the Queen, and who must by a few scraps assist his memory.'

By the end of the session, although its labours had not

been on the level of either 1881 or 1882, Mr. Gladstone was
somewhat strained. On Aug. 22 he writes to Mrs. Gladstone
at Hawarden: 'Yesterday at $4\frac{1}{2}$ I entered the House hoping to get out soon and write you a letter, when the Speaker
told me Northcote was going to raise a debate on the Appro-
priation bill, and I had to wait, listen, and then to speak for
more than an hour, which tired me a good deal, finding me
weak after sitting till 2.30 the night before, and a long cabinet in the interval. Rough work for 73!'

II

In September he took a holiday in a shape that, though he
was no hearty sailor, was always a pleasure and a relief to
him. Three letters to the Queen tell the story, and give a
glimpse of court punctilio: —

On the North Sea, Sept. 15. Posted at Copenhagen, Sept. 16, 1883.
— Mr. Gladstone presents his humble duty to your Majesty, and
has to offer his humble apology for not having sought from your
Majesty the usual gracious permission before setting foot on
a foreign shore. He embarked on the 8th in a steamer of the
Castles Company under the auspices of Sir Donald Currie, with
no more ambitious expectation than that of a cruise among the
Western Isles. But the extraordinary solidity, so to call it, of a
very fine ship (the Pembroke Castle, 4000 tons, 410 feet long) on
the water, rendering her in no small degree independent of
weather, encouraged his fellow-voyagers, and even himself, though
a most indifferent sailor, to extend their views, and the vessel is
now on the North Sea running over to Christiansand in Norway,
from whence it is proposed to go to Copenhagen, with the expectation, however, of again touching British soil in the middle
of next week. Mr. Gladstone humbly trusts that, under these
circumstances, his omission may be excused.

Mr. Tennyson, who is one of the party, is an excellent sailor,
and seems to enjoy himself much in the floating castle, as it may
be termed in a wider sense than that of its appellation on the
register. The weather has been variable with a heavy roll from
the Atlantic at the points not sheltered; but the stormy North
Sea has on the whole behaved extremely well as regards its two
besetting liabilities to storm and fog.

Ship ' Pembroke Castle,' Mouth of the Thames.   Sept. 20, 1883. —
Mr. Gladstone with his humble duty reports to your Majesty his
return this evening from Copenhagen to London. The passage
was very rapid, and the weather favourable. He had the
honour, with his wife and daughter and other companions of his
voyage, to receive an invitation to dine at Fredensborg on Monday. He found there the entire circle of illustrious personages who
have been gathered for some time in a family party, with a very
few exceptions. The singularly domestic character of this remarkable assemblage, and the affectionate intimacy which appeared to
pervade it, made an impression upon him not less deep than
the demeanour of all its members, which was so kindly and so
simple, that even the word condescending could hardly be applied
to it. Nor must Mr. Gladstone allow himself to omit another
striking feature of the remarkable picture, in the unrestrained and
unbounded happiness of the royal children, nineteen in number,
who appeared like a single family reared under a single roof.

[*The royal party, forty in number, visit the ship.*]

The Emperor of Russia proposed the health of your Majesty.
Mr. Gladstone by arrangement with your Majesty's minister at
this court, Mr. Vivian, proposed the health of the King and
Queen of Denmark, and the Emperor and Empress of Russia,
and the King and Queen of the He.lenes. The King of Denmark did Mr. Gladstone the honour to propose his health; and
Mr. Gladstone in acknowledging this toast, thought he could not
do otherwise, though no speeches had been made, than express
the friendly feeling of Great Britain towards Denmark, and the
satisfaction with which the British people recognised the tie of
race which unites them with the inhabitants of the Scandinavian
countries. Perhaps the most vigorous and remarkable portion of
the British nation had, Mr. Gladstone said, been drawn from
these countries. After luncheon, the senior imperial and royal
personages crowded together into a small cabin on the deck to
hear Mr. Tennyson read two of his poems, several of the younger
branches clustering round the doors. Between 2 and 3, the illustrious party left the *Pembroke Castle,* and in the midst of an
animated scene, went on board the King of Denmark's yacht,
which steamed towards Elsinore.

Mr. Gladstone was much pleased to observe that the Emperor of Russia appeared to be entirely released from the immediate pressure of his anxieties supposed to weigh much upon his mind. The Empress of Russia has the genial and gracious manners which on this, and on every occasion, mark H.R.H. the Princess of Wales.

CHAP. VII.

Æt. 74.

Sept. 22, 1883. — Mr. Gladstone presents his humble duty to your Majesty, and has to acknowledge your Majesty's letter of the 20th 'giving him full credit for not having reflected at, the time' when he decided, as your Majesty believes, to extend his recent cruise to Norway and Denmark.

He may humbly state that he had no desire or idea beyond a glance, if only for a few hours, at a little of the fine and peculiar scenery of Norway. But he is also responsible for having acquiesced in the proposal (which originated with Mr. Tennyson) to spend a day at Copenhagen, where he happens to have some associations of literary interest; for having accepted an unexpected invitation to dine with the king some thirty miles off; and for having promoted the execution of a wish, again unexpectedly communicated to him, that a visit of the illustrious party to the *Pembroke Castle* should be arranged. Mr. Gladstone ought probably to have foreseen all these things. With respect to the construction put upon his act abroad, Mr. Gladstone ought again, perhaps, to have foreseen that, in countries habituated to more important personal meetings, which are uniformly declared to be held in the interests of general peace, his momentary and unpremeditated contact with the sovereigns at Fredensborg would be denounced, or suspected of a mischievous design. He has, however, some consolation in finding that, in England at least, such a suspicion appears to have been confined to two secondary journals, neither of which has ever found (so far as he is aware) in any act of his anything but guilt and folly.

Thus adopting, to a great extent, your Majesty's view, Mr. Gladstone can confirm your Majesty's belief that (with the exception of a sentence addressed by him to the King of the Hellenes singly respecting Bulgaria), there was on all hands an absolute silence in regard to public affairs. . . .

In proposing at Kirkwall the health of the poet who was

his fellow-guest on the cruise, Mr. Gladstone let fall a hint
— a significant and perhaps a just one — on the comparative
place of politics and letters, the difference between the
statesman and orator and the poet. ' Mr. Tennyson's life
and labour,' he said, ' correspond in point of time as nearly
as possible to my own; but he has worked in a higher field,
and his work will be more durable. We public men play
a part which places us much in view of our countrymen,
but the words which we speak have wings and fly away and
disappear. . . . But the Poet Laureate has written his own
song on the hearts of his countrymen that can never die.'

III

It was said in 1884 that the organisation of Egypt was a
subject, whether regarded from the English or the European
point of view, that was probably more complicated and more
fraught with possible dangers in the future, than any question of foreign policy with which England had had to deal
for the last fifty years or more.

The arguments against prolonged English occupation were
tolerably clear. It would freeze all cordiality between ourselves and the French. It would make us a Mediterranean
military power. In case of war, the necessity of holding
Egypt would weaken us. In diplomacy it would expose
fresh surface to new and hostile combinations. Yet, giving
their full weight to every one of these considerations, a
British statesman was confronted by one of those intractable
dilemmas that make up the material of a good half of
human history. The Khedive could not stand by himself.
The Turk would not, and ought not to be endured for his
protector. Some other European power would step in and
block the English road. Would common prudence in such
a case suffer England to acquiesce and stand aside? Did
not subsisting obligations also confirm the precepts of policy and self-interest? In many minds this reasoning was
clenched and clamped by the sacrifices that England had
made when she took, and took alone, the initial military
step.

Egyptian affairs were one of the heaviest loads that

weighed upon Mr. Gladstone during the whole of 1884.
One day in the autumn of this year, towards the end of the
business before the cabinet, a minister asked if there was
anything else. 'No,' said Mr. Gladstone with sombre irony
as he gathered up his papers, 'we have done our Egyptian
business, and we are an Egyptian government.' His general
position was sketched in a letter to Lord Granville (Mar. 22,
1884): 'In regard to the Egyptian question proper, I am
conscious of being moved by three powerful considerations.
(1) Respect for European law, and for the peace of eastern
Europe, essentially connected with its observance. (2) The
just claims of the Khedive, who has given us no case against
him, and his people as connected with him. (3) Indisposition to extend the responsibilities of this country. On the
first two I feel very stiff. On the third I should have due
regard to my personal condition as a vanishing quantity.'

The question of the continuance of the old dual control by
England and France was raised almost immediately after
the English occupation began, but English opinion supported or stimulated the cabinet in refusing to restore a
form of co-operation that had worked well originally in the
hands of Baring and de Blignières, but had subsequently
betrayed its inherent weakness. France resumed what is
diplomatically styled liberty of action in Egypt; and many
months were passed in negotiations, the most entangled in
which a British government was ever engaged. Why did
not England, impatient critics of Mr. Gladstone and his
cabinet inquire, at once formally proclaim a protectorate?
Because it would have been a direct breach of her moral
obligations of good faith to Europe. These were undisputed
and indisputable. It would have brought her within instant
reach of a possible war with France, for which the sinister
and interested approval of Germany would have been small
compensation.

The issue lay between annexation and withdrawal, —
annexation to be veiled and indirect, withdrawal to be
cautious and conditional. No member of the cabinet at
this time seems to have listened with any favour whatever to the mention of annexation. Apart from other

objections, it would undeniably have been a flagrant breach of solemn international engagements. The cabinet was pledged up to the lips to withdrawal, and when Lord Hartington talked to the House of Commons of the last British soldier quitting Egypt in a few months, nobody ever doubted then or since that he was declaring the sincere intention of the cabinet. Nor was any doubt possible that the intention of the cabinet entirely coincided at that time with the opinion and wishes of the general public. The operations in Egypt had not been popular,[1] and the national temper was still as hostile to all expansion as when it cast out Lord Beaconsfield. Withdrawal, however, was beset with inextricable difficulties. Either withdrawal or annexation would have simplified the position and brought its own advantages. Neither was possible. The British government after Tel-el-Kebir vainly strove to steer a course that would combine the advantages of both. Say what they would, military occupation was taken to make them responsible for everything that happened in Egypt. This encouraged the view that they should give orders to Egypt, and make Egypt obey. But then direct and continuous interference with the Egyptian administration was advance in a path that could only end in annexation. To govern Egypt from London through a native ministry, was in fact nothing but annexation, and annexation in its clumsiest and most troublesome shape. Such a policy was least of all to be reconciled with the avowed policy of withdrawal. To treat native ministers as mere ciphers and puppets, and then to hope to leave them at the end with authority enough to govern the country by themselves, was pure delusion.

So much for our relations with Egypt internally. Then came Europe and the Powers, and the regulation of a financial situation of indescribable complexity. 'I sometimes fear,' Mr. Gladstone wrote to Lord Granville (Dec. 8,

---

[1] Many indications of this could be cited, if there were room. A parade of the victors of Tel-el-Kebir through the streets of London stirred little excitement. Two ministers went to make speeches at Liverpool, and had to report on returning to town that references to Egypt fell altogether flat.

1884), 'that some of the foreign governments have the same notion of me that Nicholas was supposed to have of Lord Aberdeen. But there is no one in the cabinet less disposed than I am to knuckle down to them in this Egyptian matter, about which they, except Italy, behave so ill, some of them without excuse.' 'As to Bismarck,' he said, 'it is a case of sheer audacity, of which he has an unbounded stock.' Two months before he had complained to Lord Granville of the same powerful personage : 'Ought not some notice to be taken of Bismarck's impudent reference to the 'English exchequer? Ought you to have such a remark in your possession without protest? He coolly assumes in effect that we are responsible for all the financial wants and occasions of Egypt.'

The sensible reader would resist any attempt to drag him into the Serbonian bog of Egyptian finance. Nor need I describe either the protracted conference of the European Powers, or the mission of Lord Northbrook. To this able colleague, Mr. Gladstone wrote on the eve of his departure (Aug. 29, 1884) : —

I cannot let you quit our shores without a word of valediction. Your colleagues are too deeply interested to be impartial judges of your mission. But they certainly cannot be mistaken in their appreciation of the generosity and courage which could alone have induced you to undertake it. Our task in Egypt generally may not unfairly be called an impossible task, and with the impossible no man can successfully contend. But we are well satisfied that whatever is possible, you will achieve; whatever judgment, experience, firmness, gentleness can do, will be done. Our expectations from the nature of the case must be moderate; but be assured, they will not be the measure of our gratitude. All good go with you.

Lord Northbrook's report when in due time it came, engaged the prime minister's anxious consideration, but it could not be carried further. What the Powers might agree to, parliament would not look at. The situation was one of the utmost delicacy and danger, as anybody who is aware of the diplomatic embarrassments of it knows. An agreement with France about the Suez Canal came to nothing. A conference upon finance came to nothing. Bismarck was out of humour with England, partly from his dislike of certain exalted English personages and influences at his own court, partly because it suited him that France and England should be bad friends, partly because, as he complained, whenever he tried to found a colony, we closed in upon him. He preached a sermon on *do ut des*, and while scouting the idea of any real differences with this country, he hinted that if we could not accommodate him in colonial questions, he might not find it in his power to accommodate us in European questions. Mr. Gladstone declared for treating every German claim in an equitable spirit, but said we had our own colonial communities to consider.

In March 1885, after negotiations that threatened to be endless, the London Convention was signed and the riddle of the financial sphinx was solved. This made possible the coming years of beneficent reform. The wonder is, says a competent observer, how in view of the indifference of most of the Powers to the welfare of Egypt and the bitter annoyance of France at our position in that country, the English government ever succeeded in inducing all the parties concerned to agree to so reasonable an arrangement.[1]

Meanwhile, as we shall see all too soon, the question of Egypt proper, as it was then called, had brought up the question of the Soudan, and with it an incident that made what Mr. Gladstone called 'the blackest day since the Phœnix Park.' In 1884 the government still seemed prosperous. The ordinary human tendency to croak never dies, especially in the politics of party. Men talked of humiliation abroad, ruin at home, agricultural interests doomed, trade at a standstill — calamities all obviously due to a government without spirit, and a majority with no independence. But then humiliation, to be sure, only meant jealousy in other countries because we declined to put ourselves in the wrong, and to be hoodwinked into unwise alliances. Ruin only meant reform without revolution. Doom meant an inappreciable falling off in the vast volume of our trade.

[1] Milner's *England in Egypt*, p. 185.

CHAPTER VIII

REFORM

(*1884*)

DECISION by majorities is as much an expedient as lighting by gas. In adopting it as a rule, we are not realising perfection, but bowing to an imperfection. It has the great merit of avoiding, and that by a test perfectly definite, the last resort to violence ; and of making force itself the servant instead of the master of authority. But our country rejoices in the belief that she does not decide all things by majorities. — GLADSTONE (1858).

' THE word procedure,' said Mr. Gladstone to a club of young political missionaries in 1884, 'has in it something homely, and it is difficult for any one, except those who pass their lives within the walls of parliament, to understand how vital and urgent a truth it is, that there is no more urgent demand, there is no aim or purpose more absolutely essential to the future victories and the future efficiency of the House of Commons, than that it should effect, with the support of the nation — for it can be effected in no other way — some great reform in the matter of its procedure.' He spoke further of the ' absolute and daily-growing necessity of what I will describe as a great internal reform of the House of Commons, quite distinct from that reform beyond its doors on which our hearts are at present especially set.' Reform from within and reform from without were the two tasks, neither of them other than difficult in themselves and both made supremely difficult by the extraordinary spirit of faction at that time animating the minority. The internal reform had been made necessary, as Mr. Gladstone expressed it, by systematised obstruction, based upon the abuse of ancient and generous rules, under which system the House of Commons ' becomes more and more the slave of some of the poorest

123

and most insignificant among its members.' Forty years
before he told the provost of Oriel, 'The forms of parliament
are little more than a mature expression of the principles of
justice in their application to the proceedings of deliberative
bodies, having it for their object to secure freedom and
reflection, and well fitted to attain that object.' These high
ideals had been gradually lowered, for Mr. Parnell had found
out that the rules which had for their object the security of
freedom and reflection, could be still more effectually wrested
to objects the very opposite.

In Mr. Gladstone's first session (1833) 395 members (the
speaker excluded) spoke, and the total number of speeches
was 5765. Fifty years later, in the session of 1883, the total
number of speeches had risen to 21,160. The remedies proposed from time to time in this parliament by Mr. Gladstone
were various, and were the occasion of many fierce and
stubborn conflicts. But the subject is in the highest degree
technical, and only intelligible to those who, as Mr. Gladstone
said, 'pass their lives within the walls of parliament' —
perhaps not by any means to all even of them. His papers
contain nothing of interest or novelty upon the question
either of devolution or of the compulsory stoppage of debate.
We may as well, therefore, leave it alone, only observing that
the necessity for the closure was probably the most unpalatable of all the changes forced on Mr. Gladstone by change
in social and political circumstance. To leave the subject
alone is not to ignore its extreme importance, either in the
effect of revolution in procedure upon the character of the
House, and its power of despatching and controlling national
business; or as an indication that the old order was yielding
in the political sphere as everywhere else to the conditions
of a new time.

II

The question of extending to householders in the country
the franchise that in 1867 had been conferred on householders in boroughs, had been first pressed with eloquence
and resolution by Mr. Trevelyan. In 1876 he introduced two
resolutions, one for extended franchise, the other for a new

arrangement of seats, made necessary by the creation of the new voters. In a tory parliament he had, of course, no chance. Mr. Gladstone, not naturally any more ardent for change in political machinery than Burke or Canning had been, was in no hurry about it, but was well aware that the triumphant parliament of 1880 could not be allowed to expire without the effective adoption by the government of proposals in principle such as those made by Mr. Trevelyan in 1876. One wing of the cabinet hung back. Mr. Gladstone himself, reading the signs in the political skies, felt that the hour had struck ; the cabinet followed, and the bill was framed. Never, said Mr. Gladstone, was a bill so large in respect of the numbers to have votes ; so innocent in point of principle, for it raised no new questions and sprang from no new principles. It went, he contended and most truly contended, to the extreme of consideration for opponents, and avoided several points that had especial attractions for friends. So likewise, the general principles on which redistribution of seats would be governed, were admittedly framed in a conservative spirit.

The comparative magnitude of the operation was thus described by Mr. Gladstone (Feb. 28, 1884) : —

In 1832 there was passed what was considered a Magna Charta of British liberties ; but that Magna Charta of British liberties added, according to the previous estimate of Lord John Russell, 500,000, while according to the results considerably less than 500,000 were added to the entire constituency of the three countries. After 1832 we come to 1866. At that time the total constituency of the United Kingdom reached 1,364,000. By the bills which were passed between 1867 and 1869 that number was raised to 2,448,000. Under the action of the present law the constituency has reached in round numbers what I would call 3,000,000. This bill, if it passes as presented, will add to the English constituency over 1,300,000 persons. It will add to the Scotch constituency, Scotland being at present rather better provided in this respect than either of the other countries, over 200,000, and to the Irish constituency over 400,000; or in the main, to the present aggre-

gate constituency of the United Kingdom taken at 3,000,000 it
will add 2,000,000 more, nearly twice as much as was added
since 1867, and more than four times as much as was added in
1832.

The bill was read a second time (April 7) by the overwhelming majority of 340 against 210. Even those who
most disliked the measure admitted that a majority of this
size could not be made light of, though they went on in
charity to say that it did not represent the honest opinion
of those who composed it. It was in fact, as such persons
argued, the strongest proof of the degradation brought into
our politics by the Act of 1867. ' All the bribes of Danby or
of Walpole or of Pelham,' cried one excited critic, 'all the
bullying of the Tudors, all the lobbying of George III., would
have been powerless to secure it in the most corrupt or the
most servile days of the ancient House of Commons.' [1]
On the third reading the opposition disappeared from the
House, and on Mr. Gladstone's prompt initiative it was
placed on record in the journals that the bill had been
carried by a unanimous verdict. It went to the Lords, and
by a majority, first of 59 and then of 50, they put what Mr.
Gladstone mildly called ' an effectual stoppage on the bill, or
in other words did practically reject it.' The plain issue, if
we can call it plain, was this. What the tories, with different
degrees of sincerity, professed to dread was that the election
might take place on the new franchise, but with an unaltered
disposition of parliamentary seats. At heart the bulk of
them were as little friendly to a lowered franchise in the
counties, as they had been in the case of the towns before Mr.
Disraeli educated them. But this was a secret dangerous
to let out, for the enfranchised workers in the towns would
never understand why workers in the villages should not
have a vote. Apart from this, the tory leaders believed that
unless the allotment of seats went with the addition of a
couple of million new voters, the prospect would be ruinously
unfavourable to their party, and they offered determined
resistance to the chance of a jockeying operation of this

[1] *Saturday Review*, April 12, 1884.

kind. At least one very eminent man among them had
privately made up his mind that the proceeding supposed to
be designed by their opponents — their distinct professions
notwithstanding — would efface the tory party for thirty years
to come. Mr. Gladstone and his government on the other
hand agreed, on grounds of their own and for reasons of
their own, that the two changes should come into operation
together. What they contended was, that to tack redistribution on to franchise, was to scotch or kill franchise. 'I do
not hesitate to say,' Mr. Gladstone told his electors, 'that
those who are opposing us, and making use of this topic of
redistribution of seats as a means for defeating the franchise
bill, know as well as we do that, had we been such idiots and
such dolts as to present to parliament a bill for the combined
purpose, or to bring in two bills for the two purposes as one
measure — I say, they know as well as we do, that a disgraceful failure would have been the result of our folly, and that
we should have been traitors to you, and to the cause we
had in hand.'[1] Disinterested onlookers thought there ought
to be no great difficulty in securing the result that both sides
desired. As the Duke of Argyll put it to Mr. Gladstone, if
in private business two men were to come to a breach, when
standing so near to one another in aim and profession, they
would be shut up in bedlam. This is just what the judicious
reader will think to-day.

The controversy was transported from parliament to the
platform, and a vigorous agitation marked the autumn
recess. It was a double agitation. What began as a campaign on behalf of the rural householder, threatened to end
as one against hereditary legislators. It is a well-known
advantage in movements of this sort to be not only for,
but also against, somebody or something ; against a minister,
by preference, or if not an individual, then against a body.
A hereditary legislature in a community that has reached the
self-governing stage is an anachronism that makes the easiest
of all marks for mockery and attack, so long as it lasts.
Nobody can doubt that if Mr. Gladstone had been the
frantic demagogue or fretful revolutionist that his opponents

[1] Edinburgh, August 30, 1884.

CHAP.
VIII.

Æt. 75.

thought, he now had an excellent chance of bringing the
question of the House of Lords irresistibly to the front.
As it was, in the midst of the storm raised by his lieutenants
and supporters all over the country, he was the moderating
force, elaborately appealing, as he said, to the reason rather
than the fears of his opponents.

One reproachful passage in his speeches this autumn
acquires a rather peculiar significance in the light of the
events that were in the coming years to follow. He is dealing
with the argument that the hereditary House protects the
nation against fleeting opinions : —

How is it with regard to the solid and permanent opinion of the
nation? We have had twelve parliaments since the Reform Act,
— I have a right to say so, as I have sat in every one of them, —
and the opinion, the national opinion, has been exhibited in the
following manner. Ten of those parliaments have had a liberal
majority. The eleventh parliament was the one that sat from
1841 to 1847. It was elected as a tory parliament; but in 1846
it put out the conservative government of Sir Robert Peel, and
put in and supported till its dissolution, the liberal government of
Lord John Russell. That is the eleventh parliament. But then
there is the twelfth parliament, and that is one that you and I
know a good deal about [Lord Beaconsfield's parliament], for we
talked largely on the subject of its merits and demerits, whichever
they may be, at the time of the last election. That parliament
was, I admit, a tory parliament from the beginning to the end.
But I want to know, looking back for a period of more than fifty
years, which represented the solid permanent conviction of the
nation? — the ten parliaments that were elected upon ten out of
the twelve dissolutions, or the one parliament that chanced to be
elected from the disorganized state of the liberal party in the early
part of the year 1874 ? Well, here are ten parliaments on the one
side; here is one parliament on the other side. . . . The House of
Lords was in sympathy with the one parliament, and was in
opposition . . . to the ten parliaments. And yet you are told,
when — we will say for forty-five years out of fifty — practically
the nation has manifested its liberal tendencies by the election of
liberal parliaments, and once only has chanced to elect a thoroughly

tory parliament, you are told that it is the thoroughly tory parliament that represents the solid and permanent opinion of the country.[1]

In time a curious thing, not yet adequately explained, fell out, for the extension of the franchise in 1867 and now in 1884 resulted in a reversal of the apparent law of things that had ruled our political parties through the epoch that Mr. Gladstone has just sketched. The five parliaments since 1884 have not followed the line of the ten parliaments preceding, notwithstanding the enlargement of direct popular power.

III

In August Mr. Gladstone submitted to the Queen a memorandum on the political situation. It was much more elaborate than the ordinary official submissions. Lord Granville was the only colleague who had seen it, and Mr. Gladstone was alone responsible for laying it before the sovereign. It is a masterly statement of the case, starting from the assumption for the sake of argument that the tories were right and the liberals wrong as to the two bills; then proceeding on the basis of a strongly expressed desire to keep back a movement for organic change; next urging the signs that such a movement would go forward with irresistible force if the bill were again rejected; and concluding thus : —

I may say in conclusion that there is no personal act if it be compatible with personal honour and likely to contribute to an end which I hold very dear, that I would not gladly do for the purpose of helping to close the present controversy, and in closing it to prevent the growth of one probably more complex and more formidable.

This document, tempered, unrhetorical, almost dispassionate, was the starting-point of proceedings that, after enormous difficulties had been surmounted by patience and perseverance, working through his power in parliament and his authority in the country, ended in final pacification and a sound political settlement. It was Mr. Gladstone's statesmanship that brought this pacification into sight and within reach.

[1] Corn Exchange, Edinburgh, August 30, 1884.

The Queen was deeply struck both by the force of his arguments and the earnest tone in which they were pressed. Though doubting whether there was any strong desire for a change in the position of the House of Lords, still she ' did not shut her eyes to the possible gravity of the situation ' (Aug. 31). She seemed inclined to take some steps for ascertaining the opinion of the leaders of opposition, with a view to inducing them to modify their programme. The Duke of Richmond visited Balmoral (Sept. 13), but when Mr. Gladstone, then himself on Deeside, heard what had passed in the direction of compromise, he could only say, ' Waste of breath ! ' To all suggestions of a dissolution on the case in issue, Mr. Gladstone said to a confidential emissary from Balmoral : —

Never will I be a party to dissolving in order to determine whether the Lords or the Commons were right upon the Franchise bill. If I have anything to do with dissolution, it will be a dissolution upon organic change in the House of Lords. Should this bill be again rejected in a definite manner, there will be only two courses open to me, one to cut out of public life, which I shall infinitely prefer ; the other to become a supporter of organic change in the House of Lords, which I hate and which I am making all this fuss in order to avoid. We have a few weeks before us to try and avert the mischief. After a second rejection it will be too late. There is perhaps the alternative of advising a large creation of peers; but to this there are great objections, even if the Queen were willing. I am not at present sure that I could bring myself to be a party to the adoption of a plan like that of 1832.

When people talked to him of dissolution as a means of bringing the Lords to account, he replied in scorn : ' A marvellous conception ! On such a dissolution, if the country disapproved of the conduct of its representatives, it would cashier them ; but, if it disapproved of the conduct of the peers, it would simply have to see them resume their place of power, to employ it to the best of their ability as opportunity might serve, in thwarting the desires of the country expressed through its representatives.'

It was reported to Mr. Gladstone that his speeches in

Scotland (though they were marked by much restraint) created some displeasure at Balmoral. He wrote to Lord Granville (Sept. 26) : —

The Queen does not know the facts. If she did, she would have known that while I have been compelled to deviate from the intention of speaking only to constituents which (with much difficulty) I kept until Aberdeen, I have thereby (and again with much difficulty in handling the audiences, every one of which would have wished a different course of proceeding) been enabled to do much in the way of keeping the question of organic change in the House of Lords out of the present stage of the controversy.

Sir Henry Ponsonby, of course at the Queen's instigation, was indefatigable and infinitely ingenious in inventing devices of possible compromise between Lords and Commons, or between Lords and ministers, such as might secure the passing of franchise and yet at the same time secure the creation of new electoral areas before the extended franchise should become operative. The Queen repeated to some members of the opposition — she did not at this stage communicate directly with Lord Salisbury — the essence of Mr. Gladstone's memorandum of August, and no doubt conveyed the impression that it had made upon her own mind. Later correspondence between her secretary and the Duke of Richmond set up a salutary ferment in what had not been at first a very promising quarter.

Meanwhile Mr. Gladstone was hard at work in other directions. He was urgent (Oct. 2) that Lord Granville should make every effort to bring more peers into the fold to save the bill when it reappeared in the autumn session. He had himself 'garnered in a rich harvest' of bishops in July. On previous occasions he had plied the episcopal bench with political appeals, and this time he wrote to the Archbishop of Canterbury : —

July 2, 1884. — I should have felt repugnance and scruple about addressing your Grace at any time on any subject of a political nature, if it were confined within the ordinary limits of such subjects. But it seems impossible to refuse credit to the accounts, which assure us that the peers of the opposition, under Lord

Salisbury and his coadjutors, are determined to use all their strength and influence for the purpose of throwing out the Franchise bill in the House of Lords; and thus of entering upon a conflict with the House of Commons, from which at each step in the proceeding it may probably become more difficult to retire, and which, if left to its natural course, will probably develop itself into a constitutional crisis of such an order, as has not occurred since 1832. . . .

To Tennyson, the possessor of a spiritual power even more than archiepiscopal, who had now a place among peers temporal, he addressed a remonstrance (July 6) : —

. . . Upon consideration I cannot help writing a line, for I must hope you will reconsider your intention. The best mode in which I can support a suggestion seemingly so audacious is by informing you, that all sober-minded conservative peers are in great dismay at this wild proceeding of Lord Salisbury; that the ultra-radicals and Parnellites, on the other hand, are in a state of glee, as they believe, and with good reason, that the battle once begun will end in some great humiliation to the House of Lords, or some important change in its composition. That (to my knowledge) various bishops of conservative leanings are, on this account, going to vote with the government — as may be the case with lay peers also. That you are the *only* peer, so far as I know, associated with liberal ideas or the liberal party, who hesitates to vote against Lord Salisbury.

In the later stage of this controversy, Tennyson shot the well-known lines at him —

> Steersman, be not precipitate in thine act
> Of steering, for the river here, my friend,
> Parts in two channels, moving to one end —
> This goes straight forward to the cataract:
> That streams about the bend.
> But tho' the cataract seems the nearer way,
> Whate'er the crowd on either bank may say,
> Take thou "the bend," 'twill save thee many a day.

To a poet who made to his generation such exquisite gifts of beauty and pleasure, the hardest of party-men may pardon unseasonable fears about franchise and one-horse constituencies. As matter of fact and in plain prose, this taking of the bend was exactly what the steersman had been doing, so as to keep other people out of cataracts.

'Then why should not Lord Granville try his hand on ambassadors, pressing them to save their order from a tempest that must strain and might wreck it?' To Mr. Chamberlain, who was in his element, or in one of his elements, Mr. Gladstone wrote (Oct. 8) : —

I see that Salisbury by his declaration in the *Times* of Saturday, that the Lords are to contend for the simultaneous passing of the two bills, has given you an excellent subject for denunciation, and you may safely denounce him to your heart's content. But I earnestly hope that you will leave us all elbow room on other questions which *may* arise. If you have seen my letters (virtually) to the Queen, I do not think you will have found reason for alarm in them. I am sorry that Hartington the other day used the word compromise, a word which has never passed my lips, though I believe he meant nothing wrong. If we could find anything which, though surrendering nothing substantial, would build a bridge for honourable and moderate men to retreat by, I am sure you would not object to it. But I have a much stronger plea for your reserve than any request of my own. It is this, that the cabinet has postponed discussing the matter until Wednesday simply in order that you may be present and take your share. They meet at twelve. I shall venture to count on your doing nothing to narrow the ground left open to us, which is indeed but a stinted one.

Three days later (Oct. 11) the Queen writing to the prime minister was able to mark a further stage : —

Although the strong expressions used by ministers in their recent speeches have made the task of conciliation undertaken by the Queen a most difficult one, she is so much impressed with the importance of the issue at stake, that she has persevered in her endeavours, and has obtained from the leaders of the opposition an expression of their readiness to negotiate on the basis of Lord Hartington's speech at Hanley. In the hope that this *may* lead to a compromise, the Queen has suggested that Lord Hartington may enter into communication with Lord Salisbury, and she trusts, from Mr. Gladstone's telegram received this morning, that he will empower Lord Hartington to discuss the possibility of an agreement with Lord Salisbury.

In acknowledgment, Mr. Gladstone offered his thanks for all her Majesty's ' well-timed efforts to bring about an accommodation.' He could not, however, he proceeded, feel sanguine as to obtaining any concession from the leaders, but he is very glad that Lord Hartington should try.

Happily, and as might have been expected by anybody who remembered the action of the sensible peers who saved the Reform bill in 1832, the rash and headstrong men in high places in the tory party were not allowed to have their own way. Before the autumn was over, prudent members of the opposition became uneasy. They knew that in substance the conclusion was foregone, but they knew also that just as in their own body there was a division between hothead and moderate, so in the cabinet they could count upon a whig section, and probably upon the prime minister as well. They noted his words spoken in July, ' It is not our desire to see the bill carried by storm and tempest. It is our desire to see it win its way by persuasion and calm discussion to the rational minds of men.' [1]

Meanwhile Sir Michael Hicks Beach had already, with the knowledge and without the disapproval of other leading men on the tory side, suggested an exchange of views to Lord Hartington, who was warmly encouraged by the cabinet to carry on communications, as being a person peculiarly fitted for the task, ' enjoying full confidence on one side,' as Mr. Gladstone said to the Queen, ' and probably more on the other side than any other minister could enjoy.' These two cool and able men took the extension of county franchise for granted, and their conferences turned pretty exclusively on redistribution. Sir Michael pressed the separation of urban from rural areas, and what was more specifically important was his advocacy of single-member or one-horse constituencies. His own long experience of a scattered agricultural division had convinced him that such areas with household suffrage would be unworkable. Lord Hartington knew the advantage of two-member constituencies

[1] Dinner of the Eighty Club, July 11, 1884.

for his party, because they made an opening for one whig candidate and one radical. But he did not make this a question of life or death, and the ground was thoroughly well hoed and raked. Lord Salisbury, to whom the nature of these communications had been made known by the colleague concerned, told him of the suggestion from the Queen, and said that he and Sir Stafford Northcote had unreservedly accepted it. So far the cabinet had found the several views in favour with their opponents as to electoral areas, rather more sweeping and radical than their own had been, and they hoped that on the basis thus informally laid, they might proceed to the more developed conversation with the two official leaders. Then the tory ultras interposed.

IV

On the last day of October the Queen wrote to Mr. Gladstone from Balmoral : —

The Queen thinks that it would be a means of arriving at some understanding if the leaders of the parties in both Houses could exchange their views personally. The Duke of Argyll or any other person unconnected for the present with the government or the opposition might be employed in bringing about a meeting, and in assisting to solve difficulties. The Queen thinks the government should in any project forming the basis of resolutions on redistribution to be proposed to the House, distinctly define their plans at such a personal conference. The Queen believes that were assurance given that the redistribution would not be wholly inimical to the prospects of the conservative party, their concurrence might be obtained. The Queen feels most strongly that it is of the utmost importance that in this serious crisis such means, even if unusual, should be tried, and knowing how fully Mr. Gladstone recognises the great danger that might arise by prolonging the conflict, the Queen *earnestly* trusts that he will avail himself of such means to obviate it.

The Queen then wrote to Lord Salisbury in the same sense in which she had written to the prime minister. Lord Salisbury replied that it would give him great pleasure to consult with anybody the Queen might desire, and that in

obedience to her commands he would do all that lay in him
to bring the controversy finally to a just and honourable
issue. He went on however to say, in the caustic vein that
was one of his ruling traits, that while cheerfully com-
plying with the Queen's wishes, he thought it right to add
that, so far as his information went, no danger attached
to the prolongation of the controversy for a considerable
time, nor did he believe that there was any real excitement
in the country about it. The Queen in replying (Nov. 5)
said that she would at once acquaint Mr. Gladstone with
what he had said.

The autumn session began, and the Franchise bill was
introduced again. Three days later, in consequence of
a communication from the other camp, the debate on
the second reading was conciliatory, but the tories won a
bye-election, and the proceedings in committee became
menacing and clouded. Discrepancies abounded in the
views of the opposition upon redistribution. When the
third reading came (Nov. 11), important men on the tory
side insisted on the production of a Seats bill, and declared
there must be no communication with the enemy. Mr.
Gladstone was elaborately pacific. If he could not get
peace, he said, at least let it be recorded that he desired
peace. The parleys of Lord Hartington and Sir Michael
Hicks Beach came to an end.

Mr. Gladstone, late one night soon after this (Nov. 14),
had a long conversation with Sir Stafford Northcote at the
house of a friend. He had the authority of the cabinet (not
given for this special interview) to promise the introduction
of a Seats bill before the committee stage of the Franchise
bill in the Lords, provided he was assured that it could be
done without endangering or retarding franchise. Northcote and Mr. Gladstone made good progress on the principles
of redistribution. Then came an awkward message from
Lord Salisbury that the Lords could not let the Franchise
bill through, until they got the Seats bill from the Commons.
So negotiations were again broken off.

The only hope now was that a sufficient number of Lord
Salisbury's adherents would leave him in the lurch, if he

did not close with what was understood to be Mr. Gladstone's

engagement, to procure and press a Seats bill as soon as ever franchise was out of danger.   So it happened,.and the door that had thus been shut, speedily opened.   Indirect communication reached the treasury bench that seemed to show the leaders of opposition to be again alive.   There were many surmises, everybody was excited, and two great tory leaders in the Lords called on Lord Granville one day, anxious for a *modus vivendi*.   Mr. Gladstone in the Commons, in conformity with a previous decision of the cabinet, declared the willingness of the government to produce a bill or explain its provisions, on receiving a reasonable guarantee that the Franchise bill would be passed before the end of the sittings.   The ultras of the opposition still insisted on making bets all round that the Franchise bill would not become law; besides betting, they declared they would die on the floor of the House in resisting an accommodation. A meeting of the party was summoned at the Carlton club for the purpose of declaring war to the knife, and Lord Salisbury was reported to hold to his determination.   This resolve, however, proved to have been shaken by Mr. Gladstone's language on a previous day.   The general principles of redistribution had been sufficiently sifted, tested, and compared to show that there was no insuperable discrepancy of view.   It was made clear to Lord Salisbury circuitously, that though the government required adequate assurances of the safety of franchise before presenting their scheme upon seats, this did not preclude private and confidential illumination.   So the bill was read a second time.

All went prosperously forward.   On November 19, Lord Salisbury and Sir S. Northcote came to Downing Street in the afternoon, took tea with the prime minister, and had a friendly conversation for an hour in which much ground was covered.   The heads of the government scheme were discussed and handed to the opposition leaders.   Mr. Gladstone was well satisfied.   He was much struck, he said after, with the quickness of the tory leader, and found it a pleasure to deal with so acute a man.   Lord Salisbury, for his part, was interested in the novelty of the proceeding, for no

precedent could be found in our political or party history
for the discussion of a measure before its introduction
between the leaders of the two sides.   This novelty stirred
his curiosity, while he also kept a sharp eye on the main
party chance.   He proved to be entirely devoid of respect for
tradition, and Mr. Gladstone declared himself to be a strong
conservative in comparison.   The meetings went on for
several days through the various parts of the questions, Lord
Hartington, Lord Granville, and Sir Charles Dilke being also
taken into council — the last of the three being unrivalled
master of the intricate details.

The operation was watched with jealous eyes by the
radicals, though they had their guardians in the cabinet.
To Mr. Bright who, having been all his life denounced as a
violent republican, was now in the view of the new school
hardly even so much as a sound radical, Mr. Gladstone
thought it well to write (Nov. 25) words of comfort, if
comfort were needed : —

I wish to give you the assurance that in the private communications which are now going on, liberal principles such as we
should conceive and term them, are in no danger.   Those with
whom we confer are thinking without doubt of party interests, as
affected by this or that arrangement, but these are a distinct
matter, and I am not so good at them as some others; but the
general proposition which I have stated is I think one which I can
pronounce with some confidence. . . . The whole operation is
essentially delicate and slippery, and I can hardly conceive any
other circumstance in which it would be justified, but in the
present very peculiar case I think it is not only warranted, but
called for.

On November 27 all was well over ; and Mr. Gladstone
was able to inform the Queen that 'the delicate and novel
communications' between the two sets of leaders had been
brought to a happy termination.   'His first duty,' he said,
'was to tender his grateful thanks to your Majesty for the
wise, gracious, and steady influence on your Majesty's part,
which has so powerfully contributed to bring about this
accommodation, and to avert a serious crisis of affairs.'   He

adds that 'his cordial acknowledgments are due to Lord Salisbury and Sir Stafford Northcote for the manner in which they have conducted their difficult communications.' The Queen promptly replied : ' I gladly and thankfully return your telegrams. To be able to be of use is all I care to live for now.' By way of winding up negotiations so remarkable, Mr. Gladstone wrote to Lord Salisbury to thank him for his kindness, and to say that he could have desired nothing better in candour and equity. Their conversation on the Seats bill would leave him none but the most agreeable recollections.

The Queen was in high good humour, as she had a right to be. She gave Mr. Gladstone ample credit for his conciliatory spirit. The last two months had been very trying to her, she said, but she confessed herself repaid by the thought that she had assisted in a settlement. Mr. Gladstone's severest critics on the tory side confessed that ' they did not think he had it in him.' Some friends of his in high places even suggested that this would be a good moment for giving him the garter. He wrote to Sir Arthur Gordon (Dec. 5) : ' The time of this government has been on the whole the most stormy and difficult that I have known in office, and the last six weeks have been perhaps the most anxious and difficult of the government.'

v

One further episode deserves a section, if the reader will turn back for a moment or two. The question whether the extension of the parliamentary franchise to rural householders should be limited to Great Britain or should apply to the whole kingdom, had been finally discussed in a couple of morning sittings in the month of May. Nobody who heard it can forget the speech made against Irish inclusion by Mr. Plunket, the eloquent grandson of the most eloquent of all the orators whom Ireland has sent to the imperial senate. He warned the House that to talk of assimilating the franchise in Ireland to the franchise in England, was to use language without meaning ; that out of seven hundred and sixty thousand inhabited houses in

Ireland, no fewer than four hundred and thirty-five thousand were rated at one pound and under; that those whom the bill would enfranchise would be taken from a class of whom more than forty per cent. could neither read nor write; that the measure would strengthen the hands of that disloyal party who boasted of their entire indifference to English opinion, and their undivided obligation to influences which Englishmen were wholly unable to realise. Then in a lofty strain Mr. Plunket foretold that the measure which they were asked to pass would lead up to, and would precipitate, the establishment of a separate Irish nationality. He reminded his hearers that the empire had been reared not more by the endurance of its soldiers and sailors than by the sagacity and firmness, the common sense and patriotism, of that ancient parliament; and he ended with a fervid prayer that the historian of the future might not have to tell that the union of these three kingdoms on which rested all its honour and all its power — a union that could never be broken by the force of domestic traitor or foreign foe — yielded at last under the pressure of the political ambitions and party exigencies of British statesmen.

The orator's stately diction, his solemn tone, the depth of his conviction, made a profound impression. Newer parliamentary hands below the government gangway, as he went on, asked one another by what arts of parliamentary defence the veteran minister could possibly deal with this searching appeal. Only a quarter of an hour remained. In two or three minutes Mr. Gladstone had swept the solemn impression entirely away. Contrary to his wont, he began at once upon the top note. With high passion in his voice, and mastering gesture in his uplifted arm, he dashed impetuously upon the foe. What weighs upon my mind is this, he said, that when the future historian speaks of the greatness of this empire, and traces the manner in which it has grown through successive generations, he will say that in that history there was one chapter of disgrace, and that chapter of disgrace was the treatment of Ireland. It is the scale of justice that will determine the issue of the conflict with Ireland, if conflict there is to be. There is nothing we can do, cried the orator, turning to the Irish members, except the imprudence of placing in your hands evidence that will show that we are not acting on principles of justice towards you, that can render you for a moment formidable in our eyes, should the day unfortunately arise when you endeavour to lay hands on this great structure of the British empire. Let us be as strong in right as we are in population, in wealth, and in historic traditions, and then we shall not fear to do justice to Ireland. There is but one mode of making England weak in the face of Ireland — that is by applying to her principles of inequality and principles of injustice.

As members sallied forth from the House to dine, they felt that this vehement improvisation had put the true answer. Mr. Plunket's fine appeal to those who had been comrades of the Irish loyalists in guarding the union was well enough, yet who but the Irish loyalists had held Ireland in the hollow of their hands for generation upon generation, and who but they were answerable for the odious and dishonouring failure, so patent before all the world, to effect a true incorporation of their country in a united realm? And if it should happen that Irish loyalists should suffer from extension of equal civil rights to Irishmen, what sort of reason was that why the principle of exclusion and ascendency which had worked such mischief in the past, should be persisted in for a long and indefinite future? These views, it is important to observe, were shared, not only by the minister's own party, but by a powerful body among his opponents. Some of the gentlemen who had been most furious against the government for not stopping Irish meetings in the autumn of 1883, were now most indignant at the bare idea of refusing or delaying a proposal for strengthening the hands of the very people who promoted and attended such meetings. It is true also that only two or three months before, Lord Hartington had declared that it would be most unwise to deal with the Irish franchise. Still more recently, Mr. W. H. Smith had declared that any extension of the suffrage in Ireland would draw after it 'confiscation of property, ruin of industry, withdrawal of capital, — misery, wretchedness, and war.' The valour of the platform, however, often expires in the keener air of cabinet and parliament. It became Lord Hartington's duty now to move the second reading of provisions which he had just described as most unwise provisions, and Mr. Smith found himself the object of brilliant mockery from the daring leader below the gangway on his own side.

Lord Randolph produced a more serious, though events soon showed it to be not any more solid an argument, when he said that the man who lives in a mud cabin very often has a decent holding, and has money in the savings' bank besides, and more than that, he is often more fit to take an interest in politics, and to form a sound view about them, than the English agricultural labourer. The same speaker proceeded to argue that the Fenian proclivities of the towns would be more than counterbalanced by the increased power given to the peasantry. The incidents of agricultural life, he observed, are unfavourable to revolutionary movements, and the peasant is much more under the proper and legitimate influence of the Roman catholic priesthood than the lower classes of the towns. On the whole, the extension of the franchise to the peasantry of Ireland would not be unfavourable to the landlord interest. Yet Lord Randolph, who regaled the House with these chimerical speculations, had had far better opportunities than almost any other Englishman then in parliament of knowing something about Ireland.

What is certain is that English and Scotch members acted with their eyes open. Irish tories and Irish nationalists agreed in menacing predictions. The vast masses of Irish people, said the former, had no sense of loyalty and no love of order to which a government could appeal. In many districts the only person who was unsafe was the peace officer or the relatives of a murdered man. The effect of the change would be the utter annihilation of the political power of the most orderly, the most loyal, the most educated classes of Ireland, and the swamping of one-fourth of the community, representing two-thirds of its property. A representative of the great house of Hamilton in the Commons, amid a little cloud of the dishevelled prophecies

too common in his class, assured the House that everybody
knew that if the franchise in Ireland were extended, the days
of home rule could not be far distant. The representative
of the great house of Beresford in the Lords, the resident
possessor of a noble domain, an able and determined man,
with large knowledge of his country, so far as large knowledge can be acquired from a single point of view, expressed
his strong conviction that after the passage of this bill
the Irish outlook would be blacker than it had ever been
before.[1]

Another person, far more powerful than any Hamilton or
Beresford, was equally explicit. With characteristic frigidity,
precision, and confidence, the Irish leader had defined his
policy and his expectations. 'Beyond a shadow of doubt,'
he had said to a meeting in the Rotunda at Dublin, 'it will
be for the Irish people in England — separated, isolated as
they are — and for your independent Irish members, to determine at the next general election whether a tory or a liberal
English ministry shall rule England. This is a great force
and a great power. If we cannot rule ourselves, we can at
least cause them to be ruled as we choose. This force has
already gained for Ireland inclusion in the coming Franchise
bill. We have reason to be proud, hopeful, and energetic.' [2]
In any case, he informed the House of Commons, even if
Ireland were not included in the bill, the national party
would come back seventy-five strong. If household suffrage
were conceded to Ireland, they would come back ninety
strong.[3] That was the only difference. Therefore, though
he naturally supported inclusion,[4] it was not at all indispensable to the success of his policy, and he watched the
proceedings in the committee as calmly as he might have
watched a battle of frogs and mice.

[1] Lord Waterford, July 7, 1884.
[2] December 11, 1883.
[3] ' I am not at all sure,' Mr. Forster
rashly said (March 31, 1884), 'that
Mr. Parnell will increase his followers
by means of this bill.'

[4] This was only the second occasion
on which his party in cardinal divisions voted with the government.

CHAPTER IX

THE SOUDAN

(*1884–1885*)

You can only govern men by imagination: without imagination
they are brutes. . . . 'Tis by speaking to the soul that you electrify
men. — NAPOLEON.

BOOK
VIII.

1884. IN the late summer of 1881 a certain native of Dongola,
proclaiming himself a heaven-inspired Mahdi, began to
rally to his banner the wild tribes of the southern Soudan.
His mission was to confound the wicked, the hypocrite, the
unbeliever, and to convert the world to the true faith in the one
God and his prophet. The fame of the Mahdi's eloquence,
his piety, his zeal, rapidly spread. At his ear he found a counsellor, so well known to us after as the khalifa, and this man
soon taught the prophet politics. The misrule of the Soudan
by Egypt had been atrocious, and the combination of a
religious revival with the destruction of that hated yoke
swelled a cry that was irresistible. The rising rapidly
extended, for fanaticism in such regions soon takes fire, and
the Egyptian pashas had been sore oppressors, even judged
by the rude standards of oriental states. Never was insurrection more amply justified. From the first, Mr. Gladstone's
curious instinct for liberty disclosed to him that here was a
case of 'a people rightly struggling to be free.' The phrase
was mocked and derided then and down to the end of the
chapter. Yet it was the simple truth. 'During all my
political life,' he said at a later stage of Soudanese affairs,
'I am thankful to say that I have never opened my lips in
favour of a domination such as that which has been exercised upon certain countries by certain other countries, and

144

I am not going now to begin.' 'I look upon the possession of the Soudan,' he proceeded, 'as the calamity of Egypt. It has been a drain on her treasury, it has been a drain on her men. It is estimated that 100,000 Egyptians have laid down their lives in endeavouring to maintain that barren conquest.' Still stronger was the Soudanese side of the case. The rule of the Mahdi was itself a tyranny, and tribe fought with tribe, but that was deemed an easier yoke than the sway of the pashas from Cairo. Every vice of eastern rule flourished freely under Egyptian hands. At Khartoum whole families of Coptic clerks kept the accounts of plundering raids supported by Egyptian soldiers, and 'this was a government collecting its taxes.' The function of the Egyptian soldiers 'was that of honest countrymen sharing in the villainy of the brigands from the Levant and Asia Minor, who wrung money, women, and drink from a miserable population.'[1] Yet the railing against Mr. Gladstone for saying that the 'rebels' were rightly struggling to be free could not have been more furious if the Mahdi had been for dethroning Marcus Aurelius or Saint Louis of France.

The ministers at Cairo, however, naturally could not find in their hearts to withdraw from territory that had been theirs for over sixty years,[2] although in the winter of 1882-3 Colonel Stewart, an able British officer, had reported that the Egyptian government was wholly unfit to rule the Soudan; it had not money enough, nor fighting men enough, nor administrative skill enough, and abandonment at least of large portions of it was the only reasonable course. Such counsels found no favour with the khedive's advisers and agents, and General Hicks, an Indian officer, appointed on the staff of the Egyptian army in the spring of 1883, was now despatched by the government of the khedive from Khartoum, for the recovery of distant and formidable regions. If his operations had been limited to the original intention of clearing Sennaar

[1] Wingate, pp. 50, 51.
[2] The Soudan was conquered in 1819 by Ismail Pasha, the son of Mehemet Ali, and from that date Egypt had a more or less insecure hold over the country. In 1870 Sir Samuel Baker added the equatorial provinces to the Egyptian Soudan.

of rebels and protecting Khartoum, all might have been well. Unluckily some trivial successes over the Mahdi encouraged the Cairo government to design an advance into Kordofan, and the reconquest of all the vast wildernesses of the Soudan. Lord Dufferin, Sir E. Malet, Colonel Stewart, were all of them clear that to attempt any such task with an empty chest and a worthless army was madness, and they all argued for the abandonment of Kordofan and Darfur. The cabinet in London, fixed in their resolve not to accept responsibility for a Soudan war, and not to enter upon that responsibility by giving advice for or against the advance of Hicks, stood aloof.[1] In view of all that followed later, and of their subsequent adoption of the policy of abandoning the Soudan, British ministers would evidently have been wiser if they had now forbidden an advance so pregnant with disaster. Events showed this to have been the capital miscalculation whence all else of misfortune followed. The sounder the policy of abandonment, the stronger the reasons for insisting that the Egyptian government should not undertake operations inconsistent with that policy. The Soudan was not within the sphere of our responsibility, but Egypt was; and just because the separation of Egypt from the Soudan was wise and necessary, it might have been expected that England would peremptorily interpose to prevent a departure from the path of separation. What Hicks himself, a capable and dauntless man, thought of the chances we do not positively know, but he was certainly alive to the risks of such a march with such material. On November 5 (1883) the whole force was cut to pieces, the victorious dervishes were free to advance northwards, and the loose fabric of Egyptian authority was shattered to the ground.

[1] Mr. Gladstone said on Nov. 2, 1882 : 'It is no part of the duty incumbent upon us to restore order in the Soudan. It is politically connected with Egypt in consequence of its very recent conquest ; but it has not been included within the sphere of our operations, and we are by no means disposed to admit without qualification that it is within the sphere of our responsibility.' Lord Granville, May 7, 1883 : ' H.M. government are in no way responsible for the operations in the Soudan, which have been undertaken under the authority of the Egyptian government, or for the appointment or actions of General Hicks.'

II

The three British military officers in Cairo all agreed that the Egyptian government could not hold Khartoum if the Mahdi should draw down upon it ; and unless a British, an Indian, or a Turkish force came to the rescue, abandonment of the Soudan was the only possible alternative. The London cabinet decided that they would not employ British or Indian troops in the Soudan, and though they had no objection to the resort to the Turks by Egypt, if the Turks would pay their own expenses (a condition fatal to any such resort), they strongly recommended the khedive to abandon all territory south of Assouan or Wady-Halfa. Sir Evelyn Baring, who had now assumed his post upon a theatre where he was for long years to come to play the commanding part, concurred in thinking that the policy of complete abandonment was the best admitted by the circumstances. It is the way of the world to suppose that because a given course is best, it must therefore be possible and ought to be simple. Baring and his colleagues at Cairo were under no such illusion, but it was the foundation of most of the criticism that now broke forth in the English press.

The unparalleled difficulties that ultimately attended the evacuation of the Soudan naturally led inconsiderate critics, — and such must ever be the majority, — to condemn the policy and the cabinet who ordered it. So apt are men in their rough judgments on great disputable things, to mistake a mere impression for a real opinion; and we must patiently admit that the Result — success or failure in the Event — is the most that they have time for, and all that they can go by. Yet two remarks are to be made upon this facile censure. The first is that those who knew the Soudan best, approved most. On January 22, 1884, Gordon wrote to Lord Granville that the Soudan ever was and ever would be a useless possession, and that he thought the Queen's ministers 'fully justified in recommending evacuation, inasmuch as the sacrifices necessary towards securing good government would be far too onerous to admit of such an attempt being made.' Colonel Stewart quite agreed, and added the exclamation that nobody who had ever visited the Soudan could escape the reflection, 'What a useless possession and what a huge encumbrance on Egypt!' As we shall see, the time soon came when Gordon accepted the policy of evacuation, even with an emphasis of his own. The second remark is that the reconquest of the Soudan and the holding of Khartoum were for the Egyptian government, if left to its own resources, neither more nor less than impossible; these objects, whether they were good objects or bad, not only meant recourse to British troops for the first immense operations, but the retention of them in a huge and most inhospitable region for an indefinite time. A third consideration will certainly not be overlooked by anybody who thinks on the course of the years of Egyptian reform that have since elapsed, and constitute so remarkable a chapter of British administration, — namely, that this beneficent achievement would have been fatally clogged, if those who conducted it had also had the Soudan on their hands. The renovation or reconstruction of what is called Egypt proper, its finances, its army, its civil rule, would have been absolutely out of reach, if at the same time its guiding statesmen had been charged with the responsibilities of recovering and holding that vaster tract which had been so rashly acquired and so mercilessly misgoverned. This is fully admitted by those who have had most to do with the result.

III

The policy of evacuation was taken as carrying with it the task of extricating the Egyptian garrisons. This aim induced Mr. Gladstone's cabinet once more to play an active military part, though Britain had no share in planting these garrisons where they were. Wise men in Egypt were of the same mind as General Gordon, that in the eastern Soudan it would have been better for the British government to keep quiet, and 'let events work themselves out.' Unfortunately the ready clamour of headlong philanthropists, political party men, and the men who think England humiliated if she ever lets slip an excuse for drawing her sword, drove the cabinet on to the rocks. When the decision of the cabinet was taken (Feb. 12, 1883) to send troops to Suakin, Mr. Gladstone stood alone in objecting. Many thousands of savages were slaughtered under humanitarian pressure, not a few English lives were sacrificed, much treasure flowed, and yet Sinkat fell, and Tokar fell, and our labours in the eastern Soudan were practically fruitless.[1] The operations had no effect upon the roll of the fierce mahdi wave over the Soudan.

In England, excitement of the unsound sort that is independent of knowledge, consideration, or deliberation; independent of any weighing of the actual facts and any forecast of latent possibilities, grew more and more vociferous. Ministers quailed. Twice they inquired of their agent in Egypt[2] whether General Gordon might not be of use, and twice they received an adverse reply, mainly on the ground that the presence in authority of a Christian officer was a dubious mode of confronting a sweeping outbreak of moslem fanaticism, and would inevitably alienate tribes that were still not caught by the Mahdi.[3] Unhappily a third application from London at last prevailed, and Sir E. Baring, supported by Nubar, by Sir Evelyn Wood, by Colonel Watson, who had served with Gordon and knew him well, all agreed that Gordon would be the best man if he would pledge himself to carry out the policy of withdrawing from the Soudan as quickly as possible. 'Whoever goes,' said Sir E. Baring in pregnant words to Lord Granville, will 'undertake a service of great difficulty and danger.' This was on January 16th. Two days later the die was cast. Mr. Gladstone was at Hawarden. Lord Granville submitted the question (Jan. 14, 1884) to him in this form : 'If Gordon says he

[1] It was a general mistake at that time to suppose that wherever a garrison fell into the hands of the Mahdi, they were massacred. At Tokar, for instance, the soldiers were incorporated by the victors. See Wingate, p. 553.

[2] Granville to Baring, Dec. 1, 1883; Jan. 10, 1884.

[3] Gordon had suppressed the Taiping rising in China in 1863. In 1874 he was appointed by the Egyptian government governor-general of the equatorial provinces of central Africa. In 1876 he resigned owing to trouble with the governor-general of the Soudan upon the suppression of the slave trade, but was appointed (1877) governor-general of the Soudan, Darfur, the equatorial provinces, and the Red Sea littoral. He held this position till the end of 1879, suppressing the slave trade with a strong hand and improving the means of communication throughout the Soudan. He succeeded in establishing comparative order. Then the new Egyptian government reversed Gordon's policy, and the result of his six years' work soon fell to pieces.

believes he could by his personal influence excite the tribes
to escort the Khartoum garrison and inhabitants to Suakin, a
little pressure on Baring might be advisable. The destruction
of these poor people will be a great disaster.' Mr. Gladstone
telegraphed that to this and other parts of the same letter,
he agreed. Granville then sent him a copy of the telegram
putting 'a little pressure on Baring.' To this Mr. Gladstone
replied (Jan. 16) in words that, if they had only been taken
to heart, would have made all the difference : —

I can find no fault with your telegram to Baring re Chinese
Gordon, and the main point that strikes me is this : While his
opinion on the Soudan may be of great value, must we not be
very careful in any instruction we give, that he does not shift the
centre of gravity as to political and military responsibility for that
country? In brief, if he reports what should be done, he should not
be the judge who should do it, nor ought he to commit us on that
point by advice officially given. It would be extremely difficult
after sending him to reject such advice, and it should therefore,
I think, be made clear that he is not our agent for the purpose
of advising on that point.

On January 18, Lord Hartington (then secretary of state
for war), Lord Granville, Lord Northbrook, and Sir Charles
Dilke met at the war office in Pall Mall. The summons
was sudden. Lord Wolseley brought Gordon and left
him in the ante-room. After a conversation with the
ministers, he came out and said to Gordon, 'Government
are determined to evacuate the Soudan, for they will not
guarantee the future government. Will you go and do it?'
'I said, "Yes." He said, "Go in." I went in and saw them.
They said, "Did Wolseley tell you our orders?" I said, "Yes."
I said, "You will not guarantee future government of the
Soudan, and you wish me to go up and evacuate now." They
said, "Yes," and it was over, and I left at 8 p.m. for Calais.' [1]
This graphic story does not pretend to be a full version of
all that passed, though it puts the essential point unmistak-
ably enough. Lord Granville seems to have drawn Gordon's

[1] Gordon's Letters to Barnes, 1885.
Lord Granville took his ticket, Lord
Wolseley carried the General's bag,
and the Duke of Cambridge held open
the carriage door.

special attention to the measures to be taken for the security of the Egyptian garrisons (plural) still holding positions in the Soudan and to the best mode of evacuating the interior.[1] On the other hand, according to a very authentic account that I have seen, Gordon on this occasion stated that the danger at Khartoum was exaggerated, and that he would be able to bring away the garrisons without difficulty.

CHAP. IX.

ÆT. 75.

Thus in that conclave of sober statesmen a tragedy began. The next day one of the four ministers met another; 'We were proud of ourselves yesterday — are you sure we did not commit a gigantic folly?' The prime minister had agreed at once on receiving the news of what was done at the war office, and telegraphed assent the same night.[2] The whole cabinet met four days later, Mr. Gladstone among them, and the decision was approved. There was hardly a choice, for by that time Gordon was at Brindisi. Gordon, as Mr. Gladstone said, was a hero of heroes. He was a soldier of infinite personal courage and daring; of striking military energy, initiative, and resource; a high, pure, and single character, dwelling much in the region of the unseen. But as all who knew him admit, and as his own records testify, notwithstanding an under-current of shrewd common-sense, he was the creature, almost the sport, of impulse; his impressions and purposes changed with the speed of lightning; anger often mastered him; he went very often by intuitions and inspirations rather than by cool inference from carefully surveyed fact: with many variations of mood he mixed, as we often see in people less famous, an invincible faith in his own rapid prepossessions while they lasted. Everybody now discerns that to despatch a soldier of this temperament on a piece of business that was not only difficult and dangerous, as Sir E. Baring said, but profoundly obscure, and needing vigilant sanity and self-control, was little better than to call in a wizard with his magic. Mr. Gladstone always professed perplexity in understanding why the violent end of the gallant Cavagnari in Afghanistan,

[1] Baring's Instructions to Gordon (Jan. 25, 1884).
[2] Gladstone to Granville, Jan. 19, 1884. — 'I telegraphed last night my concurrence in your proceedings about Gordon : but Chester would not awake and the message only went on this morning.'

stirred the world so little in comparison with the fate of Gordon. The answer is that Gordon seized the imagination of England, and seized it on its higher side. His religion was eccentric, but it was religion; the Bible was the rock on which he founded himself, both old dispensation and new; he was known to hate forms, ceremonies, and all the 'solemn plausibilities'; his speech was sharp, pithy, rapid, and ironic; above all, he knew the ways of war and would not bear the sword for nought. All this was material enough to make a popular ideal, and this is what Gordon in an ever-increasing degree became, to the immense inconvenience of the statesmen, otherwise so sensible and wary, who had now improvidently let the genie forth from the jar.

IV

It has been sometimes contended that all the mischief that followed was caused by the diversion of Gordon from Suakin, his original destination. If he had gone to the Red Sea, as originally intended, there to report on the state and look of things in the Soudan, instead of being waylaid and brought to Cairo, and thence despatched to Khartoum, they say, no catastrophe would have happened. This is not certain, for the dervishes in the eastern Soudan were in the flush of open revolt, and Gordon might either have been killed or taken prisoner, or else he would have come back without performing any part of his mission. In fact, on his way from London to Port Said, Gordon had suggested that with a view to carrying out evacuation, the khedive should make him governor-general of the Soudan. Lord Granville authorised Baring to procure the nomination, and this Sir Evelyn did, 'for the time necessary to accomplish the evacuation.' The instructions were thus changed, in an important sense, but the change was suggested by Gordon and sanctioned by Lord Granville.[1]

[1] Dilke in House of Commons, Feb. 14, 1884. See also Lord Granville to Sir E. Baring, March 28, 1884. In recapitulating the instructions given to General Gordon, Lord Granville says: '*His* (Gordon's) *first proposal* was to proceed to Suakin with the object of reporting from thence on the best method of effecting the evacuation of the Soudan. . . . His instructions, *drawn up in accordance with his own views*, were to report to her Majesty's government on the military situation in the Soudan,' etc.

When Gordon left London his instructions, drafted in fact by himself, were that he should 'consider and report upon the best mode of effecting the evacuation of the interior of the Soudan.' He was also to perform such duties as the Egyptian government might wish to entrust to him, and as might be communicated to him by Sir E. Baring.[1] At Cairo, Baring and Nubar, after discussion with Gordon, altered the mission from one of advice and report to an executive mission—a change that was doubtless authorised and covered by the original reference to duties to be entrusted to him by Egypt. But there was no change in the policy either at Downing Street or Cairo. Whether advisory or executive, the only policy charged upon the mission was abandonment. When the draft of the new instructions was read to Gordon at Cairo, Sir E. Baring expressly asked him whether he entirely concurred in 'the policy of abandoning the Soudan,' and Gordon not only concurred, but suggested the strengthening words, that he thought 'it should on no account be changed.'[2] This despatch, along with the instructions to Gordon making this vast alteration, was not received in London until Feb. 7. By this time Gordon was crossing the desert, and out of reach of the English foreign office.

On his way from Brindisi, Gordon had prepared a memorandum for Sir E. Baring, in which he set out his opinion that the Soudan had better be restored to the different petty sultans in existence before the Egyptian conquest, and an attempt should be made to form them into some sort of confederation. These petty rulers might be left to accept the Mahdi for their sovereign or not, just as they pleased. But in the same document he emphasised the policy of abandonment. 'I understand,' he says, 'that H.M.'s government have come to the irrevocable decision not to incur the very onerous duty of granting to the peoples of the Soudan a just future government.' Left to their independence, the sultans 'would doubtless fight among themselves.' As for future good government, it was evident that 'this we could not

[1] For the full text of these instructions, see Appendix.

[2] Baring to Granville, January 28, 1884.

secure them without an inordinate expenditure of men and
money. The Soudan is a useless possession; ever was so,
and ever will be so. No one who has ever lived in the
Soudan can escape the reflection, What a useless possession
is this land.' Therefore — so he winds up — 'I think H.M.'s
government are fully justified in recommending the evacuation, inasmuch as the sacrifices necessary towards securing
a good government would be far too onerous to admit of any
such attempt being made. Indeed, one may say it is impracticable at any cost. *H.M.'s government will now leave them as
God has placed them.*' [1]

It was, therefore, and it is, pure sophistry to contend that
Gordon's policy in undertaking his disastrous mission was
evacuation but not abandonment. To say that the Soudanese
should be left in the state in which God had placed them,
to fight it out among themselves, if they were so minded,
is as good a definition of abandonment as can be invented,
and this was the whole spirit of the instructions imposed by
the government of the Queen and accepted by Gordon.

Gordon took with him instruments from the khedive into
which, along with definite and specific statements that
evacuation was the object of his mission, two or three loose
sentences are slipped about 'establishing organised government in the different provinces of the Soudan,' maintaining
order, and the like. It is true also that the British cabinet
sanctioned the extension of the area of evacuation from
Khartoum to the whole Soudan.[2] Strictly construed, the
whole body of instructions, including firmans and khedive's
proclamations, is not technically compact nor coherent. But
this is only another way of saying that Gordon was to have
the widest discretionary powers as to the manner of carrying
out the policy, and the best time and mode of announcing
it. The policy itself, as well understood by Gordon as by
everybody else, was untouched, and it was: to leave the
Soudanese in the state in which God had placed them.

The hot controversy on this point is idle and without
substance — the idlest controversies are always the hottest

---

[1] Dated, *Steamship 'Tanjore,'* at *Sea, Jan.* 22, 1884.
[2] Granville to Baring, March 28.

— for not only was Gordon the last man in all the world CHAP.
to hold himself bound by official instructions, but the IX.
actual conditions of the case were too little known, too ÆT. 75.
shifting, too unstable, to permit of hard and fast directions beforehand how to solve so desperate a problem. Two
things at any rate were clear — one, that Gordon should faithfully adhere to the policy of evacuation and abandonment
which he had formally accepted; the other, that the British
government should leave him a free hand. Unhappily
neither of these two clear things was accepted by either
of the parties.

V

Gordon's policies were many and very mutable. Viewing
the frightful embarrassments that enveloped him, we cannot wonder. Still the same considerateness that is always
so bounteously and so justly extended to the soldier in the
field, is no less due in its measure to the councillor in the
cabinet. This is a bit of equity often much neglected both
by contemporaries and by history.

He had undertaken his mission without any serious and
measured forecast, such as his comrade, Colonel Stewart,
was well fitted to supply. His first notion was that he could
restore the representatives of the old rulers, but when he got
into the country, he found that there were none; with one
by no means happy exception, they had all disappeared.
When he reached Berber, he learned more clearly how the
question of evacuation was interlaced with other questions.
Once at Khartoum, at first he thought himself welcome as
a deliverer, and then when new light as to the real feelings
of the Soudanese broke upon him, he flung the policy of his
mission overboard. Before the end of February, instead of the
suzerainty of Egypt, the British government should control
Soudanese administration, with Zobeir as their governor-
general. 'When Gordon left this country,' said Mr. Gladstone, 'and when he arrived in Egypt, he declared it to be,
and I have not the smallest doubt that it was — a fixed
portion of his policy, that no British force should be
employed in aid of his mission.' [1] When March came, he

[1] Feb. 23, 1885.

flung himself with ardour into the policy of 'smashing up' the Mahdi, with resort to British and Indian troops. This was a violent reversal of all that had been either settled or dreamed of, whether in London or at Cairo. A still more vehement stride came next. He declared that to leave outlying garrisons to their fate would be an 'indelible disgrace.' Yet, as Lord Hartington said, the government 'were under no moral obligation to use the military resources of this empire for the relief of those garrisons.' As for Gordon's opinion that 'indelible disgrace' would attach to the British government if they were not relieved, 'I do not admit,' said the minister very sensibly, 'that General Gordon is on this point a better authority than anybody else.' [1] All this illustrates the energy of Gordon's mental movements, and also, what is more important, the distracting difficulties of the case before him. In one view and one demand he strenuously persevered, as we shall now see.

Mr. Gladstone at first, when Gordon set all instructions at defiance, was for recalling him. A colleague also was for recalling him on the first instant when he changed his policy. Another important member of the cabinet was, on the contrary, for an expedition. 'I cannot admit,' wrote a fourth leading minister, 'that either generals or statesmen who have accepted the offer of a man to lead a forlorn hope, are in the least bound to risk the lives of thousands for the uncertain chance of saving the forlorn hope.' Some think that this was stern common sense, others call it ignoble. The nation, at any rate, was in one of its high idealising humours, though Gordon had roused some feeling against himself in this country (unjustly enough) by his decree formally sanctioning the holding of slaves.

The general had not been many hours in Khartoum (February 18) before he sent a telegram to Sir E. Baring, proposing that on his withdrawal from Khartoum, Zobeir Pasha should be named his successor as governor-general of the Soudan: he should be made a K.C.M.G., and have presents given to him. This request was strenuously pressed by Gordon. Zobeir had been a prime actor in the

[1] May 13, 1884.

devastations of the slave trade; it was he who had acquired Darfur for Egypt; he was a first-rate fighting man, and the ablest leader in the Soudan. He is described by the English officer who knows the Soudan best, as a far-seeing, thoughtful man of iron will — a born ruler of men.[1] The Egyptian government had desired to send him down to aid in the operations at Suakin in 1883, but the government in London vetoed him, as they were now to veto him a second time. The Egyptian government was to act on its own responsibility, but not to do what it thought best. So now with Gordon.

Gordon in other days had caused Zobeir's son to be shot, and this was supposed to have set up an unquenchable blood-feud between them. Before reaching Cairo, he had suggested that Zobeir should be sent to Cyprus, and there kept out of the way. This was not done. On Gordon's way through Cairo, the two men met in what those present describe as a highly dramatic interview. Zobeir bitterly upbraided Gordon: 'You killed my son, whom I entrusted to you. He was as your son. You brought my wives and women and children in chains to Khartoum.' Still even after that incident, Gordon declared that he had 'a mystical feeling' that Zobeir and he were all right.[2] What inspired his reiterated demand for the immediate despatch of Zobeir is surmised to have been the conviction forced upon him during his journey to Khartoum, that his first idea of leaving the various petty sultans to fight it out with the Mahdi, would not work; that the Mahdi had got so strong a hold that he could only be met by a man of Zobeir's political capacity, military skill, and old authority. Sir E. Baring, after a brief interval of hesitation, now supported Gordon's request. So did the shrewd and expert Colonel Stewart. Nubar too favoured the idea. The cabinet could not at once assent; they were startled by the change of front

[1] Wingate's *Mahdism*, p. 109.
[2] Baring to Granville, Jan. 28. — 'I had a good deal of conversation with General Gordon as to the manner in which Zobeir Pasha should be treated. Gen. Gordon entertains a high opinion of Zobeir Pasha's en- ergy and ability. He possesses great influence in the Soudan, and General Gordon is of opinion that *circumstances might arise which would render it desirable that he should be sent back to the Soudan.*'

as to total withdrawal from the Soudan — the very object of
Gordon's mission, and accepted by him as such. On February 21 Mr. Gladstone reported to the Queen that the
cabinet were of opinion that there would be the gravest
objection to nominating by an assumption of British
authority a successor to General Gordon in the Soudan, nor
did they as yet see sufficient reasons for going beyond
Gordon's memorandum of January 25, by making special
provision for the government of that country. But at first
it looked as if ministers might yield, if Baring, Gordon, and
Nubar persisted.

As ill-fortune had it, the Zobeir plan leaked out at home by
Gordon's indiscretion before the government decided. The
omnipotent though not omniscient divinity called public
opinion intervened. The very men who had most loudly
clamoured for the extrication of the Egyptian garrisons, who
had pressed with most importunity for the despatch of
Gordon, who had been most urgent for the necessity of
giving him a free hand, now declared that it would be a
national degradation and a European scandal to listen to
Gordon's very first request. He had himself unluckily given
them a capital text, having once said that Zobeir was alone
responsible for the slave trade of the previous ten years.
Gordon's idea was, as he explained, to put Zobeir into
a position like that of the Ameer of Afghanistan, as a buffer
between Egypt and the Mahdi, with a subsidy, moral support, and all the rest of a buffer arrangement. The idea may
or may not have been a good one; nobody else had a better.

It was not at all surprising that the cabinet should ask
what new reason had come to light why Zobeir should be
trusted; why he should oppose the Mahdi whom at first he
was believed to have supported; why he should turn the
friend of Egypt; why he should be relied upon as the faithful
ally of England. To these and other doubts Gordon had
excellent answers (March 8). Zobeir would run straight,
because it was his interest. If he would be dangerous, was
not the Mahdi dangerous, and whom save Zobeir could you
set up against the Mahdi? You talked of slave-holding
and slave-hunting, but would slave-holding and slave-hunting

stop with your own policy of evacuation? Slave-holding CHAP.
you cannot interfere with, and as for slave-hunting, that IX.
depended on the equatorial provinces, where Zobeir could ÆT. 75.
be prevented from going, and besides he would have his
hands full in consolidating his power elsewhere. As for
good faith towards Egypt, Zobeir's stay in Cairo had taught
him our power, and being a great trader, he would rather
seek Egypt's close alliance. Anyhow, said Gordon, 'if you
do not send Zobeir, you have no chance of getting the
garrisons away.'

The matter was considered at two meetings of the cabinet,
but the prime minister was prevented by his physician from
attending.[1] A difference of opinion showed itself upon the
despatch of Zobeir; viewed as an abstract question, three
of the Commons members inclined to favour it, but on the
practical question, the Commons members were unanimous
that no government from either side of the House could
venture to sanction Zobeir. Mr. Gladstone had become a
strong convert to the plan of sending Zobeir. 'I am better
in chest and generally,' he wrote to Lord Granville, 'but unfortunately not in throat and voice, and Clark interdicts my
appearance at cabinet; but I am available for any necessary
communication, say with you, or you and Hartington.' One
of the ministers went to see him in his bed, and they con-
versed for two hours. The minister, on his return, reported
with some ironic amusement that Mr. Gladstone considered
it very likely that they could not bring parliament to swallow
Zobeir, but believed that he himself could. Whether his
confidence in this was right or wrong, he was unable to turn
his cabinet. The Queen telegraphed her agreement with
the prime minister. But this made no difference. 'On
Saturday 15,' Mr. Gladstone notes, 'it seemed as if by
my casting vote Zobier was to be sent to Gordon. But

[1] (*From his diary.*) *March* 9. —
. . . At night recognised the fact of
a cold, and began to deal with it.
10th. Kept my bed all day. 11th.
The cabinet sat, and Granville came
to and fro with the communications,
Clark having prohibited my attendance. Read *Sybil.* 12th. Bed as
yesterday. 13th. Got to my sitting-
room in the evening. It has, however, taken longer this time to clear
the chest, and Clark reports the pulse
still too high by ten. Saw Granville.
Conclave, 7½ to 8½, on telegram to
Baring for Gordon. I was not allowed to attend the cabinet.

on Sunday —— and —— receded from their ground,
and I gave way. The nature of the evidence on which
judgments are formed in this most strange of all cases,
precludes (in reason) pressing all conclusions, which are but
preferences, to extremes.' 'It is well known,' said Mr. Gladstone in the following year when the curtain had fallen on
the catastrophe, 'that if, when the recommendation to send
Zobeir was made, we had complied with it, an address from
this House to the crown would have paralysed our action ;
and though it was perfectly true that the decision arrived
at was the judgment of the cabinet, it was also no less
the judgment of parliament and the people.' So Gordon's
request was refused.

It is true that, as a minister put it at the time, to send
Zobeir would have been a gambler's throw. But then what
was it but a gambler's throw to send Gordon himself? The
Soudanese chieftain might possibly have done all that
Gordon and Stewart, who knew the ground and were watching the quick fluctuation of events with elastic minds, now
positively declared that he would have the strongest motives
not to do. Even then, could the issue have been worse?
To run all the risks involved in the despatch of Gordon, and
then immediately to refuse the request that he persistently
represented as furnishing him his only chance, was an inco-
herence that the parliament and people of England have not
often surpassed.[1] All through this critical month, from the
10th until the 30th, Mr. Gladstone was suffering more or less
from indisposition which he found it difficult to throw off.

VI

The chance, whatever it may have been, passed like a
flash. Just as the proposal inflamed many in England, so
it did mischief in Cairo. Zobeir like other people got wind
of it; enemies of England at Cairo set to work with him ; Sir
E. Baring might have found him hard to deal with. It was
Gordon's rashness that had made the design public. Gordon,
too, as it happened, had made a dire mistake on his way
up. At Berber he had shown the khedive's secret firman,

[1] The case of the government was
stated with all the force and reason
of which it admitted, in Lord Granville's despatch of March 28, 1884.

announcing the intended abandonment of the Soudan. The news spread; it soon reached the Mahdi himself, and the Mahdi made politic use of it. He issued a proclamation of his own, asking all the sheikhs who stood aloof from him or against him, what they had to gain by supporting a pasha who was the next day going to give the Soudan up. Gordon's argument for this unhappy proceeding was that, the object of his mission being to get out of the country and leave them to their independence, he could have put no sharper spur into them to make them organise their own government. But he spoke of it after as the fatal proclamation, and so it was.[1]

What happened was that the tribes round Khartoum almost at once began to waver. From the middle of March, says a good observer, one searches in vain for a single circumstance hopeful for Gordon. 'When the eye wanders over the huge and hostile Soudan, notes the little pin-point garrisons, each smothered in a cloud of Arab spears, and remembers that Gordon and Stewart proceeded to rule this vast empire, already given away to others, one feels that the Soudanese view was marked by common sense.'[2] Gordon's too sanguine prediction that the men who had beaten Hicks, and the men who afterwards beat Baker, would never fight beyond their tribal limits, did not come true. Wild forces gathered round the Mahdi as he advanced northwards. The tribes that had wavered joined them. Berber fell on May 26. The pacific mission had failed, and Gordon and his comrade Stewart — a more careful and clear-sighted man than himself — were shut up in Khartoum.

[1] In the light of this proceeding, the following is curious: 'There is one subject which I cannot imagine any one differing about. That is the impolicy of announcing our intention to evacuate Khartoum. Even if we were bound to do so we should have said nothing about it. The moment it is known we have given up the game, every man will go over to the Mahdi. All men worship the rising sun. The difficulties of evacuation will be enormously increased, if, indeed, the withdrawal of our garrison is not rendered impossible.' — Interview with General Gordon, *Pall Mall Gazette*, Jan. 8, 1884.

. . . 'In the afternoon of Feb. 13 Gordon assembled all the influential men of the province and showed them the secret firman. The reading of this document caused great excitement, but at the same time its purport was received evidently with much gratification. It is worthy of note that the whole of the notables present at this meeting subsequently threw in their cause with the Mahdi.' — Henry William Gordon's *Events in the Life of Charles George Gordon*, p. 340.

[2] Wingate, p. 110.

Distractions grew thicker upon the cabinet, and a just reader, now far away from the region of votes of censure, will bear them in mind. The Queen, like many of her subjects, grew impatient, but Mr. Gladstone was justified in reminding her of the imperfect knowledge, and he might have called it blank ignorance, with which the government was required on the shortest notice to form conclusions on a remote and more than half-barbarous region.

Gordon had told them that he wanted to take his steam vessels to Equatoria and serve the king of the Belgians. This Sir Evelyn Baring refused to allow, not believing Gordon to be in immediate danger (March 26). From Gordon himself came a telegram (March 28), ' I think we are now safe, and that, as the Nile rises, we shall account for the rebels.' Mr. Gladstone was still unwell and absent. Through Lord Granville he told the cabinet (March 15) that, with a view to speedy departure from Khartoum, he would not even refuse absolutely to send cavalry to Berber, much as he disliked it, provided the military authorities thought it could be done, and provided also that it was declared necessary for Gordon's safety, and was strictly confined to that object. The cabinet decided against an immediate expedition, one important member vowing that he would resign if an expedition were not sent in the autumn, another vowing that he would resign if it were. On April 7, the question of an autumn expedition again came up. Six were favourable, five the other way, including the prime minister.

Almost by the end of March it was too probable that no road of retreat was any longer open. If they could cut no way out, either by land or water, what form of relief was possible? A diversion from Suakin to Berber — one of Gordon's own suggestions? But the soldiers differed. Fierce summer heat and little water; an Indian force might stand it; even they would find it tough. A dash by a thousand cavalry across two hundred miles of desert — one hundred of them without water; without communication with its base, and with the certainty that whatever might befall, no reinforcements could reach it for months? What would be your feelings, and your language, asked Lord

Hartington, if besides having Gordon and Stewart beleaguered
in Khartoum, we also knew that a small force of British
cavalry unable to take the offensive was shut up in the
town of Berber?[1] Then the government wondered whether
a move on Dongola might not be advantageous. Here again
the soldiers thought the torrid climate a fatal objection, and
the benefits doubtful. Could not Gordon, some have asked,
have made his retreat at an early date after reaching
Khartoum, by way of Berber? Answer — the Nile was too
low. All this it was that at a later day, when the time had
come to call his government to its account, justified Mr.
Gladstone in saying that in such enterprises as these in the
Soudan, mistakes and miscarriages were inevitable, for they
were the proper and certain consequences of undertakings
that lie beyond the scope of human means and of rational
and prudent human action, and are a war against nature.[2]
If anybody now points to the victorious expedition to
Khartoum thirteen years later, as falsifying such language as
this, that experience so far from falsifying entirely justifies.
A war against nature demands years of study, observation,
preparation, and those who are best acquainted with the
conditions at first hand all agree that neither the tribes nor
the river nor the desert were well known enough in 1885, to
guarantee that overthrow in the case of the Mahdi, which
long afterwards destroyed his successor.

On April 14 Sir E. Baring, while as keenly averse as
anybody in the world to an expedition for the relief of
Khartoum if such an expedition could be avoided, still
watching events with a clear and concentrated gaze, assured
the government that it was very likely to be unavoidable;
it would be well therefore, without loss of time, to prepare
for a move as soon as ever the Nile should rise. Six days
before, Lord Wolseley also had written to Lord Hartington
at the war office, recommending immediate and active
preparations for an exclusively British expedition to Khartoum. Time, he said, is the most important element in this

---

[1] Lord Hartington, House of Commons, May 13, 1884. An admirable speech, and the best defence of min- isters up to this date.
[2] Address to the electors of Midlothian, September 17, 1885.

question; and in truth it was, for time was flying, and so were events. The cabinet were reported as feeling that Gordon, 'who was despatched on a mission essentially pacific, had found himself, from whatever cause, unable to prosecute it effectually, and now proposed the use of military means, which might fail, and which, even if they should succeed, might be found to mean a new subjugation of the Soudan — the very consummation which it was the object of Gordon's mission to avert.' On June 27 it was known in London that Berber had fallen a month before.

VII

Lord Hartington, as head of the war department, had a stronger leaning towards the despatch of troops than some of his colleagues, but, says Mr. Gladstone to Lord Granville in a letter of 1888, 'I don't think he ever came to any sharp issue (like mine about Zobeir) ; rather that in the main he got what he wanted.' Wherever the fault lay, the issue was unfortunate. The generals in London fought the battle of the routes with unabated tenacity for month after month. One was for the approach to Khartoum by the Nile ; another by Suakin and Berber ; a third by the Korosko desert. A departmental committee reported in favour of the Nile as the easiest, safest, and cheapest, but they did not report until July 29. It was not until the beginning of August that the House of Commons was asked for a vote of credit, and Lord Hartington authorised General Stephenson at Cairo to take measures for moving troops southward. In his despatch of August 8, Lord Hartington still only speaks of operations for the relief of Gordon, 'should they become necessary' ; he says the government were still unconvinced that Gordon could not secure the withdrawal of the garrison from Khartoum ; but 'they are of opinion that the time had arrived for obtaining accurate information as to his position,' and, 'if necessary, for rendering him assistance.'[1] As soon as the decision was taken, preparations were carried out with rapidity and skill. In the same month Lord Wolseley was

[1] See the official *History of the Soudan Campaign*, by Colonel Colvile, Part I. pp. 45-9.

appointed to command the expedition, and on September 9 CHAP.
he reached Cairo. The difficulties of a military decision had IX.
been great, said Lord Hartington, and there was besides, he Æт. 75.
added, a difference of opinion among the military authorities.[1]
It was October 5 before Lord Wolseley reached Wady-
Halfa, and the Nile campaign began.

Whatever decision military critics may ultimately form
upon the choice of the Nile route, or upon the question
whether the enterprise would have been any more successful if the route had been by Suakin or Korosko, it is at
least certain that no position, whether strategically false
or no, has ever evoked more splendid qualities in face of
almost preterhuman difficulties, hardship, and labour. The
treacherous and unknown river, for it was then unknown,
with its rapids, its shifting sandbanks and tortuous channels
and rocky barriers and heart-breaking cataracts; the
Bayuda desert, haunted by fierce and stealthy enemies; the
trying climate, the heat, the thirst, all the wearisome
embarrassments of transport on camels emaciated by lack
of food and water — such scenes exacted toil, patience, and
courage as worthy of remark and admiration as if the
advance had successfully achieved its object. Nobody lost
heart. 'Everything goes on swimmingly,' wrote Sir Herbert
Stewart to Lord Wolseley, 'except as to time.' This was on
January 14, 1885. Five days later, he was mortally wounded.

The end of it all, in spite of the gallantry of Abu Klea and
Kirbekan, of desert column and river column, is only too
well known. Four of Gordon's small steamers coming down
from Khartoum met the British desert column at Gubat on
January 21. The general in command at once determined
to proceed to Khartoum, but delayed his start until the
morning of the 24th. The steamers needed repairs, and Sir
Charles Wilson deemed it necessary for the safety of his troops
to make a reconnaissance down the river towards Berber
before starting up to Khartoum. He took with him on two
of Gordon's steamers — described as of the dimensions of the
penny boats upon the Thames, but bullet proof — a force of
twenty-six British, and two hundred and forty Soudanese.

[1] February 27, 1885.

He had also in tow a nugger laden with dhura. This was what, when Khartoum came in sight (Jan. 28) the 'relief force' actually amounted to. As the two steamers ran slowly on, a solitary voice from the river-bank now and again called out to them that Khartoum was taken, and Gordon slain. Eagerly searching with their glasses, the officers perceived that the government-house was a wreck, and that no flag was flying. Gordon, in fact, had met his death two days before.

Mr. Gladstone afterwards always spoke of the betrayal of Khartoum. But Major Kitchener, who prepared the official report, says that the accusations of treachery were all vague, and to his mind, the outcome of mere supposition. 'In my opinion,' he says, 'Khartoum fell from sudden assault, when the garrison were too exhausted by privations to make proper resistance.' [1] The idea that the relieving force was only two days late is misleading. A nugger's load of dhura would not have put an end to the privations of the fourteen thousand people still in Khartoum; and even supposing that the handful of troops at Gubat could have effected their advance upon Khartoum many days earlier, it is hard to believe that they were strong enough either to drive off the Mahdi, or to hold him at bay until the river column had come up.

VIII

The prime minister was on a visit to the Duke of Devonshire at Holker, where he had many long conversations with Lord Hartington, and had to deal with heavy post-bags. On Thursday, Feb. 5, after writing to the Queen and others, he heard what had happened on the Nile ten days before. 'After 11 A.M.,' he records, 'I learned the sad news of the fall or betrayal of Khartoum. H[artington] and I, with C [his wife], went off by the first train, and reached Downing Street soon after 8.15. The circumstances are sad and trying. It is one of the least points about them that they may put an end to this government.' [2] The next day the cabinet met;

---

[1] Colvile, ii., Appendix 47, p. 274. Apart from the authority of Kitchener, Gordon's own language shows that he knew himself to be in extremis by the end of December.

[2] The story that he went to the theatre the same night is untrue.

discussions 'difficult but harmonious.' The Queen sent to CHAP.
him and to Lord Hartington at Holker an angry telegram IX.
— blaming her ministers for what had happened — a telegram ÆT. 76.
not in cipher as usual, but open. Mr. Gladstone addressed
to the Queen in reply (Feb. 5, 1885) a vindication of the
course taken by the cabinet; and it may be left to close an
unedifying and a tragic chapter : —

To the Queen.

Mr. Gladstone has had the honour this day to receive your
Majesty's telegram en clair, relating to the deplorable intelligence
received this day from Lord Wolseley, and stating that it is too
fearful to consider that the fall of Khartoum might have been
prevented and many precious lives saved by earlier action. Mr.
Gladstone does not presume to estimate the means of judgment
possessed by your Majesty, but so far as his information and
recollection at the moment go, he is not altogether able to
follow the conclusion which your Majesty has been pleased
thus to announce. Mr. Gladstone is under the impression that
Lord Wolseley's force might have been sufficiently advanced to
save Khartoum, had not a large portion of it been detached by a
circuitous route along the river, upon the express application of
General Gordon, to occupy Berber on the way to the final destination. He speaks, however, with submission on a point of this
kind. There is indeed in some quarters a belief that the river
route ought to have been chosen at an earlier period, and had the
navigation of the Nile in its upper region been as well known as
that of the Thames, this might have been a just ground of reproach.
But when, on the first symptoms that the position of General
Gordon in Khartoum was not secure, your Majesty's advisers at
once sought from the most competent persons the best information
they could obtain respecting the Nile route, the balance of testimony and authority was decidedly against it, and the idea of the
Suakin and Berber route, with all its formidable difficulties, was
entertained in preference; nor was it until a much later period
that the weight of opinion and information warranted the defini-
tive choice of the Nile route. Your Majesty's ministers were well
aware that climate and distance were far more formidable than the
sword of the enemy, and they deemed it right, while providing

adequate military means, never to lose from view what might have proved to be the destruction of the gallant army in the Soudan. It is probable that abundant wrath and indignation will on this occasion be poured out upon them. Nor will they complain if so it should be; but a partial consolation may be found on reflecting that neither aggressive policy, nor military disaster, nor any gross error in the application of means to ends, has marked this series of difficult proceedings, which, indeed, have greatly redounded to the honour of your Majesty's forces of all ranks and arms. In these remarks which Mr. Gladstone submits with his humble devotion, he has taken it for granted that Khartoum has fallen through the exhaustion of its means of defence. But your Majesty may observe from the telegram that this is uncertain. Both the correspondent's account and that of Major Wortley refer to the delivery of the town by treachery, a contingency which on some previous occasions General Gordon has treated as far from improbable; and which, if the notice existed, was likely to operate quite independently of the particular time at which a relieving force might arrive. The presence of the enemy in force would naturally suggest the occasion, or perhaps even the apprehension of the approach of the British army. In pointing to these considerations, Mr. Gladstone is far from assuming that they are conclusive upon the whole case; in dealing with which the government has hardly ever at any of its stages been furnished sufficiently with those means of judgment which rational men usually require. It may be that, on a retrospect, many errors will appear to have been committed. There are many reproaches, from the most opposite quarters, to which it might be difficult to supply a conclusive answer. Among them, and perhaps among the most difficult, as far as Mr. Gladstone can judge, would be the reproach of those who might argue that our proper business was the protection of Egypt, that it never was in military danger from the Mahdi, and that the most prudent course would have been to provide it with adequate frontier defences, and to assume no responsibility for the lands beyond the desert.

One word more. Writing to one of his former colleagues long after Mr. Gladstone says : —

Jan. 10, '90. — In the Gordon case we all, and I rather prominently, must continue to suffer in silence. Gordon was a hero, and a hero of heroes; but we ought to have known that a hero of heroes is not the proper person to give effect at a distant point, and in most difficult circumstances, to the views of ordinary men. It was unfortunate that he should claim the hero's privilege by turning upside down and inside out every idea and intention with which he had left England, and for which he had obtained our approval. Had my views about Zobeir prevailed, it would not have removed our difficulties, as Forster would certainly have moved, and with the tories and the Irish have carried, a condemnatory address. My own opinion is that it is harder to justify our doing so much to rescue him, than our not doing more. Had the party reached Khartoum in time, he would not have come away (as I suppose), and the dilemma would have arisen in another form.

CHAP.
IX.

Æt. 76.

In 1890 an application was made to Mr. Gladstone by a certain foreign writer who had undertaken an article on Gordon and his mission. Mr. Gladstone's reply (Jan. 11, '90) runs to this effect : —

I am much obliged by your kind letter and enclosure. I hope you will not think it belies this expression when I say that I feel myself precluded from supplying any material or entering upon any communications for the purpose of self-defence against the charges which are freely made and I believe widely accepted against myself and against the cabinet of 1880–5 in connection with General Gordon. It would be felt in this country, by friends I think in many cases as well as adversaries, that General Gordon's much-lamented death ought to secure him, so far as we are concerned, against the counter-argument which we should have to present on his language and proceedings. On this account you will, I hope, excuse me from entering into the matter. I do not doubt that a true and equitable judgment will eventually prevail.[1]

---

[1] *Belford's Magazine* (New York), Sept. 1890. A French translation of this letter will be found in *L'Égypte et ses Provinces Perdues*, by the recipient, Colonel C. Chaillé-Long Bey (1892), pp. 196–7. He was chief of the staff to Gordon in the Soudan, and consular-agent for the United States at Alexandria. Another book of his, published in 1884, is *The Three Prophets; Chinese Gordon, El Mahdi, and Arabi Pasha.* Burton reviewed Gordon's Khartoum Journals, *Academy*, June 11, 1885.

CHAPTER X

INTERIOR OF THE CABINET

(*1885*)

I AM aware that the age is not what we all wish, but I am sure that the only means to check its degeneracy is heartily to concur in whatever is best in our time. — BURKE.

BOOK VIII.

1885.

THE year 1885 must be counted as in some respects the severest epoch of Mr. Gladstone's life. The previous twelve months had not ended cheerfully. Sleep, the indispensable restorer, and usually his constant friend, was playing him false. The last entry in his diary was this : —

The year closed with a bad night, only one hour and a half of sleep, which will hardly do to work upon. There is much that I should like to have recorded. . . . But the pressure on me is too great for the requisite recollection. It is indeed a time of *Sturm und Drang*. What with the confusion of affairs, and the disturbance of my daily life by the altered character of my nights, I cannot think in calm, but can only trust and pray.

He was unable to be present at the dinner of the tenants, and his eldest son in his absence dwelt once more on his father's wish to retire, whenever occasion should come, from the public service, or at least from that kind of service to the public which imposed on him such arduous efforts. One great element of confusion was the sphinx's riddle of Egyptian finance. On his birthday, among a dozen occupations, he says: 'A little woodcraft for helping sleep ; wrote mem. on Egyptian finance which I hope may help to clear my brain and nerves.' And this was a characteristic way of seeking a cure ; for now and at every time, any task that demanded close thought and firm expression was his surest

sedative. More perplexing even than the successive prob- CHAP.
lems of the hour, was the threatened disorganisation, not only X.
of his cabinet, but of the party and its future. On January 20 Æt. 76.
he was forced to London for two Egyptian cabinets, but he
speedily returned to Hawarden, whence he immediately wrote
a letter to Lord Granville: —

January 22, 1885. — Here I am after a journey of 5½ hours from
door to door, through the unsought and ill-deserved kindness of
the London and North-Western railway, which entirely spoils me
by special service.

There was one part of my conversation of to-day with Hartington which I should like not to leave in any case without record.
He referred to the difficulties he had had, and he 'gratefully'
acknowledged the considerateness of the cabinet. He said the
point always urged upon him was, not to break up the liberal
party. But, he said, can we avoid its breaking up, within a very
short time after you retire, and ought this consideration therefore
to be regarded as of such very great force? I said, my reply is in
two sentences. First, I admit that from various symptoms it is
not improbable there may be a plan or intention to break up the
party. But if a rupture of that kind comes, — this is my second
sentence — it will come upon matters of principle, known and
understood by the whole country, and your duty will probably be
clear and your position unembarrassed. But I entreat you to use
your utmost endeavour to avoid bringing about the rupture on
one of the points of this Egyptian question, which lies outside
the proper business of a government and is beyond its powers,
which does not turn upon clear principles of politics, and about
which the country understands almost nothing, and cares, for the
most part, very little. All this he took without rejoinder.

P.S. — We are going to Holker next week, and Hartington said
he would try to come and see me there.

As we have already seen,[1] Mr. Gladstone paid his visit to
Holker (January 30), where he found the Duke of Devonshire
'wonderfully well, and kind as ever,' where he was joined by
Lord Hartington, and where they together spelled out the

[1] Above, p. 166.

cipher telegram (on February 5) bringing the evil news of the fall of Khartoum.

It is not uninteresting to see how the notion of Mr. Gladstone's retirement, now much talked of in his family, affected a friendly, philosophic, and most observant onlooker. Lord Acton wrote to him (February 2): —

You mean that the new parliament, the first of our democratic constitution, shall begin its difficult and perilous course without the services of a leader who has greater experience and authority than any other man. You design to withdraw your assistance when most urgently needed, at the moment of most conservative apprehension and most popular excitement. By the choice of this particular moment for retirement you increase the danger of the critical transition, because nobody stands as you do between the old order of things and the new, or inspires general confidence; and the lieutenants of Alexander are not at their best. Next year's change will appear vast and formidable to the suspicious foreigner, who will be tempted to doubt our identity. It is in the national interest to reduce the outer signs of change, to bridge the apparent chasm, to maintain the traditional character of the state. The unavoidable elements of weakness will be largely and voluntarily aggravated by their untimely coincidence with an event which must, at any time, be a blow to the position of England among the Powers. Your absence just then must grievously diminish our credit. . . . You alone inspire confidence that what is done for the great masses shall be done with a full sense of economic responsibility. . . . A divided liberal party and a weak conservative party mean the supremacy of the revolutionary Irish. . . .'

To this Mr. Gladstone replied: —

10 *Downing Street, Feb.* 11, 1885. . . . Your argument against letting the outworn hack go to grass, depends wholly on a certain proposition, namely this, that there is about to be a crisis in the history of the constitution, growing out of the extension of the franchise, and that it is my duty to do what I can in aiding to steer the ship through the boiling waters of this crisis. My answer is simple. There is no crisis at all in view. There is a process of slow modification and development mainly in directions which

I view with misgiving. 'Tory democracy,' the favourite idea on that side, is no more like the conservative party in which I was bred, than it is like liberalism. In fact less. It is demagogism, only a demagogism not ennobled by love and appreciation of liberty, but applied in the worst way, to put down the pacific, law-respecting, economic elements which ennobled the old conservatism, living upon the fomentation of angry passions, and still in secret as obstinately attached as ever to the evil principle of class interests. The liberalism of to-day is better in what I have described as ennobling the old conservatism; nay, much better, yet far from being good. Its pet idea is what they call construc-tion, — that is to say, taking into the hands of the state the busi-ness of the individual man. Both the one and the other have much to estrange me, and have had for many, many years. But, with all this, there is no crisis. I have even the hope that while the coming change may give undue encouragement to ' construction,' it will be favourable to the economic, pacific, law-regarding elements; and the sense of justice which abides tenaciously in the masses will never knowingly join hands with the fiend of Jingoism. On the whole, I do not abandon the hope that it may mitigate the chronic distemper, and have not the smallest fear of its bringing about an acute or convulsive action. You leave me therefore rooted in my evil mind. . . .

The activity of the left wing, acute, perhaps, but not con-vulsive, became much more embarrassing than the desire of the right wing to be inactive. Mr. Chamberlain had been rapidly advancing in public prominence, and he now showed that the agitation against the House of Lords was to be only the beginning and not the end. At Ipswich (January 14), he said this country had been called the paradise of the rich, and warned his audience no longer to allow it to remain the purgatory of the poor. He told them that reform of local government must be almost the first reform of the next parliament, and spoke in favour of allotments, the creation of small proprietors, the placing of a small tax on the total property of the taxpayer, and of free education. Mr. Gladstone's attention was drawn from Windsor to these utterances, and he replied (January 22) that though he

thought some of them were 'on various grounds open to
grave objection,' yet they seemed to raise no 'definite point
on which, in his capacity of prime minister, he was entitled
to interfere and lecture the speaker.' A few days later,
more terrible things were said by Mr. Chamberlain at
Birmingham. He pronounced for the abolition of plural
voting, and in favour of payment of members, and manhood suffrage. He also advocated a bill for enabling local
communities to acquire land, a graduated income-tax, and
the breaking up of the great estates as the first step in land
reform. This deliverance was described by not unfriendly
critics as 'a little too much the speech of the agitator of the
future, rather than of the minister of the present.' Mr.
Gladstone made a lenient communication to the orator, to the
effect that 'there had better be some explanations among
them when they met.' To Lord Granville he wrote (January
31) : —

Upon the whole, weak-kneed liberals have caused us more
trouble in the present parliament than radicals. But I think
these declarations by Chamberlain upon matters which cannot,
humanly speaking, become practical before the next parliament,
can hardly be construed otherwise than as having a remote and
(in that sense) far-sighted purpose which is ominous enough.
The opposition can hardly fail in their opportunity, I must add
in their duty, to make them matter of attack. Such things will
happen casually from time to time, and always with inconvenience
— but there is here a degree of method and system which seem to
give the matter a new character.

It will be seen from his tone that Mr. Gladstone, in all the
embarrassments arising from this source, showed complete
freedom from personal irritation. Like the lofty-minded man
he was, he imputed no low motives to a colleague because
the colleague gave him trouble. He recognised by now
that in his cabinet the battle was being fought between old
time and new. He did not allow his dislike of some of the
new methods of forming public opinion, to prevent him from
doing full justice to the energetic and sincere public spirit
behind them. He had, moreover, quite enough to do with

the demands of the present, apart from signs that were ominous for the future. A year before, in a letter to Lord Granville (March 24, 1884), he had attempted a definition that will, perhaps, be of general interest to politicians of either party complexion. It is, at any rate, characteristic of his subtlety, if that be the right word, in drawing distinctions: —

What are divisions in a cabinet? In my opinion, differences of views stated, and if need be argued, and then advisedly surrendered with a view to a common conclusion are not 'divisions in a cabinet.' By that phrase I understand unaccommodated differences on matters standing for immediate action.

It was unaccommodated differences of this kind that cost Mr. Disraeli secessions on the Reform bill, and secessions no less serious on his eastern policy, and it is one of the wonders of his history that Mr. Gladstone prevented secession on the matters now standing for immediate action before his own cabinet. During the four months between the meeting of parliament and the fall of the government, the two great difficulties of the government — Egypt and Ireland — reached their climax.

II

The news of the fall of Khartoum reached England on February 5. One of the least points, as Mr. Gladstone wrote on the day, was that the grievous news would put an end to the government, and so it very nearly did. As was to be expected, Sir Stafford Northcote moved a vote of censure. Mr. Gladstone informed the Queen, on the day before the division, that the aspect of the House was 'dubious and equivocal.' If there was a chance of overthrowing the ministry, he said, the nationalists were pretty sure to act and vote as a body with Sir Stafford. Mr. Forster, Mr. Goschen, and some members of the whig section of the liberal party, were likely either to do the same, or else to abstain. These circumstances looked towards an unfavourable issue, if not in the shape of an adverse majority, yet in the form of a majority too small to enable the govern-

ment to carry on with adequate authority and efficiency.
In the debate, said Mr. Gladstone, Lord Hartington re-stated
with measured force the position of the government, and
overthrew the contention that had taken a very forward
place in the indictment against ministers, that their great
offence was the failure to send forward General Graham's
force to relieve General Gordon. In the course of this
debate Mr. Goschen warned the government that if they
flinched from the policy of smashing the Mahdi at Khartoum,
he should vote against them. A radical below the gangway
upon this went to the party whip and declared, with equal
resolution, that if the government insisted on the policy,
then it would be for him and others to vote against them.
Sir William Harcourt, in a speech of great power, satisfied
the gentlemen below the gangway, and only a small handful
of the party went into the lobby with the opposition and
the Irish. The division was taken at four in the morning
(February 28), and the result was that the government which
had come in with morning radiance five years ago, was worn
down to an attenuated majority of fourteen.[1]

When the numbers were declared, Mr. Gladstone said
to a colleague on the bench, ' *That will do.*' Whether this
delphic utterance meant that the size of the majority
would justify resignation or retention, the colleague was
not sure. When the cabinet met at a more mellowed
hour in the day, the question between going out of office
and staying in, was fully discussed. Mere considerations
of ease all pointed one way, for, if they held on, they
would seem to be dependent on tory support; trouble
was brewing with Russia, and the Seats bill would not be
through in a hurry. On the other hand, fourteen was
majority enough to swear by, the party would be surprised
by resignation and discouraged, and retirement would
wear the look of a false position. In fact Mr. Gladstone,
in spite of his incessant sighs for a hermit's calm, was
always for fighting out every position to the last trench.
I can think of no exception, and even when the time came
ten years later, he thought his successors pusillanimous for

[1] For the censure, 288 ; against, 302.

retiring on a small scratch defeat on cordite.[1] So now
he acted on the principle that with courage cabinets may
weather almost any storm. No actual vote was taken, but
the numbers for and against retirement were equal, until
Mr. Gladstone spoke. He thought that they should try
to go on, at least until the Seats bill was through. This was
the final decision.

All this brought once more into his mind the general
consideration that now naturally much haunted him. He
wrote to the Queen (February 27) : —

Mr. Gladstone believes that circumstances independent of his
own will enable him to estimate, with some impartiality, future
political changes, and he is certainly under the impression that,
partly from the present composition and temper of the liberal
party, and still more, and even much more, from the changes
which the conservative party has been undergoing during the
last forty years (especially the last ten or fifteen of them), the
next change of government may possibly form the introduction to
a period presenting some new features, and may mean more than
what is usually implied in the transfer of power from one party
to another.

Mr. Bright has left a note of a meeting with him at this
time : —

March 2, 1885. — Dined with Mrs. Gladstone. After dinner,
sat for half an hour or more with Mr. Gladstone, who is ill with
cold and hoarseness. Long talk on Egypt. He said he had
suffered torment during the continuance of the difficulty in that
country. The sending Gordon out a great mistake, — a man
totally unsuited for the work he undertook. Mr. Gladstone never
saw Gordon. He was appointed by ministers in town, and
Gladstone concurred, but had never seen him.

At this moment clouds began to darken the remote
horizon on the north-west boundary of our great Indian
possessions. The entanglement in the deserts of the Soudan
was an obvious temptation to any other Power with policies
of its own, to disregard the susceptibilities or even the solid

---

[1] I often tried to persuade him that
our retreat was to be explained apart
from pusillanimity, but he would not
listen.

interests of Great Britain. As we shall see, Mr. Gladstone
was as little disposed as Chatham or Palmerston to shrink
from the defence of the legitimate rights or obligations of
his country. But the action of Russia in Afghanistan became an added and rather poignant anxiety.

As early as March 12 the cabinet found it necessary to
consider the menacing look of things on the Afghan frontier.
Military necessities in India, as Mr. Gladstone described to
the Queen what was in the mind of her ministers, 'might
conceivably at this juncture come to overrule the present
intentions as to the Soudan as part of them, and it would
consequently be imprudent to do anything which could
practically extend our obligations in that quarter; as it is the
entanglement of the British forces in Soudanese operations,
which would most powerfully tempt Russia to adopt aggressive measures.' Three or four weeks later these considerations
came to a head. The question put by Mr. Gladstone to his
colleagues was this: 'Apart from the defence of Egypt,
which no one would propose to abandon, does there appear
to be any obligation of honour or any inducement of policy
(for myself I should add, is there any moral warrant?) that
should lead us in the present state of the demands on the
empire, to waste a large portion of our army in fighting
against nature, and I fear also fighting against liberty (such
liberty as the case admits) in the Soudan?' The assumptions
on which the policy had been founded had all broken
down. Osman Digna, instead of being readily crushed, had
betaken himself to the mountains and could not be got at.
The railway from Suakin to Berber, instead of serving
the advance on Khartoum in the autumn, could not possibly be ready in time. Berber, instead of being taken before the hot season, could not be touched. Lord Wolseley,
instead of being able to proceed with his present forces
or a moderate addition, was already asking for twelve
more battalions of infantry, with a proportion of other
arms.

Mr. Gladstone's own view of this crisis is to be found in
a memorandum dated April 9, circulated to the cabinet three
or four days before the question came up for final settle-

ment. It is long, but then the case was intricate and the CHAP.
stages various. The reader may at least be satisfied to know   X.
that he will have little more of it.[1]   Æt. 76.
Three cabinets were held on three successive days (April
13–15). On the evening of the first day Mr. Gladstone sent
a telegram to the Queen, then abroad, informing her that
in the existing state of foreign affairs, her ministers felt
bound to examine the question of the abandonment of
offensive operations in the Soudan and the evacuation of
the territory. The Queen, in reply, was rather vehement
against withdrawal, partly on the ground that it would
seriously affect our position in India. The Queen had
throughout made a great point that the fullest powers
should be granted to those on the spot, both Wolseley and
Baring having been selected by the government for the
offices they held. No question cuts deeper in the art of
administering a vast system like that of Great Britain, than
the influence of the agent at a distant place ; nowhere is the
balance of peril between too slack a rein from home and
a rein too tight, more delicate. Mr. Gladstone, perhaps
taught by the experience of the Crimean war, always
strongly inclined to the school of the tight rein, though
I never heard of any representative abroad with a right
to complain of insufficient support from a Gladstone
cabinet.[2] On this aspect of matters, so raised by the Queen,
Mr. Gladstone had (March 15) expressed his view to Sir
Henry Ponsonby : —

Sir Evelyn Baring was appointed to carry onwards a declared
and understood policy in Egypt, when all share in the management of the Soudan was beyond our province. To Lord
Wolseley as general of the forces in Egypt, and on account
of the arduous character of the work before him, we are bound
to render in all military matters a firm and ungrudging support.
We have accordingly not scrupled to counsel, on his recommendation, very heavy charges on the country, and military

1 See Appendix.
2 For instance when Mr. Gladstone
fell from office in 1874, Lord Odo
Russell wrote to him, ' how sorry
I feel at your retirement, and how

grateful I am to you for the great
advantage and encouragement I have
enjoyed while serving under your
great administration, in Rome and
Berlin.'

operations of the highest importance. But we have no right to
cast on him any responsibility beyond what is strictly military.
It is not surely possible that he should decide policy, and that
we should adopt and answer for it, even where it is in conflict
with the announcements we have made in parliament.

By the time of these critical cabinets in April Sir Evelyn
Baring had spontaneously expressed his views, and with a
full discussion recommended abandonment of the expedition to Khartoum.

On the second day the matter was again probed and sifted
and weighed.

At the third cabinet the decision was taken to retire
from the Soudan, and to fix the southern frontier of Egypt
at the line where it was left for twelve years, until apprehension of designs of another European power on the
upper waters of the Nile was held to demand a new policy.
Meanwhile, the policy of Mr. Gladstone's cabinet was adopted
and followed by Lord Salisbury when he came into office.
He was sometimes pressed to reverse it, and to overthrow the
dervish power at Khartoum. To any importunity of this
kind, Lord Salisbury's answer was until 1896 unwavering.[1]

It may be worth noting that, in the course of his correspondence with the Queen on the change of policy in the
Soudan, Mr. Gladstone casually indulged in the luxury of a
historical parallel. 'He must assure your Majesty,' he
wrote in a closing sentence (April 20), 'that at least he has
never in any cabinet known any question more laboriously
or more conscientiously discussed; and he is confident that
the basis of action has not been the mere change in the
public view (which, however, is in some cases imperative, as

[1] 'We do not depart in any degree
from the policy of leaving the Soudan.
As to the civilisation which the noble
and gallant earl [Lord Dundonald]
would impose upon us the duty of
restoring, it could only be carried
out by a large and costly expedition,
entailing enormous sacrifice of blood
and treasure, and for the present a
continuous expenditure, which I do
not think the people of this country
would sanction. . . . The defence
of our retention of Suakin is that
it is a very serious obstacle to the
renewal and the conduct of that
slave trade which is always trying
to pass over from Africa into Asia.
I do not think that the retention
of Suakin is of any advantage to
the Egyptian government. If I
were to speak purely from the
point of view of that government's
own interest, I should say, "Abandon
Suakin at once."' — Lord Salisbury,
in the House of Lords, March 16, 1888.

it was with King George III. in the case of the American CHAP.
war), but a deep conviction of what the honour and interest   X.
of the empire require them as faithful servants of your Æt. 76.
Majesty to advise.' The most harmless parallel is apt to
be a challenge to discussion, and the parenthesis seems to
have provoked some rejoinder from the Queen, for on April
28 Mr. Gladstone wrote to her secretary a letter which takes
him away from Khartoum to a famous piece of the world's
history: —

To Sir Henry Ponsonby.

In further prosecution of my reply to your letter of the 25th,
I advert to your remarks upon Lord North. I made no reference
to his conduct, I believe, in writing to her Majesty. What I
endeavoured to show was that King George III., without changing his opinion of the justice of his war against the colonies, was
obliged to give it up on account of a change of public opinion,
and was not open to blame for so doing.

You state to me that Lord North never flinched from his task
till it became hopeless, that he then resigned office, but did not
change his opinions to suit the popular cry. The implied contrast
to be drawn with the present is obvious. I admit none of your
three propositions. Lord North did not, as I read history, require
to change his opinions to suit the popular cry. They were already
in accordance with the popular cry ; and it is a serious reproach
against him that without sharing his master's belief in the propriety of the war, he long persisted in carrying it on, through
subserviency to that master.

Lord North did not resign office for any reason but because
he could not help it, being driven from it by some adverse votes
of the House of Commons, to which he submitted with great
good humour, and probably with satisfaction.

Lord North did not, so far as I know, state the cause to be
hopeless. Nor did those who were opposed to him. The movers
of the resolution that drove him out of office did not proceed
upon that ground. General Conway in his speech advised the
retention of the ground we held in the colonies, and the resolution, which expressed the sense of the House as a body, bears a
singular resemblance to the announcement we have lately made,

as it declares, in its first clause, that the further prosecution of offensive war (on the continent of America) 'will be the means of weakening the efforts of this country against her European enemies,' February 27, 1782. This was followed, on March 4, by an address on the same basis ; and by a resolution declaring that any ministers who should advise or attempt to frustrate it should be considered 'as enemies to his Majesty and to this country.' I ought, perhaps, to add that I have never stated, and I do not conceive, that a change in the public opinion of the country is the ground on which the cabinet have founded the change in their advice concerning the Soudan.

III

The reader has by this time perhaps forgotten how Mr. Gladstone good-humouredly remonstrated with Lord Palmerston for associating him as one of the same school as Cobden and Bright.[1] The twenty intervening years had brought him more and more into sympathy with those two eminent comrades in good causes, but he was not any less alive to the inconvenience of the label. Speaking in Midlothian after the dissolution in 1880, he denied the cant allegation that to instal the liberals in power would be to hand over the destinies of the country to the Manchester school.[2] 'Abhorring all selfishness of policy,' he said, 'friendly to freedom in every country of the earth attached, to the modes of reason, detesting the ways of force, this Manchester school, this peace-party, has sprung prematurely to the conclusion that wars may be considered as having closed their melancholy and miserable history, and that the affairs of the world may henceforth be conducted by methods more adapted to the dignity of man, more suited both to his strength and to his weakness, less likely to lead him out of the ways of duty, to stimulate his evil passions, to make him guilty before God for inflicting misery on his fellow-creatures.' Such a view, he said, was a serious error, though it was not only a respectable, it was even a noble error. Then he went on, 'However much you may detest war — and you cannot detest it too much — there is

[1] Above, vol. ii. p. 49.   [2] Edinburgh, March 17, 1880.

no war — except one, the war for liberty — that does not CHAP.
contain in it elements of corruption, as well as of misery, X.
that are deplorable to recollect and to consider; but however Æт. 76.
deplorable wars may be, they are among the necessities of
our condition; and there are times when justice, when faith,
when the welfare of mankind, require a man not to shrink
from the responsibility of undertaking them. And if you
undertake war, so also you are often obliged to undertake
measures that may lead to war.'[1]

It is also, if not one of the necessities, at least one of
the natural probabilities of our imperfect condition, that
when a nation has its forces engaged in war, that is
the moment when other nations may press inconvenient
questions of their own. Accordingly, as I have already
mentioned, when Egyptian distractions were at their
height, a dangerous controversy arose with Russia in
regard to the frontier of Afghanistan. The question had
been first raised a dozen years before without effect, but
it was now sharpened into actuality by recent advances of
Russia in Central Asia, bringing her into close proximity
to the territory of the Ameer. The British and Russian
governments appointed a commission to lay down the precise line of division between the Turcoman territory recently
annexed by Russia and Afghanistan. The question of instructions to the commission led to infinite discussion, of
which no sane man not a biographer is now likely to read
one word. While the diplomatists were thus teasing one
another, Russian posts and Afghan pickets came closer
together, and one day (March 30, 1885) the Russians broke
in upon the Afghans at Penjdeh. The Afghans fought gal-
lantly, their losses were heavy, and Penjdeh was occupied
by the Russians. 'Whose was the provocation,' as Mr.
Gladstone said later, ' is a matter of the utmost consequence. We only know that the attack was a Russian
attack. We know that the Afghans suffered in life, in
spirit, and in repute. We know that a blow was struck at

[1] In the letter to Mr. Bright his agreement with Bright in believ-
(July 14, 1882) already given, Mr. ing most wars to have been sad
Gladstone went somewhat nearer to errors.
the Manchester school, and expressed

the credit and the authority of a sovereign — our protected ally — who had committed no offence. All I say is, we cannot in that state of things close this book and say, "We will look into it no more." We must do our best to have right done in the matter.'

Here those who were most adverse to the Soudan policy stood firmly with their leader, and when Mr. Gladstone proposed a vote of credit for eleven millions, of which six and a half were demanded to meet 'the case for preparation,' raised by the collision at Penjdeh, he was supported with much more than a mechanical loyalty, alike by the regular opposition and by independent adherents below his own gangway. The speech in which he moved this vote of a war supply (April 27) was an admirable example both of sustained force and lucidity in exposition, and of a combined firmness, dignity, reserve, and right human feeling, worthy of a great minister dealing with an international situation of extreme delicacy and peril. Many anxious moments followed; for the scene of quarrel was far off, details were hard to clear up, diplomacy was sometimes ambiguous, popular excitement was heated, and the language of faction was unmeasured in its violence. The preliminary resolution on the vote of credit had been received with acclamation, but a hostile motion was made from the front opposition bench (May 11), though discord on a high imperial matter was obviously inconvenient enough for the public interest. The mover declared the government to have murdered so many thousand men and to have arranged a sham arbitration, and this was the prelude to other speeches in the same key. Sir S. Northcote supported the motion — one to displace the ministers on a bill that it was the declared intention not to oppose. The division was taken at half-past two in the morning, after a vigorous speech from the prime minister, and the government only counted 290 against 260. In the minority were 42 followers of Mr. Parnell. This premature debate cleared the air. Worked with patience and with vigorous preparations at the back of conciliatory negotiation, the question was prosecuted to a happy issue, and those who had done their best to denounce Mr. Gladstone and Lord Granville for trampling the interests and honour of their country underfoot thought themselves very lucky, when the time came for them to take up the threads, in being able to complete the business by adopting and continuing the selfsame line. With justifiable triumph Mr. Gladstone asked how they would have confronted Russia if 'that insane policy — for so I still must call it' — of Afghan occupation which he had brought to an end in 1880, had been persevered in. In such a case, when Russia came to advance her claim so to adjust boundaries as to make her immediate neighbour to Afghanistan, she would have found the country full of friends and allies, ready to join her in opposing the foreigner and the invader; and she would have been recognised as the liberator.[1]

IV

In some respects Mr. Gladstone was never more wonderful than in the few weeks that preceded the fall of his second administration. Between the middle of April and the middle of May, he jots down with half-rueful humour the names of no fewer than nine members of the cabinet who within that period, for one reason or another and at one moment or another, appeared to contemplate resignation; that is to say a majority. Of one meeting he said playfully to a colleague, 'A very fair cabinet to-day — only three resignations.' The large packets of copious letters of this date, written and received, show him a minister of unalterable patience, unruffled self-command; inexhaustible in resource, catching at every straw from the resource of others, indefatigable in bringing men of divergent opinions within friendly reach of one another; of tireless ingenuity in minimising differences and convincing recalcitrants that what they took for a yawning gulf was in fact no more than a narrow trench that any decent political gymnast ought to be ashamed not to be able to vault over. Though he takes it all as being in the day's work, in the confidence of the old jingle, that be the day short or never so long,

[1] West Calder, November 17, 1885.

at length it ringeth to evensong, he does not conceal the burden. To Mrs. Gladstone he writes from Downing Street on May-day: —

Rather oppressed and tired with the magnitude and the complication of subjects on my mind, I did not think of writing by the first post, but I will now supply the omission by making use of the second. As to all the later history of this ministry, which is now entering on its sixth year, it has been a wild romance of politics, with a continual succession of hairbreadth escapes and strange accidents pressing upon one another, and it is only from the number of dangers we have passed through already, that one can be bold enough to hope we may pass also through what yet remain. Some time ago I told you that dark as the sky was with many a thunder-cloud, there were the possibilities of an admirable situation and result, and *for me* a wind-up better than at any time I could have hoped. Russia and Ireland are the two *great* dangers remaining. The 'ray' I mentioned yesterday for the first is by no means extinct to-day, but there is nothing new of a serious character; what there is, is good. So also upon the Irish complications there is more hope than there was yesterday, although the odds may still be heavily against our getting forward unitedly in a satisfactory manner.

On May 2, as he was looking at the pictures in the Academy, Lord Granville brought him tidings of the Russian answer, which meant peace. His short entries tell a brave story: —

May 3, Sunday. — Dined at Marlborough House. They were most kind and pleasant. But it is so unsundaylike and unrestful. I am much fatigued in mind and body. Yet very happy. *May* 4. — Wrote to Lord Spencer, Mr. Chamberlain, Sir C. Dilke, Lord Granville. Conclave. H. of C., 4¾-8½ and 9½-2½. Spoke on Russian question. A heavy day. Much knocked up. *May* 5. — ... Another anxious, very anxious day, and no clearing of the sky as yet. But after all that has come, what may not come ? *May* 14, *Ascension Day.* — Most of the day was spent in anxious interviews, and endeavours to bring and keep the members of the cabinet together. *May* 15. — Cabinet 2-4½. Again stiff. But I must not lose heart.

Difference of opinion upon the budget at one time wore a threatening look, for the radicals disliked the proposed increase of the duty on beer; but Mr. Gladstone pointed out in compensation that on the other hand the equalisation of the death duties struck at the very height of class preference. Mr. Childers was, as always, willing to accommodate difficulties; and in the cabinet the rising storm blew over. Ireland never blows over.

The struggle had gone on for three years. Many murderers had been hanged, though more remained undetected; conspirators had fled; confidence was restored to public officers; society in all its various grades returned externally to the paths of comparative order; and the dire emergency of three years before had been brought to an apparent close. The gratitude in this country to the viceroy who had achieved this seeming triumph over the forces of disorder was such as is felt to a military commander after a hazardous and successful campaign. The country was once more half-conquered, but nothing was advanced, and the other half of the conquest was not any nearer. The scene was not hopeful. There lay Ireland, — squalid, dismal, sullen, dull, expectant, sunk deep in hostile intent. A minority with these misgivings and more felt that the minister's pregnant phrase about the government 'having no moral force behind them' too exactly described a fatal truth.

CHAPTER XI

DEFEAT OF MINISTERS

(*May–June 1885*)

Οὔπω
τὰν Διὸς ἁρμονίαν
θνατῶν παρεξίασι βουλαί.
— ÆSCH. *Prom.* v. 548.

Never do counsels of mortal men thwart the ordered purpose
of Zeus.

WHAT was to be the Irish policy? The Crimes Act would
expire in August, and the state of parties in parliament and
of sections within the cabinet, together with the approach
of the general election, made the question whether that Act
should be renewed, and if so on what terms, an issue of
crucial importance.   There were good grounds for suspecting
that tories were even then intimating to the Irish that if
Lord Salisbury should come into office, they would drop
coercion, just as the liberals had dropped it when they
came into office in 1880, and like them would rely upon
the ordinary law.   On May 15 Mr. Gladstone announced in
terms necessarily vague, because the new bill was not settled,
that they proposed to continue what he described as certain
clauses of a valuable and equitable description in the existing
Coercion Act.

No parliamentary situation could be more tempting to an
astute opposition.   The signs that the cabinet was not united
were unmistakable.   The leader of the little group of four
clever men below the gangway on the tory side gave signs
that he espied an opportunity.   This was one of the occasions
that disclosed the intrepidity of Lord Randolph Churchill.
He made a speech after Mr. Gladstone's announcement of a

renewal of portions of the Crimes Act, not in his place but at a tory club. He declared himself profoundly shocked that so grave an announcement should have been taken as a matter of course. It was really a terrible piece of news. Ireland must be in an awful state, or else the radical members of the cabinet would never have assented to such unanswerable evidence that the liberal party could not govern Ireland without resort to that arbitrary force which their greatest orators had so often declared to be no remedy. It did not much matter whether the demand was for large powers or for small. Why not put some kind thoughts towards England in Irish minds, by using the last days of this unlucky parliament to abrogate all that harsh legislation which is so odious to England, and which undoubtedly abridges the freedom and insults the dignity of a sensitive and imaginative race? The tory party should be careful beyond measure not to be committed to any act or policy which should unnecessarily wound or injure the feelings of our brothers on the other side of the channel of St. George.[1]

The key to an operation that should at once, with the aid of the disaffected liberals and the Irish, turn out Mr. Gladstone and secure the English elections, was an understanding with Mr. Parnell. The price of such an understanding was to drop coercion, and that price the tory leaders resolved to pay. The manœuvre was delicate. If too plainly disclosed, it might outrage some of the tory rank and file who would loathe an Irish alliance, and it was likely, moreover, to deter some of the disaffected liberals from joining in any motion for Mr. Gladstone's overthrow. Lord Salisbury and his friends considered the subject with 'immense deliberation some weeks before the fall of the government.' They came to the conclusion that in the absence of official information, they could see nothing to warrant a government in applying for a renewal of exceptional powers. That conclusion they profess to have kept sacredly in their own bosoms. Why they should give immense deliberation to a decision that in their view must be worthless without official information, and that was to remain for an indefinite time in mysterious

[1] May 20, 1885.

darkness, was never explained when this secret decision some
months later was revealed to the public.[1] If there was no
intention of making the decision known to the Irishmen,
the purpose of so unusual a proceeding would be inscrutable.
Was it made known to them? Mr. McCarthy, at the time
acting for his leader, has described circumstantially how
the Irish were endeavouring to obtain a pledge against
coercion; how two members of the tory party, one of them
its recognised whip, came to him in succession declaring
that they came straight from Lord Salisbury with certain
propositions; how he found the assurance unsatisfactory,
and asked each of these gentlemen in turn on different
nights to go back to Lord Salisbury, and put further questions to him; and how each of them professed to have gone
back to Lord Salisbury, to have conferred with him, and to
have brought back his personal assurance.[2] On the other
hand, it has been uniformly denied by the tory leaders that
there was ever any compact whatever with the Irishmen at
this moment. We are not called upon here to decide in a
conflict of testimony which turns, after all, upon words so
notoriously slippery as pledge, compact, or understanding.
It is enough to mark what is not denied, that Lord Salisbury
and his confidential friends had resolved, subject to official
information, to drop coercion, and that the only visible
reason why they should form the resolution at that particular
moment was its probable effect upon Mr. Parnell.

II

Let us now return to the ministerial camp. There the
whig wing of the cabinet, adhering to Lord Spencer, were
for a modified renewal of the Coercion Act, with the balm
of a land purchase bill and a limited extension of self-
government in local areas. The radical wing were averse
to coercion, and averse to a purchase bill, but they were
willing to yield a milder form of coercion, on condition that
the cabinet would agree not merely to small measures of
self-government in local areas, but to the erection of a

[1] The story was told by Lord R.
Churchill in a speech at Sheffield,
Sept 4, 1885.   [2] Mr. McCarthy's speech at Hull,
Dec. 15, 1887.

central board clothed with important administrative functions for the whole of Ireland. In the House of Commons
it was certain that a fairly strong radical contingent would
resist coercion in any degree, and a liberal below the gangway, who had not been long in parliament but who had been
in the press a strong opponent of the coercion policy of 1881,
at once gave notice that if proposals were made for the
renewal of exceptional law, he should move their rejection.
Mr. Gladstone had also to inform the Queen that in what
is considered the whig or moderate section of the House
there had been recent indications of great dislike to special
legislation, even of a mild character, for Ireland. These
proceedings are all of capital importance in an eventful
year, and bear pretty directly upon the better known crisis
of the year following.

A memorandum by Mr. Gladstone of a conversation
between himself and Lord Granville (May 6) will best
show his own attitude at this opening of a momentous
controversy : —

. . . I told him [Granville] I had given no pledge or indication
of my future conduct to Mr. Chamberlain, who, however, knew
my opinions to be strong in favour of some plan for a Central
Board of Local Government in Ireland on something of an elective
basis. . . . Under the circumstances, while the duty of the hour
evidently was to study the means of possible accommodation, the
present aspect of affairs was that of a probable split, *independently*
of the question what course I might individually pursue. My
opinions, I said, were very strong and inveterate. I did not
calculate upon Parnell and his friends, nor upon Manning and his
bishops. Nor was I under any obligation to follow or act with
Chamberlain. But independently of all questions of party, of
support, and of success, I looked upon the extension of a strong
measure of local government like this to Ireland, now that the
question is effectually revived by the Crimes Act, as invaluable
itself, and as the only hopeful means of securing crown and state
from an ignominious surrender in the next parliament after a
mischievous and painful struggle. (I did not advert to the
difficulties which will in this session be experienced in carrying on

a great battle for the Crimes Act.)   My difficulty would lie not in my pledges or declarations (though these, of a public character, are serious), but in my opinions.

Under these circumstances, I said, I take into view the freedom of my own position.   My engagements to my colleagues are fulfilled; the great Russian question is probably settled; if we stand firm on the Soudan, we are now released from that embarrassment; and the Egyptian question, if the financial convention be safe, no longer presents any very serious difficulties.   I am entitled to lay down my office as having done my work.

Consequently the very last thing I should contemplate is opening the Irish difficulty in connection with my resignation, should I resign.   It would come antecedently to any parliamentary treatment of that problem.   If thereafter the secession of some members should break up the cabinet, it would leave behind it an excellent record at home and abroad.   Lord Granville, while ready to resign his office, was not much consoled by this presentation of the case.

Late in the month (May 23) Mr. Gladstone wrote a long letter to the Queen, giving her 'some idea of the shades of opinion existing in the cabinet with reference to legislation for Ireland.'   He thought it desirable to supply an outline of this kind, because the subject was sure to recur after a short time, and was 'likely to exercise a most important influence in the coming parliament on the course of affairs.'   The two points on which there was considerable divergence of view were the expiry of the Crimes Act, and the concession of local government.   The Irish viceroy was ready to drop a large portion of what Mr. Gladstone called coercive provisions, while retaining provisions special to Ireland, but favouring the efficiency of the law.   Other ministers were doubtful whether any special legislation was needed for Irish criminal law.   Then on the point whether the new bill should be for two years or one, some, including Mr. Gladstone and Lord Spencer, were for the longer term, others, including Mr. Chamberlain and Sir Charles Dilke, for the shorter.   At last the whole cabinet agreed to two years.   Next for local government, — some held that a liberal move in this region

would possibly obviate all need for special criminal legislation, and would at any rate take the sting out of it. To
this 'vastly important subject' the prime minister presumed
to draw the Queen's special attention, as involving great
and far-reaching questions. He did not, he said, regard the
differences of leaning in the cabinet upon these matters
with either surprise or dismay. Such difficulties were due
to inherent difficulties in the matters themselves, and were
to be expected from the action of independent and energetic
minds in affairs so complex.

There were two main opinions. One favoured the erection
of a system of representative county government in Ireland.
The other view was that besides the county boards, there
should be in addition a central board for all Ireland,
essentially municipal and not political; in the main executive
and administrative, but also with a power to make bye-laws,
raise funds, and pledge public credit in such modes as
parliament should provide. The central board would take
over education, primary, in part intermediate, and perhaps
even higher; poor law and sanitary administration; and
public works. The whole charge of justice, police, and
prisons would remain with the executive. This board would
not be directly elective by the whole Irish people; it would
be chosen by the representative county boards. Property,
moreover, should have a representation upon it distinct from
numbers. This plan, 'first made known to Mr. Gladstone
by Mr. Chamberlain,' would, he believed, be supported by
six out of the eight Commons ministers. But a larger
number of ministers were not prepared to agree to any plan
involving the principle of an elective central board as the
policy of the cabinet. On account of this preliminary bar,
the particular provisions of the policy of a central board
were not discussed.

All this, however, was for the moment retrospective and
historic, because a fortnight before the letter was written,
the policy of the central board, of which Mr. Gladstone
so decisively approved, had been killed. A committee
of the cabinet was appointed to consider it; some remained stubbornly opposed; as the discussion went on,

some changed their minds and, having resisted, at last inclined to acquiesce. Ministers were aware from the correspondence of one of them with an eminent third person, that Mr. Parnell approved the scheme, and in consideration of it would even not oppose a very limited Crimes bill. This, however, was no temptation to all of them; perhaps it had the contrary effect. When it came to the full cabinet, it could not be carried. All the peers except Lord Granville were against it. All the Commoners except Lord Hartington were for it. As the cabinet broke up (May 9), the prime minister said to one colleague, 'Ah, they will rue this day'; and to another, 'Within six years, if it please God to spare their lives, they will be repenting in sackcloth and ashes.' Later in the day he wrote to one of them, 'The division of opinion in the cabinet on the subject of local government with a central board for Ireland was so marked, and if I may use the expression, so diametrical, that I dismissed the subject from my mind, and sorrowfully accepted the negative of what was either a majority, or a moiety of the entire cabinet.'

This decision, more profoundly critical than anybody excepting Mr. Gladstone and perhaps Mr. Chamberlain seemed to be aware, left all existing difficulties as acute as ever. In the middle of May things looked very black. The scheme for a central board was dead, though, wrote Mr. Gladstone to the viceroy, 'for the present only. *It will quickly rise again, as I think, perhaps in larger dimensions.*' Some members of the cabinet, he knew not how many, would resign rather than demand from parliament, without a Central Board bill, the new Coercion Act. If such resignations took place, how was a Coercion bill to be fought through the House, when some liberals had already declared that they would resist it?

On May 15 drafts not only of a Coercion bill, but of a bill for land purchase, came before the cabinet. Much objection was taken to land purchase, especially by the two radical leaders, and it was agreed to forego such a bill for the present session. The viceroy gravely lamented this decision, and Mr. Gladstone entered into communication with Mr.

Chamberlain and Sir C. Dilke. From them he understood that their main anxiety sprang from a fear lest the future handling of local government should be prejudiced by premature disposal of the question of land purchase, but that in the main they thought the question of local government would not be prejudiced if the purchase bill only provided funds for a year. Under this impression and with a full belief that he was giving effect to the real desire of his colleagues in general to meet the views of Lord Spencer, and finding the prospects of such a bill favourable, Mr. Gladstone proceeded (May 20) to give notice of its introduction. Mr. Chamberlain and Sir C. Dilke took this to be a reversal of the position to which they had agreed, and would not assent to land purchase unless definitely coupled with assurances as to local government. They immediately resigned. The misapprehension was explained, and though the resignations were not formally withdrawn, they were suspended. But the two radical leaders did not conceal their view of the general state of the case, and in very direct terms told Mr. Gladstone that they differed so completely on the questions that were to occupy parliament for the rest of the session, as to feel the continuance of the government of doubtful advantage to the country. In Mr. Chamberlain's words, written to the prime minister at the time of the misunderstanding (May 21) —

I feel there has been a serious misapprehension on both sides with respect to the Land Purchase bill, and I take blame to myself if I did not express myself with sufficient clearness. . . . I doubt very much if it is wise or was right to cover over the serious differences of principle that have lately disclosed themselves in the cabinet. I think it is now certain that they will cause a split in the new parliament, and it seems hardly fair to the constituencies that this should only be admitted, after they have discharged their function and are unable to influence the result.

III

Still the prime minister altogether declined, in his own phrase, to lose heart, and new compromises were invented. Meanwhile he cheerfully went for the Whitsuntide recess to Hawarden, and dived into Lechler's *Wycliffe*, Walpole's *George III.*, Conrad on German Union, Cooper on the Atonement, and so forth. Among other guests at Hawarden came Lord Wolverton, ' with much conversation ; we opened rather a new view as to my retirement.' What the new view was we do not know, but the conversation was resumed and again resumed, until the unwelcome day (June 4) for return to Downing Street. Before returning, however, Mr. Gladstone set forth his view of the internal crisis in a letter to Lord Hartington : —

To Lord Hartington.

May 30, 1885. — I am sorry but not surprised that your rather remarkable strength should have given way under the pressure of labour or anxiety or both. Almost the whole period of this ministry, particularly the year and a half since the defeat of Hicks, and most particularly of all, the four months since the morning when you deciphered the Khartoum telegram at Holker, have been without example in my experience, as to the gravity and diversity of difficulties which they have presented. What I hope is that they will not discourage you, or any of our colleagues, in your anticipations of the future. It appears to me that there is not one of them, viewed in the gross, which has been due to our own action. By viewing in the gross, I mean taking the Egyptian question as one. When we subdivide between Egypt proper and the Soudan, I find what seem to me two grave errors in our management of the Soudan business : the first our *landing* at Suakin, the second the mission of Gordon, or rather the choice of Gordon for that mission. But it sometimes happens that the errors gravest in their consequences are also the most pardonable. And these errors were surely pardonable enough in themselves, without relying on the fact that they were approved by the public opinion of the day and by the opposition. Plenty of other and worse errors have been urged upon us which we have refused or avoided. I do not remember a single good measure recommended by opponents, which we have declined to adopt (or indeed any good measure which they have recommended at all). We certainly have worked hard. I believe that according to the measure of human infirmity, we have done fairly well, but the duties we have

had to discharge have been duties, I mean in Egypt and the CHAP.
Soudan, which it was impossible to discharge with the ordinary XI.
measure of credit and satisfaction, which were beyond human Æt. 76.
strength, and which it was very unwise of our predecessors to
saddle upon the country.

At this moment we have but two great *desiderata :* the Egyptian
Convention and the Afghan settlement (the evacuation of the Soudan
being in principle a thing done). Were these accomplished, we
should have attained for the empire at home and abroad a
position in most respects unusually satisfactory, and both of them
ought to be near accomplishment. With the Egyptian Convention
fairly at work, I should consider the Egyptian question as within
a few comparatively easy stages of satisfactory solution.

Now as regards the immediate subject. What if Chamberlain
and Dilke, as you seem to anticipate, raise the question of a prospective declaration about local government in Ireland as a
condition of their remaining in the cabinet? I consider that
question as disposed of for the present (much against my will),
and I do not see that any of us, having accepted the decision, can
attempt to disturb it. Moreover, their ground will be very weak
and narrow; for their actual reason of going, if they go, will be
the really small question arising upon the Land Purchase bill.

I think they will commit a great error if they take this course.
It will be straining at the gnat. No doubt it will weaken the
party at the election, but I entertain no fear of the immediate
effect. Their error will, however, in my view go beyond this.
Forgive me if I now speak with great frankness on a matter, one
of few, in which I agree with them, and not with you. I am
firmly convinced that on local government for Ireland they
hold a winning position; which by resignation now they will
greatly compromise. You will all, I am convinced, have to give
what they recommend; at the least what they recommend.

There are two differences between them and me on this subject.
First as to the matter; I go rather further than they do ; for I
would undoubtedly make a *beginning* with the Irish police.
Secondly as to the *ground;* here I differ seriously. I do not reckon
with any confidence upon Manning or Parnell; I have never
looked much in Irish matters at negotiation or the conciliation of

leaders. I look at the question in itself, and I am deeply convinced that the measure in itself will (especially if accompanied with similar measures elsewhere, *e.g.* in Scotland) be good for the country and the empire; I do not say unmixedly good, but with advantages enormously outweighing any drawbacks.

Apart from these differences, and taking their point of view, I think they ought to endeavour to fight the election with you ; and in the *new state of affairs* which will be presented after the dissolution, try and see what effect may be produced upon your mind, and on other minds, when you have to look at the matter *cominus* and not *eminus*, as actual, and not as hypothetical. I gave Chamberlain a brief hint of these speculations when endeavouring to work upon him ; otherwise I have not mentioned them to any one.

IV

On the day of his return to London from Hawarden Mr. Gladstone had an interview with the two ministers with whom on the merits he was most disposed to agree, though he differed strongly from them as to tactics. Resignations were still only suspended, yet the prospects of compromise were hopeful. At a cabinet held on the following day (June 5) it was agreed that he should in the course of a week give notice of a bill to take the place of the expiring Crimes Act. The point left open was whether the operative provisions of such an Act — agreed on some time before — should not be brought into operation without some special act of the executive government, by proclamation, order in council, or otherwise. Local government was still left open. Lord Spencer crossed over from Ireland on the night of June 7, and the cabinet met next day. All differences were narrowed down to the point whether the enactments against intimidation should be inoperative unless and until the lord lieutenant should waken them into life by proclamation. As it happened, intimidation had been for a considerable time upon the increase — from which it might be inferred either, on the one side, that coercion failed in its object, or, on the other, that more coercion was still indispensable. The precise state in which matters were left at the eleventh hour before the crisis, now swiftly advancing, was set out by Mr. Gladstone in a letter written by him to the Queen in the autumn (October 5), when he was no longer her Majesty's minister: —

To the Queen.

. . . He has perceived that in various quarters misapprehension prevails as to the point at which the deliberations of the late cabinet on the question of any renewal of, or substitution for, the Crimes Act in Ireland had arrived when their financial defeat on the 8th of June caused the tender of their resignation.

Mr. Gladstone prays your Majesty's gracious permission to remove this misapprehension by simply stating that which occurred in the cabinet at its latest meetings, with reference to this particular question. Substantially it would be a repetition, or little more (and without any mention of names), of his latest reports to your Majesty, to the effect —

1. That the cabinet had long before arrived at the conclusion that the coercion clauses of the Act, properly so called, might be safely abandoned.

2. With regard to the other clauses, which might be generally described as procedure clauses, they intended as a rule to advise, not their absolute re-enactment, but that the viceroy should be empowered to bring them into action, together or separately, as and when he might see cause.

3. But that, with respect to the intimidation or boycotting provisions, it still remained for consideration whether they should thus be left subject to executive discretion, or whether, as the offence had not ceased, they should, as an effective instrument of repression, remain in direct and full operation.

It is worth noticing here as a signal instance of Mr. Gladstone's tenacious and indomitable will after his defeat, that in a communication to the Queen four days later (June 12), he stated that the single outstanding point of difference on the Crimes bill was probably in a fair way of settlement, but that even if the dissent of the radical members of the cabinet had become operative, it was his firm intention to make new arrangements for filling the vacant offices and carrying on the government. The overthrow came in a different way. The deliberations thus summarised had been held under the shadow of a possibility, mentioned to the Queen in the report of this last cabinet, of a coalition between the tories and the Irish nationalists, in order to put an end to the existence of the government on their budget. This cloud at last burst, though Mr. Gladstone at any rate with his usual invincible adherence to the salutary rule never to bid good morrow to the devil until you meet him, did not strongly believe in the risk. The diary sheds no light on the state of his expectations : —

June 6. . . . Read Amiel's *Journal Intime.* Queen's birthday dinner, 39; went very well. Much conversation with the Prince of Wales, who was handy and pleasant even beyond his wont. Also had some speech of his son, who was on my left. *June* 7, *Trinity Sunday.* — Chapel Royal at noon and 5.30. Wrote. . . . Saw Lord Granville; ditto *cum* Kimberley. Read Amiel. Edersheim on Old Testament. *June* 8. — Wrote, etc. . . . Pitiless rain. Cabinet, 2–3¾. . . . Spoke on budget. Beaten by 264: 252. Adjourned the House. This is a considerable event.

The amendment that led to this ' considerable event ' was moved by Sir Michael Hicks Beach. The two points raised by the fatal motion were, first, the increased duty on beer and spirits without a corresponding increase on wine ; and, second, the increase of the duty on real property while no relief was given to rates. The fiscal issue is not material. What was ominous was the alliance that brought about the result.

The defeat of the Gladstone government was the first success of a combination between tories and Irish, that proved of cardinal importance to policies and parties for several critical months to come. By a coincidence that cut too deep to be mere accident, divisions in the Gladstone cabinet found their counterpart in insurrection among the tory opposition. The same general forces of the hour, working through the energy, ambition, and initiative of individuals, produced the same effect in each of the two parties; the radical programme of Mr. Chamberlain was matched by the tory democracy of Lord Randolph Churchill; each saw that the final transfer of power from the ten-pound householder to artisans and labourers would rouse new social demands; each was aware that Ireland was the electoral pivot of the day, and while one of them was wrestling with those whom he stigmatised as whigs, the other by dexterity and resolution overthrew his leaders as ' the old gang.'

CHAPTER XII

ACCESSION OF LORD SALISBURY

(*1885*)

Politics are not a drama where scenes follow one another according to a methodical plan, where the actors exchange forms of speech, settled beforehand : politics are a conflict of which chance is incessantly modifying the whole course. — Sorel.

BOOK VIII.

1885.

In tendering his resignation to the Queen on the day following his parliamentary defeat (June 9), and regretting that he had been unable to prepare her for the result, Mr. Gladstone explained that though the government had always been able to cope with the combined tory and nationalist oppositions, what had happened on this occasion was the silent withdrawal, under the pressure of powerful trades, from the government ranks of liberals who abstained from voting, while six or seven actually voted with the majority. ' There was no previous notice,' he said, ' and it was immediately before the division that Mr. Gladstone was apprised for the first time of the likelihood of a defeat.' The suspicious hinted that ministers, or at least some of them, unobtrusively contrived their own fall. Their supporters, it was afterwards remarked, received none of those imperative adjurations to return after dinner that are usual on solemn occasions ; else there could never have been seventy-six absentees. The majority was composed of members of the tory party, six liberals, and thirty-nine nationalists. Loud was the exultation of the latter contingent at the prostration of the coercion system. What was natural exultation in them, may have taken the form of modest satisfaction among many liberals, that they could go to the country without the obnoxious label of coercion tied round their necks. As for ministers, it was observed that if in the streets you saw a man coming along with a particularly elastic step and a joyful frame of

countenance, ten to one on coming closer you would find CHAP.
that it was a member of the late cabinet.[1] XII.

The ministerial crisis of 1885 was unusually prolonged, Æt. 76.
and it was curious. The victory had been won by a coalition
with the Irish; its fruits could only be reaped with Irish
support; and Irish support was to the tory victors both
dangerous and compromising. The normal process of a
dissolution was thought to be legally impossible, because by
the redistribution bill the existing constituencies were for the
most part radically changed; and a new parliament chosen
on the old system of seats and franchise, even if it were
legally possible, would still be empty of all semblance of
moral authority. Under these circumstances, some in the
tory party argued that instead of taking office, it would be
far better for them to force Mr. Gladstone and his cabinet
to come back, and leave them to get rid of their internal
differences and their Irish embarrassments as they best could.
Events were soon to demonstrate the prudence of these wary
counsels. On the other hand, the bulk of the tory party
like the bulk of any other party was keen for power, because
power is the visible symbol of triumph over opponents, and
to shrink from office would discourage their friends in the
country in the electoral conflict now rapidly approaching.

The Queen meanwhile was surprised (June 10) that Mr.
Gladstone should make his defeat a vital question, and asked
whether, in case Lord Salisbury should be unwilling to form
a government, the cabinet would remain. To this Mr. Gladstone replied that to treat otherwise an attack on the budget,
made by an ex-cabinet minister with such breadth of front
and after all the previous occurrences of the session, would be
contrary to every precedent, — for instance, the notable case of
December 1852, — and it would undoubtedly tend to weaken
and lower parliamentary government.[2] If an opposition

---

[1] Duke of Argyll, July 10, 1885.

[2] As the reader will remember (vol.
i. pp. 436–440), on Dec. 16, 1852,
Mr. Disraeli's motion for imposing a
house duty of a shilling in the pound
was rejected by 305 to 286. Mr.
Gladstone also referred to the case of
the expulsion of the whigs by Peel.
On May 13, 1841, after eight nights'
debate, the government were defeated
by a majority of 36 on their budget
proposals in regard to sugar. Ministers not resigning, Sir Robert Peel
moved a vote of want of confidence
on May 27, which was carried by
a majority of 1 (312–311), June 4,
1841. Parliament thereupon was dissolved.

defeated a government, they must be prepared to accept
the responsibility of their action. As to the second question, he answered that a refusal by Lord Salisbury would obviously change the situation. On this, the Queen accepted
the resignations (June 11), and summoned Lord Salisbury to
Balmoral. The resignations were announced to parliament
the next day. Remarks were made at the time, indeed by
the Queen herself, at the failure of Mr. Gladstone to seek the
royal presence. Mr. Gladstone's explanation was that, viewing
' the probably long reach of Lord Hartington's life into the
future,' he thought that he would be more useful in conversation with her Majesty than ' one whose ideas might be uncon-
sciously coloured by the limited range of the prospect before
him,' and Lord Hartington prepared to comply with the
request that he should repair to Balmoral. The visit was
eventually not thought necessary by the Queen.

In his first audience Lord Salisbury stated that though he
and his friends were not desirous of taking office, he was
ready to form a government; but in view of the difficulties
in which a government formed by him would stand, confronted by a hostile majority and unable to dissolve, he
recommended that Mr. Gladstone should be invited to reconsider his resignation. Mr. Gladstone, however (June 13),
regarded the situation and the chain of facts that had led
up to it, as being so definite, when coupled with the readiness
of Lord Salisbury to undertake an administration, that it
would be a mere waste of valuable time for him to consult
his colleagues as to the resumption of office. Then Lord
Salisbury sought assurances of Mr. Gladstone's support, as
to finance, parliamentary time, and other points in the
working of executive government. These assurances neither
Mr. Gladstone's own temperament, nor the humour of his
friends and his party — for the embers of the quarrel with
the Lords upon the franchise bill were still hot — allowed him
to give, and he founded himself on the precedent of the
communications of December 1845 between Peel and Russell.
In this default of assurances, Lord Salisbury thought that he
should render the Queen no useful service by taking office.
So concluded the first stage.

Though declining specific pledges, Mr. Gladstone now wrote to the Queen (June 17) that in the conduct of the necessary business of the country, he believed there would be no disposition to embarrass her ministers. Lord Salisbury, however, and his colleagues were unanimous in thinking this general language insufficient. The interregnum continued. On the day following (June 18), Mr. Gladstone had an audience at Windsor, whither the Queen had now returned. It lasted over three-quarters of an hour. 'The Queen was most gracious and I thought most reasonable.' (*Diary.*) He put down in her presence some heads of a memorandum to assist her recollection, and the one to which she rightly attached most value was this: 'In my opinion,' Mr. Gladstone wrote, 'the whole value of any such declaration as at the present circumstances permit, really depends upon the spirit in which it is given and taken. For myself and any friend of mine, I can only say that the spirit in which we should endeavour to interpret and apply the declaration I have made, would be the same spirit in which we entered upon the recent conferences concerning the Seats bill.' To this declaration his colleagues on his return to London gave their entire and marked approval, but they would not compromise the liberty of the House of Commons by further and particular pledges.

It was sometimes charged against Mr. Gladstone that he neglected his duty to the crown, and abandoned the Queen in a difficulty. This is wholly untrue. On June 20, Sir Henry Ponsonby called and opened one or two aspects of the position, among them these : —

1. Can the Queen do anything more ?

I answered, As you ask me, it occurs to me that it might help Lord Salisbury's going on, were she to make reference to No. 2 of my memorandum [the paragraph just quoted], and to say that in her judgment he would be safe in receiving it in a spirit of trust.

2. If Lord Salisbury fails, may the Queen rely on you ?

I answered that on a previous day I had said that if S. failed, the situation would be altered. I hoped, and on the whole thought, he would go on. But if he did not ? I could not promise or expect smooth water. The movement of questions such as the Crimes Act and Irish Local Government might be accelerated. But my desire would be to do my best to prevent the Queen being left without a government.[1]

Mr. Gladstone's view of the position is lucidly stated in the following memorandum, like the others, in his own hand, (June 21) : —

1. I have endeavoured in my letters (*a*) to avoid all controversial matter ; (*b*) to consider not what the incoming ministers had a right to ask, but what it was possible for us in a spirit of conciliation to give.

2. In our opinion there was no right to demand from us anything whatever. The declarations we have made represent an extreme of concession. The conditions required, *e.g.* the first of them [control of time], place in abeyance the liberties of parliament, by leaving it solely and absolutely in the power of the ministers to determine on what legislative or other questions (except supply) it shall be permitted to give a judgment. The House of Commons may and ought to be disposed to facilitate the progress of all necessary business by all reasonable means as to supply and otherwise, but would deeply resent any act of ours by which we agreed beforehand to the extinction of its discretion.

The difficulties pleaded by Lord Salisbury were all in view when his political friend, Sir M. H. Beach, made the motion which, as we apprised him, would if carried eject us from office, and are simply the direct consequences of their own action. If it be true that Lord Salisbury loses the legal power to advise and the crown to grant a dissolution, that cannot be a reason for leaving in the hands of the executive an absolute power to stop the action (except as to supply) of the legislative and corrective power of the House of Commons. At the same time these conditions do not appear to me to attain the end proposed by Lord Salisbury, for it would still be left in the power of the House to refuse supplies, and thereby to bring about in its worst form the difficulty which he apprehends.

It looked for a couple of days as if he would be compelled

[1] Memo. by Mr. Gladstone, on a sheet of notepaper, June 20, 1885.

to return, even though it would almost certainly lead to CHAP. disruption of the liberal cabinet and party.[1] The Queen, XII. acting apparently on Mr. Gladstone's suggestion of June 20, Æt. 76. was ready to express her confidence in Mr. Gladstone's assurance that there would be no disposition on the part of himself or his friends to embarrass new ministers. By this expression of confidence, the Queen would thus make herself in some degree responsible as it were for the action of the members of the defeated Gladstone government in the two Houses. Still Lord Salisbury's difficulties — and some difficulties are believed to have arisen pretty acutely within the interior conclaves of his own party — remained for forty-eight hours insuperable. His retreat to Hatfield was taken to mark a second stage in the interregnum.

June 22 is set down in the diary as 'a day of much stir and vicissitude.' Mr. Gladstone received no fewer than six visits during the day from Sir Henry Ponsonby, whose activity, judgment, and tact in these duties of infinite delicacy were afterwards commemorated by Lord Granville in the House of Lords.[2] He brought up from Windsor the draft of a letter that might be written by the Queen to Lord Salisbury, testifying to her belief in the sincerity and loyalty of Mr. Gladstone's words. Sir Henry showed the draft to Mr. Gladstone, who said that he could not be party to certain passages in it, though willing to agree to the rest. The draft so altered was submitted to Lord Salisbury; he demanded modification, placing a more definite interpretation on the words of Mr. Gladstone's previous letters to the Queen. Mr. Gladstone was immovable throughout the day in declining to admit any modifications in the sense desired; nor would he consent to be privy to any construction or interpretation placed upon his words which Lord Salisbury, with no less tenacity than his own, desired to extend.

At 5.40 [June 22] Sir H. Ponsonby returned for a fifth interview, his infinite patience not yet exhausted. . . . He said the Queen believed the late government did not wish to come back.

[1] Mr. Gladstone was reminded by a colleague that when Sir Robert Peel resumed office in 1845, at the request of the Queen, he did so before and without consultation with his colleagues. In the end they all, excepting Lord Stanley, supported him.
[2] June 25, 1885.

I simply reminded him of my previous replies, which he remembered, nearly as follows: — That if Lord Salisbury failed, the situation would be altered. That I could not in such a case promise her Majesty smooth water. That, however, a great duty in such circumstances lay upon any one holding my situation, to use his best efforts so as, *quoad* what depended upon him, not to leave the Queen without a government. I think he will now go to Windsor. — *June 22, '85*, 6 P.M.

The next day (June 23), the Queen sent on to Lord Salisbury the letter written by Mr. Gladstone on June 21, containing his opinion that facilities of supply might reasonably be provided, without placing the liberties of the House of Commons in abeyance, and further, his declaration that he felt sure there was no idea of withholding ways and means, and that there was no danger to be apprehended on that score. In forwarding this letter, the Queen expressed to Lord Salisbury her earnest desire to bring to a close a crisis calculated to endanger the best interests of the state ; and she felt no hesitation in further communicating to Lord Salisbury her opinion that he might reasonably accept Mr. Gladstone's assurances. In deference to these representations from the Queen, Lord Salisbury felt it his duty to take office, the crisis ended, and the tory party entered on the first portion of a term of power that was destined, with two rather brief interruptions, to be prolonged for many years.[1] In reviewing this interesting episode in the annals of the party system, it is impossible not to observe the dignity in form, the patriotism in substance, the common-sense in result, that marked the proceedings alike of the sovereign and of her two ministers.

II

After accepting Mr. Gladstone's resignation the Queen, on June 13, proffered him a peerage : —

[1] The correspondence with the Queen up to June 21 was read by Mr. Gladstone in the House of Commons on June 24, and Lord Salisbury made his statement in the House of Lords on the next day. Mr. Gladstone told the House of Commons that he omitted one or two sentences from one of his letters, as having hardly any bearing on the real points of the correspondence. The omitted sentences related to the Afghan frontier, and the state of the negotiations with Russia.

The Queen to Mr. Gladstone.

Mr. Gladstone mentioned in his last letter but one, his intention of proposing some honours. But before she considers these, she wishes to offer him an Earldom, as a mark of her recognition of his long and distinguished services, and she believes and thinks he will thereby be enabled still to render great service to his sovereign and country — which if he retired, as he has repeatedly told her of late he intended to do shortly, — he could not. The country would doubtless be pleased at any signal mark of recognition of Mr. Gladstone's long and eminent services, and the Queen believes that it would be beneficial to his health, — no longer exposing him to the pressure from without, for more active work than he ought to undertake. Only the other day — without reference to the present events — the Queen mentioned to Mrs. Gladstone at Windsor the advantage to Mr. Gladstone's health of a removal from one House to the other, in which she seemed to agree. The Queen trusts, therefore, that Mr. Gladstone will accept the offer of an earldom, which would be very gratifying to her.

The outgoing minister replied on the following day : —

Mr. Gladstone offers his humble apology to your Majesty. It would not be easy for him to describe the feelings with which he has read your Majesty's generous, most generous letter. He prizes every word of it, for he is fully alive to all the circumstances which give it value. It will be a precious possession to him and to his children after him. All that could recommend an earldom to him, it already has given him. He remains, however, of the belief that he ought not to avail himself of this most gracious offer. Any service that he can render, if small, will, however, be greater in the House of Commons than in the House of Lords ; and it has never formed part of his views to enter that historic chamber, although he does not share the feeling which led Sir R. Peel to put upon record what seemed a perpetual or almost a perpetual self-denying ordinance for his family.

When the circumstances of the state cease, as he hopes they may ere long, to impose on him any special duty, he will greatly covet that interval between an active career and death, which the profession of politics has always appeared to him especially to require. There are circumstances connected with the position of his family, which he will not obtrude upon your Majesty, but which, as he conceives, recommend in point of prudence the personal intention from which he has never swerved. He might hesitate to act upon the motives to which he has last adverted, grave as they are, did he not feel rooted in the persuasion that the small good he may hope hereafter to effect, can best be prosecuted without the change in his position. He must beg your Majesty to supply all that is lacking in his expression from the heart of profound and lasting gratitude.

To Lord Granville, the nearest of his friends, he wrote on the same day : —

I send you herewith a letter from the Queen which moves and almost upsets me. It must have cost her much to write, and it is really a pearl of great price. Such a letter makes the subject of it secondary — but though it would take me long to set out my reasons, I remain firm in the intention to accept nothing for myself.

Lord Granville replied that he was not surprised at the decision. ‘I should have greatly welcomed you,’ he said, ‘and under some circumstances it might be desirable, but I think you are right now.’

Here is Mr. Gladstone’s letter to an invaluable occupant of the all-important office of private secretary : —

To Mr. E. W. Hamilton.

June 30, 1885. — Since you have in substance (and in form ?) received the appointment [at the Treasury], I am unmuzzled, and may now express the unbounded pleasure which it gives me, together with my strong sense (not disparaging any one else) of your desert. The modesty of your letter is as remarkable as its other qualities, and does you the highest honour. I can accept no tribute from you, or from any one, with regard to the office of private secretary under me except this, that it has always been made by me a strict and severe office, and that this is really the only favour I have ever done you, or any of your colleagues to whom in their several places and measures I am similarly obliged.

As to your services to me they have been simply indescribable. No one I think could dream, until by experience he knew, to what an extent in these close personal relations devolution can be carried, and how it strengthens the feeble knees and thus also sustains the fainting heart.

III

The declaration of the Irish policy of the new government was made to parliament by no less a personage than the lord-lieutenant.[1] The prime minister had discoursed on frontiers in Asia and frontiers in Africa, but on Ireland he was silent. Lord Carnarvon, on the contrary, came forward voluntarily with a statement of policy, and he opened it on the broadest general lines. His speech deserves as close attention as any deliverance of this memorable period. It laid down the principles of that alternative system of government, with which the new ministers formally challenged their predecessors. Ought the Crimes Act to be re-enacted as it stood; or in part; or ought it to be allowed to lapse? These were the three courses. Nobody, he thought, would be for the first, because some provisions had.never been put in force; others had been put in force but found useless; and others again did nothing that might not be done just as well under the ordinary law. The re-enactment of the whole statute, therefore, was dismissed. But the powers for changing venue at the discretion of the executive ; for securing special juries at the same discretion; for holding secret inquiry without an accused person; for dealing summarily with charges of intimidation — might they not be continued? They were not unconstitutional, and they were not opposed to legal instincts. No, all quite true; but then the Lords should not conceal from themselves that their re-enactment would be in the nature of special or exceptional legislation. He had been looking through coercion Acts, he continued, and had been astonished to find that ever since 1847, with some very short intervals hardly worth mentioning, Ireland

---

[1] This proceeding was so unusual as to be almost without a precedent. Lord Mulgrave had addressed the House of Lords in 1837, and Lord Clarendon in 1850. But on each of these occasions the viceroy's administration had been the object of vigorous attack, and no one but the viceroy himself was capable of making an effective parliamentary defence.

had lived under exceptional and coercive legislation. What sane man could admit this to be a satisfactory or a wholesome state of things? Why should not they try to extricate themselves from this miserable habit, and aim at some better solution? ' Just as I have seen in English colonies across the sea a combination of English, Irish, and Scotch settlers bound together in loyal obedience to the law and the crown, and contributing to the general prosperity of the country, so I cannot conceive that there is any irreconcilable bar here in their native home and in England to the unity and the amity of the two nations.' He went to his task individually with a perfectly free, open, and unprejudiced mind, to hear, to question, and, as far as might be, to understand. ' My Lords, I do not believe that with honesty and single-mindedness of purpose on the one side, and with the willingness of the Irish people on the other, it is hopeless to look for some satisfactory solution of this terrible question. My Lords, these I believe to be the opinions and the views of my colleagues.' [1]

This remarkable announcement, made in the presence of the prime minister, in the name of the cabinet as a whole, and by a man of known purity and sincerity of character, was taken to be an express renunciation, not merely of the policy of which notice had been given by the outgoing administration, but of coercion as a final instrument of imperial rule. It was an elaborate repudiation in advance of that panacea of firm and resolute government, which became so famous before twelve months were over. It was the suggestion, almost in terms, that a solution should be sought in that policy which had brought union both within our colonies, and between the colonies and the mother country, and men did not forget that this suggestion was being made by a statesman who had carried federation in Canada, and tried to carry it in South Africa. We cannot wonder that upon leading members of the late government, and especially upon the statesman who had been specially responsible for Ireland, the impression was startling and profound. Important members of the tory party hurried

[1] July 6, 1885.   *Hans.* 298, p. 1659.

from Ireland to Arlington Street, and earnestly warned their
leader that he would never be able to carry on with the
ordinary law. They were coldly informed that Lord Salisbury had received quite different counsel from persons well
acquainted with the country.

The new government were not content with renouncing
coercion for the present. They cast off all responsibility for
its practice in the past. Ostentatiously they threw overboard the viceroy with whom the only fault that they had
hitherto found, was that his sword was not sharp enough.
A motion was made by the Irish leader calling attention to
the maladministration of the criminal law by Lord Spencer.
Forty men had been condemned to death, and in twenty-one
of these cases the capital sentence had been carried out. Of
the twenty-one executions six were savagely impugned, and
Mr. Parnell's motion called for a strict inquiry into these
and some other convictions, with a view to the full
discovery of truth and the relief of innocent persons. The
debate soon became famous from the principal case adduced,
as the Maamtrasna debate. The topic had been so copiously
discussed as to occupy three full sittings of the House in the
previous October. The lawyer who had just been made
Irish chancellor, at that time pronounced against the
demand. In substance the new government made no fresh
concession. They said that if memorials or statements were
laid before him, the viceroy would carefully attend to them.
No minister could say less. But incidental remarks fell from
the government that created lively alarm in tories and deep
disgust in liberals. Sir Michael Hicks Beach, then leader of
the House, told them that while believing Lord Spencer to be
a man of perfect honour and sense of duty, ' he must say very
frankly that there was much in the Irish policy of the late
government which, though in the absence of complete
information he did not condemn, he should be very sorry to
make himself responsible for.' [1] An even more important
minister emphasised the severance of the new policy from
the old. ' I will tell you,' cried Lord Randolph Churchill,
' how the present government is foredoomed to failure.

[1] Sir M. H. Beach, July 17, 1885. *Hans.* 299, p. 1085.

They will be foredoomed to failure if they go out of their way unnecessarily to assume one jot or tittle of the responsibility for the acts of the late administration. It is only by divesting ourselves of all responsibility for the acts of the late government, that we can hope to arrive at a successful issue.'[1]

Tory members got up in angry fright, to denounce this practical acquiescence by the heads of their party in what was a violent Irish attack not only upon the late viceroy, but upon Irish judges, juries, and law officers. They remonstrated against 'the pusillanimous way' in which their two leaders had thrown over Lord Spencer. 'During the last three years,' said one of these protesting tories, ' Lord Spencer has upheld respect for law at the risk of his life from day to day, with the sanction, with the approval, and with the acknowledgment inside and outside of this House, of the country, and especially of the conservative party. Therefore I for one will not consent to be dragged into any implied, however slight, condemnation of Lord Spencer, because it happens to suit the exigencies of party warfare.'[2] This whole transaction disgusted plain men, tory and liberal alike; it puzzled calculating men; and it had much to do with the silent conversion of important and leading men.

The general sentiment about the outgoing viceroy took the form of a banquet in his honour (July 24), and some three hundred members of the two Houses attended, including Lord Hartington, who presided, and Mr. Bright. The two younger leaders of the radical wing who had been in the late cabinet neither signed the invitation nor were present. But on the same evening in another place, Mr. Chamberlain recognised the high qualities and great services of Lord Spencer, though they had not always agreed upon details. He expressed, however, his approval both of the policy and of the arguments which had led the new government to drop the Crimes Act. At the same time he denounced the 'astounding tergiversation' of ministers, and energetically declared that ' a strategic movement of that kind, executed in opposition to the notorious convictions of

[1] *Hans.* 299, p. 1098.   [2] *Ibid.* p. 1119.

the men who effected it, carried out for party purposes and party purposes alone, is the most flagrant instance of political dishonesty this country has ever known.' Lord Hartington a few weeks later told his constituents that the conduct of the government, in regard to Ireland, had dealt a heavy blow 'both at political morality, and at the cause of order in Ireland.' The severity of such judgments from these two weighty statesmen testifies to the grave importance of the new departure.

The enormous change arising from the line adopted by the government was visible enough even to men of less keen vision than Mr. Gladstone, and it was promptly indicated by him in a few sentences in a letter to Lord Derby on the very day of the Maamtrasna debate : —

Within the last two or three weeks, he wrote, the situation has undergone important changes. I am not fully informed, but what I know looks as if the Irish party so-called in parliament, excited by the high biddings of Lord Randolph, had changed what was undoubtedly Parnell's ground until within a very short time back. It is now said that a central board will not suffice, and that there must be a parliament. This I suppose may mean the repeal of the Act of Union, or may mean an Austro-Hungarian scheme, or may mean that Ireland is to be like a great colony such as Canada. Of all or any of these schemes I will now only say that, of course, they constitute an entirely new point of departure and raise questions of an order totally different to any that are involved in a central board appointed for local purposes.

Lord Derby recording his first impressions in reply (July 19) took the rather conventional objection made to most schemes on all subjects, that it either went too far or did not go far enough. Local government he understood, and home rule he understood, but a quasi-parliament in Dublin, not calling itself such though invested with most of the authority of a parliament, seemed to him to lead to the demand for fuller recognition. If we were forced, he said, to move beyond local government as commonly understood, he would rather have Ireland treated like Canada. 'But the difficulties every way are enormous.' On this Mr. Gladstone wrote a little later to Lord Granville (Aug. 6) : —

As far as I can learn, both you and Derby are on the same lines as Parnell, in rejecting the smaller and repudiating the larger scheme. It would not surprise me if he were to formulate something on the subject. For my own part I have seen my way pretty well as to the particulars of the minor and rejected plan, but the idea of the wider one puzzles me much. At the same time, *if* the election gives a return of a decisive character, the sooner the subject is dealt with the better.

So little true is it to say that Mr. Gladstone only thought of the possibility of Irish autonomy after the election.

IV

Apart from public and party cares, the bodily machinery gave trouble, and the fine organ that had served him so nobly for so long showed serious signs of disorder.

To Lord Richard Grosvenor.

July 14. — After two partial examinations, a thorough examination of my throat (larynx *versus* pharynx) has been made to-day by Dr. Semon in the presence of Sir A. Clark, and the result is rather bigger than I had expected. It is, that I have a fair chance of real recovery provided I keep silent almost like a Trappist, but all treatment would be nugatory without this rest; that the other alternative is nothing dangerous, but merely the constant passage of the organ from bad to worse. He asked what demands the H. of C. would make on me. I answered about three speeches of about five minutes each, but he was not satisfied and wished me to get rid of it altogether, which I must do, perhaps saying instead a word by letter to some friend. Much time has almost of necessity been lost, but I must be rigid for the future, and even then I shall be well satisfied if I get back before winter to a natural use of the voice in conversation. This imports a considerable change in the course of my daily life. Here it is difficult to organise it afresh. At Hawarden I can easily do it, but there I am at a distance from the best aid. I am disposed to 'top up,' with a sea voyage, but this is No. 3 — Nos. 1 and 2 being rest and then treatment.

The sea voyage that was to 'top up' the rest of the treatment began on August 8, when the Gladstones became the guests of Sir Thomas and Lady Brassey on the *Sunbeam*. They sailed from Greenhithe to Norway, and after a three weeks' cruise, were set ashore at Fort George on September 1. Mr. Gladstone made an excellent tourist; was full of interest in all he saw ; and, I dare say, drew some pleasure from the demonstrations of curiosity and admiration that attended his presence from the simple population wherever he moved. Long expeditions with much climbing and scrambling were his delight, and he let nothing beat him. One of these excursions, the ascent to the Vöringfos, seems to deserve a word of commemoration, in the interest either of physiology or of philosophic musings after Cicero's manner upon old age. 'I am not sure,' says Lady Brassey in her most agreeable diary of the cruise,[1] ' that the descent did not seem rougher and longer than our journey up had been, although, as a matter of fact, we got over the ground much more quickly. As we crossed the green pastures on the level ground near the village of Sæbö we met several people taking their evening stroll, and also a tourist apparently on his way up to spend the night near the Vöringfos. The wind had gone down sin ;e the morning, and we crossed the little lake with fair rapid ty, admiring as we went the glorious effects of the setting sun upon the tops of the precipitous mountains, and the wondei ful echo which was aroused for our benefit by the boatmen. An extremely jolty drive, in springless country carts, soon brought us to the little inn at Vik, and by half-past eight we were once more on board the *Sunbeam*, exactly ten hours after setting out upon our expedition, which had included a ride or walk, as the case might be, of eighteen miles, independently of the journey by boat and cart — a hardish day's work for any one, but really a wonderful undertaking for a man of seventy-five, who disdained all proffered help, and insisted on walking the whole distance. No one who saw Mr. Gladstone that evening

[1] In *The Contemporary Review*, October 1885, p. 491.

at dinner in the highest spirits, and discussing subjects both grave and gay with the greatest animation, could fail to admire his marvellous pluck and energy, or, knowing what he had shown himself capable of doing in the way of physical exertion, could feel much anxiety on the score of the failure of his strength.'

He was touched by a visit from the son of an old farmer, who brought him as an offering from his father to Mr. Gladstone a curiously carved Norwegian bowl three hundred years old, with two horse-head handles. Strolling about Aalesund, he was astonished to find in the bookshop of the place a Norse translation of Mill's *Logic*. He was closely observant of all religious services whenever he had the chance, and noticed that at Laurvig all the tombstones had prayers for the dead. He read perhaps a little less voraciously than usual, and on one or two days, being unable to read, he 'meditated and reviewed' — always, I think, from the same point of view — the point of view of Bunyan's *Grace Abounding*, or his own letters to his father half a century before. Not seldom a vision of the coming elections flitted before the mind's eye, and he made notes for what he calls an *abbozzo* or sketch of his address to Midlothian.

Book IX

1885-1886

CHAPTER I

LEADERSHIP AND THE GENERAL ELECTION

(1885)

Our understanding of history is spoiled by our knowledge of the event. — Helps.

Mr. Gladstone came back from his cruise in the *Sunbeam* at the beginning of September; leaving the yacht at Fort George and proceeding to Fasque to celebrate his elder brother's golden wedding. From Fasque he wrote to Lord Hartington (Sept. 3): ' I have returned to terra firma extremely well in general health, and with a better throat; in full expectation of having to consider anxious and doubtful matters, and now finding them rather more anxious and doubtful than I had anticipated. As yet I am free to take a share or not in the coming political issues, and I must weigh many things before finally surrendering this freedom.' His first business, he wrote to Sir W. Harcourt (Sept.12), was to throw his thoughts into order for an address to his constituents, framed only for the dissolution, and ' written with my best care to avoid treading on the toes of either the right or the left wing.' He had communicated, he said, with Granville, Hartington, and Chamberlain; by both of the two latter he had been a good deal buffeted; and having explained the general idea with which he proposed to write, he asked each of the pair whether upon the whole their wish was that he should go on or cut out. 'To this question I have not yet got a clear affirmative answer from either of them.'

219

'The subject of Ireland,' he told Lord Hartington, 'has
perplexed me much even on the North Sea,' and he expressed
some regret that in a recent speech his correspondent had
felt it necessary at this early period to join issue in so
pointed a manner with Mr. Parnell and his party. Parnell's
speech was, no doubt, he said, 'as bad as bad could be, and
admitted of only one answer. But the whole question of
the position which Ireland will assume after the general
election is so new, so difficult, and as yet, I think, so little
understood, that it seems most important to reserve until
the proper time all possible liberty of examining it.'

The address to his electors, of which he had begun to
think on board the *Sunbeam*, was given to the public on
September 17. It was, as he said, as long as a pamphlet,
and a considerable number of politicians doubtless passed
judgment upon it without reading it through. The whigs,
we are told, found it vague, the radicals cautious, the
tories crafty; but everybody admitted that it tended to
heal feuds. Mr. Goschen praised it, and Mr. Chamberlain,
though raising his own flag, was respectful to his leader's
manifesto.[1]

The surface was thus stilled for the moment, yet the
waters ran very deep. What were 'the anxious and doubtful
matters,' what 'the coming political issues,' of which Mr.
Gladstone had written to Lord Hartington? They were, in
a word, twofold: to prevent the right wing from breaking
with the left; and second, to make ready for an Irish crisis,
which as he knew could not be averted. These were the
two keys to all his thoughts, words, and deeds during the
important autumn of 1885 — an Irish crisis, a solid party.
He was not the first great parliamentary leader whose
course lay between two impossibilities.

All his letters during the interval between his return
from the cruise in the *Sunbeam* and the close of the general
election disclose with perfect clearness the channels in
which events and his judgment upon them were moving.
Whigs and radicals alike looked to him, and across him
fought their battle. The Duke of Argyll, for example,

[1] See *Spectator*, Sept. 26, 1885.

taking advantage of a lifelong friendship to deal faithfully
with him, warned him that the long fight with 'Beacons-
fieldism' had thrown him into antagonism with many
political conceptions and sympathies that once had a steady
hold upon him. Yet they had certainly no less value and
truth than they ever had, and perhaps were more needed
than ever in face of the present chaos of opinion. To this
Mr. Gladstone replied at length:—

To the Duke of Argyll.

Sept. 30, 1885.—I am very sensible of your kind and sympathetic
tone, and of your indulgent verdict upon my address. It was
written with a view to the election, and as a practical document,
aiming at the union of all, it propounds for immediate action what
all are supposed to be agreed on. This is necessarily somewhat
favourable to the moderate section of the liberal party. You will
feel that it would not have been quite fair to the advanced men
to add some special reproof to them. And reproof, if I had presumed upon it, would have been two-sided. Now as to your suggestion that I should say something in public to indicate that I am
not too sanguine as to the future. If I am unable to go in this
direction—and something I may do—it is not from want of
sympathy with much that you say. But my first and great cause
of anxiety is, believe me, the condition of the tory party. As at
present constituted, or at any rate moved, it is destitute of all the
effective qualities of a respectable conservatism. . . . For their
administrative spirit I point to the Beaconsfield finance. For their
foreign policy they have invented Jingoism, and at the same time
by their conduct *re* Lord Spencer and the Irish nationalists, they
have thrown over—and they formed their government only by
means of throwing over—those principles of executive order and
caution which have hitherto been common to all governments. . . .

There are other chapters which I have not time to open. I
deeply deplore the oblivion into which public economy has fallen;
the prevailing disposition to make a luxury of panics, which multitudes seem to enjoy as they would a sensational novel or a highly
seasoned cookery; and the leaning of both parties to socialism,
which I radically disapprove. I must lastly mention among my
causes of dissatisfaction the conduct of the timid or reactionary

whigs. They make it day by day more difficult to maintain that most valuable characteristic of our history, which has always exhibited a good proportion of our great houses at the head of the liberal movement. If you have ever noted of late years a too sanguine and high-coloured anticipation of our future, I should like to be reminded of it. I remain, and I hope always to be, your affectionate friend.

The correspondence with Lord Granville sets out more clearly than anything else could do Mr. Gladstone's general view of the situation of the party and his own relation to it, and the operative words in this correspondence, in view of the maelstrom to which they were all drawing nearer, will be accurately noted by any reader who cares to understand one of the most interesting situations in the history of party. To Lord Granville he says (September 9, 1885), 'The problem for me is to make if possible a statement which will hold through the election and not to go into conflict with either the right wing of the party for whom Hartington has spoken, or the left wing for whom Chamberlain, I suppose, spoke last night. I do not say they are to be treated as on a footing, but I must do no act disparaging to Chamberlain's wing.' And again to Lord Granville a month later (Oct. 5) : —

You hold a position of great impartiality in relation to any divergent opinions among members of the late cabinet. No other person occupies ground so thoroughly favourable. I turn to myself for one moment. I remain at present in the leadership of the party, first with a view to the election, and secondly with a view to being, by a bare possibility, of use afterwards in the Irish question if it should take a favourable turn ; but as you know, with the intention of taking no part in any schism of the party should it arise, and of avoiding any and all official responsibility, should the question be merely one of liberal v. conservative and not one of commanding imperial necessity, such as that of Irish government may come to be after the dissolution.

He goes on to say that the ground had now been sufficiently laid for going to the election with a united front, that ground being the common profession of a limited creed or programme in the liberal sense, with an entire freedom for those so inclined, to travel beyond it, but not to impose their own sense upon all other people. No one, he thought, was bound to determine at that moment on what conditions he would join a liberal government. If the party and its leaders were agreed as to immediate measures on local government, land, and registration, were not these enough to find a liberal administration plenty of work, especially with procedure, for several years? If so, did they not supply a ground broad enough to start a government, that would hold over, until the proper time should come, all the questions on which its members might not be agreed, just as the government of Lord Grey held over, from 1830 to 1834, the question whether Irish church property might or might not be applied to secular uses?

As for himself, in the event of such a government being formed (of which I suppose Lord Granville was to be the head), ' My desire would be,' he says, ' to place myself in your hands for all purposes, except that of taking office; to be present or absent from the House, and to be absent for a time or for good, as you might on consultation and reflection think best.' In other words Mr. Gladstone would take office to try to settle the Irish question, but for nothing else. Lord Granville held to the view that this was fatal to the chances of a liberal government. No liberal cabinet could be constructed unless Mr. Gladstone were at its head. The indispensable chief, however, remained obdurate.

An advance was made at this moment in the development of a peculiar situation by important conversations with Mr. Chamberlain. Two days later the redoubtable leader of the left wing came to Hawarden for a couple of days, and Mr. Gladstone wrote an extremely interesting account of what passed to Lord Granville:[1] —

[1] Mr. Chamberlain has been good enough to read these two letters, and he assents to their substantial accuracy, with a demurrer on two or three points, justly observing that anybody reporting a very long and varied conversation is almost certain, however scrupulous in intention, to insert in places what were thoughts much in his own mind, rather than words actually spoken. In inserting these two letters, it may tend to prevent controversy if we print such corrective hints as are desired.

To Lord Granville.

Hawarden, Oct. 8, 1885. — Chamberlain came here yesterday and I have had a great deal of conversation with him. He is a good man to talk to, not only from his force and clearness, but because he speaks with reflection, does not misapprehend or (I think) suspect, or make unnecessary difficulties, or endeavour to maintain pedantically the uniformity and consistency of his argument throughout.

As to the three points of which he was understood to say that they were indispensable to the starting of a liberal government, I gather that they stand as follows : —

1. As to the authority of local authorities for compulsory expropriation.[1] To this he adheres ; though I have said I could not see the justification for withholding countenance from the formation of a government with considerable and intelligible plans in view, because it would not at the first moment bind all its members to this doctrine. He intimates, however, that the form would be simple, the application of the principle mild ; that he does not expect wide results from it, and that Hartington, he conceives, is not disposed wholly to object to everything of the kind.

2. As regards readjustment of taxation, he is contented with the terms of my address, and indisposed to make any new terms.

3. As regards free education, he does not ask that its principle be adopted as part of the creed of a new cabinet. He said it would be necessary to reserve his right individually to vote for it. I urged that he and the new school of advanced liberals were not sufficiently alive to the necessity of refraining when in government from declaring by *vote* all their individual opinions ; that a vote founded upon time, and the engagements of the House at the moment with other indispensable business, would imply no disparagement to the principle, which might even be expressly saved ('without prejudice') by an amending resolution ; that he could hardly carry this point to the rank of a *sine quâ non.* He said, — That the sense of the country might bind the liberal majority (presuming it to exist) to declare its opinion, eve hough unable

---

[1] In connection with a local government bill for small holdings and allotments, subsequently passed.

to give effect to it at the moment; that he looked to a single
declaration, not to the sustained support of a measure; and he
seemed to allow that if the liberal sense were so far divided as
not to show a unanimous front, in that case it might be a
question whether some plan other than, and short of, a direct
vote might be pursued.[1]

The question of the House of Lords and disestablishment he
regards as still lying in the remoter distance.

All these subjects I separated entirely from the question of
Ireland, on which I may add that he and I are pretty well agreed;
unless upon a secondary point, namely, whether Parnell would be
satisfied to acquiesce in a County Government bill, good so far as
it went, maintaining on other matters his present general attitude.[2] We agreed, I think, that a prolongation of the present
relations of the Irish party would be a national disgrace, and the
civilised world would scoff at the political genius of countries
which could not contrive so far to understand one another as to
bring their differences to an accommodation.

All through Chamberlain spoke of reducing to an absolute
minimum his idea of necessary conditions, and this conversation
so far left untouched the question of men, he apparently assuming (wrongly) that I was ready for another three or four years'
engagement.

Hawarden, Oct. 8, 1885. — In another 'private,' but less private
letter, I have touched on measures, and I have now to say what
passed in relation to men.

He said the outline he had given depended on the supposition
of my being at the head of the government. He did not say he
could adhere to it on no other terms, but appeared to stipulate for
a new point of departure.

I told him the question of my time of life had become such, that
in any case prudence bound him, and all who have a future, to
think of what is to follow me. That if a big Irish question should
arise, and arise in such a form as to promise a possibility of settle-

---

[1] He suggested, for instance, the
appointment of a committee.
[2] Mr. Chamberlain puts it that he
proposed to exclude home rule as impossible, and to offer a local government bill which he thought that

Parnell might accept. Mr. Gladstone's
statement that he and his visitor
were 'pretty well agreed' on Ireland,
cannot mean therefore that the visitor
was in favour of home rule.

ment, that would be a crisis with a beginning and an end, and perhaps one in which from age and circumstances I might be able to supply aid and service such as could not be exactly had without me.[1] Apart from an imperious demand of this kind the question would be that of dealing with land laws, with local government, and other matters, on which I could render *no* special service, and which would require me to enter into a new contest for several years, a demand that ought not to be made, and one to which I could not accede. I did not think the adjustment of personal relations, or the ordinary exigencies of party, constituted a call upon me to continue my long life in a course of constant pressure and constant contention with half my fellow-countrymen, until nothing remained but to step into the grave.

He agreed that the House of Lords was not an available resort. He thought I might continue at the head of the government, and leave the work of legislation to others.[2] I told him that all my life long I had had an essential and considerable share in the legislative work of government, and to abandon it would be an essential change, which the situation would not bear.

He spoke of the constant conflicts of opinion with Hartington in the late cabinet, but I reverted to the time when Hartington used to summon and lead meetings of the leading commoners, in which he was really the least antagonistic of men.

He said Hartington might lead a whig government aided by the tories, or might lead a radical government. . . . I recommended his considering carefully the personal composition of the group of leading men, apart from a single personality on which reliance could hardly be placed, except in the single contingency to which I have referred as one of a character probably brief.

He said it might be right for him to look as a friend on the formation of a liberal government, having (as I understood) moderate but intelligible plans, without forming part of it. I think this was the substance of what passed.

Interesting as was this interview, it did not materially alter Mr. Gladstone's disposition. After it had taken place he wrote to Lord Granville (Nov. 10) : —

---

[1] This is not remembered.   [2] " Some misunderstanding here."

To Lord Granville.

I quite understand how natural it is that at the present juncture pressure, and even the whole pressure, should from both quarters be brought to bear upon me. Well, if a special call of imperial interest, such as I have described, should arise, I am ready for the service it may entail, so far as my will is concerned. But a very different question is raised. Let us see how matters stand.

A course of action for the liberals, moderate but substantial, has been sketched. The party in general have accepted it. After the late conversations, there is no reason to anticipate a breach upon any of the conditions laid down anywhere for immediate adoption, between the less advanced and the more advanced among the leaders. It must occupy several years, and it may occupy the whole parliament. According to your view they will, unless on a single condition [*i.e.* Mr. Gladstone's leadership], refuse to combine in a cabinet, and to act, with a majority at their back; and will make over the business voluntarily to the tories in a minority, at the commencement of a parliament. Why? They agree on the subjects before them. Other subjects, unknown as yet, may arise to split them. But this is what may happen to any government, and *it* can form no reason.

But what *is* the condition demanded? It is that a man of seventy-five,[1] after fifty-three years' service, with *no* particular qualification for the questions in view should enter into a fresh contract of service in the House of Commons, reaching according to all likelihood over three, four, or five years, and without the smallest reasonable prospect of a break. And this is not to solve a political difficulty, but to soothe and conjure down personal misgivings and apprehensions. I have not said jealousies, because I do *not* believe them to be the operative cause; perhaps they do not exist at all.

I firmly say this is not a reasonable condition, or a tenable demand, in the circumstances supposed. Indeed no one has endeavoured to show that it is. Further, abated action in the House of Commons is out of the question. We cannot have, in these times, a figurehead prime minister. I have gone a very long way in what I have said, and I really cannot go further.

---

[1] That is, in his seventy-sixth year.

Lord Aberdeen, taking office at barely seventy in the House of
Lords, apologised in his opening speech for doing this at a time
when his mind ought rather to be given to 'other thoughts.'
Lord Palmerston in 1859 did not speak thus. But he was bound
to no plan of any kind; and he was seventy-four, *i.e.* in his
seventy-fifth year.

II

It is high time to turn to the other deciding issue in
the case. Though thus stubborn against resuming the
burden of leadership merely to compose discords between
Chatsworth and Birmingham, Mr. Gladstone was ready to
be of use in the Irish question, 'if it should take a favourable turn.' As if the Irish question ever took a favourable
turn. We have seen in the opening of the present chapter,
how he spoke to Lord Hartington of a certain speech
of Mr. Parnell's in September, 'as bad as bad could be.'
The secret of that speech was a certain fact that must be
counted a central hinge of these far-reaching transactions. In July, a singular incident had occurred, nothing
less strange than an interview between the new lord-
lieutenant and the leader of the Irish party. To realise
its full significance, we have to recall the profound odium
that at this time enveloped Mr. Parnell's name in the
minds of nearly all Englishmen. For several years and at
that moment he figured in the public imagination for all
that is sinister, treasonable, dark, mysterious, and unholy.
He had stood his trial for a criminal conspiracy, and was
supposed only to have been acquitted by the corrupt connivance of a Dublin jury. He had been flung into prison
and kept there for many months without trial, as a person
reasonably suspected of lawless practices. High treason was
the least dishonourable of the offences imputed to him and
commonly credited about him. He had been elaborately
accused before the House of Commons by one of the most
important men in it, of direct personal responsibility for
outrages and murders, and he left the accusation with scant
reply. He was constantly denounced as the apostle of
rapine and rebellion. That the viceroy of the Queen should

without duress enter into friendly communication with such CHAP. a man, would have seemed to most people at that day incredible and abhorrent. Yet the incredible thing hap- Æt. 76. pened, and it was in its purpose one of the most sensible things that any viceroy ever did.[1]

The interview took place in a London drawing-room. Lord Carnarvon opened the conversation by informing Mr. Parnell, first, that he was acting of himself and by himself, on his own exclusive responsibility; second, that he sought information only, and that he had not come for the purpose of arriving at any agreement or understanding however shadowy; third, that he was there as the Queen's servant, and would neither hear nor say one word that was inconsistent with the union of the two countries. Exactly what Mr. Parnell said, and what was said in reply, the public were never authentically told. Mr. Parnell afterwards spoke [2] as if Lord Carnarvon had given him to understand that it was the intention of the government to offer Ireland a statutory legislature, with full control over taxation, and that a scheme of land purchase was to be coupled with it. On this, the viceroy denied that he had communicated any such intention. Mr. Parnell's story was this : —

Lord Carnarvon proceeded to say that he had sought the interview for the purpose of ascertaining my views regarding — should he call it ? — a constitution for Ireland. But I soon found out that

[1] This episode was first mentioned in the House of Commons, June 7, 1886. Lord Carnarvon explained in the Lords, June 10. Mr. Parnell replied in a letter to the Times, June 12. He revived the subject in the House of Commons, Feb. 13, 1888, and Lord Carnarvon explained a second time in the Lords on May 3. On Lord Carnarvon's first explanation, the Duke of Argyll, while placing the utmost reliance on his personal honour and accuracy, 'felt bound to observe that the statement did not appear to be complete, for he had omitted to explain what the nature of the communication [with Mr. Parnell] absolutely was.' Neither then nor two years later was the omission made good. Curiously enough on the first occasion Lord Carnarvon did not even mention that Lord Salisbury in any way shared his responsibility for the interview, and in fact his language pointed the other way. What remains is his asseveration, supported by Lord Salisbury, that he had made no formal bargain with Mr. Parnell, and gave him no sort of promise, assurance, or pledge. This is not only entirely credible, it is certain ; for the only body that could carry out such a promise had not been consulted. 'I may at least say this of what went on outside the cabinet — that I had no communication on the subject, no authorisation, and that I never communicated to them even that which I had done.' — Hansard, 306, p. 1258.

[2] E.g. Hans. 306, pp. 1181, 1199.

he had brought me there in order that he might communicate his own views upon the matter, as well as ascertain mine. . . . In reply to an inquiry as to a proposal which had been made to build up a central legislative body upon the foundation of county boards, I told him I thought this would be working in the wrong direction, and would not be accepted by Ireland; that the central legislative body should be a parliament in name and in fact. . . . Lord Carnarvon assured me that this was his own view also, and he strongly appreciated the importance of giving due weight to the sentiment of the Irish in this matter. . . . He had certain suggestions to this end, taking the colonial model as a basis, which struck me as being the result of much thought and knowledge of the subject. . . . At the conclusion of the conversation, which lasted for more than an hour, and to which Lord Carnarvon was very much the larger contributor, I left him, believing that I was in complete accord with him regarding the main outlines of a settlement conferring a legislature upon Ireland.[1]

It is certainly not for me to contend that Mr. Parnell was always an infallible reporter, but if closely scrutinised the discrepancy in the two stories as then told was less material than is commonly supposed. To the passage just quoted, Lord Carnarvon never at any time in public offered any real contradiction. What he contradicted was something different. He denied that he had ever stated to Mr. Parnell that it was the intention of the government, if they were successful at the polls, to establish the Irish legislature, with limited powers and not independent of imperial control, which he himself favoured. He did not deny, any more than he admitted, that he had told Mr. Parnell that on opinion and policy they were very much at one. How could he deny it, after his speech when he first took office? Though the cabinet was not cognisant of the nature of these proceedings, the prime minister was. To take so remarkable a step without the knowledge and assent of the head of the government, would have been against the whole practice and principles of our ministerial system. Lord Carnarvon informed Lord Salisbury of his intention of meeting Mr.

[1] Letter to the *Times*, June 12, 1886.

Parnell, and within twenty-four hours after the meeting, both in writing and orally, he gave Lord Salisbury as careful and accurate a statement as possible of what had passed. We can well imagine the close attention with which the prime minister followed so profoundly interesting a report, and at the end of it he told the viceroy that 'he had conducted the conversation with Mr. Parnell with perfect discretion.' The knowledge that the minister responsible for the government of Ireland was looking in the direction of home rule, and exchanging home rule views with the great home rule leader, did not shake Lord Salisbury's confidence in his fitness to be viceroy.

This is no mere case of barren wrangle and verbal recrimination. The transaction had consequences, and the Carnarvon episode was a pivot. The effect upon the mind of Mr. Parnell was easy to foresee. Was I not justified, he asked long afterwards, in supposing that Lord Carnarvon, holding the views that he now indicated, would not have been made viceroy unless there was a considerable feeling in the cabinet that his views were right?[1] Could he imagine that the viceroy would be allowed to talk home rule to him — however shadowy and vague the words — unless the prime minister considered such a solution to be at any rate well worth discussing? Why should he not believe that the alliance formed in June to turn Mr. Gladstone out of office and eject Lord Spencer from Ireland, had really blossomed from being a mere lobby manœuvre and election expedient, into a serious policy adopted by serious statesmen? Was it not certain that in such remarkable circumstances Mr. Parnell would throughout the election confidently state the national demand at its very highest?

In 1882 and onwards up to the Reform Act of 1885, Mr. Parnell had been ready to advocate the creation of a central council at Dublin for administrative purposes merely. This he thought would be a suitable achievement for a party that numbered only thirty-five members. But the assured increase of his strength at the coming election made all the difference. When semi-official soundings were

[1] *Hans.* 332, p. 336.

taken from more than one liberal quarter after the fall of
the Gladstone government, it was found that Mr. Parnell no
longer countenanced provisional reforms.   After the interview with Lord Carnarvon, the mercury rose rapidly to the
top of the tube.   Larger powers of administration were not
enough. • The claim for legislative power must now be
brought boldly to the front.   In unmistakable terms, the
Irish leader stated the Irish demand, and posed both
problem and solution.   He now declared his conviction
that the great and sole work of himself and his friends in
the new parliament would be the restoration of a national
parliament of their own, to do the things which they had
been vainly asking the imperial parliament to do for
them.[1]

III

When politicians ruminate upon the disastrous schism
that followed Mr. Gladstone's attempt to deal with the Irish
question in 1886, they ought closely to study the general
election of 1885.   In that election, though leading men foresaw the approach of a marked Irish crisis, and awaited the
outcome of events with an overshadowing sense of pregnant
issues, there was nothing like general concentration on the
Irish prospect.   The strife of programmes and the rivalries
of leaders were what engrossed the popular attention.
The main body of the British electors were thinking mainly
of promised agrarian booms, fair trade, the church in danger,
or some other of their own domestic affairs.

Few forms of literature or history are so dull as the narrative of political debates.   With a few exceptions, a political
speech like the manna in the wilderness loses its savour on
the second day.   Three or four marked utterances of this
critical autumn, following all that has been set forth already,
will enable the reader to understand the division of counsel
that prevailed immediately before the great change of
policy in 1886, and the various strategic evolutions, masked
movements, and play of mine, sap, and countermine, that
led to it.   As has just been described, and with good reason,

[1] August 24, 1885.

for he believed that he had the Irish viceroy on his side,
Mr. Parnell stood inflexible.   In his speech of August 24
already mentioned, he had thrown down his gauntlet.

Much the most important answer to the challenge, if we
regard the effect upon subsequent events, was that of Lord
Salisbury two months later.   To this I shall have to return.
The two liberal statesmen, Lord Hartington and Mr. Chamberlain, who were most active in this campaign, and whose
activity was well spiced and salted by a lively political
antagonism, agreed in a tolerably stiff negative to the
Irish demand.   The whig leader with a slow mind, and
the radical leader with a quick mind, on this single
issue of the campaign spoke with one voice.   The whig
leader [1] thought Mr. Parnell had made a mistake and
ensured his own defeat: he overestimated his power in
Ireland and his power in parliament ; the Irish would not
for the sake of this impossible and impracticable undertaking, forego without duress all the other objects which
parliament was ready to grant them; and it remained to be
seen whether he could enforce his iron discipline upon his
eighty or ninety adherents, even if Ireland gave him so
many.

The radical leader was hardly less emphatic, and his
utterance was the more interesting of the two, because
until this time Mr. Chamberlain had been generally taken
throughout his parliamentary career as leaning strongly in
the nationalist direction.   He had taken a bold and energetic part in the proceedings that ended in the release of
Mr. Parnell from Kilmainham.   He had with much difficulty
been persuaded to acquiesce in the renewal of any part of the
Coercion Act, and had absented himself from the banquet
in honour of Lord Spencer.   Together with his most
intimate ally in the late government, he had projected a
political tour in Ireland with Mr. Parnell's approval and
under his auspices.   Above all, he had actually opened his
electoral campaign with that famous declaration which was
so long remembered: ' The pacification of Ireland at this
moment depends, I believe, on the concession to Ireland of

[1] Lord Hartington at Waterfoot, August 29.

the right to govern itself in the matter of its purely domestic business. Is it not discreditable to us that even now it is only by unconstitutional means that we are able to secure peace and order in one portion of her Majesty's dominions? It is a system as completely centralised and bureaucratic as that with which Russia governs Poland, or as that which prevailed in Venice under the Austrian rule. An Irishman at this moment cannot move a step — he cannot lift a finger in any parochial, municipal, or educational work, without being confronted with, interfered with, controlled by, an English official, appointed by a foreign government, and without a shade or shadow of representative authority. I say the time has come to reform altogether the absurd and irritating anachronism which is known as Dublin Castle. That is the work to which the new parliament will be called.'[1] Masters of incisive speech must pay the price of their gifts, and the sentence about Poland and Venice was long a favourite in many a debate. But when the Irish leader now made his proposal for removing the Russian yoke and the Austrian yoke from Ireland, the English leader drew back. 'If these,' he said, 'are the terms on which Mr. Parnell's support is to be obtained, I will not enter into the compact.' This was Mr. Chamberlain's response.[2]

IV

The language used by Mr. Gladstone during this eventful time was that of a statesman conscious of the magnitude of the issue, impressed by the obscurity of the path along which parties and leaders were travelling, and keenly alive to the perils of a premature or unwary step. Nothing was easier for the moment either for quick minds or slow minds, than to face the Irish demand beforehand with a bare, blank, wooden *non possumus*. Mr. Gladstone had pondered the matter more deeply. His gift of political imagination, his wider experience, and his personal share in some chapters of the modern history of Europe and its changes, planted him on a height whence he commanded a view of possibili-

[1] June 17, 1885.   [2] Warrington, September 8.

ties and necessities, of hopes and of risks, that were unseen by
politicians of the beaten track. Like a pilot amid wandering
icebergs, or in waters where familiar buoys had been taken
up and immemorial beacons put out, he scanned the scene
with keen eyes and a glass sweeping the horizon in every
direction. No wonder that his words seemed vague, and
vague they undoubtedly were. Suppose that Cavour had
been obliged to issue an election address on the eve of
the interview at Plombières, or Bismarck while he was on his
visit to Biarritz. Their language would hardly have been
pellucid. This was no moment for ultimatums. There
were too many unascertained elements. Yet some of those,
for instance, who most ardently admired President Lincoln
for the caution with which he advanced step by step to the
abolition proclamation, have most freely censured the English
statesman because he did not in the autumn of 1885 come
out with either a downright Yes or a point-blank No. The
point-blank is not for all occasions, and only a simpleton can
think otherwise.

In September Mr. Childers — a most capable administrator,
a zealous colleague, wise in what the world regards as the
secondary sort of wisdom, and the last man to whom one
would have looked for a plunge — wrote to Mr. Gladstone to
seek his approval of a projected announcement to his constituents at Pontefract, which amounted to a tolerably full-
fledged scheme of home rule.[1] In view of the charitable
allegation that Mr. Gladstone picked up home rule after the
elections had placed it in the power of the Irish either to put
him into office or to keep him out of office, his reply to Mr.
Childers deserves attention : —

To Mr. Childers.

Sept. 28, 1885. — I have a decided sympathy with the general
scope and spirit of your proposed declaration about Ireland. If I
offer any observations, they are meant to be simply in furtherance
of your purpose.

1. I would disclaim giving any exhaustive list of Imperial
subjects, and would not 'put my foot down' as to revenue, but

[1] *Life of Childers*, ii. p. 230.

would keep plenty of elbow-room to keep all customs and excise, which would probably be found necessary.

2. A general disclaimer of particulars as to the form of any local legislature might suffice, without giving the Irish expressly to know it might be decided mainly by their wish.

3. I think there is no doubt Ulster would be able to take care of itself in respect to education, but a question arises and forms, I think, the most difficult part of the whole subject, whether some defensive provisions for the owners of land and property should not be considered.

4. It is evident you have given the subject much thought, and my sympathy goes largely to your details as well as your principle. But considering the danger of placing confidence in the leaders of the national party at the present moment, and the decided disposition they have shown to raise their terms on any favourable indication, I would beg you to consider further whether you should *bind* yourself at present to any details, or go beyond general indications. If you say in terms (and this I do not dissuade) that you are ready to consider the question whether they can have a legislature for all questions not Imperial, this will be a great step in advance; and anything you may say beyond it, I should like to see veiled in language not such as to commit you.

The reader who is now acquainted with Mr. Gladstone's strong support of the Chamberlain plan in 1885, and with the bias already disclosed, knows in what direction the main current of his thought must have been setting. The position taken in 1885 was in entire harmony with all these premonitory notes. Subject, said Mr. Gladstone, to the supremacy of the crown, the unity of the empire, and all the authority of parliament necessary for the conservation of that unity, every grant to portions of the country of enlarged powers for the management of their own affairs, was not a source of danger, but a means of averting it. As to the legislative union, I believe history and posterity will consign to disgrace the name and memory of every man, be he who he may, and on whichever side of the Channel he may dwell, that having the power to aid in an equitable settlement between Ireland and Great Britain, shall use that power not to aid, but to prevent or retard it.'[1] These and all the other large and profuse sentences of the Midlothian address were undoubtedly open to more than one construction, and they either admitted or excluded home rule, as might happen. The fact that, though it was running so freely in his own mind, he did not put Irish autonomy into the forefront of his address, has been made a common article of charge against him. As if the view of Irish autonomy now running in his mind were not dependent on a string of hypotheses. And who can imagine a party leader's election address that should have run thus? — 'If Mr. Parnell returns with a great majority of members, and if the minority is not weighty enough, and if the demand is constitutionally framed, and if the Parnellites are unanimous, then we will try home rule. And this possibility of a hypothetical experiment is to be the liberal cry with which to go into battle against Lord Salisbury, who, so far as I can see, is nursing the idea of the same experiment.'

Some weeks later, in speaking to his electors in Midlothian, Mr. Gladstone instead of minimising magnified the Irish case, pushed it into the very forefront, not in one speech, but in nearly all ; warned his hearers of the gravity of the questions soon to be raised by it, and assured them that it would probably throw into the shade the other measures that he had described as ripe for action. He elaborated a declaration, of which much was heard for many months and years afterwards. What Ireland, he said, may deliberately and constitutionally demand, unless it infringes the principles connected with the honourable maintenance of the unity of the empire, will be a demand that we are bound at any rate to treat with careful attention. To stint Ireland in power which might be necessary or desirable for the management of matters purely Irish, would be a great error: and if she was so stinted, the end that any such measure might contemplate could not be attained. Then came the memorable appeal: 'Apart from the term of whig and tory, there is one thing I will say and will endeavour to impress upon you, and it is this. It will be a vital danger to the country and to the empire, if at a time when a demand from Ireland for larger powers

CHAP. I.

Æt. 76.

[1] Sept. 18, 1885.

of self-government is to be dealt with, there is not in parliament a party totally independent of the Irish vote.'[1]   Loud and long sustained have been the reverberations of this clanging sentence. It was no mere passing dictum. Mr. Gladstone himself insisted upon the same position again and again, that 'for a government in a minority to deal with the Irish question would not be safe.' This view, propounded in his first speech, was expanded in his second. There he deliberately set out that the urgent expediency of a liberal majority independent of Ireland did not foreshadow the advent of a liberal government to power. He referred to the settlement of household suffrage in 1867. How was the tory government enabled to effect that settlement? Because there was in the House a liberal majority which did not care to eject the existing ministry.[2]   He had already reminded his electors that tory governments were sometimes able to carry important measures, when once they had made up their minds to it, with greater facility than liberal governments could. For instance, if Peel had not been the person to propose the repeal of the corn laws, Lord John would not have had fair consideration from the tories ; and no liberal government could have carried the Maynooth Act.[3]

The plain English of the abundant references to Ireland in the Midlothian speeches of this election is, that Mr. Gladstone foresaw beyond all shadow of doubt that the Irish question in its largest extent would at once demand the instant attention of the new parliament; that the best hope of settling it would be that the liberals should have a majority of their own; that the second best hope lay in its settlement by the tory government with the aid of the liberals; but that, in any case, the worst of all conditions under which a settlement could be attempted — an attempt that could not be avoided — would be a situation in which Mr. Parnell should hold the balance between parliamentary parties.

The precise state of Mr. Gladstone's mind at this moment is best shown in a very remarkable letter written by him to Lord Rosebery, under whose roof at Dalmeny he was staying at the time : —

[1] Nov. 9, 1885.   [2] Midlothian Speeches, p. 49.   [3] Ibid. p. 39.

To Lord Rosebery.

Dalmeny Park, 13th *Nov.* 1885. — You have called my attention to the recent speech of Mr. Parnell, in which he expresses the desire that I should frame a plan for giving to Ireland, without prejudice to imperial unity and interests, the management of her own affairs. The subject is so important that, though we are together, I will put on paper my view of this proposal. For the moment I assume that such a plan can be framed. Indeed, if I had considered this to be hopeless, I should have been guilty of great rashness in speaking of it as a contingency that should be kept in view at the present election. I will first give reasons, which I deem to be of great weight, against my producing a scheme, reserving to the close one reason, which would be conclusive in the absence of every other reason.

1. It is not the province of the person leading the party in opposition, to frame and produce before the public detailed schemes of such a class.

2. There are reasons of great weight, which make it desirable that the party now in power should, if prepared to adopt the principle, and if supported by an adequate proportion of the coming House of Commons, undertake the construction and proposal of the measure.

3. The unfriendly relations between the party of nationalists and the late government in the expiring parliament, have of necessity left me and those with whom I act in great ignorance of the interior mind of the party, which has in parliament systematically confined itself to very general declarations.

4. That the principle and basis of an admissible measure have been clearly declared by myself, if not by others, before the country; more clearly, I think, than was done in the case of the Irish disestablishment; and that the particulars of such plans in all cases have been, and probably must be, left to the discretion of the legislature acting under the usual checks.

But my final and paramount reason is, that the production at this time of a plan by me would not only be injurious, but would destroy all reasonable hope of its adoption. Such a plan, proposed by the heads of the liberal party, is so certain to have the opposition of the tories *en bloc,* that every computation must be founded on this anticipation. This opposition, and the appeals with which it will be accompanied, will render the carrying of the measure difficult even by a united liberal party ; hopeless or most difficult, should there be serious defection.

Mr. Parnell is apprehensive of the opposition of the House of Lords. That idea weighs little with me. I have to think of something nearer, and more formidable. The idea of constituting a legislature for Ireland, whenever seriously and responsibly proposed, will cause a mighty heave in the body politic. It will be as difficult to carry the liberal party and the two British nations in favour of a legislature for Ireland, as it was easy to carry them in the case of Irish disestablishment. I think that it may possibly be done ; but only by the full use of a great leverage. That leverage can only be found in their equitable and mature consideration of what is due to the fixed desire of a nation, clearly and constitutionally expressed. Their prepossessions will not be altogether favourable ; and they cannot in this matter be bullied.

I have therefore endeavoured to lay the ground by stating largely the possibility and the gravity, even the solemnity, of that demand. I am convinced that this is the only path which can lead to success. With such a weapon, one might go hopefully into action. But I well know, from a thousand indications past and present, that a new project of mine launched into the air, would have no *momentum* which could carry it to its aim. So, in my mind, stands the case. . . .

Three days before this letter, Mr. Gladstone had replied to one from Lord Hartington : —

To Lord Hartington.

Dalmeny, Nov. 10, 1885. — I made a beginning yesterday in one of my conversation speeches, so to call them, on the way, by laying it down that I was particularly bound to prevent, if I could, the domination of sectional opinion over the body and action of the party.

I wish to say something about the modern radicalism. But I must include this, that if it is rampant and ambitious, the two most prominent causes of its forwardness have been : 1. Tory

democracy. 2. The gradual disintegration of the liberal aristo-
cracy. On both these subjects my opinions are strong. I think
the conduct of the Duke of Bedford and others has been as
unjustifiable as it was foolish, especially after what we did
to save the House of Lords from itself in the business of the
franchise.

Nor can I deny that the question of the House of Lords, of the
church, or both, will probably split the liberal party. But let it
split decently, honourably, and for cause. That it should split
now would, so far as I see, be ludicrous.

So far I have been writing in great sympathy with you, but
now I touch a point where our lines have not been the same.
You have, I think, courted the hostility of Parnell. Salisbury
has carefully avoided doing this, and last night he simply confined himself to two conditions, which you and I both think vital;
namely, the unity of the empire and an honourable regard to the
position of the 'minority,' i.e. the landlords. You will see in the
newspapers what Parnell, *making* for himself an opportunity, is
reported to have said about the elections in Ulster now at hand.
You have 'opened a vista which appears to terminate in a possible
concession to Ireland of full power to manage her own local affairs.
But I own my leaning to the opinion that, if that consummation is
in any way to be contemplated, action at a stroke will be more
honourable, less unsafe, less uneasy, than the jolting process of a
series of partial measures. This is my opinion, but I have no
intention, as at present advised, of signifying it. I have all along
in public declarations avoided offering anything to the nationalists,
beyond describing the limiting rule which must govern the question.
It is for them to ask, and for us, as I think, to leave the space so
defined as open and unencumbered as possible. I am much struck
by the increased breadth of Salisbury's declaration last night; he
dropped the 'I do not see how.'

We shall see how these great and difficult matters develop themselves. Meantime be assured that, with a good deal of misgiving
as to the future, I shall do what little I can towards enabling all
liberals at present to hold together with credit and good
conscience.

V

Mr. Gladstone's cardinal deliverance in November had been preceded by an important event. On October 7, 1885, Lord Salisbury made that speech at Newport, which is one of the tallest and most striking landmarks in the shifting sands of this controversy. It must be taken in relation to Lord Carnarvon's declaration of policy on taking office, and to his exchange of views with Mr. Parnell at the end of July. Their first principle, said Lord Salisbury, was to extend to Ireland, so far as they could, all the institutions of this country. But one must remember that in Ireland the population is on several subjects deeply divided, and a government is bound 'on all matters of essential justice' to protect a minority against a majority. Then came remarkable sentences: 'Local authorities are more exposed to the temptation of enabling the majority to be unjust to the minority when they obtain jurisdiction over a small area, than is the case when the authority derives its sanction and extends its jurisdiction over a wider area. In a large central authority, the wisdom of several parts of the country will correct the folly and mistakes of one. In a local authority, that correction is to a much greater extent wanting, and it would be impossible to leave that out of sight, in any extension of any such local authority in Ireland.' This principle was often used in the later controversy as a recognition by Lord Salisbury that the creation of a great central body would be a safer policy than the mere extension of self-government in Irish counties. In another part of the speech, it is true, the finger-post or weather-vane pointed in the opposite direction. 'With respect to the larger organic questions connected with Ireland,' said Lord Salisbury, 'I cannot say much, though I can speak emphatically. I have nothing to say but that the traditions of the party to which we belong, are on this point clear and distinct, and you may rely upon it our party will not depart from them.' Yet this emphatic refusal to depart from the traditions of the tory party did not prevent Lord Salisbury from retaining at that moment in his cabinet an Irish viceroy, with whom he

was in close personal relations, and whose active Irish policy
he must have known to be as wide a breach in tory tradition
as the mind of man can imagine. So hard is it in distracted
times, the reader may reflect, even for men of honourable
and lofty motive to be perfectly ingenuous.

The speaker next referred to the marked way in which
Mr. Parnell, a day or two before, had mentioned the position
of Austro-Hungary. 'I gathered that some notion of imperial federation was floating in his mind. With respect to
Ireland, I am bound to say that I have never seen any plan
or any suggestion which gives me at present the slightest
ground for anticipating that it is in that direction that we
shall find any substantial solution of the difficulties of the
problem.' In an electric state of the political atmosphere, a
statesman who said that at present he did not think federal
home rule possible, was taken to imply that he might think
it possible by-and-by. No door was closed.

It was, however, Lord Salisbury's language upon social
order that gave most scandal to simple consciences in his
own ranks. You ask us, he said, why we did not renew the
Crimes Act. There are two answers: we could not, and
it would have done no good if we could. To follow the
extension of the franchise by coercion, would have been a
gross inconsistency. To show confidence by one act, and
the absence of confidence by a simultaneous act, would be
to stultify parliament. Your inconsistency would have provoked such intense exasperation, that it would have led to
ten times more evil, ten times more resistance to the law,
than your Crimes Act could possibly have availed to check.
Then the audience was favoured with a philosophic view of
boycotting. This, said the minister, is an offence which
legislation has very great difficulty in reaching. The provisions of the Crimes Act against it had a very small effect.
It grew up under that Act. And, after all, look at boycotting. An unpopular man or his family go to mass. The
congregation with one accord get up and walk out. Are you
going to indict people for leaving church? The plain fact
is that boycotting 'is more like the excommunication or
interdict of the middle ages, than anything that we know

now.' 'The truth about boycotting is that it depends on the passing humour of the population.'

It is important to remember that in the month immediately preceding this polished apologetic, there were delivered some of the most violent boycotting speeches ever made in Ireland.[1] These speeches must have been known to the Irish government, and their occurrence and the purport of them must presumably have been known therefore to the prime minister. Here was indeed a removal of the ancient buoys and beacons that had hitherto guided English navigation in Irish waters. There was even less of a solid ultimatum at Newport, than in those utterances in Midlothian which were at that time and long afterwards found so culpably vague, blind, and elusive. Some of the more astute of the minister's own colleagues were delighted with his speech, as keeping the Irishmen steady to the tory party. They began to hope that they might even come within five-and-twenty of the liberals when the polling began.

The question on which side the Irish vote in Great Britain should be thrown seems not to have been decided until after Mr. Gladstone's speech. It was then speedily settled. On Nov. 21 a manifesto was issued, handing over the Irish vote in Great Britain solid to the orator of the Newport speech. The tactics were obvious. It was Mr. Parnell's interest to bring the two contending British parties as near as might be to a level, and this he could only hope to do by throwing his strength upon the weaker side. It was from the weaker side, if they could be retained in office, that he would get the best terms.[2] The document was composed with vigour and astuteness. But the phrases of the manifesto were the least important part of it. It was enough that the hard word was passed. Some estimated the loss to the liberal party in this island at twenty seats, others at forty. Whether twenty or forty, these lost seats made a fatal difference in the division on the Irish bill a few months later, and when

---

[1] Some of them are set out in Special Commission *Report*, pp. 99, 100.
[2] See Mr. Gladstone upon these tactics in his fifth Midlothian speech, Nov. 24, 1885. Also in the seventh, Nov. 28, pp. 159-60.

that day had come and gone, Mr. Parnell sometimes ruefully asked himself whether the tactics of the electoral manifesto were not on the whole a mistake. But this was not all and was not the worst of it. The Irish manifesto became a fiery element in a sharp electioneering war, and threw the liberals in all constituencies where there was an Irish vote into a direct and angry antagonism to the Irish cause and its leaders ; passions were roused, and things were said about Irishmen that could not at once be forgotten ; and the great task of conversion in 1886, difficult in any case, was made a thousand times more difficult still by the arguments and antipathies of the electoral battle of 1885. Meanwhile it was for the moment, and for the purposes of the moment, a striking success.

CHAPTER II

THE POLLS IN 1885

(*1885*)

I WOULD say that civil liberty can have no security without political
power. — C. J. Fox.

BOOK
IX.

1885.
THE election ran a chequered course (Nov. 23–Dec. 19).
It was the first trial of the whole body of male householders,
and it was the first trial of the system of single-member
districts. This is not the place for a discussion of the change
of electoral area. As a scheme for securing representation of
minorities it proved of little efficacy, and many believe that
the substitution of a smaller constituency for a larger one has
tended to slacken political interest, and to narrow political
judgment. Meanwhile some of those who were most deeply
concerned in establishing the new plan, were confident that
an overwhelming liberal triumph would be the result. Many
of their opponents took the same view, and were in despair.
A liberal met a tory minister on the steps of a club in Pall
Mall, as they were both going to the country for their
elections. 'I suppose,' said the tory, 'we are out for twenty
years to come.' *O pectora cœca!* He has been in office for
nearly fifteen of the eighteen years since. In September one
of the most authoritative liberal experts did not see how the
tories were to have more than 210 out of the 670 seats,
including the tory contingent from Ireland. Two months
later the expert admitted that the tory chances were improving, mainly owing to what in electioneering slang was called
the church scare. Fair trade, too, had made many converts
in Lancashire. On the very eve of the polls the estimate
at liberal headquarters was a majority of forty over tories
and Irishmen combined.

II

As I should have told the reader on an earlier page, Mr. Gladstone had proceeded to his own constituency on November 9. The previous month had found, as usual, endless other interests to occupy him, quite apart from politics. These are the ordinary entries. 'Worked, say, five hours on books. Three more hours reduced my books and rooms to apparent order, but much detail remains. Worked mildly on books.' In this region he would have said of disorder and disarray what Carlyle said to dirt, 'Thou shalt not abide with me.' As to the insides of books, his reading was miscellaneous: Madame d'Arblay, Bodley's *Remains*, Bachaumont's *Anecdotes*, Cuvier's *Theory of the Earth*, Whewell on *Astronomy*, the *Life of B. Gilpin*, Hennell's *Inquiry*, Schmidt's *Social Effects of Christianity*, Miss Martineau's *Autobiography*, Anderson on *Glory of the Bible*, Barrow's *Towards the Truth*, and so on — many of the books now stone-dead. Besides such reading as this, he 'made a beginning of a paper on Hermes, and read for it,' and worked hard at a controversial article, in reply to M. Réville, upon the Dawn of Creation and Worship. When he corrected the proof, he found it ill-written, and in truth we may rather marvel at, than admire, the hardihood that handled such themes amid such distractions.[1] Much company arrived. 'Count Münster came to luncheon; long walk and talk with him. The Derby-Bedford party came and went. I had an hour's good conversation with Lord D. Tea in the open air. *Oct*. 7. — Mr. Chamberlain came. Well, and much conversation. *Oct*. 8. — Mr. Chamberlain. Three hours of conversation.

Before the end of the month the doctors reported excellently of the condition of his vocal cords, and when he started for Dalmeny and the scene of the exploits of 1880 once more, he was in spirits to enjoy 'an animated journey,' and the vast enthusiasm with which Edinburgh again received him. His speeches were marked by undiminished fire. He boldly challenged a verdict on policy in the Soudan, while freely admitting that in some points, not immaterial, his cabinet had fallen into error, though in every case the error was fostered by the party opposite; and he pointed to the vital

[1] *Nineteenth Century*, November 1885; reprinted in *Later Gleanings*.

fact that though the party opposite were in good time, they never dreamed of altering the policy. He asked triumphantly how they would have fared in the Afghan dispute, if the policy anterior to 1880 had not been repudiated. In his address he took the same valiant line about South Africa. 'In the Transvaal,' he said, 'we averted a war of European and Christian races throughout South African states, which would have been alike menacing to our power, and scandalous in the face of civilisation and of Christendom. As this has been with our opponents a favourite subject of unmeasured denunciation, so I for one hail and reciprocate their challenge, and I hope the nation will give a clear judgment on our refusal to put down liberty by force, and on the measures that have brought about the present tranquillity of South Africa.' His first speech was on Ireland, and Ireland figured, as we have seen, largely and emphatically to the last. Disestablishment was his thorniest topic, for the scare of the church in danger was working considerable havoc in England, and every word on Scottish establishment was sure to be translated to establishment elsewhere. On the day on which he was to handle it, his entry is : 'Much rumination, and made notes which in speaking I could not manage to see. Off to Edinburgh at 2.30. Back at 6. Spoke seventy minutes in Free Kirk Hall : a difficult subject. The present agitation does not strengthen in my mind the principle of establishment.' His leading text was a favourite and a salutary maxim of his, that 'it is a very serious responsibility to take political questions out of their proper time and their proper order,' and the summary of his speech was that the party was agreed upon certain large and complicated questions, such as were enough for one parliament to settle, and that it would be an error to attempt to thrust those questions aside, to cast them into the shade and the darkness, 'for the sake of a subject of which I will not undervalue the importance, but of which I utterly deny the maturity at the present moment.'[1]

On Nov. 27 the poll was taken ; 11,241 electors out of 12,924, or 87 per cent., recorded their votes, and of these 7879 voted for Mr. Gladstone, and 3248 for Mr. Dalrymple, or a majority of 4631. So little impression had been made

[1] Speech in the Free Assembly Hall, Nov. 11, 1885.

in Midlothian by Kilmainham, Majuba, Khartoum, Penjdeh,
and the other party cries of a later period.

III

Let us turn to the general result, and the final composition of Mr. Gladstone's thirteenth parliament. The
polls of the first three or four days were startling. It
looked, in the phrases of the time, as if there were conservative reaction all round, as if the pendulum had swung
back to the point of tory triumph in 1874, and as if early
reverses would wind up in final rout. Where the tories did
not capture the seat, their numbers rose and the liberal
majorities fell. At the end of four days the liberals in
England and Wales had scored 86 against 109 for their
adversaries. When two-thirds of the House had been
elected, the liberals counted 196, the tories 179, and the
Irish nationalists 37. In spite of the early panic or exultation, it was found that in boroughs of over 100,000 the
liberals had after all carried seventeen, against eight for
their opponents. But the tories were victorious in a solid
Liverpool, save one Irish seat; they won all the seats in
Manchester save one; and in London, where liberals had
been told by those who were believed to know, that they
would make a clean sweep, there were thirty-six tories
against twenty-six liberals. Two members of the late liberal
cabinet and three subordinate ministers were thrown out.
'The verdict of the English borough constituencies,' cried
the *Times*, 'will be recorded more emphatically than was
even the case in 1874 in favour of the conservatives. The
opposition have to thank Mr. Chamberlain not only for
their defeat at the polls, but for the irremediable disruption
and hopeless disorganisation of the liberal party with its high
historic past and its high claims to national gratitude. His
achievement may give him such immortality as was won by
the man who burned down the temple of Diana at Ephesus.' [1]
The same writers have ever since ascribed the irremediable disruption to Mr. Gladstone and the Irish question.

Now came the counties with their newly enfranchised

[1] November 26, 1885.

hosts.   Here the tide flowed strong and steady.   Squire and
parson were amazed to see the labourer, of whose stagnant
indifference to politics they had been so confident, trudging
four or five miles to a political meeting, listening without
asking for a glass of beer to political speeches, following
point upon point, and then trudging back again dumbly
chewing the cud.   Politicians with gifts of rhetoric began to
talk of the grand revolt of the peasants, and declared that it
was the most remarkable transformation since the conversion
of the Franks.   Turned into prose, this meant that the
liberals had extended their area into large rural provinces
where hitherto tory supremacy had never been disputed.
Whether or no Mr. Chamberlain had broken the party in
the boroughs, his agrarian policy together with the natural
uprising of the labourer against the party of squire and
farmer, had saved it in the counties.   The nominees of
such territorial magnates as the Northumberlands, the
Pembrokes, the Baths, the Bradfords, the Watkin Wynns,
were all routed, and the shock to territorial influence was
felt to be profound.   An ardent agrarian reformer, who later
became a conspicuous unionist, writing to Mr. Gladstone in
July a description of a number of great rural gatherings, told
him, ' One universal feature of these meetings is the joy,
affection, and unbounded applause with which your name is
received by these earnest men.   Never in all your history had
you so strong a place in the hearts of the common people,
as you have to-day.   It requires to be seen to be realised.'

All was at last over.   It then appeared that so far from
there being a second version of the great tory reaction
of 1874, the liberals had now in the new parliament a
majority over tories of 82, or thirty under the corresponding
majority in the year of marvel, 1880.   In great Britain
they had a majority of 100, being 333 against 233.[1]   But

---

[1] *Result of General Election of* 1885: —

	L.	C.	P.
English and Welsh boroughs and universities,	93	86	1
Metropolis, ...	26	36	0
English and Welsh counties, . . .	152	101	0
Scottish boroughs, ...	30	3	0
" counties, ...	32	7	0
Ireland, ...	0	18	85
	333	251	86

they had no majority over tories and Irishmen combined. That hopeful dream had glided away through the ivory gate. Shots between right wing and left of the liberal party were exchanged to the very last moment. When the borough elections were over, the Birmingham leader cried that so far from the loss in the boroughs being all the fault of the extreme liberals, it was just because the election had not been fought on their programme, but was fought instead on a manifesto that did not include one of the points to which the extreme liberals attached the greatest importance. For the sake of unity, they had put aside their most cherished principles, disestablishment for instance, and this, forsooth, was the result.[1] The retort came as quickly as thunder after the flash. Lord Hartington promptly protested from Matlock, that the very crisis of the electoral conflict was an ill-chosen moment for the public expression of doubt by a prominent liberal as to the wisdom of a policy accepted by the party, and announced by the acknowledged leader of the whole party. When the party had found some more tried, more trusted, more worthy leader, then might perhaps be the time to impugn the policy. These reproachful ironies of Lord Hartington boded ill for any prospect of the heroes of this fratricidal war of the platform smoothing their wrinkled fronts in a liberal cabinet.

IV

In Ireland the result shed a strong light on the debating prophecies that the extension of the county franchise would

The following figures may also be found interesting : —

Election of 1868 —

English and Welsh Liberals, ...		267
" " Tories, ...		225
	Majority, . .	42

In 1880 —

English and Welsh Liberals, ...		284
" " Tories, ...		205
	Majority, . .	79

In 1885 —

English and Welsh Liberals, ...		270
" " Tories, ...		223
	Majority, . .	47

[1] Mr. Chamberlain at Leicester, December 3, 1885.

not be unfavourable to the landlord interest ; that it would enable the deep conservative interest of the peasantry to vindicate itself against the nationalism of the towns ; that it would prove beyond all doubt that the Irish leader did not really speak the mind of a decided majority of the people of Ireland. Relying on the accuracy of these abstract predictions, the Irish tories started candidates all over the country. Even some of them who passed for shrewd and candid actually persuaded themselves that they were making an impression on the constituencies. The effect of their ingenuous operations was to furnish such a measure of nationalist strength, as would otherwise have seemed incredible almost to the nationalists themselves. An instance or two will suffice. In two divisions of Cork, the tories polled 300 votes against nearly 10,000 for the nationalists. In two divisions of Mayo, the tories polled 200 votes against nearly 10,000 for the nationalists. In one division of Kilkenny there were 4000 nationalist votes against 170 for the tory, and in another division 4000 against 220. In a division of Kerry the nationalist had over 3000 votes against 30 for the tory, — a hundred to one. In prosperous counties with resident landlords and a good class of gentry such as Carlow and Kildare, in one case the popular vote was 4800 against 750, and in the other 3169 against 467. In some fifty constituencies the popular majorities ranged in round numbers from 6500 the highest, to 2400 the lowest. Besides these constituencies where a contest was so futile, were those others in which no contest was even attempted.

In Ulster a remarkable thing happened. This favoured province had in the last parliament returned nine liberals. Lord Hartington attended a banquet at Belfast (Nov. 5) just before the election. It was as unlucky an affair as the feast of Belshazzar. His mission was compared by Orange wits to that of the Greek hero who went forth to wrestle with Death for the body of an old woman. The whole of the liberal candidates in Ulster fell down as dead men. Orangemen and catholics, the men who cried damnation to King William and the men who cried ' To hell with the Pope,' joined hands against them. In Belfast itself, nationalists were

seen walking to the booths with orange cards in their hats
to vote for orangemen against liberals.[1] It is true that the
paradox did not last, and that the Pope and King William
were speedily on their old terms again. Within six months,
the two parties atoned for this temporary backsliding into
brotherly love, by one of the most furious and protracted
conflagrations that ever raged even in the holy places of
Belfast. Meanwhile nationalism had made its way in the
south of the province, partly by hopes of reduced rents,
partly by the energy of the catholic population, who had not
tasted political power for two centuries. The adhesion of
their bishops to the national movement in the Monaghan
election had given them the signal three years before.
Fermanagh, hitherto invariably Orange, now sent two
nationalists. Antrim was the single county out of the
thirty-two counties of Ireland that was solid against home
rule, and even in Antrim in one contest the nationalist was
beaten only by 35 votes.

Not a single liberal was returned in the whole of Ireland.
To the last parliament she had sent fourteen. They were
all out bag and baggage. Ulster now sent eighteen nationalists and seventeen tories. Out of the eighty-nine contests
in Ireland, Mr. Parnell's men won no fewer than eighty-five,
and in most of them they won by such overwhelming
majorities as I have described. It was noticed that twenty-
two of the persons elected, or more than one-fourth of the
triumphant party, had been put in prison under the Act of
1881. A species of purge, moreover, had been performed.
All half-hearted nationalists, the doubters and the faithless,
were dismissed, and their places taken by men pledged
either to obey or else go.

The British public now found out on what illusions they
had for the last four years been fed. Those of them who
had memories, could recollect how the Irish secretary of
the day, on the third reading of the first Coercion bill in
1881, had boldly appealed from the Irish members to the
people of Ireland. 'He was sure that he could appeal with
confidence from gentlemen sitting below the gangway
opposite to their constituents.'[2] They remembered all the

---

[1] Macknight's *Ulster as it Is*, ii. p. 108.   [2] Mr. Forster, March 11, 1881.

talk about Mr. Parnell and his followers being a mere handful of men and not a political party at all, and the rest of it.
They had now a revelation what a fool's paradise it had been.
As a supreme electoral demonstration, the Irish elections
of 1885 have never been surpassed in any country. They
showed that neither remedial measures nor repressive measures had made even the fleeting shadow of an impression
on the tenacious sentiment of Ireland, or on the powerful
organisation that embodied and directed it. The Land Act
had made no impression. The two Coercion Acts had made
none. The imperial parliament had done its best for five
years. Some of the ablest of its ministers had set zealous
and intrepid hands to the task, and this was the end.
Whether you counted seats or counted votes, the result
could not be twisted into anything but what it was — the
vehement protest of one of the three kingdoms against the
whole system of its government, and a strenuous demand for
its reconstruction on new foundations.

Endeavours were made to discredit so startling and unwelcome a result. It was called 'the carefully prepared
verdict of a shamefully packed jury.' Much was made of
the number of voters who declared themselves illiterate,
said to be compelled so to do in order that the priest or
other intimidatory person might see that they voted right.
As a matter of fact the percentage of illiterate voters
answered closely to the percentage of males over twenty-one
in the census returns, who could neither read nor write.
Only two petitions followed the general election, one at
Belfast against a nationalist, and the other at Derry against
a tory, and in neither of the two was undue influence or
intimidation alleged. The routed candidates in Ireland, like
the same unlucky species elsewhere, raised the usual chorus
of dolorous explanation. The register, they cried, was in
a shameful condition; the polling stations were too few or
too remote ; the loyalists were afraid, and the poll did not
represent their real numbers ; people did not believe that
the ballot was really secret ; the percentage of illiterates was
monstrous ; promises and pledges went for nothing. Such
are ever the too familiar voices of mortified electioneering

There was also the best known of all the conclusive topics from tory Ireland. It was all done, vowed the tories, by the bishops and clergy; they were indefatigable; they canvassed at the houses and presided at meetings; they exhorted their flocks from the altar, and they drilled them at the polling-booths. The spiritual screw of the priest and the temporal screw of the league — there was the whole secret. Such was the story, and it was not wholly devoid of truth ; but then what balm, what comfort, had even the truth of it for British rulers ?

Some thousands of voters stayed away from the polls. It was ingeniously explained that their confidence in British rule had been destroyed by the Carnarvon surrender ; a shopkeeper would not offend his customers for the sake of a Union Jack that no longer waved triumphant in the breeze. They were like the Arab sheikhs at Berber, who, when they found that the Egyptian pashas were going to evacuate, went over to the Mahdi. The conventions appointed to select the candidates were denounced as the mere creatures of Mr. Parnell, the Grand Elector. As if anything could have shown a more politic appreciation of the circumstances. There are situations that require a dictator, not to impose an opinion, but to kindle an aspiration ; not to shape a demand, but to be the effective organ of opinion and demand. Now in the Irish view was one of those situations. In the last parliament twenty-six seats were held by persons designated nominal home rulers ; in the new parliament, not one. Every new nationalist member pledged himself to resign whenever the parliamentary party should call upon him. Such an instrument grasped in a hand of iron was indispensable, first to compel the British government to listen, and second, to satisfy any British government disposed to listen, that in dealing with Mr. Parnell they were dealing with nationalist Ireland, and with a statesman who had the power to make his engagements good. You need greater qualities, said Cardinal De Retz, to be a good party leader than to be emperor of the universe. Ireland is not that portion of the universe in which this is least true.

CHAPTER III

A CRITICAL MONTH

(*December 1885*)

WHOEVER has held the post of minister for any considerable time can never absolutely, unalterably maintain and carry out his original opinions. He finds himself in the presence of situations that are not always the same — of life and growth — in, connection with which he must take one course one day, and then, perhaps, another on the next day. I could not always run straight ahead like a cannon ball. — BISMARCK.

BOOK
IX.

1885.
THE month of December was passed by Mr. Gladstone at Hawarden, in such depth of meditation as it is easy for us to conjecture. The composition of his party, the new situation in parliament, the mutual relations of important individuals, the Irish case, his own share in respect of the Irish case, the strange new departure in Irish policy announced and acted upon by the subsisting cabinet — from all these points of view it was now his business to survey the extraordinary scene. The knot to be unravelled in 1886 was hardly less entangled than that which engaged the powerful genius of Pitt at the opening of the century. Stripped of invidious innuendo, the words of Lord Salisbury a few weeks later state with strength and truth the problem that now confronted parliament and its chief men. ' Up to the time,' said the tory prime minister, ' when Mr. Gladstone took office, be it for good or evil, for many generations Ireland had been governed through the influence and the action of the landed gentry. I do not wish to defend that system. There is a good deal to be said for it, and a good deal to be said against it. What I wish to insist upon is, not that that system was good, but that the statesman who undertook to overthrow it, should have had something to put in its place.

He utterly destroyed it. By the Land Act of 1870, by the CHAP.
Ballot Act of 1872, by the Land Act of 1881, and last of all III.
by the Reform bill of 1884, the power of the landed gentry Æт. 76.
in Ireland is absolutely shattered ; and he now stands before
the formidable problem of a country deprived of a system of
government under which it had existed for many generations, and absolutely without even a sketch of a substitute
by which the ordinary functions of law and order can be
maintained. Those changes which he introduced into the
government of Ireland were changes that were admirable
from a parliamentary point of view. They were suited to
the dominant humour of the moment. But they were
barren of any institutions by which the country could be
governed and kept in prosperity for the future.'[1] This is
a statement of the case that biographer and historian alike
should ponder. Particularly should they remember that
both parties had renounced coercion.

Mr. Gladstone has publicly explained the working of his
mind, and both his private letters at the time, and many a
conversation later, attest the hold which the new aspect,
however chimerical it may now seem to those who do not
take long views, had gained upon him. He could not be
blind to the fact that the action and the language of the
tory ministers during the last six months had shown an
unquestionable readiness to face the new necessities of a complex situation with new methods. Why should not a solution
of the present difficulties be sought in the same co-operation
of parties, that had been as advantageous as it was indispensable in other critical occasions of the century? He
recalled other leading precedents of national crisis. There
was the repeal of the Test Act in 1828; catholic emancipation in 1829 ; the repeal of the corn law in 1846 ; the
extension of the franchise in 1867. In the history of these
memorable transactions, Mr. Gladstone perceived it to be
extremely doubtful whether any one of these measures, all
carried as they were by tory governments, could have become
law except under the peculiar conditions which secured for

[1] Lord Salisbury, at a dinner given   members for Hertfordshire, February
in London to the four conservative   17, 1886.

each of them both the aid of the liberal vote in the House of Commons, and the authority possessed by all tory governments in the House of Lords. What was the situation? The ministerial party just reached the figure of two hundred and fifty-one. Mr. Gladstone had said in the course of the election that for a government in a minority to deal with the Irish question would not be safe, such an operation could not but be attended by danger; but the tender of his support to Lord Salisbury was a demonstration that he thought the operation might still properly be undertaken.[1]

To Herbert Gladstone.

December 10, 1885. — 1. The nationalists have run in political alliance with the tories for years; more especially for six months; most of all at the close during the elections, when *they* have made us 335 (say) against 250 [conservatives] instead of 355 against 230. This alliance is therefore at its zenith. 2. The question of Irish government ought for the highest reasons to be settled at once, and settled by the allied forces, (1) because they have the government, (2) because their measure will have fair play from all, most, or many of us, which a measure of ours would not have from the tories. 3. As the allied forces are half the House, so that there is not a majority against them, no constitutional principle is violated by allowing the present cabinet to continue undisturbed for the purpose in view. 4. The plan for Ireland ought to be produced by the government of the day. Principles may be laid down by others, but not the detailed interpretation of them in a measure. I have publicly declared I produce no plan until the government has arrived at some issue with the Irish, as I hope they will. 5. If the moment ever came when a plan had to be considered with a view to production on behalf of the liberal party, I do not at present see how such a question could be dissociated from another vital question, namely, who are to be the government. For a government alone can carry a measure, though some outline of essentials might be put out in a motion or resolution.

Happening in these days to meet in the neighbouring

_____
[1] *Special Aspects of the Irish Question*, p. 18.

palace of a whig magnate, Mr. Balfour, a young but even
then an important member of the government, with whom
as a veteran with a junior of high promise he had long
been on terms of friendly intimacy, Mr. Gladstone began
an informal conversation with him upon the condition of
Ireland, on the stir that it was making in men's minds,
and on the urgency of the problem. The conversation he
followed up by a letter (Dec. 20). Every post, he said, bore
him testimony to the growing ferment. In urging how
great a calamity it would be if so vast a question should
fall into the lines of party conflict, he expressed his desire
to see it taken up by the government, and to be able, with
reserve of necessary freedom, to co-operate in their design.
Mr. Balfour replied with courteous scepticism, but promised
to inform Lord Salisbury. The tactical computation was
presumably this, that Lord Salisbury would lose the Orange
group from Ireland and the extreme tories in England, but
would keep the bulk of his party. On the other hand, Mr.
Gladstone in supporting a moderate home rule would drop
some of the old whigs and some of the extreme radicals, but
he too would keep the bulk of the liberal party. Therefore,
even if Mr. Parnell and his followers should find the scheme
too moderate to be endurable, still Lord Salisbury with Mr.
Gladstone's help would settle the Irish question as Peel
with the help of the whigs settled the question of corn.

Both at the time and afterwards Mr. Gladstone was wont
to lay great stress upon the fact that he had opened this suggestion and conveyed this proffer of support. For instance,
he writes to Lord Hartington (Dec. 20): 'On Tuesday I
had a conversation with Balfour at Eaton, which in conformity with my public statements, I think, conveyed informally
a hope that they would act, as the matter is so serious, and
as its becoming a party question would be a great national
calamity. I have written to him to say (without speaking
for others) that if they can make a proposal for the purpose
of settling definitely the question of Irish government, I
shall wish with proper reserves to treat it in the spirit in
which I have treated Afghanistan and the Balkan Peninsula.'

The language of Lord Carnarvon when he took office and

of Lord Salisbury at Newport, coupled with the more substantial fact of the alliance between tories and nationalists
before and during the election, no doubt warranted Mr.
Gladstone's assumption that the alliance might continue,
and that the talk of a new policy had been something more
than an electioneering manœuvre. Yet the importance that
he always attached to his offer of support for a definite
settlement, or in plainer English, some sort of home rule,
implies a certain simplicity. He forgot in his patriotic zeal
the party system. The tory leader, capable as his public
utterances show of piercing the exigencies of Irish government to the quick, might possibly, in the course of responsible consultations with opponents for a patriotic purpose,
have been drawn by argument and circumstance on to the
ground of Irish autonomy, which he had hitherto considered,
and considered with apparent favour, only in the dim distance of abstract meditation or through the eyes of Lord
Carnarvon. The abstract and intellectual temperament is
sometimes apt to be dogged and stubborn; on the other
hand, it is often uncommonly elastic. Lord Salisbury's clear
and rationalising understanding might have been expected
to carry him to a thoroughgoing experiment to get rid of a
deep and inveterate disorder. If he thought it politic to
assent to communication with Mr. Parnell, why should he
not listen to overtures from Mr. Gladstone? On the other
hand, Lord Salisbury's hesitation in facing the perils of
an Irish settlement in reliance upon the co-operation of
political opponents is far from being unintelligible. His
inferior parliamentary strength would leave him at the
mercy of an extremely formidable ally. He may have
anticipated that, apart from the ordinary temptations of
every majority to overthrow a minority, all the strong
natural impulses of the liberal leader, his vehement sympathy with the principle of nationality, the irresistible
attraction for him of all the grand and eternal commonplaces of liberty and self-government, would inevitably
carry him much further on the Irish road than either Lord
Salisbury himself may have been disposed to travel, or than
he could be sure of persuading his party to follow. He may

well have seen grounds for pause before committing himself
to so delicate and precarious an enterprise.

II

Early in December Lord Granville was at Hawarden, and
the two discussed the crucial perplexities of the hour, not
going further than agreement that responsibility lay with
the government, and that the best chance for settlement
lay in large concession. From Hawarden Lord Granville
went to Chatsworth, where he found Lord Spencer on his
way to visit Mr. Gladstone ; but nothing important passed
among the three leaders thus brought together under the
roof of Lord Hartington. Lord Granville imparted to Lord
Spencer and Lord Hartington that Mr. Gladstone was full
of Ireland in the direction of some large concession of self-
government. The host discussed the thing dispassionately
without much expression of opinion. Proceeding to Hawarden, Lord Spencer was there joined by Lord Rosebery. Their
chief repeated to them the propositions already stated
(p. 258). Mr. Gladstone wrote to Lord Granville (Dec. 9):

You have, I think, acted very prudently in not returning here.
It would have been violently canvassed. Your report is as
favourable as could be expected. I think my conversations with
Rosebery and Spencer have also been satisfactory. What I expect
is a healthful, slow fermentation in many minds, working towards
the final product. It is a case of between the devil and the deep
sea. But our position is a bed of roses, compared with that of
the government. . . .

Lord Spencer was hardly second in weight to Mr. Gladstone
himself. His unrivalled experience of Irish administration,
his powers of firm decision in difficult circumstances, and
the impression of high public spirit, uprightness, and fortitude, which had stamped itself deep upon the public mind,
gave him a force of moral authority in an Irish crisis that
was unique. He knew the importance of a firm and continuous system in Ireland. Such a system he had inflexibly
carried out. Extreme concessions had been extorted from
him by the radicals in the cabinet, and when the last moment

of the eleventh hour had arrived, it looked as if he would
break up the government by insisting.   Then the government was turned out, and the party of 'law and order' came
in.   He saw his firm and continuous system at the first
opportunity flouted and discarded.   He was aware, as
officials and as the public were aware, that his successor
at Dublin Castle made little secret that he had come over
to reverse the policy.   Lord Spencer, too, well knew in the
last months of his reign at Dublin that his own system,
in spite of outward success, had made no mark upon Irish
disaffection.   It is no wonder that after his visit to Hawarden, he laboured hard at consideration of the problem
that the strange action of government on the one hand,
and the speculations of a trusted leader on the other, had
forced upon him.   On Mr. Gladstone he pressed the question
whether a general support should be given to Irish autonomy
as a principle, before particulars were matured.   In any case
he perceived that the difficulty of governing Ireland might
well be increased by knowledge of the mere fact that Mr.
Gladstone and himself, whether in office or in opposition,
were looking in the direction of autonomy.   Somebody said
to Mr. Gladstone, people talked about his turning Spencer
round his thumb.   'It would be more true,' he replied, 'that
he had turned me round his.'   That is, I suppose, by the
lessons of Lord Spencer's experience.

In the middle of the month Lord Hartington asked Mr.
Gladstone for information as to his views and intentions on
the Irish question as developed by the general election.   The
rumours in the newspapers, he said, as well as in private
letters, were so persistent that it was hard to believe them
without foundation.   Mr. Gladstone replied to Lord Hartington in a letter of capital importance in its relation to the
prospects of party union (Dec. 17): —

To Lord Hartington.

The whole stream of public excitement is now turned upon me,
and I am pestered with incessant telegrams which I have no
defence against, but either suicide or Parnell's method of self-con-
cealment.   The truth is, I have more or less of opinions and ideas,

but no intentions or negotiations. In these ideas and opinions there is, I think, little that I have not more or less conveyed in public declarations; in principle nothing. I will try to lay them before you. I consider that Ireland has now spoken; and that an effort ought to be made *by the government* without delay to meet her demands for the management by an Irish legislative body of Irish as distinct from imperial affairs. Only a government can do it, and a tory government can do it more easily and safely than any other. There is first a postulate that the state of Ireland shall be such as to warrant it. The conditions of an admissible plan are —

1. Union of the empire and due supremacy of parliament.

2. Protection for the minority — a difficult matter on which I have talked much with Spencer, certain points, however, remaining to be considered.

3. Fair allocation of imperial charges.

4. A statutory basis seems to me better and safer than the revival of Grattan's parliament, but I wish to hear much more upon this, as the minds of men are still in so crude a state on the whole subject.

5. Neither as opinions nor as instructions have I to any one alive promulgated these ideas as decided on by me.

6. As to intentions, I am determined to have none at present, to leave space to the government — I should wish to encourage them if I properly could — above all, on no account to say or do anything which would enable the nationalists to establish rival biddings between us. If this storm of rumours continues to rage, it may be necessary for me to write some new letter to my constituents, but I am desirous to do nothing, simply leaving the field open for the government until time makes it necessary to decide. Of our late colleagues I have had most communication with Granville, Spencer, Rosebery. Would you kindly send this on to Granville?

I think you will find this in conformity with my public declarations, though some blanks are filled up. I have in truth thought it my duty without in the least committing myself or any one else, to think through the subject as well as I could, being equally convinced of its urgency and bigness. If H. and N. are with you, pray show them this letter, which is a very hasty one, for I am so battered with telegrams that I hardly know whether I stand on my head or my heels. . . .

With regard to the letter I sent you, my opinion is that there is a Parnell party and a separation or civil war party, and the question which is to have the upper hand will have to be decided in a limited time. My earnest recommendation to everybody is not to commit himself. Upon this rule, under whatever pressure, I shall act as long as I can. There shall be no private negotiation carried on by me, but the time may come when I shall be obliged to speak publicly. Meanwhile I hope you will keep in free and full communication with old colleagues. Pray put questions if this letter seems ambiguous. . . .

Pray remember that I am at all times ready for personal communication, should you think it desirable.

III

Before receiving this letter, Lord Hartington was startled, as all the world was, to come on something in the newspapers that instantly created a new situation. Certain prints published on December 17 what was alleged to be Mr. Gladstone's scheme for an Irish settlement.[1] It proposed in terms the creation of an Irish parliament. Further particulars were given in detail, but with these we need not concern ourselves. The Irish parliament was enough. The public mind, bewildered as it was by the situation that the curious issue of the election had created, was thrown by this announcement into extraordinary commotion. The facts are these. Mr. Herbert Gladstone visited London at this time (Dec. 14), partly in consequence of a speech made a few days before by Sir C. Dilke, and of the club talk which the speech had set going. It was taken to mean that he and Mr. Chamberlain, the two radical leaders, thought that such an Irish policy as might be concocted between Mr. Gladstone and Mr. Parnell would receive no general support from the liberal party, and that it would be much safer to

[1] These statements first appeared in the *Leeds Mercury* and the *Standard* on Dec. 17, and in a communication from the National Press Agency issued on the night of Dec. 16. They were not published in the *Times* and other London morning papers until Dec. 18. Mr. Gladstone's telegram was printed in the evening papers on Dec. 17.

leave the tories in power, in the expectation that some
moderate measures of reform might be got from them, and
that meanwhile they would become committed with the
Irishmen. Tactics of this kind were equivalent to the
exclusion of Mr. Gladstone, for in every letter that he wrote
he pronounced the Irish question urgent. Mr. Herbert
Gladstone had not been long in London before the impression became strong upon him, that in the absence of a
guiding hint upon the Irish question, the party might be
drifting towards a split. Under this impression he had a
conversation with the chief of an important press agency,
who had previously warned him that the party was all at
sea. To this gentleman, in an interview at which no notes
were taken and nothing read from papers — so little formal
was it — he told his own opinions on the assumed opinions
of Mr. Gladstone, all in general terms, and only with the
negative view of preventing friendly writers from falling
into traps. Unluckily it would seem to need at least the
genius of a Bismarck, to perform with precision and success the delicate office of inspiring a modern oracle on
the journalistic tripod. Here, what was intended to be a
blameless negative soon swelled, as the oracular fumes are
wont to do, into a giant positive. In conversations with
another journalist, who was also his private friend (Dec. 15),
he used language which the friend took to justify the pretty
unreserved announcement that Mr. Gladstone was about to
set to work in earnest on home rule.

'With all these matters,' Mr. Herbert Gladstone wrote to a
near relative at the time, 'my father had no more connection
than the man in the moon, and until each event occurred, he
knew no more of it than the man in the street.' Mr. Gladstone on the same day (Dec. 17) told the world by telegraph
that the statement was not an accurate representation of
his views, but a speculation upon them; he added that it
had not been published with his knowledge or authority.
There can be no doubt, whatever else may be said, that
the publication was neither to his advantage, nor in conformity with his view of the crisis. No statesman in our
history has ever been more careful of the golden rule of

political strategy — to neglect of which Frederick the Great traced the failure of Joseph II. — not to take the second step before you have taken the first. Neither scheme nor intention had yet crystallised in his mind. Never was there a moment when every consideration of political prudence more imperatively counselled silence. Mr. Gladstone's denial of all responsibility was not found to be an explicit contradiction ; it was a repudiation of the two newspapers, but it was not a repudiation of an Irish parliament. Therefore people believed the story the more. Friends and foes became more than ever alert, excited, alarmed, and in not a few cases vehemently angry. This unauthorised publication with the qualified denial, placed Mr. Gladstone in the very position which he declared that he would not take up ; it made him a trespasser on ground that belonged to the government. Any action on his part would in his own view not only be unnecessary ; it would be unwarrantable ; it would be in the highest degree injurious and mischievous.[1] Yet whatever it amounted to, some of this very injury and mischief followed.

Lord Hartington no sooner saw what was then called the Hawarden kite flying in the sky, than he felt its full significance. He at once wrote to Mr. Gladstone, partly in reply to the letter of the 17th already given, and pointed with frankness to what would follow. No other subject would be discussed until the meeting of parliament, and it would be discussed with the knowledge, or what would pass for knowledge, that in Mr. Gladstone's opinion the time for concession to Ireland had arrived, and that concession was practicable. In replying to his former letter Mr. Gladstone had invited personal communication, and Lord Hartington thought that he might in a few days avail himself of it, though (December 18) he feared that little advantage would follow. In spite of urgent arguments from wary friends, Lord Hartington at once proceeded to write to his chairman in Lancashire (December 20), informing the public that no proposals of liberal policy on the Irish demand had been communicated to him; for his own part he stood to what

[1] Speech on the Address, January 21, 1886.

he said at the election.   This letter was the first bugle note
of an inevitable conflict between Mr. Gladstone and those
who by and by became the whig dissentients.

To Lord Hartington resistance to any new Irish policy
came easily, alike by temperament and conviction.   Mr.
Chamberlain was in a more embarrassing position; and his
first speech after the election showed it.   'We are face to
face,' he said, 'with a very remarkable demonstration by
the Irish people.   They have shown that as far as regards
the great majority of them, they are earnestly in favour of
a change in the administration of their government, and of
some system which would give them a larger control of their
domestic affairs.   Well, we ourselves by our public declarations and by our liberal principles are pledged to acknowledge the justice of this claim.'   What was the important
point at the moment, Mr. Chamberlain declared that in his
judgment the time had hardly arrived when the liberal party
could interfere safely or with advantage to settle this great
question.   'Mr. Parnell has appealed to the tories.   Let
him settle accounts with his new friends.   Let him test
their sincerity and goodwill; and if he finds that he has
been deceived, he will approach the liberal party in a spirit
of reason and conciliation.' [1]

Translated into the language of parliamentary action, this
meant that the liberals, with a majority of eighty-two over
the tories, were to leave the tory minority undisturbed in
office, on the chance of their bringing in general measures
of which liberals could approve, and making Irish proposals
to which Mr. Parnell, in the absence of competition for his
support, might give at least provisional assent.   In principle, these tactics implied, whether right or wrong, the old-
fashioned union of the two British parties against the
Irish.   Were the two hundred and fifty tories to be left
in power, to carry out all the promises of the general
election, and fulfil all the hopes of a new parliament chosen
on a new system?   The Hawarden letter-bag was heavy
with remonstrances from newly elected liberals against any
such course.

[1] At the Birmingham Reform Club, Dec. 17, 1885.

Second only to Mr. Gladstone in experience of stirring
and perilous positions, Lord Granville described the situation to one of his colleagues as nothing less than 'thoroughly
appalling.' A great catastrophe, he said, might easily result
from any of the courses open : from the adoption of coercion
by either government or opposition; from the adoption by
either of concession; from the attempt to leave the state of
Ireland as it was. If, as some think, a great catastrophe
did in the end result from the course that Mr. Gladstone
was now revolving in his own mind at Hawarden, and that
he had commended to the meditations of his most important
colleagues, what alternative was feasible?

IV

The following letters set out the various movements in a
drama that was now day by day, through much confusion
and bewilderment, approaching its climax.

To Lord Granville.

December 18, '85. —. . . Thinking incessantly about the matter,
speaking freely and not with finality to you, and to Rosebery and
Spencer — the only colleagues I have seen — I have trusted to
writing to Hartington (who had had Harcourt and Northbrook
with him) and to you for Derby.

If I have made *any* step in advance at all, which I am not sure of,
it has most certainly been in the direction of leaving the field open
for the government, encouraging them to act, and steadily refusing to say or do *anything* like negotiation on my own behalf. So
I think Derby will see that in the main I am certainly with him.
. . . What will Parnell do? What will the government do?
How can we decide without knowing or trying to know, both if
we can, but at any rate the second ? This letter is at your discretion to use in proper quarters.

December 22. — In the midst of these troubles, I look to you as
the great feud-composer, and your note just received is just what
I should have hoped and expected. Hartington wrote to me on
Saturday that he was going up to see Goschen, but as I thought
inviting a letter from me, which I wrote [December 17, above],
and it was with no small surprise that I read him yesterday in

the *Times*. However, I repeated yesterday to R. Grosvenor all
that I have said to you about what seems to me the plain duty of
the *party*, in the event of a severance between nationalists and
tories. Meantime I care not who knows my anxiety to prevent that
severance, and for that reason among others to avoid all communications of ideas and intentions which could tend to bring it about.

On December 27, Lord Granville wrote to Mr. Gladstone
at Hawarden : —

I have been asked to request you to call a cabinet of your late
colleagues to discuss the present state of affairs. I have declined,
giving my reasons, which appear to me to be good. At the same
time, I think it would calm some fussiness that exists, if you let
it be known to a few that you will be in town and ready for consultation, before the actual meeting.

Mr. Gladstone answered, as those acquainted with his
modes of mind might have been sure that he would : —

December 28. — Thank you for stopping the request to which
your letter of yesterday refers. A cabinet does not exist out of
office, and no one in his senses could covenant to call *the late
cabinet* together, I think, even if there were something on which
it was ready to take counsel, which at this moment there is not.
On the other hand, you will have seen from my letter that the
idea before me has been that of going unusual lengths in the way
of consulting beforehand, not only leading men but the party, or
undertaking some special obligation to be assured of their concurrence generally, before undertaking new responsibilities.

The one great difficulty in proceeding to consult now, I think,
is that we cannot define the situation for ourselves, as an essential
element of it is the relation between nationalists and tories, which
they — not we — have to settle. If we meet on Tuesday 12th to
choose a Speaker, so far as I can learn, regular business will not
begin before the 19th. By the 12th we shall have given ourselves
a much better chance of knowing how the two parties stand together; and there will be plenty of time for our consultations.
Thus at least I map out the time; pray give me any comments
you think required.

I begged you to keep Derby informed; would you kindly do the same with Harcourt? Rosebery goes to London to-morrow.

Two days before this resistance to the request for a meeting, he had written to Lord Granville with an important enclosure : —

December 26, 1885. — I have put down on paper in a memorandum as well as I can, the possible forms of the question which may have to be decided at the opening of the session. I went over the ground in conversation with you, and afterwards with R. Grosvenor, and I requested R. Grosvenor, who was going to London, to speak to Hartington in that sense. After his recent act of publication, I should not like to challenge him by sending him the written paper. Please, however, to send it on to Spencer, who will send it back to me.

The memorandum itself must here be quoted, for it sets out in form, succinct, definite, and exhaustive, the situation as Mr. Gladstone at that time regarded it : —

Secret.   *Hawarden Castle, Chester, Dec.* 26, 1885.

1. Government should act.

2. Nationalists should support them in acting.

3. I have done what I can to bring about (1). I am confident the nationalists know my desire. They also publicly know there can be no plan from me in the present circumstances.

4. If (1) and (2) come about, we, who are half the House of Commons, may under the circumstances be justified in waiting for the production of a plan.

5. This would be in every sense the best situation.

6. But if ministers refuse to take up the question — or if from their not actually taking it up, or on any grounds, the nationalists publicly dissolve their alliance with them, the government then have a party of 250 in the face of 420, and in the face of 335 who were elected to oppose them.

7. The basis of our system is that the ministry shall have the confidence of the House of Commons. The exception is, when it is about to appeal to the people. The rule applies most strongly when an election has just taken place. Witness 1835, 1841, 1859,

and the *three* last elections, after each of which the rule has been acted upon, silent inference standing instead of a vote.

8. The present circumstances warrant, I think, an understanding as above, between ministers and the nationalists; but not one between us and the nationalists.

9. If from any cause the alliance of the tories and nationalists which did exist, and presumably does exist, should be known to be dissolved, I do not see how it is possible for what would then be the liberal majority to shrink from the duty appertaining to it as such, and to leave the business of government to the 250 men whom it was elected to oppose.

10. This looks towards an amendment to the Address, praying her Majesty to choose ministers possessed of the confidence of the House of Commons.

11. Which under the circumstances should, I think, have the sanction of a previous meeting of the party.

12. An attempt would probably be made to traverse the proceeding by drawing me on the Irish question.

13. It is impossible to justify the contention that *as a condition previous* to asserting the right and duty of a parliamentary majority, the party or the leaders should commit themselves on a measure about which they can form no final judgment, until by becoming the government they can hold all the necessary communications.

14. But in all likelihood jealousy will be stronger than logic; and to obviate such jealousy, it might be right for me [to go] to the very farthest allowable point.

15. The case supposed is, the motion made — carried — ministers resign — Queen sends for me.

Might I go so far as to say at the first meeting that in the case supposed, I should only accept the trust if assured of the adequate, that is of the general, support of the party to a plan of duly guarded home rule ?

16. If that support were withheld, it would be my duty to stand aside.

17. In that event it would, I consider, become the duty of that portion of the party, which was not prepared to support me in an effort to frame a plan of duly guarded home rule, to form a government itself if invited by the Queen to do so.

18. With me the Irish question would of course remain paramount; but preferring a liberal government without an adequate Irish measure to a tory government similarly lacking, such a liberal government would be entitled to the best general support I could give it.

The reference of this memorandum to Lords Granville and Spencer was regarded as one of the first informal steps towards a consultation of leaders. On receiving Lord Spencer's reply on the point of procedure Mr. Gladstone wrote to him (December 30) : —

To Lord Spencer.

I understand your idea to be that inasmuch as leaders of the party are likely to be divided on the subject of a bold Irish measure, and a divergence might be exhibited in a vote on the Address, it may be better to allow the tory government, with 250 supporters in a house of 670, to assume the direction of the session and continue the administration of imperial affairs. I do not undervalue the dangers of the other course. But let us look at this one —

1. It is an absolute novelty.

2. Is it not a novelty which strikes at the root of our parliamentary government ? under which the first duty of a majority freshly elected, according to a uniform course of precedent and a very clear principle, is to establish a government which has its confidence.

3. Will this abdication of primary duty avert or materially postpone the (apprehended) disruption of the party ? Who can guarantee us against an Irish or independent amendment to the Address ? The government must in any case produce at once their Irish plan. What will have been gained by waiting for it ? The Irish will know three things — (1) That I am conditionally in favour of at least examining their demand. (2) That from the nature of the case, I must hold this question paramount to every interest of party. (3) That a part, to speak within bounds, of the liberal party will follow me in this respect. Can it be supposed that in these circumstances they will long refrain, or possibly refrain at all ? With their knowledge of possibilities behind them,

dare they long refrain ? An immense loss of dignity in a great crisis of the empire would attend the forcing of our hands by the Irish or otherwise. There is no necessity for an instant decision. My desire is thoroughly to shake up all the materials of the question. The present leaning of my mind is to consider the faults and dangers of abstention greater than those of a more decided course. Hence, in part, my great anxiety that the present government should move. Please send this on to Granville.

Finding Mr. Gladstone immovable at Hawarden, four of the members of the last liberal cabinet of both wings met at Devonshire House on New Year's day. All, save one, found themselves hopeless, especially after the Hawarden revelations, as to the possibility of governing Ireland by mere repression. Lord Hartington at once communicated the desires of the conclave for information of his views and designs. Mr. Gladstone replied (January 2, 1886) : —

On the 17th December I communicated to you *all* the opinions I had formed on the Irish question. But on the 21st you published in the *Times* a re-affirmation of opposite opinions. On the Irish question, I have not a word to add to that letter. I am indeed doing what little the pressure of correspondence permits, to prepare myself by study and reflection. My object was to facilitate study by you and others — I cannot say it was wholly gained. But I have done nothing, and shall do nothing, to convert those opinions into intentions, for I have not the material before me. I do not know whether my 'postulate' is satisfied. . . . I have taken care by my letter of the 17th that you should know my opinions *en bloc*. You are quite welcome to show it, if you think fit, to those whom you met. But Harcourt has, I believe, seen it, and the others, if I mistake not, know the substance. . . . There is no doubt that a very grave situation is upon us, a little sooner or a little later. All my desire and thought was how to render it less grave, for next to the demands of a question far higher than all or any party interests, is my duty to labour for the consolidation of the party. . . . Pray show this letter, if you think fit, to those on whose behalf you write. I propose to be available in London about 4 P.M., for any who wish to see me.

V

Signals and intimations were not wholly wanting from
the Irish camp. It was known among the subalterns in that
rather impenetrable region, partly by the light of nature,
partly by the indiscretions of dubiously accredited ambassadors, that Mr. Gladstone was not disposed on any terms to
meet the Irish demand by more coercion. For the liberal
party as a whole the Irish had a considerable aversion. The
violent scenes that attended the Coercion bill of 1881, the
interchange of hard words, the suspensions, the imprisonments — all mechanically acquiesced in by the ministerial
majority — had engendered both bitterness and contempt.
The Irishmen did not conceal the satisfaction with which
they saw the defeat of some of those liberals who had
openly gloated over their arrests and all the rest of their
humiliations. Mr. Gladstone, it is true, had laid a heavy
and chastening hand upon them. Yet, even when the
struggle had been fiercest, with the quick intuition of a
people long oppressed, they detected a note of half-sym-
pathetic passion which convinced them that he would be
their friend if he could, and would help them when he might.

Mr. Parnell was not open to impressions of this order. He
had a long memory for injuries, and he had by no means
satisfied himself that the same injuries might not recur.
As soon as the general election was over, he had at once
set to work upon the result. Whatever might be right for
others, his line of tactics was plain — to ascertain from which
of the two English parties he was most likely to obtain the
response that he desired to the Irish demand, and then to
concert the procedure best fitted to place that party in
power. He was at first not sure whether Lord Salisbury
would renounce the Irish alliance after it had served the
double purpose of ousting the liberals from office, and then
reducing their numbers at the election. He seems also to
have counted upon further communications with Lord
Carnarvon, and this expectation was made known to Mr.
Gladstone, who expressed his satisfaction at the news, though
it was also made known to him that Mr. Parnell doubted

Lord Carnarvon's power to carry out his unquestionably
favourable dispositions. He at the same time very naturally
did his best to get some light as to Mr. Gladstone's own
frame of mind. If neither party would offer a solution of the
problem of Irish government, Mr. Parnell would prefer to
keep the tories in office, as they would at least work out
gradually a solution of the problems of Irish land. To all
these indirect communications Mr. Gladstone's consistent
reply was that Mr. Parnell's immediate business was with
the government of the day, first, because only the government could handle the matter; second, because a tory
government with the aid that it would receive from liberals,
might most certainly, safely, and quickly settle it. He
declined to go beyond the ground already publicly taken by
him, unless by way of a further public declaration. On to
this new ground he would not go, until assured that the
government had had a fair opportunity given them.

By the end of December Mr. Parnell decided that there
was not the slightest possibility of any settlement being
offered by the conservatives under the existing circumstances. ' Whatever chance there was,' he said, ' disappeared
when the seemingly authoritative statements of Mr. Gladstone's intention to deal with the question were published.'
He regarded it as quite probable that in spite of a direct
refusal from the tories, the Irish members might prefer to
pull along with them, rather than run the risk of fresh
coercion from the liberals, should the latter return to power.
' Supposing,' he argued, ' that the liberals came into office,
and that they offered a settlement of so incomplete a character that we could not accept it, or that owing to defections
they could not carry it, should we not, if any long interval
occurred before the proposal of a fresh settlement, incur considerable risk of further coercion?' At any rate, they had
better keep the government in, rather than oust them in
order to admit Lord Hartington or Mr. Chamberlain with a
new coercion bill in their pockets.

Foreseeing these embarrassments, Mr. Gladstone wrote in
a final memorandum (December 24) of this eventful year,
' I used every effort to obtain a clear majority at the election,

and failed.   I am therefore at present a man in chains.   Will
ministers bring in a measure ?   If " Aye," I see my way.   If
" No " : that I presume puts an end to all relations of confidence between nationalists and tories.   If that is done, I
have then upon me, as is evident, the responsibilities of
the leader of a majority.   But what if neither Aye nor No can
be had — will the nationalists then continue their support
and thus relieve me from responsibility, or withdraw their
support [from the government] and thus change essentially
my position?   Nothing but a public or published dissolution
of a relation of amity publicly sealed could be of any avail.'

So the year ended.

CHAPTER IV

FALL OF THE FIRST SALISBURY GOVERNMENT

(*January 1886*)

HISTORIANS coolly dissect a man's thoughts as they please; and label them like specimens in a naturalist's cabinet. Such a thing, they argue, was done for mere personal aggrandizement; such a thing for national objects; such a thing from high religious motives. In real life we may be sure it was not so. — GARDINER.

MINISTERS meanwhile hesitated, balanced, doubted, and wavered. Their party was in a minority, and so they had a fair plea for resigning and not meeting the new parliament. On the other hand, they had a fair plea for continuing in office, for though they were in a minority, no other party had a majority. Nobody knew what the Hartington whigs would do, or what the Irish would do. There seemed to be many chances for expert angling. Then with what policy were they to meet the House of Commons? They might adhere to the conciliatory policy of the summer and autumn, keep clear of repressive legislation, and make a bold attempt in the direction of self-government. Taking the same courageous plunge as was taken by Wellington and Peel in 1829, by Peel in the winter of 1845, by Disraeli in 1867, they might carry the declarations made by Lord Carnarvon on behalf of the government in July to their only practical conclusion. But then they would have broken up their party, as Wellington and Peel broke it up; and Lord Salisbury may have asked himself whether the national emergency warranted the party risk.

Resistance then to the Irish demand being assumed, various tactics came under review. They might begin by asking for a vote of confidence, saying plainly that if they were turned out and Mr. Gladstone were put in, he would propose home rule. In that case a majority was not wholly impossible, for the whig wing might come over, nor was it quite certain that the Irish would help to put the government out. At any rate the debate would force Mr. Gladstone into the open, and even if they did not have a majority, they would be in a position to advise immediate dissolution on the issue of home rule.

The only other course open to the cabinet was to turn their backs upon the professions of the summer; to throw overboard the Carnarvon policy as a cargo for which there was no longer a market; to abandon a great experiment after a ludicrously short trial; and to pick up again the old instrument of coercion, which not six months before they had with such elaborate ostentation condemned and discarded. This grand manœuvre was kept carefully in the background, until there had been time for the whole chapter of accidents to exhaust itself, and it had become certain that no trump cards were falling to the ministerial hand. Not until this was quite clear, did ministers reveal their poignant uneasiness about the state of Ireland.

In the middle of October (1885) Lord Randolph Churchill visited the viceroy in Dublin, and found him, as he afterwards said, extremely anxious and alarmed at the growing power of the National League. Yet the viceroy was not so anxious and alarmed as to prevent Lord Randolph from saying at Birmingham a month after, on November 20, that up to the present time their decision to preserve order by the same laws as in England had been abundantly justified, and that on the whole crime and outrage had greatly diminished. This was curious, and shows how tortuous was the crisis. Only a fortnight later the cabinet met (December 2), and heard of the extraordinary development and unlimited resources of the league. All the rest of the month of December, — so the public were by and by informed, — the condition of Ireland was the subject of the most anxious consideration. With great deliberation, a decision was at length reached. It was that ordinary law had broken down, and that exceptional means of repression were indispensable. Then a

serious and embarrassing incident occurred. Lord Carnarvon 'threw up the government of Ireland,' and was
followed by Sir William Hart Dyke, the chief secretary.[1] A
measure of coercion was prepared, its provisions all drawn
in statutory form, but who was to warrant the necessity for
it to parliament?[2]

Though the viceroy's retirement was not publicly known
until the middle of January, yet so early as December 17 the
prime minister had applied to Mr. Smith, then secretary of
state for war, to undertake the duties of Irish government.[3]
This was one of the sacrifices that no man of public spirit can
ever refuse, and Mr. Smith, who had plenty of public spirit,
became Irish secretary. Still when parliament assembled
more than a month after Lord Salisbury's letter to his new
chief secretary, no policy was announced. Even on the
second night of the session Mr. Smith answered questions
for the war office. The parliamentary mystification was
complete. Who, where, and what was the Irish government?

The parliamentary session was rapidly approaching, and
Mr. Gladstone had good information of the various quarters
whence the wind was blowing. Rumours reached him
(January 9) from the purlieus of Parliament Street, that
general words of confidence in the government would be
found in the Queen's Speech. Next he was told of the
report that an amendment would be moved by the ultras of
law and order, — the same who had mutinied on the Maamtrasna debate, — censuring ministers for having failed to
uphold the authority of the Queen. The same correspondent (January 15), who was well able to make his words
good, wrote to Mr. Gladstone that even though home
rule might perhaps not be in a parliamentary sense before
the House, it was in a most distinct manner before the
country, and no political party could avoid expressing an
opinion upon it. On the same day another colleague of
hardly less importance drew attention to an article in a

[1] Correspondence between Lord
Salisbury and Lord Carnarvon, *Times*,
Jan. 16, 1886.
[2] *Hans.* 302, pp. 1929-1993, March
4, 1886. See also Lord Randolph
Churchill at Paddington, Feb. 13,
1886.
[3] Maxwell's *Life of W. H. Smith*,
ii. p. 163.

journal supposed to be inspired by Lord Randolph, to the effect that conciliation in Ireland had totally failed, that Lord Carnarvon had retired because that policy was to be reversed and he was not the man for the rival policy of vigour, and finally, that the new policy would probably be announced in the Queen's Speech; in no circumstances would it be possible to avoid a general action on the Address.

II

The current of domestic life at Hawarden, in the midst of all these perplexities, flowed in its usual ordered channels. The engagement of his second daughter stirred Mr. Gladstone's deepest interest. He practised occasional woodcraft with his sons, though ending his seventy-sixth year. He spends a morning in reviewing his private money affairs, the first time for three years. He never misses church. He corrects the proofs of an article on Huxley; carries on tolerably profuse correspondence, coming to very little; he works among his books, and arranges his papers; reads Beaconsfield's *Home Letters*, Lord Stanhope's *Pitt*, Macaulay's *Warren Hastings*, which he counts the most brilliant of all that illustrious man's performances; Maine on *Popular Government; King Solomon's Mines;* something of Tolstoy; Dicey's *Law of the Constitution*, where a chapter on semi-sovereign assemblies made a deep impression on him in regard to the business that now absorbed his mind. Above all, he nearly every day reads Burke: '*December* 18. — Read Burke; what a magazine of wisdom on Ireland and America. *January* 9. — Made many extracts from Burke — *sometimes almost divine.*'[1] We may easily imagine how the heat from that profound and glowing furnace still further inflamed strong purposes and exalted resolution in Mr. Gladstone. The Duke of Argyll wrote to say that he was sorry to hear of the study of Burke: 'Your *perfervidum ingenium Scoti* does not need being touched with a live coal from that Irish altar. Of course your reference to Burke indicates a tendency to

[1] If this seems hyperbole, let the reader remember an entry in Macaulay's diary : 'I have now finished reading again most of Burke's works. Admirable! The greatest man since Milton.' Trevelyan's *Life*, ii. p. 377.

compare our position as regards Ireland to the position of George III. towards the colonies. I deny that there is any parallelism or even analogy.' It was during these months that he renewed his friendly intercourse with Cardinal Manning, which had been suspended since the controversy upon the Vatican pamphlets. In November Mr. Gladstone sent Manning his article on the ' Dawn of Creation.' The cardinal thanked him for the paper — ' still more for your words, which revive the memories of old days. Fifty-five years are a long reach of life in which to remember each other. We have twice been parted, but as the path declines, as you say, it narrows, and I am glad that we are again nearing each other as we near our end. . . . If we cannot unite in the realm where " the morning stars sang together " we should be indeed far off.' Much correspondence followed on the articles against Huxley. Then his birthday came : —

Postal deliveries and other arrivals were seven hundred. Immeasurable kindness almost overwhelmed us. There was also the heavy and incessant weight of the Irish question, which offers daily phases more or less new. It was a day for intense thankfulness, but, alas, not for recollection and detachment. When will that day come ? Until then, why string together the commonplaces and generalities of great things, really unfelt ? . . . I am certain there is one keen and deep desire to be extricated from the life of contention in which a chain of incidents has for the last four years detained me against all my will. Then, indeed, I should reach an eminence from which I could look before and after. But I know truly that I am not worthy of this liberty with which Christ makes free his elect. In his own good time, something, I trust, will for me too be mercifully devised.

III

At the end of this long travail, which anybody else would have found all the sorer for the isolation and quietude that it was ever Mr. Gladstone's fashion in moments of emergency to seek, he reached London on January 11th ; two days later he took the oath in the new parliament, whose life was destined to be so short ; and then he found himself on the edge of the whirlpool. Three days before formalities were over, and the House assembled for the despatch of business, he received a communication that much perturbed him, and shed an ominous light on the prospect of liberal unity. This communication he described to Lord Granville : —

21 Carlton House Terrace, Jan. 18, 1886. — Hartington writes to me a letter indicating the possibility that on Thursday, while I announce with reasons a policy of silence and reserve, he may feel it his duty to declare his determination 'to maintain the legislative union,' that is to proclaim a policy (so I understand the phrase) of absolute resistance without examination to the demand made by Ireland through five-sixths of her members. This is to play the tory game with a vengeance. They are now, most rashly not to say more, working the Irish question to split the liberal party.

It seems to me that if a gratuitous declaration of this kind is made, it must produce an explosion ; and that in a week's time Hartington will have to consider whether he will lead the liberal party himself, or leave it to chaos. He will make my position impossible. When, in conformity with the wishes expressed to me, I changed my plans and became a candidate at the general election, my motives were two. The *first,* a hope that I might be able to contribute towards some pacific settlement of the Irish question. The *second,* a desire to prevent the splitting of the party, of which there appeared to be an immediate danger. The second object has thus far been attained. But it may at any moment be lost, and the most disastrous mode of losing it perhaps would be that now brought into view. It would be certainly opposed to my convictions and determination, to attempt to lead anything like a home rule opposition, and to make this subject — the strife of nations — the dividing line between parties. This being so, I do not see how I could as leader survive a gratuitous declaration of opposition to me such as Hartington appears to meditate. If he still meditates it, ought not the party to be previously informed ?

Pray, consider whether you can bring this subject before him, less invidiously than I. I have explained to you and I believe to him, and I believe you approve, my general idea, that we ought

not to join issue with the government on what is called home
rule (which indeed the social state of Ireland may effectually
thrust aside for the time); and that still less ought we to join
issue among ourselves, if we have a choice, unless and until we
are called upon to consider whether or not to take the government. I for one will have nothing to do with ruining the party
if I can avoid it.

This letter discloses with precision the critical state of
facts on the eve of action being taken. Issue was not
directly joined with ministers on home rule; no choice was
found to exist as to taking the government; and this
brought deep and long-standing diversities among the
liberal leaders to the issue that Mr. Gladstone had strenuously laboured to avoid from the beginning of 1885 to
the end.

IV

The Irish paragraphs in the speech from the throne
(January 21, 1886) were abstract, hypothetical, and vague.
The sovereign was made to say that during the past year
there had been no marked increase of serious crime, but there
was in many places a concerted resistance to the enforcement
of legal obligations, and the practice of intimidation continued
to exist. 'If,' the speech went on, 'as my information leads
me to apprehend, the existing provisions of the law should
prove to be inadequate to cope with these growing evils, I
look with confidence to your willingness to invest my government with all necessary powers.' There was also an abstract paragraph about the legislative union between the two
islands.

In a fragment composed in the autumn of 1897, Mr. Gladstone has described the anxiety with which he watched the
course of proceedings on the Address : —

I had no means of forming an estimate how far the bulk of the
liberal party could be relied on to support a measure of home
rule, which should constitute an Irish parliament subject to the
supremacy of the parliament at Westminster. I was not sanguine
on this head. Even in the month of December, when rumours of
my intentions were afloat, I found how little I could reckon on a

general support. Under the circumstances I certainly took upon myself a grave responsibility. I attached value to the acts and language of Lord Carnarvon, and the other favourable manifestations. Subsequently we had but too much evidence of a deliberate intention to deceive the Irish, with a view to their support at the election. But in the actual circumstances I thought it my duty to encourage the government of Lord Salisbury to settle the Irish question, so far as I could do this by promises of my personal support. Hence my communication with Mr. Balfour, which has long been in the hands of the public.

It has been unreasonably imputed to me, that the proposal of home rule was a bid for the Irish vote. But my desire for the adjustment of the question by the tories is surely a conclusive answer. The fact is that I could not rely upon the collective support of the liberals; but I could and did rely upon the support of so many of them as would make the success of the measure certain, in the event of its being proposed by the tory administration. It would have resembled in substance the liberal support given to Roman catholic emancipation in 1829, and the repeal of the corn laws in 1846. Before the meeting of parliament, I had to encounter uncomfortable symptoms among my principal friends, of which I think —— was the organ.

I was, therefore, by no means eager for the dismissal of the tory government, though it counted but 250 supporters out of 670, as long as there were hopes of its taking up the question, or at all events doing nothing to aggravate the situation.

When we came to the debate on the Address I had to face a night of extreme anxiety. The speech from the throne referred in a menacing way to Irish disturbances, and contained a distinct declaration in support of the legislative union. On referring to the clerks at the table to learn in what terms the Address in reply to the speech was couched, I found it was a 'thanking' address, which did not commit the House to an opinion. What I dreaded was lest some one should have gone back to the precedent of 1833, when the Address in reply to the speech was virtually made the vehicle of a solemn declaration in favour of the Act of Union.[1]

[1] In 1833 the King's Speech represented the state of Ireland in words that might be used at the present time, and expressed confidence that parliament would entrust the King with 'such additional powers

Home rule, rightly understood, altered indeed the terms of the Act
of Union, but adhered to its principle, which was the supremacy
of the imperial parliament. Still [it] was pretty certain that any
declaration of a substantive character, at the epoch we had now
reached, would in its moral effect shut the doors of the existing
parliament against home rule.

In a speech of pronounced clearness, Mr. Arthur Elliot endeavoured to obtain a movement in this direction. I thought it would
be morally fatal if this tone were extensively adopted on the liberal
side; so I determined on an effort to secure reserve for the time,
that our freedom might not be compromised. I, therefore, ventured upon describing myself as an 'old parliamentary hand,' and
in that capacity strongly advised the party to keep its own
counsel, and await for a little the development of events. Happily
this counsel was taken; had it been otherwise, the early formation
of a government favourable to home rule would in all likelihood
have become an impossibility. For although our Home Rule bill
was eventually supported by more than 300 members, I doubt
whether, if the question had been prematurely raised on the night
of the Address, as many as 200 would have been disposed to act
in that sense.

In the debate on the Address the draft Coercion bill
reposing in the secret box was not mentioned. Sir Michael
Hicks Beach, the leader of the House, described the mischiefs
then afoot, and went on to say that whether they could be
dealt with by ordinary law, or would require exceptional
powers, were questions that would receive the new chief
secretary's immediate attention.[1] Parliament was told that

as may be necessary for punishing the
disturbers of the public peace and for
preserving and strengthening the
legislative union between the two
countries, which with your support
and under the blessing of divine Providence I am determined to maintain
by all the means in my power.'
The Address in answer assured his
Majesty that his confidence should
not be disappointed, and that 'we
shall be ready to entrust to H.M. such
additional measures, etc., for preserving and strengthening the legislative
union which we have determined,'
etc. This was the address that Mr.

O'Connell denounced as a 'bloody
and brutal address,' and he moved as
an amendment that the House do
resolve itself into a committee of the
whole House to consider of an humble
address to his Majesty. Feb. 8.
Amendment negatived, Ayes being
428, Noes 40. — *Memo.* by Sir T. E.
May for Mr. Gladstone, Jan. 18,
1886. O'Connell, that is to say, did
not move an amendment in favour of
repeal, but proposed the consideration of the Address in committee of
the whole House.

[1] *Hans.* 302, p. 128.

the minister had actually gone to Ireland to make anxious inquiry into these questions. Mr. Smith arrived in Dublin at six o'clock on the morning of January 24, and he quitted it at six o'clock on the evening of the 26th. He was sworn in at the Castle in the forenoon of that day.[1] His views must have reached the cabinet in London not later than the morning of the 26th. Not often can conclusions on such a subject have been ripened with such electrifying precocity.

'I intend to reserve my own freedom of action,' Mr. Gladstone said; 'there are many who have taken their seats for the first time upon these benches, and I may avail myself of the privilege of old age to offer a recommendation. I would tell them of my own intention to keep my counsel and reserve my own freedom, until I see the moment and the occasion when there may be a prospect of public benefit in endeavouring to make a movement forward, and I will venture to recommend them, as an old parliamentary hand, to do the same.'[2] Something in this turn of phrase kindled lively irritation, and it drew bitter reproaches from more than one of the younger whigs. The angriest of these remonstrances was listened to from beginning to end without a solitary cheer from the liberal benches. The great bulk of the party took their leader's advice. Of course the reserve of his speech was as significant of Irish concession, as the most open declaration would have been. Yet there was no rebellion. This was felt by ministers to be a decisive omen of the general support likely to be given to Mr. Gladstone's supposed policy by his own party. Mr. Parnell offered some complimentary remarks on the language of Mr. Gladstone, but he made no move in the direction of an amendment. The public outside looked on with stupefaction. For two or three days all seemed to be in suspense. But the two ministerial leaders in the Commons knew how to read the signs. What Sir Michael

[1] Lord Carnarvon left Ireland on Jan. 28, and Lord Justices were then appointed. But the lawyers seem to hold that there cannot be Lord Justices without a viceroy, and Lord Carnarvon was therefore technically viceroy out of the kingdom (of Ireland), until Lord Aberdeen was sworn in upon Feb. 10, 1886. He must, accordingly, have signed the minute appointing Mr. Smith chief secretary, though of course Mr. Smith had gone over to reverse the Carnarvon policy.

[2] *Hans.* 302, p. 112.

Hicks Beach and Lord Randolph foresaw, for one thing was an understanding between Mr. Gladstone and the Irishmen, and for another, they foresaw the acquiescence of the mass of the liberals. This twofold discovery cleared the ground for a decision. After the second night's debate ministers saw that the only chance now was to propose coercion. Then it was that the ephemeral chief secretary had started on his voyage for the discovery of something that had already been found.

V

On the afternoon of the 26th, the leader of the House gave notice that two days later the new Irish secretary would ask leave to introduce a bill dealing with the National League, with intimidation, and with the protection of life, property, and public order. This would be followed by a bill dealing with land, pursuing in a more extensive sense the policy of the Ashbourne Act of the year before. The great issue was thus at last brought suddenly and nakedly into view. When the Irish secretary reached Euston Square on the morning of the 27th, he found that his government was out.

The crucial announcement of the 26th of January compelled a prompt determination, and Mr. Gladstone did not shrink. A protest against a return to coercion as the answer of the British parliament to the extraordinary demonstration from Ireland, carried with it the responsibility of office, and this responsibility Mr. Gladstone had resolved to undertake.

The determining event of these transactions, — he says in the fragment already cited, — was the declaration of the government that they would propose coercion for Ireland. This declaration put an end to all the hopes and expectations associated with the mission of Lord Carnarvon. Not perhaps in mere logic, but practically, it was now plain that Ireland had no hope from the tories. This being so, my rule of action was changed at once, and I determined on taking any and every legitimate opportunity to remove the existing government from office. Immediately on making up my mind about the rejection of the government, I went to call upon Sir William Harcourt and informed him as to my intentions and the grounds of them. He said, 'What! Are you prepared to go forward without either Hartington or Chamberlain?' I answered, 'Yes.' I believe it was in my mind to say, if I did not actually say it, that I was prepared to go forward without anybody. That is to say without any known and positive assurance of support. This was one of the great imperial occasions which call for such resolutions.

An amendment stood upon the notice-paper in the name of Mr. Collings, regretting the omission from the speech of measures for benefiting the rural labourer; and on this motion an immediate engagement was fought. Time was important. An exasperating debate on coercion with obstruction, disorder, suspensions, would have been a damning prologue to any policy of accommodation. The true significance of the motion was not concealed. On the agrarian aspect of it, the only important feature was the adhesion of Mr. Gladstone, now first formally declared, to the policy of Mr. Chamberlain. The author of the agrarian policy fought out once more on the floor of the House against Lord Hartington and Mr. Goschen the battle of the platform. It was left for Sir Michael Hicks Beach to remind the House that, whatever the honest mover might mean, the rural labourer had very little to do with the matter, and he implored the gentlemen in front of him to think twice and thrice before they committed the future of this country to the gravest dangers that ever awaited it.

The debate was not prolonged. The discussion opened shortly before dinner, and by one o'clock the division was taken. The government found itself in a minority of 79. The majority numbered 331, composed of 257 liberals and 74 Irish nationalists. The ministerialist minority was 252, made up of 234 tories and 18 liberals. Besides the fact that Lord Hartington, Mr. Goschen, and Sir Henry James voted with ministers, there was a still more ominous circumstance. No fewer than 76 liberals were absent, including among them the imposing personality of Mr. Bright. In a memorandum written for submission to the Queen a few days later, Mr. Gladstone said, 'I must express my personal con-

viction that had the late ministers remained in office and proceeded with their proposed plan of repression, and even had
that plan received my support, it would have ended in a disastrous parliamentary failure.'[1]

The next day (Jan. 28) ministers of course determined to
resign. A liberal member of parliament was overtaken by
Lord Randolph on the parade ground, walking away from the
cabinet. 'You look a little pensive,' said the liberal. 'Yes;
I was thinking. I have plenty to think of. Well, we are
out, and you are in.' 'I suppose so,' the liberal replied, 'we
are in for six months; we dissolve; you are in for six years.'
'Not at all sure,' said Lord Randolph; 'let me tell you one
thing most solemnly and most surely: the conservative party
are not going to be made the instrument of the Irish for
turning out Mr. Gladstone, if he refuses repeal.' 'Nobody,'
observed the sententious liberal, 'should so often as the politician say the prayer not to be led into temptation. Remember your doings last summer.'

---

[1] Mr. Gladstone was often taunted with having got in upon the question of allotments, and then throwing the agricultural labourer overboard. 'The proposition,' he said, 'is not only untrue but ridiculous. If true, it would prove that Lord Grey in 1830 came in upon the pension list, and Lord Derby in 1852 on the militia. . . . For myself, I may say personally that I made my public declaration on behalf of allotments in 1832, when Mr. Jesse Collings was just born.'—To Mr. C. A. Fyffe, May 6, 1890.

CHAPTER V

THE NEW POLICY

(1886)

In reason all government without the consent of the governed is
the very definition of slavery; but in fact eleven men well armed
will certainly subdue one single man in his shirt. . . . Those who
have used to cramp liberty have gone so far as to resent even
the liberty of complaining; although a man upon the rack was
never known to be refused the liberty of roaring as loud as he
thought fit. — JONATHAN SWIFT.

BOOK
IX.

1886.
THE tory government was defeated in the sitting of Tuesday (Jan. 26). On Friday, 'at a quarter after midnight, in
came Sir H. Ponsonby, with verbal commission from her
Majesty, which I at once accepted.'[1] The whole of Saturday
was spent in consultations with colleagues. On Sunday, Mr.
Gladstone records, 'except church, my day from one to
eight was given to business. I got only fragmentary reading of the life of the admirable Mr. Suckling and other
books. At night came a painful and harassing succession of
letters, and my sleep for once gave way; yet for the soul it
was profitable, driving me to the hope that the strength of
God might be made manifest in my weakness.' On Monday,
Feb. 1, he went to attend the Queen. 'Off at 9.10 to Osborne.
Two audiences: an hour and half in all. Everything good
in the main points. Large discourse upon Ireland in particular. Returned at 7¾. I kissed hands and am thereby prime
minister for the third time. But, as I trust, for a brief time
only. Slept well, *D.G.*'

The first question was, how many of his colleagues in the
liberal cabinet that went out of office six months before,
would now embark with him in the voyage into stormy and
unexplored seas. I should suppose that no such difficulties

[1] *Diary.*

had ever confronted the attempt at making a cabinet since Canning's in 1827.

Mr. Gladstone begins the fragment from which I have already quoted with a sentence or two of retrospect, and then proceeds : —

In 1885 (I think) Chamberlain had proposed a plan accepted by Parnell (and supported by me) which, without establishing in Ireland a national parliament, made very considerable advances towards self-government. It was rejected by a small majority of the cabinet — Granville said at the time he would rather take home rule. Spencer thought it would introduce confusion into executive duties.

On the present occasion a full half of the former ministers declined to march with me. Spencer and Granville were my main supports. Chamberlain and Trevelyan went with me, their basis being that we were to seek for some method of dealing with the Irish case other than coercion. What Chamberlain's motive was I do not clearly understand. It was stated that he coveted the Irish secretaryship. . . . To have given him the office would at that time have been held to be a declaration of war against the Irish party.

Selborne nibbled at the offer, but I felt that it would not work, and did not use great efforts to bring him in.[1] . . .

When I had accepted the commission, Ponsonby brought me a message from the Queen that she hoped there would not be any Separation in the cabinet. The word had not at that time acquired the offensive meaning in which it has since been stereotyped by the so-called unionists; and it was easy to frame a reply in general but strong words. I am bound to say that at Osborne in the course of a long conversation, the Queen was frank and free, and showed none of the 'armed neutrality,' which as far as I know has been the best definition of her attitude in the more recent years towards a liberal minister. Upon the whole, when I look back upon 1886, and consider the inveterate sentiment of hostility flavoured with contempt towards Ireland, which has from time

[1] 'When the matter was finally adjusted by Chamberlain's retirement, we had against us — Derby, Northbrook, Carlingford, Selborne, Dodson, Chamberlain, Hartington, Trevelyan, Bright ; and for — Granville, Spencer, Kimberley, Ripon, Rosebery, Harcourt, Childers, Lefevre, Dilke (unavailable).' Mr. Goschen was not in the cabinet of 1880.

immemorial formed the basis of English tradition, I am much
more disposed to be thankful for what we then and afterwards
accomplished, than to murmur or to wonder at what we did not.

What Mr. Gladstone called the basis of his new government was set out in a short memorandum, which he read to
each of those whom he hoped to include in his cabinet:
'I propose to examine whether it is or is not practicable
to comply with the desire widely prevalent in Ireland, and
testified by the return of eighty-five out of one hundred and
three representatives, for the establishment by statute of a
legislative body to sit in Dublin, and to deal with Irish
as distinguished from imperial affairs; in such a manner
as would be just to each of the three kingdoms, equitable
with reference to every class of the people of Ireland, conducive to the social order and harmony of that country,
and calculated to support and consolidate the unity of the
empire on the continued basis of imperial authority and
mutual attachment.'

No definite plan was propounded or foreshadowed, but only
the proposition that it was a duty to seek a plan. The
cynical version was that a cabinet was got together on the
chance of being able to agree. To Lord Hartington, Mr.
Gladstone applied as soon as he received the Queen's commission. The invitation was declined on reasoned grounds
(January 30). Examination and inquiry, said Lord Hartington, must mean a proposal. If no proposal followed inquiry,
the reaction of Irish disappointment would be severe, as it
would be natural. His adherence, moreover, would be of
little value. He had already, he observed, in the government of 1880 made concessions on other subjects that might
be thought to have shaken public confidence in him; he
could go no further without destroying that confidence
altogether. However that might be, he could not depart
from the traditions of British statesmen, and he was opposed
to a separate Irish legislature. At the same time he concluded, in a sentence afterwards pressed by Mr. Gladstone on
the notice of the Queen: 'I am fully convinced that the alternative policy of governing Ireland without large concessions

to the national sentiment, presents difficulties of a tremendous character, which in my opinion could now only be
faced by the support of a nation united by the consciousness that the fullest opportunity had been given for the production and consideration of a conciliatory policy.'

A few days later (February 5) Lord Hartington wrote:
'I have been told that I have been represented as having
been in general agreement with you on your Irish policy,
and having been prevented joining your government solely
by the declarations which I made to my constituents; and
as not intending to oppose the government even on home
rule. On looking over my letter I think that the general
intention is sufficiently clear, but there is part of one sentence
which, taken by itself, might be understood as committing me
beyond what I intended or wished. The words I refer to are
those in which I say that it may be possible for me as a
private member to prevent obstacles being placed in the way
of a fair trial being given to the policy of the new government. But I think that the commencement of the sentence
in which these words occur sufficiently reserves my liberty,
and that the whole letter shows that what I desire is that the
somewhat undefined declarations which have hitherto been
made should now assume a practical shape.' [1]

The decision was persistently regarded by Mr. Gladstone as
an important event in English political history. With a small
number of distinguished individual exceptions, it marked
the withdrawal from the liberal party of the aristocratic
element. Up to a very recent date this had been its governing element. Until 1868, the whig nobles and their connections held the reins and shaped the policy. After the
accession of a leader from outside of the caste in 1868, when
Mr. Gladstone for the first time became prime minister, they
continued to hold more than their share of the offices, but

---

[1] A few weeks later, Lord Hartington said on the point of Mr. Gladstone's consistency: 'When I look
back to the declarations that Mr.
Gladstone made in parliament, which
have not been infrequent; when I
look back to the increased definite-
ness given to these declarations in
his address to the electors of Midlothian and in his Midlothian speeches;
when I consider all these things, I
feel that I have not, and that no one
has, any right to complain of the
declaration that Mr. Gladstone has
recently made.'—Speech at the Eighty
Club, March 5, 1886.

in cabinet they sank to the position of what is called a moderating force. After 1880 it became every day more clear that even this modest function was slipping away. Lord Hartington found that the moderating force could no longer moderate. If he went on, he must make up his mind to go under the Caudine forks once a week. The significant reference, among his reasons for not joining the new ministry, to the concessions that he had made in the last government for the sake of party unity, and to his feeling that any further moves of the same kind for the same purpose would destroy all public confidence in him, shows just as the circumstances of the election had shown, and as the recent debate on the Collings amendment had shown, how small were the chances, quite apart from Irish policy, of uniting whig and radical wings in any durable liberal government.

Mr. Goschen, who had been a valuable member of the great ministry of 1868, was invited to call, but without hopes that he would rally to a cause so startling; the interview, while courteous and pleasant, was over in a very few minutes. Lord Derby, a man of still more cautious type, and a rather recent addition to the officers of the liberal staff, declined, not without good nature. Lord Northbrook had no faith in a new Irish policy, and his confidence in his late leader had been shaken by Egypt. Most lamented of all the abstentions was the honoured and trusted name of Mr. Bright.

Mr. Trevelyan agreed to join, in the entirely defensible hope that they 'would knock the measure about in the cabinet, as cabinets do,' and mould it into accord with what had until now been the opinion of most of its members.[1] Mr. Chamberlain, who was destined to play so singular and versatile a part in the eventful years to come, entered the cabinet with reluctance and misgiving. The Admiralty was first proposed to him and was declined, partly on the ground that the chief of the fighting and spending departments was not the post for one who had just given to domestic reforms the paramount place in his stirring addresses to

[1] *Hans.* 304, p. 1106.

the country. Mr. Chamberlain, we may be sure, was not much concerned about the particular office. Whatever its place in the hierarchy, he knew that he could trust himself to make it as important as he pleased, and that his weight in the cabinet and the House would not depend upon the accident of a department. Nobody's position was so difficult. He was well aware how serious a thing it would be for his prospects, if he were to join a confederacy of his arch enemies, the whigs, against Mr. Gladstone, the commanding idol of his friends, the radicals. If, on the other hand, by refusing to enter the government he should either prevent its formation or should cause its speedy overthrow, he would be left planted with a comparatively ineffective group of his own, and he would incur the deep resentment of the bulk of those with whom he had hitherto been accustomed to act.

All these were legitimate considerations in the mind of a man with the instinct of party management. In the end he joined his former chief. He made no concealment of his position. He warned the prime minister that he did not believe it to be possible to reconcile conditions as to the security of the empire and the supremacy of parliament, with the establishment of a legislative body in Dublin. He declared his own preference for an attempt to come to terms with the Irish members on the basis of a more limited scheme of local government, coupled with proposals about land and about education. At the same time, as the minister had been good enough to leave him unlimited liberty of judgment and rejection, he was ready to give unprejudiced examination to more extensive proposals.[1] Such was Mr. Chamberlain's excuse for joining. It is hardly so intelligible as Lord Hartington's reasons for not joining. For the new government could only subsist by Irish support. That support notoriously depended on the concession of more than a limited scheme of local government. The administration would have been overthrown in a week, and to form a cabinet on such a basis as was here proposed would be the idlest experiment that ever was tried.

The appointment of the writer of these pages to be Irish

[1] January 30, 1886. *Hans.* 304, p. 1185.

secretary was at once generally regarded as decisive of Mr.
Gladstone's ultimate intention, for during the election and
afterwards I had spoken strongly in favour of a colonial type
of government for Ireland.   It was rightly pressed upon Mr.
Gladstone by at least one of his most experienced advisers,
that such an appointment to this particular office would
be construed as a declaration in favour of an Irish parliament, without any further examination at all.[1]   And so, in
fact, it was generally construed.

Nobody was more active in aiding the formation of the
new ministry than Sir William Harcourt, in whose powerful
composition loyalty to party and conviction of the value of
party have ever been indestructible instincts.   ' I must not
let the week absolutely close,' Mr. Gladstone wrote to him
from Mentmore (February 6), ' without emphatically thanking you for the indefatigable and effective help which you
have rendered to me during its course, in the difficult work
now nearly accomplished.'

At the close of the operation, he writes from Downing
Street to his son Henry, then in India : —

February 12, 1886.   You see the old date has reappeared at the
head of my letter.   The work last week was extremely hard from
the mixture of political discussions on the Irish question, by way
of preliminary condition, with the ordinary distribution of offices,
which while it lasts is of itself difficult enough.

Upon the whole I am well satisfied with its composition.   It is

[1] As for the story of my being concerned in Mr. Gladstone's conversion to home rule, it is, of course,
pure moonshine.   I only glance at it
because in politics people are ready
to believe anything.   At the general
election of 1880, I had declined to
support home rule.   In the press,
however, I had strenuously opposed
the Forster Coercion bill of the
following winter, as involving a
radical misapprehension of the nature
and magnitude of the case.   In
the course of that controversy, arguments pressed themselves forward
which led much further than mere
resistance to the policy of coercion.   Without having had the advantage of any communication whatever with Mr. Gladstone upon Irish
subjects for some years before, I had
still pointed out to my constituents
at Newcastle in the previous November, that there was nothing in Mr.
Gladstone's electoral manifesto to
prevent him from proposing a colonial
plan for Ireland, and I had expressed
my own conviction that this was the
right direction in which to look.   A
few days before the fall of the tory
government, I had advocated the
exclusion of Irish members from
Westminster, and the production of
measures dealing with the land. —
Speech at Chelmsford, January 7,
1886.

not a bit more radical than the government of last year; perhaps a little less. And we have got some good young hands, which please me very much. Yet short as the Salisbury government has been, it would not at all surprise me if this were to be shorter still, such are the difficulties that bristle round the Irish question. But the great thing is to be right; and as far as matters have yet advanced, I see no reason to be apprehensive in this capital respect. I have framed a plan for the land and for the finance of what must be a very large transaction. It is necessary to see our way a little on these at the outset, for, unless these portions of anything we attempt are sound and well constructed, we cannot hope to succeed. On the other hand, if we fail, as I believe the late ministers would have failed even to pass their plan of repressive legislation, the consequences will be deplorable in every way. There seems to be no doubt that some, and notably Lord R. Churchill, fully reckoned on my failing to form a government.[1]

II

The work pressed, and time was terribly short. The new ministers had barely gone through their re-elections before the opposition began to harry them for their policy, and went so far, before the government was five weeks old, as to make the extreme motion for refusing supply. Even if the opposition had been in more modest humour, no considerable delay could be defended. Social order in Ireland was in a profoundly unsatisfactory phase. That

---

[1] The cabinet was finally composed as follows: —

Mr. Gladstone, ...	*First lord of the treasury.*
Lord Herschell, . . .	*Lord chancellor.*
Lord Spencer, ...	*President of council.*
Sir W. Harcourt, . . .	*Chancellor of exchequer.*
Mr. Childers, ...	*Home secretary.*
Lord Rosebery, . . .	*Foreign* "
Lord Granville, . . .	*Colonial* "
Lord Kimberley, . . .	*Indian* "
Mr. Campbell-Bannerman, .	*War* "
Lord Ripon, ...	*Admiralty.*
Mr. Chamberlain, . . .	*Local government.*
Mr. Morley, ...	*Irish secretary.*
Mr. Trevelyan, ...	*Scotch secretary.*
Mr. Mundella, ...	*Board of trade.*

The Lord chancellor, Mr. C.-Bannerman, Mr. Mundella, and myself now sat in cabinet for the first time. After the two resignations at the end of March, Mr. Stansfeld came in as head of the Local government board, and we sat with the ominous number of thirteen at table.

fact was the starting-point of the reversal of policy which the government had come into existence to carry out. You cannot announce a grand revolution, and then beg the world to wait. The very reason that justified the policy commanded expedition. Anxiety and excitement were too intense out of doors for anything but a speedy date, and it was quite certain that if the new plan were not at once propounded, no other public business would have much chance.

The new administration did not meet parliament until after the middle of February, and the two Irish bills, in which their policy was contained, were ready by the end of the first week of April. Considering the enormous breadth and intricacy of the subjects, the pressure of parliamentary business all the time, the exigencies of administrative work in the case of at least one of the ministers principally concerned, and the distracting atmosphere of party perturbation and disquiet that daily and hourly harassed the work, the despatch of such a task within such limits of time was at least not discreditable to the industry and concentration of those who achieved it. I leave it still open to the hostile critic to say, as Molière's Alceste says of the sonnet composed in a quarter of an hour, that time has nothing to do with the business.

All through March Mr. Gladstone laboured in what he called 'stiff conclaves' about finance and land, attended drawing rooms, and 'observed the variations of H.M.'s *accueils*'; had an audience of the Queen, 'very gracious, but avoided serious subjects'; was laid up with cold, and the weather made Sir Andrew Clark strict; then rose up to fresh grapples with finance and land and untoward colleagues, and all the 'inexorable demands of my political vocation.' His patience and self-control were as marvellous as his tireless industry. Sorely tried by something or another at a cabinet, he enters, — 'Angry with myself for not bearing it better. I ought to have been thankful for it all the time.' On a similar occasion, a junior colleague showed himself less thankful than he should have been for purposeless antagonism. 'Think of it as discipline,' said Mr.

Gladstone. 'But why,' said the unregenerate junior, 'should
we grudge the blessings of discipline to some other people?'
Mr. Gladstone was often blamed even by Laodiceans
among his supporters, not wise but foolish after the event,
because he did not proceed by way of resolution, instead of
by bill. Resolutions, it was argued, would have smoothed the
way. General propositions would have found readier access
to men's minds. Having accepted the general proposition,
people would have found it harder to resist the particular
application. Devices that startled in the precision of a
clause, would in the vagueness of a broad and abstract
principle have soothed and persuaded. Mr. Gladstone was
perfectly alive to all this, but his answer to it was plain.
Those who eventually threw out the bill would insist on
unmasking the resolution. They would have exhausted all
the stereotyped vituperation of abstract motions. They
would have ridiculed any general proposition as mere plati-
tude, and pertinaciously clamoured for working details.
What would the resolution have affirmed? The expediency
of setting up a legislative authority in Ireland to deal with
exclusively Irish affairs. But such a resolution would
be consistent equally with a narrow scheme on the one
hand, such as a plan for national councils, and a broad
scheme on the other, giving to Ireland a separate exchequer,
separate control over customs and excise, and practically
an independent and co-ordinate legislature.[1] How could the
government meet the challenge to say outright whether they
intended broad or narrow? Such a resolution could hardly
have outlived an evening's debate, and would not have postponed the evil day of schism for a single week.

Precedents lent no support. It is true that the way was
prepared for the Act of Union in the parliament of Great
Britain, by the string of resolutions moved by Mr. Pitt in
the beginning of 1799. But anybody who glances at them,
will at once perceive that if resolutions on their model had
been framed for the occasion of 1886, they would have covered
the whole ground of the actual bill, and would instantly have

[1] See Mr. Chamberlain's speech,   Also Lord Hartington at Bradford,
June 1, 1886. *Hans.* 306, p. 677.   May 18, 1886.

raised all the formidable objections and difficulties exactly
as the bill itself raised them.   The Bank Charter Act of
1833 was founded on eight resolutions, and they also set
forth in detail the points of the ministerial plan.[1]   The
renewal of the East India Company's charter in the same
year went on by way of resolutions, less abundant in particulars than the Bank Act, but preceded by correspondence
and papers which had been exhaustively canvassed and discussed.[2]   The question of Irish autonomy was in no position
of that sort.

The most apt precedent in some respects is to be found
on a glorious occasion, also in the year 1833.   Mr. Stanley
introduced the proposals of his government for the emancipation of the West Indian slaves in five resolutions.   They
furnished a key not only to policy and general principles,
but also to the plan by which these were to be carried out.[3]
Lord Howick followed the minister at once, raising directly
the whole question of the plan.   Who could doubt that Lord
Hartington would now take precisely the same course towards
Irish resolutions of similar scope?   The procedure on the
India bill of 1858 was just as little to the point.   The general
disposition of the House was wholly friendly to a settlement of the question of Indian government by the existing ministry.   No single section of the opposition wished to
take it out of their hands, for neither Lord Russell nor the
Peelites nor the Manchester men, and probably not even
Lord Palmerston himself, were anxious for the immediate
return of the last-named minister to power.   Who will
pretend that in the House of Commons in February 1886,
anything at all like the same state of facts prevailed?   As
for the resolutions in the case of the Irish church, they
were moved by Mr. Gladstone in opposition, and he thought
it obvious that a policy proposed in opposition stands on a
totally different footing from a policy laid before parliament
on the responsibility of a government, and a government
bound by every necessity of the situation to prompt action.[4]

---

[1] June 1, 1833.   *Hans.* 18, p. 186.
[2] June 13, 1833.   *Ibid.* p. 700.
[3] May 14, 1833.   *Hans.* 17, p. 1230.
[4] There is also the case of the

Reform bill of 1867.   Disraeli laid
thirteen resolutions on the table.
Lowe and Bright both agreed in
urging that the resolutions should be

At a later stage, as we shall see, it was actually proposed that a vote for the second reading of the bill should be taken to mean no more than a vote for its principle. Every one of the objections that instantly sprang out of their ambush against this proposal would have worked just as much mischief against an initial resolution. In short, in opening a policy of this difficulty and extent, the cabinet was bound to produce to parliament not merely its policy but its plan for carrying the policy out. By that course only could parliament know what it was doing. Any other course must have ended in a mystifying, irritating, and barren confusion, alike in the House of Commons and in the country.[1]

The same consideration that made procedure by resolution unadvisable told with equal force within the cabinet. Examination into the feasibility of some sort of plan was most rapidly brought to a head by the test of a particular plan. It is a mere fable of faction that a cast iron policy was arbitrarily imposed upon the cabinet ; as matter of fact, the plan originally propounded did undergo large and radical modifications.

The policy as a whole shaped itself in two measures. First, a scheme for creating a legislative body, and defining its powers ; second, a scheme for opening the way to a settlement of the land question, in discharge of an obligation of honour and policy, imposed upon this country by its active share in all the mischiefs that the Irish land system had produced. The introduction of a plan for dealing with the land was not very popular even among ministers, but it was pressed by Lord Spencer and the Irish secretary, on the double ground that the land was too burning a question to be left where it then stood, and next that it was unfair to a new and untried legislature in Ireland to find itself confronted by such a question on the very threshold.

The plan was opened by Mr. Gladstone in cabinet on

dropped and the bill at once printed. A meeting of liberal members at Mr. Gladstone's house unanimously resolved to support an amendment setting aside the resolutions. Disraeli at once abandoned them.

[1] Lord Hartington's argument on the second reading shows how a resolution would have fared. *Hans.* 305, p. 610.

March 13th, and Mr. Chamberlain and Mr. Trevelyan at once wished to resign. He remonstrated in a vigorous correspondence. ' I have seen many and many a resignation,' he said, ' but never one based upon the intentions, nay the immature intentions, of the prime minister, and on a pure intuition of what may happen. Bricks and rafters are prepared for a house, but are not themselves a house.' The evil hour was postponed, but not for long. The Cabinet met again a few days later (March 26) and things came to a sharp issue. The question was raised in a sufficiently definite form by the proposition from the prime minister for the establishment of a statutory body sitting in Dublin with legislative powers. No difficulty was made about the bare proposition itself. Every one seemed to go as far as that. It needed to be tested, and tests were at once forthcoming. Mr. Trevelyan could not assent to the control of the immediate machinery of law and order being withdrawn from direct British authority, among other reasons because it was this proposal that created the necessity for buying out the Irish landlords, which he regarded as raising a problem absolutely insoluble.[1] Mr. Chamberlain raised four points. He objected to the cesser of Irish representation ; he could not consent to the grant of full rights of taxation to Ireland ; he resisted the surrender of the appointment of judges and magistrates ; and he argued strongly against proceeding by enumeration of the things that an Irish government might not do, instead of by a specific delegation of the things that it might do.[2] That these four objections were not in themselves incapable of accommodation was shown by subsequent events. The second was very speedily, and the first was ultimately allowed, while the fourth was held by good authority to be little more than a question of drafting. Even the third was not a point either way on which to break up a government, destroy a policy, and split a party. But everybody who is acquainted with either the great or the small conflicts of human history, knows how little the mere terms of a principle or of an objection are to be trusted as a clue either to its practical significance, or

[1] *Hans.* 304, p. 1116.   [2] *Hans.* 304, p. 1190.

to the design with which it is in reality advanced. The CHAP.

design here under all the four heads of objection, was the V.

dwarfing of the legislative body, the cramping and con- Æt. 77.

striction of its organs, its reduction to something which

the Irish could not have even pretended to accept, and

which they would have been no better than fools if they

had ever attempted to work.

Some supposed then, and Mr. Chamberlain has said since,

that when he entered the cabinet room on .this memorable

occasion, he intended to be conciliatory. Witnesses of the

scene thought that the prime minister made little attempt

in that direction. Yet where two men of clear mind and

firm will mean two essentially different things under the

same name, whether autonomy or anything else, and each

intends to stand by his own interpretation, it is childish to

suppose that arts of deportment will smother or attenuate

fundamental divergence, or make people who are quite

aware how vitally they differ, pretend that they entirely

agree. Mr. Gladstone knew the giant burden that he had

taken up, and when he went to the cabinet of March 26, his

mind was no doubt fixed that success, so hazardous at best,

would be hopeless in face of personal antagonisms and

bitterly divided counsels. This, in his view, and in his

own phrase, was one of the 'great imperial occasions' that

call for imperial resolves. The two ministers accordingly

resigned.

Besides these two important secessions, some ministers

out of the cabinet resigned, but they were of the whig

complexion.[1] The new prospect of the whig schism extend-

ing into the camp of the extreme radicals created natural

alarm but hardly produced a panic. So deep were the roots

of party, so immense the authority of a veteran leader. It

used to be said of the administration of 1880, that the world

would never really know Mr. Gladstone's strength in par-

liament and the country, until every one of his colleagues

[1] Faint hopes were nourished that Mr. Bright might be induced to join, but there was unfortunately no ground for them. Mr. Whitbread was invited, but preferred to lend staunch and important support outside. Lord Dalhousie, one of the truest hearts that ever was attracted to public life, too early lost to his country, took the Scottish secretaryship, not in the cabinet.

had in turn abandoned him to his own resources. Certainly the secessions of the end of March 1886 left him undaunted. Every consideration of duty and of policy bound him to persevere. He felt, justly enough, that a minister who had once deliberately invited his party and the people of the three kingdoms to follow him on so arduous and bold a march as this, had no right on any common plea to turn back until he had exhausted every available device to 'bring the army of the faithful through.'

III

From the first the Irish leader was in free and constant communication with the chief secretary. Proposals were once or twice made, not I think at Mr. Parnell's desire, for conversations to be held between Mr. Gladstone and himself, but they were always discouraged by Mr. Gladstone, who was never fond of direct personal contentions, or conversations when the purpose could be as well served otherwise, and he had a horror of what he called multiplying channels of communication. 'For the moment,' he replied, 'I think we may look to Mr. M. alone, and rely on all he says for accuracy as well as fidelity. I have been hard at work, and to-day I mean to have a further and full talk with Mr. M., who will probably soon after wish for some renewed conversation with Mr. Parnell.' Mr. Parnell showed himself acute, frank, patient, closely attentive, and possessed of striking though not rapid insight. He never slurred over difficulties, nor tried to pretend that rough was smooth. On the other hand, he had nothing in common with that desperate species of counsellor, who takes all the small points, and raises objections instead of helping to contrive expedients. He measured the ground with a slow and careful eye, and fixed tenaciously on the thing that was essential at the moment. Of constructive faculty he never showed a trace. He was a man of temperament, of will, of authority, of power; not of ideas or ideals, or knowledge, or political maxims, or even of the practical reason in any of its higher senses, as Hamilton, Madison, and Jefferson had practical reason. But he knew what he wanted.

He was always perfectly ready at this period to acquiesce in Irish exclusion from Westminster, on the ground that they would want all the brains they had for their own parliament. At the same time he would have liked a provision for sending a delegation to Westminster on occasion, with reference to some definite Irish questions such as might be expected to arise. As to the composition of the upper or protective order in the Irish parliament, he was wholly unfamiliar with the various utopian plans that have been advanced for the protection of minorities, and he declared himself tolerably indifferent whether the object should be sought in nomination by the crown, or through a special and narrower elective body, or by any other scheme. To such things he had given no thought. He was a party chief, not a maker of constitutions. He liked the idea of both orders sitting in one House. He made one significant suggestion : he wished the bill to impose the same disqualification upon the clergy as exists in our own parliament. But he would have liked to see certain ecclesiastical dignitaries included by virtue of their office in the upper or protective branch. All questions of this kind, however, interested him much less than finance. Into financial issues he threw himself with extraordinary energy, and he fought for better terms with a keenness and tenacity that almost baffled the mighty expert with whom he was matched. They only met once during the weeks of the preparation of the bill, though the indirect communication was constant. Here is my scanty note of the meeting : —

April 5. — Mr. Parnell came to my room at the House at 8.30, and we talked for two hours. At 10.30 I went to Mr. Gladstone next door, and told him how things stood. He asked me to open the points of discussion, and into my room we went. He shook hands cordially with Mr. Parnell, and sat down between him and me. We at once got to work. P. extraordinarily close, tenacious, and sharp. It was all finance. At midnight, Mr. Gladstone rose in his chair and said, 'I fear I must go; I cannot sit as late as I used to do.' 'Very clever, very clever,' he muttered to me as I held open the door of his room for him. I returned to Parnell, who went on repeating his points in his impenetrable way, until the policeman mercifully came to say the House was up.

Mr. Gladstone's own note must also be transcribed: —

April 5. — Wrote to Lord Spencer. The Queen and ministers. Four hours on the matter for my speech. 1½ hours with Welby and Hamilton on the figures. Saw Lord Spencer, Mr. Morley, Mr. A. M. H. of C., 5-8. Dined at Sir Thomas May's.

1½ hours with Morley and Parnell on the root of the matter; rather too late for me, 10½-12. A hard day. (*Diary.*)

On more than one financial point the conflict went perilously near to breaking down the whole operation. 'If we do not get a right budget,' said Mr. Parnell, 'all will go wrong from the very first hour.' To the last he held out that the just proportion of Irish contribution to the imperial fund was not one-fourteenth or one-fifteenth, but a twentieth or twenty-first part. He insisted all the more strongly on his own more liberal fraction, as a partial compensation for their surrender of fiscal liberty and the right to impose customs duties. Even an hour or two before the bill was actually to be unfolded to the House, he hurried to the Irish office in what was for him rather an excited state, to make one more appeal to me for his fraction. It is not at all improbable that if the bill had gone forward into committee, it would have been at the eleventh hour rejected by the Irish on this department of it, and then all would have been at an end. Mr. Parnell never concealed this danger ahead.

In the cabinet things went forward with such ups and downs as are usual when a difficult bill is on the anvil. In a project of this magnitude, it was inevitable that some minister should occasionally let fall the consecrated formula that if this or that were done or not done, he must reconsider his position. Financial arrangements, and the protection of the minority, were two of the knottiest points, — the first from the contention raised on the Irish side, the second from misgiving in some minds as to the possibility of satisfying protestant sentiment in England and Scotland. Some kept the colonial type more strongly in view than others, and the bill no doubt ultimately bore that cast.

The draft project of surrendering complete taxing-power to the Irish legislative body was eventually abandoned. It was soon felt that the bare possibility of Ireland putting duties on British goods — and it was not more than a bare possibility in view of Britain's position as practically Ireland's only market — would have destroyed the bill in every manufacturing and commercial centre in the land. Mr. Parnell agreed to give up the control of customs, and also to give up direct and continuous representation at Westminster. On this cardinal point of the cesser of Irish representation, Mr. Gladstone to the last professed to keep an open mind, though to most of the cabinet, including especially three of its oldest hands and coolest heads, exclusion was at this time almost vital. Exclusion was favoured not only on its merits. Mr. Bright was known to regard it as large compensation for what otherwise he viewed as pure mischief, and it was expected to win support in other quarters generally hostile. So in truth it did, but at the cost of support in quarters that were friendly. On April 30, Mr. Gladstone wrote to Lord Granville, 'I scarcely see how a cabinet could have been formed, if the inclusion of the Irish members had been insisted on; and now I do not see how the scheme and policy can be saved from shipwreck, if the exclusion is insisted on.'

The plan was bound to be extensive, as its objects were extensive, and it took for granted in the case of Ireland the fundamental probabilities of civil society. He who looks with 'indolent and kingly gaze' upon all projects of written constitutions need not turn to the Appendix unless he will. Two features of the plan were cardinal.

The foundation of the scheme was the establishment in Ireland of a domestic legislature to deal with Irish as distinguished from imperial affairs. It followed from this that if Irish members and representative peers remained at Westminster at all, though they might claim a share in the settlement of imperial affairs, they could not rightly control English or Scotch affairs. This was from the first, and has ever since remained, the Gordian knot. The cabinet on a review of all the courses open determined to propose the

plan of total exclusion, save and unless for the purpose of
revising this organic statute.

The next question was neither so hard nor so vital.
Ought the powers of the Irish legislature to be specifically
enumerated? Or was it better to enumerate the branches
of legislation from which the statutory parliament was to be
shut out? Should we enact the things that they might do,
or the things that they might not do, leaving them the
whole residue of law-making power outside of these exceptions and exclusions? The latter was the plan adopted in
the bill. Disabilities were specified, and everything not so
specified was left within the scope of the Irish authority.
These disabilities comprehended all matters affecting the
crown. All questions of defence and armed force were
shut out; all foreign and colonial relations; the law of
trade and navigation, of coinage and legal tender. The
new legislature could not meddle with certain charters, nor
with certain contracts, nor could it establish or endow any
particular religion.[1]

IV

Among his five spurious types of courage, Aristotle names
for one the man who seems to be brave, only because he
does not see his danger. This, at least, was not Mr. Gladstone's case. No one knew better than the leader in the
enterprise, how formidable were the difficulties that lay in
his path. The giant mass of secular English prejudice
against Ireland frowned like a mountain chain across the
track. A strong and proud nation had trained itself for
long courses of time in habits of dislike for the history, the
political claims, the religion, the temperament, of a weaker
nation. The violence of the Irish members in the last
parliament, sporadic barbarities in some of the wilder portions of the island, the hideous murders in the Park, had all
deepened and vivified the scowling impressions nursed by
large bodies of Englishmen for many ages past about unfortunate Ireland. Then the practical operation of shaping
an Irish constitution, whether on colonial, federal, or any

[1] See Appendix.

other lines, was in itself a task that, even if all external
circumstance had been as smiling as it was in fact the
opposite, still abounded in every kind of knotty, intricate, and
intractable matter.

It is true that elements could be discovered on the other
side.   First, was Mr. Gladstone's own high place in the confidence of great masses of his countrymen, the result of a
lifetime of conspicuous service and achievement.   Next, the
lacerating struggle with Ireland ever since 1880, and the
confusion into which it had brought our affairs, had bred
something like despair in many minds, and they were ready
to look in almost any direction for relief from an intolerable
burden.   Third, the controversy had not gone very far before
opponents were astounded to find that the new policy, which
they angrily scouted as half insanity and half treason, gave
comparatively little shock to the new democracy.   This was
at first imputed to mere ignorance and raw habits of political
judgment.   Wider reflection might have warned them that
the plain people of this island, though quickly roused against
even the shadow of concession when the power or the greatness of their country is openly assailed, seem at the same
time ready to turn to moral claims of fair play, of conciliation, of pacific truce.   With all these magnanimous sentiments the Irish case was only too easily made to associate
itself.   The results of the Irish elections and the force of the
constitutional demand sank deep in the popular mind.   The
grim spectre of Coercion as the other alternative wore its
most repulsive look in the eyes of men, themselves but
newly admitted to full citizenship.   Rash experiment in
politics has been defined as raising grave issues without
grave cause.   Nobody of any party denied in this crisis the
gravity of the cause.

CHAPTER VI

INTRODUCTION OF THE BILL

(*1886*)

Much have I seen and known; cities of men
And manners, climates, councils, governments,
Myself not least, but honour'd of them all. . . .
There lies the port; the vessel puffs her sail;
There gloom the dark broad seas.
— TENNYSON, *Ulysses*.

It was not within the compass either of human effort or
human endurance even for the most practised and skilful
of orators to unfold the whole plan, both government and
land, in a single speech. Nor was public interest at all
equally divided. Irish land had devoured an immense
amount of parliamentary time in late years; it is one of the
most technical and repulsive of all political subjects; and to
many of the warmest friends of Irish self-government, any
special consideration for the owners of Irish land was bitterly
unpalatable. Expectation was centred upon the plan for
general government. This was introduced on April 8. Here
is the entry in the little diary : —

The message came to me this morning: 'Hold thou up my
goings in thy path, that my footsteps slip not.' Settled finally my
figures with Welby and Hamilton; other points with Spencer and
Morley. Reflected much. Took a short drive. H. of C., $4\frac{1}{2}$–$8\frac{1}{4}$.
Extraordinary scenes outside the House and in. My speech, which
I have sometimes thought could never end, lasted nearly $3\frac{1}{2}$ hours.
Voice and strength and freedom were granted to me in a degree
beyond what I could have hoped. But many a prayer had gone
up for me, and not I believe in vain.

No such scene had ever been beheld in the House of
Commons. Members came down at break of day to secure
their places; before noon every seat was marked, and

310

crowded benches were even arrayed on the floor of the
House from the mace to the bar. Princes, ambassadors,
great peers, high prelates, thronged the lobbies. The fame
of the orator, the boldness of his exploit, curiosity as to the
plan, poignant anxiety as to the party result, wonder
whether a wizard had at last actually arisen with a spell
for casting out the baleful spirits that had for so many
ages made Ireland our torment and our dishonour, all these
things brought together such an assemblage as no minister
before had ever addressed within those world-renowned
walls. The parliament was new. Many of its members had
fought a hard battle for their seats, and trusted they were
safe in the haven for half a dozen good years to come.
Those who were moved by professional ambition, those
whose object was social advancement, those who thought
only of upright public service, the keen party men, the men
who aspired to office, the men with a past and the men who
looked for a future, all alike found themselves adrift on
dark and troubled waters. The secrets of the bill had been
well kept. To-day the disquieted host were first to learn
what was the great project to which they would have to say
that Aye or No on which for them and for the state so
much would hang.

Of the chief comrades or rivals of the minister's own
generation, the strong administrators, the eager and accomplished debaters, the sagacious leaders, the only survivor
now comparable to him in eloquence or in influence was
Mr. Bright. That illustrious man seldom came into the
House in those distracted days ; and on this memorable
occasion his stern and noble head was to be seen in dim
obscurity. Various as were the emotions in other regions
of the House, in one quarter rejoicing was unmixed.
There, at least, was no doubt and no misgiving. There
pallid and tranquil sat the Irish leader, whose hard insight,
whose patience, energy, and spirit of command, had achieved
this astounding result, and done that which he had vowed
to his countrymen that he would assuredly be able to do.
On the benches round him, genial excitement rose almost to
tumult. Well it might. For the first time since the union,

the Irish case was at last to be pressed in all its force and strength, in every aspect of policy and of conscience, by the most powerful Englishman then alive.

More striking than the audience was the man ; more striking than the multitude of eager onlookers from the shore was the rescuer with deliberate valour facing the floods ready to wash him down ; the veteran Ulysses, who after more than half a century of combat, service, toil, thought it not too late to try a further ' work of noble note.' In the hands of such a master of the instrument, the theme might easily have lent itself to one of those displays of exalted passion which the House had marvelled at in more than one of Mr. Gladstone's speeches on the Turkish question, or heard with religious reverence in his speech on the Affirmation bill in 1883. What the occasion now required was that passion should burn low, and reasoned persuasion hold up the guiding lamp. An elaborate scheme was to be unfolded, an unfamiliar policy to be explained and vindicated. Of that best kind of eloquence which dispenses with declamation, this was a fine and sustained example. There was a deep, rapid, steady, onflowing volume of argument, exposition, exhortation. Every hard or bitter stroke was avoided. Now and again a fervid note thrilled the ear and lifted all hearts. But political oratory is action, not words, — action, character, will, conviction, purpose, personality. As this eager muster of men underwent the enchantment of periods exquisite in their balance and modulation, the compulsion of his flashing glance and animated gesture, what stirred and commanded them was the recollection of national service, the thought of the speaker's mastering purpose, his unflagging resolution and strenuous will, his strength of thew and sinew well tried in long years of resounding war, his unquenched conviction that the just cause can never fail. Few are the heroic moments in our parliamentary politics, but this was one.

II

The first reading of the bill was allowed to pass without a division. To the second, Lord Hartington moved an amendment in the ordinary form of simple rejection.[1] His two speeches[2] present the case against the policy and the bill in its most massive form. The direct and unsophisticated nature of his antagonism, backed by a personal character of uprightness and plain dealing beyond all suspicion, gave a momentum to his attack that was beyond any effect of dialectics. It was noticed that he had never during his thirty years of parliamentary life spoken with anything like the same power before. The debates on the two stages occupied sixteen nights. They were not 'unworthy of the gravity of the issue, nor of the fame of the House of Commons. Only one speaker held the magic secret of Demosthenic oratory. Several others showed themselves masters of the higher arts of parliamentary discussion. One or two transient spurts of fire in the encounters of orange and green, served to reveal the intensity of the glow behind the closed doors of the furnace. But the general temper was good. The rule against irritating language was hardly ever broken. Swords crossed according to the strict rules of combat. The tone was rational and argumentative. There was plenty of strong, close, and acute reasoning ; there was some learning, a considerable acquaintance both with historic and contemporary, foreign and domestic fact, and when fact and reasoning broke down, their place was abundantly filled by eloquent prophecy of disaster on one side, or blessing on the other. Neither prophecy was demonstrable ; both could be made plausible.

Discussion was adorned by copious references to the mighty shades who had been the glory of the House in a great parliamentary age. We heard again the Virgilian hexameters in which Pitt had described the spirit of his policy at the union : —

> ' Paribus se legibus ambæ
> Invictæ gentes æterna in fœdera mittant.'

We heard once more how Grattan said that union of the legislatures was severance of the nations ; that the ocean

CHAP.
VI.

Æt. 77.

---

[1] First reading, April 13. Motion made for second reading and amendment, May 10. Land bill introduced and first reading, April 16.
[2] April 9, May 10.

forbade union, the channel forbade separation; that England
in her government of Ireland had gone to hell for her principles and to bedlam for her discretion.   There was, above
all, a grand and copious anthology throughout the debate
from Burke, the greatest of Irishmen and the largest master
of civil wisdom in our tongue.

The appearance of a certain measure of the common form
of all debates was inevitable.   No bill is ever brought in of
which its opponents do not say that it either goes too far, or
else it does not go far enough ; no bill of which its defenders
do not say as to some crucial flaw pounced upon and
paraded by the enemy, that after all it is a mere question of
drafting, or can be more appropriately discussed in committee.   There was the usual evasion of the strong points of
the adversary's case, the usual exaggeration of its weak ones.
That is debating.   Perorations ran in a monotonous mould ;
integrity of the empire on one side, a real, happy, and in-
dissoluble reconciliation between English and Irish on the
other.

One side dwelt much on the recall of Lord Fitzwilliam in
1795, and the squalid corruption of the union ; the other, on
the hopeless distraction left by the rebellion of 1798, and
the impotent confusion of the Irish parliament.   One
speaker enumerated Mr. Pitt's arguments for the union —
the argument about the regency and about the commercial
treaty, the argument about foreign alliances and confeder-
acies and the army, about free trade and catholic emancipation ; he showed that under all these six heads the new
bill carefully respected and guarded the grounds taken by
the minister of the union.   He was bluntly answered by
the exclamation that nobody cared a straw about what Mr.
Pitt said, or what Sir Ralph Abercromby said ; what we had
to deal with were the facts of the case in the year 1886.
You show your mistrust of the Irish by inserting all these
safeguards in the bill, said the opposition.   No, replied
ministers ; the safeguards are to meet no mistrusts of ours,
but those entertained or feigned by other people.   You had
no mandate for home rule, said the opposition.   Still less,
ministers retorted, had you a mandate for coercion.

Such a scheme as this, exclaimed the critics, with all
its checks and counterchecks, its truncated functions, its
vetoes, exceptions, and reservations, is degrading to Ireland,
and every Irish patriot with a spark of spirit in his bosom
must feel it so. As if, retorted the defenders, there were
no degradation to a free people in suffering twenty years of
your firm and resolute coercion. One side argued that the
interests of Ireland and Great Britain were much too closely
intertwined to permit a double legislature. The other
argued that this very interdependence was just what made
an Irish legislature safe, because it was incredible that they
should act as if they had no benefit to receive from us, and
no injury to suffer from injury inflicted upon us. Do you,
asked some, blot out of your minds the bitter, incendiary,
and rebellious speech of Irish members ? But do you then,
the rejoinder followed, suppose that the language that came
from men's hearts when a boon was refused, is a clue to the
sentiment in their hearts when the boon shall have been
granted ? Ministers were bombarded with reproachful
quotations from their old speeches. They answered the
fire by taunts about the dropping of coercion, and the
amazing manœuvres of the autumn of 1885. The device of
the two orders was denounced as inconsistent with the
democratic tendencies of the age. A very impressive argument forsooth from you, was the reply, who are either
stout defenders of the House of Lords as it is, or else stout
advocates for some of the multifarious schemes for mixing
hereditary peers with fossil officials, all of them equally
alien to the democratic tendencies whether of this age or
any other. So, with stroke and counter-stroke, was the
ball kept flying.

Much was made of foreign and colonial analogies ; of the
union between Austria and Hungary, Norway and Sweden,
Denmark and Iceland ; how in forcing legislative union on
North America we lost the colonies ; how the union of legislatures ended in the severance of Holland from Belgium.
All this carried little conviction. Most members of parliament like to think with pretty large blinkers on, and though
it may make for narrowness, this is consistent with much

BOOK
IX.

1886.

practical wisdom. Historical parallels in the actual politics of the day are usually rather decorative than substantial. If people disbelieve premisses, nothing can be easier than to ridicule conclusions ; and what happened now was that critics argued against this or that contrivance in the machinery, because they insisted that no machinery was needed at all, and that no contrivance could ever be made to work, because the Irish mechanicians would infallibly devote all their infatuated energy and perverse skill, not to work it, but to break it in pieces. The Irish, in Mr. Gladstone's ironical paraphrase of these singular opinions, had a double dose of original sin ; they belonged wholly to the kingdoms of darkness, and therefore the rules of that probability which wise men have made the guide of life can have no bearing in any case of theirs. A more serious way of stating the fundamental objection with which Mr. Gladstone had to deal was this. Popular government is at the best difficult to work. It is supremely difficult to work in a statutory scheme with limits, reservations, and restrictions lurking round every corner. Finally, owing to history and circumstance, no people in all the world is less fitted to try a supremely difficult experiment in government than the people who live in Ireland. Your superstructure, they said, is enormously heavy, yet you are going to raise it on foundations that are a quaking bog of incapacity and discontent. This may have been a good answer to the policy of the bill. But to criticise its provisions from such a point of view was as inevitably unfruitful as it would be to set a hardened agnostic to revise the Thirty-nine articles or the mystic theses of the Athanasian creed.

On the first reading, Mr. Chamberlain astounded allies and opponents alike by suddenly revealing his view, that the true solution of the question was to be sought in some form of federation. It was upon the line of federation, and not upon the pattern of the self-governing colonies, that we should find a way out of the difficulty.[1] Men could hardly trust their ears. On the second reading, he startled us once more by declaring that he was perfectly prepared, the very

[1] *Hans.* 304, pp. 1204-6.

next day if we pleased, to establish between this country CHAP.
and Ireland the relations subsisting between the provincial VI.
legislatures and the dominion parliament of Canada.[1] As Æt. 77.
to the first proposal, anybody could see that federation was
a vastly more revolutionary operation than the delegation of
certain legislative powers to a local parliament. Moreover
before federating an Irish legislature, you must first create
it. As to the second proposal, anybody could see on turning
for a quarter of an hour to the Dominion Act of 1867, that
in some of the particulars deemed by Mr. Chamberlain to be
specially important, a provincial legislature in the Canadian
system had more unfettered powers than the Irish legislature
would have under the bill. Finally, he urged that inquiry
into the possibility of satisfying the Irish demand should
be carried on by a committee or commission representing
all sections of the House.[2] In face of projects so strangely
fashioned as this, Mr. Gladstone had a right to declare that
just as the subject held the field in the public mind — for
never before had been seen such signs of public absorption
in the House and out of the House — so the ministerial plan
held the field in parliament. It had many enemies, but it
had not a single serious rival.

The debate on the second reading had hardly begun when
Lord Salisbury placed in the hands of his adversaries a
weapon with which they took care to do much execution.
Ireland, he declared, is not one nation, but two nations.
There were races like the Hottentots, and even the Hindoos,
incapable of self-government. He would not place confidence in people who had acquired the habit of using knives
and slugs. His policy was that parliament should enable
the government of England to govern Ireland. 'Apply that
recipe honestly, consistently, and resolutely for twenty years,
and at the end of that time you will find that Ireland will
be fit to accept any gifts in the way of local government or
repeal of coercion laws that you may wish to give her.'[3] In
the same genial vein, Lord Salisbury told his Hottentot
fellow-citizens — one of the two *invictæ gentes* of Mr. Pitt's
famous quotation — that if some great store of imperial

[1] *Hans.* 306, p. 697.   [2] *Hans.* 304, p. 1202.   [3] May 15, 1886.

treasure were going to be expended on Ireland, instead of
buying out landlords, it would be far more usefully employed in providing for the emigration of a million Irishmen.
Explanations followed this inconvenient candour, but explanations are apt to be clumsy, and the pungency of the
indiscretion kept it long alive. A humdrum speaker, who
was able to contribute nothing better to the animation of
debate, could always by insinuating a reference to Hottentots,
knives and slugs, the deportation of a million Irishmen, and
twenty years of continuous coercion, make sure of a roar
of angry protest from his opponents, followed by a lusty
counter-volley from his friends.

V

The· reception of the bill by the organs of Irish opinion
was easy to foretell. The nationalists accepted it in sober
and rational language, subject to amendments on the head
of finance and the constabulary clauses. The tories said it
was a bill for setting up an Irish republic. It is another
selfish English plan, said the moderates. Some Irishmen
who had played with home rule while it was a phrase, drew
back when they saw it in a bill. Others, while holding to
home rule, objected to being reduced to the status of
colonists. The body of home rulers who were protestant was
small, and even against them it was retorted that for every
protestant nationalist there were ten catholic unionists.
The Fenian organs across the Atlantic, while quarrelling
with such provisions as the two orders, 'one of which
would be Irish and the other English,' did justice to the
bravery of the attempt, and to the new moral forces which
it would call out. The florid violence which the Fenians
abandoned was now with proper variations adopted by
Orangemen in the north. The General Assembly of the
presbyterian church in Ireland passed strong resolutions
against a parliament, in favour of a peasant proprietary, in
favour of loyalty, and of coercion. A few days later the
general synod of the protestant episcopal church followed
suit, and denounced a parliament. The Orange print in
Belfast drew up a Solemn League and Covenant for Ulster,

to ignore and resist an Irish national government. Unionist prints in Dublin declared and indignantly repelled ' the selfish English design to get rid of the Irish nuisance from Westminster, and reduce us to the position of a tributary dependency.' [1]

The pivot of the whole policy was the acceptance of the bill by the representatives of Ireland. On the evening when the bill was produced, Mr. Parnell made certain complaints as to the reservation of the control of the constabulary, as to the power of the first order to effect a deadlock, and as to finance. He explicitly and publicly warned the government from the first that, when the committee stage was reached, he would claim a large decrease in the fraction named for the imperial contribution. There was never any dissembling as to this. In private discussion, he had always held that the fair proportion of Irish contribution to imperial charges was not a fifteenth but a twentieth, and he said no more in the House than he had persistently said in the Irish secretary's room. There too he had urged what he also declared in the House : that he had always insisted that due representation should be given to the minority ; that he should welcome any device for preventing ill-considered legislation, but that the provision in the bill, for the veto of the first order, would lead to prolonged obstruction and delay. Subject to modification on these three heads, he accepted the bill. ' I am convinced,' he said in concluding, ' that if our views are fairly met in committee regarding the defects to which I have briefly alluded, — the bill will be cheerfully accepted by the Irish people, and by their representatives, as a solution of the long-standing dispute between the two countries.' [2]

It transpired at a later date that just before the introduction of the bill, when Mr. Parnell had been made acquainted with its main proposals, he called a meeting of eight of his leading colleagues, told them what these proposals were, and asked them whether they would take the

---

[1] See for instance, *Irish Times*, May 8, and *Belfast Newsletter*, May 17, 18, 21, 1886.   [2] *Hans.* 304, p. 1134.   Also 305, p. 1252.

bill or leave it.[1] Some began to object to the absence of certain provisions, such as the immediate control of the constabulary, and the right over duties of customs. Mr. Parnell rose from the table, and clenched the discussion by informing them that if they declined the bill, the government would go. They at once agreed 'to accept it *pro tanto*, reserving for committee the right of enforcing and, if necessary, reconsidering their position with regard to these important questions.' This is neither more nor less than the form in which Mr. Parnell made his declaration in parliament. There was complete consistency between the terms of this declaration, and the terms of acceptance agreed to by his colleagues, as disclosed in the black days of December four years later. The charge of bad faith and hypocrisy so freely made against the Irishmen is wholly unwarranted by a single word in these proceedings. If the whole transaction had been known to the House of Commons, it could not have impaired by one jot or tittle the value set by the supporters of the bill on the assurances of the Irishmen that, in principle and subject to modification on points named, they accepted the bill as a settlement of the question, and would use their best endeavours to make it work.[2]

[1] When the bill was practically settled, he asked if he might have a draft of the main provisions, for communication to half a dozen of his confidential colleagues. After some demur, the Irish secretary consented, warning him of the damaging consequences of any premature divulgation. The draft was duly returned, and not a word leaked out. Some time afterwards Mr. Parnell recalled the incident to me. 'Three of the men to whom I showed the draft were newspaper men, and they were poor men, and any newspaper would have given them a thousand pounds for it. No very wonderful virtue, you may say. But how many of your House of Commons would believe it?'

[2] For this point, see the *Times* report of the famous proceedings in Committee-room Fifteen, collected in the volume entitled *The Parnellite Split* (1891).

CHAPTER VII

THE POLITICAL ATMOSPHERE. DEFEAT OF THE BILL

(*1886*)

EVERYTHING on every side was full of traps and mines. . . . It was
in the midst of this chaos of plots and counterplots . . . that the
firmness of that noble person [Lord Rockingham] was put to the
proof. He never stirred from his ground ; no, not an inch. —
BURKE (1766).

THE atmosphere in London became thick and hot with
political passion. Veteran observers declared that our
generation had not seen anything like it. Distinguished
men of letters and, as it oddly happened, men who had won
some distinction either by denouncing the legislative union,
or by insisting on a decentralisation that should satisfy Irish
national aspirations, now choked with anger because they
were taken at their word. Just like irascible scholars of old
time who settled controversies about corrupt texts by im-
puting to rival grammarians shameful crimes, so these writers
could find no other explanation for an opinion that was
not their own about Irish government, except moral turpi-
tude and personal degradation. One professor of urbanity
compared Mr. Gladstone to a desperate pirate burning his
ship, or a gambler doubling and trebling his stake as luck
goes against him. Such strange violence in calm natures,
such pharisaic pretension in a world where we are all fallen,
remains a riddle. Political differences were turned into
social proscription. Whigs who could not accept the new
policy were specially furious with whigs who could. Great
ladies purified their lists of the names of old intimates.
Amiable magnates excluded from their dinner-tables and
their country houses once familiar friends who had fallen
into the guilty heresy, and even harmless portraits of the

321

heresiarch were sternly removed from the walls. At some of the political clubs it rained blackballs. It was a painful demonstration how thin after all is our social veneer, even when most highly polished.

When a royal birthday was drawing near, the prime minister wrote to Lord Granville, his unfailing counsellor in every difficulty political and social: 'I am becoming seriously perplexed about my birthday dinner. Hardly any peers of the higher ranks will be available, and not many of the lower. Will the seceding colleagues come if they are asked? (Argyll, to whom I applied privately on the score of old friendship, has already *refused* me.) I am for asking them; but I expect refusal. Lastly, it has become customary for the Prince of Wales to dine with me on that day, and he brings his eldest son now that the young Prince is of age. But his position would be very awkward, if he comes and witnesses a great nakedness of the land. What do you say to all this? If you cannot help me, who can?' Most of the seceding colleagues accepted, and the dinner came off well enough, though as the host wrote to a friend beforehand, 'If Harting-ton were to get up and move a vote of want of confidence after dinner, he would almost carry it.' The Prince was unable to be present, and so the great nakedness was by him unseen, but Prince Albert Victor, who was there instead, is described by Mr. Gladstone as 'most kind.'

The conversion of Peel to free trade forty years before had led to the same species of explosion, though Peel had the court strongly with him. Both then and now it was the case of a feud within the bosom of a party, and such feuds like civil wars have ever been the fiercest. In each case there was a sense of betrayal — at least as unreasonable in 1886 as it was in 1846. The provinces somehow took things more rationally than the metropolis. Those who were stunned by the fierce moans of London over the assured de-cline in national honour and credit, the imminence of civil war, and the ultimate destruction of British power, found their acquaintances in the country excited and interested, but still clothed and in their right minds. The gravity of the question was fully understood, but in taking sides ordinary men did not talk as if they were in for the battle of Armageddon. The attempt to kindle the torch of religious fear or hate was in Great Britain happily a failure. The mass of liberal presbyterians in Scotland, and of nonconformists in England and Wales, stood firm, though some of their most eminent and able divines resisted the new project, less on religious grounds than on what they took to be the balance of political arguments. Mr. Gladstone was able to point to the conclusive assurances he had received that the kindred peoples in the colonies and America regarded with warm and fraternal sympathy the present effort to settle the long-vexed and troubled relations between Great Britain and Ireland : —

We must not be discouraged if at home and particularly in the upper ranks of society, we hear a variety of discordant notes, notes alike discordant from our policy and from one another. You have before you a cabinet determined in its purpose and an intelligible plan. I own I see very little else in the political arena that is determined or that is intelligible.

Inside the House subterranean activity was at its height all through the month of May. This was the critical period. The regular opposition spoke little and did little ; with composed interest they watched others do their work. On the ministerial side men wavered and changed and changed again, from day to day and almost from hour to hour. Never were the motions of the pendulum so agitated and so irregular. So novel and complex a problem was a terrible burden for a new parliament. About half its members had not sat in any parliament before. The whips were new, some of the leaders on the front benches were new, and those of them who were most in earnest about the policy were too heavily engrossed in the business of the measure, to have much time for the exercises of explanation, argument, and persuasion with their adherents. One circumstance told powerfully for ministers. The great central organisation of the liberal party came decisively over to Mr. Gladstone (May 5), and was followed by nearly all the local associations in the country. Neither whig secession nor radical dubitation shook the strength inherent in such machinery, in a community where the principle of government by party has solidly established itself. This was almost the single consolidating and steadying element in that hour of dispersion. A serious move in the opposite direction had taken place three weeks earlier. A great meeting was held at the Opera House, in the Haymarket, presided over by the accomplished whig nobleman who had the misfortune to be Irish viceroy in the two dismal years from 1880, and it was attended both by Lord Salisbury on one side and Lord Hartington on the other. This was the first broad public mark of liberal secession, and of that practical fusion between whig and tory which the new Irish policy had actually precipitated, but to which all the signs in the political heavens had been for three or four years unmistakably pointing.

The strength of the friends of the bill was twofold : first, it lay in the dislike of coercion as the only visible alternative ; and second, it lay in the hope of at last touching the firm ground of a final settlement with Ireland. Their weakness was also twofold : first, misgivings about the exclusion of the Irish members ; and second, repugnance to the scheme for land purchase. There were not a few, indeed, who pronounced the exclusion of Irish members to be the most sensible part of the plan. Mr. Gladstone retained his impartiality, but knew that if we proposed to keep the Irishmen, we should be run in upon quite as fiercely from the other side. Mr. Parnell stood to his original position. Any regular and compulsory attendance at Westminster, he said, would be highly objectionable to his friends. Further, the right of Irish members to take part in purely English as well as imperial business would be seized upon by English politicians, whenever it should answer their purpose, as a pretext for interfering in Irish affairs. In short, he foresaw, as all did, the difficulties that would inevitably arise from retention. But the tide ran more and more strongly the other way. Scotland grew rather restive at a proposal which, as she apprehended, would make a precedent for herself when her turn for extension of local powers should come, and Scotchmen had no intention of being shut out

from a voice in imperial affairs. In England, the catholics
professed alarm at the prospect of losing the only catholic
force in the House of Commons. ' We cannot spare one of
you,' cried Cardinal Manning. Some partisans of imperial
federation took it into their heads that the plan for Ireland
would be fatal to a plan for the whole empire, though others
more rationally conceived that if there was to be a scheme
for the empire, schemes for its several parts must come first.
Some sages, while pretending infinite friendship to home
rule, insisted that the parliament at Westminster should
retain a direct and active veto upon legislation at Dublin,
and that Irish members should remain as they were in
London. That is to say, every precaution should be taken
to ensure a stiff fight at Westminster over every Irish
measure of any importance that had already been fought on
College Green. Speaking generally, the feeling against this
provision was due less to the anomaly of taxation without
representation, than to fears for the unity of the empire and
the supremacy of parliament.

The Purchase bill proved from the first to be an almost
intolerable dose. Vivid pictures were drawn of a train of
railway trucks two miles long, loaded with millions of bright
sovereigns, all travelling from the pocket of the British son of
toil to the pocket of the idle Irish landlord. The nationalists
from the first urged that the scheme for home rule should
not be weighted with a land scheme, though they were willing
to accept it so long as it was not used to prejudice the larger
demand. On the other side the Irish landlords themselves
peremptorily rejected the plan that had been devised for
their protection.

The air was thick with suggestions, devices, contrivances,
expedients, possible or madly impossible. Proposals or
embryonic notions of proposals floated like motes in a sunbeam. Those to whom lobby diplomacy is as the breath of
their nostrils, were in their element. So were the worthy
persons who are always ready with ingenious schemes for
catching a vote or two here, at the cost of twenty votes elsewhere. Intrigue may be too dark a word, but coaxing, bullying, managing, and all the other arts of party emergency, went

on at an unprecedented rate.   Of these arts, the supervising angels will hardly record that any section had a monopoly. The legerdemain that makes words pass for things, and liquefies things into words, achieved many flashes of success. But they were only momentary, and the solid obstacles remained.   The foundations of human character are much the same in all historic ages, and every public crisis brings out the same types.

Much depended on Mr. Bright, the great citizen and noble orator, who had in the last five-and-forty years fought and helped to win more than one battle for wise and just government ;   whose constancy had confronted storms of public obloquy without yielding an inch of his ground ;   whose eye for the highest questions of state had proved itself singularly sure ;   and whose simplicity, love of right, and unsophisticated purity of public and private conduct, commanded the trust and the reverence of nearly all the better part of his countrymen.   To Mr. Bright the eyes of many thousands were turned in these weeks of anxiety and doubt.   He had in public kept silence, though in private he made little secret of his disapproval of the new policy.   Before the bill was produced he had a prolonged conversation (March 20) with Mr. Gladstone at Downing Street.   ' Long and weighty ' are the words in the diary.   The minister sketched his general design.   Mr. Bright stated his objections much in the form in which, as we shall see, he stated them later.   Of the exclusion of the Irish members he approved.   The Land bill he thought quite wrong, for why should so enormous an effort be made for one interest only ?   He expressed his sympathy with Mr. Gladstone in his great difficulties, could not but admire his ardour, and came away with the expectation that the obstacles would be found invincible, and that the minister would retire and leave others to approach the task on other lines.   Other important persons, it may be observed, derived at this time a similar impression from Mr. Gladstone's language to them : that he might discern the impossibility of his policy, that he would admit it, and would then hand the responsibility over to Lord Hartington, or whoever else might be willing to face it.

On the other hand, Mr. Bright left the minister himself CHAP.
VII. not without hopes that as things went forward he might count on this potent auxiliary. So late as the middle of Æt. 77. May, though he could not support, it was not certain that he would actively oppose. The following letter to Mr. Glad-stone best describes his attitude at this time : —

Mr. Bright to Mr. Gladstone.

Rochdale, May 13th, 1886.

MY DEAR GLADSTONE, — Your note just received has put me in a great difficulty. To-day is the anniversary of the greatest sorrow of my life, and I feel pressed to spend it at home. I sent a message to Mr. Arnold Morley last evening to say that I did not intend to return to town before Monday next — but I shall now arrange to go to-morrow — although I do not see how I can be of service in the great trouble which has arisen.

I feel outside all the contending sections of the liberal party — for I am not in favour of home rule, or the creation of a Dublin parliament — nor can I believe in any scheme of federation as shadowed forth by Mr. Chamberlain.

I do not believe that with regard to the Irish question 'the resources of civilisation are exhausted'; and I think the plan of your bill is full of complexity, and gives no hope of successful working in Ireland or of harmony between Westminster and Dublin.   I may say that my regard for you and my sympathy with you have made me silent in the discussion on the bills before the House.   I cannot consent to a measure which is so offensive to the whole protestant population of Ireland, and to the whole sentiment of the province of Ulster so far as its loyal and pro-testant people are concerned.   I cannot agree to exclude them from the protection of the imperial parliament.   I would do much to clear the rebel party from Westminster, and I do not sympathise with those who wish to retain them, but admit there is much force in the arguments on this point which are opposed to my views upon it.

Up to this time I have not been able to bring myself to the point of giving a vote in favour of your bills.   I am grieved to have to say this.   As to the Land bill, if it comes to a second reading, I fear I must vote against it.   It may be that my hostility to the rebel party, looking at their conduct since your government was formed six years ago, disables me from taking an impartial view of this great question.   If I could believe them loyal, if they were honourable and truthful men, I could yield them much; but I suspect that your policy of surrender to them will only place more power in their hands, to war with greater effect against the unity of the three kingdoms with no increase of good to the Irish people.

How then can I be of service to you or to the real interests of Ireland if I come up to town ?   I cannot venture to advise you, so superior to me in party tactics and in experienced statesmanship, and I am not so much in accord with Mr. Chamberlain as to make it likely that I can say anything that will affect his course. One thing I may remark, that it appears to me that measures of the gravity of those now before parliament cannot and ought not to be thrust through the House by force of a small majority. The various reform bills, the Irish church bill, the two great land bills, were passed by very large majorities.   In the present case, not only the whole tory party oppose, but a very important section of the liberal party; and although numerous meetings of clubs and associations have passed resolutions of confidence in you, yet generally they have accepted your Irish government bill as a 'basis' only, and have admitted the need of important changes in the bill — changes which in reality would destroy the bill.   Under these circumstances it seems to me that more time should be given for the consideration of the Irish question. Parliament is not ready for it, and the intelligence of the country is not ready for it.   If it be possible, I should wish that no division should be taken upon the bill.   If the second reading should be carried only by a *small* majority, it would not forward the bill ; but it would strengthen the rebel party in their future agitation, and make it more difficult for another session or another parliament to deal with the question with some sense of independence of that party.   In any case of a division, it is I suppose certain that a considerable majority of British members will oppose the bill.   Thus, whilst it will have the support of the rebel members, it will be opposed by a majority from Great Britain and by a most hostile vote from all that is loyal in Ireland.   The result will

be, if a majority supports you it will be one composed in effect
of the men who for six years past have insulted the Queen, have
torn down the national flag, have declared your lord lieutenant
guilty of deliberate murder, and have made the imperial parliament an assembly totally unable to manage the legislative business for which it annually assembles at Westminster.

Pray forgive me for writing this long letter. I need not assure
you of my sympathy with you, or my sorrow at being unable to
support your present policy in the House or the country. The
more I consider the question, the more I am forced in a direction
contrary to my wishes.

For thirty years I have preached justice to Ireland. I am as
much in her favour now as in past times, but I do not think it
justice or wisdom for Great Britain to consign her population,
including Ulster and all her protestant families, to what there is
of justice and wisdom in the Irish party now sitting in the parliament in Westminster.

Still, if you think I can be of service, a note to the Reform
Club will, I hope, find me there to-morrow evening. — Ever most
sincerely yours,   JOHN BRIGHT.

An old parliamentary friend, of great weight and authority, went to Mr. Bright to urge him to support a proposal to read the bill a second time, and then to hang it
up for six months. Bright suffered sore travail of spirit.
At the end of an hour the peacemaker rose to depart.
Bright pressed him to continue the wrestle. After three-
quarters of an hour more of it, the same performance
took place. It was not until a third hour of discussion
that Mr. Bright would let it come to an end, and at the
end he was still uncertain. The next day the friend met
him, looking worn and gloomy. 'You may guess,' Mr.
Bright said, 'what sort of a night I have had.' He had
decided to vote against the second reading. The same person went to Lord Hartington. He took time to deliberate,
and then finally said, 'No; Mr. Gladstone and I do not
mean the same thing.'

II

The centre of interest lay in the course that might be finally taken by those who declared that they accepted the principle of the bill, but demurred upon detail. It was upon the group led from Birmingham that the issue hung. 'There are two principles in the bill,' said Mr. Chamberlain at this time, 'which I regard as vital. The first is the principle of autonomy, to which I am able to give a hearty assent. The second is involved in the method of giving effect to this autonomy. In the bill the government have proceeded on the lines of separation or of colonial independence, whereas, in my humble judgment, they should have adopted the principle of federation as the only one in accordance with democratic aspirations and experience.'[1] He was even so strong for autonomy, that he was ready to face all the immense difficulties of federation, whether on the Canadian or some other pattern, rather than lose autonomy. Yet he was ready to slay the bill that made autonomy possible. To kill the bill was to kill autonomy. To say that they would go to the country on the plan, and not on the principle, was idle. If the election were to go against the government, that would destroy not only the plan which they disliked, but the principle of which they declared that they warmly approved. The new government that would in that case come into existence, would certainly have nothing to say either to plan or principle.

Two things, said Mr. Chamberlain on the ninth night of the debate, had become clear during the controversy. One was that the British democracy had a passionate devotion to the prime minister. The other was the display of a sentiment out of doors, 'the universality and completeness of which, I dare say, has taken many of us by surprise, in favour of some form of home rule to Ireland, which will give to the Irish people some greater control over their own affairs.'[2] It did not need so acute a strategist as Mr. Chamberlain to perceive that the only hope of rallying any

[1] Letter to Mr. T. H. Bolton, M.P. *Times*, May 8, 1886.
[2] *Hans.* 306, p. 698.

considerable portion of the left wing of the party to the dissentient flag, in face of this strong popular sentiment embodied in a supereminent minister, was to avoid as much
as possible all irreconcilable language against either the
minister or the sentiment, even while taking energetic steps
to unhorse the one and to nullify the other.

The prime minister meanwhile fought the battle as a
battle for a high public design once begun should be fought.
He took few secondary arguments, but laboured only to hold
up to men's imagination, and to burn into their understanding, the lines of central policy, the shame and dishonour
from which it would relieve us, the new life with which it
would inspire Ireland, the ease that it would bring to parliament in England. His tenacity, his force and resource, were
inexhaustible. He was harassed on every side. The Irish
leader pressed him hard upon finance. Old adherents urged
concession about exclusion. The radicals disliked the two
orders. Minor points for consideration in committee rained
in upon him, as being good reasons for altering the bill
before it came in sight of committee. Not a single constructive proposal made any way in the course of the debate.
All was critical and negative. Mr. Gladstone's grasp was
unshaken, and though he saw remote bearings and interde-
pendent consequences where others supposed all to be plain
sailing, yet if the principle were only saved he professed
infinite pliancy. He protested that there ought to be no
stereotyping of our minds against modifications, and that
the widest possible variety of modes of action should be
kept open ; and he 'hammered hard at his head,' as he put
it, to see what could be worked out in the way of admitting
Irish members without danger, and without intolerable inconvenience. If anybody considered, he continued to repeat
in endless forms, that there was another set of provisions by
which better and fuller effect could be given to the principle
of the bill, they were free to displace all the particulars that
hindered this better and fuller effect being given to the
principle.[1]

[1] *Hans.* 306, p. 1218.

III

At the beginning of May the unionist computation was that 119 on the ministerial side of the House had, with or without qualification, promised to vote against the second reading. Of these, 70 had publicly committed themselves, and 23 more were supposed to be absolutely certain. If the whole House voted, this estimate of 93 would give a majority of 17 against the bill.[1] The leader of the radical wing, however, reckoned that 55 out of the 119 would vote with him for the second reading, if he pronounced the ministerial amendments of the bill satisfactory. The amendments demanded were the retention of the Irish members, a definite declaration of the supremacy of the imperial parliament, a separate assembly for Ulster, and the abolition of the restrictive devices for the representation of minorities. Less than all this might have been taken in committee, provided that the government would expressly say before the second reading, that they would retain the Irish representation on its existing footing. The repeated offer by ministers to regard this as an open question was derided, because it was contended that if the bill were once safe through its second reading, Mr. Bright and the whigs would probably vote with ministers against Irish inclusion.

Even if this ultimatum had been accepted, there would still have remained the difficulty of the Land bill, of which Mr. Chamberlain had announced that he would move the rejection. In the face of ever-growing embarrassments and importunities, recourse was had to the usual device of a meeting of the party at the foreign office (May 27). The circular calling the meeting was addressed to those liberals who, while retaining full freedom on all particulars in the bill, were 'in favour of the establishment of a legislative body in Dublin for the management of affairs specifically and exclusively Irish.' This was henceforth to be the test of party membership. A man who was for an Irish legislative body was expected to come to the party meeting, and a man who was against it was expected to stay

---

[1] In the end exactly 93 liberals did vote against the bill.

away.   Many thought this discrimination a mistake.   Some
two hundred and twenty members attended.   The pith of
the prime minister's speech, which lasted for an hour, came
to this: that the government would not consent to emascu-
late the principle of the bill, or turn it into a mockery, a
delusion, and a snare; that members who did not wholly
agree with the bill, might still in accordance with the strict
spirit of parliamentary rules vote for the second reading
with a view to its amendment in committee; that such a
vote would not involve support of the Land bill; that he
was ready to consider any plan for the retention of the
Irish members, provided that it did not interfere with the
liberty of the Irish legislative body, and would not introduce
confusion into the imperial parliament.   Finally, as to procedure—and here his anxious audience fell almost breathless
—they could either after a second reading hang up the bill,
and defer committee until the autumn ; or they could wind
up the session, prorogue, and introduce the bill afresh with
the proper amendments in October.   The cabinet, he told
them, inclined to the later course.

Before the meeting Mr. Parnell had done his best to
impress upon ministers the mischievous effect that would
be produced on Irish members and in Ireland, by any
promise to withdraw the bill after the second reading.   On
the previous evening, I received from him a letter of unusual
length.   'You of course,' he said, 'are the best judges of what
the result may be in England, but if it be permitted me to
express an opinion, I should say that withdrawal could
scarcely fail to give great encouragement to those whom it
cannot conciliate, to depress and discourage those who are
now the strongest fighters for the measure, to produce doubt
and wonder in the country and to cool enthusiasm; and
finally, when the same bill is again produced in the autumn,
to disappoint and cause reaction among those who may
have been temporarily disarmed by withdrawal, and to
make them at once more hostile and less easy to appease.'
This letter I carried to Mr. Gladstone the next morning, and
read aloud to him a few minutes before he was to cross over
to the foreign office.   For a single instant—the only occasion

that I can recall during all these severe weeks — his patience broke. The recovery was as rapid as the flash, for he knew the duty of the lieutenant of the watch to report the signs of rock or shoal. He was quite as conscious of all that was urged in Mr. Parnell's letter as was its writer, but perception of risks on one side did not overcome risks on the other. The same evening they met for a second time : —

May 27. — . . . Mr. Gladstone and Parnell had a conversation in my room. Parnell courteous enough, but depressed and gloomy. Mr. Gladstone worn and fagged. . . . When he was gone, Parnell repeated moodily that he might not be able to vote for the second reading, if it were understood that after the second reading the bill was to be withdrawn. 'Very well,' said I, 'that will of course destroy the government and the policy; but be that as it may, the cabinet, I am positive, won't change their line.'

The proceedings at the foreign office brought to the supporters of government a lively sense of relief. In the course of the evening a score of the waverers were found to have been satisfied, and were struck off the dissentient lists. But the relief did not last for many hours. The opposition instantly challenged ministers (May 28) to say plainly which of the two courses they intended to adopt. Though short, this was the most vivacious debate of all. Was the bill to be withdrawn, or was it to be postponed ? If it was to be withdrawn, then, argued the tory leader (Sir M. H. Beach) in angry tones, the vote on the second reading would be a farce. If it was to be postponed, what was that but to paralyse the forces of law and order in Ireland in the meantime ? Such things were trifling with parliament, trifling with a vital constitutional question, and trifling with the social order which the government professed to be so anxious to restore. A bill read a second time on such terms as these would be neither more nor less than a Continuance-in-Office bill.

This biting sally raised the temper of the House on both sides, and Mr. Gladstone met it with that dignity which did not often fail to quell even the harshest of his adversaries. 'You pronounce that obviously the motive of the government is to ensure their own continuance in office. They prefer that to all the considerations connected with the great issue before them, and their minds in fact are of such a mean and degraded order, that they can only be acted upon, not by motives of honour and duty, but simply by those of selfishness and personal interest. Sir, I do not condescend to discuss that imputation. The dart aimed at our shield, being such a dart as that, is *telum imbelle sine ictu.*[1]

The speaker then got on to the more hazardous part of the ground. He proceeded to criticise the observation of the leader of the opposition that ministers had undertaken to remodel the bill. 'That happy word,' he said, 'as applied to the structure of the bill, is a pure invention.' Lord Randolph interjected that the word used was not 're-modelled,' but 'reconstructed.' 'Does the noble lord dare to say,' asked the minister, 'that it was used in respect of the bill?' 'Yes,' said the noble lord. 'Never, never,' cried the minister, with a vehemence that shook the hearts of doubting followers; 'it was used with respect to one particular clause, and one particular point of the bill, namely so much of it as touches the future relation of the representatives of Ireland to the imperial parliament.' Before the exciting episode was over, it was stated definitely that if the bill were read a second time, ministers would advise a prorogation and re-introduce the bill with amendments. The effect of this couple of hours was to convince the House that the government had made up their minds that it was easier and safer to go to the country with the plan as it stood, than to agree to changes that would entangle them in new embarrassments, and discredit their confidence in their own handiwork. Ingenious negotiators perceived that their toil had been fruitless. Every man now knew the precise situation that he had to face, in respect alike of the Irish bill and liberal unity.

On the day following this decisive scene (May 29), under the direction of the radical leader an invitation to a conference was issued to those members 'who being in favour

[1] *Hans.* 306, p. 322.

of some sort of autonomy for Ireland, disapproved of the government bills in their present shape.' The form of the invitation is remarkable in view of its ultimate effect on Irish autonomy. The meeting was held on May 31, in the same committee room upstairs that four years later became associated with the most cruel of all phases of the Irish controversy. Mr. Chamberlain presided, and some fifty-five gentlemen attended. Not all of them had hitherto been understood to be in favour either of some sort, or of any sort, of autonomy for Ireland. The question was whether they should content themselves with abstention from the division, or should go into the lobby against the government. If they abstained, the bill would pass, and an extension of the party schism would be averted. The point was carried, as all great parliamentary issues are, by considerations apart from the nice and exact balance of argument on the merits. In anxious and distracting moments like this, when so many arguments tell in one way and so many tell in another, a casting vote often belongs to the moral weight of some particular person. The chairman opened in a neutral sense. It seems to have been mainly the moral weight of Mr. Bright that sent down the scale. He was not present, but he sent a letter. He hoped that every man would use his own mind, but for his part he must vote against the bill. This letter was afterwards described as the death-warrant of the bill and of the administration. The course of the men who had been summoned because they were favourable to some sort of home rule was decided by the illustrious statesman who opposed every sort of home rule. Their boat was driven straight upon the rocks of coercion by the influence of the great orator who had never in all his career been more eloquent than when he was denouncing the mischief and futility of Irish coercion, and protesting that force is no remedy.

One of the best speakers in the House, though not at that time in the cabinet, was making an admirably warm and convinced defence alike of the policy and the bill while these proceedings were going on. But Mr. Fowler was listened to by men of pre-occupied minds. All knew what

momentous business was on foot in another part of the
parliamentary precincts.   Many in the ranks were confident
that abstention would carry the day.   Others knew that the
meeting had been summoned for no such purpose, and they
made sure that the conveners would have their way.   The
quiet inside the House was intense and unnatural.   As
at last the news of the determination upstairs to vote
against the bill ran along the benches before the speaker
sat down, men knew that the ministerial day was lost.   It
was estimated by the heads of the 'Chamberlain group'
that if they abstained, the bill would pass by a majority
of five.   Such a bill carried by such a majority could of
course not have proceeded much further.   The principle of
autonomy would have been saved, and time would have
been secured for deliberation upon a new plan.   More than
once Mr. Gladstone observed that no decision taken from
the beginning of the crisis to the end was either more
incomprehensible or more disastrous.

IV

The division was taken a little after one o'clock on the
morning of the 8th of June.   The Irish leader made one
of the most masterly speeches that ever fell from him.
Whether agreeing with or differing from the policy, every unprejudiced listener felt that this was not the mere dialectic
of a party debater, dealing smartly with abstract or verbal
or artificial arguments, but the utterance of a statesman
with his eye firmly fixed upon the actual circumstances of
the nation for whose government this bill would make him
responsible.   As he dealt with Ulster, with finance, with the
supremacy of parliament, with the loyal minority, with the
settlement of education in an Irish legislature, — soberly,
steadily, deliberately, with that full, familiar, deep insight
into the facts of a country, which is only possible to a man
who belongs to it and has passed his life in it, the effect of
Mr. Parnell's speech was to make even able disputants on
either side look little better than amateurs.

The debate was wound up for the regular opposition by
Sir Michael Hicks Beach, who was justly regarded through-

out the session as having led his party with remarkable skill and judgment. Like the Irish leader, he seemed to be inspired by the occasion to a performance beyond his usual range, and he delivered the final charge with strong effect. The bill, he said, was the concoction of the prime minister and the Irish secretary, and the cabinet had no voice in the matter. The government had delayed the progress of the bill for a whole long and weary month, in order to give party wirepullers plenty of time in which to frighten waverers. To treat a vote on the second reading as a mere vote on a principle, without reference to the possibility of applying it, was a mischievous farce. Could anybody dream that if he supported the second reading now, he would not compromise his action in the autumn, and would not be appealed to as having made a virtual promise to Ireland, of which it would be impossible to disappoint her? As for the bill itself, whatever lawyers might say of the theoretic maintenance of supremacy, in practice it would have gone. All this side of the case was put by the speaker with the straight and vigorous thrust that always works with strong effect in this great arena of contest.

Then came the unflagging veteran with the last of his five speeches. He was almost as white as the flower in his coat, but the splendid compass, the flexibility, the moving charm and power of his voice, were never more wonderful. The construction of the speech was a masterpiece, the temper of it unbroken, its freedom from taunt and bitterness and small personality incomparable. Even if Mr. Gladstone had been in the prime of his days, instead of a man of seventy-six years all struck; even if he had been at his ease for the last four months, instead of labouring with indomitable toil at the two bills, bearing all the multifarious burdens of the head of a government, and all the weight of the business of the leader of the House, undergoing all the hourly strain and contention of a political situation of unprecedented difficulty, — much of the contention being of that peculiarly trying and painful sort which means the parting of colleagues and friends, — his closing speech would still have been a surprising effort of free, argumentative, and fervid appeal. With the fervid

appeal was mingled more than one piece of piquant mockery.
Mr. Chamberlain had said that a dissolution had no terrors
for him. 'I do not wonder at it. I do not see how a dissolution can have any terrors for him. He has trimmed his
vessel, and he has touched his rudder in such a masterly
way, that in whichever direction the winds of heaven may
blow they must fill his sails. Supposing that at an election
public opinion should be very strong in favour of the bill,
my right hon. friend would then be perfectly prepared to
meet that public opinion, and tell it, "I declared strongly
that I adopted the principle of the bill." On the other
hand, if public opinion were very adverse to the bill, he
again is in complete armour, because he says, "Yes, I voted
against the bill." Supposing, again, public opinion is in
favour of a very large plan for Ireland, my right hon. friend
is perfectly provided for that case also. The government
plan was not large enough for him, and he proposed in his
speech on the introduction of the bill that we should have a
measure on the basis of federation, which goes beyond this
bill. Lastly — and now I have very nearly boxed the compass — supposing that public opinion should take quite a
different turn, and instead of wanting very large measures
for Ireland, should demand very small measures for Ireland,
still the resources of my right hon. friend are not exhausted,
because he is then able to point out that the last of his plans
was for four provincial circuits controlled from London.'
All these alternatives and provisions were visibly 'creations
of the vivid imagination, born of the hour and perishing
with the hour, totally unavailable for the solution of a great
and difficult problem.'

Now, said the orator, was one of the golden moments of
our history, one of those opportunities which may come and
may go, but which rarely return, or if they return, return at
long intervals, and under circumstances which no man can
forecast. There was such a golden moment in 1795, on the
mission of Lord Fitzwilliam. At that moment the parliament of Grattan was on the point of solving the Irish problem. The cup was at Ireland's lips, and she was ready to
drink it, when the hand of England rudely and ruthlessly

dashed it to the ground in obedience to the wild and
dangerous intimations of an Irish faction. There had been
no great day of hope for Ireland since, no day when you
might completely and definitely hope to end the controversy
till now — more than ninety years. The long periodic time
had at last run out, and the star had again mounted into
the heavens.

This strain of living passion was sustained with all its fire
and speed to the very close. ' Ireland stands at your bar
expectant, hopeful, almost suppliant. Her words are the
words of truth and soberness. She asks a blessed oblivion
of the past, and in that oblivion our interest is deeper even
than hers. You have been asked to-night to abide by the
traditions of which we are the heirs. What traditions ? By
the Irish traditions ? Go into the length and breadth of the
world, ransack the literature of all countries, find if you
can a single voice, a single book, in which the conduct of
England towards Ireland is anywhere treated except with
profound and bitter condemnation. Are these the traditions
by which we are exhorted to stand ? No, they are a sad
exception to the glory of our country. They are a broad
and black blot upon the pages of its history, and what we
want to do is to stand by the traditions of which we are the
heirs in all matters except our relations with Ireland, and
to make our relation with Ireland to conform to the other
traditions of our country. So we treat our traditions, so we
hail the demand of Ireland for what I call a blessed oblivion
of the past. She asks also a boon for the future ; and that
boon for the future, unless we are much mistaken, will be a
boon to us in respect of honour, no less than a boon to her
in respect of happiness, prosperity and peace. Such, sir, is
her prayer. Think, I beseech you ; think well, think wisely,
think, not for the moment, but for the years that are to
come, before you reject this bill.'

The question was put, the sand glass was turned upon the
table, the division bells were set ringing. Even at this
moment, the ministerial whips believed that some were still
wavering. A reference made by Mr. Parnell to harmonious
communications in the previous summer with a tory minister,

inclined them to vote for the bill. On the other hand, the prospect of going to an election without a tory opponent was no weak temptation to a weak man. A common impression was that the bill would be beaten by ten or fifteen. Others were sure that it would be twice as much as either figure. Some on the treasury bench, perhaps including the prime minister himself, hoped against hope that the hostile majority might not be more than five or six. It proved to be thirty. The numbers were 343 against 313. Ninety-three liberals voted against the bill. These with the two tellers were between one-third and one-fourth of the full liberal strength from Great Britain. So ended the first engagement in this long campaign. As I passed into his room at the House with Mr. Gladstone that night, he seemed for the first time to bend under the crushing weight of the burden that he had taken up.

V

When ministers went into the cabinet on the following day, three of them inclined pretty strongly towards resignation as a better course than dissolution ; mainly on the ground that the incoming government would then have to go to the country with a policy of their own. Mr. Gladstone, however, entirely composed though pallid, at once opened the case with a list of twelve reasons for recommending dissolution, and the reasons were so cogent that his opening of the case was also its closing. They were entirely characteristic, for they began with precedent and the key was courage. He knew of no instance where a ministry defeated under circumstances like ours, upon a great policy or on a vote of confidence, failed to appeal to the country. Then with a view to the enthusiasm of our friends in this country, as well as to feeling in Ireland, it was essential that we should not let the flag go down. We had been constantly challenged to a dissolution, and not to take the challenge up would be a proof of mistrust, weakness, and a faint heart. ' My conclusion is,' he said, ' a dissolution is formidable, but resignation would mean for the present juncture abandonment of the cause.' His conclusion was accepted without comment. The experts outside the cabinet were convinced that a bold front was the best way of securing the full fighting power of the party. The white feather on such an issue, and with so many minds wavering, would be a sure provocative of defeat.

Mr. Gladstone enumerated to the Queen what he took to be the new elements in the case. There were on the side of the government, 1. The transfer of the Irish vote from the tories, 2. The popular enthusiasm in the liberal masses which he had never seen equalled. But what was the electoral value of enthusiasm against (a) anti-Irish prejudices, (b) the power of rank, station, and wealth, (c) the kind of influence exercised by the established clergy, 'perversely applied as of course Mr. Gladstone thinks in politics, but resting upon a very solid basis as founded on the generally excellent and devoted work which they do in their parishes'? This remained to be proved. On the other side there was the whig defection, with the strange and unnatural addition from Birmingham. 'Mr. Gladstone himself has no skill in these matters, and dare not lay an opinion before your Majesty on the probable general result.' He thought there was little chance, if any, of a tory majority in the new parliament. Opinion taken as a whole seemed to point to a majority not very large, whichever way it may be.

No election was ever fought more keenly, and never did so many powerful men fling themselves with livelier activity into a great struggle. The heaviest and most telling attack came from Mr. Bright, who had up to now in public been studiously silent. Every word, as they said of Daniel Webster, seemed to weigh a pound. His arguments were mainly those of his letter already given, but they were delivered with a gravity and force that told powerfully upon the large phalanx of doubters all over the kingdom. On the other side, Mr. Gladstone's plume waved in every part of the field. He unhorsed an opponent as he flew past on the road ; his voice rang with calls as thrilling as were ever heard in England ; he appealed to the individual, to his personal responsibility, to the best elements in him, to the sense of justice, to the powers of hope and of sympathy ; he

displayed to the full that rare combination of qualities that
had always enabled him to view affairs in all their range,
at the same time from the high commanding eminence
and on the near and sober level.

He left London on June 17 on his way to Edinburgh, and
found ' wonderful demonstrations all along the road; many
little speeches; could not be helped.' ' The feeling here,'
he wrote from Edinburgh (June 21), ' is truly wonderful,
especially when the detestable state of the press is considered.' Even Mr. Goschen, whom he described as
' supplying in the main, soul, brains, and movement to the
dissentient body,' was handsomely beaten in one of the
Edinburgh divisions, so fatal was the proximity of Achilles.
' *June* 22. Off to Glasgow, 12¾. Meeting at 3. Spoke an
hour and twenty minutes. Off at 5.50. Reached Hawarden
at 12.30 or 40. Some speeches by the way; others I declined.
The whole a scene of triumph. God help us, His poor
creatures.' At Hawarden, he found chaos in his room, and
he set to work upon it, but he did not linger. On June 25,
' off to Manchester; great meeting in the Free Trade Hall.
Strain excessive. Five miles through the streets to Mr.
Agnew's; a wonderful spectacle half the way.' From Manchester he wrote, ' I have found the display of enthusiasm
far beyond all former measure,' and the torrid heat of the
meeting almost broke him down, but friends around him
heard him murmur, ' I must do it,' and bracing himself with
tremendous effort he went on. Two days later (June 28) he
wound up the campaign in a speech at Liverpool, which
even old and practised political hands who were there, found
the most magnificent of them all. Staying at Courthey, the
residence of his nephews, in the morning he enters, ' Worked
up the Irish question once more for my last function. Seven
or eight hours of processional uproar, and a speech of an
hour and forty minutes to five or six thousand people in
Hengler's Circus. Few buildings give so noble a presentation of an audience. Once more my voice held out in a
marvellous manner. I went in bitterness, in the heat of my
spirit, but the hand of the Lord was strong upon me.'

He had no sooner returned to Hawarden, than he wrote to

tell Mrs. Gladstone (July 2) of a stroke which was thought
to have a curiously dæmonic air about it : —

The Leith business will show you I have not been inactive here.
—— former M.P. *attended my meeting in the Music Hall,* and was
greeted by me accordingly (he had voted against us after wobbling
about much). Hearing by late post yesterday that waiting to the
last he had then declared against us, I telegraphed down to Edinburgh in much indignation, that they might if they liked put me
up against him, and I would go down again and speak if they
wished it. They seem to have acted with admirable pluck and
promptitude. Soon after mid-day to-day I received telegrams to
say I am elected for Midlothian,[1] and *also for Leith,* —— having
retired rather than wait to be beaten. I told them instantly to
publish this, as it may do good.

The Queen, who had never relished these oratorical
crusades whether he was in opposition or in office, did
not approve of the first minister of the crown addressing
meetings outside of his own constituency. In reply to a
gracious and frank letter from Balmoral, Mr. Gladstone
wrote : —

He must state frankly what it is that has induced him thus to
yield [to importunity for speeches]. It is that since the death
of Lord Beaconsfield, in fact since 1880, the leaders of the opposition, Lord Salisbury and Lord Iddesleigh (he has not observed the
same practice in the case of Sir M. H. Beach) have established
a rule of what may be called popular agitation, by addressing public
meetings from time to time at places with which they were not
connected. This method was peculiarly marked in the case of
Lord Salisbury as a peer, and this change on the part of the
leaders of opposition has induced Mr. Gladstone to deviate on
this critical occasion from the rule which he had (he believes)
generally or uniformly observed in former years. He is,
as he has previously apprised your Majesty, aware of the immense responsibility he has assumed, and of the severity of just
condemnation which will be pronounced upon him, if he should
eventually prove to have been wrong. But your Majesty will be

[1] He was returned without opposition.

the first to perceive that, even if it had been possible for him to
decline this great contest, it was not possible for him having
entered upon it, to conduct it in a half-hearted manner, or to omit
the use of any means requisite in order to place (what he thinks)
the true issue before the country.

Nature, however, served the royal purpose. Before his
speech at Liverpool, he was pressed to speak in the
metropolis : —

As to my going to London, — he wrote in reply, — I have twice had
my chest rather seriously strained, and I have at this moment a sense
of internal fatigue within it which is quite new to me, from the
effects of a bad arrangement in the hall at Manchester. Should anything like it be repeated at Liverpool to-morrow I shall not be fit
physically to speak for a week, if then. Mentally I have never
undergone such an uninterrupted strain as since January 30 of
this year. The forming and reforming of the government, the
work of framing the bills, and *studying the subject* (which none of
the opponents would do), have left me almost stunned, and I have
the autumn in prospect with, perhaps, most of the work to do
over again if we succeed.

But this was not to be. The incomparable effort was in
vain. The sons of Zeruiah were too hard for him, and
England was unconvinced.

The final result was that the ministerialists or liberals of
the main body were reduced from 235 to 196, the tories rose
from 251 to 316, the dissentient liberals fell to 74, and Mr.
Parnell remained at his former strength. In other words,
the opponents of the Irish policy of the government were
390, as against 280 in its favour; or a unionist majority of
110. Once more no single party possessed an independent
or absolute majority. An important member of the tory
party said to a liberal of his acquaintance (July 7), that he
was almost sorry the tories had not played the bold game
and fought independently of the dissentient liberals. 'But
then,' he added, 'we could not have beaten you on the bill,
without the compact to spare unionist seats.'

England had returned opponents of the liberal policy in

the proportion of two and a half to one against its friends;
but Scotland approved in the proportion of three to two,
Wales approved by five to one, and Ireland by four and a
half to one. Another fact with a warning in it was that,
taking the total poll for Great Britain, the liberals had
1,344,000, the seceders 397,000, and the tories 1,041,000.
Therefore in contested constituencies the liberals of the
main body were only 76,000 behind the forces of tories
and seceders combined. Considering the magnitude and
the surprise of the issue laid before the electors, and in
view of the confident prophecies of even some peculiar
friends of the policy, that both policy and its authors
would be swept out of existence by a universal explosion
of national anger and disgust, there was certainly no final
and irrevocable verdict in a hostile British majority of no
more than four per cent. of the votes polled. Apart from
electoral figures, coercion loomed large and near at hand,
and coercion tried under the new political circumstances
that would for the first time attend it, might well be trusted
to do much more than wipe out the margin at the polls.
'There is nothing in the recent defeat,' said Mr. Gladstone,
'to abate the hopes or to modify the anticipations of those
who desire to meet the wants and wishes of Ireland.'

VI

The question now before Mr. Gladstone was whether to
meet the new parliament or at once to resign. For a short
time he wavered, along with an important colleague, and
then he and all the rest came round to resignation. The
considerations that guided him were these. It is best for
Ireland that the party strongest in the new parliament
should be at once confronted with its responsibilities. Again,
we were bound to consider what would most tend to reunite
the liberal party, and it was in opposition that the chances of
such reunion would be likely to stand highest, especially in
view of coercion which many of the dissidents had refused to
contemplate. If he could remodel the bill or frame a new
one, that might be a possible ground for endeavouring to
make up a majority, but he could not see his way to any

such process, though he was ready for certain amendments. Finally, if we remained, an amendment would be moved definitely committing the new House against home rule. The conclusion was for immediate resignation, and his colleagues were unanimous in assent. The Irish view was different and impossible. Returning from a visit to Ireland I wrote to Mr. Gladstone (July 19): —

You may perhaps care to see what —— [not a secular politician] thinks, so I enclose you a conversation between him and ——. He does not show much strength of political judgment, and one can understand why Parnell never takes him into counsel. Parnell, of course, is anxious for us to hold on to the last moment. Our fall will force him without delay to take up a new and difficult line. But his letters to me, especially the last, show a desperate willingness to blink the new parliamentary situation.

Mr. Parnell, in fact, pressed with some importunity that we should meet the new parliament, on the strange view that the result of the election was favourable on general questions, and indecisive only on Irish policy. We were to obtain the balance of supply in an autumn sitting, in January to attack registration reform, and then to dissolve upon that, without making any Irish proposition whatever. This curious suggestion left altogether out of sight the certainty that an amendment referring to Ireland would be at once moved on the Address, such as must beyond all doubt command the whole of the tories and a large part, if not all, of the liberal dissentients. Only one course was possible for the defeated ministers, and they resigned.

On July 30, Mr. Gladstone had his final audience of the Queen, of which he wrote the memorandum following: —

Conversation with the Queen, August 2, 1886.

The conversation at my closing audience on Friday was a singular one, when regarded as the probable last word with the sovereign after fifty-five years of political life, and a good quarter of a century's service rendered to her in office.

The Queen was in good spirits; her manners altogether pleasant. She made me sit at once. Asked after my wife as we began, and sent a kind message to her as we ended. About me personally, I think, her single remark was that I should require some rest. I remember that on a closing audience in 1874 she said she felt sure I might be reckoned upon to support the throne. She did not say anything of the sort to-day. Her mind and opinions have since that day been seriously warped, and I respect her for the scrupulous avoidance of anything which could have seemed to indicate a desire on her part to claim anything in common with me.

Only at three points did the conversation touch upon anything even faintly related to public affairs. . . . The second point was the conclusion of some arrangement for appanages or incomes on behalf of the third generation of the royal house. I agreed that there ought at a suitable time to be a committee on this subject, as had been settled some time back, she observing that the recent circumstances had made the time unsuitable. I did not offer any suggestion as to the grounds of the affair, but said it seemed to me possible to try some plan under which intended marriages should be communicated without forcing a reply from the Houses. Also I agreed that the amounts were not excessive. I did not pretend to have a solution ready : but said it would, of course, be the duty of the government to submit a plan to the committee. The third matter was trivial : a question or two from her on the dates and proceedings connected with the meeting. The rest of the conversation, not a very long one, was filled up with nothings. It is rather melancholy. But on neither side, given the conditions, could it well be helped.

On the following day she wrote a letter, making it evident that, so far as Ireland was concerned, she could not trust herself to say what she wanted to say. . . .

Among the hundreds of letters that reached him every week was one from an evangelical lady of known piety, enclosing him a form of prayer that had been issued against home rule. His acknowledgment (July 27) shows none of the impatience of the baffled statesman : —

I thank you much for your note ; and though I greatly deplored the issue, and the ideas of the prayer in question, yet, from the moment when I heard it was your composition, I knew

perfectly well that it was written in entire good faith, and had no
relation to political controversy in the ordinary sense. I cannot
but think that, in bringing the subject of Irish intolerance before
the Almighty Father, we ought to have some regard to the fact
that down to the present day, as between the two religions, the
offence has been in the proportion of perhaps a hundred to one
on the protestant side, and the suffering by it on the Roman side.
At the present hour, I am pained to express my belief that there
is far more of intolerance in action from so-called protestants
against Roman catholics, than from Roman catholics against
protestants. It is a great satisfaction to agree with you, as I feel
confident that I must do, in the conviction that of prayers we
cannot possibly have too much in this great matter, and for my
own part I heartily desire that, unless the policy I am proposing
be for the honour of God and the good of His creatures, it may
be trampled under foot and broken into dust. Of your most
charitable thoughts and feelings towards me I am deeply sensible,
and I remain with hearty regard.

As he wrote at this time to R. H. Hutton (July 2), one of
the choice spirits of our age, 'Rely upon it, I can never
quarrel with you or with Bright. What vexes me is when
differences disclose baseness, which sometimes happens.'

Book X

1886–1892

CHAPTER I

THE MORROW OF DEFEAT

(1886–1887)

> CHARITY rendereth a man truly great, enlarging his mind into a
> vast circumference, and to a capacity nearly infinite ; so that it by
> a general care doth reach all things, by an universal affection doth
> embrace and grace the world. . . . Even a spark of it in generosity
> of dealing breedeth admiration ; a glimpse of it in formal courtesy
> of behaviour procureth much esteem, being deemed to accomplish
> and adorn a man. — BARROW.

AFTER the rejection of his Irish policy in the summer of
1886, Mr. Gladstone had a period of six years before him,
the life of the new parliament. Strangely dramatic years
they were, in some respects unique in our later history. The
party schism among liberals grew deeper and wider. The
union between tories and seceders became consolidated and
final. The alternative policy of coercion was passed through
parliament in an extreme form and with violent strain on
the legislative machinery, and it was carried out in Ireland
in a fashion that pricked the consciences of many thousands
of voters who had resisted the proposals of 1886. A fierce
storm rent the Irish phalanx in two, and its leader vanished
from the field where for sixteen years he had fought so bold
and uncompromising a fight. During this period Mr. Gladstone stood in the most trying of all the varied positions of
his life, and without flinching he confronted it in the strong
faith that the national honour as well as the assuagement

of the inveterate Irish wound in the flank of his country,
were the issues at stake.

This intense pre-occupation in the political struggle did
not for a single week impair his other interests, nor stay his
ceaseless activity in controversies that were not touched by
politics. Not even now, when the great cause to which he
had so daringly committed himself was in decisive issue,
could he allow it to dull or sever what had been the
standing concerns of life and thought to him for so long a
span of years. As from his youth up, so now behind the
man of public action was the diligent, eager, watchful
student, churchman, apologist, divine. And what is curious
and delightful is that he never set a more admirable example
of the tone and temper in which literary and religious controversy should be conducted, than in these years when in
politics exasperation was at its worst. It was about this
time that he wrote: ' Certainly one of the lessons life has
taught me is that where there is known to be a common
object, the pursuit of truth, there should also be a studious
desire to interpret the adversary in the best sense his words
will fairly bear; to avoid whatever widens the breach; and
to make the most of whatever tends to narrow it. These I
hold to be part of the laws of knightly tournament.' And to
these laws he sedulously conformed. Perhaps at some happy
time before the day of judgment they may be transferred
from the tournament to the battle-fields of philosophy,
criticism, and even politics.

II

After the defeat in which his tremendous labours had for
the moment ended, he made his way to what was to him the
most congenial atmosphere in the world, to the company of
Döllinger and Acton, at Tegernsee in Bavaria. ' Tegernsee,'
Lord Acton wrote to me (Sept. 7), ' is an out-of-the-way
place, peaceful and silent, and as there is a good library in
the house, I have taken some care of his mind, leading in
the direction of little French comedies, and away from the
tragedy of existence. It has done him good, and he has
just started with Döllinger to climb a high mountain in the
neighbourhood.'

To Mrs. Gladstone.

Tegernsee, Aug. 28, 1886. — We found Döllinger reading in the garden. The course of his life is quite unchanged. His constitution does not appear at all to have given way. He beats me utterly in standing, but that is not saying much, as it never was one of my gifts; and he is not conscious (eighty-seven last February) of any difficulty with the heart in going up hill. His deafness has increased materially, but not so that he cannot carry on very well conversation with a single person. We have talked much together even on disestablishment which he detests, and Ireland as to which he is very apprehensive, but he never seems to shut up his mind by prejudice. I had a good excuse for giving him my pamphlet,[1] but I do not know whether he will tell us what he thinks of it. He was reading it this morning. He rises at six and breakfasts alone. Makes a *good* dinner at two and has nothing more till the next morning. He does not appear after dark. On the whole one sees no reason why he should not last for several years yet.

'When Dr. Döllinger was eighty-seven,' Mr. Gladstone wrote later, 'he walked with me seven miles across the hill that separates the Tegernsee from the next valley to the eastward. At that time he began to find his sleep subject to occasional interruptions, and he had armed himself against them by committing to memory the first three books of the *Odyssey* for recital.'[2] Of Mr. Gladstone Döllinger had said in 1885, 'I have known Gladstone for thirty years, and would stand security for him any day; his character is a very fine one, and he possesses a rare capability for work. I differ from him in his political views on many points, and it is difficult to convince him, for he is clad in triple steel.'[3]

Another high personage in the Roman catholic world sent him letters through Acton, affectionately written and with signs of serious as well as sympathising study of his Irish policy. A little later (Sept. 21) Mr. Gladstone writes to his wife at Hawarden : —

Bishop Strossmayer may make a journey all the way to

---

[1] On the Irish Question — 'The History of an Idea and the Lesson of the Elections,' a fifty-page pamphlet prepared before leaving England.

[2] *Speaker*, Jan. 1, 1890.

[3] *Conversations of Döllinger*. By L. von Köbell, pp. 100, 102.

Hawarden, and it seems that Acton may even accompany him,
which would make it much more manageable. His coming would
be a great compliment, and cannot be discouraged or refused. It
would, however, be a serious affair, for he speaks no language
with which as a spoken tongue we are familiar, his great cards
being Slavonic and Latin. Unfortunately I have a very great
increase of difficulty in *hearing* the words in foreign tongues, a
difficulty which I hope has hardly begun with you as yet.

Like a good host, Lord Acton kept politics out of his way
as well as he could, but some letter of mine 'set him on fire,
and he is full of ——'s blunder and of Parnell's bill.' Parliamentary duty was always a sting to him, and by September
20 he was back in the House of Commons, speaking on the
Tenants Relief (Ireland) bill. Then to the temple of peace
at Hawarden for the rest of the year, to read the *Iliad* 'for
the twenty-fifth or thirtieth time, and every time richer and
more glorious than before'; to write elaborately on Homeric
topics; to receive a good many visitors; and to compose the
admirable article on Tennyson's second *Locksley Hall*. On
this last let us pause for an instant. The moment was hardly
one in which, from a man of nature less great and powerful
than Mr. Gladstone, we should have counted on a buoyant
vindication of the spirit of his time. He had just been
roughly repulsed in the boldest enterprise of his career; his
name was a target for infinite obloquy; his motives were
largely denounced as of the basest; the conflict into which he
had plunged and from which he could not withdraw was hard;
friends had turned away from him; he was old; the issue was
dubious and dark. Yet the personal, or even what to him
were the national discomfitures of the hour, were not allowed
to blot the sun out of the heavens. His whole soul rose in
challenge against the tragic tones of Tennyson's poem, as
he recalled the solid tale of the vast improvements, the
enormous mitigation of the sorrows and burdens of mankind,
that had been effected in the land by public opinion and
public authority, operative in the exhilarating sphere of self-
government during the sixty years between the first and
second *Locksley Hall*.

The sum of the matter seems to be that upon the whole, and in a degree, we who lived fifty, sixty, seventy years back, and are living now, have lived into a gentler time; that the public conscience has grown more tender, as indeed was very needful; and that in matters of practice, at sight of evils formerly regarded with indifference or even connivance, it now not only winces but rebels; that upon the whole the race has been reaping, and not scattering; earning and not wasting; and that without its being said that the old Prophet is wrong, it may be said that the young Prophet was unquestionably right.

Here is the way in which a man of noble heart and high vision as of a circling eagle, transcends his individual chagrins. All this optimism was the natural vein of a statesman who had lived a long life of effort in persuading opinion in so many regions, in overcoming difficulty upon difficulty, in content with a small reform where men would not let him achieve a great one, in patching where he could not build anew, in unquenchable faith, hope, patience, endeavour. Mr. Gladstone knew as well as Tennyson that 'every blessing has its drawbacks, and every age its dangers'; he was as sensitive as Tennyson or Ruskin or any of them, to the implacable tragedy of industrial civilisation — the city children 'blackening soul and sense in city slime,' progress halting on palsied feet 'among the glooming alleys,' crime and hunger casting maidens on the street, and all the other recesses of human life depicted by the poetic prophet in his sombre hours. But the triumphs of the past inspired confidence in victories for the future, and meanwhile he thought it well to remind Englishmen that 'their country is still young as well as old, and that in these latest days it has not been unworthy of itself.' [1]

On his birthday he enters in his diary: —

Dec. 29, 1886. — This day in its outer experience recalls the Scotch usage which would say, 'terrible pleasant.' In spite of the ruin of telegraph wires by snow, my letters and postal arrivals of to-day have much exceeded those of last year. Even my share of

[1] *Nineteenth Century*, January 1887. See also speech at Hawarden, on the Queen's Reign, August 30, 1887. The reader will remember Mr. Gladstone's contrast between poet and active statesman at Kirkwall in 1883.

the reading was very heavy. The day was gone before it seemed to have begun, all amidst stir and festivity. The estimate was nine hundred arrivals. O for a birthday of recollection. It is long since I have had one. There is so much to say on the soul's history, but bracing is necessary to say it, as it is for reading Dante. It has been a year of shock and strain. I think a year of some progress; but of greater absorption in interests which, though profoundly human, are quite off the line of an old man's direct preparation for passing the River of Death. I have not had a chance given me of creeping from this whirlpool, for I cannot abandon a cause which is so evidently that of my fellow-men, and in which a particular part seems to be assigned to me. Therefore am I not disturbed 'though the hills be carried into the middle of the sea.'

III

To Lord Acton.

Hawarden, Jan. 13, 1887. — It is with much pleasure that I read your estimate of Chamberlain. His character is remarkable, as are in a very high degree his talents. It is one of my common sayings that to me characters of the political class are the most mysterious of all I meet, so that I am obliged to travel the road of life surrounded by an immense number of judgments more or less in suspense, and getting on for practical purposes as well as I can.

I have with a clear mind and conscience not only assented to but promoted the present conferences, and I had laboured in that sense long before Mr. Chamberlain made his speech at Birmingham. It will surprise as well as grieve me if they do harm; if indeed they do not do some little good. Large and final arrangements, it would be rash I think to expect.

The tide is flowing, though perhaps not rapidly, in our favour. Without our lifting a finger, a crumbling process has begun in both the opposite parties. 'In quietness and in confidence shall be your strength' is a blessed maxim, often applicable to temporals as well as spirituals. I have indeed one temptation to haste, namely, that the hour may come for me to say farewell and claim my retirement; but inasmuch as I remain *in situ* for the Irish question only, I cannot be so foolish as to allow myself to ruin by precipitancy my own purpose. Though I am writing a paper on the Irish question for Mr. Knowles, it is no trumpet-blast, but is meant to fill and turn to account a season of comparative quietude.

The death of Iddesleigh has shocked and saddened us all. He was full of excellent qualities, but had not the backbone and strength of fibre necessary to restore the tone of a party demoralised by his former leader. In gentleness, temper, sacrifice of himself to the common purpose of his friends, knowledge, quickness of perception, general integrity of intention, freedom from personal aims, he was admirable. . . . I have been constantly struggling to vindicate a portion of my time for the pursuits I want to follow, but with very little success indeed. Some rudiments of Olympian religion have partially taken shape. I have a paper ready for Knowles probably in his March number on the Poseidon of Homer, a most curious and exotic personage. . . . Williams and Norgate got me the books I wanted, but alack for the time to read them! In addition to want of time, I have to deplore my slowness in reading, declining sight, and declining memory; all very serious affairs for one who has such singular reason to be thankful as to general health and strength.

I wish I could acknowledge duly or pay even in part your unsparing, untiring kindness in the discharge of your engagements as 'Cook.' Come early to England — and stay long. We will try what we can to bind you.

A few months later, he added to his multifarious exercises in criticism and controversy, a performance that attracted especial attention.[1] 'Mamma and I,' he wrote to Mrs. Drew, ' are each of us still separately engaged in a death-grapple with *Robert Elsmere*. I complained of some of the novels you gave me to read as too stiff, but they are nothing to this. It is wholly out of the common order. At present I regard with doubt and dread the idea of doing anything on it, but cannot yet be sure whether your observations will be verified or not. In any case it is a tremendous book.' And on April 1 (1888), he wrote, 'By hard work I have finished and am correcting my article on *Robert Elsmere*.

[1] *Robert Elsmere: the Battle of Belief* (1888). Republished from the *Nineteenth Century* in *Later Gleanings*, 1898.

It is rather stiff work. I have had two letters from her.
She is much to be liked personally, but is a fruit, I think,
of what must be called Arnoldism.'

To Lord Acton.

Aston Clinton, Tring, Easter Day, April 1, '88. — I do not like to
let too long a time elapse without some note of intercourse, even
though that season approaches which brings you back to the shores
of your country. Were you here I should have much to say on
many things; but I will now speak, or first speak, of what is
uppermost, and would, if a mind is like a portmanteau, be taken
or tumble out first.

You perhaps have not heard of *Robert Elsmere*, for I find without surprise, that it makes its way slowly into public notice. It is
not far from twice the length of an ordinary novel; and the labour
and effort of reading it all, I should say, sixfold; while one could
no more stop in it than in reading Thucydides. The idea of the
book, perhaps of the writer, appears to be a movement of retreat
from Christianity upon Theism : a Theism with a Christ glorified,
always in the human sense, but beyond the ordinary measure. It
is worked out through the medium of a being — one ought to say
a character, but I withhold the word, for there is no sufficient sub-
stratum of character to uphold the qualities — gifted with much
intellectual subtlety and readiness, and almost every conceivable
moral excellence. He finds vent in an energetic attempt to carry
his new gospel among the skilled artisans of London, whom the
writer apparently considers as supplying the *norm* for all right
human judgment. He has extraordinary success, establishes a new
church under the name of the new Christian brotherhood, kills
himself with overwork, but leaves his project flourishing in
a certain 'Elgood Street.' It is in fact (like the Salvation Army),
a new Kirche der Zukunft.

I am always inclined to consider this Theism as among the least
defensible of the positions alternative to Christianity. Robert
Elsmere, who has been a parish clergyman, is upset entirely, as it
appears, by the difficulty of accepting miracles, and by the suggestion that the existing Christianity grew up in an age specially
predisposed to them.

I want as usual to betray you into helping the lame dog over the stile; and I should like to know whether you would think me violently wrong in holding that the period of the Advent was a period when the appetite for, or disposition to, the supernatural was declining and decaying; that in the region of human thought, speculation was strong and scepticism advancing; that if our Lord were a mere man, armed only with human means, His whereabouts was in this and many other ways misplaced by Providence; that the gospels and the New Testament must have much else besides miracle torn out of them, in order to get us down to the *caput mortuum* òf Elgood Street. This very remarkable work is in effect identical with the poor, thin, ineffectual production published with some arrogance by the Duke of Somerset, which found a quack remedy for difficulties in what he considered the impregnable citadel of belief in God.

Knowles has brought this book before me, and being as strong as it is strange, it cannot perish still-born. I am tossed about with doubt as to writing upon it.

To Lord Acton.

Oxford, April 8, '88. — I am grateful for your most interesting letter, which contains very valuable warnings. On the other side is copied what I have written on two of the points raised by the book. Have I said too much of the Academy? I have spoken only of the first century. You refer to (apparently) about 250 A.D. as a time of great progress? But I was astonished on first reading the census of Christian clergy in Ròme *temp.* St. Cyprian, it was so slender. I am not certain, but does not Beugnot estimate the Christians, before Constantine's conversion, in the west at one-tenth of the population? Mrs. T. Arnold died yesterday here. Mrs. Ward had been summoned and she is coming to see me this evening. It is a very singular phase of the controversy which she has opened. When do you *repatriate?*

I am afraid that my kindness to the Positivists amounts only to a comparative approval of their not dropping the great human tradition out of view; *plus* a very high appreciation of the personal qualities of our friend ——.

To Lord Acton.

Dollis Hill, May 13, '88. — Your last letter was one of extreme interest. It raised such a multitude of points, after your perusal of my article on R. Elsmere, as to stimulate in the highest degree my curiosity to know how far you would carry into propositions, the ideas which you for the most part obliquely put forward. I gave the letter to Mary, who paid us a flying visit in London, that she might take it to Hawarden for full digestion. For myself I feed upon the hope that when (when ?) you come back to England we may go over the points, and I may reap further benefits from your knowledge. I will not now attempt anything of the kind. But I will say this generally, that I am not so much oppressed as you appear to be, with the notion that great difficulties have been imported by the researches of scientists into the religious and theological argument. As respects cosmogony and *geogony*, the Scripture has, I think, taken much benefit from them. Whatever be the date of the early books, Pentateuch or Hexateuch in their present *edition*, the Assyriological investigations seem to me to have fortified and accredited their substance by producing similar traditions in variant forms inferior to the Mosaic forms, and tending to throw them back to a higher antiquity, a fountainhead nearer the source. Then there is the great chapter of the Dispersal: which Renan (I think) treats as exhibiting the marvellous genius (!) of the Jews. As to unbroken sequences in the physical order, they do not trouble me, because we have to do not with the natural but the moral order, and over this science, or as I call it natural science, does not wave her sceptre. It is no small matter, again (if so it be, as I suppose), that, after warring for a century against miracle as unsustained by experience, the assailants should now have to abandon that ground, stand only upon sequence, and controvert the great facts of the New Testament only by raising to an extravagant and unnatural height the demands made under the law of testimony in order to [justify] a rational belief. One admission has to be made, that death did not come into the world by sin, namely the sin of Adam, and this sits inconveniently by the declaration of Saint Paul.

Mrs. Ward wrote to thank me for the tone of my article. Her

first intention was to make some reply in the *Nineteenth Century* itself. It appears that —— advised her not to do it. But Knowles told me that he was labouring to bring her up to the scratch again. There, I said, you show the cloven foot; you want to keep the *Nineteenth Century* pot boiling.

I own that your reasons for not being in England did not appear to me cogent, but it would be impertinent to make myself a judge of them. The worst of it was that you did not name *any* date. But I must assume that you are coming; and surely the time cannot now be far. Among other things, I want to speak with you about French novels, a subject on which there has for me been quite recently cast a most lurid light.

Acton's letters in reply may have convinced Mr. Gladstone that there were depths in this supreme controversy that he had hardly sounded; and adversaria that he might have mocked from a professor of the school or schools of unbelief, he could not in his inner mind make light of, when coming from the pen of a catholic believer. Before and after the article on *Robert Elsmere* appeared, Acton, the student with his vast historic knowledge and his deep penetrating gaze, warned the impassioned critic of some historic point overstated or understated, some dangerous breach left all unguarded, some lack of nicety in definition. Acton's letters will one day see the light, and the reader may then know how candidly Mr. Gladstone was admonished as to the excess of his description of the moral action of Christianity; as to the risk of sending modern questions to ancient answers, for the apologists of an age can only meet the difficulties of their age ; that there are leaps and bounds in the history of thought; how well did Newman once say that in theology you have to meet questions that the Fathers could hardly have been made to understand; how if you go to St. Thomas or Leibnitz or Paley for rescue from Hegel or Haeckel your apologetics will be a record of disaster. You insist broadly, says Acton, on belief in the divine nature of Christ as the soul, substance, and creative force of Christian religion; you assign to it very much of the good the church has done; all this with little or no qualification or drawback from the other side : —

Enter Martineau or Stephen or —— (unattached), and loq. : —
Is this the final judgment of the chief of liberals ? the pontiff of
a church whose fathers are the later Milton and the later Penn,
Locke, Bayle, Toland, Franklin, Turgot, Adam Smith, Washington,
Jefferson, Bentham, Dugald Stewart, Romilly, Tocqueville,
Channing, Macaulay, Mill ?   These men and others like them
disbelieved that doctrine established freedom, and they undid the
work of orthodox Christianity, they swept away that appalling
edifice of intolerance, tyranny, cruelty, which believers in Christ
built up to perpetuate their belief.

The philosophy of liberal history, Acton proceeds, which
has to acknowledge the invaluable services of early
Christianity, feels the anti-liberal and anti-social action of
later Christianity, before the rise of the sects that rejected,
some of them the divinity of Christ ; others, the institutions
of the church erected upon it.   Liberalism if it admits these
things as indifferent, surrenders its own *raison d'être*, and
ceases to strive for an ethical cause.   If the doctrine of
Torquemada make us condone his morality, there can be no
public right and no wrong, no political sin, no secular cause
to die for.   So it might be said that —

You do not work really from the principle of liberalism, but
from the cognate, though distinct principles of democracy,
nationality, progress, etc.   To some extent, I fear, you will
estrange valued friends, not assuredly by any expression of
theological belief, but by seeming to ignore the great central
problem of Christian politics.   If I had to put my own doubts,
instead of the average liberal's, I should state the case in other
words, but not altogether differently.[1]

[1] May 2, 1888.

CHAPTER II

THE ALTERNATIVE POLICY IN ACT

(*1886-1888*)

> THOSE who come over hither to us from England, and some weak
> people among ourselves, whenever in discourse we make mention of
> liberty and property, shake their heads, and tell us that 'Ireland is
> a depending kingdom,' as if they would seem by this phrase to
> intend, that the people of Ireland are in some state of slavery or
> dependence different from those of England. — JONATHAN SWIFT.

BOOK
X.

1886.

IN the ministry that succeeded Mr. Gladstone in 1886,
Sir Michael Hicks Beach undertook for the second time the
office of Irish secretary, while Lord Randolph Churchill
filled his place at the exchequer and as leader of the House.
The new Irish policy was to open with the despatch of a
distinguished soldier to put down moonlighters in Kerry ;
the creation of one royal commission under Lord Cowper,
to inquire into land rents and land purchase ; and another
to inquire into the country's material resources. The two
commissions were well-established ways of marking time.
As for Irish industries and Irish resources, a committee of
the House of Commons had made a report in a blue book of
a thousand pages only a year before. On Irish land there
had been a grand commission in 1880, and a committee of
the House of Lords in 1882-3. The latest Purchase Act was
hardly yet a year old. Then to commission a general to hunt
down little handfuls of peasants who with blackened faces
and rude firearms crept stealthily in the dead of night
round lonely cabins in the remote hillsides and glens of
Kerry, was hardly more sensible than it would be to send
a squadron of life-guards to catch pickpockets in a London
slum.

A question that exercised Mr. Gladstone at least as
sharply as the proceedings of ministers, was the attitude

to be taken by those who had quitted him, ejected him in the short parliament of 1886, and fought the election against him. We have seen how much controversy arose long years before as to the question whereabouts in the House of Commons the Peelites should take their seats.[1] The same perplexity now confronted the liberals who did not agree with Mr. Gladstone upon Irish government. Lord Hartington wrote to him, and here is his reply : —

August 2, 1886. — I fully appreciate the feeling which has prompted your letter, and I admit the reality of the difficulties you describe. It is also clear, I think, that so far as title to places on the front opposition bench is concerned, your right to them is identical with ours. I am afraid, however, that I cannot materially contribute to relieve you from embarrassment. The choice of a seat is more or less the choice of a symbol; and I have no such acquaintance with your political views and intentions, as could alone enable me to judge what materials I have before me for making an answer to your inquiry. For my own part, I earnestly desire, subject to the paramount exigencies of the Irish question, to promote in every way the reunion of the liberal party ; a desire in which I earnestly trust that you participate. And I certainly could not directly or indirectly dissuade you from any step which you may be inclined to take, and which may appear to you to have a tendency in any measure to promote that end.

A singular event occurred at the end of the year (1886), that produced an important change in the relations of this group of liberals to the government that they had placed and maintained in power. Lord Randolph, the young minister who with such extraordinary rapidity had risen to ascendency in the councils of the government, suddenly in a fatal moment of miscalculation or caprice resigned (Dec. 23). Political suicide is not easy to a man with energy and resolution, but this was one of the rare cases. In a situation so strangely unstable and irregular, with an administration resting on the support of a section sitting on benches opposite, and still declaring every day that they adhered to old liberal

---

[1] See vol. i. p. 423.

principles and had no wish to sever old party ties, the withdrawal of Lord Randolph Churchill created boundless perturbation. It was one of those exquisite moments in which excited politicians enjoy the ineffable sensation that the end of the world has come. Everything seemed possible. Lord Hartington was summoned from the shores of the Mediterranean, but being by temperament incredulous of all vast elemental convulsions, he took his time. On his return he declined Lord Salisbury's offer to make way for him as head of the government. The glitter of the prize might have tempted a man of schoolboy ambition, but Lord Hartington was too experienced in affairs not to know that to be head of a group that held the balance was, under such equivocal circumstances, far the more substantial and commanding position of the two. Mr. Goschen's case was different, and by taking the vacant post at the exchequer he saved the prime minister from the necessity of going back under Lord Randolph's yoke. As it happened, all this gave a shake to both of the unionist wings. The ominous clouds of coercion were sailing slowly but discernibly along the horizon, and this made men in the unionist camp still more restless and uneasy. Mr. Chamberlain, on the very day of the announcement of the Churchill resignation, had made a speech that was taken to hold out an olive branch to his old friends. Sir William Harcourt, ever holding stoutly in fair weather and in foul to the party ship, thought the break-up of a great political combination to be so immense an evil, as to call for almost any sacrifices to prevent it. He instantly wrote to Birmingham to express his desire to co-operate in re-union, and in the course of a few days five members of the original liberal cabinet of 1886 met at his house in what was known as the Round Table Conference.[1]

A letter of Mr. Gladstone's to me puts some of his views on the situation created by the retirement of Lord Randolph : —

Hawarden, Christmas Day, 1886. — Between Christmas services, a flood of cards and congratulations for the season, and many

[1] Sir W. Harcourt, Mr. Chamberlain, Lord Herschell, Sir George Trevelyan, and myself.

interesting letters, I am drowned in work to-day, having just at
1¼ P.M. ascertained what my letters *are*. So forgive me if, first
thanking you very much for yours, I deal with some points
rather abruptly.

1. Churchill has committed an outrage as against the Queen, and
also the prime minister, in the method of resigning and making
known his resignation. This, of course, they will work against
him. 2. He is also entirely wrong in supposing that the finance
minister has any ruling authority on the great estimates of
defence. If he had, he would be the master of the country.
But although he has no right to demand the concurrence of his
colleagues in his view of the estimates, he has a rather special
right, because these do so much towards determining budget and
taxation, to indicate his own views by resignation. I have
repeatedly fought estimates to the extremity, with an intention
of resigning in *case*. But to send in a resignation makes it
impossible for his colleagues as men of honour to recede. 3. I
think one of his best points is that he had made before taking
office recent and formal declarations on behalf of economy, of
which his colleagues must be taken to have been cognisant, and
Salisbury in particular. He may plead that he could not reduce
these all at once to zero. 4. Cannot something be done, without
reference to the holes that may be picked, to give him some
support as a champion of economy? This talk about the continental war, I for one regard as pure nonsense when aimed at
magnifying our estimates.

5. With regard to Hartington. What he will do I know not,
and our wishes could have no weight with him. . . . The position
is one of such difficulty for H. that I am very sorry for him,
though it was never more true that he who makes his own bed
in a certain way must lie in it. Chamberlain's speech hits him
very hard in case of acceptance. I take it for granted that he
will not accept to sit among thirteen tories, but will have to
demand an entry by force, *i.e.* with three or four friends. To
accept upon that footing would, I think, be the logical consequence of all he has said and done since April. In logic, he ought
to go forward, *or*, as Chamberlain has done, backward. The
Queen will, I have no doubt, be brought to bear upon him, and

the nine-tenths of his order. If the Irish question rules all others, all he has to consider is whether he (properly flanked) can serve his view of the Irish question. But with this logic we have nothing to do. The question for us also is (I think), what is best for our view of the Irish question? I am tempted to wish that he should accept; it would clear the ground. But I do not yet see my way with certainty.

6. With regard to Chamberlain. From what has already passed between us you know that, apart from the new situation and from his declaration, I was very desirous that everything honourable should be done to conciliate and soothe. Unquestionably his speech is a new fact of great weight. He is again a liberal, *quand même*, and will not on all points (as good old Joe Hume used to say) swear black is white for the sake of his views on Ireland. We ought not to waste this new fact, but take careful account of it. On the other hand, I think he will see that the moment for taking account of it has not come. Clearly the first thing is to see who are the government. When we see this, we shall also know something of its colour and intentions. I do not think Randolph can go back. He would go back at a heavy discount. If he wants to minimise, the only way I see is that he should isolate his vote on the estimates, form no *clique*, and proclaim strong support in Irish matters and general policy. Thus he might pave a roundabout road of return. . . . In *many* things Goschen is more of a liberal than Hartington, and he would carry with him next to nobody.

7. On the whole, I rejoice to think that, come what may, this affair will really effect progress in the Irish question.

A happy Christmas to you. It will be happier than that of the ministers.

Mr. Gladstone gave the Round Table his blessing, his 'general idea being that he had better meddle as little as possible with the conference, and retain a free hand.' Lord Hartington would neither join the conference, nor deny that he thought it premature. While negotiation was going on, he said, somebody must stay at home, guard the position, and keep a watch on the movements of the enemy, and this duty was his. In truth, after encouraging or pressing Mr.

Goschen to join the government, it was obviously impossible to do anything that would look like desertion either of him or of them. On the other side, both English liberals and Irish nationalists were equally uneasy lest the unity of the party should be bought by the sacrifice of fundamentals. The conference was denounced from this quarter as an attempt to find a compromise that would help a few men sitting on the fence to salve ' their consciences at the expense of a nation's rights.' Such remarks are worth quoting, to illustrate the temper of the rank and file. Mr. Parnell, though alive to the truth that when people go into a conference it usually means that they are ready to give up something, was thoroughly awake to the satisfactory significance of the Birmingham overtures.

Things at the round table for some time went smoothly enough. Mr. Chamberlain gradually advanced the whole length. He publicly committed himself to the expediency of establishing some kind of legislative authority in Dublin in accordance with Mr. Gladstone's principle, with a preference in his own mind for a plan on the lines of Canada. This he followed up, also in public, by the admission that of course the Irish legislature must be allowed to organise their own form of executive government, either by an imitation on a small scale of all that goes on at Westminster and Whitehall, or in whatever other shape they might think proper.[1] To assent to an Irish legislature for such affairs as parliament might determine to be distinctively Irish, with an executive responsible to it, was to accept the party credo on the subject. Then the surface became mysteriously ruffled. Language was used by some of the plenipotentiaries in public, of which each side in turn complained as inconsistent with conciliatory negotiation in private. At last on the very day on which the provisional result of the conference was laid before Mr. Gladstone, there appeared in a print called the *Baptist*[2] an article from Mr. Chamberlain, containing an ardent plea for the disestablishment of the Welsh church, but warning the Welshmen that they and the Scotch crofters and the English

[1] See speeches at Hawick, Jan. 22, and at Birmingham, Jan. 29, 1887.

[2] *Baptist* article, in *Times*, Feb. 25, 1887.

labourers, thirty-two millions of people, must all go without much-needed legislation because three millions were disloyal, while nearly six hundred members of parliament would be reduced to forced inactivity, because some eighty delegates, representing the policy and receiving the pay of the Chicago convention, were determined to obstruct all business until their demands had been conceded. Men naturally asked what was the use of continuing a discussion, when one party to it was attacking in this peremptory fashion the very persons and the policy that in private he was supposed to accept. Mr. Gladstone showed no implacability. Viewing the actual character of the *Baptist* letter, he said to Sir W. Harcourt, 'I am inclined to think we can hardly do more now, than to say we fear it has interposed an unexpected obstacle in the way of any attempt at this moment to sum up the result of your communications, which we should otherwise hopefully have done; but on the other hand we are unwilling that so much ground apparently gained should be lost, that a little time may soften or remove the present ruffling of the surface, and that we are quite willing that the subject should stand over for resumption at a convenient season.'

The resumption never happened. Two or three weeks later, Mr. Chamberlain announced that he did not intend to return to the round table.[1] No other serious and formal attempt was ever made on either side to prevent the liberal unionists from hardening into a separate species. When they became accomplices in coercion, they cut off the chances of re-union. Coercion was the key to the new situation. Just as at the beginning of 1886, the announcement of it by the tory government marked the parting of the ways, so was it now.

II

We must now with reasonable cheerfulness turn our faces back towards Ireland. On the day of his return from

---

[1] If anybody should ever wish further to disinter the history of this fruitless episode, he will find all the details in a speech by Sir William Harcourt at Derby, Feb. 27, 1889. See also Sir G. O. Trevelyan, *Times*, July 26, 1887, Mr. Chamberlain's letter to Mr. Evelyn Ashley, *Times*, July 29, 1887, and a speech of my own at Wolverhampton, April 19, 1887.

Ireland (August 17, 1886) Mr. Parnell told me that he CHAP.
was quite sure that rents could not be paid in the II.
coming winter, and if the country was to be kept quiet, Æt. 77.
the government would have to do something. He hoped
that they would do something; otherwise there would be
disturbance, and that he did not want. He had made up
his mind that his interests would be best served by a quiet
winter. For one thing he knew that disturbance would be
followed by coercion, and he knew and often said that of
course strong coercion must always in the long run win the
day, little as the victory might be worth. For another thing
he apprehended that disturbance might frighten away his new
political allies in Great Britain, and destroy the combination
which he had so dexterously built up. This was now a
dominant element with him. He desired definitely that the
next stage of his movement should be in the largest sense
political and not agrarian. He brought two or three sets of
proposals in this sense before the House, and finally produced
a Tenants Relief bill. It was not brilliantly framed. For in
truth it is not in human nature, either Irish or any other, to
labour the framing of a bill which has no chance of being
seriously considered.

The golden secret of Irish government was always to begin
by trying to find all possible points for disagreement with
anything that Mr. Parnell said or proposed, instead of seeking
whether what he said or proposed might not furnish a basis
for agreement. The conciliatory tone was soon over, and the
Parnell bill was thrown out. The Irish secretary denounced
it as permanently upsetting the settlement of 1881, as giving
a death-blow to purchase, and as produced without the proof
of any real grounds for a general reduction in judicial rents.
Whatever else he did, said Sir Michael Hicks Beach, he would
never agree to govern Ireland by a policy of blackmail.[1]

A serious movement followed the failure of the government
to grapple with arrears of rent. The policy known as the
plan of campaign was launched. The plan of campaign was
this. The tenants of a given estate agreed with one another
what abatement they thought just in the current half-year's

[1] *Hans.* 309, Sept. 21, 1886.

rent. This in a body they proffered to landlord or agent. If it was refused as payment in full, they handed the money to a managing committee, and the committee deposited it with some person in whom they had confidence, to be used for the purpose of the struggle.[1] That such proceeding constituted an unlawful conspiracy nobody doubts, any more than it can be doubted that before the Act of 1875 every trade combination of a like kind in this island was a conspiracy.

At an early stage the Irish leader gave his opinion to the present writer: —

Dec. 7, 1886. — Mr. Parnell called, looking very ill and worn. He wished to know what I thought of the effect of the plan of campaign upon public opinion. 'If you mean in Ireland,' I said, 'of course I have no view, and it would be worth nothing if I had. In England, the effect is wholly bad; it offends almost more even than outrages.' He said he had been very ill and had taken no part, so that he stands free and uncommitted. He was anxious to have it fully understood that the fixed point in his tactics is to maintain the alliance with the English liberals. He referred with much bitterness, and very justifiable too, to the fact that when Ireland seemed to be quiet some short time back, the government had at once begun to draw away from all their promises of remedial legislation. If now rents were paid, meetings abandoned, and newspapers moderated, the same thing would happen over again as usual. However, he would send for a certain one of his lieutenants, and would press for an immediate cessation of the violent speeches.

December 12. — Mr. Parnell came, and we had a prolonged conversation. The lieutenant had come over, and had defended the plan of campaign. Mr. Parnell persevered in his dissent and disapproval, and they parted with the understanding that the meetings should be dropped, and the movement calmed as much as could be. I told him that I had heard from Mr. Gladstone, and that he could not possibly show any tolerance for illegalities.

That his opponents should call upon Mr. Gladstone to denounce the plan of campaign and cut himself off from its authors, was to be expected. They made the most of it.

---

[1] See *United Ireland*, Oct. 23, 1886.

But he was the last man to be turned aside from the prosecution of a policy that he deemed of overwhelming
moment, by any minor currents. Immediately after the
election, Mr. Parnell had been informed of his view that it
would be a mistake for English and Irish to aim at uniform
action in parliament. Motives could not be at all points the
same. Liberals were bound to keep in view (next to what
the Irish question might require) the reunion of the liberal
party. The Irish were bound to have special regard to the
opinion and circumstances of Ireland. Common action up
to a certain degree would arise from the necessities of the
position. Such was Mr. Gladstone's view. He was bent on
bringing a revolutionary movement to what he confidently
anticipated would be a good end; to allow a passing phase
of that movement to divert him, would be to abandon his
own foundations. No reformer is fit for his task who suffers
himself to be frightened off by the excesses of an extreme
wing.

In reply to my account of the conversation with Mr.
Parnell, he wrote to me:—

Hawarden, December 8, 1886. — I have received your very clear
statement and reply in much haste for the post — making the same
request as yours for a return. I am glad to find the —— speech
is likely to be neutralised, I hope effectually. It was really very
bad. I am glad you write to ——. 2. As to the campaign in Ireland, I do not at present feel the force of Hartington's appeal to
me to speak out. I do not recollect that he ever spoke out about
Churchill, of whom he is for the time the enthusiastic follower.[1]
3. But all I say and do must be kept apart from the slightest
countenance direct or indirect to illegality. We too suffer under
the power of the landlord, but we cannot adopt this as a method
of breaking it. 4. I am glad you opened the question of intermediate measures. . . . 5. Upon the whole I suppose he sees he
cannot have countenance from us in the plan of campaign. The
question rather is how much disavowal. I have contradicted
a tory figment in Glasgow that I had approved.

At a later date (September 16, 1887) he wrote to me as to

[1] Lord Randolph had encouraged a plan of campaign in Ulster against
home rule.

an intended speech at Newcastle : 'You will, I have no doubt, press even more earnestly than before on the Irish people the duty and policy of maintaining order, and in these instances I shall be very glad if you will associate me with yourself.'

'The plan of campaign,' said Mr. Gladstone, 'was one of those devices that cannot be reconciled with the principles of law and order in a civilised country. Yet we all know that such devices are the certain result of misgovernment. With respect to this particular instance, if the plan be blameable (I cannot deny that I feel it difficult to acquit any such plan) I feel its authors are not one-tenth part so blameable as the government whose contemptuous refusal of what they have now granted, was the parent and source of the mischief.'[1] This is worth looking at.

The Cowper Commission, in February 1887, reported that refusal by some landlords explained much that had occurred in the way of combination, and that the growth of these combinations had been facilitated by the fall in prices, restriction of credit by the banks, and other circumstances making the payment of rent impossible.[2] Remarkable evidence was given by Sir Redvers Buller. He thought there should be some means of modifying and redressing the grievance of rents being still higher than the people can pay. 'You have got a very ignorant poor people, and the law should look after them, instead of which it has only looked after the rich.'[3] This was exactly what Mr. Parnell had said. In the House the government did not believe him ; in Ireland they admitted his case to be true. In one instance General Buller wrote to the agents of the estate that he believed it was impossible for the tenants to pay the rent that was demanded ; there might be five or six rogues among them, but in his opinion the greater number of them were nearer famine than paying rent.[4] In this very case ruthless evictions followed. The same scenes were enacted elsewhere. The landlords were within their rights, the courts were bound by the law, the police had no choice but to back

[1] Speech at the Memorial Hall, July 29, 1887.
[2] Report, p. 8, sect. 15.
[3] *Freeman*, Jan. 1887.
[4] Questions 16, 473–5.

the courts. The legal case was complete. The moral case
remained, and it was through these barbarous scenes that in
a rough and non-logical way the realities of the Irish land
system for the first time gained access to the minds of the
electors of Great Britain. Such devices as the plan of campaign came to be regarded in England and Scotland as what
they were, incidents in a great social struggle. In a vast
majority of cases the mutineers succeeded in extorting
a reduction of rent, not any more immoderate than the
reduction voluntarily made by good landlords, or decreed in
the land-courts. No agrarian movement in Ireland was ever
so unstained by crime.

Some who took part in these affairs made no secret of
political motives. Unlike Mr. Parnell, they deliberately
desired to make government difficult. Others feared that
complete inaction would give an opening to the Fenian
extremists. This section had already shown some signs both
of their temper and their influence in certain proceedings
of the Gaelic association at Thurles. But the main spring
was undoubtedly agrarian, and the force of the spring came
from mischiefs that ministers had refused to face in time.
'What they call a conspiracy now,' said one of the insurgent
leaders, 'they will call an Act of parliament next year.' So
it turned out.

The Commission felt themselves 'constrained to recommend an earlier revision of judicial rents, on account
of the straitened circumstances of Irish farmers.' What
the commissioners thus told ministers in the spring was
exactly what the Irish leader had told them in the previous autumn. They found that there were 'real grounds'
for some legislation of the kind that the chief secretary,
unconscious of what his cabinet was so rapidly to come to,
had stigmatised as the policy of blackmail.

On the last day of March 1887, the government felt the
necessity of introducing a measure based on facts that they
had disputed, and on principles that they had repudiated.
Leaseholders were admitted, some hundred thousand of
them. That is, the more solemn of the forms of agrarian
contract were set aside. Other provisions we may pass over.

But this was not the bill to which the report of the Commission pointed. The pith of that report was the revision and abatement of judicial rents, and from the new bill this vital point was omitted. It could hardly have been otherwise after a curt declaration made by the prime minister in the previous August. 'We do not contemplate any revision of judicial rents,' he said — immediately, by the way, after appointing a commission to find out what it was that they ought to contemplate. 'We do not think it would be honest in the first place, and we think it would be exceedingly inexpedient.'[1] He now repeated that to interfere with judicial rents because prices had fallen, would be to 'lay your axe to the root of the fabric of civilised society.'[2] Before the bill was introduced, Mr. Balfour, who had gone to the Irish office on the retirement of Sir M. H. Beach in the month of March, proclaimed in language even more fervid, that it would be folly and madness to break these solemn contracts.[3]

For that matter, the bill even as it first stood was in direct contravention to all such high doctrine as this, inasmuch as it clothed a court with power to vary solemn contracts by fixing a composition for outstanding debt, and spreading the payment of it over such a time as the judge might think fit. That, however, was the least part of what finally overtook the haughty language of the month of April. In May the government accepted a proposal that the court should not only settle the sum due by an applicant for relief for outstanding debt, but should fix a reasonable rent for the rest of the term. This was the very power of variation that ministers had, as it were only the day before, so roundly denounced. But then the tenants in Ulster were beginning to growl. In June ministers withdrew the power of variation, for now it was the landlords who were growling. Then at last in July the prime minister called his party together, and told them that if the bill were not altered, Ulster would be lost to the unionist cause, and that after all he must put into the bill a general revision of judicial rents for three years. So finally, as it was put by a speaker of that time,

[1] *Hans.* August 19, 1886. [3] *Ibid.* 312, April 22, 1887.
[2] *Ibid.* 313, March 22, 1887.

you have the prime minister rejecting in April the policy
which in May he accepts; rejecting in June the policy which
he had accepted in May; and then in July accepting the
policy which he had rejected in June, and which had been
within a few weeks declared by himself and his colleagues to
be inexpedient and dishonest, to be madness and folly, and
to be a laying of the axe to the very root of the fabric of
civilised society. The simplest recapitulation made the
bitterest satire.

The law that finally emerged from these singular operations dealt, it will be observed in passing, with nothing less
than the chief object of Irish industry and the chief form
of Irish property. No wonder that the landlords lifted up
angry voices. True, the minister the year before had laid it
down that if rectification of rents should be proved necessary,
the landlords ought to be compensated by the state. Of this
consolatory balm it is needless to say no more was ever
heard; it was only a graceful sentence in a speech, and
proved to have little relation to purpose or intention. At
the Kildare Street club in Dublin members moodily asked
one another whether they might not just as well have had
the policy of Mr. Parnell's bill adopted on College Green, as
adopted at Westminster.

III

The moment had by this time once more come for
testing the proposition from which Mr. Gladstone's policy
had first started. The tory government had been turned
out at the beginning of 1886 upon coercion, and Mr.
Gladstone's government had in the summer of that year
been beaten upon conciliation. 'I ventured to state in
1886,' said Mr. Gladstone a year later,[1] 'that we had arrived
at the point where two roads met, or rather where two roads
parted; one of them the road that marked the endeavour to
govern Ireland according to its constitutionally expressed
wishes; the other the road principally marked by ultra-
constitutional measures, growing more and more pronounced in character.' Others, he said, with whom we had

[1] Speech on Criminal Law Amendment (Ireland) bill, March 29, 1887.

been in close alliance down to that date, considered that a third course was open, namely liberal concession, stopping short of autonomy, but upon a careful avoidance of coercion. Now it became visible that this was a mistake, and that in default of effective conciliation, coercion was the inevitable alternative. So it happened.

The government again unlocked the ancient armoury, and brought out the well-worn engines. The new Crimes bill in most particulars followed the old Act, but it contained one or two serious extensions, including a clause afterwards dropped, that gave to the crown a choice in cases of murder or certain other aggravated offences of carrying the prisoner out of his own country over to England and trying him before a Middlesex jury at the Old Bailey — a puny imitation of the heroic expedient suggested in 1769, of bringing American rebels over for trial in England under a slumbering statute of King Henry VIII. The most startling innovation of all was that the new Act was henceforth to be the permanent law of Ireland, and all its drastic provisions were to be brought into force whenever the executive government pleased.[1] This Act was not restricted as every former law of the kind had been in point of time, to meet an emergency; it was made a standing instrument of government. Criminal law and procedure is one of the most important of all the branches of civil rule, and certainly is one of the most important of all its elements. This was now in Ireland to shift up and down, to be one thing to-day and another thing to-morrow at executive discretion. Acts would be innocent or would be crimes, just as it pleased the Irish minister. Parliament did not enact that given things were criminal, but only that they should be criminal when an Irish minister should choose to say so.[2] Persons charged with them would have the benefit of a jury or would be deprived of a jury, as the Irish minister might think proper.

[1] This vital feature of the bill was discussed in the report stage, on a motion limiting the operation of the Act to three years. June 27, 1887. *Hans.* 316, p. 1013. The clause was rejected by 180 to 119, or a majority of 61.

[2] See Palles, C. B., in Walsh's case. *Judgments of Superior Courts in cases under the Criminal Law and Procedure Amendment Act*, 1887, p. 110.

Mr. Parnell was in bad health and took little part, but he made more than one pulverising attack in that measured and frigid style which, in a man who knows his case at first hand, may be so much more awkward for a minister than more florid onslaughts. He discouraged obstruction, and advised his followers to select vital points and to leave others alone. This is said to have been the first Coercion bill that a majority of Irish members voting opposed.

It was at this point that the government suddenly introduced their historic proposal for closure by guillotine. They carried (June 10) a resolution that at ten o'clock on that day week the committee stage should be brought compulsorily to an end, and that any clauses remaining undisposed of should be put forthwith without amendment or debate. The most remarkable innovation upon parliamentary rule and practice since Cromwell and Colonel Pride, was introduced by Mr. Smith in a characteristic speech, well larded with phrases about duty, right, responsibility, business of the country, and efficiency of the House. These 'solemnising complacencies' did not hide the mortifying fact that if it had really been one of the objects of Irish members for ten years past to work a revolution in the parliament where they were forced against their will to sit, they had at least, be such a revolution good or bad, succeeded in their design.

Perhaps looking forward with prophetic eye to a day that actually arrived six years later, Mr. Gladstone, while objecting to the proposal as unjustified, threw the responsibility of it upon the government, and used none of the flaming colours of defiance. The bulk of the liberals abstained from the division. This practical accord between the two sets of leading men made the parliamentary revolution definite and finally clenched it. It was not without something of a funereal pang that members with a sense of the old traditions of the power, solemnity, and honour of the House of Commons came down on the evening of the seventeenth of June. Within a week they would be celebrating the fiftieth year of the reign of the Queen, and that night's business was the strange and unforeseen goal at which a journey of little more than the same period of time

along the high democratic road had brought the commonalty
of the realm since 1832. Among the provisions that went
into the bill without any discussion in committee were those
giving to the Irish executive the power of stamping an association as unlawful; those dealing with special juries and
change of the place of trial; those specifying the various
important conditions attaching to proclamations, which lay at
the foundation of the Act; those dealing with rules, procedure,
and the limits of penalty. The report next fell under what
Burke calls the accursed slider. That stage had taken three
sittings, when the government moved (June 30) that it must
close in four days. So much grace, however, was not needed;
for after the motion had been carried the liberals withdrew
from the House, and the Irishmen betook themselves to the
galleries, whence they looked down upon the mechanical
proceedings below.

IV

In Ireland the battle now began in earnest. The Irish
minister went into it with intrepid logic. Though very
different men in the deeper parts of character, Macaulay's
account of Halifax would not be an ill-natured account of Mr.
Balfour. 'His understanding was keen, sceptical, inexhausti-
bly fertile in distinctions and objections, his taste refined, his
sense of the ludicrous exquisite; his temper placid and for-
giving, but fastidious, and by no means prone either to male-
volence or to enthusiastic admiration.' His business was to
show disaffected Ireland that parliament was her master.
Parliament had put the weapon into his hands, and it was
for him to smite his antagonists to the ground. He made
no experiments in judicious mixture, hard blows and soft
speech, but held steadily to force and fear. His apologists
argued that after all substantial justice was done even in
what seemed hard cases, and even if the spirit of law were
sometimes a trifle strained. Unluckily the peasant with the
blunderbuss, as he waits behind the hedge for the tyrant or
the traitor, says just the same. The forces of disorder were
infinitely less formidable than they had been a hundred
times before. The contest was child's play compared with

the violence and confusion with which Mr. Forster or Lord Spencer had to deal. On the other hand the alliance between liberals and Irish gave to the struggle a parliamentary complexion, by which no coercion struggle had ever been marked hitherto. In the dialectic of senate and platform, Mr. Balfour displayed a strength of wrist, a rapidity, an instant readiness for combat, that took his foes by surprise, and roused in his friends a delight hardly surpassed in the politics of our day.

There was another important novelty this time. To England hitherto Irish coercion had been little more than a word of common form, used without any thought what the thing itself was like to the people coerced. Now it was different. Coercion had for once become a flaming party issue, and when that happens all the world awakes. Mr. Gladstone had proclaimed that the choice lay between conciliation and coercion. The country would have liked conciliation, but did not trust his plan. When coercion came, the two British parties rushed to their swords, and the deciding body of neutrals looked on with anxiety and concern. There has never been a more strenuously sustained contest in the history of political campaigns. No effort was spared to bring the realities of repression vividly home to the judgment and feelings of men and women of our own island. English visitors trooped over to Ireland, and brought back stories of rapacious landlords, violent police, and famishing folk cast out homeless upon the wintry roadside. Irishmen became the most welcome speakers on British platforms, and for the first time in all our history they got a hearing for their lamentable tale. To English audiences it was as new and interesting as the narrative of an African explorer or a navigator in the Pacific. Our Irish instructors even came to the curious conclusion that ordinary international estimates must be revised, and that Englishmen are in truth far more emotional than Irishmen. Ministerial speakers, on the other hand, diligently exposed inaccuracy here or over-colouring there. They appealed to the English distaste for disorder, and to the English taste for mastery, and they did not overlook the slumbering jealousy of popery and priestcraft.   But the course of affairs was too rapid for them, the strong harsh doses to the Irish patient were too incessant.   The Irish convictions in cases where the land was concerned rose to 2805, and of these rather over one-half were in cases where in England the rights of the prisoner would have been guarded by a jury.   The tide of common popular feeling in this island about the right to combine, the right of public meeting, the frequent barbarities of eviction, the jarring indignities of prison treatment, flowed stronger and stronger.   The general impression spread more and more widely that the Irish did not have fair play, that they were not being treated about speeches and combination and meetings as Englishmen or Scotchmen would be treated. Even in breasts that had been most incensed by the sudden reversal of policy in 1886, the feeling slowly grew that it was perhaps a pity after all that Mr. Gladstone had not been allowed to persevere on the fair-shining path of conciliation.

V

The proceedings under exceptional law would make an instructive chapter in the history of the union.   Mr. Gladstone followed them vigilantly, once or twice without his usual exercise of critical faculty, but always bringing into effective light the contrast between this squalid policy and his anticipations of his own.   Here we are only concerned with what affected British opinion on the new policy.   One set of distressing incidents, not connected with the Crimes Act, created disgust and even horror in the country and set Mr. Gladstone on fire.   A meeting of some six thousand persons assembled in a large public square at Mitchelstown in the county of Cork.[1]   It was a good illustration of Mr. Gladstone's habitual strategy in public movements, that he should have boldly and promptly seized on the doings at Mitchelstown as an incident well fitted to arrest the attention of the country. ' Remember   Mitchelstown '   became   a   watchword.   The chairman, speaking from a carriage that did duty for a platform, opened the proceedings.   Then a file of police endeavoured to force a way through the densest part of the

[1] On September 9, 1887.

crowd for a government note-taker. Why they did not
choose an easier mode of approach from the rear, or by the
side ; why they had not got their reporter on to the platform
before the business began; and why they had not beforehand
asked for accommodation as was the practice, were three
points never explained. The police unable to make a way
through the crowd retired to the outskirt. The meeting
went on. In a few minutes a larger body of police pressed
up through the thick of the throng to the platform. A
violent struggle began, the police fighting their way through
the crowd with batons and clubbed rifles. The crowd flung
stones and struck out with sticks, and after three or four
minutes the police fled to their barracks — some two hundred
and fifty yards away. So far there is no material discrepancy
in the various versions of this dismal story. What followed
is matter of conflicting testimony. One side alleged that a
furious throng rushed after the police, attacked the barrack,
and half murdered a constable outside, and that the constables inside in order to save their comrade and to beat off
the assailing force, opened fire from an upper window. The
other side declared that no crowd followed the retreating
police at all, that the assault on the barrack was a myth,
and that the police fired without orders from any responsible
officer, in mere blind panic and confusion. One old man
was shot dead, two others were mortally wounded and died
within a week.

Three days later the affray was brought before the House
of Commons. Any one could see from the various reports
that the conduct of the police, the resistance of the crowd,
and the guilt or justification of the bloodshed, were all
matters in the utmost doubt and demanding rigorous
inquiry. Mr. Balfour pronounced instant and peremptory
judgment. The thing had happened on the previous Friday.
The official report, however rapidly prepared, could not have
reached him until the morning of Sunday. His officers at
the Castle had had no opportunity of testing their official
report by cross-examination of the constables concerned, nor
by inspection of the barrack, the line of fire, and other
material elements of the case. Yet on the strength of this

hastily drawn and unsifted report received by him from
Ireland on Sunday, and without even waiting for any information that eye-witnesses in the House might have to
lay before him in the course of the discussion, the Irish
minister actually told parliament once for all, on the afternoon of Monday, that he was of opinion, 'looking at the
matter in the most impartial spirit, that the police were in
no way to blame, and that no responsibility rested upon any
one except upon those who convened the meeting under
circumstances which they knew would lead to excitement
and might lead to outrage.'[1] The country was astounded to
see the most critical mind in all the House swallow an
untested police report whole ; to hear one of the best judges
in all the country of the fallibility of human testimony, give
offhand, in what was really a charge of murder, a verdict of
Not Guilty, after he had read the untested evidence on one
side.

The rest was all of a piece. The coroner's inquest was
held in due course. The proceedings were not more happily
conducted than was to be expected where each side followed
the counsels of ferocious exasperation. The jury, after some
seventeen days of it, returned a verdict of wilful murder
against the chief police officer and five of his men. This
inquisition was afterwards quashed (February 10, 1888) in
the Queen's bench, on the ground that the coroner had
perpetrated certain irregularities of form. Nobody has
doubted that the Queen's bench was right ; it seemed as if
there had been a conspiracy of all the demons of human
stupidity in this tragic bungle, from the first forcing of the
reporter through the crowd, down to the inquest on the
three slain men and onwards. The coroner's inquest having
broken down, reasonable opinion demanded that some other
public inquiry should be held. Even supporters of the
government demanded it. If three men had been killed by
the police in connection with a public meeting in England
or Scotland, no home secretary would have dreamed for five
minutes of resisting such a demand. Instead of a public
inquiry, what the chief secretary did was to appoint a

[1] Sept. 12, 1887. *Hans.* 321, p. 327.

confidential departmental committee of policemen privately to examine, not whether the firing was justified by the circumstances, but how it came about that the police were so handled by their officers that a large force was put to flight by a disorderly mob. The three deaths were treated as mere accident and irrelevance. The committee was appointed to correct the discipline of the force, said the Irish minister, and in no sense to seek justification for actions which, in his opinion, required no justification.[1] Endless speeches were made in the House and out of it; members went over to Mitchelstown to measure distances, calculate angles, and fire imaginary rifles out of the barrack window; all sorts of theories of ricochet shots were invented, photographs and diagrams were taken. Some held the police to be justified, others held them to be wholly unjustified. But without a judicial inquiry, such as had been set up in the case of Belfast in 1886, all these doings were futile. The government remained stubborn. The slaughter of the three men was finally left just as if it had been the slaughter of three dogs. No other incident of Irish administration stirred deeper feelings of disgust in Ireland, or of misgiving and indignation in England.

Here was, in a word, the key to the new policy. Every act of Irish officials was to be defended. No constable could be capable of excess. No magistrate could err. No prison rule was over harsh. Every severity technically in order must be politic.

VI

Among other remarkable incidents, the Pope came to the rescue, and sent an emissary to inquire into Irish affairs. The government had lively hopes of the emissary, and while they beat the Orange drum in Ulster with one hand, with the other they stealthily twitched the sleeve of Monsignor Persico. It came to little. The Congregation at Rome were directed by the Pope to examine whether it was lawful to resort to the plan of campaign. They answered that it was contrary both to natural justice and Christian charity. The papal rescript, embodying this conclusion, was received in

[1] Dec. 3, 1888. *Hans.* 331, p. 916.

Ireland with little docility.   Unwisely the cardinals had given reasons, and the reasons, instead of springing in the mystic region of faith and morals, turned upon issues of fact as to fair rents.   But then the Irish tenant thought himself a far better judge of a fair rent, than all the cardinals that ever wore red hats.   If he had heard of such a thing as Jansenism, he would have known that he was in his own rude way taking up a position not unlike that of the famous teachers of Port Royal two hundred and thirty years before, that the authority of the Holy See is final as to doctrine, but may make a mistake as to fact.

Mr. Parnell spoke tranquilly of ' a document from a distant country,' and publicly left the matter to his catholic countrymen.[1]   Forty catholic members of parliament met at the Mansion House in Dublin, and signed a document in which they flatly denied every one of the allegations and implications about fair rents, free contract, the land commission and all the rest, and roundly declared the Vatican circular to be an instrument of the unscrupulous foes both of the Holy See and of the people of Ireland.   They told the Pope, that while recognising unreservedly as catholics the spiritual jurisdiction of the Holy See, they were bound solemnly to affirm that Irish catholics recognise no rights in Rome to interfere in their political affairs.   A great meeting in the Phœnix Park ratified the same position by acclamation.   At Cork, under the presidency of the mayor, and jealously watched by forces of horse and foot, a great gathering in a scene of indescribable excitement protested that they would never allow the rack-renters of Ireland to grind them down at the instigation of intriguers at Rome.   Even in many cities in the United States the same voice was heard.   The bishops knew well that the voice was strongly marked by the harsh accent of their Fenian adversaries.   They issued a declaration of their own, protesting to their flocks that the rescript was confined within the spiritual sphere, and that his holiness was far from wishing to prejudice the nationalist movement.   In the closing week of the year, the Pope himself judged that the time had come for him to make known

[1] May 8, 1888.

that the action which had been 'so sadly misunderstood,' had been prompted by the desire to keep the cause in which Ireland was struggling from being weakened by the introduction of anything that could justly be brought in reproach against it.[1] The upshot of the intervention was that the action condemned by the rescript was not materially affected within the area already disturbed ; but the rescript may have done something to prevent its extension elsewhere.

VII

Among the entries for 1887 there occur : —

Sandringham, Jan. 29. — A large party. We were received with the usual delicacy and kindness. Much conversation with the Prince of Wales. . . . Walk with ——, who charmed me much. _Jan._ 31. — Off by 11 A.M. to Cambridge. . . . Dined with the master of Trinity in hall. Went over the Newnham buildings : greatly pleased. Saw Mr. Sidgwick. Evening service at King's. . . . _Feb._ 2. — Hawarden at 5.30. Set to work on papers. Finished Greville's Journals. _Feb._ 3. — Wrote on Greville. _Feb._ 5. — Felled a chestnut. _Feb._ 27. — Read Lord Shaftesbury's _Memoirs_ — an excellent discipline for me. _March_ 5. — Dollis Hill [a house near Willesden often lent to him in these times by Lord and Lady Aberdeen] a refuge from my timidity, unwilling at 77 to begin a new London house. _March_ 9. — Windsor [to dine and sleep]. The Queen courteous as always ; somewhat embarrassed, as I thought. _March_ 29. — Worked on Homer, Apollo, etc. Then turned to the Irish business and revolved much, with extreme difficulty in licking the question into shape. Went to the House and spoke 1½ hours as carefully and with as much measure as I could. Conclave on coming course of business. _April_ 5. — Conversation with Mr. Chamberlain — ambiguous result, but some ground made. _April_ 18. — H. of C. 4½–8¼ and 10–2. Spoke 1¼ h. My voice did its duty but with great effort. _April_ 25. — Spoke for an hour upon the budget. R. Churchill excellent. Conclave on the forged letters. _May_ 4. — Read earlier speeches of yesterday with care, and worked up the subject of Privilege. Spoke 1¼ h.

[1] _Tablet_, Jan. 5, 1889.

In June (1887) Mr. Gladstone started on a political campaign in South Wales, where his reception was one of the most triumphant in all his career. Ninety-nine hundredths of the vast crowds who gave up wages for the sake of seeing him and doing him honour were strong protestants, yet he said to a correspondent, 'they made this demonstration in order to secure firstly and mainly justice to catholic Ireland. It is not after all a bad country in which such things take place.'

It was at Swansea that he said what he had to say about the Irish members. He had never at any time from the hour when he formed his government, set up their exclusion as a necessary condition of home rule. All that he ever bargained for was that no proposal for inclusion should be made a ground for impairing real and effective self-government. Subject to this he was ready to adjourn the matter and to leave things as they were, until experience should show the extent of the difficulty and the best way of meeting it. Provisional exclusion had been suggested by a member of great weight in the party in 1886. The new formula was provisional inclusion. This announcement restored one very distinguished adherent to Mr. Gladstone, and it appeased the clamour of the busy knot who called themselves imperial federationists. Of course it opened just as many new difficulties as it closed old ones, but both old difficulties and new fell into the background before the struggle in Ireland.

June 2, 1887. — Off at 11.40. A tumultuous but interesting journey to Swansea and Singleton, where we were landed at 7.30. Half a dozen speeches on the way. A small party to dinner. 3. — A 'quiet day.' Wrote draft to the associations on the road, as model. Spent the forenoon in settling plans and discussing the lines of my meditated statement to-morrow with Sir Hussey Vivian, Lord Aberdare, and Mr. Stuart Rendel. In the afternoon we went to the cliffs and the Mumbles, and I gave some hours to writing preliminary notes on a business where all depends on the manner of handling. Small party to dinner. Read Cardiff and Swansea guides. 4. — More study and notes. 12–4½ the astonishing procession. Sixty thousand ! Then spoke for near an hour. Dinner at 8, near an hundred, arrangements perfect. Spoke for nearly another hour; got through a most difficult business as well as I could expect. 5. — Church 11 A.M., notable sermon and H. C. (service long), again 6½ P.M., good sermon. Wrote to Sir W. Harcourt, Mr. Morley, etc. Walked in the garden. Considered the question of a non-political address 'in council'; we all decided against it. 6. — Surveys in the house, then 12–4 to Swansea for the freedom and opening the town library. I was rather jealous of a non-political affair at such a time, but could not do less than speak for thirty or thirty-five minutes for the two occasions. 4–8 to Park Farm, the beautiful vales, breezy common and the curious chambered cairn. Small dinner-party. 7. — Off at 8.15 and a hard day to London, the occasion of processions, hustles, and speeches; that at Newport in the worst atmosphere known since the Black Hole. Poor C. too was an invalid. Spoke near an hour to 3000 at Cardiff; about ¼ hour at Newport; more briefly at Gloucester and Swindon. Much enthusiasm even in the English part of the journey. Our party was reduced at Newport to the family, at Gloucester to our two selves. C. H. Terrace at 6.20. Wrote to get off the House of Commons. It has really been a 'progress,' and an extraordinary one.

In December 1887, under the pressing advice of his physician, though 'with a great lazy reluctance,' Mr. Gladstone set his face with a family party towards Florence. He found the weather more northern than at Hawarden, but it was healthy. He was favourably impressed by all he saw of Italian society (English being cultivated to a degree that surprised him), but he did his best to observe Sir Andrew Clark's injunction that he should practise the Trappist discipline of silence, and the condition of his voice improved in consequence. He read Scartazzini's book on Dante, and found it fervid, generally judicial, and most unsparing in labour ; and he was much interested in Beugnot's *Chute du Paganisme*. And as usual, he returned homeward as unwillingly as he had departed. During the session he fought his Irish battle with unsparing tenacity, and the most conspicuous piece of his activity out of parliament was a pilgrimage to Birmingham (November 1888). It was a great gathering of lieutenants and leading supporters from every part of the country. Here is a note of mine : —

On the day of the great meeting in Bingley Hall, somebody came to say that Mr. Gladstone wanted to know if I could supply him with a certain passage from a speech of Lord Hartington's. I found him in his dressing-gown, conning his notes and as lively as youth. He jumped up and pressed point after point on me, as if I had been a great public meeting. I offered to go down to the public library and hunt for the passage; he deprecated this, but off I went, and after some search unearthed the passage, and copied it out. In the evening I went to dine with him before the meeting. He had been out for a short walk to the Oratory in the afternoon to call on Cardinal Newman. He was not allowed, he told me, to see the cardinal, but he had had a long talk with Father Neville. He found that Newman was in the habit of reading with a reflector candle, but had not a good one. ' So I said I had a good one, and I sent it round to him.' He was entirely disengaged in mind during dinner, ate and drank his usual quantity, and talked at his best about all manner of things. At the last moment he was telling us of John Hunter's confirmation, from his own medical observation, of Homer's remark about Dolon; a bad fellow, whose badness Homer explains by the fact that he was a brother brought up among sisters only : —

αὐτὰρ ὃ μοῦνος ἔην μετὰ πέντε κασιγνήτῃσιν.[1]

Oliver Cromwell, by the way, was an only surviving boy among seven sisters, so we cannot take either poet or surgeon for gospel. Time was up, and bore us away from Homer and Hunter. He was perfectly silent in the carriage, as I remembered Bright had been when years before I drove with him to the same hall. The sight of the vast meeting was almost appalling, from fifteen to seventeen thousand people. He spoke with great vigour and freedom; the fine passages probably heard all over; many other passages certainly not heard, but his gestures so strong and varied as to be almost as interesting as the words would have been. The speech lasted an hour and fifty minutes; and he was not at all

[1] *Iliad*, x. 317. See *Homer and Homeric Age*, iii. 467 n.

exhausted when he sat down. The scene at the close was absolutely
indescribable and incomparable, overwhelming like the sea.

He took part in parliamentary business at the beginning
of December. On December 3rd he spoke on Ireland with
immense fervour and passion. He was roused violently by
the chairman's attempt to rule out strong language from
debate, and made a vehement passage on that point. The
substance of the speech was rather thin and not new, but
the delivery magnificent. The Irish minister rose to reply
at 7.50, and Mr. Gladstone reluctantly made up his mind
to dine in the House. A friend by his side said No, and
at 8.40 hurried him down the back-stairs to a hospitable
board in Carlton Gardens. He was nearly voiceless, until
it was time for the rest of us to go back. A speedy meal
revived him, and he was soon discoursing on O'Connell
and many other persons and things, with boundless force
and vivacity.

A few days later he was carried off to Naples. Hereto, he
told Lord Acton, 'we have been induced by three circumstances. First, a warm invitation from the Dufferins to
Rome; as to which, however, there are *cons* as well as *pros*
for a man who like me is neither Italian nor Curial in the
view of present policies. Secondly, our kind friend Mr.
Stuart Rendel has actually offered to be our conductor
thither and back, to perform for us the great service which
you rendered us in the trip to Munich and Saint Martin.
Thirdly, I have the hope that the stimulating climate of
Naples, together with an abstention from speech greater than
any I have before enjoyed, may act upon my " vocal cord,"
and partially at least restore it.'

CHAPTER III

THE SPECIAL COMMISSION

(1887-1890)

> MY Lords, it appears to me that the measure is unfortunate in its
> origin, unfortunate in its scope and object, and unfortunate in the
> circumstances which accompanied its passage through the other
> House. It appears to me to establish a precedent most novel, and
> fraught with the utmost danger. — LORD HERSCHELL.[1]

BOOK
X.

1887.

MR. GLADSTONE'S ceaseless attention to the many phases of
the struggle that was now the centre of his public life, was
especially engaged on what remains the most amazing of
them. I wish it were possible to pass it over, or throw it
into a secondary place; but it is too closely connected with
the progress of Mr. Gladstone's Irish policy in British opinion
at a critical stage, and it is still the subject of too many
perversions that affect his name. Transactions are to be
found in our annals where wrong was done by government
to individuals on a greater scale, where a powerful majority
devised engines for the proscription of a weak minority
with deadlier aim, and where the omnipotence of parliament
was abused for the purpose of faction with more ruthless
result. But whether we look at the squalid fraud in which
the incident began, or at the tortuous parliamentary pre-
tences by which it was worked out, or at the perversion of
fundamental principles of legal administration involved in
sending men to answer the gravest charges before a tribunal
specially constituted at the absolute discretion of their
bitterest political opponents — at the moment engaged in
a fierce contest with them in another field — from whatever
point of view we approach, the erection of the Special Commission of 1888 stands out as one of the ugliest things done
in the name and under the forms of law in this island during
the century.

[1] House of Lords, August 10, 1888.

In the spring of 1887 the conductors of *The Times*, intending to strengthen the hands of the government in their new and doubtful struggle, published a series of articles, in which old charges against the Irish leader and his men were served up with fresh and fiery condiments. The allegations of crime were almost all indefinite; the method was by allusion, suggestion, innuendo, and the combination of ingeniously selected pieces, to form a crude and hideous mosaic. Partly from its extravagance, partly because it was in substance stale, the thing missed fire.

On the day on which the division was to be taken on the second reading of the Coercion bill, a more formidable bolt was shot. On that morning (April 18th, 1887), there appeared in the newspaper, with all the fascination of facsimile, a letter alleged to be written by Mr. Parnell. It was dated nine days after the murders in the Phœnix Park, and purported to be an apology, presumably to some violent confederate, for having as a matter of expediency openly condemned the murders, though in truth the writer thought that one of the murdered men deserved his fate.[1] Special point was given to the letter by a terrible charge, somewhat obliquely but still unmistakably made, in an article five or six weeks before, that Mr. Parnell closely consorted with the leading Invincibles when he was released on parole in April 1882 ; that he probably learned from them what they were about; and that he recognised the murders in the Phœnix Park as their handiwork.[2] The significance of the letter therefore was that, knowing the bloody deed to be theirs, he wrote for his own safety to qualify, recall, and make a humble apology for the condemnation which he had thought it politic publicly to pronounce. The town was

---

[1] Here is the text of this once famous piece : —

'15/5/82.

'DEAR SIR, — I am not surprised at your friend's anger, but he and you should know that to denounce the murders was the only course open to us. To do that promptly was plainly our best policy. But you can tell him and all others concerned, that though I regret the accident of Lord F. Cavendish's death, I cannot refuse to admit that Burke got no more than his deserts. You are at liberty to show him this, and others whom you can trust also, but let not my address be known. He can write to the House of Commons. — Yours very truly,

'CHAS. S. PARNELL.'

[2] The three judges held this to be a correct interpretation of the language used in the article of March 10th, 1887. Report, pp. 57-8.

thrown into a great ferment. At the political clubs and in the lobbies, all was complacent jubilation on the one side, and consternation on the other. Even people with whom politics were a minor interest were shocked by such an exposure of the grievous depravity of man.

Mr. Parnell did not speak until one o'clock in the morning, immediately before the division on the second reading of the bill. He began amid the deepest silence. His denial was scornful but explicit. The letter, he said, was an audacious fabrication. It is fair to admit that the ministerialists were not without some excuse of a sort for the incredulous laughter with which they received this repudiation. They put their trust in the most serious, the most powerful, the most responsible, newspaper in the world; greatest in resources, in authority, in universal renown. Neglect of any possible precaution against fraud and forgery in a document to be used for the purpose of blasting a great political opponent would be culpable in no common degree. Of this neglect people can hardly be blamed for thinking that the men of business, men of the world, and men of honour who were masters of the *Times*, must be held absolutely incapable.

Those who took this view were encouraged in it by the prime minister. Within four-and-twenty hours he publicly took the truth of the story, with all its worst innuendoes, entirely for granted. He went with rapid stride from possibility to probability, and from probability to certainty. In a speech, of which precipitate credulity was not the only fault, Lord Salisbury let fall the sentence: 'When men who knew gentlemen who intimately knew Mr. Parnell murdered Mr. Burke.' He denounced Mr. Gladstone for making a trusted friend of such a man — one who had 'mixed on terms of intimacy with those whose advocacy of assassination was well known.' Then he went further. 'You may go back,' he said, 'to the beginning of British government, you may go back from decade to decade, and from leader to leader, but you will never find a man who has accepted a position, in reference to an ally tainted with the strong presumption of conniving at assassination, which

has been accepted by Mr. Gladstone at the present time.'[1]
Seldom has party spirit led eminent personages to greater
lengths of dishonouring absurdity.

Now and afterwards people asked why Mr. Parnell did
not promptly bring his libellers before a court of law. The
answer was simple. The case would naturally have been
tried in London. In other words, not only the plaintiff's
own character, but the whole movement that he represented,
would have been submitted to a Middlesex jury, with all the
national and political prejudices inevitable in such a body,
and with all the twelve chances of a disagreement, that
would be almost as disastrous to Mr. Parnell as an actual
verdict for his assailants. The issues were too great to be
exposed to the hazards of a cast of the die. Then, why not
lay the venue in Ireland? It was true that a favourable
verdict might just as reasonably be expected from the prepossessions of Dublin, as an unfavourable one from the
prepossessions of London. But the moral effect of an Irish
verdict upon English opinion would be exactly as worthless,
as the effect of an English verdict in a political or international case would be upon the judgment and feeling of
Ireland. To procure a condemnation of the *Times* at the
Four Courts, as a means of affecting English opinion, would
not be worth a single guinea. Undoubtedly the subsequent
course of this strange history fully justified the advice that
Mr. Parnell received in this matter from the three persons
in the House of Commons with whom on this point he took
counsel.

II

The prudent decision against bringing a fierce political
controversy before an English judge and jury was in a few
months brought to nought, from motives that have remained
obscure, and with results that nobody could foresee. The
next act in the drama was the institution of proceedings
for libel against the *Times* in November 1887, by an Irishman who had formerly sat in parliament as a political
follower of Mr. Parnell. The newspaper met him by denying
that the articles on *Parnellism and Crime* related to him.

[1] April 20, 1887.

It went on to plead that the statements in the articles were true in substance and in fact. The action was tried before Lord Coleridge in July 1888, and the newspaper was represented by the advocate who happened to be the principal law officer of the crown. The plaintiff's counsel picked out certain passages, said that his client was one of the persons intended to be libelled, and claimed damages. He was held to have made an undoubted *prima facie* case on the two libels in which he had been specifically named. This gave the enemy his chance. The attorney general, speaking for three days, opened the whole case for the newspaper; repeated and enlarged upon the charges and allegations in its articles; stated the facts which he proposed to give in evidence; sought to establish that the fac-simile letter was really signed by Mr. Parnell; and finally put forward other letters, now produced for the first time, which carried complicity and connivance to a further point. These charges he said that he should prove. On the third day he entirely changed his tack. Having launched this mass of criminating imputation, he then suddenly bethought him, so he said, of the hardships which his course would entail upon the Irishmen, and asked that in that action he should not be called upon to prove anything at all. The Irishmen and their leader remained under a load of odium that the law officer of the crown had cast upon them, and declined to substantiate.

The production of this further batch of letters stirred Mr. Parnell from his usual impassiveness. His former determination to sit still was shaken. The day after the attorney general's speech, he came to the present writer to say that he thought of sending a paragraph to the newspapers that night, with an announcement of his intention to bring an action against the *Times*, narrowed to the issue of the letters. The old arguments against an action were again pressed upon him. He insisted, on the other side, that he was not afraid of cross-examination; that they might cross-examine as much as ever they pleased, either about the doings of the land league or the letters; that his hands would be found to be clean, and the letters to be gross forgeries. The question between us was adjourned; and meanwhile he fell in with my suggestion that he should the next day make a personal statement to the House. The personal statement was made in his most frigid manner, and it was as frigidly received. He went through the whole of the letters, one by one ; showed the palpable incredibility of some of them upon their very face, and in respect of those which purported to be written by himself, he declared, in words free from all trace of evasion, that he had never written them, never signed them, never directed nor authorised them to be written.

So the matter was left on the evening of Friday (July 6, 1888). On Monday Mr. Parnell came to the House with the intention to ask for a select committee. The feeling of the English friend to whom he announced his intention in the lobby, still was that the matter might much better be left where it stood. The new batch of letters had strengthened his position, for the Kilmainham letter was a fraud upon the face of it, and a story that he had given a hundred pounds to a fugitive from justice after the murders, had been demolished. The press throughout the country had treated the subject very coolly. The government would pretty certainly refuse a select committee, and what would be the advantage to him in the minds of persons inclined to think him guilty, of making a demand which he knew beforehand would be declined? Such was the view now pressed upon Mr. Parnell. This time he was not moved. He took his own course, as he had a paramount right to do. He went into the House and asked the ministers to grant a select committee to inquire into the authenticity of the letters read at the recent trial. Mr. Smith replied, as before, that the House was absolutely incompetent to deal with the charges. Mr. Parnell then gave notice that he would that night put on the paper the motion for a committee, and on Thursday demand a day for its discussion.

When Thursday arrived, either because the hot passion of the majority was irresistible, or from a cool calculation of policy, or simply because the situation was becoming intolerable, a new decision had been taken, itself

far more intolerable than the scandal that it was to dis-
sipate. The government met the Irish leader with a refusal
and an offer. They would not give a committee, but they
were willing to propose a commission to consist wholly
or mainly of judges, with statutory power to inquire into
'the allegations and charges made against members of
parliament by the defendants in the recent action.' If the
gentlemen from Ireland were prepared to accept the offer,
the government would at once put on the paper for the
following Monday, notice of motion for leave to bring in a
bill.[1]

When the words of the notice of motion appeared in
print, it was found amid universal astonishment that the
special commission was to inquire into the charges and
allegations generally, not only against certain members of
parliament, but also against 'other persons.' The enormity
of this sudden extension of the operation was palpable. A
certain member is charged with the authorship of incrimi-
nating letters. To clear his character as a member of
parliament, he demands a select committee. We decline to
give a committee, says the minister, but we offer you a commission of judges, and you may take our offer or refuse, as
you please; only the judges must inquire not merely into
your question of the letters, but into all the charges and
allegations made against all of you, and not these only, but
into the charges and allegations made against other people
as well. This was extraordinary enough, but it was not all.

It is impossible to feel much surprise that Mr. Parnell
was ready to assent to any course, however unconstitutional
that course might be, if only it led to the exposure of an
insufferable wrong. The credit of parliament and the
sanctity of constitutional right were no supreme concern of
his. He was burning to get at any expedient, committee or
commission, which should enable him to unmask and smite
his hidden foes. Much of his private language at this time
was in some respects vague and ineffectual, but he was
naturally averse to any course that might, in his own words,
look like backing down. 'Of course,' he said, 'I am not

[1] *Hans.* July 12, 1888, p. 1102.

sure that we shall come off with flying colours. But I think we shall. I am never sure of anything.' He was still confident that he had the clue.

On the second stage of the transaction, Mr. Smith, in answer to various questions in the early part of the sitting, made a singular declaration. The bill, he said, of which he had given notice, was a bill to be introduced in accordance with the offer already made. ' I do not desire to debate the proposal; and I have put it in this position on the Order Book, in order that it may be rejected or accepted by the honourable member in the form in which it stands.' Then in the next sentence, he said, ' If the motion is received and accepted by the House, the bill will be printed and circulated, and I will then name a day for the second reading. But I may say frankly that I do not anticipate being able to make provision for a debate on the second reading of a measure of this kind. It was an offer made by the government to the honourable gentleman and his friends, to be either accepted or rejected.'[1] The minister treated his bill as lightly as if it were some small proposal of ordinary form and of even less than ordinary importance. It is not inconceivable that there was design in this, for Mr. Smith concealed under a surface of plain and homely worth a very full share of parliamentary craft, and he knew well enough that the more extraordinary the measure, the more politic it always is to open with an air of humdrum.

The bill came on at midnight July 16, in a House stirred with intense excitement, closely suppressed. The leader of the House made the motion for leave to introduce the most curious innovation of the century, in a speech of half-a-minute. It might have been a formal bill for a provisional order, to be taken as of course. Mr. Parnell, his ordinary pallor made deeper by anger, and with unusual though very natural vehemence of demeanour, at once hit the absurdity of asking him whether he accepted or rejected the bill, not only before it was printed but without explanation of its contents. He then pressed in two or three weighty sentences the deeper absurdity of leaving him any option at

[1] *Hans.* July 16, p. 1410.

all. The attorney general had said of the story of the fac-simile letter, that if it was not genuine, it was the worst libel ever launched on a public man. If the first lord believed his attorney, said Mr. Parnell, instead of talking about making a bargain with me, he ought to have come down and said, 'The government are determined to have this investigation, whether the honourable member, this alleged criminal, likes it or not.'[1]

That was in fact precisely what the government had determined. The profession that the bill was a benevolent device for enabling the alleged criminals to extricate themselves was very soon dropped. The offer of a boon to be accepted or declined at discretion was transformed into a grand compulsory investigation into the connection of the national and land leagues with agrarian crime, and the members of parliament were virtually put into the dock along with all sorts of other persons who chanced to be members of those associations. The effect was certain. Any facts showing criminality in this or that member of the league would be taken to show criminality in the organisation as a whole, and especially in the political leaders. And the proceeding could only be vindicated by the truly outrageous principle that where a counsel in a suit finds it his duty as advocate to make grave charges against members of parliament in court, then it becomes an obligation on the government to ask for an Act to appoint a judicial commission to examine those charges, if only they are grave enough.

The best chance of frustrating the device was lost when the bill was allowed to pass its first reading unopposed. Three of the leaders of the liberal opposition — two in the Commons, one in the Lords — were for making a bold stand against the bill from the first. Mr. Gladstone, on the contrary, with his lively instinct for popular feeling out of doors, disliked any action indicative of reluctance to face inquiry; and though holding a strong view that no case had been made out for putting aside the constitutional and convenient organ of a committee, yet he thought that an

[1] *Hans.* July 16, 1888, p. 1495.

inquiry under thoroughly competent and impartial judges, CHAP.
after the right and true method of proceeding had been III.
refused, was still better than no proceeding at all. This much ÆT. 79.
of assent, however, was qualified. 'I think,' he said, 'that
an inquiry under thoroughly competent and impartial judges
is better than none. But that inquiry must, I think, be put
into such a shape as shall correspond with the general law
and principles of justice.' As he believed, the first and most
indispensable conditions of an effective inquiry were wanting, and without them he 'certainly would have no responsibility whatever.'[1]

For the first few days politicians were much adrift. They
had moments of compunction. Whether friends or foes of
the Irish, they were perplexed by the curious double aspect
of the measure. Mr. Parnell himself began to feel misgivings, as he came to realise the magnitude of the inquiry,
its vast expense, its interminable length, its unfathomable
uncertainties. On the day appointed for the second reading
of the bill appointing the commission (July 23), some other
subject kept the business back until seven o'clock. Towards
six, Mr. Parnell who was to open the debate on his own side,
came to an English friend, to ask whether there would be
time for him to go away for an hour; he wished to examine
some new furnace for assaying purposes, the existence of
gold in Wicklow being one of his fixed ideas. So steady
was the composure of this extraordinary man. The English
friend grimly remarked to him that it would perhaps be
rather safer not to lose sight of the furnace in which at any
moment his own assaying might begin. His speech on this
critical occasion was not one of his best. Indifference to his
audience often made him meagre, though he was scarcely
ever other than clear, and in this debate there was only one
effective point which it was necessary for him to press. The
real issue was whether the reference to the judges should be
limited or unlimited; should be a fishing inquiry at large
into the history of an agrarian agitation ten years old, or
an examination into definite and specified charges against
named members of parliament. The minister, in moving

[1] *Hans.* 329, July 23, 1888, p. 263.

the second reading, no longer left it to the Irish members to accept or reject; it now rested, he said, with the House to decide. It became evident that the acuter members of the majority, fully awakened to the opportunities for destroying the Irishmen which an unlimited inquisition might furnish, had made up their minds that no limit should be set to the scope of the inquisition. Boldly they tramped through a thick jungle of fallacy and inconsistency. They had never ceased to insist, and they insisted now, that Mr. Parnell ought to have gone into a court of law. Yet they fought as hard as they could against every proposal for making the procedure of the commission like the procedure of a law court. In a court there would have been a specific indictment. Here a specific indictment was what they most positively refused, and for it they substituted a roving inquiry, which is exactly what a court never undertakes. They first argued that nothing but a commission was available to test the charges against members of parliament. Then, when they had bethought themselves of further objects, they argued round that it was unheard of and inconceivable to institute a royal commission for members of parliament alone.

All arguments, however unanswerable, were at this stage idle, because Mr. Parnell had reverted to his original resolution to accept the bill, and at his request the radicals sitting below him abandoned their opposition. The bill passed the second reading without a division. This circumstance permitted the convenient assertion, made so freely afterwards, that the bill, irregular, unconstitutional, violent, as it might be, at any rate received the unanimous assent of the House of Commons.

Stormy scenes marked the progress of the bill through committee. Seeing the exasperation produced by their shifting of the ground, and the delay which it would naturally entail, ministers resolved on a bold step. It was now August. Government remembered the process by which they had carried the Coercion bill, and they improved upon it. After three days of committee, they moved that at one o'clock in the morning on the fourth sitting the chairman should break off discussion, put forthwith the question already proposed from the chair, then successively put forthwith all the remaining clauses, and so report the bill to the House. This process shut out all amendments not reached at the fatal hour, and is the most drastic and sweeping of all forms of closure. In the case of the Coercion bill, resort to the guillotine was declared to be warranted by the urgency of social order in Ireland. That plea was at least plausible. No such plea of urgency could be invoked for a measure, which only a few days before the government had considered to be of such secondary importance, that the simple rejection of it by Mr. Parnell was to be enough to induce them to withdraw it. The bill that had been proffered as a generous concession to Irish members, was now violently forced upon them without debate. Well might Mr. Gladstone speak of the most extraordinary series of proceedings that he had ever known.[1]

III

The three judges first met on September 17, 1888, to settle their procedure. They sat for one hundred and twenty-eight days, and rose for the last time on November 22, 1889. More than four hundred and fifty witnesses were examined. One counsel spoke for five days, another for seven, and a third for nearly twelve. The mammoth record of the proceedings fills eleven folio volumes, making between seven and eight thousand pages. The questions put to witnesses numbered ninety-eight thousand.

It was a strange and fantastic scene. Three judges were trying a social and political revolution. The leading actors in it were virtually in the dock. The tribunal had been specially set up by their political opponents, without giving them any effective voice either in its composition or upon the character and scope of its powers. For the first time in England since the Great Rebellion, men were practically put upon their trial on a political charge, without giving them the protection of a jury. For the first time in that period judges were to find a verdict upon the facts of crime. The

[1] *Hans.* Aug. 2, 1888, p. 1282.

charge placed in the forefront was a charge of conspiracy. But to call a combination a conspiracy does not make it a conspiracy or a guilty combination, unless the verdict of a jury pronounces it to be one. A jury would have taken all the large attendant circumstances into account. The three judges felt themselves bound expressly to shut out those circumstances. In words of vital importance, they said, 'We must leave it for politicians to discuss, and for statesmen to determine, in what respects the present laws affecting land in Ireland are capable of improvement. *We have no commission to consider whether the conduct of which they are accused can be palliated by the circumstances of the time, or whether it should be condoned in consideration of benefits alleged to have resulted from their action.*' [1] When the proceedings were over, Lord Salisbury applauded the report as 'giving a very complete view of a very curious episode of our internal history.' [2] A very complete view of an agrarian rising — though it left out all palliating circumstances and the whole state of agrarian law!

Instead of opening with the letters, as the country expected, the accusers began by rearing a prodigious accumulation of material, first for the Irish or agrarian branch of their case, and then for the American branch. The government helped them to find their witnesses, and so varied a host was never seen in London before. There was the peasant from Kerry in his frieze swallow-tail and knee-breeches, and the woman in her scarlet petticoat who runs barefoot over the bog in Galway. The convicted member of a murder club was brought up in custody from Mountjoy prison or Maryborough. One of the most popular of the Irish representatives had been fetched from his dungeon, and was to be seen wandering through the lobbies in search of his warders. Men who had been shot by moonlighters limped into the box, and poor women in their blue-hooded cloaks told pitiful tales of midnight horror. The sharp spy was there, who disclosed sinister secrets from cities across the Atlantic, and the uncouth informer who betrayed or invented the history of rude and ferocious plots hatched at the country cross-roads

---

[1] *Report*, p. 5.　　　　　　[2] *Hans.* 342, p. 1357.

or over the peat fire in desolate cabins in western Ireland.

Divisional commissioners with their ledgers of agrarian offences, agents with bags full of figures and documents, landlords, priests, prelates, magistrates, detectives, smart members of that famous constabulary force which is the arm, eye, and ear of the Irish government — all the characters of the Irish melodrama were crowded into the corridors, and in their turn brought out upon the stage of this surprising theatre.

The proceedings speedily settled down into the most wearisome drone that was ever heard in a court of law. The object of the accusers was to show the complicity of the accused with crime by tracing crime to the league, and making every member of the league constructively liable for every act of which the league was constructively guilty. Witnesses were produced in a series that seemed interminable, to tell the story of five-and-twenty outrages in Mayo, of as many in Cork, of forty-two in Galway, of sixty-five in Kerry, one after another, and all with immeasurable detail. Some of the witnesses spoke no English, and the English of others was hardly more intelligible than Erse. Long extracts were read out from four hundred and forty speeches. The counsel on one side produced a passage that made against the speaker, and then the counsel on the other side found and read some qualifying passage that made as strongly for him. The three judges groaned. They had already, they said plaintively, ploughed through the speeches in the solitude of their own rooms. Could they not be taken as read ? No, said the prosecuting counsel ; we are building up an argument, and it cannot be built up in a silent manner. In truth it was designed for the public outside the court,[1] and not a touch could be spared that might deepen the odium. Week after week the ugly tale went on — a squalid ogre let loose among a population demoralised by ages of wicked neglect, misery, and oppression. One side strove to show that the ogre had been wantonly raised by the land league for political objects of their own ; the other, that it was the progeny of distress and wrong, that

[1] *Evidence*, iv. p. 219.

the league had rather controlled than kindled its ferocity, and that crime and outrage were due to local animosities for which neither league nor parliamentary leaders were answerable.

On the forty-fourth day (February 5) came a lurid glimpse from across the Atlantic. The Irish emigration had carried with it to America the deadly passion for the secret society. A spy was produced, not an Irishman this time for a wonder, but an Englishman. He had been for eight-and-twenty years in the United States, and for more than twenty of them he had been in the pay of Scotland Yard, a military spy, as he put it, in the service of his country. There is no charge against him that he belonged to that foul species who provoke others to crime and then for a bribe betray them. He swore an oath of secrecy to his confederates in the camps of the Clan-na-Gael, and then he broke his oath by nearly every post that went from New York to London. It is not a nice trade, but then the dynamiter's is not a nice trade either.[1] The man had risen high in the secret brotherhood. Such an existence demanded nerves of steel; a moment of forgetfulness, an accident with a letter, the slip of a phrase in the two parts that he was playing, would have doomed him in the twinkling of an eye. He now stood a rigorous cross-examination like iron. There is no reason to think that he told lies. He was perhaps a good deal less trusted than he thought, for he does not appear on any occasion to have forewarned the police at home of any of the dynamite attempts that four or five years earlier had startled the English capital. The pith of his week's evidence was his account of an interview between himself and Mr. Parnell in the corridors of the House of Commons in April 1881. In this interview, Mr. Parnell, he said, expressed his desire to bring the Fenians in Ireland into line with his own constitutional movement, and to that end requested the spy to invite a notorious leader of the physical force party in America to come over to Ireland, to arrange a harmonious understanding. Mr. Parnell had no recollection of the inter-

[1] The common-sense view of the employment of such a man seems to be set out in the speech of Sir Henry James (Cassell and Co.), pp 149–51, and 494–5.

view, though he thought it very possible that an interview might have taken place. It was undoubtedly odd that the spy having once got his line over so big a fish, should never afterwards have made any attempt to draw him on. The judges, however, found upon a review of 'the probabilities of the case,' that the conversation in the corridor really took place, that the spy's account was correct, and that it was not impossible that in conversation with a supposed revolutionist, Mr. Parnell may have used such language as to leave the impression that he agreed with his interlocutor. Perhaps a more exact way of putting it would be that the spy talked the Fenian doctrine of physical force, and that Mr. Parnell listened.

IV

At last, on the fiftieth day (February 14, 1889), and not before, the court reached the business that had led to its own creation. Three batches of letters had been produced by the newspaper. The manager of the newspaper told his story, and then the immediate purveyor of the letters told his. Marvellous stories they were.

The manager was convinced from the beginning, as he ingenuously said, quite independently of handwriting, that the letters were genuine. Why? he was asked. Because he felt they were the sort of letters that Mr. Parnell would be likely to write. He counted, not wholly without some reason, on the public sharing this inspiration of his own in-dwelling light. The day was approaching for the division on the Coercion bill. Every journalist, said the manager, must choose his moment. He now thought the moment suitable for making the public acquainted with the character of the Irishmen. So, with no better evidence of authority than his firm faith that it was the sort of letter that Mr. Parnell would be likely to write, on the morning of the second reading of the Coercion bill, he launched the fac-simile letter. In the early part of 1888 he received from the same hand a second batch of letters, and a third batch a few days later. His total payments amounted to over two thousand five hundred pounds. He still asked no questions as to the source of these expensive documents. On the contrary he particularly avoided the subject. So much for the cautious and experienced man of business.

The natural course would have been now to carry the inquiry on to the source of the letters. Instead of that, the prosecutors called an expert in handwriting. The court expostulated. Why should they not hear at once where the letters came from ; and then it might be proper enough to hear what an expert had to say ? After a final struggle the prolonged tactics of deferring the evil day, and prejudicing the case up to the eleventh hour, were at last put to shame. The second of the two marvellous stories was now to be told.

The personage who had handed the three batches of letters to the newspaper, told the Court how he had in 1885 compiled a pamphlet called *Parnellism Unmasked*, partly from materials communicated to him by a certain broken-down Irish journalist. To this unfortunate sinner, then in a state of penury little short of destitution, he betook himself one winter night in Dublin at the end of 1885. Long after, when the game was up and the whole sordid tragi-comedy laid bare, the poor wretch wrote : ' I have been in difficulties and great distress for want of money for the last twenty years, and in order to find means of support for myself and my large family, I have been guilty of many acts which must for ever disgrace me.'[1] He had now within reach a guinea a day, and much besides, if he would endeavour to find any documents that might be available to sustain the charges made in the pamphlet. After some hesitation the bargain was struck, a guinea a day, hotel and travelling expenses, and a round price for documents. Within a few months the needy man in clover pocketed many hundreds of pounds. Only the author of the history of *Jonathan Wild the Great* could do justice to such a story of the Vagabond in Luck — a jaunt to Lausanne, a trip across the Atlantic, incessant journeys backward and forward to Paris, the jingling of guineas, the rustle of hundred-pound notes, and now and then perhaps a humorous thought of simple and solemn people in newspaper offices in London, or a moment's meditation on that perplexing law of human affairs by which the weak things

[1] Feb. 24, 1889. *Evidence*, vi. p. 20.

of the world are chosen to confound the things that are CHAP.
mighty.

The moment came for delivering the documents in Paris, Ær. 80.
and delivered they were with details more grotesque than
anything since the foolish baronet in Scott's novel was
taken by Dousterswivel to find the buried treasure in Saint
Ruth's. From first to last not a test or check was applied
by anybody to hinder the fabrication from running its course
without a hitch or a crease. When men have the demon of
a fixed idea in their cerebral convolutions, they easily fall
victims to a devastating credulity, and the victims were now
radiant as, with microscope and calligraphic expert by their
side, they fondly gazed upon their prize. About the time
when the judges were getting to work, clouds arose on
this smiling horizon. It is good, says the old Greek, that
men should carry a threatening shadow in their hearts
even under the full sunshine. Before this, the manager
learned for the first time, what was the source of the letters.
The blessed doctrine of intrinsic certainty, however, which
has before now done duty in far graver controversy, prevented him from inquiring as to the purity of the source.

The toils were rapidly enclosing both the impostor and the
dupes. He was put into the box at last (Feb. 21). By the
end of the second day, the torture had become more than
he could endure. Some miscalled the scene dramatic. That
is hardly the right name for the merciless hunt of an abject
fellow-creature through the doublings and windings of a
thousand lies. The breath of the hounds was on him, and
he could bear the chase no longer. After proceedings not
worth narrating, except that he made a confession and then
committed his last perjury, he disappeared. The police
traced him to Madrid. When they entered his room with
their warrant (March 1), he shot himself dead. They found
on his corpse the scapulary worn by devout catholics as a
visible badge and token of allegiance to the heavenly powers.
So in the ghastliest wreck of life, men still hope and seek for
some mysterious cleansing of the soul that shall repair all.

This damning experience was a sharp mortification to
the government, who had been throughout energetic con-

federates in the attack. Though it did not come at once formally into debate, it exhilarated the opposition, and Mr. Gladstone himself was in great spirits, mingled with intense indignation and genuine sympathy for Mr. Parnell as a man who had suffered an odious wrong.

VI

The report of the commission was made to the crown on February 13, 1890. It reached the House of Commons about ten o'clock the same evening. The scene was curious, — the various speakers droning away in a House otherwise profoundly silent, and every member on every bench, including high ministers of state, plunged deep and eager into the blue-book. The general impression was that the findings amounted to acquittal, and everybody went home in considerable excitement at this final explosion of the damaged blunderbuss. The next day Mr. Gladstone had a meeting with the lawyers in the case, and was keen for action in one form or another; but on the whole it was agreed that the government should be left to take the initiative.

The report was discussed in both Houses, and strong speeches were made on both sides. The government (Mar. 3) proposed a motion that the House adopted the report, thanked the judges for their just and impartial conduct, and ordered the report to be entered on the journals. Mr. Gladstone followed with an amendment, that the House deemed it to be a duty to record its reprobation of the false charges of the gravest and most odious description, based on calumny and on forgery, that had been brought against members of the House; and, while declaring its satisfaction at the exposure of these calumnies, the House expressed its regret at the wrong inflicted and the suffering and loss endured through a protracted period by reason of these acts of flagrant iniquity. After a handsome tribute to the honour and good faith of the judges, he took the point that some of the opinions in the report were in no sense and no degree judicial. How, for instance, could three judges, sitting ten years after the fact (1879–80), determine better than anybody else that distress and extravagant rents had nothing to do with crime? Why should the House of Commons declare its adoption of this finding without question or correction? Or of this, that the rejection of the Disturbance bill by the Lords in 1880 had nothing to do with the increase of crime? Mr. Forster had denounced the action of the Lords with indignation, and was not he, the responsible minister, a better witness than the three judges in no contact with contemporary fact? How were the judges authorised to affirm that the Land bill of 1881 had not been a great cause in mitigating the condition of Ireland? Another conclusive objection was that — on the declaration of the judges themselves, rightly made by them — what we know to be essential portions of the evidence were entirely excluded from their view.

He next turned to the findings, first of censure, then of acquittal. The findings of censure were in substance three. First, seven of the respondents had joined the league with a view of separating Ireland from England. The idea was dead, but Mr. Gladstone was compelled to say that in his opinion to deny the moral authority of the Act of Union was for an Irishman no moral offence whatever. Here the law-officer sitting opposite to him busily took down a note. 'Yes, yes,' Mr. Gladstone exclaimed, 'you may take my words down. I heard you examine your witness from a pedestal, as you felt, of the greatest elevation, endeavouring to press home the monstrous guilt of an Irishman who did not allow moral authority to the Act of Union. In my opinion the Englishman has far more cause to blush for the means by which that Act was obtained.' As it happened, on the only occasion on which Mr. Gladstone paid the Commission a visit, he had found the attorney general cross-examining a leading Irish member, and this passage of arms on the Act of Union between counsel and witness then occurred.

The second finding of censure was that the Irish members incited to intimidation by speeches, knowing that intimidation led to crime. The third was that they never placed themselves on the side of law and order; they did not assist the administration, and did not denounce the party of physical force. As if this, said Mr. Gladstone, had not been the subject of incessant discussion and denunciation in parliament at the time ten years ago, and yet no vote of condemnation was passed upon the Irish members then. On the contrary, the tory party, knowing all these charges, associated with them for purposes of votes and divisions; climbed into office on Mr. Parnell's shoulders; and through the viceroy with the concurrence of the prime minister, took Mr. Parnell into counsel upon the devising of a plan for Irish government. Was parliament now to affirm and record a finding that it had scrupulously abstained from ever making its own, and without regard to the counter-allegation that more crime and worse crime was prevented by agitation? It was the duty of parliament to look at the whole of the facts of the great crisis of 1880–1 — to the distress, to the rejection of the Compensation bill, to the growth of evictions, to the prevalence of excessive rents. The judges expressly shut out this comprehensive survey. But the House was not a body with a limited commission; it was a body of statesmen, legislators, politicians, bound to look at the whole range of circumstances, and guilty of misprision of justice if they failed so to do. 'Suppose I am told,' he said in notable and mournful words, 'that without the agitation Ireland would never have had the Land Act of 1881, are you prepared to deny that? I hear no challenges upon that statement, for I think it is generally and deeply felt that without the agitation the Land Act would not have been passed. As the man responsible more than any other for the Act of 1881 — as the man whose duty it was to consider that question day and night during nearly the whole of that session — I must record my firm opinion that it would not have become the law of the land, if it had not been for the agitation with which Irish society was convulsed.'[1]

This bare table of his leading points does nothing to convey the impression made by an extraordinarily fine performance. When the speaker came to the findings of acquittal, to the dismissal of the infamous charges of the forged letters, of intimacy with the Invincibles, of being

[1] See above, vol. iii. p. 56.

accessory to the assassinations in the Park, glowing passion in voice and gesture reached its most powerful pitch, and the moral appeal at its close was long remembered among the most searching words that he had ever spoken. It was not forensic argument, it was not literature; it had every note of true oratory — a fervid, direct and pressing call to his hearers as 'individuals, man by man, not with a responsibility diffused and severed until it became inoperative and worthless, to place himself in the position of the victim of this frightful outrage; to give such a judgment as would bear the scrutiny of the heart and of the conscience of every man when he betook himself to his chamber and was still.'

The awe that impressed the House from this exhortation to repair an enormous wrong soon passed away, and debate in both Houses went on the regular lines of party. Everything that was found not to be proved against the Irishmen, was assumed against them. Not proven was treated as only an evasive form of guilty. Though the three judges found that there was no evidence that the accused had done this thing or that, yet it was held legitimate to argue that evidence must exist — if only it could be found. The public were to nurse a sort of twilight conviction and keep their minds in a limbo of beliefs that were substantial and alive — only the light was bad.

In truth, the public did what the judges declined to do. They took circumstances into account. The general effect of this transaction was to promote the progress of the great unsettled controversy in Mr. Gladstone's sense. The abstract merits of home rule were no doubt untouched, but it made a difference to the concrete argument, whether the future leader of an Irish parliament was a proved accomplice of the Park murderers or not. It presented moreover the chameleon Irish case in a new and singular colour. A squalid insurrection awoke parliament to the mischiefs and wrongs of the Irish cultivators. Reluctantly it provided a remedy. Then in the fulness of time, ten years after, it dealt with the men who had roused it to its duty. And how? It brought them to trial before a special tribunal, invented for the purpose, and with no jury; it allowed them no voice in the constitution of the tribunal; it exposed them to long and harassing proceedings; and it thereby levied upon them a tremendous pecuniary fine. The report produced a strong 'recoil against the flagrant violence, passion, and calumny, that had given it birth; and it affected that margin of men, on the edge of either of the two great parties by whom electoral decisions are finally settled.

CHAPTER IV

THE nobler a soul is, the more objects of compassion it hath.
— BACON.

AT the end of 1888 Mr. Gladstone with his wife and others
of his house was carried off by Mr. Rendel's friendly care to
Naples. Hereto, he told Lord Acton, 'we have been induced
by three circumstances. First, a warm invitation from the
Dufferins to Rome; as to which, however, there are *cons* as
well as *pros*, for a man who like me is neither Italian nor
Curial in the view of present policies. Secondly, our kind
friend Mr. Stuart Rendel has actually offered to be our conductor thither and back, to perform for us the great service
which you rendered us in the trip to Munich and Saint-
Martin. Thirdly, I have the hope that the stimulating
climate of Naples, together with an abstention from speech
greater than any I have before enjoyed, might act upon my
" vocal cord," and partially at least restore it.'
At Naples he was much concerned with Italian policy.

To Lord Granville.

Jan. 13, 1889. — My stay here where the people really seem
to regard me as not a foreigner, has brought Italian affairs
and policy very much home to me, and given additional force and
vividness to the belief I have always had, that it was sadly impolitic
for Italy to make enemies for herself beyond the Alps. Though
I might try and keep back this sentiment in Rome, even my silence
might betray it and I could not promise to keep silence altogether.
I think the impolicy amounts almost to madness especially for a

413

country which carries with her, nestling in her bosom, the 'stand-ing menace' of the popedom. . . .

To J. Morley.

Jan. 10. — I hope you have had faith enough not to be troubled about my supposed utterances on the temporal power. . . . I will not trouble you with details, but you may rest assured I have never said the question of the temporal power was anything except an Italian question. I have a much greater anxiety than this about the Italian alliance with Germany. It is in my opinion an awful error and constitutes the great danger of the country. It may be asked, 'What have you to do with it?' More than people might suppose. I find myself hardly regarded here as a foreigner. They look upon me as having had a real though insignificant part in the Liberation. It will hardly be possible for me to get through the affair of this visit without making my mind known. On this account mainly I am verging towards the conclusion that it will be best for me not to visit Rome, and my wife as it happens is not anxious to go there. If you happen to see Granville or Rosebery please let them know this.

We have had on the whole a good season here thus far. Many of the days delicious. We have been subjected here as well as in London to a course of social kindnesses as abundant as the waters which the visitor has to drink at a watering place, and so enervat-ing from the abstraction of cares that I am continually thinking of the historical Capuan writer. I am in fact totally demoralised, and cannot wish not to continue so. Under the circumstances Fortune has administered a slight, a very slight physical correction. A land-slip, or rather a Tufo rock-slip of 50,000 tons, has come down and blocked the proper road between us and Naples.

To Lord Acton.

Jan. 23, 1889. — Rome is I think definitely given up. I shall be curious to know your reasons for approving this *gran rifiuto.* Meantime I will just glance at mine. I am not so much afraid of the Pope as of the Italian government and court. My sentiments are so very strong about the present foreign policy. The foreign policy of the government but not I fear of the government only. If I went to Rome, and saw the King and the minister, as I must,

I should be treading upon eggs all the time with them. I could
not speak out uninvited; and it is not satisfactory to be silent
in the presence of those interested, when the feelings are very
strong. . . .

These feelings broke out in time in at least one anonymous article.[1] He told Lord Granville how anxious he was
that no acknowledgment of authorship, direct or indirect,
should come from any of his friends. 'Such an article of
necessity lectures the European states. As one of a public
of three hundred and more millions, I have a right to do
this, but not in my own person.' This strange simplicity
rather provoked his friends, for it ignored two things —
first, the certainty that the secret of authorship would get
out; second, if it did not get out, the certainty that the
European states would pay no attention to such a lecture
backed by no name of weight — perhaps even whether it
were so backed or not. Faith in lectures, sermons, articles,
even books, is one of the things most easily overdone.

Most of my reading, he went on to Acton, has been about the Jews
and the Old Testament. I have not looked at the books you kindly
sent me, except a little before leaving Hawarden ; but I want to get
a hold on the broader side of the Mosaic dispensation and the Jewish
history. The great historic features seem to me in a large degree
independent of the critical questions which have been raised about
the *redaction* of the Mosaic books. Setting aside Genesis, and the
Exodus proper, it seems difficult to understand how either Moses
or any one else could have advisedly published them in their
present form; and most of all difficult to believe that men going
to work deliberately after the captivity would not have managed
a more orderly execution. My thoughts are always running back
to the parallel question about Homer. In that case, those who
hold that Peisistratos or some one of his date was the compiler,
have at least this to say, that the poems in their present form are
such as a compiler, having liberty of action, might have aimed
at putting out from his workshop. Can that be said of the
Mosaic books ? Again, are we not to believe in the second and

[1] 'The Triple Alliance and Italy's Place in It.' By Outidanos. *Contemporary Review*, October 1889. See Appendix.

third Temples as centres of worship because there was a temple at Leontopolis, as we are told? Out of the frying-pan, into the fire.

When he left Amalfi (Feb. 14) for the north, he found himself, he says, in a public procession, with great crowds at the stations, including Crispi at Rome, who had once been his guest at Hawarden.

After his return home, he wrote again to Lord Acton: —

April 28, 1889. — I have long been wishing to write to you. But as a rule I never can write any letters that I wish to write. My volition of that kind is from day to day exhausted by the worrying demand of letters that I do not wish to write. Every year brings me, as I reckon, from three to five thousand new correspondents, of whom I could gladly dispense with 99 per cent. May you never be in a like plight.

Mary showed me a letter of recent date from you, which referred to the idea of my writing on the Old Testament. The matter stands thus: An appeal was made to me to write something on the general position and claims of the holy scriptures for the working men. I gave no pledge but read (what was for me) a good deal on the laws and history of the Jews with only two results: first, deepened impressions of the vast interest and importance attaching to them, and of their fitness to be made the subject of a telling popular account; secondly, a discovery of the necessity of reading much more. But I have never in this connection thought much about what is called the criticism of the Old Testament, only seeking to learn how far it impinged upon the matters that I really was thinking of. It seems to me that it does not impinge much. . . . It is the fact that among other things I wish to make some sort of record of my life. You say truly it has been very full. I add fearfully full. But it has been in a most remarkable degree the reverse of self-guided and self-suggested, with reference I mean to all its best known aims. Under this surface, and in its daily habit no doubt it has been selfish enough. Whether anything of this kind will ever come off is most doubtful. Until I am released from politics by the solution of the Irish problem, I cannot even survey the field.

I turn to the world of action. It has long been in my mind to found something of which a library would be the nucleus. I incline to begin with a temporary building here. Can you, who have built a library, give me any advice? On account of fire I have half a mind to corrugated iron, with felt sheets to regulate the temperature.

Have you read any of the works of Dr. Salmon? I have just finished his volume on Infallibility, which fills me with admiration of its easy movement, command of knowledge, singular faculty of disentanglement, and great skill and point in argument; though he does not quite make one love him. He touches much ground trodden by Dr. Döllinger; almost invariably agreeing with him.

II

July 25, 1889, was the fiftieth anniversary of his marriage. The Prince and Princess of Wales sent him what he calls a beautiful and splendid gift. The humblest were as ready as the highest with their tributes, and comparative strangers as ready as the nearest. Among countless others who wrote was Bishop Lightfoot, great master of so much learning : —

I hope you will receive this tribute from one who regards your private friendship as one of the great privileges of his life.

And Döllinger : —

If I were fifteen years younger than I am, how happy I would be to come over to my beloved England once more, and see you surrounded by your sons and daughters, loved, admired, I would almost say worshipped, by a whole grateful nation.

On the other side, a clever lady having suggested to Browning that he should write an inscription for her to some gift for Mr. Gladstone, received an answer that has interest, both by the genius and fame of its writer, and as a sign of widespread feeling in certain circles in those days : —

Surely your kindness, even your sympathy, will be extended to me when I say, with sorrow indeed, that I am unable now conscientiously to do what, but a few years ago, I would have at least attempted with such pleasure and pride as might almost promise success. I have received much kindness from that extraordinary personage, and what my admiration for his transcendent abilities was and ever will be, there is no need to speak of. But I am forced to altogether deplore his present attitude with respect to the liberal party, of which I, the humblest unit, am still a member, and as such grieved to the heart by every fresh utterance of his which comes to my knowledge. Were I in a position to explain publicly how much the personal feeling is independent of the political aversion, all would be easy ; but I am a mere man of letters, and by the simple inscription which would truly testify to what is enduring, unalterable in my esteem, I should lead people — as well those who know me as those who do not — to believe my approbation extended far beyond the bounds which unfortunately circumscribe it now. All this — even more — was on my mind as I sat, last evening, at the same table with the brilliantly-gifted man whom once — but that 'once' is too sad to remember.

At a gathering at Spencer House in the summer of 1888, when this year of felicitation opened, Lord Granville, on behalf of a number of subscribers, presented Mr. and Mrs. Gladstone with two portraits, and in his address spoke of the long span of years through which they had enjoyed 'the unclouded blessings of the home.' The expression was a just one. The extraordinary splendour and exalted joys of an outer life so illustrious were matched in the inner circle of the hearth by a happy order, affectionate reciprocal attachments, a genial round of kindliness and duty, that from year to year went on untarnished, unstrained, unbroken. Visitors at Hawarden noticed that, though the two heads of the house were now old, the whole atmosphere seemed somehow to be alive with the freshness and vigour of youth ; it was one of the youngest of households in its interests and activities. The constant tension of his mind never impaired his tenderness and wise solicitude for family and kinsfolk, and for all about him ; and no man ever had such observance of decorum with such entire freedom from pharisaism. Nor did the order and moral prosperity of his own home leave him complacently forgetful of fellow-creatures to whom life's cup had been dealt in another measure. On his first entry upon the field of responsible life, he had formed a serious and solemn engagement with a friend — I suppose it was Hope-Scott — that each would devote himself to active service in some branch of religious work.[1] He could not, without treason to his gifts, go forth like Selwyn or Patteson to Melanesia to convert the savages. He sought a missionary field at home, and he found it among the unfortunate ministers to ' the great sin of great cities.' In these humane efforts at reclamation he persevered all through his life, fearless of misconstruction, fearless of the levity or baseness of men's tongues, regardless almost of the possible mischiefs to the public policies that depended on him. Greville [2] tells the story how in 1853 a man made an attempt one night to extort money from Mr. Gladstone, then in office as chancellor of the exchequer, by threats of exposure ; and how he instantly gave the offender into custody, and met the case at the police office. Greville could not complete the story. The man was committed for trial. Mr. Gladstone directed his solicitors to see that the accused was properly defended. He was convicted and sent to prison. By and by Mr. Gladstone inquired from the governor of the prison how the delinquent was conducting himself. The report being satisfactory, he next wrote to Lord Palmerston, then at the home office, asking that the prisoner should be let out. There was no worldly wisdom in it, we all know. But then what are people Christians for ?

We have already seen [3] his admonition to a son, and how much importance he attached to the dedication of a certain portion of our means to purposes of charity and religion. His example backed his precept. He kept detailed accounts under these heads from 1831 to 1897, and from these it appears that from 1831 to the end of 1890 he had devoted to objects of charity and religion upwards of seventy thousand pounds, and in the remaining years of his life the figure in this account stands at thirteen thousand five

[1] See above, vol. i. pp. 99, 568.   [2] Third Part, vol. i. p. 62.
[3] Vol. i. p. 206.

hundred — this besides thirty thousand pounds for his
cherished object of founding the hostel and library at Saint
Deiniol's. His friend of early days, Henry Taylor, says in
one of his notes on life that if you know how a man deals
with money, how he gets it, spends it, keeps it, shares it, you
know some of the most important things about him. His
old chief at the colonial office in 1846 stands the test most
nobly.

III

Near the end of 1889 among the visitors to Hawarden
was Mr. Parnell. His air of good breeding and easy composure pleased everybody. Mr. Gladstone's own record is
simple enough, and contains the substance of the affair as
he told me of it later : —

Dec. 18, 1889. — Reviewed and threw into form all the points
of possible amendment or change in the plan of Irish government,
etc., for my meeting with Mr. Parnell. He arrived at 5.30, and
we had two hours of satisfactory conversation ; but he put off the
gros of it.   19. — Two hours more with Mr. P. on points in Irish
government plans. He is certainly one of the very best people to
deal with that I have ever known. Took him to the old castle.
He seems to notice and appreciate everything.

Thinking of all that had gone before, and all that was so
soon to come after, anybody with a turn for imaginary
dialogue might easily upon this theme compose a striking
piece.

In the spring of 1890 Mr. Gladstone spent a week at
Oxford of which he spoke with immense enthusiasm. He
was an honorary fellow of All Souls, and here he went into
residence in his own right with all the zest of a virtuous
freshman bent upon a first class. Though, I daresay, pretty
nearly unanimous against his recent policies, they were all
fascinated by his simplicity, his freedom from assumption
or parade, his eagerness to know how leading branches of
Oxford study fared, his naturalness and pleasant manners.
He wrote to Mrs. Gladstone (Feb. 1) : —

Here I am safe and sound, and launched anew on my university career, all my days laid out and occupied until the morning of this day week, when I am to return to London. They press me to stay over the Sunday, but this cannot be thought of. I am received with infinite kindness, and the rooms they have given me are delightful. Weather dull, and light a medium between London and Hawarden. I have seen many already, including Liddon and Acland, who goes up to-morrow for a funeral early on Monday. Actually I have engaged to give a kind of Homeric lecture on Wednesday to the members of the union. The warden and his sisters are courteous and hospitable to the last degree. He is a unionist. The living here is very good, perhaps some put on for a guest, but I like the tone of the college; the fellows are men of a high class, and their conversation is that of men with work to do. I had a most special purpose in coming here which will be more than answered. It was to make myself safe so far as might be, in the articles [1] which eighteen months ago I undertook to write about the Old Testament. This, as you know perhaps, is now far more than the New, the battle-ground of belief. There are here most able and instructed men, and I am already deriving great benefit.

Something that fell from him one morning at breakfast in the common room led in due time to the election of Lord Acton to be also an honorary member of this distinguished society. 'If my suggestion,' Mr. Gladstone wrote to one of the fellows, 'really contributed to this election, then I feel that in the dregs of my life I have at least rendered one service to the college. My ambition is to visit it and Oxford in company with him.'

IV

In 1890 both Newman and Döllinger died.

I have been asked from many quarters, Mr. Gladstone said to Acton, to write about the Cardinal. But I dare not. First, I do not know enough. Secondly, I should be puzzled to use the little knowledge that I have. I was not a friend of his, but only an

---

[1] These articles appeared in *Good Words* (March–November 1900), and were subsequently published in vol-ume form under the title of *The Impregnable Rock of Holy Scripture*.

acquaintance treated with extraordinary kindness whom it would ill become to note what he thinks defects, while the great powers and qualities have been and will be described far better by others. Ever since he published his University Sermons in 1843, I have thought him unsafe in philosophy, and no Butlerian though a warm admirer of Butler. No; it was before 1843, in 1841 when he published Tract XC. The *general* argument of that tract was unquestionable; but he put in sophistical matter without the smallest necessity. What I recollect is about General Councils: where in treating the declaration that they may err he virtually says, 'No doubt they may — unless the Holy Ghost prevents them.' But he was a wonderful man, a holy man, a very refined man, and (to me) a most kindly man.

Of Dr. Döllinger he contributed a charming account to a weekly print,[1] and to Acton he wrote : —

I have the fear that my Döllinger letters will disappoint you. When I was with him, he spoke to me with the utmost freedom; and so I think he wrote, but our correspondence was only occasional. I think nine-tenths of my intercourse with him was oral; with Cardinal Newman nothing like one-tenth. But with neither was the mere *corpus* of my intercourse great, though in D.'s case it was very precious, most of all the very first of it in 1845. . . . With my inferior faculty and means of observation, I have long adopted your main proposition. His attitude of mind was more historical than theological. When I first knew him in 1845, and he honoured me with very long and interesting conversations, they turned very much upon theology, and I derived from him what I thought very valuable and steadying knowledge. Again in 1874 during a long walk, when we spoke of the shocks and agitation of our time, he told me how the Vatican decrees had required him to reperuse and retry the whole circle of his thought. He did not make known to me any general result; but he had by that time found himself wholly detached from the Council of Trent, which was indeed a logical necessity from his preceding action. The Bonn Conference appeared to show him nearly at the standing point of anglican theology. I thought him more liberal as a

[1] *Speaker*, Aug. 30, 1890.

theologian than as a politician.   On the point of church establishment he was as impenetrable as if he had been a Newdegate.   He
would not see that there were two sides to the question.   I long
earnestly to know what progress he had made at the last towards
redeeming the pledge given in one of his letters to me, that the
evening of his life was to be devoted to a great theological construction. . . .   I should have called him an anti-Jesuit, but in
no other sense, that is in no sense, a Jansenist.   I never saw the
least sign of leaning in that direction.

V

Here the reader may care to have a note or two of talk
with him in these days : —

At Dollis Hill, Sunday, Feb. 22, 1891. . . .   A few minutes after
eight Mr. and Mrs. Gladstone came in from church, and we
three sat down to dinner.   A delightful talk, he was in full
force, plenty of energy without vehemence.   The range of topics
was pretty wide, yet marvellous to say, we had not a single
word about Ireland.   Certainly no harm in that.

J. M. — A friend set me on a hunt this morning through
Wordsworth for the words about France standing on the top
of golden hours.   I did not find them, but I came across a good
line of Hartley Coleridge's about the Thames : —

> ' And the thronged river toiling to the main.'

Mr. G. — Yes, a good line.   Toiling to the main recalls
Dante : —
> ' Su la marina, dove 'l Po discende,
>   Per aver pace co' seguaci sui.' [1]

J. M. — Have you seen Symonds's re-issued volume on Dante ?
'Tis very good.   Shall I lend it to you ?

Mr. G. — Sure to be good, but not in the session.   I never look
at Dante unless I can have a great continuous draught of him.
He's too big, he seizes and masters you.

J. M. — Oh, I like the picturesque bits, if it's only for half-an-
hour before dinner ; the bird looking out of its nest for the

[1] *Inf.* v. 98 : ' Where Po descends for rest with his tributary streams.'

dawn, the afternoon bell, the trembling of the water in the morning light, and the rest that everybody knows.

Mr. G. — No, I cannot do it. By the way, ladies nowadays keep question books, and among other things ask their friends for the finest line in poetry. I think I'm divided between three, perhaps the most glorious is Milton's — [*Somehow this line slipped from memory, but the reader might possibly do worse than turn over Milton in search for his finest line.*] Or else Wordsworth's — 'Or hear old Triton blow his wreathèd horn.' Yet what so splendid as Penelope's about not rejoicing the heart of anybody less than Odysseus?

μηδέ τι χείρονος ἀνδρὸς ἐϋφραίνοιμι νόημα.[1]

He talked a great deal to-night about Homer; very confident that he had done something to drive away the idea that Homer was an Asiatic Greek. Then we turned to Scott, whom he held to be by far the greatest of his countrymen. I suggested John Knox. 'No, the line must be drawn firm between the writer and the man of action; no comparisons there.'

J. M. — Well, then, though I love Scott so much that if any man chooses to put him first, I won't put him second, yet is there not a vein of pure gold in Burns that gives you pause?

Mr. G. — Burns very fine and true, no doubt; but to imagine a whole group of characters, to marshal them, to set them to work, to sustain the action — I must count that the test of highest and most diversified quality.

We spoke of the new Shakespeare coming out. I said I had been taking the opportunity of reading vol. i., and should go over it all in successive volumes. *Mr. G.* — 'Falstaff is wonderful — one of the most wonderful things in literature.'

Full of interest in *Hamlet*, and enthusiasm for it — comes closer than any other play to some of the strangest secrets of human nature — what *is* the key to the mysterious hold of this play on the world's mind? I produced my favourite proposition that *Measure for Measure* is one of the most modern of all the plays; the profound analysis of Angelo and his moral catastrophe, the strange figure of the duke, the deep irony of our modern time in it all. But I do not think he cared at all for this sort of criticism.

[1] *Od.* xx. 82.

He is too healthy, too objective, too simple, for all the complexities of modern morbid analysis.

Talked of historians; Lecky's two last volumes he had not yet read, but — had told him that, save for one or two blots due to contemporary passion, they were perfectly honourable to Lecky in every way. Lecky, said Mr. G., 'has real insight into the motives of statesmen. Now Carlyle, so mighty as he is in flash and penetration, has no eye for motives. Macaulay, too, is so caught by a picture, by colour, by surface, that he is seldom to be counted on for just account of motive.'

He had been reading with immense interest and satisfaction Sainte-Beuve's *History of Port Royal*, which for that matter deserves all his praise and more, though different parts of it are written from antagonistic points of view. Vastly struck by Saint-Cyran. When did the notion of the spiritual director make its appearance in Europe? Had asked both Döllinger and Acton on this curious point. For his own part, he doubted whether the office existed before the Reformation.

J. M. — Whom do you reckon the greatest Pope?

Mr. G. — I think on the whole, Innocent III. But his greatness was not for good. What did he do? He imposed the dogma of transubstantiation; he is responsible for the Albigensian persecutions; he is responsible for the crusade which ended in the conquest of Byzantium. Have you ever realised what a deadly blow was the ruin of Byzantium by the Latins, how wonderful a fabric the Eastern Empire was?

J. M. — Oh, yes, I used to know my Finlay better than most books. Mill used to say a page of Finlay was worth a chapter of Gibbon : he explains how decline and fall came about.

Mr. G. — Of course. Finlay has it all.

He tried then to make out that the eastern empire was more wonderful than anything done by the Romans; it stood out for eleven centuries, while Rome fell in three. I pointed out to him that the whole solid framework of the eastern empire was after all built up by the Romans. But he is philhellene all through past and present.

CHAPTER V

BREACH WITH MR. PARNELL

(*1890-1891*)

Fortuna vitrea est, — tum quum splendet frangitur. — PUBLIL. SYRUS.
Brittle like glass is fortune, — bright as light, and then the crash.

BOOK
X.

1890.

IT would have been a miracle if the sight of all the methods of coercion, along with the ignominy of the forged letters, had not worked with strong effect upon the public mind. Distrust began to creep at a very rapid pace even into the ministerial ranks. The tory member for a large northern borough rose to resent 'the inexpedient treatment of the Irishmen from a party point of view,' to protest against the 'straining and stretching of the law' by the resident magistrates, to declare his opinion that these gentlemen were not qualified to exercise the jurisdiction entrusted to them, 'and to denounce the folly of making English law unpopular in Ireland, and provoking the leaders of the Irish people by illegal and unconstitutional acts.'[1] These sentiments were notoriously shared to the full by many who sat around him. Nobody in those days, discredited as he was with his party, had a keener scent for the drift of popular feeling than Lord Randolph Churchill, and he publicly proclaimed that this sending of Irish members of parliament to prison in such numbers was a feature which he did not like. Further, he said that the fact of the government not thinking it safe for public meetings of any sort to be held, excited painful feelings in English minds.[2] All this was after the system had been in operation for two years. Even strong unionist organs in the Irish press could not stand it.[3] They declared that if

[1] Mr. Hanbury, August 1, 1889. *Hans.* 339, p. 98.
[2] At Birmingham, July 30, 1889.
[3] *E.g. Northern Whig*, February 21, 1889.

426

the Irish government wished to make the coercive system appear as odious as possible, they would act just as they were acting. They could only explain all these doings, not by 'wrong-headedness or imbecility,' but by a strange theory that there must be deliberate treachery among the government agents.

Before the end of the year 1889 the electoral signs were unmistakable. Fifty-three bye-elections had been contested since the beginning of the parliament. The net result was the gain of one seat for ministers and of nine to the opposition. The Irish secretary with characteristic candour never denied the formidable extent of these victories, though he mourned over the evils that such temporary successes might entail, and was convinced that they would prove to be dearly bought.[1] A year later the tide still flowed on ; the net gain of the opposition rose to eleven. In 1886 seventy-seven constituencies were represented by forty-seven unionists and thirty liberals. By the beginning of October in 1890 the unionist members in the same constituencies had sunk to thirty-six, and the liberals had risen to forty-one. Then came the most significant election of all.

There had been for some months a lull in Ireland. Government claimed the credit of it for coercion ; their adversaries set it down partly to the operation of the Land Act, partly to the natural tendency in such agitations to fluctuate or to wear themselves out, and most of all to the strengthened reliance on the sincerity of the English liberals. Suddenly the country was amazed towards the middle of September by news that proceedings under the Coercion Act had been instituted against two nationalist leaders, and others. Even strong adherents of the government and their policy were deeply dismayed, when they saw that after three years of it, the dreary work was to begin over again. The proceedings seemed to be stamped in every aspect as impolitic. In a few days the two leaders would have been on their way to America, leaving a half-empty war chest behind them and the flame of agitation burning low. As

[1] Mr. Balfour at Manchester. *Times*, October 21, 1889.

the offences charged had been going on for six months, there was clearly no pressing emergency. A critical bye-election was close at hand at the moment in the Eccles division of Lancashire. The polling took place four days after a vehement defence of his policy by Mr. Balfour at Newcastle. The liberal candidate at Eccles expressly declared from his election address onwards, that the great issue on which he fought was the alternative between conciliation and coercion. Each candidate increased the party vote, the tory by rather more than one hundred, the liberal by nearly six hundred. For the first time the seat was wrested from the tories, and the liberal triumphed by a substantial majority.[1] This was the latest gauge of the failure of the Irish policy to conquer public approval, the last indication of the direction in which the currents of public opinion were steadily moving.[2] Then all at once a blinding sandstorm swept the ground.

II

One of those events now occurred that with their stern irony so mock the statesman's foresight, and shatter political designs in their most prosperous hour. As a mightier figure than Mr. Parnell remorsefully said on a grander stage, a hundred years before, cases sometimes befall in the history of nations where private fault is public disaster.

At the end of 1889, the Irish leader had been made a party in a suit for divorce. He betrayed no trace in his demeanour, either to his friends or to the House, of embarrassment at the position. His earliest appearance after the evil news, was in the debate on the first night of the session (February 11, '90), upon a motion about the publication of the forged letter. Some twenty of

[1] October 22, 1890.
[2] See Mr. Roby's speech at the Manchester Reform Club, Oct. 24, and articles in *Manchester Guardian*, Oct. 16 and 25, 1890. The *Times* (Oct. 23), while denying the inference that the Irish question was the question most prominent in the minds of large numbers of the elec- tors, admitted that this was the vital question really before the constituency, and says generally, 'The election, like so many other bye-elections, has been decided by the return to their party allegiance of numbers of Gladstonians who in 1886 absented themselves from the polling booths.'

his followers being absent, he wished the discussion to be prolonged into another sitting. Closely as it might be supposed to concern him, he listened to none of the debate. He had a sincere contempt for speeches in themselves, and was wont to set down most of them to vanity. A message was sent that he should come upstairs and speak. After some indolent remonstrance, he came. His speech was admirable; firm without emphasis, penetrating, dignified, freezing, and unanswerable. Neither now nor on any later occasion did his air of composure in public or in private give way.

Mr. Gladstone was at Hawarden, wide awake to the possibility of peril. To Mr. Arnold Morley he wrote on November 4 : — 'I fear a thundercloud is about to burst over Parnell's head, and I suppose it will end the career of a man in many respects invaluable.' On the 13th he was told by the present writer that there were grounds for an impression that Mr. Parnell would emerge as triumphantly from the new charge, as he had emerged from the obloquy of the forged letters. The case was opened two days later, and enough came out upon the first day of the proceedings to point to an adverse result. A Sunday intervened, and Mr. Gladstone's self-command under storm-clouds may be seen in a letter written on that day to me : —

Nov. 16, 1890. — 1. It is, after all, a thunder-clap about Parnell. Will he ask for the Chiltern Hundreds ? He cannot continue to lead ? What could he mean by his language to you ? The Pope has now clearly got a commandment under which to pull him up. It surely cannot have been always thus; for he represented his diocese in the church synod. 2. I thank you for your kind scruple, but in the country my Sundays are habitually and largely invaded. 3. Query, whether if a bye-seat were open and chanced to have a large Irish vote W— might not be a good man there. 4. I do not think my Mem. is worth circulating but perhaps you would send it to Spencer. I sent a copy to Harcourt. 5. [A small parliamentary point, not related to the Parnell affair, nor otherwise significant.] 6. Most warmly do I agree with you about the Scott *Journal.* How one loves him. 7. Some day I hope to inflict on you a talk about Homer and Homerology (as I call it).

The court pronounced a condemnatory decree on Monday, November 17th. Parliament was appointed to meet on Tuesday, the 25th. There was only a week for Irish and English to resolve what effect this condemnation should have upon Mr. Parnell's position as leader of one and ally of the other. Mr. Parnell wrote the ordinary letter to his parliamentary followers. The first impulses of Mr. Gladstone are indicated in a letter to me on the day after the decree : —

Nov. 18, 1890. — Many thanks for your letter. I had noticed the Parnell circular, not without misgiving. I read in the *P. M. G.* this morning a noteworthy article in the *Daily Telegraph*,[1] or rather from it, with which I very much agree. But I think it plain that we have nothing to say and nothing to do in the matter. The party is as distinct from us as that of Smith or Hartington. I own to some surprise at the apparent facility with which the R. C. bishops and clergy appear to take the continued leadership, but they may have tried the ground and found it would not *bear*. It is the Irish parliamentary party, and that alone to which we have to look. . . .

Such were Mr. Gladstone's thoughts when the stroke first fell.

III

In England and Scotland loud voices were speedily lifted up. Some treated the offence itself as an inexpiable disqualification. Others argued that, even if the offence could be passed over as lying outside of politics, it

---

[1] 'That the effect of this trial will be to relegate Mr. Parnell for a time, at any rate, to private life, must we think be assumed. . . . Special exemptions from penalties which should apply to all public men alike cannot possibly be made in favour of exceptionally valuable politicians to suit the convenience of their parties. He must cease, for the present at any rate, to lead the nationalist party ; and conscious as we are of the loss our opponents will sustain by his resignation, we trust that they will believe us when we say that we are in no mood to exult in it. . . . It is no satisfaction to us to feel that a political adversary whose abilities and prowess it was impossible not to respect, has been overthrown by irrelevant accident, wholly unconnected with the struggle in which we are engaged.' — *Daily Telegraph*, Nov. 17, 1890.

had been surrounded by incidents of squalor and deceit that betrayed a character in which no trust could ever be placed again. In some English quarters all this was expressed with a strident arrogance that set Irishmen on fire. It is ridiculous, if we remember what space Mr. Parnell filled in Irish imagination and feeling, how popular, how mysterious, how invincible he had been, to blame them because in the first moment of shock and bewilderment they did not instantly plant themselves in the judgment seat, always so easily ascended by Englishmen with little at stake. The politicians in Dublin did not hesitate. A great meeting was held at Leinster Hall in Dublin on the Thursday (November 20th). The result was easy to foresee. Not a whisper of revolt was heard. The chief nationalist newspaper stood firm for Mr. Parnell's continuance. At least one ecclesiastic of commanding influence was supposed to be among the journal's most ardent prompters. It has since been stated that the bishops were in fact forging bolts of commination. No lurid premonitory fork or sheet flashed on the horizon, no rumble of the coming thunders reached the public ear.

Three days after the decree in the court, the great English liberal organization chanced to hold its annual meeting at Sheffield (November 20–21). In reply to a request of mine as to his views upon our position, Mr. Gladstone wrote to me as follows : —

Nov. 19, 1890. — Your appeal as to your meeting of to-morrow gives matter for thought. I feel (1) that the Irish have abstractedly a right to decide the question; (2) that on account of Parnell's enormous services — he has done for home rule something like what Cobden did for free trade, set the argument on its legs — they are in a position of immense difficulty; (3) that we, the liberal party as a whole, and especially we its leaders, have for the moment nothing to say to it, that we must be passive, must wait and watch. But I again and again say to myself, I say I mean in the interior and silent forum, 'It'll na dee.' I should not be surprised if there were to be rather painful manifestations in the House on Tuesday. It is yet to be seen what our Nonconformist friends, such a man as —, for example, or such a man as — will say. . . . If I recollect right, Southey's *Life of Nelson* was in my early days published and circulated by the Society for Promoting Christian Knowledge. It would be curious to look back upon it and see how the biographer treats his narrative at the tender points. What I have said under figure 3 applies to me beyond all others, and notwithstanding my prognostications I shall maintain an extreme reserve in a position where I can do no good (in the present tense), and might by indiscretion do much harm. You will doubtless communicate with Harcourt and confidential friends only as to anything in this letter. The thing, one can see, is not a *res judicata*. It may ripen fast. Thus far, there is a total want of moral support from this side to the Irish judgment.

A fierce current was soon perceived to be running. All the elements so powerful for high enthusiasm, but hazardous where an occasion demands circumspection, were in full blast. The deep instinct for domestic order was awake. Many were even violently and irrationally impatient that Mr. Gladstone had not peremptorily renounced the alliance on the very morrow of the decree. As if, Mr. Gladstone himself used to say, it could be the duty of any party leader to take into his hands the intolerable burden of exercising the rigours of inquisition and private censorship over every man with whom what he judged the highest public expediency might draw him to co-operate. As if, moreover, it could be the duty of Mr. Gladstone to hurry headlong into action, without giving Mr. Parnell time or chance of taking such action of his own as might make intervention unnecessary. Why was it to be assumed that Mr. Parnell would not recognise the facts of the situation? 'I determined,' said Mr. Gladstone 'to watch the state of feeling in this country. I made no public declaration, but the country made up its mind. I was in some degree like the soothsayer Shakespeare introduces into one of his plays. He says, " I do not make the facts; I only foresee them." I did not foresee the facts even; they were present before me.' [1]

[1] Speech at Retford, Dec. 11, 1890. *Antony and Cleopatra*, Act I. Sc. 2.

The facts were plain, and Mr. Gladstone was keenly alive to the full purport of every one of them. Men, in whose hearts religion and morals held the first place, were strongly joined by men accustomed to settle political action by political considerations. Platform-men united with pulpit-men in swelling the whirlwind. Electoral calculation and moral faithfulness were held for once to point the same way. The report from every quarter, every letter to a member from a constituent, all was in one sense. Some, as I have said, pressed the point that the misconduct itself made co-operation impossible; others urged the impossibility of relying upon political understandings with one to whom habitual duplicity was believed to have been brought home. We may set what value we choose upon such arguments. Undoubtedly they would have proscribed some of the most important and admired figures in the supreme doings of modern Europe. Undoubtedly some who have fallen into shift and deceit in this particular relation, have yet been true as steel in all else. For a man's character is a strangely fitted mosaic, and it is unsafe to assume that all his traits are of one piece, or inseparable in fact because they ought to be inseparable by logic. But people were in no humour for casuistry, and whether all this be sophistry or sense, the volume of hostile judgment and obstinate intention could neither be mistaken, nor be wisely breasted if home rule was to be saved in Great Britain.

Mr. Gladstone remained at Hawarden during the week. To Mr. Arnold Morley he wrote (Nov. 23): 'I have a bundle of letters every morning on the Parnell business, and the bundles increase. My own opinion has been the same from the first, and I conceive that the time for action has now come. All my correspondents are in unison.' Every post-bag was heavy with admonitions, of greater cogency than such epistles sometimes possess; and a voluminous bundle of letters still at Hawarden bears witness to the emotions of the time. Sir William Harcourt and I, who had taken part in the proceedings at Sheffield, made our reports. The acute manager of the liberal party came to announce that three of our candidates had bolted already, that more were sure to follow, and that this indispensable commodity in elections would become scarcer than ever. Of the general party opinion, there could be no shadow of doubt. It was no application of special rigour because Mr. Parnell was an Irishman. Any English politician of his rank would have fared the same or worse, and retirement, temporary or for ever, would have been inevitable. Temporary withdrawal, said some; permanent withdrawal, said others; but for withdrawal of some sort, almost all were inexorable.

IV

Mr. Gladstone did not reach London until the afternoon of Monday, November 24. Parliament was to assemble on the next day. Three members of the cabinet of 1886, and the chief whip of the party,[1] met him in the library of Lord Rendel's house at Carlton Gardens. The issue before the liberal leaders was a plain one. It was no question of the right of the nationalists to choose their own chief. It was no question of inflicting political ostracism on a particular kind of moral delinquency. The question was whether the present continuance of the Irish leadership with the silent assent of the British leaders, did not involve decisive abstention at the polls on the day when Irish policy could once more be submitted to the electors of Great Britain? At the best the standing difficulties even to sanguine eyes, and under circumstances that had seemed so promising, were still formidable. What chance was there if this new burden were superadded? Only one conclusion was possible upon the state of facts, and even those among persons responsible for this decision who were most earnestly concerned in the success of the Irish policy, reviewing all the circumstances of the dilemma, deliberately hold to this day that though a catastrophe followed, a worse catastrophe was avoided. It is one of the commonest of all secrets of cheap misjudgment in human affairs, to start by assuming that there is always some good way out of a bad case. Alas for us all, this is not so. Situations arise alike

---

[1] Lord Granville, Sir W. Harcourt, Mr. Arnold Morley, and myself.

for individuals, for parties, and for states, from which no
good way out exists, but only choice between bad way and
worse. Here was one of those situations. The mischiefs
that followed the course actually taken, we see; then, as is
the wont of human kind, we ignore the mischiefs that as
surely awaited any other.

Mr. Gladstone always steadfastly resisted every call to
express an opinion of his own that the delinquency itself had
made Mr. Parnell unfit and impossible. It was vain to tell
him that the party would expect such a declaration, or that
his reputation required that he should found his action on
moral censure all his own. 'What!' he cried, 'because a
man is what is called leader of a party, does that constitute
him a censor and a judge of faith and morals? I will not
accept it. It would make life intolerable.' He adhered
tenaciously to political ground. 'I have been for four
years,' Mr. Gladstone justly argued, 'endeavouring to persuade voters to support Irish autonomy. Now the voter
says to me, "If a certain thing happens — namely, the retention of the Irish leadership in its present hands — I will
not support Irish autonomy." How can I go on with the
work? We laboriously rolled the great stone up to the
top of the hill, and now it topples down to the bottom
again, unless Mr. Parnell sees fit to go.' From the point
of view of Irish policy this was absolutely unanswerable.
It would have been just as unanswerable, even if all the
dire confusion that afterwards came to pass had then been
actually in sight. Its force was wholly independent, and
necessarily so, of any intention that might be formed by
Mr. Parnell.

As for that intention, let us turn to him for a moment.
Who could dream that a man so resolute in facing facts as
Mr. Parnell, would expect all to go on as before? Substantial people in Ireland who were preparing to come round
to home rule at the prospect of a liberal victory in Great
Britain, would assuredly be frightened back. Belfast would
be more resolute than ever. A man might estimate as he
pleased either the nonconformist conscience in England, or
the catholic conscience in Ireland. But the most cynical

of mere calculators, — and I should be slow to say that this was Mr. Parnell, — could not fall a prey to such a hallucination as to suppose that a scandal so frightfully public, so impossible for even the most mild-eyed charity to pretend not to see, and which political passion was so interested in keeping in full blaze, would instantly drop out of the mind of two of the most religious communities in the world ; or that either of these communities could tolerate without effective protest so impenitent an affront as the unruffled continuity of the stained leadership. All this was independent of anything that Mr. Gladstone might do or might not do. The liberal leaders had a right to assume that the case must be as obvious to Mr. Parnell as it was to everybody else, and unless loyalty and good faith have no place in political alliances, they had a right to look for his spontaneous action. Was unlimited consideration due from them to him and none from him to them ?

The result of the consultation was the decisive letter addressed to me by Mr. Gladstone, its purport to be by me communicated to Mr. Parnell. As any one may see, its language was courteous and considerate. Not an accent was left that could touch the pride of one who was known to be as proud a man as ever lived. It did no more than state an unquestionable fact, with an inevitable inference. It was not written in view of publication, for that it was hoped would be unnecessary. It was written with the expectation of finding the personage concerned in his usual rational frame of mind, and with the intention of informing him of what it was right that he should know. The same evening Mr. McCarthy was placed in possession of Mr. Gladstone's views, to be laid before Mr. Parnell at the earliest moment.

'1 *Carlton Gardens, Nov.* 24, 1890. — MY DEAR MORLEY. — Having arrived at a certain conclusion with regard to the continuance, at the present moment, of Mr. Parnell's leadership of the Irish party, I have seen Mr. McCarthy on my arrival in town, and have inquired from him whether I was likely to receive from Mr. Parnell himself any communication on the subject. Mr. McCarthy replied that he was unable to give me any information on the subject. I mentioned to him that in 1882, after the terrible murder in the Phœnix Park, Mr. Parnell, although totally removed from any idea of responsibility, had spontaneously written to me, and offered to take the Chiltern Hundreds, an offer much to his honour but one which I thought it my duty to decline.

While clinging to the hope of a communication from Mr. Parnell, to whomsoever addressed, I thought it necessary, viewing the arrangements for the commencement of the session to-morrow, to acquaint Mr. McCarthy with the conclusion at which, after using all the means of observation and reflection in my power, I had myself arrived. It was that notwithstanding the splendid services rendered by Mr. Parnell to his country, his continuance at the present moment in the leadership would be productive of consequences disastrous in the highest degree to the cause of Ireland. I think I may be warranted in asking you so far to expand the conclusion I have given above, as to add that the continuance I speak of would not only place many hearty and effective friends of the Irish cause in a position of great embarrassment, but would render my retention of the leadership of the liberal party, based as it has been mainly upon the prosecution of the Irish cause, almost a nullity. This explanation of my views I begged Mr. McCarthy to regard as confidential, and not intended for his colleagues generally, if he found that Mr. Parnell contemplated spontaneous action; but I also begged that he would make known to the Irish party, at their meeting to-morrow afternoon, that such was my conclusion, if he should find that Mr. Parnell had not in contemplation any step of the nature indicated. I now write to you, in case Mr. McCarthy should be unable to communicate with Mr. Parnell, as I understand you may possibly have an opening to-morrow through another channel. Should you have such an opening, I beg you to make known to Mr. Parnell the conclusion itself, which I have stated in the earlier part of this letter. I have thought it best to put it in terms simple and direct, much as I should have desired had it lain within my power, to alleviate the painful nature of the situation. As respects the manner of conveying what my public duty has made it an obligation to say, I rely entirely on your good feeling, tact, and judgment. — Believe me sincerely yours, W. E. GLADSTONE.

No direct communication had been possible, though every effort to open it was made. Indirect information had been received. Mr. Parnell's purpose was reported to have shifted during the week since the decree. On the Wednesday he had been at his stiffest, proudest, and coldest, bent on holding on at all cost. He thought he saw a way of getting something done for Ireland; the Irish people had given him a commission; he should stand to it, so long as ever they asked him. On the Friday, however (Nov. 21), he appeared, so I had been told, to be shaken in his resolution. He had bethought him that the government might possibly seize the moment for a dissolution; that if there were an immediate election, the government would under the circumstances be not unlikely to win; if so, Mr. Gladstone might be thrown for four or five years into opposition; in other words, that powerful man's part in the great international transaction would be at an end. In this mood he declared himself alive to the peril and the grave responsibility of taking any course that could lead to consequences so formidable. That was the last authentic news that reached us. His Irish colleagues had no news at all. After this glimpse the curtain had fallen, and all oracles fell dumb.

If Mr. Gladstone's decision was to have the anticipated effect, Mr. Parnell must be made aware of it before the meeting of the Irish party (Nov. 25). This according to custom was to be held at two o'clock in the afternoon, to choose their chairman for the session. Before the choice was made, both the leader and his political friends should know the view and the purpose that prevailed in the camp of their allies. Mr. Parnell kept himself invisible and inaccessible alike to English and Irish friends until a few minutes before the meeting. The Irish member who had seen Mr. Gladstone the previous evening, at the last moment was able to deliver the message that had been confided to him. Mr. Parnell replied that he should stand to his guns. The other members of the Irish party came together, and, wholly ignorant of the attitude taken by Mr. Gladstone, promptly and with hardly a word of discussion re-elected their leader to his usual post. The gravity of the unfortunate error

committed in the failure to communicate the private message
to the whole of the nationalist members, with or without
Mr. Parnell's leave, lay in the fact that it magnified and
distorted Mr. Gladstone's later intervention into a humili-
ating public ultimatum. The following note, made at the
time, describes the fortunes of Mr. Gladstone's letter : —

Nov. 25. — I had taken the usual means of sending a message to
Mr. Parnell, to the effect that Mr. Gladstone was coming to town
on the following day, and that I should almost certainly have
a communication to make to Mr. Parnell on Tuesday morning.
It was agreed at my interview with his emissary on Sunday
night (November 23) that I should be informed by eleven on
Tuesday forenoon where I should see him. I laid special stress
on my seeing him before the party met. At half-past eleven,
or a little later, on that day I received a telegram from the
emissary that he could not reach his friend.[1] I had no difficulty
in interpreting this. It meant that Mr. Parnell had made up
his mind to fight it out, whatever line we might adopt; that
he guessed that my wish to see him must from his point of
view mean mischief; and that he would secure his re-election as
chairman before the secret was out. Mr. McCarthy was at this
hour also entirely in the dark, and so were all the other members of the Irish party supposed to be much in Mr. Parnell's
confidence. When I reached the House a little after three, the
lobby was alive with the bustle and animation usual at the
opening of a session, and Mr. Parnell was in the thick of it,
talking to a group of his friends. He came forward with much
cordiality. 'I am very sorry,' he said, 'that I could not make
an appointment, but the truth is I did not get your message
until I came down to the House, and then it was too late.' I
asked him to come round with me to Mr. Gladstone's room. As
we went along the corridor he informed me in a casual way that
the party had again elected him chairman. When we reached
the sunless little room, I told him I was sorry to hear that the
election was over, for I had a communication to make to him
which might, as I hoped, still make a difference. I then read out

[1] If anybody cares to follow all   and a full reply of mine sent to the
this up, he may read a speech of Mr.   press, Aug. 17.
Parnell's at Kells, Aug. 16, 1891,

to him Mr. Gladstone's letter. As he listened, I knew the look on his face quite well enough to see that he was obdurate. The conversation did not last long. He said the feeling against him was a storm in a teacup, and would soon pass. I replied that he might know Ireland, but he did not half know England; that it was much more than a storm in a teacup; that if he set British feeling at defiance and brazened it out, it would be ruin to home rule at the election; that if he did not withdraw for a time, the storm would not pass; that if he withdrew from the actual leadership now as a concession due to public feeling in this country, this need not prevent him from again taking the helm when new circumstances might demand his presence; that he could very well treat his re-election as a public vote of confidence by his party; that, having secured this, he would suffer no loss of dignity or authority by a longer or shorter period of retirement. I reminded him that for two years he had been practically absent from active leadership. He answered, in his slow dry way, that he must look to the future; that he had made up his mind to stick to the House of Commons and to his present position in his party, until he was convinced, and he would not soon be convinced, that it was impossible to obtain home rule from a British parliament; that if he gave up the leadership for a time, he should never return to it; that if he once let go, it was all over. There was the usual iteration on both sides in a conversation of the kind, but this is the substance of what passed. His manner throughout was perfectly cool and quiet, and his unresonant voice was unshaken. He was paler than usual, and now and then a wintry smile passed over his face. I saw that nothing would be gained by further parley, so I rose and he somewhat slowly did the same. 'Of course,' he said, as I held the door open for him to leave, 'Mr. Gladstone will have to attack me. I shall expect that. He will have a right to do that.' So we parted.

I waited for Mr. Gladstone, who arrived in a few minutes. It was now four o'clock. 'Well?' he asked eagerly the moment the door was closed, and without taking off cape or hat. 'Have you seen him?' 'He is obdurate,' said I. I told him shortly what had passed. He stood at the table, dumb for some instants, looking at me as if he could not believe what I had said. Then he burst out that we must at once publish his letter to me; at once, that very afternoon. I said, ''Tis too late now.' 'Oh, no,' said he, 'the *Pall Mall* will bring it out in a special edition.' 'Well, but,' I persisted, 'we ought really to consider it a little.' Reluctantly he yielded, and we went into the House. Harcourt presently joined us on the bench, and we told him the news. It was by and by decided that the letter should be immediately published. Mr. Gladstone thought that I should at once inform Mr. Parnell of this. There he was at that moment, pleasant and smiling, in his usual place on the Irish bench. I went into our lobby, and sent somebody to bring him out. Out he came, and we took three or four turns in the lobby. I told him that it was thought right, under the new circumstances, to send the letter to the press. 'Yes,' he said amicably, as if it were no particular concern of his, 'I think Mr. Gladstone will be quite right to do that; it will put him straight with his party.'

The debate on the address had meanwhile been running its course. Mr. Gladstone had made his speech. One of the newspapers afterwards described the liberals as wearing pre-occupied countenances. 'We were pre-occupied with a vengeance,' said Mr. Gladstone, 'and even while I was speaking I could not help thinking to myself, Here am I talking about Portugal and about Armenia, while every single creature in the House is absorbed in one thing only, and that is an uncommonly long distance from either Armenia or Portugal.' News of the letter, which had been sent to the reporters about eight o'clock, swiftly spread. Members hurried to ex-ministers in the dining-room to ask if the story of the letter were true. The lobbies were seized by one of those strange and violent fevers to which on such occasions the House of Commons is liable. Unlike the clamour of the Stock Exchange or a continental Chamber, there is little noise, but the perturbation is profound. Men pace the corridors in couples and trios, or flit from one knot to another, listening to an oracle of the moment modestly retailing a rumour false on the face of it, or evolving monstrous hypotheses to explain incredible occurrences. This, however, was no common crisis of lobby or gallery.

One party quickly felt that, for them at least, it was an affair of life or death. It was no wonder that the Irish members were stirred to the very depths. For five years they had worked on English platforms, made active friendships with English and Scottish liberals in parliament and out of it, been taught to expect from their aid and alliance that deliverance which without allies must remain out of reach and out of sight; above all, for nearly five years they had been taught to count on the puissant voice and strong right arm of the leader of all the forces of British liberalism.

They suddenly learned that if they took a certain step in respect of the leadership of their own party, the alliance was broken off, the most powerful of Englishmen could help them no more, and that all the dreary and desperate marches since 1880 were to be faced once again in a blind and endless campaign, against the very party to whose friendship they had been taught to look for strength, encouragement, and victory. Well might they recoil. More astounded still, they learned at the same time that they had already taken the momentous step in the dark, and that the knowledge of what they were doing, the pregnant meanings and the tremendous consequences of it, had been carefully concealed from them. Never were consternation, panic, distraction, and resentment better justified.

The Irishmen were anxious to meet at once. Their leader sat moodily in the smoking-room downstairs. His faculty of concentrated vision had by this time revealed to him the certainty of a struggle, and its intensity. He knew in minute detail every element of peril both at Westminster and in Ireland. A few days before, he mentioned to the present writer his suspicion of designs on foot in ecclesiastical quarters, though he declared that he had no fear of them. He may have surmised that the demonstration at the Leinster Hall was superficial and impulsive. On the other hand, his confidence in the foundations of his dictatorship was unshaken. This being so, if deliberate calculation were the universal mainspring of every statesman's action — as it assuredly is not nor can ever be — he would have spontaneously withdrawn for a season, in the

assurance that if signs of disorganisation were to appear
among his followers, his prompt return from Elba would
be instantly demanded in Ireland, whether or no it were
acquiesced in by the leaders and main army of liberals
in England. That would have been both politic and decent,
even if we conceive his mind to have been working in
another direction. He may, for instance, have believed that
the scandal had destroyed the chances of a liberal victory
at the election, whether he stayed or withdrew. Why
should he surrender his position in Ireland and over contending factions in America, in reliance upon an English
party to which, as he was well aware, he had just dealt a
smashing blow? These speculations, however, upon the
thoughts that may have been slowly moving through his
mind, are hardly worth pursuing. Unluckily, the stubborn
impulses of defiance that came naturally to his temperament were aroused to their most violent pitch and swept all
calculations of policy aside. He now proceeded passionately
to dash into the dust the whole fabric of policy which he
had with such infinite sagacity, patience, skill, and energy
devised and reared.

Two short private memoranda from his own hand on this
transaction, I find among Mr. Gladstone's papers. He read
them to me at the time, and they illustrate his habitual
practice of shaping and clearing his thought and recollection
by committal to black and white : —

Nov. 26, 1890. — Since the month of December 1885 my whole
political life has been governed by a supreme regard to the Irish
question. For every day, I may say, of these five, we have been
engaged in laboriously rolling up hill the stone of Sisyphus. Mr.
Parnell's decision of yesterday means that the stone is to break
away from us and roll down again to the bottom of the hill. I
cannot recall the years which have elapsed. It was daring, perhaps, to begin, at the age I had then attained, a process which it
was obvious must be a prolonged one.

Simply to recommence it now, when I am within a very few
weeks of the age at which Lord Palmerston, the marvel of parliamentary longevity, succumbed, and to contemplate my accompany-

ing the cause of home rule to its probable triumph a rather long course of years hence, would be more than daring; it would be presumptuous. My views must be guided by rational probabilities, and they exclude any such anticipation. My statement, therefore, that my leadership would, under the contemplated decision of Mr. Parnell, be almost a nullity, is a moderate statement of the case. I have been endeavouring during all these years to reason with the voters of the kingdom, and when the voter now tells me that he cannot give a vote for making the Mr. Parnell of to-day the ruler of Irish affairs under British sanction, I do not know how to answer him, and I have yet to ask myself formally the question what under those circumstances is to be done. I must claim entire and absolute liberty to answer that question as I may think right.

Nov. 28, 1890. — The few following words afford a key to my proceedings in the painful business of the Irish leadership.

It was at first my expectation, and afterwards my desire, that Mr. Parnell would retire by a perfectly spontaneous act. As the likelihood of such a course became less and less, while time ran on, and the evidences of coming disaster were accumulated, I thought it would be best that he should be impelled to withdraw, but by an influence conveyed to him, at least, from within the limits of his own party. I therefore begged Mr. Justin McCarthy to acquaint Mr. Parnell of what I thought as to the consequences of his continuance; I also gave explanations of my meaning, including a reference to myself; and I begged that my message to Mr. Parnell might be made known to the Irish party, in the absence of a spontaneous retirement.

This was on Monday afternoon. But there was no certainty either of finding Mr. Parnell, or of an impression on him through one of his own followers. I therefore wrote the letter to Mr. Morley, as a more delicate form of proceeding than a direct communication from myself, but also as a stronger measure than that taken through Mr. McCarthy, because it was more full, and because, as it was in writing, it admitted of the ulterior step of immediate publication. Mr. Morley could not find Mr. Parnell until after the first meeting of the Irish party on Monday. When we found that Mr. McCarthy's representation had had no effect, that the Irish party had not been informed, and that Mr. Morley's making known the material parts of my letter was likewise without result, it at once was decided to publish the letter; just too late for the *Pall Mall Gazette*, it was given for publication to the morning papers, and during the evening it became known in the lobbies of the House.

v

Mr. Parnell took up his new ground in a long manifesto to the Irish people (November 29). It was free of rhetoric and ornament, but the draught was skilfully brewed. He charged Mr. Gladstone with having revealed to him during his visit at Hawarden in the previous December, that in a future scheme of home rule the Irish members would be cut down from 103 to 32, land was to be withdrawn from the competency of the Irish legislature, and the control of the constabulary would be reserved to the Imperial authority for an indefinite period, though Ireland would have to find the money all the time. This perfidious truncation of self-government by Mr. Gladstone was matched by an attempt on my part as his lieutenant only a few days before, to seduce the Irish party into accepting places in a liberal government, and this gross bribe of mine was accompanied by a despairing avowal that the hapless evicted tenants must be flung overboard. In other words, the English leaders intended to play Ireland false, and Mr. Parnell stood between his country and betrayal. Such a story was unluckily no new one in Irish history since the union. On that theme Mr. Parnell played many adroit variations during the eventful days that followed. Throw me to the English wolves if you like, he said, but at any rate make sure that real home rule and not its shadow is to be your price, and that they mean to pay it. This was to awaken the spectre of old suspicions, and to bring to life again those forces of violence and desperation which it had been the very crown of his policy to exorcise.

The reply on the Hawarden episode was prompt. Mr. Gladstone asserted that the whole discussion was one of those informal exchanges of view which go to all political action, and in which men feel the ground and discover the leanings of one another's minds. No single proposal was made, no proposition was mentioned to which a binding assent was sought. Points of possible improvement in the bill of 1886 were named as having arisen in Mr. Gladstone's mind, or been suggested by others, but no positive conclusions were asked for or were expected or were possible. Mr. Parnell quite agreed that the real difficulty lay in finding the best form in which Irish representation should be retained at Westminster, but both saw the wisdom and necessity of leaving deliberation free until the time should come for taking practical steps. He offered no serious objection on any point ; much less did he say that they augured any disappointment of Irish aspirations. Apart from this denial, men asked themselves how it was that if Mr. Parnell knew that the cause was already betrayed, he yet for a year kept the black secret to himself, and blew Mr. Gladstone's praise with as loud a trumpet as before ?[1] As for my own guilty attempt at corruption in proposing an absorption of the Irish party in English politics by means of office and emolument, I denied it with reasonable emphasis at the time, and it does not concern us here, nor in fact anywhere else.

VI

We now come to what was in its day the famous story of Committee Room Fifteen, so called from the chamber in which the next act of this dismal play went on.[2] The proceedings between the leader and his party were watched with an eagerness that has never been surpassed in this kingdom or in America. They were protracted, intense, dramatic, and the issue for a time hung in poignant doubt. The party interest of the scene was supreme, for if the Irishmen should rally to their chief, then the English alliance was at an end, Mr. Gladstone would virtually close

---

[1] On the day after leaving Hawarden Mr. Parnell spoke at Liverpool, calling on Lancashire to rally to their 'grand old leader.' 'My countrymen rejoice,' he said, 'for we are on the safe path to our legitimate freedom and our future prosperity.' Decem-

ber 19, 1889.

[2] See *The Parnell Split*, reprinted from the *Times* in 1891. Especially also *The Story of Room 15*, by Donal Sullivan, M.P., the accuracy of which seems not to have been challenged.

his illustrious career, the rent in the liberal ranks might
be repaired, and leading men and important sections would
all group themselves afresh. ' Let us all keep quiet,' said
one important unionist, ' we may now have to revise our
positions.' Either way, the serpent of faction would raise
its head in Ireland, and the strong life of organised and
concentrated nationalism would perish in its coils. The
personal interest was as vivid as the political, — the spectacle
of a man of infinite boldness, determination, astuteness, and
resource, with the will and pride of Lucifer, at bay with
fortune and challenging a malignant star. Some talked of
the famous Ninth Thermidor, when Robespierre fought inch
by inch the fierce struggle that ended in his ruin. Others
talked of the old mad discord of Zealot and Herodian in
face of the Roman before the walls of Jerusalem. The
great veteran of English politics looked on, wrathful and
astounded at a preternatural perversity for which sixty years
of public life could furnish him no parallel. The sage public
looked on, some with the same interest that would in ancient
days have made them relish a combat of gladiators ; others
with glee at the mortification of political opponents ; others
again with honest disgust at what threatened to be the
ignoble rout of a beneficent policy.

It was the fashion for the moment in fastidious reactionary
quarters to speak of the actors in this ordeal as ' a hustling
group of yelling rowdies.' Seldom have terms so censorious
been more misplaced. All depends upon the point of view.
Men on a raft in a boiling sea have something to think of
besides deportment and the graces of serenity. As a matter
of fact, even hostile judges then and since agreed that no
case was ever better opened within the walls of Westminster
than in the three speeches made on the first day by Mr.
Sexton and Mr. Healy on the one side, and Mr. Redmond
on the other. In gravity, dignity, acute perception, and
that good faith which is the soul of real as distinct from
spurious debate, the parliamentary critic recognises them
as all of the first order. So for the most part things continued. It was not until a protracted game had gone
beyond limits of reason and patience, that words sometimes

flamed high. Experience of national assemblies gives no reason to suppose that a body of French, German, Spanish, Italian, or even of English, Scotch, Welsh, or American politicians placed in circumstances of equal excitement, arising from an incident in itself at once so squalid and so provocative, would have borne the strain with any more self-control.

Mr. Parnell presided, frigid, severe, and lofty, 'as if,' said one present, 'it were we who had gone astray, and he were sitting there to judge us.' Six members were absent in America, including Mr. Dillon and Mr. O'Brien, two of the most important of all after Mr. Parnell himself. The attitude of this pair was felt to be a decisive element. At first, under the same impulse as moved the Leinster Hall meeting, they allowed their sense of past achievement to close their eyes ; they took for granted the impossible, that religious Britain and religious Ireland would blot what had happened out of their thoughts ; and so they stood for Mr. Parnell's leadership. The grim facts of the case were rapidly borne in upon them. The defiant manifesto convinced them that the leadership could not be continued. Travelling from Cincinnati to Chicago, they read it, made up their minds, and telegraphed to anxious colleagues in London. They spoke with warmth of Mr. Parnell's services, but protested against his unreasonable charges of servility to liberal wirepullers ; they described the 'endeavours to fasten the responsibility for what had happened upon Mr. Gladstone and Mr. Morley' as reckless and unjust ; and they foresaw in the position of isolation, discredit, and international ill-feeling which Mr. Parnell had now created, nothing but ruin for the cause. This deliverance from such a quarter (November 30) showed that either abdication or deposition was inevitable.

The day after Mr. Parnell's manifesto, the bishops came out of their shells. Cardinal Manning had more than once written most urgently to the Irish prelates the moment the decree was known, that Parnell could not be upheld in London, and that no political expediency could outweigh the moral sense. He knew well enough that the bishops in

Ireland were in a very difficult strait, but insisted 'that plain and prompt speech was safest.' It was now a case, he said to Mr. Gladstone (November 29), of *res ad triarios*, and it was time for the Irish clergy to speak out from the house-tops. He had also written to Rome. 'Did I not tell you,' said Mr. Gladstone when he gave me this letter to read, 'that the Pope would now have one of the ten commandments on his side?' 'We have been slow to act,' Dr. Walsh telegraphed to one of the Irish members (November 30), 'trusting that the party will act manfully. Our considerate silence and reserve are being dishonestly misinterpreted.' 'All sorry for Parnell,' telegraphed Dr. Croke, the Archbishop of Cashel — a manly and patriotic Irishman if ever one was — 'but still, in God's name, let him retire quietly and with good grace from the leadership. If he does so, the Irish party will be kept together, the honourable alliance with Gladstonian liberals maintained, success at general election secured, home rule certain. If he does not retire, alliance will be dissolved, election lost, Irish party seriously damaged if not wholly broken up, home rule indefinitely postponed, coercion perpetuated, evicted tenants hopelessly crushed, and the public conscience outraged. Manifesto flat and otherwise discreditable.' This was emphatic enough, but many of the flock had already committed themselves before the pastors spoke. To Dr. Croke, Mr. Gladstone wrote (Dec. 2): 'We in England seem to have done our part within our lines, and what remains is for Ireland itself. I am as unwilling as Mr. Parnell himself could be, to offer an interference from without, for no one stands more stoutly than I do for the independence of the Irish national party as well as for its unity.'

A couple of days later (Dec. 2) a division was taken in Room Fifteen upon a motion made in Mr. Parnell's interest, to postpone the discussion until they could ascertain the views of their constituents, and then meet in Dublin. It was past midnight. The large room, dimly lighted by a few lamps and candles placed upon the horse-shoe tables, was more than half in shadow. Mr. Parnell, his features barely discernible in the gloom, held a printed list of the party in

CHAP. V.

Æt. 81.

his hand, and he put the question in cold, unmoved tones. The numbers were 29 for the motion — that is to say, for him, and 44 against him. Of the majority, many had been put on their trial with him in 1880; had passed months in prison with him under the first Coercion Act and suffered many imprisonments besides ; they had faced storm, obloquy, and hatred with him in the House of Commons, a place where obloquy stings through tougher than Hibernian skins; they had undergone with him the long ordeal of the three judges; they had stood by his side with unswerving fidelity from the moment when his band was first founded for its mortal struggle down to to-day, when they saw the fruits of the struggle flung recklessly away, and the policy that had given to it all its reason and its only hope, wantonly brought to utter foolishness by a suicidal demonstration that no English party and no English leader could ever be trusted. If we think of even the least imaginative of them as haunted by such memories of the past, such distracting fears for the future, it was little wonder that when they saw Mr. Parnell slowly casting up the figures, and heard his voice through the sombre room announcing the ominous result, they all sat, both ayes and noes, in profound and painful stillness. Not a sound was heard, until the chairman rose and said without an accent of emotion that it would now be well for them to adjourn until the next day.

This was only the beginning. Though the ultimate decision of the party was quite certain, every device of strategy and tactics was meanwhile resolutely employed to avert it. His supple and trenchant blade was still in the hands of a consummate swordsman. It is not necessary to recapitulate all the moves in Mr. Parnell's grand manœuvre for turning the eyes of Ireland away from the question of leadership to the question of liberal good faith and the details of home rule. Mr. Gladstone finally announced that only after the question of leadership had been disposed of — one belonging entirely to the competence of the Irish party — could he renew former relations, and once more enter into confidential communications with any of them. There was only one guarantee, he said, that could be of any value to Ireland, namely the assured and unalterable fact that no English leader and no party could ever dream of either proposing or carrying any scheme of home rule which had not the full support of Irish representatives. This was obvious to all the world. Mr. Parnell knew it well enough, and the members knew it, but the members were bound to convince their countrymen that they had exhausted compliance with every hint from their falling leader, while Mr. Parnell's only object was to gain time, to confuse issues, and to carry the battle over from Westminster to the more buoyant and dangerously charged atmosphere of Ireland.

The majority resisted as long as they could the evidence that Mr. Parnell was audaciously trifling with them and openly abusing his position as chairman. On the evening of Friday (December 5) Mr. Sexton and Mr. Healy went to Mr. Parnell after the last communication from Mr. Gladstone. They urged him to bend to the plain necessities of the case. He replied that he would take the night to consider. The next morning (December 6) they returned to him. He informed them that his responsibility to Ireland would not allow him to retire. They warned him that the majority would not endure further obstruction beyond that day, and would withdraw. As they left, Mr. Parnell wished to shake hands, 'if it is to be the last time.' They all shook hands, and then went once more to the field of action.

It was not until after some twelve days of this excitement and stress that the scene approached such disorder as has often before and since been known in the House of Commons. The tension at last had begun to tell upon the impassive bronze of Mr. Parnell himself. He no longer made any pretence of the neutrality of the chair. He broke in upon one speaker more than forty times. In a flash of rage he snatched a paper from another speaker's hand. The hours wore away, confusion only became worse confounded, and the conclusion on both sides was foregone. Mr. McCarthy at last rose, and in a few moderate sentences expressed his opinion that there was no use in continuing a discussion that must be barren of anything but reproach, bitterness, and indignity, and he would therefore suggest that those who were of the same mind should withdraw. Then he moved from the table, and his forty-four colleagues stood up and silently followed him out of the room. In silence they were watched by the minority who remained, in number twenty-six.[1]

VII

A vacancy at Bassetlaw gave Mr. Gladstone an opportunity of describing the grounds on which he had acted. His speech was measured and weighty, but the result showed the effect of the disaster. The tide, that a few weeks before had been running so steadily, now turned. The unionist vote remained almost the same as in 1885; the liberal vote showed a falling off of over 400 and the unionist majority was increased from 295 to 728.

About this time having to go to Ireland, on my way back I stopped at Hawarden, and the following note gives a glimpse of Mr. Gladstone at this evil moment (Dec. 17) : —

I found him in his old corner in the 'temple of peace.' He was only half recovered from a bad cold, and looked in his worsted jacket, and dark tippet over his shoulders, and with his white, deep-furrowed face, like some strange Ancient of Days : so different from the man whom I had seen off at King's Cross less than a week before. He was cordial as always, but evidently in some perturbation. I sat down and told him what I had heard from different quarters about the approaching Kilkenny election. I mentioned X. as a Parnellite authority. 'What,' he flamed up with passionate vehemence, 'X. a Parnellite! Are they mad, then ? Are they clean demented ? ' etc. etc.

I gave him my general impression as to the future. The bare idea that Parnell might find no inconsiderable following came upon him as if it had been a thunder-clap. He listened, and catechised, and knit his brow.

---

[1] The case for the change of mind which induced the majority who had elected Mr. Parnell to the chair less than a fortnight before, now to depose him, was clearly put by Mr. Sexton at a later date. To the considerations adduced by him nobody has ever made a serious political answer. The reader will find Mr. Sexton's argument in the reports of these proceedings already referred to.

Mr. G. — What do you think we should do in case (1) of a divided Ireland, (2) of a Parnellite Ireland?

J. M. — It is too soon to settle what to think. But, looking to Irish interests, I think a Parnellite Ireland infinitely better than a divided Ireland. Anything better than an Ireland divided, so far as she is concerned.

Mr. G. — Bassetlaw looks as if we were going back to 1886. For me that is notice to quit. Another five years' agitation at my age would be impossible — *ludicrous* (with much emphasis).

J. M. — I cannot profess to be surprised that in face of these precious dissensions men should have misgivings, or that even those who were with us, should now make up their minds to wait a little.

I said what there was to be said for Parnell's point of view; that, in his words to me of Nov. 25, he 'must look to the future'; that he was only five and forty; that he might well fear that factions would spring up in Ireland if he were to go; that he might have made up his mind, that whether he went or stayed, we should lose the general election when it came. The last notion seemed quite outrageous to Mr. G., and he could not suppose that it had ever entered Parnell's head.

Mr. G. — You have no regrets at the course we took?

J. M. — None — none. It was inevitable. I have never doubted. That does not prevent lamentation that it was inevitable. It is the old story. English interference is always at the root of mischief in Ireland. But how could we help what we did? We had a right to count on Parnell's sanity and his sincerity. . . .

Mr. G. then got up and fished out of a drawer the memorandum of his talk with Parnell at Hawarden on Dec. 18, 1889, and also a memorandum written for his own use on the general political position at the time of the divorce trial. The former contained not a word as to the constabulary, and in other matters only put a number of points, alternative courses, etc., without a single final or definite decision. While he was fishing in his drawer, he said, as if speaking to himself, 'It looks as if I should get my release even sooner than I had expected.'

'That,' I said, 'is a momentous matter which will need immense deliberation.' So it will, indeed.

Mr. G. — Do you recall anything in history like the present distracted scenes in Ireland?

J. M. — Florence, Pisa, or some other Italian city, with the French or the Emperor at the gates?

Mr. G. — I'll tell you what is the only thing that I can think of as at all like it. Do you remember how it was at the siege of Jerusalem — the internecine fury of the Jewish factions, the Ζηλωταί, and the rest — while Titus and the legions were marching on the city!

We went in to luncheon. Something was said of our friend ——, and the new found malady, Renault's disease.

J. M. — Joseph de Maistre says that in the innocent primitive ages men died of diseases without names.

Mr. G. — Homer never mentions diseases at all.

J. M. — Not many of them die a natural death in Homer.

Mr. G. — Do you not recollect where Odysseus meets his mother among the shades, and she says : —

> Οὔτε τις οὖν μοι νοῦσος ἐπήλυθεν . . .
> ἀλλά με σός τε πόθος σά τε μήδεα, φαίδιμ' 'Οδυσσεῦ,
> σή τ' ἀγανοφροσύνη μελιηδέα θυμὸν ἀπηύρα.[1]

J. M. — Beautiful lines. Πόθος such a tender word, and it is untranslatable.

Mr. G. — Oh, *desiderium.*

> ' Quis desiderio sit pudor aut modus
> Tam cari capitis.' [2]

J. M. — The Scotch word '*wearying*' for somebody. And *Sehnsucht.*

Then Mr. G. went off to his library to hunt up the reference, and when I followed him, I found the worn old *Odyssey* open at the passage in the eleventh book. As he left the room, he looked at me and said, ' Ah, this is very different stuff for talking about, from all the wretched work we were speaking of just now. Homer's fellows would have cut a very different figure, and made short work in that committee room last week!' We had a few more words on politics. . . . So I bade him good-bye. . . .

---

[1] *Od.* xi. 200. ' It was not sickness that came upon me ; it was wearying for thee and thy lost counsels, glorious Odysseus, and for all thy gentle kindness, this it was that broke the heart within me.'

[2] Hor. *Carm.* i. 24.

In view of the horrors of dissension in Ireland, well-meaning attempts were made at the beginning of the year to bring about an understanding. The Irish members, returning from America where the schism at home had quenched all enthusiasm and killed their operations, made their way to Boulogne, for the two most important among them were liable to instant arrest if they were found in the United Kingdom. They thought that Mr. Parnell was really desirous to withdraw on such terms as would save his self-respect, and if he could plead hereafter that before giving way he had secured a genuine scheme of home rule. Some suspicion may well have arisen in their minds when a strange suggestion came from Mr. Parnell that the liberal leaders should enter into a secret engagement about constabulary and the other points. He had hardly given such happy evidence of his measure of the sanctity of political confidences, as to encourage further experiments. The proposal was absurd on the face of it. These suspicions soon became certainties, and the Boulogne negotiations came to an end. I should conjecture that those days made the severest ordeal through which Mr. Gladstone, with his extreme sensibility and his abhorrence of personal contention, ever passed. Yet his facility and versatility of mood was unimpaired, as a casual note or two of mine may show : —

. . . Mr. G.'s confabulation [with an Irish member] proved to have been sought for the purpose of warning him that Parnell was about to issue a manifesto in which he would make all manner of mischief. Mr. G. and I had a few moments in the room at the back of the chair; he seemed considerably perturbed, pale, and concentrated. We walked into the House together; he picked up the points of the matter in hand (a motion for appropriating all the time) and made one of the gayest, brightest, and most delightful speeches in the world — the whole House enjoying it consumedly. Who else could perform these magic transitions ?

Mr. G. came into the House, looking rather anxious; gave us an account of his interview with the Irish deputation; and in the midst of it got up to say his few sentences of condolence with the Speaker on the death of Mrs. Peel — the closing phrases admirably chosen, and the tones of his voice grave, sincere, sonorous, and compassionate. When he sat down, he resumed his talk with H. and me. He was so touched, he said, by those 'poor wretches' on the deputation, that he would fain, if he could, make some announcement that would ease their unlucky position.

[A question of a letter in reply to some application prompted by Mr. Parnell. Mr. Gladstone asked two of us to try our hands at a draft.] At last we got it ready for him and presently we went to his room. It was now six o'clock. Mr. G. read aloud in full deep voice the letter he had prepared on the base of our short draft. We suggested this and that, and generally argued about phrases for an hour, winding up with a terrific battle on two prodigious points: (1) whether he ought to say, 'after this statement of my views,' or 'I have now fully stated my views on the points you raise'; (2) 'You will *doubtless* concur,' or '*probably* concur.' Most characteristic, most amazing. It was past seven before the veteran would let go — and then I must say that he looked his full years. Think what his day had been, in mere intellectual strain, apart from what strains him far more than that — his strife with persons and his compassion for the unlucky Irishmen. I heard afterwards that when he got home, he was for once in his life done up, and on the following morning he lay in bed. All the same, in the evening he went to see *Antony and Cleopatra*, and he had a little ovation. As he drove away the crowd cheered him with cries of 'Bravo, don't you mind Parnell!' Plenty of race feeling left, in spite of union of hearts!

No leader ever set a finer example under reverse than did Mr. Gladstone during these tedious and desperate proceedings. He was steadfastly loyal, considerate, and sympathetic towards the Irishmen who had trusted him; his firm patience was not for a moment worn out; in vain a boisterous wave now and again beat upon him from one quarter or another. Not for a moment was he shaken; even under these starless skies his faith never drooped. 'The public mischief,' he wrote to Lord Acton (Dec. 27, 1890), 'ought to put out of view every private thought. But the blow to me is very heavy — the heaviest I ever

have received.   It is a great and high call to work by faith
and not by sight.'

Occasion had already offered for testing the feeling of
Ireland.   There was a vacancy in the representation of
Kilkenny, and the Parnellite candidate had been defeated.

To J. Morley.

Hawarden, Dec. 23, 1890. — Since your letter arrived this morning, the Kilkenny poll has brightened the sky.   It will have a
great effect in Ireland, although it is said not to be a representative constituency, but one too much for us.   It is a great gain;
and yet sad enough to think that even here one-third of the voters
should be either rogues or fools.   I suppose the ballot has largely
contributed to save Kilkenny.   It will be most interesting to
learn how the tories voted.

I return your enclosure. . . .   I have ventured, without asking
your leave, on keeping a copy of a part.   Only in one proposition
do I differ from you.   I would rather see Ireland disunited than
see it Parnellite.

I think that as the atmosphere is quiet for the moment we had
better give ourselves the benefit of a little further time for reflection.   Personally, I am hard hit.   My course of life was daring
enough as matters stood six weeks ago.   How it will shape in the
new situation I cannot tell.   But this is the selfish part.   Turning
for a moment to the larger outlook, I am extremely indisposed to
any harking back in the matter of home rule; we are now, I
think, freed from the enormous danger of seeing P. master in
Ireland; division and its consequences in diminishing force, are
the worst we have to fear.   What my mind leans to in a way still
vague is to rally ourselves by some affirmative legislation taken up
by and on behalf of the party.   Something of this kind would be
the best source to look to for reparative strength.

To Lord Acton.

Jan. 9, 1891. — To a greybeard in a hard winter the very name
of the south is musical, and the kind letters from you and Lord
Hampden make it harmony as well as melody.   But I have been
and am chained to the spot by this Parnell business, and every

day have to consider in one shape or other what ought to be said by myself or others. . . . I consider the Parnell chapter of politics finally closed for us, the British liberals, at least during my time. He has been even worse since the divorce court than he was in it. The most astounding revelation of my lifetime.

To J. Morley.

Hawarden, Dec. 30, 1890. — I must not longer delay thanking you for your most kind and much valued letter on my birthday — a birthday more formidable than usual, on account of the recent disasters, which, however, may all come to good. If I am able to effect in the world anything useful, be assured I know how much of it is owed to the counsel and consort of my friends.

It is not indeed the common lot of man to make serious additions to the friendships which so greatly help us in this pilgrimage, after seventy-six years old; but I rejoice to think that in your case it has been accomplished for me.

VIII

A few more sentences will end this chapter in Mr. Gladstone's life. As we have seen, an election took place in the closing days of December 1890. Mr. Parnell flung himself into the contest with frantic activity. A fierce conflict ended in the defeat of his candidate by nearly two to one.[1] Three months later a contest occurred in Sligo. Here again, though he had strained every nerve in the interval as well as in the immediate struggle, his candidate was beaten.[2] Another three months, then a third election at Carlow, — with the same result, the rejection of Mr. Parnell's man by a majority of much more than two to one.[3] It was in vain that his adherents denounced those who had left him as mutineers and helots, and exalted him as 'truer than Tone, abler than Grattan, greater than O'Connell, full of love for Ireland as Thomas Davis himself.' On the other side, he encountered antagonism in every key, from pathetic remonstrance or earnest reprobation, down to an unsparing fury that savoured

[1] December 23, 1890.   [2] April 3, 1891.   [3] July 8, 1891.

of the ruthless factions of the Seine. In America almost every name of consideration was hostile.

Yet undaunted by repulse upon repulse, he tore over from England to Ireland and back again, week after week and month after month, hoarse and haggard, seamed by sombre passions, waving the shreds of a tattered flag. Ireland must have been a hell on earth to him. To those Englishmen who could not forget that they had for so long been his fellow-workers, though they were now the mark of his attack, these were dark and desolating days. No more lamentable chapter is to be found in all the demented scroll of aimless and untoward things, that seem as if they made up the history of Ireland. It was not for very long. The last speech that Mr. Parnell ever made in England was at Newcastle-on-Tyne in July 1891, when he told the old story about the liberal leaders, of whom he said that there was but one whom he trusted. A few weeks later, not much more than ten months after the miserable act had opened, the Veiled Shadow stole upon the scene, and the world learned that Parnell was no more.[1]

[1] October 6. He was in his forty-sixth year (b. June 1846), and had been sixteen years in parliament.

CHAPTER VI

BIARRITZ

(*1891-1892*)

OMNIUM autem ineptiarum, quæ sunt innumerabiles, haud sciam
an nulla sit major, quam, ut illi solent, quocunque in loco,
quoscunque inter homines visum est, de rebus aut difficillimis
aut non necessariis argutissime disputare. — CICERO.

Of all the numberless sorts of bad taste and want of tact, perhaps
the worst is to insist, no matter where you are or with whom
you are, on arguing about the hardest subjects to the full pitch
of elaboration and detail.

BOOK
X.

1891.

WE have seen how in 1889 Mr. and Mrs. Gladstone celebrated the fiftieth anniversary of one of the most devoted
and successful marriages that ever was made, and the
unbroken felicity of their home. In 1891, after the shadows
of approaching calamity had for many months hung doubt-
fully over them, a heavy blow fell, and their eldest son died.
Not deeply concerned in ordinary politics, he was a man of
many virtues and some admirable gifts ; he was an accomplished musician, and I have seen letters of his to his father,
marked by a rare delicacy of feeling and true power of
expression. 'I had known him for nearly thirty years,' one
friend wrote, 'and there was no man, until his long illness,
who had changed so little, or retained so long the best
qualities of youth, and my first thought was that the greater
the loss to you, the greater would be the consolation.'

To Archbishop Benson, Mr. Gladstone wrote (July 6) : —

It is now forty-six years since we lost a child,[1] and he who
has now passed away from our eyes, leaves to us only blessed
recollections. I suppose all feel that those deaths which reverse
the order of nature have a sharpness of their own. But setting

[1] Vol. i. p. 387.

460

this apart, there is nothing lacking to us in consolations human or divine. I can only wish that I may become less unworthy to have been his father.

To me he wrote (July 10) : —

We feel deeply the kindness and tenderness of your letter. It supplies one more link in a long chain of recollection which I deeply prize. Yes, ours is a tribulation, and a sore one, but yet we feel we ought to find ourselves carried out of ourselves by sympathy with the wife whose noble and absorbing devotion had become like an entire life of itself, and who is now face to face with the void. The grief of children too, which passes, is very sharp while it remains. The case has been very remarkable. Though with abatement of some powers, my son has not been without many among the signs and comforts of health during a period of nearly two and a half years. All this time the terrible enemy was lodged in the royal seat, and only his healthy and unyielding constitution kept it at defiance, and maintained his mental and inward life intact. . . . And most largely has human, as well as divine compassion, flowed in upon us, from none more conspicuously than from yourself, whom we hope to count among near friends for the short remainder of our lives.

To another correspondent who did not share his own religious beliefs, he said (July 5) : —

When I received your last kind note, I fully intended to write to you with freedom on the subject of *The Agnostic Island*. But since then I have been at close quarters, so to speak, with the dispensations of God, for yesterday morning my dearly beloved eldest son was taken from the sight of our eyes. At this moment of bleeding hearts, I will only say what I hope you will in consideration of the motives take without offence, namely this : I would from the bottom of my heart that whenever the hour of bereavement shall befall you or those whom you love, you and they may enjoy the immeasurable consolation of believing, with all the mind and all the heart, that the beloved one is gone into eternal rest, and that those who remain behind may through the same mighty Deliverer hope at their appointed time to rejoin him.

All this language on the great occasions of human life was not with him the tone of convention. Whatever the synthesis, as they call it, — whatever the form, whatever the creed and faith may be, he was one of that high and favoured household who, in Emerson's noble phrase, 'live from a great depth of being.'

Earlier in the year Lord Granville, who so long had been his best friend, died. The loss by his death was severe. As Acton, who knew of their relations well and from within, wrote to Mr. Gladstone (April 1) : —

There was an admirable fitness in your union, and I had been able to watch how it became closer and easier, in spite of so much to separate you, in mental habits, in early affinities, and even in the form of fundamental convictions, since he came home from your budget, overwhelmed, thirty-eight years ago. I saw all the connections which had their root in social habit fade before the one which took its rise from public life and proved more firm and more enduring than the rest.

II

In September he paid a visit to his relatives at Fasque, and thence he went to Glenalmond — spots that in his tenacious memory must have awakened hosts of old and dear associations. On October 1, he found himself after a long and busy day, at Newcastle-on-Tyne, where he had never stayed since his too memorable visit in 1862.[1] Since the defeat of the Irish policy in 1886, he had attended the annual meeting of the chief liberal organisation at Nottingham (1887), Birmingham (1888), and Manchester (1889). This year it was the turn of Newcastle. On October 2, he gave his blessing to various measures that afterwards came to be known as the Newcastle programme. After the shock caused by the Irish quarrel, every politician knew that it would be necessary to balance home rule by reforms expected in England and Scotland. No liberal, whatever his particular shade, thought that it would be either honourable or practical to throw the Irish policy overboard, and if there

[1] See above, vol. ii. p. 76.

were any who thought such a course honourable, they knew
it would not be safe. The principle and expediency of home
rule had taken a much deeper root in the party than it
suited some of the trimming tribe later to admit. On the
other hand, after five years of pretty exclusive devotion to
the Irish case, to pass by the British case and its various
demands for an indefinite time longer, would have been
absurd.

III

In the eighties Mr. Gladstone grew into close friendship
with one who had for many years been his faithful supporter
in the House of Commons as member for Dundee. Nobody
ever showed him devotion more considerate, loyal, and
unselfish than did Mr. Armitstead, from about the close of
the parliament of 1880 down to the end of this story.[1] In
the middle of December 1891 Mr. Armitstead planned a
foreign trip for his hero, and persuaded me to join. Biarritz
was to be our destination, and the expedition proved a
wonderful success. Some notes of mine, though intended
only for domestic consumption, may help to bring Mr.
Gladstone in his easiest moods before the reader's eye.
No new ideas struck fire, no particular contribution was
made to grand themes. But a great statesman on a holiday
may be forgiven for not trying to discover bran-new keys
to philosophy, history, and 'all the mythologies.' As a
sketch from life of the veteran's buoyancy, vigour, genial
freshness of heart and brain, after four-score strenuous
years, these few pages may be found of interest.

We left Paris at nine in the morning (Dec. 16), and were
listening to the swell of the mighty Bay resounding under
our windows at Biarritz soon after midnight.

The long day's journey left no signs of fatigue on either
Mr. or Mrs. Gladstone, and his only regret was that we had

[1] Once Mr. Gladstone presented
him with a piece of plate, and set
upon it one of those little Latin inscriptions to which he was so much
addicted, and which must serve here
instead of further commemoration of
a remarkable friendship : Georgio
Armitstead, Armigero, D.D. Gul. E.
Gladstone. Amicitiæ Benevolentiæ
Beneficiorum delatorum Valde me-
mor Mense Augusti A.D., 1894.

not come straight through instead of staying a night in Paris. I'm always for going straight on, he said. For some odd reason in spite of the late hour he was full of stories of American humour, which he told with extraordinary verve and enjoyment. I contributed one that amused him much, of the Bostonian who, having read Shakespeare for the first time, observed, 'I call that a very clever book. Now, I don't suppose there are twenty men in Boston to-day who could have written that book!'

Thursday, Dec. 17. — Splendid morning for making acquaintance with a new place. Saw the western spur of the Pyrenees falling down to the Bidassoa and the first glimpse of the giant wall, beyond which, according to Michelet, Africa begins, and our first glimpse of Spain.

After breakfast we all sallied forth to look into the shops and to see the lie of the land. Mr. G. as interested as a child in all the objects in the shops — many of them showing that we are not far from Spain. The consul very polite, showed us about, and told us the hundred trifles that bring a place really into one's mind. Nothing is like a first morning's stroll in a foreign town. By afternoon the spell dissolves, and the mood comes of Dante's lines, '*Era già l'ora*,' etc.[1]

Some mention was made of Charles Austin, the famous lawyer: it brought up the case of men who are suddenly torn from lives of great activity to complete idleness.

Mr. G. — I don't know how to reconcile it with what I've always regarded as the foundation of character — Bishop Butler's view of habit. How comes it that during the hundreds of years in which priests and fellows of Eton College have retired from hard work to college livings and leisure, not one of them has ever done anything whatever for either scholarship or divinity — not one?

Mr. G. did not know Mazzini, but Armellini, another of the Roman triumvirs, taught him Italian in 1832.

---

[1] Era già l'ora, che volge 'l disio
A' naviganti, e 'ntenerisce 'l cuore
Lo dì ch' han detto a' dolci amici addio, etc.
Purg. viii.
Byron's rendering is well enough known.

I spoke a word for Gambetta, but he would not have it. 'Gambetta was *autoritaire;* I do not feel as if he were a true liberal in the old and best sense. I cannot forget how hostile he was to the movement for freedom in the Balkans.'

Said he only once saw Lord Liverpool. He went to call on Canning at Glos'ter House (close to our Glos'ter Road Station), and there through a glass door he saw Canning and Lord Liverpool talking together.

Peel. — Had a good deal of temper; not hot; but perhaps sulky. Not a farsighted man, but fairly clear-sighted. 'I called upon him after the election in 1847. The Janissaries, as Bentinck called us, that is the men who had stood by Peel, had been 110 before the election; we came back only 50. Peel said to me that what he looked forward to was a long and fierce struggle on behalf of protection. I must say I thought this foolish. If Bentinck had lived, with his strong will and dogged industry, there might have been a wide rally for protection, but everybody knew that Dizzy did not care a straw about it, and Derby had not constancy and force enough.'

Mr. G. said Disraeli's performances against Peel were quite as wonderful as report makes them. Peel altogether helpless in reply. Dealt with them with a kind of 'righteous dulness.' The Protectionist secession due to three men : Derby contributed prestige; Bentinck backbone; and Dizzy parliamentary brains.

The golden age of administrative reform was from 1832 to the Crimean War; Peel was always keenly interested in the progress of these reforms.

Northcote. — 'He was my private secretary; and one of the very best imaginable; pliant, ready, diligent, quick, acute, with plenty of humour, and a temper simply perfect. But as a leader, I think ill of him; you had a conversation; he saw the reason of your case; and when he left, you supposed all was right. But at the second interview, you always found that he had been unable to persuade his friends. What could be weaker than his conduct on the Bradlaugh affair! You could not wonder that the rank and file of his men should be caught by the proposition that an atheist ought not to sit in parliament. But what is a leader good for, if he dare not tell his party that in a matter like this they are wrong, and of course nobody knew better than N. that they were wrong. A clever, quick man with fine temper. By the way, how is it that we have no word, no respectable word, for backbone?'

J. M. — Character?

Mr. G. — Well, character; yes; but that's vague. It means will, I suppose. (I ought to have thought of Novalis's well-known definition of character as 'a completely fashioned will.')

J. M. — Our inferiority to the Greeks in discriminations of language shown by our lack of precise equivalents for φρόνησις, σοφία, σωφροσύνη, etc., of which we used to hear so much when coached in the *Ethics*.

Mr. G. went on to argue that because the Greeks drew these fine distinctions in words, they were superior in conduct. 'You cannot beat the Greeks in noble qualities.'

Mr. G. — I admit there is no Greek word of good credit for the virtue of humility.

J. M. — ταπεινότης? But that has an association of meanness.

Mr. G. — Yes; a shabby sort of humility. Humility as a sovereign grace is the creation of Christianity.

Friday, December 18. — Brilliant sunshine, but bitterly cold; an east wind blowing straight from the Maritime Alps. Walking, reading, talking. Mr. G. after breakfast took me into his room, where he is reading Heine, Butcher on Greek genius, and Marbot. Thought Thiers's well-known remark on Heine's death capital, — 'To-day the wittiest Frenchman alive has died.'

Mr. G. — We have talked about the best line in poetry, etc. How do you answer this question — Which century of English history produced the greatest men?

J. M. — What do you say to the sixteenth?

Mr. G. — Yes, I think so. Gardiner was a great man. Henry VIII. was great. But bad. Poor Cranmer. Like Northcote, he'd no backbone. Do you remember Jeremy Collier's sentence about his bravery at the stake, which

I count one of the grandest in English prose—'He seemed to repel the force of the fire and to overlook the torture, by strength of thought.'[1] Thucydides could not beat that.

The old man twice declaimed the sentence with deep sonorous voice, and his usual incomparable modulation.

Mr. G. talked of a certain General ——. He was thought to be a first-rate man ; neglected nothing, looked to things himself, conceived admirable plans, and at last got an important command. Then to the universal surprise, nothing came of it ; —— they said, 'could do everything that a commander should do, except say, *Quick march.*' There are plenty of politicians of that stamp, but Mr. G. decidedly not one of them. I mentioned a farewell dinner given to —— in the spring, by some rich man or other. It cost £560 for forty-eight guests ! Flowers alone £150. Mr. G. on this enormity, recalled a dinner to Talfourd about copyright at the old Clarendon Hotel in Bond Street, and the price was £2, 17s. 6d. a head. The old East India Company used to give dinners at a cost of seven guineas a head. He has a wonderfully lively interest for these matters, and his curiosity as to the prices of things in the shop-windows is inexhaustible. We got round to Goethe. Goethe, he said, never gave prominence to duty.

J. M. — Surely, surely in that fine psalm of life, *Das Göttliche ?*

Mr. G. — Döllinger used to confront me with the *Iphigenie* as a great drama of duty.

He wished that I had known Döllinger —' a man thoroughly from beginning to end of his life *purged of self.*' Mistook the nature of the Irish questions, from the erroneous view that Irish catholicism is ultramontane, which it certainly is not.

Saturday, Dec. 19. — *   *   *   *   *

What is extraordinary is that all Mr. G.'s versatility, buoyancy, and the rest goes with the most profound accuracy and intense concentration when any point of public business

---

[1] On some other occasion he set this against Macaulay's praise of a passage in Barrow mentioned above, ii. p. 536.

is raised. Something was said of the salaries of bishops. He was ready in an instant with every figure and detail, and every circumstance of the history of the foundation of the Ecclesiastical Commission in 1835–6. Then his *savoir faire* and wisdom of parliamentary conduct. 'I always made it a rule in the H. of C. to allow nobody to suppose that I did not like him, and to say as little as I could to prevent anybody from liking me. Considering the intense friction and contention of public life, it is a saving of wear and tear that as many as possible even among opponents should think well of one.'

Sunday, Dec. 20.—At table, a little discussion as to the happiness and misery of animal creation. Outside of man Mr. G. argued against Tennyson's description of Nature as red in tooth and claw. Apart from man, he said, and the action of man, sentient beings are happy and not miserable. But Fear? we said. No; they are unaware of impending doom; when hawk or kite pounces on its prey, the small bird has little or no apprehension; 'tis death, but death by appointed and unforeseen lot.

J. M.—There is Hunger. Is not the probability that most creatures are always hungry, not excepting Man?

To this he rather assented. Of course optimism like this is indispensable as the basis of natural theology.

Talked to Mr. G. about Michelet's Tableau de la France, which I had just finished in vol. 2 of the history. A brilliant tour de force, but strains the relations of soil to character; compels words and facts to be the slaves of his phantasy ; the modicum of reality overlaid with violent paradox and foregone conclusion. Mr. G. not very much interested — seems only to care for political and church history.

Monday, Dec. 31. — Mr. G. did not appear at table to-day, suffering from a surfeit of wild strawberries the day before. But he dined in his dressing gown, and I had some chat with him in his room after lunch.

Mr. G. — ' 'Tis a hard law of political things that if a man shows special competence in a department, that is the very thing most likely to keep him there, and prevent his promotion.'

Mr. G.—I consider Burke a tripartite man : America, France, Ireland—right as to two, wrong in one.

J. M.—Must you not add home affairs and India? His *Thoughts on the Discontents* is a masterpiece of civil wisdom, and the right defence in a great constitutional struggle. Then he gave fourteen years of industry to Warren Hastings, and teaching England the rights of the natives, princes and people, and her own duties. So he was right in four out of five.

Mr. G.—Yes, yes—quite true. Those two ought to be added to my three. There is a saying of Burke's from which I must utterly dissent. ' Property is sluggish and inert.' Quite the contrary. Property is vigilant, active, sleepless ; if ever it seems to slumber, be sure that one eye is open.

Marie Antoinette. I once read the three volumes of letters from Mercy d'Argenteau to Maria Theresa. He seems to have performed the duty imposed upon him with fidelity.

J. M.—Don't you think the Empress comes out well in the correspondence?

Mr. G.—Yes, she shows always judgment and sagacity.

J. M.—Ah, but besides sagacity, worth and as much integrity as those slippery times allowed.

Mr. G.—Yes (but rather reluctantly, I thought). As for Marie Antoinette, she was not a striking character in any sense, she was horribly frivolous ; and, I suppose, we must say she was, what shall I call it—a very considerable flirt ?

J. M.—The only case with real foundation seems to be that of the *beau Fersen*, the Swedish secretary. He too came to as tragic an end as the Queen.

Tuesday, Dec. 22.—Mr. G. still somewhat indisposed—but reading away all day long. Full of Marbot. Delighted with the story of the battle of Castiglione : how when Napoleon held a council of war, and they all said they were hemmed in, and that their only chance was to back out, Augereau roughly cried that they might all do what they liked, but he would attack the enemy cost what it might. ' Exactly like a place in the *Iliad;* when Agamemnon and the rest sit sorrowful in the assembly arguing that it was useless to withstand the sovereign will of Zeus, and that they had better flee into their ships, Diomed bursts out that whatever others think, in any event he and Sthenelus, his squire, will hold firm, and never desist from the onslaught until they have laid waste the walls of Troy.'[1] A large dose of Diomed in Mr. G. himself.

Talk about the dangerous isolation in which the monarchy will find itself in England if the hereditary principle goes down in the House of Lords; 'it will stand bare, naked, with no shelter or shield, only endured as the better of two evils.' 'I once asked,' he said, 'who besides myself in the party cares for the hereditary principle? The answer was, That perhaps —— cared for it !!' — naming a member of the party supposed to be rather sapient than sage.

News in the paper that the Comte de Paris in his discouragement was about to renounce his claims, and break up his party. Somehow this brought us round to Tocqueville, of whom Mr. G. spoke as the nearest French approach to Burke.

J. M. — But pale and without passion. Who was it that said of him that he was an aristocrat who accepted his defeat? That is, he knew democracy to be the conqueror, but he doubted how far it would be an improvement, he saw its perils, etc.

Mr. G. — I have not much faith in these estimates, whether in favour of progress or against it. I don't believe in comparisons of age with age. How can a man strike a balance between one government and another? How can he place himself in such an attitude, and with such comprehensive sureness of vision, as to say that the thirteenth century was better or higher or worse or lower than the nineteenth?

Thursday, Dec. 24. — At lunch we had the news of the Parnellite victory at Waterford. A disagreeable reverse for us. Mr. G. did not say many words about it, only that it would give heart to the mischief makers — only too certain. But we said no more about it. He and I took a walk on the sands in the afternoon, and had a curious talk (considering), about the prospects of the church of England. He was

[1] *Iliad*, ix. 32.

anxious to know about my talk some time ago with the
Bishop of —— whom I had met at a feast at Lincoln's Inn.
I gave him as good an account as I could of what had
passed. Mr. G. doubted that this prelate was fundamentally
an Erastian, as Tait was. Mr. G. is eager to read the signs
of the times as to the prospects of Anglican Christianity, to
which his heart is given ; and he fears the peril of Erastianism to the spiritual life of the church, which is naturally
the only thing worth caring about. Hence, he talked with
much interest of the question whether the clever fellows at
Oxford and Cambridge now take orders. He wants to know
what kind of defenders his church is likely to have in days
to come. Said that for the first time interest has moved
away both from politics and theology, towards the vague
something which they call social reform ; and he thinks
they won't make much out of that in the way of permanent
results. The establishment he considers safer than it has
been for a long time.

As to Welsh disestablishment, he said it was a pity that
where the national sentiment was so unanimous as it was in
Wales, the operation itself should not be as simple as
in Scotland. In Scotland sentiment is not unanimous, but
the operation is easy. In Wales sentiment is all one way,
but the operation difficult — a good deal more difficult than
people suppose, as they will find out when they come to
tackle it.

[Perhaps it may be mentioned here that, though we
always talked freely and abundantly together upon ecclesiastical affairs and persons, we never once exchanged a word
upon theology or religious creed, either at Biarritz or anywhere else.]

Pitt.—A strong denunciation of Pitt for the French war.
People don't realise what the French war meant. In 1812
wheat at Liverpool was 20s. (?) the imperial bushel of
65 pounds (?) ! Think of that, when you bring it into
figures of the cost of a loaf. And that was the time when
Eaton, Eastnor, and other great palaces were built by the
landlords out of the high rents which the war and war prices
enabled them to exact.

Wished we knew more of Melbourne. He was in many ways a very fine fellow. ' In two of the most important of all the relations of a prime minister, he was perfect ; I mean first, his relations to the Queen, second to his colleagues.'

Somebody at dinner quoted a capital description of the perverse fashion of talking that prevailed at Oxford soon after my time, and prevails there now, I fancy — 'hunting for epigrammatic ways of saying what you don't think.' —— was the father of this pestilent mode.

Rather puzzled him by repeating a saying of mine that used to amuse Fitzjames Stephen, that Love of Truth is more often than we think only a fine name for Temper. I think Mr. G. has a thorough dislike for anything that has a cynical or sardonic flavour about it. I wish I had thought, by the way, of asking him what he had to say of that piece of Swift's, about all objects being insipid that do not come by delusion, and everything being shrunken as it appears in the glass of nature, so that if it were not for artificial mediums, refracted angles, false lights, varnish and tinsel, there would be pretty much of a level in the felicity of mortal man.

Am always feeling how strong is his aversion to seeing more than he can help of what is sordid, mean, ignoble. He has not been in public life all these years without rubbing shoulders with plenty of baseness on every scale, and plenty of pettiness in every hue, but he has always kept his eyes well above it. Never was a man more wholly free of the starch of the censor, more ready to make allowance, nor more indulgent even ; he enters into human nature in all its compass. But he won't linger a minute longer than he must in the dingy places of life and character.

Christmas Day, 1891. — A divine day, brilliant sunshine, and mild spring air. Mr. G. heard what he called an admirable sermon from an English preacher, 'with a great command of his art.' A quietish day, Mr. G. no doubt engaged in φρονεῖν τὰ ὅσια.

Saturday, *Dec*. 26. — Once more a noble day. We started in a couple of carriages for the Négress station, a couple of miles away or more, I with the G.'s. Occasion produced the Greek epitaph of the nameless drowned sailor

who wished for others kinder seas.[1] Mr. G. felt its pathos
and its noble charm — so direct and simple, such benignity,
such a good lesson to men to forget their own misdeeds and
mischance, and to pray for the passer-by a happier star.
He repaid me by two epigrams of a different vein, and one
admirable translation into Greek, of Tennyson on Sir John
Franklin, which I do not carry in my mind ; another on a
boisterous Eton fellow —

> Didactic, dry, declamatory, dull,
> The bursar —— bellows like a bull.

Just in the tone of Greek epigram, a sort of point, but not
too much point.

Parliamentary Wit. — Thought Disraeli had never been
surpassed, nor even equalled, in this line. He had a contest
with General Grey, who stood upon the general merits of
the whig government, after both Lord Grey and Stanley had
left it. D. drew a picture of a circus man who advertised
his show with its incomparable team of six grey horses.
One died, he replaced it by a mule. Another died, and he
put in a donkey, still he went on advertising his team of
greys all the same. Canning's wit not to be found conspicuously in his speeches, but highly agreeable pleasantries,
though many of them in a vein which would jar horribly on
modern taste.

Some English redcoats and a pack of hounds passed us
as we neared the station. They saluted Mr. G. with a
politeness that astonished him, but was pleasant. Took the
train for Irun, the fields and mountain slopes delightful
in the sun, and the sea on our right a superb blue such
as we never see in English waters. At Irun we found
carriages waiting to take us on to Fuentarabia. From the
balcony of the church had a beautiful view over the scene of
Wellington's operations when he crossed the Bidassoa, in the
presence of the astonished Soult. A lovely picture, made
none the worse by this excellent historic association. The

[1] ναυτίλε, μὴ πεύθου τίνος ἐνθάδε τύμβος ὅδ' εἰμί,
ἀλλ αὐτὸς πόντου τύγχανε χρηστοτέρου.

'Ask not, mariner, whose tomb I am here, but be thine own fortune a
kinder sea.' — MACKAIL.

alcalde was extremely polite and intelligent. The consul who was with us showed a board on the old tower, in which *v* in some words was *b*, and I noted that the alcalde spoke of Viarritz. I reminded Mr. G. of Scaliger's epigram—

> Haud temere antiquas mutat Vasconia voces,
> Cui nihil est aliud vivere quam bibere.

Pretty cold driving home, but Mr. G. seemed not to care. He found both the churches at St. Jean and at Fuentarabia very noteworthy, though the latter very popish, but both, he felt, 'had a certain association with grandeur.'

Sunday, Dec. 27. — After some quarter of an hour of travellers' topics, we plunged into one of the most interesting talks we have yet had. *Apropos* of I do not know what, Mr. G. said that he had not advised his son to enter public life. 'No doubt there are some men to whom station, wealth, and family traditions make it a duty. But I have never advised any individual, as to whom I have been consulted, to enter the H. of C.'

J. M. — But isn't that rather to encourage self-indulgence? Nobody who cares for ease or mental composure would seek public life?

Mr. G. — Ah, I don't know that. Surely politics open up a great field for the natural man. Self-seeking, pride, domination, power — all these passions are gratified in politics.

J. M. — You cannot be sure of achievement in politics, whether personal or public?

Mr. G. — No; to use Bacon's pregnant phrase, they are too immersed in matter. Then as new matter, that is, new details and particulars, come into view, men change their judgment.

J. M. — You have spoken just now of somebody as a thorough good tory. You know the saying that nobody is worth much who has not been a bit of a radical in his youth, and a bit of a tory in his fuller age.

Mr. G. (laughing) — Ah, I'm afraid that hits me rather hard. But for myself, I think I can truly put up all the change that has come into my politics into a sentence; I was brought up to distrust and dislike liberty, I learned to believe in it. That is the key to all my changes.

J. M. — According to my observation, the change in my own generation is different. They have ceased either to trust or to distrust liberty, and have come to the mind that it matters little either way. Men are disenchanted. They have got what they wanted in the days of their youth, yet what of it, they ask? France has thrown off the Empire, but the statesmen of the republic are not a great breed. Italy has gained her unity, yet unity has not been followed by thrift, wisdom, or large increase of public virtue or happiness. America has purged herself of slavery, yet life in America is material, prosaic, — so say some of her own rarest sons. Don't think that I say all these things. But I know able and high-minded men who suffer from this disenchantment.

Mr. G. — Italy would have been very different if Cavour had only lived — and even Ricasoli. Men ought not to suffer from disenchantment. They ought to know that *ideals in politics are never realised.* And don't let us forget in eastern Europe the rescue in our time of some ten millions of men from the harrowing domination of the Turk. (On this he expatiated, and very justly, with much energy.)

We turned to our own country. Here he insisted that democracy had certainly not saved us from a distinct decline in the standard of public men. . . . Look at the whole conduct of opposition from '80 to '85 — every principle was flung overboard, if they could manufacture a combination against the government. For all this deterioration one man and one man alone is responsible, Disraeli. He is the grand corrupter. He it was who sowed the seed.

J. M. — Ought not Palmerston to bear some share in this?

Mr. G. — No, no; Pam. had many strong and liberal convictions. On one subject Dizzy had them too — the Jews. There he was much more than rational, he was fanatical. He said once that Providence would deal good or ill fortune to nations, according as they dealt well or ill by the Jews. I remember once sitting next to John Russell when D. was

BOOK
X.

1891.

making a speech on Jewish emancipation. 'Look at him,'
said J. R., 'how manfully he sticks to it, tho' he knows that
every word he says is gall and wormwood to every man who
sits around him and behind him.' A curious irony, was it
not, that it should have fallen to me to propose a motion
for a memorial both to Pam. and Dizzy?

A superb scene upon the ocean, with a grand wind from
the west. Mr. G. and I walked on the shore; he has a
passion for tumultuous seas. I have never seen such huge
masses of water shattering themselves among the rocks.

In the evening Mr. G. remarked on our debt to Macaulay,
for guarding the purity of the English tongue. I recalled
a favourite passage from Milton, that next to the man
who gives wise and intrepid counsels of government, he
places the man who cares for the purity of his mother
tongue. Mr. G. liked this. Said he only knew Bright once
slip into an error in this respect, when he used 'transpire'
for 'happen.' Macaulay of good example also in rigorously
abstaining from the inclusion of matter in footnotes.
Hallam an offender in this respect. I pointed out that he
offended in company with Gibbon.

Monday, Dec. 28. — We had an animated hour at breakfast.

Oxford and Cambridge. — Curious how, like two buckets,
whenever one was up, the other was down. Cambridge has
never produced four such men of action in successive ages
as Wolsey, Laud, Wesley, and Newman.

J. M. — In the region of thought Cambridge has produced
the greatest of all names, Newton.

Mr. G. — In the earlier times Oxford has it—with Wycliff,
Occam, above all Roger Bacon. And then in the eighteenth
century, Butler.

J. M. — But why not Locke, too, in the century before?

This brought on a tremendous tussle, for Mr. G. was of
the same mind, and perhaps for the same sort of reason, as
Joseph de Maistre, that contempt for Locke is the beginning
of knowledge. All very well for De Maistre, but not for a
man in line with European liberalism. I pressed the very
obvious point that you must take into account not only a
man's intellectual product or his general stature, but also

his influence as a historic force. From the point of view of
influence Locke was the origin of the emancipatory movement of the eighteenth century abroad, and laid the philosophic foundations of liberalism in civil government at home.
Mr. G. insisted on a passage of Hume's which he believed
to be in the history, disparaging Locke as a metaphysical
thinker.[1] 'That may be,' said I, 'though Hume in his
Essays is not above paying many compliments to "the
great reasoner," etc., to whom, for that matter, I fancy that
he stood in pretty direct relation. But far be it from me to
deny that Hume saw deeper than Locke into the metaphysical millstone. That is not the point. I'm only
thinking of his historic place, and, after all, the history of
philosophy is itself a philosophy.' To minds nursed in
dogmatic schools, all this is both unpalatable and incredible.

Somehow we slid into the freedom of the will and
Jonathan Edwards. I told him that Mill had often told
us how Edwards argued the necessarian or determinist case
as keenly as any modern.

Tuesday, Dec. 29. — Mr. G. 82 to-day. I gave him Mackail's
Greek Epigrams, and if it affords him half as much pleasure
as it has given me, he will be very grateful. Various people
brought Mr. G. bouquets and addresses. Mr. G. went to
church in the morning, and in the afternoon took a walk
with me. . . . *Land Question.* As you go through France
you see the soil cultivated by the population. In our little
dash into Spain the other day, we saw again the soil cultivated by the population. In England it is cultivated by
the capitalist, for the farmer is capitalist. Some astonishing
views recently propounded by D. of Argyll on this matter.
Unearned increment — so terribly difficult to catch it.
Perhaps best try to get at it through the death duties.
Physical condition of our people — always a subject of great
anxiety — their stature, colour, and so on. Feared the
atmosphere of cotton factories, etc., very deleterious. As
against bad air, I said, you must set good food ; the Lancashire operative in decent times lives uncommonly well, as he
deserves to do. He agreed there might be something in this.

[1] I have not succeeded in hitting on the passage in the *History*.

The day was humid and muggy, but the tumult of the sea was most majestic. Mr. G. delighted in it. He has a passion for the sound of the sea; would like to have it in his ear all day and all night. Again and again he recurred to this.

After dinner, long talk about Mazzini, of whom Mr. G. thought poorly in comparison with Poerio and the others who for freedom sacrificed their lives. I stood up for Mazzini, as one of the most morally impressive men I had ever known, or that his age knew; he breathed a soul into democracy.

Then we fell into a discussion as to the eastern and western churches. He thought the western popes by their proffered alliance with the mahometans, etc., had betrayed Christianity in the east. I offered De Maistre's view.

Mr. G. strongly assented to old Chatham's dictum that vacancy is worse than even the most anxious work. He has less to reproach himself with than most men under that head.

He repeated an observation that I have heard him make before, that he thought politicians are more *rapid* than other people. I told him that Bowen once said to me on this that he did not agree; that he thought rapidity the mark of all successful men in the practical line of life, merchants and stockbrokers, etc.

Wednesday, Dec. 30. — A very muggy day. A divine sunset, with the loveliest pink and opal tints in the sky. Mr. G. reading Gleig's *Subaltern*. Not a very entertaining book in itself, but the incidents belong to Wellington's Pyrenean campaign, and, for my own part, I rather enjoyed it on the principle on which one likes reading *Romola* at Florence, *Transformation* at Rome, *Sylvia's Lovers* at Whitby, and *Hurrish* on the northern edge of Clare.

Thursday, Dec. 31. — Down to the pier, and found all the party watching the breakers, and superb they were. Mr. G. exulting in the huge force of the Atlantic swell and the beat of the rollers on the shore, like a Titanic pulse.

After dinner Mr. G. raised the question of payment of members. He had been asked by somebody whether he meant at Newcastle to indicate that everybody should be paid, or only those who chose to take it or to ask

for it. He produced the same extraordinary plan as he
had described to me on the morning of his Newcastle
speech — *i.e.* that the Inland Revenue should ascertain from
their own books the income of every M.P., and if they
found any below the limit of exemption, should notify the
same to the Speaker, and the Speaker should thereupon
send to the said M.P. below the limit an annual cheque for,
say, £300, the name to appear in an annual return to Parliament of all the M.P.'s in receipt of public money on any
grounds whatever. I demurred to this altogether, as
drawing an invidious distinction between paid and unpaid
members; said it was idle to ignore the theory on which the
demand for paid members is based, namely, that it is desirable in the public interest that poor men should have access
to the H. of C.; and that the poor man should stand there
on the same footing as anybody else.

Friday, Jan. 1, 1892. — After breakfast Mrs. Gladstone
came to my room and said how glad she was that I had not
scrupled to put unpleasant points; that Mr. G. must not be
shielded and sheltered as some great people are, who hear
all the pleasant things and none of the unpleasant; that the
perturbation from what is disagreeable only lasts an hour. I
said I hoped that I was faithful with him, but of course
I could not be always putting myself in an attitude of
perpetual controversy. She said, 'He is never made angry
by what you say.' And so she went away, and —— and
I had a good and most useful set-to about Irish finance.

At luncheon Mr. G. asked what we had made out of our
morning's work. When we told him he showed a good deal
of impatience and vehemence, and, to my dismay, he came
upon union finance and the general subject of the treatment of Ireland by England. . . .

In the afternoon we took a walk, he and I, afterwards
joined by the rest. He was as delighted as ever with the
swell of the waves, as they bounded over one another, with
every variety of grace and tumultuous power. He wondered
if we had not more and better words for the sea than the
French — 'breaker,' 'billow,' 'roller,' as against 'flot,' 'vague,'
'onde,' 'lame,' etc.

At dinner he asked me whether I had made up my mind on the burning question of compulsory Greek for a university degree. I said, No, that as then advised I was half inclined to be against compulsory Greek, but it is so important that I would not decide before I was obliged. 'So with me,' he said, ' the question is one with many subtle and deep-reaching consequences.' He dwelt on the folly of striking Italian out of the course of modern education, thus cutting European history in two, and setting an artificial gulf between the ancient and modern worlds.

Saturday, Jan. 2. — Superb morning, and all the better for being much cooler. At breakfast somebody started the idle topic of quill pens. When they came to the length of time that so-and-so made a quill serve, ' De Retz,' said I, ' made up his mind that Cardinal Chigi was a poor creature, *maximus in minimis,* because at their first interview Chigi boasted that he had used one pen for three years.' That recalled another saying of Retz's about Cromwell's famous dictum, that nobody goes so far as the man who does not know where he is going. Mr. G. gave his deep and eager Ah ! to this. He could not recall that Cromwell had produced many dicta of such quality. 'I don't love him, but he was a mighty big fellow. But he was intolerant. He was intolerant of the episcopalians.'

Mr. G. — Do you know whom I find the most tolerant churchman of that time ? *Laud !* Laud got Davenant made Bishop of Salisbury, and he zealously befriended Chillingworth and Hales. (There was some other case, which I forget.)

The execution of Charles. — I told him of Gardiner's new volume which I had just been reading. ' Charles,' he said, ' was no doubt a dreadful liar ; Cromwell perhaps did not always tell the truth ; Elizabeth was a tremendous liar.'

J. M. — Charles was not wholly inexcusable, being what he was, for thinking that he had a good game in his hands, by playing off the parliament against the army, etc.

Mr. G. — There was less excuse for cutting off his head than in the case of poor Louis XVI., for Louis was the excuse for foreign invasion.

J. M. — Could you call foreign invasion the intervention of the Scotch?

Mr. G. — Well, not quite. I suppose it is certain that it was Cromwell who cut off Charles's head? Not one in a hundred in the nation desired it.

J. M. — No, nor one in twenty in the parliament. But then, ninety-nine in a hundred in the army.

In the afternoon we all drove towards Bayonne to watch the ships struggle over the bar at high water. As it happened we only saw one pass out, a countryman for Cardiff. A string of others were waiting to go, but a little steamer from Nantes came first, and having secured her station, found she had not force enough to make the bar, and the others remained swearing impatiently behind her. The Nantes steamer was like Ireland. The scene was very fresh and fine, and the cold most exhilarating after the mugginess of the last two or three days. Mr. G., who has a dizzy head, did not venture on the jetty, but watched things from the sands. He and I drove home together, at a good pace. 'I am inclined,' he said laughingly, 'to agree with Dr. Johnson that there is no pleasure greater than sitting behind four fast-going horses." [1] Talking of Johnson generally, 'I suppose we may take him as the best product of the eighteenth century.' Perhaps so, but is he its most characteristic product?

Wellington. — Curious that there should be no general estimate of W.'s character ; his character not merely as a general but as a man. No love of freedom. His sense of duty very strong, but military rather than civil.

Montalembert. — Had often come into contact with him. A very amiable and attractive man. But less remarkable than Rio.

Latin Poets. — Would you place Virgil first?

J. M. — Oh, no, Lucretius much the first for the greatest and sublimest of poetic qualities. Mr. G. seemed to assent to this, though disposed to make a fight for the second *Aeneid* as equal to anything. He expressed his admiration for

[1] Boswell, March 21, 1776. Repeated, with a very remarkable qualification, Sept. 19, 1777. Birkbeck Hill's edition, iii. p. 162.

Catullus, and then he was strong that Horace would run anybody else very hard, breaking out with the lines about Regulus —

> ' Atqui sciebat quæ sibi barbarus
> Tortor pararet ; ' etc.[1]

Blunders in Government. — How right Napoleon was when he said, reflecting on all the vast complexities of government, that the best to be said of a statesman is that he has avoided the biggest blunders.

It is not easy to define the charm of these conversations. Is charm the right word ? They are in the highest degree stimulating, bracing, widening. That is certain. I return to my room with the sensations of a man who has taken delightful exercise in fresh air. He is so wholly free from the *ergoteur.* There's all the difference between the *ergoteur* and the great debater. He fits his tone to the thing ; he can be as playful as anybody. In truth I have many a time seen him in London and at Hawarden not far from trivial. But here at Biarritz all is appropriate, and though, as I say, he can be playful and gay as youth, he cannot resist rising in an instant to the general point of view — to grasp the elemental considerations of character, history, belief, conduct, affairs. There he is at home, there he is most himself. I never knew anybody less guilty of the tiresome sin of arguing for victory. It is not his knowledge that attracts ; it is not his ethical tests and standards ; it is not that dialectical strength of arm which, as Mark Pattison said of him, could twist a bar of iron to its purpose. It is the combination of these with elevation, with true sincerity, with extraordinary mental force.

Sunday, Jan. 3. — Vauvenargues is right when he says that to carry through great undertakings, one must act as though one could never die. My wonderful companion is a wonderful illustration. He is like M. Angelo, who, just before he died on the very edge of ninety, made an allegorical figure, and inscribed upon it, *ancora impara,* ' still learning.'

At dinner he showed in full force.

[1] *Carm.* iii. 5.

Heroes of the Old Testament. — He could not honestly say CHAP.
that he thought there was any figure in the O. T. comparable VI.
to the heroes of Homer. Moses was a fine fellow. But the *Æt.* 83.
others were of secondary quality — not great high personages,
of commanding nature.

Thinkers. — Rather an absurd word — to call a man a
thinker (and he repeated the word with gay mockery in his
tone). When did it come into use? Not until quite our
own times, eh? I said, I believed both Hobbes and Locke
spoke of thinkers, and was pretty sure that *penseur*, as in
libre penseur, had established itself in the last century.
[Quite true; Voltaire used it, but it was not common.]

Dr. Arnold. — A high, large, impressive figure — perhaps
more important by his character and personality than his
actual work. I mentioned M. A.'s poem on his father, *Rugby
Chapel*, with admiration. Rather to my surprise, Mr. G.
knew the poem well, and shared my admiration to the full.
This brought us on to poetry generally, and he expatiated
with much eloquence and sincerity for the rest of the talk.
The wonderful continuity of fine poetry in England for
five whole centuries, stretching from Chaucer to Tennyson,
always a proof to his mind of the soundness, the sap, and
the vitality of our nation and its character. What people,
beginning with such a poet as Chaucer 500 years ago, could
have burst forth into such astonishing production of poetry
as marked the first quarter of the century, Byron, Wordsworth, Shelley, etc.

J. M. — It is true that Germany has nothing, save Goethe,
Schiller, Heine, that's her whole list. But I should say a
word for the poetic movement in France : Hugo, Gautier,
etc. Mr. G. evidently knew but little, or even nothing, of
modern French poetry. He spoke up for Leopardi, on whom
he had written an article first introducing him to the British
public, ever so many years ago — in the *Quarterly*.

Mr. G. — Wordsworth used occasionally to dine with me
when I lived in the Albany. A most agreeable man. I
always found him amiable, polite, and sympathetic. Only
once did he jar upon me, when he spoke slightingly of
Tennyson's first performance.

J. M. — But he was not so wrong as he would be now. Tennyson's Juvenilia are terribly artificial.

Mr. G. — Yes, perhaps. Tennyson has himself withdrawn some of them. I remember W., when he dined with me, used on leaving to change his silk stockings in the ante-room and put on grey worsted.

J. M. — I once said to M. Arnold that I'd rather have been Wordsworth than anybody [not exactly a modest ambition]; and Arnold, who knew him well in the Grasmere country, said, 'Oh no, you would not; you would wish you were dining with me at the Athenæum. He was too much of the peasant for you.'

Mr. G. — No, I never felt that; I always thought him a polite and an amiable man.

Mentioned Macaulay's strange judgment in a note in the *History*, that Dryden's famous lines,

> '. . . Fool'd with hope, men favour the deceit ;
> Trust on, and think to-morrow will repay.
> To-morrow's falser than the former day;
> Lies worse, and while it says we shall be blest
> With some new joys, cuts off what we possest.
> Strange cozenage ! . . .'

are as fine as any eight lines in Lucretius. Told him of an excellent remark of —— on this, that Dryden's passage wholly lacks the mystery and great superhuman air of Lucretius. Mr. G. warmly agreed.

He regards it as a remarkable sign of the closeness of the church of England to the roots of life and feeling in the country, that so many clergymen should have written so much good poetry. Who, for instance? I asked. He named Heber, Moultrie, Newman (*Dream of Gerontius*), and Faber in at least one good poem, 'The poor Labourer' (or some such title), Charles Tennyson. I doubt if this thesis has much body in it. He was for Shelley as the most musical of all our poets. I told him that I had once asked M. to get Tennyson to write an autograph line for a friend of mine, and Tennyson had sent this : —

> 'Coldly on the dead volcano sleeps the gleam of dying day.'

So I suppose the poet must think well of it himself. 'Tis

from the second *Locksley Hall*, and describes a man after passions have gone cool.

Mr. G. — Yes, in melody, in the picturesque, and as apt simile, a fine line.

Had been trying his hand at a translation of his favourite lines of Penelope about Odysseus. Said that, of course, you could translate similes and set passages, but to translate Homer as a whole, impossible. He was inclined, when all is said, to think Scott the nearest approach to a model.

Monday, Jan. 4. — At luncheon, Mr. Gladstone recalled the well-known story of Talleyrand on the death of Napoleon. The news was brought when T. chanced to be dining with Wellington. 'Quel événement!' they all cried. 'Non, ce n'est pas un événement,' said Talleyrand, 'c'est une nouvelle' — 'Tis no event, 'tis a piece of news. 'Imagine such a way,' said Mr. G., 'of taking the disappearance of that colossal man! Compare it with the opening of Manzoni's ode, which makes the whole earth stand still. Yet both points of view are right. In one sense, the giant's death was only news; in another, when we think of his history, it was enough to shake the world.' At the moment, he could not recall Manzoni's words, but at dinner he told me that he had succeeded in piecing them together, and after dinner he went to his room and wrote them down for me on a piece of paper. Curiously enough, he could not recall the passage in his own splendid translation.[1]

Talk about handsome men of the past; Sidney Herbert one of the handsomest and most attractive. But the Duke of Hamilton bore away the palm, as glorious as a Greek god. 'One day in Rotten Row, I said this to the Duchess of C. She set up James Hope-Scott against my Duke. No doubt he had an intellectual element which the Duke lacked.' Then we discussed the best-looking man in the H. of C. to-day. . . .

Duke of Wellington. — Somebody was expatiating on the incomparable position of the Duke; his popularity with kings, with nobles, with common people. Mr. G. remem-

[1] *Translations by Lyttelton and Gladstone*, p. 166.

bered that immediately after the formation of Canning's government in 1827, when it was generally thought that he had been most unfairly and factiously treated (as Mr. G. still thinks, always saving Peel) by the Duke and his friends, the Duke made an expedition to the north of England, and had an overwhelming reception. Of course, he was then only twelve years from Waterloo, and yet only four or five years later he had to put up his iron shutters.

Approved a remark that a friend of ours was not simple enough, not ready enough to take things as they come.

Mr. G. — Unless a man has a considerable gift for taking things as they come, he may make up his mind that political life will be sheer torment to him. He must meet fortune in all its moods.

Tuesday, Jan. 5. — After dinner to-day, Mr. G. extraordinarily gay. He had bought a present of silver for his wife. She tried to guess the price, and after the manner of wives in such a case, put the figure provokingly low. Mr. G. then put on the deprecating air of the tradesman with wounded feelings — and it was as capital fun as we could desire. That over, he fell to his backgammon with our host.

Wednesday, Jan. 6. — Mrs. Gladstone eighty to-day! What a marvel. . . .

Léon Say called to see Mr. G. Long and most interesting conversation about all sorts of aspects of French politics, the concordat, the schools, and all the rest of it.

He illustrated the ignorance of French peasantry as to current affairs. Thiers, long after he had become famous, went on a visit to his native region ; and there met a friend of his youth. 'Eh bien,' said his friend, 'tu as fait ton chemin.' 'Mais oui, j'ai fait un peu mon chemin. J'ai été ministre même.' 'Ah, tiens ! je ne savais pas que tu étais protestant.'

I am constantly struck by his solicitude for the well-being and right doing of Oxford and Cambridge — 'the two eyes of the country.' This connection between the higher education and the general movement of the national mind engages his profound attention, and no doubt deserves such attention

in any statesman who looks beyond the mere surface problems of the day. To perceive the bearings of such matters
as these, makes Mr. G. a statesman of the highest class, as
distinguished from men of clever expedients.

Mr. G. had been reading the Greek epigrams on religion
in Mackail; quoted the last of them as illustrating the
description of the dead as the inhabitants of the more
populous world : —

> τῶν ἄπο κῆν ζωοῖσιν ἀκηδέα, κεῦτ' ἂν ἵκηαι
> ἐς πλεόνων, ἕξεις θυμὸν ἐλαφρότερον.[1]

A more impressive epigram contains the same thought,
where the old man, leaning on his staff, likens himself to the
withered vine on its dry pole, and goes on to ask himself what
advantage it would be to warm himself for three or four more
years in the sun; and on that reflection without heroics put
off his life, and changed his home to the greater company,

> κῆς πλεόνων ἦλθε μετοικεσίην.

All the rest of the evening he kept us alive by a stock of
infinite drolleries. A scene of a dish of over-boiled tea at
West Calder after a meeting, would have made the fortune
of a comedian.

I said that in the all-important quality of co-operation,
—— was only good on condition of being in front. Mr. G.
read him in the same sense. Reminded of a mare he once
had — admirable, provided you kept off spur, curb, or whip;
show her one of these things, and she would do nothing.
Mr. G. more of a judge of men than is commonly thought.

Told us of a Chinese despatch which came under his notice
when he was at the board of trade, and gave him food for
reflection. A ship laden with grain came to Canton. The
administrator wrote to the central government at Pekin to
know whether the ship was to pay duty and land its cargo.
The answer was to the effect that the central government of
the Flowery Land was quite indifferent as a rule to the goings
and comings of the Barbarians; whether they brought a cargo
or brought no cargo was a thing of supreme unconcern. ' But
this cargo, you say, is food for the people. There ought to be

[1] Thou shalt possess thy soul with- when thou goest to the place where
out care among the living, and lighter most are.

no obstacle to the entry of food for the people. So let it in.
Your Younger Brother commends himself to you, etc. etc.'

Friday, Jan. 8. — A quiet evening. We were all rather
piano at the end of an episode which had been thoroughly
delightful. When Mr. G. bade me good-night, he said with
real feeling, ' More sorry than I can say that this is our last
evening together at Biarritz.' He is painfully grieved to
lose the sound of the sea in his ears.

Saturday, Jan. 9. — Strolled about all the forenoon. ' What
a time of blessed composure it has been,' said Mr. G. with a
heavy sigh. The distant hills covered with snow, and the
voice of the storm gradually swelling. Still the savage fury
of the sea was yet some hours off, so we had to leave Biarritz
without the spectacle of Atlantic rage at its fiercest.

Found comfortable saloon awaiting us at Bayonne, and so
under weeping skies we made our way to Pau. The landscape must be pretty, weather permitting. As it was, we
saw but little. Mr. G. dozed and read Max Müller's book on
Anthropological Religions.

Arrived at Pau towards 5.30; drenching rain: nothing to
be seen.

At tea time, a good little discussion raised by a protest
against Dante being praised for a complete survey of human
nature and the many phases of human lot. Intensity he
has, but insight over the whole field of character and life?
Mr. G. did not make any stand against this, and made the
curious admission that Dante was too optimist to be placed
on a level with Shakespeare, or even with Homer.

Then we turned to lighter themes. He had once said to
Henry Taylor, ' I should have thought he was the sort of
man to have a good strong grasp of a subject,' speaking of
Lord Grey, who had been one of Taylor's many chiefs at the
Colonial Office. ' I should have thought,' replied Taylor
slowly and with a dreamy look, ' he was the sort of man to
have a good strong *nip* of a subject.' Witty, and very
applicable to many men.

Wordsworth once gave Mr. G. with much complacency,
as an example of his own readiness and resource, this story.
A man came up to him at Rydal and said, ' Do you happen

to have seen my wife.' 'Why,' replied the Sage, 'I did not know you had a wife!' This peculiarly modest attempt at pointed repartee much tickled Mr. G., as well it might.

Tuesday, Jan. 12. — Mr. G. completely recovered from two days of indisposition. We had about an hour's talk on things in general, including policy in the approaching session. He did not expect a dissolution, at the same time a dissolution would not surprise him.

At noon they started for Périgord and Carcassonne, Nismes, Arles, and so on to the Riviera full of kind things at our parting.

CHAPTER VII

THE FOURTH ADMINISTRATION

(*1892-1894*)

Τῷ δ' ἤδη δύο μὲν γενεαὶ μερόπων ἀνθρώπων
ἐφθίαθ, οἳ οἱ πρόσθεν ἄμα τράφεν ἠδὲ γένοντο
ἐν Πύλῳ ἠγαθέῃ, μετὰ δὲ τριτάτοισιν ἄνασσεν.

Iliad, i. 250.

Two generations of mortal men had he already seen pass away, who with him of old had been born and bred in sacred Pylos, and among the third generation he held rule.

BOOK X.

1892.

IN 1892 the general election came, after a session that was not very long nor at all remarkable. Everybody knew that we should soon be dismissed, and everybody knew that the liberals would have a majority, but the size of it was beyond prognostication. Mr. Gladstone did not talk much about it, but in fact he reckoned on winning by eighty or a hundred. A leading liberal-unionist at whose table we met (May 24) gave us forty. That afternoon by the way the House had heard a speech of great power and splendour. An Irish tory peer in the gallery said afterwards, ' That old hero of yours is a miracle. When he set off in that high pitch, I said that won't last. Yet he kept it up all through as grand as ever, and came in fresher and stronger than when he began.' His sight failed him in reading an extract, and he asked me to read it for him, so he sat down amid sympathetic cheers while it was read out from the box.

After listening to a strong and undaunted reply from Mr. Balfour, he asked me to go with him into the tea-room; he was fresh, unperturbed, and in high spirits. He told me he had once sat at table with Lord Melbourne, but regretted that he had never known him. Said that of the sixty men or so who had been his colleagues in cabinet, the

very easiest and most attractive was Clarendon. Constantly
regretted that he had never met nor known Sir Walter
Scott, as of course he might have done. Thought the effect
of diplomacy to be bad on the character; to train yourself
to practise the airs of genial friendship towards men from
whom you are doing your best to hide yourself, and out of
whom you are striving to worm that which they wish to
conceal. Said that he was often asked for advice by young
men as to objects of study. He bade them study and ponder,
first, the history and working of freedom in America; second, the history of absolutism in France from Louis XIV. to
the Revolution. It was suggested that if the great thing
with the young is to attract them to fine types of character,
the Huguenots had some grave, free, heroic figures, and in
the eighteenth century Turgot was the one inspiring example : when Mill was in low spirits, he restored himself by
Condorcet's life of Turgot. This reminded him that Canning had once praised Turgot in the House of Commons,
though most likely nobody but himself knew anything at
all about Turgot. Talking of the great centuries, the thirteenth, and the sixteenth, and the seventeenth, Mr. Gladstone
let drop what for him seems the remarkable judgment
that 'Man as a type has not improved since those great
times ; he is not so big, so grand, so heroic as he has
been.' This, the reader will agree, demands a good deal
of consideration.

Then he began to talk about offices, in view of what were
now pretty obvious possibilities. After discussing more
important people, he asked whether, after a recent conversation, I had thought more of my own office, and I told him
that I fancied like Regulus I had better go back to the Irish
department. ' Yes,' he answered with a flash of his eye, ' I
think so. The truth is that we're both chained to the oar ;
I am chained to the oar ; you are chained.'

II

The electoral period, when it arrived, he passed once more
at Dalmeny. In a conversation the morning after I was

BOOK
X.
1892.

allowed to join him there, he seemed already to have a grand majority of three figures, to have kissed hands, and to be installed in Downing Street. This confidence was indispensable to him. At the end of his talk he went up to prepare some notes for the speech that he was to make in the afternoon at Glasgow. Just before the carriage came to take him to the train, I heard him calling from the library. In I went, and found him hurriedly thumbing the leaves of a Horace. 'Tell me,' he cried, 'can you put your finger on the passage about Castor and Pollux? I've just thought of something; Castor and Pollux will finish my speech at Glasgow.' 'Isn't it in the Third Book?' said I. 'No, no; I'm pretty sure it is in the First Book' — busily turning over the pages. 'Ah, here it is,' and then he read out the noble lines with animated modulation, shut the book with a bang, and rushed off exultant to the carriage. This became one of the finest of his perorations.[1] His delivery of it that afternoon, they said, was most majestic — the picture of the wreck, and then the calm that gradually brought down the towering billows to the surface of the deep, entrancing the audience like magic.

Then came a depressing week. The polls flowed in, all day long, day after day. The illusory hopes of many months faded into night. The three-figure majority by the end of the week had vanished so completely, that one wondered how it could ever have been thought of. On July 13 his own Midlothian poll was declared, and instead of his old majority of 4000, or the 3000 on which he counted, he was only in by 690. His chagrin was undoubtedly intense, for he had put forth every atom of his strength in the campaign. But with that splendid suppression of vexation which is one of the good lessons that men learn in public life, he put a brave face on it, was perfectly cheery all through the luncheon, and afterwards took me to the music-room, where instead of constructing a triumphant cabinet with a majority of a hundred, he had to try to adjust an Irish policy to a parliament with hardly a majority at all. These topics exhausted, with a curiously quiet gravity of tone he told me

[1] See Appendix, Hor. *Carm.* i. 12, 25.

that cataract had formed over one eye, that its sight was
gone, and that in the other eye he was infested with a white
speck. 'One white speck,' he said, almost laughing, 'I can
do with, but if the one becomes many, it will be a bad business. They tell me that perhaps the fresh air of Braemar
will do me good.' To Braemar the ever loyal Mr. Armitstead
piloted them, in company with Lord Acton of whose society
Mr. Gladstone could never have too much.

III

It has sometimes been made a matter of blame by friends
no less than foes, that he should have undertaken the task
of government, depending on a majority not large enough to
coerce the House of Lords. One or two short observations
on this would seem to be enough. How could he refuse to
try to work his Irish policy through parliament, after the
bulk of the Irish members had quitted their own leader four
years before in absolute reliance on the sincerity and good
faith of Mr. Gladstone and his party? After all the confidence that Ireland had shown in him at the end of 1890, how
could he in honour throw up the attempt that had been the
only object of his public life since 1886? To do this would
have been to justify indeed the embittered warnings of Mr.
Parnell in his most reckless hour. How could either refusal
of office or the postponement of an Irish bill after taking
office, be made intelligible in Ireland itself? Again, the path
of honour in Ireland was equally the path of honour and of
safety in Great Britain. Were British liberals, who had
given him a majority, partly from disgust at Irish coercion,
partly from faith that he could produce a working plan of
Irish government, and partly from hopes of reforms of their
own — were they to learn that their leaders could do nothing
for any of their special objects?

Mr. Gladstone found some consolation in a precedent. In
1835, he argued, 'the Melbourne government came in with a
British minority, swelled into a majority hardly touching
thirty by the O'Connell contingent of forty. And they staid

in for six years and a half, the longest lived government since Lord Liverpool's.[1] But the Irish were under the command of a master ; and Ireland, scarcely beginning her political life, had to be content with small mercies. Lastly, that government was rather slack, and on this ground perhaps could not well be taken as a pattern.' In the present case, the attitude of the Parnellite group who continued the schism that began in the events of the winter of 1890, was not likely to prove a grave difficulty in parliament, and in fact it did not. The mischief here was in the effect of Irish feuds upon public opinion in the country. As Mr. Gladstone put it in the course of a letter that he had occasion to write to me (November 26, 1892) : —

Until the schism arose, we had every prospect of a majority approaching those of 1868 and 1880. With the death of Mr. Parnell it was supposed that it must perforce close. But this expectation has been disappointed. The existence and working of it have to no small extent puzzled and bewildered the English people. They cannot comprehend how a quarrel, to them utterly unintelligible (some even think it discreditable), should be allowed to divide the host in the face of the enemy; and their unity and zeal have been deadened in proportion. Herein we see the main cause why our majority is not more than double what it actually numbers, and the difference between these two scales of majority represents, as I apprehend, the difference between power to carry the bill as the Church and Land bills were carried into law, and the default of such power. The main mischief has already been done; but it receives additional confirmation with the lapse of every week or month.

In forming his fourth administration Mr. Gladstone found one or two obstacles on which he had not reckoned, and perhaps could not have been expected to reckon. By that forbearance of which he was a master, they were in good time surmounted. New men, of a promise soon amply fulfilled, were taken in, including, to Mr. Gladstone's own particular satisfaction, the son of the oldest

[1] Lord Palmerston's government of 1859 was shorter by only a few days.

of all the surviving friends of his youth, Sir Thomas Acland.[1]

Mr. Gladstone remained as head of the government for a year and a few months (Aug. 1892 to March 3, 1894). In that time several decisions of pith and moment were taken, one measure of high importance became law, operations began against the Welsh establishment, but far the most conspicuous biographic element of this short period was his own incomparable display of power of every kind in carrying the new bill for the better government of Ireland through the House of Commons.

In foreign affairs it was impossible that he should forget the case of Egypt. Lord Salisbury in 1887 had pressed forward an arrangement by which the British occupation was under definite conditions and at a definite date to come to an end. If this convention had been accepted by the Sultan, the British troops would probably have been home by the time of the change of government in this country. French diplomacy, however, at Constantinople, working as it might seem against its own professed aims, hindered the ratification of the convention, and Lord Salisbury's policy was frustrated. Negotiations did not entirely drop, and they had not passed out of existence when Lord Salisbury resigned. In the autumn of 1892 the French ambassador addressed a friendly inquiry to the new government as to the reception likely to be given to overtures for re-opening the negotiations. The

---

[1] Here is the Fourth Cabinet : —

First lord of the treasury and privy seal, .	W. E. Gladstone.
Lord chancellor, ...	Lord Herschell.
President of the council and Indian secretary,	Earl of Kimberley.
Chancellor of the exchequer, ...	Sir W. V. Harcourt.
Home secretary, ...	H. H. Asquith.
Foreign secretary, ...	Earl of Rosebery.
Colonial secretary, ...	Marquis of Ripon.
Secretary for war, ...	H. Campbell-Bannerman.
First lord of the admiralty, ...	Earl Spencer.
Chief secretary for Ireland, ...	John Morley.
Secretary for Scotland, ...	Sir G. O. Trevelyan.
President of the board of trade, . .	A. J. Mundella.
President of the local government board, .	H. H. Fowler.
Chancellor of the duchy of Lancaster, .	James Bryce.
Postmaster-general, ...	Arnold Morley.
First commissioner of works, . . .	J. G. Shaw Lefevre.
Vice-president of the council, . . .	A. H. D. Acland.

answer was that if France had suggestions to offer, they would be received in the same friendly spirit in which they were tendered. When any communications were received, Mr. Gladstone said in the House of Commons, there would be no indisposition on our part to extend to them our friendly consideration. Of all this nothing came. A rather serious ministerial crisis in Egypt in January 1893, followed by a ministerial crisis in Paris in April, arrested whatever projects of negotiation France may have entertained.[1]

IV

In December (1892), at Hawarden, Mr. Gladstone said to me one day after we had been working for five or six hours at the heads of the new Home Rule bill, that his general health was good and sound, but his sight and his hearing were so rapidly declining, that he thought he might almost any day have to retire from office. It was no moment for banal deprecation. He sat silently pondering this vision in his own mind, of coming fate. It seemed like Tennyson's famous simile —

> So dark a forethought rolled about his brain,
> As on a dull day in an ocean cave
> The blind wave feeling round his long sea-hall
> In silence.

It would have been preternatural if he had shown the same overwhelming interest that had animated him when the Irish policy was fresh in 1886. Yet the instinct of a strong mind and the lifelong habit of ardent industry carried him through his Sisyphean toil. The routine business of head of a government he attended to, with all his usual assiduity, and in cabinet he was clear, careful, methodical, as always.

The preparation of the bill was carefully and elaborately worked by Mr. Gladstone through an excellent committee

[1] See Mr. Gladstone's speeches and answers to questions in the House of Commons, Jan. 1, Feb. 3, and May 1, 1893. See also the French Yellow Book for 1893, for M. Waddington's despatches of Nov. 1, 1892, May 5, 1893, and Feb. 1, 1893.

of the cabinet.[1] Here he was acute, adroit, patient, full of device, expedient, and the art of construction; now and then vehement and bearing down like a three-decker upon craft of more modest tonnage. But the vehemence was rare, and here as everywhere else he was eager to do justice to all the points and arguments of other people. He sought opportunities of deliberation in order to deliberate, and not under that excellent name to cultivate the art of the harangue, or to overwork secondary points, least of all to treat the many as made for one. That is to say, he went into counsel for the sake of counsel, and not to cajole, or bully, or insist on his own way because it was his own way. In the high article of finance, he would wrestle like a tiger. It was an intricate and difficult business by the necessity of the case, and among the aggravations of it was the discovery at one point that a wrong figure had been furnished to him by some department. He declared this truly heinous crime to be without a precedent in his huge experience.

The crucial difficulty was the Irish representation at Westminster. In the first bill of 1886, the Irish members were to come no more to the imperial parliament, except for one or two special purposes. The two alternatives to the policy of exclusion were either inclusion of the Irish members for all purposes, or else their inclusion for imperial purposes only. In his speech at Swansea in 1887, Mr. Gladstone favoured provisional inclusion, without prejudice to a return to the earlier plan of exclusion if that should be recommended by subsequent experience.[2] In the bill now introduced (Feb. 13, 1893), eighty representatives from Ireland were to have seats at Westminster, but they were not to vote upon motions or bills expressly confined to England or Scotland, and there were other limitations. This plan was soon found to be wholly intolerable to the House of Commons. Exclusion having failed, and inclusion of reduced numbers for limited purposes having failed, the only

---

[1] I hope I am not betraying a cabinet secret if I mention that this committee was composed of Mr. Gladstone, Lord Spencer, Lord Herschell, Mr. Campbell-Bannermann, Mr. Bryce, and myself.

[2] See above, p. 386.

course left open was what was called *omnes omnia*, or rather the inclusion of eighty Irish members, with power of voting on all purposes.

Each of the three courses was open to at least one single, but very direct, objection. Exclusion, along with the exaction of revenue from Ireland by the parliament at Westminster, was taxation without representation. Inclusion for all purposes was to allow the Irish to meddle in our affairs, while we were no longer to meddle in theirs. Inclusion for limited purposes still left them invested with the power of turning out a British government by a vote against it on an imperial question. Each plan, therefore, ended in a paradox. There was a fourth paradox, namely, that whenever the British supporters of a government did not suffice to build up a decisive majority, then the Irish vote descending into one or other scale of the parliamentary balance might decide who should be our rulers. This paradox — the most glaring of them all — habit and custom have made familiar, and familiarity might almost seem to have actually endeared it to us. In 1893 Mr. Gladstone and his colleagues thought themselves compelled to change clause 9 of the new bill, just as they had thought themselves forced to drop clause 24 of the old bill.

V

It was Mr. Gladstone's performances in the days of committee on the bill, that stirred the wonder and admiration of the House. If he had been fifty they would have been astonishing ; at eighty-four they were indeed a marvel. He made speeches of powerful argument, of high constitutional reasoning, of trenchant debating force. No emergency arose for which he was not ready, no demand that his versatility was not adequate to meet. His energy never flagged. When the bill came on, he would put on his glasses, pick up the paper of amendments, and running through them like lightning, would say, ' Of course, that's absurd — that will never do — we can never accept that — is there any harm in this ? ' Too many concessions made on the spur of the

moment to the unionists stirred resentment in the nationalists, and once or twice they exploded. These rapid
splendours of his had their perils. I pointed out to him the
pretty obvious drawbacks of settling delicate questions as
we went along with no chance of sounding the Irishmen,
and asked him to spare me quarter of an hour before
luncheon, when the draftsman and I, having threshed out
the amendments of the day, could put the bare points for
his consideration. He was horrified at the very thought.
'Out of the question. Do you want to kill me? I must
have the whole of the morning for general government
business. Don't ask me.'[1]

Obstruction was freely practised and without remorse.
The chief fighting debater against the government made
a long second-reading speech, on the motion that the clause
stand part of the bill. A little before eight o'clock when
the fighting debater was winding up, Mr. Gladstone was
undecided about speaking. 'What do you advise?' he asked
of a friend. 'I am afraid it will take too much out of you,'
the friend replied; 'but still, speak for twenty minutes and
no more.' Up he rose, and for half an hour a delighted
House was treated to one of the most remarkable performances that ever was known. 'I have never seen Mr.
Gladstone,' says one observer, 'so dramatic, so prolific of all
the resources of the actor's art. The courage, the audacity,
and the melodrama of it were irresistible' (May 11).

For ten minutes, writes another chronicler, Mr. Gladstone
spoke, holding his audience spell-bound by his force. Then came
a sudden change, and it seemed that he was about to collapse
from sheer physical exhaustion. His voice failed, huskiness and
indistinctness took the place of clearness and lucidity. Then
pulling himself together for a great effort, Mr. Gladstone pointing
the deprecatory finger at Mr. Chamberlain, warned the Irishmen
to beware of him; to watch the fowler who would inveigle
them in his snare. Loud and long rang the liberal cheers.

---

[1] One poor biographic item perhaps the tolerant reader will not grudge me leave to copy from Mr. Glad-stone's diary:—'*October* 6, 1892. Saw J. Morley and made him envoy to ——. He is on the whole . . . about the best stay I have.'

In plain words he told the unionists that Mr. Chamberlain's purpose was none other than obstruction, and he conveyed the intimation with a delicate expressiveness, a superabundant good feeling, a dramatic action and a marvellous music of voice that conspired in their various qualities to produce a *tour de force.* By sheer strength of enthusiasm and an overflowing wealth of eloquence, Mr. Gladstone literally conquered every physical weakness and secured an effect electric in its influence even on seasoned 'old hands.' Amidst high excitement and the sound of cheering that promised never to die away the House gradually melted into the lobbies. Mr. Gladstone, exhausted with his effort, chatted to Mr. Morley on the treasury bench. Except for these two the government side was deserted, and the conservatives had already disappeared. The nationalists sat shoulder to shoulder, a solid phalanx. They eyed the prime minister with eager intent, and as soon as the venerable statesman rose to walk out of the House, they sprang to their feet and rent the air with wild hurrahs.

No wonder if the talk downstairs at dinner among his colleagues that night, all turned upon their chief, his art and power, his union of the highest qualities of brain and heart with extraordinary practical penetration, and close watchfulness of incident and trait and personality, disclosed in many a racy aside and pungent sally. The orator was fatigued, but full of keen enjoyment. This was one of the three or four occasions when he was induced not to return to the House after dinner. It had always been his habit in taking charge of bills to work the ship himself. No wonder that he held to this habit in this case.

On another occasion ministers had taken ground that, as the debate went on, everybody saw they could not hold. An official spokesman for the bill had expressed an opinion, or intention, that, as very speedily appeared, Irish opposition would not allow to be maintained. There was no great substance in the point, but even a small dose of humiliation will make a parliamentary dish as bitter to one side as it is savoury to the other. The opposition grew more and more radiant, as it grew more certain that the official spokesman

must be thrown over. The discomfiture of the ministerialists
at the prospect of the public mortification of their leaders
was extreme in the same degree. 'I suppose we must give
it up,' said Mr. Gladstone. This was clear; and when he
rose, he was greeted with mocking cheers from the enemy,
though the enemy's chief men who had long experience of
his Protean resources were less confident. Beginning in a
tone of easy gravity and candour, he went on to points of
pleasant banter, got his audience interested and amused and
a little bewildered; carried men with him in graceful arguments on the merits; and finally, with bye-play of consummate sport, showed in triumph that the concession that
we consented to make was so right and natural, that it must
have been inevitable from the very first. Never were tables
more effectively turned; the opposition watched first with
amazement, then with excitement and delight as children
watch a wizard; and he sat down victorious. Not another
word was said or could be said. 'Never in all my parliamentary years,' said a powerful veteran on the front bench
opposite, as he passed behind the Speaker's chair, 'never have
I seen so wonderful a thing done as that.'

The state of the county of Clare was a godsend to the
obstructive. Clare was not at that moment quite as innocent as the garden of Eden before the fall, but the condition
was not serious; it had been twenty times worse before without occupying the House of Commons five minutes. Now
an evening a week was not thought too much for a hollow
debate on disorder in Clare. It was described as a definite
matter of urgent importance, though it had slept for years,
and though three times in succession the judge of assize
(travelling entirely out of his proper business) had denounced
the state of things. It was made to support five votes of
censure in eight weeks.

On one of these votes of censure on Irish administration,
moved by Mr. Balfour (March 27), Mr. Gladstone listened to
the debate. At 8 we begged him not to stay and not to take
the trouble to speak, so trumpery was the whole affair. He
said he must, if only for five minutes, to show that he
identified himself with his Irish minister. He left to dine,

and then before ten was on his feet, making what Lord Randolph Churchill rightly called 'a most impressive and entrancing speech.' He talked of Pat this and Michael that, and Father the other, as if he had pondered their cases for a month, clenching every point with extraordinary strength as well as consummate ease and grace, and winding up with some phrases of wonderful simplicity and concentration.

A distinguished member made a motion for the exclusion of Irish cabinet ministers from their chamber. Mr. Gladstone was reminded on the bench just before he rose, that the same proposal had been inserted in the Act of Settlement, and repealed in 1705. He wove this into his speech with a skill, and amplified confidence, that must have made everybody suppose that it was a historic fact present every day to his mind. The attention of a law-officer sitting by was called to this rapid amplification. 'I never saw anything like it in all my whole life,' said the law-officer; and he was a man who had been accustomed to deal with some of the strongest and quickest minds of the day as judges and advocates.

One day when a tremendous afternoon of obstruction had almost worn him down, the adjournment came at seven o'clock. He was haggard and depressed. On returning at ten we found him making a most lively and amusing speech upon procedure. He sat down as blithe as dawn. 'To make a speech of that sort,' he said in deprecation of compliment, 'a man does best to dine out; 'tis no use to lie on a sofa and think about it.'

Undoubtedly Mr. Gladstone's method in this long committee carried with it some disadvantages. His discursive treatment exposed an enormous surface. His abundance of illustration multiplied points for debate. His fertility in improvised arguments encouraged improvisation in disputants without the gift. Mr. Gladstone always supposed that a great theme needs to be copiously handled, which is perhaps doubtful, and indeed is often an exact inversion of the true state of things. However that may be, copiousness is a game at which two can play, as a patriotic opposition now and at other times has effectually disclosed. Some thought in these days that a man like Lord Althorp, for

instance, would have given the obstructives much more
trouble in their pursuits than did Mr. Gladstone.

That Mr. Gladstone's supporters should become restive at
the slow motion of business was natural enough. They came
to ministers, calling out for a drastic closure, as simple tribes
might clamour to a rain-maker. It was the end of June, and
with a reasonable opposition conducted in decent good faith,
it was computed that the bill might be through committee
in nineteen days. But the hypothesis of reason and good
faith was not thought to be substantial, and the cabinet
resolved on resort to closure on a scale like that on which it
had been used by the late government in the case of the
Crimes Act of 1887, and of the Special Commission. It has
been said since on excellent authority, that without speaking
of their good faith, Mr. Gladstone's principal opponents were
now running absolutely short of new ammunition, and having
used the same arguments and made the same speeches for
so many weeks, they were so worn out that the guillotine
was superfluous. Of these straits, however, there was little
evidence. Mr. Gladstone entered into the operation with
a good deal of chagrin. He saw that the House of Commons
in which he did his work and rose to glory was swiftly fading
out of sight, and a new institution of different habits of responsibility and practice taking its place.

The stage of committee lasted for sixty-three sittings. The
whole proceedings occupied eighty-two. It is not necessary
to hold that the time was too long for the size of the task, if
it had been well spent. The spirit of the debate was aptly
illustrated by the plea of a brilliant tory, that he voted
for a certain motion against a principle that he approved,
because he thought the carrying of the motion 'would make
the bill more detestable.' Opposition rested on a view of
Irish character and Irish feeling about England, that can
hardly have been very deeply thought out, because ten years
later the most bitter opponents of the Irish claim launched
a policy, that was to make Irish peasants direct debtors to
the hated England to the tune of one hundred million
pounds, and was to dislodge by imperial cash those who were
persistently called the only friends of the imperial connection.

The bill passed its second reading by 347 against 304, or a majority of 43. In some critical divisions, the majority ran down to 27. The third reading was carried by 301 against 267, or a majority of 34. It was estimated that excluding the Irish, there was a majority against the bill of 23. If we counted England and Wales alone, the adverse majority was 48. When it reached them, the Lords incontinently threw it out. The roll of the Lords held 560 names, beyond the peers of the royal house. Of this body of 560, no fewer than 419 voted against the bill, and only 41 voted for it.

VI

The session was protracted until it became the longest in the history of parliament. The House was sitting when Mr. Gladstone's eighty-fourth birthday arrived. ' Before putting a question,' said Mr. Balfour in a tone that, after the heat and exasperations of so many months, was refreshing to hear, ' perhaps the right honourable gentleman will allow me, on my own part and on that of my friends, to offer him our most sincere congratulations.' ' Allow me to thank him,' said Mr. Gladstone, ' for his great courtesy and kindness.' The government pressed forward and carried through the House of Commons a measure dealing with the liability of employers for accidents, and a more important measure setting up elective bodies for certain purposes in parishes. Into the first the Lords introduced such changes as were taken to nullify all the advantages of the bill, and the cabinet approved of its abandonment. Into the second they forced back certain provisions that the Commons had with full deliberation decisively rejected.

Mr. Gladstone was at Biarritz, he records, when this happened in the January of 1894. He had gone there to recruit after the incomparable exertions of the session, and also to consider at a cool distance and in changed scenes other topics that had for some weeks caused him some agitation. He now thought that there was a decisive case against the House of Lords. Apart from the Irish bill to which the

Commons had given eighty-two days, the Lords had maimed
the bill for parish councils, to which had gone the labour of
forty-one days.   Other bills they had mutilated or defeated.
Upon the whole, he argued, it was not too much to say that
for practical purposes the Lords had destroyed the work of
the House of Commons, unexampled as that work was in the
time and pains bestowed upon it.   'I suggested dissolution
to my colleagues in London, where half, or more than half,
the cabinet were found at the moment.   I received by telegraph a hopelessly adverse reply.'   Reluctantly he let the
idea drop, always maintaining, however, that a signal opportunity had been lost.   Even in my last conversation with
him in 1897, he held to his text that we ought to have
dissolved at this moment.   The case, he said, was clear,
thorough, and complete.   As has been already mentioned,
there were four occasions on which he believed that he
had divined the right moment for a searching appeal to
public opinion on a great question.[1]   The renewal of the
income tax in 1853 was the first ; the proposal of religious
equality for Ireland in 1868 was the second ; home rule
was the third, and here he was justified by the astonishing
and real progress that he had made up to the catastrophe
at the end of 1890.   The fourth case was this, of a dissolution upon the question of the relations of the two Houses.

[1] See above, ii. p. 241.

CHAPTER VIII

RETIREMENT FROM PUBLIC LIFE

(1894)

O, 'TIS a burden, Cromwell, 'tis a burden
Too heavy for a man that hopes for heaven.

Henry VIII. iii. 2.

'POLITICS,' wrote Mr. Gladstone in one of his private memoranda in March 1894, 'are like a labyrinth, from the inner intricacies of which it is even more difficult to find the way of escape, than it was to find the way into them. My age did something but not enough. The deterioration of my hearing helped, but insufficiently. It is the state of my sight which has supplied me with effectual aid in exchanging my imperious public obligations for what seems to be a free place on "the breezy common of humanity." And it has only been within the last eight months, or thereabouts, that the decay of working sight has advanced at such a pace as to present the likelihood of its becoming stringently operative at an early date. It would have been very difficult to fix that date at this or that precise point, without the appearance of making an arbitrary choice ; but then the closing of the parliamentary session (1893-4) offered a natural break between the cessation and renewal of engagements, which was admirably suited to the design. And yet I think it, if not certain, yet very highly probable at the least, that any disposition of mine to profit by this break would — but for the naval scheme of my colleagues in the naval estimates — have been frustrated by their desire to avoid the inconveniences of a change, and by the pressure which they would have brought to bear upon me in consequence. The effect of that

Walker&Cockerell.ph. sc.

William Ewart Gladstone

from a photograph by Mr L. V. Harcourt.

scheme was not to bring about the construction of an artificial cause, or pretext rather, of resignation, but to compel
me to act upon one that was rational, sufficient, and ready
to hand.'

This is the short, plain, and intelligible truth as to what
now happened. There can be no reason to-day for not stating
what was for a long time matter of common surmise, if not
of common knowledge, that Mr. Gladstone did not regard
the naval estimates, opened but not settled in December
1893, as justified by the circumstances of the time. He
made a speech that month in parliament in reply to a
motion from the front bench opposite, and there he took a
position undoubtedly antagonistic to the new scheme that
found favour with his cabinet, though not with all its
members. The present writer is of course not free to go
into details, beyond those that anybody else not a member
of the cabinet would discover from Mr. Gladstone's papers.
Nor does the public lose anything of real interest by this
necessary reserve. Mr. Gladstone said he wished to make
me 'his depositary' as things gradually moved on, and he
wrote me a series of short letters from day to day. If they
could be read aloud in Westminster Hall, no harm would be
done either to surviving colleagues or to others; they would
furnish no new reason for thinking either better or worse of
anybody; and no one with a decent sense of the value of time
would concern himself in all the minor detail of an ineffectual
controversy. The central facts were simple. Two things
weighed with him, first his infirmities, and second his disapproval of the policy. How, he asked himself, could he turn
his back on his former self by becoming a party to swollen expenditure? True he had changed from conservative to liberal
in general politics, but when he was conservative, that party
was the economic party, 'Peel its leader being a Cobdenite.'
To assent to this new outlay in time of peace was to revolu-
tionise policy. Then he would go on — 'Owing to the part
which I was drawn to take, first in Italy, then as to Greece,
then on the eastern question, I have come to be considered
not only an English but a European statesman. My name
stands in Europe as a symbol of the policy of peace, modera-

tion, and non-aggression. What would be said of my active participation in a policy that will be taken as plunging England into the whirlpool of militarism? Third, I have been in active public life for a period nearly as long as the time between the beginning of Mr. Pitt's first ministry and the close of Sir Robert Peel's; between 1783 and 1846 — sixty-two years and a half. During that time I have uniformly opposed militarism.' Thus he would put his case.

After the naval estimates were brought forward, attempts were naturally made at accommodation, for whether he availed himself of the end of the session as a proper occasion of retirement or not, he was bound to try to get the estimates down if he could. He laboured hard at the task of conversion, and though some of his colleagues needed no conversion, with the majority he did not prevail. He admitted that he had made limited concessions to scares in 1860 and in 1884, and that he had besides been repeatedly responsible for extraordinary financial provisions having reference to some crisis of the day: —

I did this, (1) By a preliminary budget in 1854; (2) By the final budget of July 1859; by the vote of credit in July 1870; and again by the vote of credit in 1884. Every one of these was special, and was shown in each case respectively to be special by the sequel: no one of them had reference to the notion of establishing dominant military or even naval power in Europe. Their amounts were various, but were adapted to the view taken, at least by me, of the exigency actually present.[1]

II

While the House after so many months of toil was still labouring manfully upon English bills, two of them of no secondary importance, it was decided by his family and their advisers that Mr. Gladstone should again try the effects of Biarritz, and thither they went on January 13. Distance, however, could not efface from his mind all thought of the decision that the end of the session would exact from him.

[1] See Appendix for further elucidation.

Rumours began to fly about in London that the prime minister upon his return intended to resign, and they were naturally clad with intrinsic probability. From Biarritz a communication was made to the press with his authority. It was to this effect, that the statement that Mr. Gladstone had definitely decided, or had decided at all, on resigning office was untrue. It was true that for many months past his age and the condition of his sight and hearing had in his judgment made relief from public cares desirable, and that accordingly his tenure of office had been at any moment liable to interruption from these causes, in their nature permanent.

Nature meanwhile could not set back the shadow on the dial. On his coming back from Biarritz (February 10) neither eyes nor ears were better. How should they be at eighty-five? The session was ending, the prorogation speech was to be composed, and the time had come for that 'natural break' between the cessation and renewal of his official obligations, of which we have already heard him speak. His colleagues carried almost to importunity their appeals to him to stay; to postpone what one of them called, and many of them truly felt to be, this 'moment of anguish.' The division of opinion on estimates remained, but even if that could have been bridged, his sight and hearing could not be made whole. The rational and sufficient cause of resignation, as he only too justly described it, was strong as ever. Whether if the cabinet had come to his view on estimates, he would in spite of his great age and infirmities have come to their view of the importance of his remaining, we cannot tell. According to his wont, he avoided decision until the time had come when decision was necessary, and then he made up his mind, 'without the appearance of an arbitrary choice,' that the time had come for accepting the natural break, and quitting office.

On Feb. 27, arriving in the evening at Euston from Ireland, I found a messenger with a note from Mr. Gladstone begging me to call on my way home. I found him busy as usual at his table in Downing Street. 'I suppose 'tis the long habit of a life,' he said cheerily, 'but even in the midst

BOOK
X.
1894.

of these passages, if ever I have half or quarter of an hour to spare, I find myself turning to my Horace translation.' He said the prorogation speech would be settled on Thursday ; the Queen would consider it on Friday ; the council would be held on Saturday, and on that evening or afternoon he should send in his letter of resignation.

The next day he had an audience at Buckingham Palace, and indirectly conveyed to the Queen what she might soon expect to learn from him. His rigorous sense of loyalty to colleagues made it improper and impossible to bring either before the Queen or the public his difference of judgment on matters for which his colleagues, not he, would be responsible, and on which they, not he, would have to take action. He derived certain impressions at his audience, he told me, one of them being that the Sovereign would not seek his advice as to a successor.

He wrote to inform the Prince of Wales of the approaching event : —

In thus making it known to your royal Highness, he concluded, I desire to convey, on my own and my wife's part our fervent thanks for the unbounded kindness which we have at all times received from your royal Highness and not less from the beloved Princess of Wales. The devotion of an old man is little worth ; but if at any time there be the smallest service which by information or suggestion your royal Highness may believe me capable of rendering, I shall remain as much at your command as if I had continued to be an active and responsible servant of the Queen. I remain with heartfelt loyalty and gratitude, etc.

The Prince expressed his sincere regret, said how deeply the Princess and he were touched by the kind words about them, and how greatly for a long number of years they had valued his friendship and that of Mrs. Gladstone. Mr. Balfour, to whom he also confidentially told the news, communicated among other graceful words, 'the special debt of gratitude that was due to him for the immense public service he had performed in fostering and keeping alive the great traditions of the House of Commons.' The day after that (March 1) was his last cabinet council, and a painful day it was. The business of the speech and other matters were discussed as usual, then came the end. In his report to the Queen — his last — he said : —

Looking forward to the likelihood that this might be the last occasion on which Mr. Gladstone and his colleagues might meet in the cabinet, Lord Kimberley and Sir William Harcourt on their own part and on that of the ministers generally, used words undeservedly kind of acknowledgment and farewell. Lord Kimberley will pray your Majesty to appoint a council for Saturday, at as early an hour as may be convenient.

Mr. Gladstone sat composed and still as marble, and the emotion of the cabinet did not gain him for an instant. He followed the ' words of acknowledgment and farewell' in a little speech of four or five minutes, his voice unbroken and serene, the tone low, grave, and steady. He was glad to know that he had justification in the condition of his senses. He was glad to think that notwithstanding difference upon a public question, private friendships would remain unaltered and unimpaired. Then hardly above a breath, but every accent heard, he said ' God bless you all.' He rose slowly and went out of one door, while his colleagues with minds oppressed filed out by the other. In his diary he enters — ' A really moving scene.'

A little later in the afternoon he made his last speech in the House of Commons. It was a vigorous assault upon the House of Lords. His mind had changed since the day in September 1884 when he had declared to an emissary from the court that he hated organic change in the House of Lords, and would do much to avert that mischief.[1] Circumstances had now altered the case ; we had come to a more acute stage. Were they to accept the changes made by the Lords in the bill for parish councils, or were they to drop it ? The question, he said, is whether the work of the House of Lords is not merely to modify, but to annihilate the whole work of the House of Commons, work which has been performed at an amount of sacrifice — of time, of labour, of convenience, and perhaps of health — but at any rate an amount

---

[1] Above, p. 130.

of sacrifice totally unknown to the House of Lords. The government had resolved that great as were the objections to acceptance of the changes made by the Lords, the arguments against rejection were still weightier. Then he struck a note of passion, and spoke with rising fire : —

We are compelled to accompany that acceptance with the sorrowful declaration that the differences, not of a temporary or casual nature merely, but differences of conviction, differences of prepossession, differences of mental habit, and differences of fundamental tendency, between the House of Lords and the House of Commons, appear to have reached a development in the present year such as to create a state of things of which we are compelled to say that, in our judgment, it cannot continue. Sir, I do not wish to use hard words, which are easily employed and as easily retorted — it is a game that two can play at — but without using hard words, without presuming to judge of motives, without desiring or venturing to allege imputations, I have felt it a duty to state what appeared to me to be indisputable facts. The issue which is raised between a deliberative assembly, elected by the votes of more than 6,000,000 people, and a deliberative assembly occupied by many men of virtue, by many men of talent, of course with considerable diversities and varieties, is a controversy which, when once raised, must go forward to an issue.

Men did not know that they were listening to his last speech, but his words fell in with the eager humour of his followers around him, and he sat down amid vehement plaudits. Then when the business was at an end, he rose, and for the last time walked away from the House of Commons. He had first addressed it sixty-one years before.

III

The following day (March 2) he busied himself in packing his papers, and working at intervals on his translation of Horace. He told me that he had now reason to suppose that the Queen might ask him for advice as to his successor. After some talk, he said that if asked he should advise her to send for Lord Spencer. As it happened, his advice was not sought. That evening he went to Windsor to dine and sleep. The next day was to be the council. Here is his memorandum of the last audience on Saturday, March 3 [1]: —

As I crossed the quadrangle at 10.20 on my way to St. George's Chapel, I met Sir H. Ponsonby, who said he was anxious to speak to me about the future. He was much impressed with the movement among a body of members of parliament against having any peer for prime minister. I signified briefly that I did not think there should be too ready a submission to such a movement. There was not time to say a great deal, and I had something serious to say, so we adjourned the conversation till half past eleven, when I should return from St. George's.

He came at that time and opened on the same lines, desiring to obtain from me whatever I thought proper to say as to persons in the arrangements for the future. I replied to him that this was in my view a most serious matter. All my thoughts on it were absolutely at the command of the Queen. And I should be equally at his command, if he inquired of me from her and in her name; but that otherwise my lips must be sealed. I knew from him that he was in search of information to report to the Queen, but this was a totally different matter.

I entered, however, freely on the general question of the movement among a section of the House of Commons. I thought it impossible to say at the moment, but I should not take for granted that it would be formidable or regard it as *in limine* disposing of the question. Up to a certain point, I thought it a duty to strengthen the hands of our small minority and little knot of ministers in the Lords, by providing these ministers with such weight as attaches to high office. All this, or rather all that touched the main point, namely the point of a peer prime minister, he without doubt reported.

The council train came down and I joined the ministers in the drawing-room. I received various messages as to the time when I was to see the Queen, and when it would be most convenient to me. I interpret this variety as showing that she was nervous. It ended in fixing the time after the council and before luncheon. I carried with me a box containing my resignation, and, the council being over, handed it to her immediately, and told her that it con-

[1] Written down, March 5.

tained my tender of resignation. She asked whether she ought then to read it. I said there was nothing in the letter to require it. It repeated my former letter of notice, with the requisite additions.

I must notice what, though slight, supplied the only incident of any interest in this perhaps rather memorable audience, which closed a service that would reach to fifty-three years on September 3, when I was sworn privy councillor before the Queen at Claremont. When I came into the room and came near to take the seat she has now for some time courteously commanded, I did think she was going to 'break down.' If I was not mistaken, at any rate she rallied herself, as I thought, by a prompt effort, and remained collected and at her ease. Then came the conversation, which may be called neither here nor there. Its only material feature was negative. There was not one syllable on the past, except a repetition, an emphatic repetition, of the thanks she had long ago amply rendered for what I had done, a service of no great merit, in the matter of the Duke of Coburg, and which I assured her would not now escape my notice if occasion should arise. There was the question of eyes and ears, of German *versus* English oculists, she believing in the German as decidedly superior. Some reference to my wife, with whom she had had an interview and had ended it affectionately, — and various nothings. No touch on the subject of the last Ponsonby conversation. Was I wrong in not tendering orally my best wishes? I was afraid that anything said by me should have the appearance of *touting*. A departing servant has some title to offer his hopes and prayers for the future; but a servant is one who has done, or tried to do, service in the past. There is in all this a great sincerity. There also seems to be some little mystery as to my own case with her. I saw no sign of embarrassment or preoccupation. The Empress Frederick was outside in the corridor. She bade me a most kind and warm farewell, which I had done nothing to deserve.

The letter tendered to the Queen in the box was this : —

Mr. Gladstone presents his most humble duty to your Majesty. The close of the session and the approach of a new one have offered Mr. Gladstone a suitable opportunity for considering the condition of his sight and hearing, both of them impaired, in relation to his official obligations. As they now place serious and also growing obstacles in the way of the efficient discharge of

those obligations, the result has been that he has found it his
duty humbly to tender to your Majesty his resignation of the
high offices which your Majesty has been pleased to intrust to
him.   His desire to make this surrender is accompanied with a
grateful sense of the condescending kindnesses, which your
Majesty has graciously shown him on so many occasions during
the various periods for which he has had the honour to serve your
Majesty.   Mr. Gladstone will not needlessly burden your Majesty
with a recital of particulars.   He may, however, say that although
at eighty-four years of age he is sensible of a diminished capacity
for prolonged labour, this is not of itself such as would justify his
praying to be relieved from the restraints and exigencies of official
life.   But his deafness has become in parliament, and even in the
cabinet, a serious inconvenience, of which he must reckon on more
progressive increase.   More grave than this, and more rapid in
its growth, is the obstruction of vision which arises from cataract
in both his eyes.   It has cut him off in substance from the newspapers, and from all except the best types in the best lights, while
even as to these he cannot master them with that ordinary facility
and despatch which he deems absolutely required for the due
despatch of his public duties.   In other respects than reading
the operation of the complaint is not as yet so serious, but this
one he deems to be vital.   Accordingly he brings together these
two facts, the condition of his sight and hearing, and the break in
the course of public affairs brought about in the ordinary way
by the close of the session.   He has therefore felt that this is the
fitting opportunity for the resignation which by this letter he
humbly prays your Majesty to accept.

In the course of the day the Queen wrote what I take to
be her last letter to him : —

Windsor Castle, March 3, 1894. — Though the Queen has already
accepted Mr. Gladstone's resignation, and has taken leave of him,
she does not like to leave his letter tendering his resignation
unanswered.   She therefore writes these few lines to say that she
thinks that after so many years of arduous labour and responsibility
he is right in wishing to be relieved at his age of these arduous
duties.   And she trusts he will be able to enjoy peace and quiet
with his excellent and devoted wife in health and happiness, and
that his eyesight may improve.

The Queen would gladly have conferred a peerage on Mr. Gladstone, but she knows he would not accept it.

His last act in relation to this closing scene of the great official drama was a letter to General Ponsonby (March 5): —

The first entrance of a man to Windsor Castle in a responsible character, is a great event in his life; and his last departure from it is not less moving. But in and during the process which led up to this transaction on Saturday, my action has been in the strictest sense sole, and it has required me in circumstances partly known to harden my heart into a flint. However, it is not even now so hard, but that I can feel what you have most kindly written; nor do I fail to observe with pleasure that you do not speak absolutely in the singular. If there were feelings that made the occasion sad, such feelings do not die with the occasion.   But this letter must not be wholly one of egotism.   I have known and have liked and admired all the men who have served the Queen in your delicate and responsible office; and have liked most, probably because I knew him most, the last of them, that most true-hearted man, General Grey. But forgive me for saying you are 'to the manner born'; and such a combination of tact and temper with loyalty, intelligence, and truth I cannot expect to see again.   Pray remember these are words which can only pass from an old man to one much younger, though trained in a long experience.

It is hardly in human nature, in spite of Charles v., Sulla, and some other historic persons, to lay down power beyond recall, without a secret pang.   In Prior's lines that came to the mind of brave Sir Walter Scott, as he saw the curtain falling on his days, —

> The man in graver tragic known,
> (Though his best part long since was done,)
> Still on the stage desires to tarry . . .
> Unwilling to retire, though weary.

Whether the departing minister had a lingering thought that in the dispensations of the world, purposes and services would still arise to which even yet he might one day be summoned, we do not know.   Those who were nearest to him believe not, and assuredly he made no outer sign.

CHAPTER IX

THE CLOSE

(*1894–1898*)

Natural death is as it were a haven and a rest to us after long navigation. And the noble Soul is like a good mariner; for he, when he draws near the port, lowers his sails and enters it softly with gentle steerage. . . . And herein we have from our own nature a great lesson of suavity; for in such a death as this there is no grief nor any bitterness: but as a ripe apple is lightly and without violence loosened from its branch, so our soul without grieving departs from the body in which it hath been. — Dante, *Convito*.[1]

After the first wrench was over, and an end had come to the demands, pursuits, duties, glories, of powerful and active station held for a long lifetime, Mr. Gladstone soon settled to the new conditions of his existence, knowing that for him all that could be left was, in the figure of his great Italian poet, 'to lower sails and gather in his ropes.'[2] He was not much in London, and when he came he stayed in the pleasant retreat to which his affectionate and ever-attached friends, Lord and Lady Aberdeen, so often invited him at Dollis Hill. Much against his will, he did not resign his seat in the House, and he held it until the dissolution of 1895.[3] In June (1895) he took a final cruise in one of Sir Donald Currie's ships, visiting Hamburg, the new North Sea canal, and Copenhagen once more. His injured sight was a far deadlier breach in the habit of his days than withdrawal from office or from parliament. His own tranquil words written in the year in which he laid down his part in the shows of the world's huge stage, tell the story : —

July 25, 1894.—For the first time in my life there has been given

[1] Dr. Carlyle's translation.
[2] *Inferno*, xxvii. 81.
[3] On July 1, 1895, he announced his formal withdrawal in a letter to Sir John Cowan, so long the loyal chairman of his electoral committee.

to me by the providence of God a period of comparative leisure, reckoning at the present date to four and a half months. Such a period drives the mind in upon itself, and invites, almost constrains, to recollection, and the rendering at least internally an account of life; further it lays the basis of a habit of meditation, to the formation of which the course of my existence, packed and crammed with occupation outwards, never stagnant, oft-times overdriven, has been extremely hostile. As there is no life which in its detail does not seem to afford intervals of brief leisure, or what is termed 'waiting' for others engaged with us in some common action, these are commonly spent in murmurs and in petulant desire for their termination. But in reality they supply excellent opportunities for brief or ejaculatory prayer.

As this new period of my life has brought with it my retirement from active business in the world, it affords a good opportunity for breaking off the commonly dry daily journal, or ledger as it might almost be called, in which for seventy years I have recorded the chief details of my outward life. If life be continued I propose to note in it henceforward only principal events or occupations. This first breach since the latter part of May in this year has been involuntary. When the operation on my eye for cataract came, it was necessary for a time to suspend all use of vision. Before that, from the beginning of March, it was only my out-of-door activity or intercourse that had been paralysed. . . . For my own part, *suave mari magno* steals upon me; or at any rate, an inexpressible sense of relief from an exhausting life of incessant contention. A great revolution has been operated in my correspondence, which had for many years been a serious burden, and at times one almost intolerable. During the last months of partial incapacity I have not written with my own hand probably so much as one letter per day. Few people have had a smaller number of *otiose* conversations probably than I in the last fifty years; but I have of late seen more friends and more freely, though without practical objects in view. Many kind friends have read books to me; I must place Lady Sarah Spencer at the head of the proficients in that difficult art; in distinctness of articulation, with low clear voice, she is supreme. Dearest Catherine has been my chaplain from morning to morning. My church-going has been almost confined to mid-day communions, which have not required my abandonment of the reclining posture for long periods of time. Authorship has not been quite in abeyance; I have been able to write what I was not allowed to read, and have composed two theological articles for the *Nineteenth Century* of August and September respectively.[1]

Independently of the days of blindness after the operation, the visits of doctors have become a noticeable item of demand upon time. Of physic I incline to believe I have had as much in 1894 as in my whole previous life. I have learned for the first time the extraordinary comfort of the aid which the attendance of a nurse can give. My health will now be matter of little interest except to myself. But I have not yet abandoned the hope that I may be permitted to grapple with that considerable armful of work, which had been long marked out for my old age; the question of my recovering sight being for the present in abeyance.

Sept. 13. — I am not yet thoroughly accustomed to my new stage of existence, in part because the remains of my influenza have not yet allowed me wholly to resume the habits of health. But I am thoroughly content with my retirement; and I cast no longing, lingering look behind. I pass onward from it *oculo irretorto.* There is plenty of work before me, peaceful work and work directed to the supreme, *i.e.* the spiritual cultivation of mankind, if it pleases God to give me time and vision to perform it.

Oct. 1. — As far as I can at present judge, all the signs of the eye being favourable, the new form of vision will enable me to get through in a given time about half the amount of work which would have been practicable under the old. I speak of reading and writing work, which have been principal with me when I had the option. In conversation there is no difference, although there are various drawbacks in what we call society. On the 20th of last month when I had gone through my crises of trials, Mr. Nettleship, [the oculist], at once declared that any further operation would be superfluous.

I am unable to continue attendance at the daily morning service, not on account of the eyesight but because I may not rise before

---

[1] 'The Place of Heresy and Schism in the Modern Christian Church' and 'The True and False Conception of the Atonement.'

ten at the earliest. And so a Hawarden practice of over fifty years is interrupted; not without some degree of hope that it may be resumed. Two evening services, one at 5 P.M. and the other at 7, afford me a limited consolation. I drive almost every day, and thus grow to my dissatisfaction more burdensome. My walking powers are limited; once I have exceeded two miles by a little. A large part of the day remains available at my table; daylight is especially precious; my correspondence is still a weary weight, though I have admirable help from children. Upon the whole the change is considerable. In early and mature life a man walks to his daily work with a sense of the duty and capacity of self-provision, a certain αὐτάρκεια [independence] (which the Greeks carried into the moral world). Now that sense is reversed; it seems as if I must, God knows how reluctantly, lay burdens upon others; and as if capacity were, so to speak, dealt out to me mercifully — but by armfuls.

Old age until the very end brought no grave changes in physical conditions. He missed sorely his devoted friend, Sir Andrew Clark, to whose worth as man and skill as healer he had borne public testimony in May 1894. But for physician's service there was no special need. His ordinary life, though of diminished power, suffered little interruption. 'The attitude,' he wrote, 'in which I endeavoured to fix myself was that of a soldier on parade, in a line of men drawn up ready to march and waiting for the word of command. I sought to be in preparation for prompt obedience, feeling no desire to go, but on the other hand without reluctance because firmly convinced that whatever He ordains for us is best, best both for us and for all.'

He worked with all his old zest at his edition of Bishop Butler, and his volume of studies subsidiary to Butler. He wrote to the Duke of Argyll (Dec. 5, 1895) : —

I find my Butler a weighty undertaking, but I hope it will be useful at least for the important improvements of form which I am making.

It is very difficult to keep one's temper in dealing with M. Arnold when he touches on religious matters. His patronage of a Christianity fashioned by himself is to me more offensive and

trying than rank unbelief. But I try, or seem to myself to try, to   CHAP.
shrink from controversy of which I have had so much. Organic   IX.
evolution sounds to me a Butlerish idea, but I doubt if he ever   Æт. 86.
employed either term, certainly he has not the phrase, and I
cannot as yet identify the passage to which you may refer.

Dec. 9. — Many thanks for your letter. The idea of evolution is
without doubt deeply ingrained in Butler. The case of the animal
creation had a charm for him, and in his first chapter he opens,
without committing himself, the idea of their possible elevation to
a much higher state. I have always been struck by the glee with
which negative writers strive to get rid of 'special creation,' as if
by that method they got the idea of God out of their way, whereas
I know not what right they have to say that the small increments
effected by the divine workman are not as truly special as the
large. It is remarkable that Butler has taken such hold both on
nonconformists in England and outside of England, especially on
those bodies in America which are descended from English nonconformists.

He made progress with his writings on the Olympian
Religion, without regard to Acton's warnings and exhorta-
tions to read a score of volumes by learned explorers with
uncouth names. He collected a new series of his *Gleanings.*
By 1896 he had got his cherished project of hostel and
library at St. Deiniol's in Hawarden village, near to its
launch. He was drawn into a discussion on the validity of
anglican orders, and even wrote a letter to Cardinal Rampolla, in his effort to realise the dream of Christian unity.
The Vatican replied in such language as might have been
expected by anybody with less than Mr. Gladstone's in-
extinguishable faith in the virtues of argumentative persuasion. Soon he saw the effects of Christian disunion
upon a bloodier stage. In the autumn of this year he was
roused to one more vehement protest like that twenty years
before against the abominations of Turkish rule, this time
in Armenia. He had been induced to address a meeting in
Chester in August 1895, and now a year later he travelled to
Liverpool (Sept. 24) to a non-party gathering at Hengler's
Circus. He always described this as the place most agreeable
to the speaker of all those with which he was acquainted.

'Had I the years of 1876 upon me,' he said to one of his sons, 'gladly would I start another campaign, even if as long as that.' To discuss, almost even to describe, the course of his policy and proceedings in the matter of Armenia, would bring us into a mixed controversy affecting statesmen now living, who played an unexpected part, and that controversy may well stand over for another, and let us hope a very distant, day. Whether we had a right to interfere single-handed; whether we were bound as a duty to interfere under the Cyprus Convention; whether our intervention would provoke hostilities on the part of other Powers and even kindle a general conflagration in Europe; whether our severance of diplomatic relations with the Sultan or our withdrawal from the concert of Europe would do any good; what possible form armed intervention could take — all these are questions on which both liberals and tories vehemently differed from one another then, and will vehemently differ again. Mr. Gladstone was bold and firm in his replies. As to the idea, he said, that all independent action on the part of this great country was to be made chargeable for producing war in Europe, 'that is in my opinion a mistake almost more deplorable than almost any committed in the history of diplomacy.' We had a right under the convention. We had a duty under the responsibilities incurred at Paris in 1856, at Berlin in 1878. The upshot of his arguments at Liverpool was that we should break off relations with the Sultan; that we should undertake not to turn hostilities to our private advantage; that we should limit our proceedings to the suppression of mischief in its aggravated form; and if Europe threatened us with war it might be necessary to recede, as France had receded under parallel circumstances from her individual policy on the eastern question in 1840, — receded without loss either of honour or power, believing that she had been right and wise and others wrong and unwise.

If Mr. Gladstone had still had, as he puts it, 'the years of 1876,' he might have made as deep a mark. As it was, his speech at Liverpool was his last great deliverance to a public audience. As the year ended this was his birthday entry: —

Dec. 29, 1896. — My long and tangled life this day concludes its 87th year. My father died four days short of that term. I know of no other life so long in the Gladstone family, and my profession has been that of politician, or, more strictly, minister of state, an extremely short-lived race when their scene of action has been in the House of Commons, Lord Palmerston being the only complete exception. In the last twelve months eyes and ears may have declined, but not materially. The occasional contraction of the chest is the only inconvenience that can be called new. I am not without hope that Cannes may have a [illegible] to act upon it. The blessings of family life continue to be poured in the largest measure upon my unworthy head. Even my temporal affairs have thriven. Still old age is appointed for the gradual loosening and succeeding snapping of the threads. I visited Lord Stratford when he was, say, 90 or 91 or thereabouts. He said to me, ' It is not a blessing.' As to politics, I think the basis of my mind is laid principally in finance and philanthropy. The prospects of the first are darker than I have ever known them. Those of the second are black also, but with more hope of some early dawn. I do not enter on interior matters. It is so easy to write, but to write honestly nearly impossible. Lady Grosvenor gave me to-day a delightful present of a small crucifix. I am rather too independent of symbol.

This is the last entry in the diaries of seventy years.

At the end of January 1897, the Gladstones betook themselves once more to Lord Rendel's *palazzetto*, as they called it, at Cannes.

I had hoped during this excursion, he journalises, to make much way with my autobiographica. But this was in a large degree frustrated, first by invalidism, next by the eastern question, on which I was finally obliged to write something.[1] Lastly, and not least, by a growing sense of decline in my daily amount of brain force available for serious work. My power to read (but to read very slowly indeed since the cataract came) for a considerable number of hours daily, thank God, continues. This is a great mercy. While on my outing, I may have read, of one kind and another, twenty volumes. Novels enter into this list

[1] *Letter to the Duke of Westminster.*

rather considerably. I have begun seriously to ask myself whether I shall ever be able to face 'The Olympian Religion.'

The Queen happened to be resident at Cimiez at this time, and Mr. Gladstone wrote about their last meeting: —

A message came down to us inviting us to go into the hotel and take tea with the Princess Louise. We repaired to the hotel, and had our tea with Miss Paget, who was in attendance. The Princess soon came in, and after a short delay we were summoned into the Queen's presence. No other English people were on the ground. We were shown into a room tolerably, but not brilliantly lighted, much of which was populated by a copious supply of Hanoverian royalties. The Queen was in the inner part of the room, and behind her stood the Prince of Wales and the Duke of Cambridge. Notwithstanding my enfeebled sight, my vision is not much impaired for practical purposes in cases such as this, where I am thoroughly familiar with the countenance and whole contour of any person to be seen. My wife preceded, and Mary followed me. The Queen's manner did not show the old and usual vitality. It was still, but at the same time very decidedly kind, such as I had not seen it for a good while before my final resignation. She gave me her hand, a thing which is, I apprehended, rather rare with men, and which had never happened with me during all my life, though that life, be it remembered, had included some periods of rather decided favour. Catherine sat down near her, and I at a little distance. For a good many years she had habitually asked me to sit. My wife spoke freely and a good deal to the Queen, but the answers appeared to me to be very slight. As to myself, I expressed satisfaction at the favourable accounts I had heard of the accommodation at Cimiez, and perhaps a few more words of routine. To speak frankly, it seemed to me that the Queen's peculiar faculty and habit of conversation had disappeared. It was a faculty, not so much the free offspring of a rich and powerful mind, as the fruit of assiduous care with long practice and much opportunity. After about ten minutes, it was signified to us that we had to be presented to all the other royalties, and so passed the remainder of this meeting.

In the early autumn of 1897 he found himself affected by

what was supposed to be a peculiar form of catarrh. He
went to stay with Mr. Armitstead at Butterstone in Perth-
shire. I saw him on several occasions afterwards, but this
was the last time when I found him with all the freedom,
full self-possession, and kind geniality of old days. He was
keenly interested at my telling him that I had seen James
Martineau a few days before, in his cottage further north in
Inverness-shire ; that Martineau, though he had now passed
his ninety-second milestone on life's road, was able to walk
five or six hundred feet up his hillside every day, was at his
desk at eight each morning, and read theology a good many
hours before he went to bed at night. Mr. Gladstone's conversation was varied, glowing, full of reminiscence. He had
written me in the previous May, hoping among other kind
things that ' we may live more and more in sympathy and
communion.' I never saw him more attractive than in the
short pleasant talks of these three or four days. He discussed
some of the sixty or seventy men with whom he had been
associated in cabinet life,[1] freely but charitably, though he
named two whom he thought to have behaved worse to him
than others. He repeated his expression of enormous admiration for Graham. Talked about his own voice. After he had
made his long budget speech in 1860, a certain member, supposed to be an operatic expert, came to him and said, ' You
must take great care, or else you will destroy the *colour* in
your voice.' He had kept a watch on general affairs. The
speech of a foreign ruler upon divine right much incensed him.
He thought that Lord Salisbury had managed to set the Turk
up higher than he had reached since the Crimean war ; and
his policy had weakened Greece, the most liberal of the
eastern communities. We fought over again some old
battles of 1886 and 1892-4. Mr. Armitstead had said to
him — ' Oh, sir, you'll live ten years to come.' ' I do trust,'
he answered as he told me this, 'that God in his mercy
will spare me that.'

II

Then came months of distress. The facial annoyance
grew into acute and continued pain, and to pain he proved

[1] For the list see Appendix.

to be exceedingly sensitive. It did not master him, but there were moments that seemed almost of collapse and defeat. At last the night was gathering

> About the burning crest
> Of the old, feeble, and day-wearied sun.[1]

They took him at the end of November (1897) to Cannes, to the house of Lord Rendel.

Sometimes at dinner he talked with his host, with Lord Welby, or Lord Acton, with his usual force, but most of the time he lay in extreme suffering and weariness, only glad when they soothed him with music. It was decided that he had better return, and in hope that change of air might even yet be some palliative, he went to Bournemouth, which he reached on February 22. For weeks past he had not written nor read, save one letter that he wrote in his journey home to Lady Salisbury upon a rather narrow escape of her husband's in a carriage accident. On March 18 his malady was pronounced incurable, and he learned that it was likely to end in a few weeks. He received the verdict with perfect serenity and with a sense of unutterable relief, for his sufferings had been cruel. Four days later he started home to die. On leaving Bournemouth before stepping into the train, he turned round, and to those who were waiting on the platform to see him off, he said with quiet gravity, 'God bless you and this place, and the land you love.' At Hawarden he bore the dreadful burden of his pain with fortitude, supported by the ritual ordinances of his church and faith. Music soothed him, the old composers being those he liked best to hear. Messages of sympathy were read to him, and he listened silently or with a word of thanks.

' The retinue of the whole world's good wishes' flowed to the ' large upper chamber looking to the sunrising, where the aged pilgrim lay.' Men and women of every communion offered up earnest prayers for him. Those who were of no communion thought with pity, sympathy, and sorrow of

> A Power passing from the earth
> To breathless Nature's dark abyss.

---

[1] *King John.*

From every rank in social life came outpourings in every
key of reverence and admiration. People appeared — as
is the way when death comes — to see his life and character as a whole, and to gather up in his personality,
thus transfigured by the descending shades, all the best
hopes and aspirations of their own best hours. A certain
grandeur overspread the moving scene. Nothing was there
for tears. It was 'no importunate and heavy load.' The
force was spent, but it had been nobly spent in devoted and
effective service for his country and his fellow-men.

From the Prince of the Black Mountain came a telegram:
'Many years ago, when Montenegro, my beloved country,
was in difficulties and in danger, your eloquent voice and
powerful pen successfully pleaded and worked on her behalf.
At this time vigorous and prosperous, with a bright future
before her, she turns with sympathetic eye to the great
English statesman to whom she owes so much, and for whose
present sufferings she feels so deeply.' And he answered by
a message that ' his interest in Montenegro had always been
profound, and he prayed that it might prosper and be blessed
in all its undertakings.'

Of the thousand salutations of pity and hope none went
so much to his heart as one from Oxford — an expression of
true feeling, in language worthy of her fame : —

At yesterday's meeting of the hebdomadal council, wrote the
vice-chancellor, an unanimous wish was expressed that I should
convey to you the message of our profound sorrow and affection at
the sore trouble and distress which you are called upon to endure.
While we join in the universal regret with which the nation
watches the dark cloud which has fallen upon the evening of a
great and impressive life, we believe that Oxford may lay claim to
a deeper and more intimate share in this sorrow. Your brilliant
career in our university, your long political connection with it,
and your fine scholarship, kindled in this place of ancient learning,
have linked you to Oxford by no ordinary bond, and we cannot
but hope that you will receive with satisfaction this expression of
deep-seated kindliness and sympathy from us.

We pray that the Almighty may support you and those near

and dear to you in this trial, and may lighten the load of suffering which you bear with such heroic resignation.

To this he listened more attentively and over it he brooded long, then he dictated to his youngest daughter sentence by sentence at intervals his reply: —

There is no expression of Christian sympathy that I value more than that of the ancient university of Oxford, the God-fearing and God-sustaining university of Oxford. I served her, perhaps mistakenly, but to the best of my ability. My most earnest prayers are hers to the uttermost and to the last.

When May opened, it was evident that the end was drawing near. On the 13th he was allowed to receive visits of farewell from Lord Rosebery and from myself, the last persons beyond his household to see him. He was hardly conscious. On the early morning of the 19th, his family all kneeling around the bed on which he lay in the stupor of coming death, without a struggle he ceased to breathe. Nature outside — wood and wide lawn and cloudless far-off sky — shone at her fairest.

III

On the day after his death, in each of the two Houses the leader made the motion, identical in language in both cases save the few final words about financial provision in the resolution of the Commons : —

That an humble Address be presented to her Majesty praying that her Majesty will be graciously pleased to give directions that the remains of the Right Hon. William Ewart Gladstone be interred at the public charge, and that a monument be erected in the Collegiate Church of St. Peter, Westminster, with an inscription expressive of the public admiration and attachment and of the high sense entertained of his rare and splendid gifts, and of his devoted labours to parliament and in great offices of state, and to assure her Majesty that this House will make good the expenses attending the same.

The language of the movers was worthy of the British parliament at its best, worthy of the station of those who

used it, and worthy of the figure commemorated. Lord
Salisbury was thought by most to go nearest to the core of
the solemnity : —

What is the cause of this unanimous feeling? Of course, he
had qualities that distinguished him from all other men; and
you may say that it was his transcendent intellect, his astonishing power of attaching men to him, and the great influence he
was able to exert upon the thought and convictions of his contemporaries. But these things, which explain the attachment, the
adoration of those whose ideas .he represented, would not explain
why it is that sentiments almost as fervent are felt and expressed
by those whose ideas were not carried out by his policy. My
Lords, I do not think the reason is to be found in anything so
far removed from the common feelings of mankind as the abstruse
and controversial questions of the policy of the day. They had
nothing to do with it. Whether he was right, or whether he
was wrong, in all the measures, or in most of the measures
which he proposed — those are matters of which the discussion
has passed by, and would certainly be singularly inappropriate
here; they are really remitted to the judgment of future generations, who will securely judge from experience what we can only
decide by forecast. It was on account of considerations more
common to the masses of human beings, to the general working
of the human mind, than any controversial questions of policy
that men recognised in him a man guided — whether under mistaken impressions or not, it matters not — but guided in all the
steps he took, in all the efforts that he made, by a high moral
ideal. What he sought were the attainments of great ideals,
and, whether they were based on sound convictions or not, they
could have issued from nothing but the greatest and the purest
moral aspirations; and he is honoured by his countrymen, because through so many years, across so many vicissitudes and
conflicts, they had recognised this one characteristic of his action,
which has never ceased to be felt. He will leave behind him,
especially to those who have followed with deep interest the
history of the later years — I might almost say the later months
of his life — he will leave behind him the memory of a great
Christian statesman. Set up necessarily on high — the sight of

his character, his motives, and his intentions would strike all the world. They will have left a deep and most salutary influence on the political thought and the social thought of the generation in which he lived, and he will be long remembered not so much for the causes in which he was engaged or the political projects which he favoured, but as a great example, to which history hardly furnishes a parallel, of a great Christian man.

Mr. Balfour, the leader in the Commons, specially spoke of him as ' the greatest member of the greatest deliberative assembly that the world has seen,' and most aptly pointed to Mr. Gladstone's special service in respect of that assembly.

One service he did, in my opinion incalculable, which is altogether apart from the judgment that we may be disposed to pass upon particular opinions, or particular lines of policy which Mr. Gladstone may from time to time have advocated. Sir, he added a dignity, as he added a weight, to the deliberations of this House by his genius, which I think it is impossible adequately to replace. It is not enough for us to keep up simply a level, though it be a high level, of probity and of patriotism. The mere average of civic virtue is not sufficient to preserve this Assembly from the fate that has overcome so many other Assemblies, products of democratic forces. More than this is required; more than this was given to us by Mr. Gladstone. He brought to our debates a genius which compelled attention, he raised in the public estimation the whole level of our proceedings, and they will be most ready to admit the infinite value of his service who realise how much of public prosperity is involved in the maintenance of the worth of public life, and how perilously difficult most democracies apparently feel it to be to avoid the opposite dangers into which so many of them have fallen.

Sir William Harcourt spoke of him as friend and official colleague : —

I have heard men who knew him not at all, who have asserted that the supremacy of his genius and the weight of his authority oppressed and overbore those who lived with him and those who worked under him. Nothing could be more untrue. Of all chiefs he was the least exacting. He was the most kind, the most tolerant, he was the most placable. How seldom in this House was the voice of personal anger heard from his lips. These are the true marks of greatness.

Lord Rosebery described his gifts and powers, his concentration, the multiplicity of his interests, his labour of every day, and almost of every hour of every day, in fashioning an intellect that was mighty by nature. And besides this panegyric on the departed warrior, he touched with felicity and sincerity a note.of true feeling in recalling to his hearers

the solitary and pathetic figure, who for sixty years, shared all the sorrows and all the joys of Mr. Gladstone's life, who received his confidence and every aspiration, who shared his triumphs with him and cheered him under his defeats; who by her tender vigilance, I firmly believe, sustained and prolonged his years.

When the memorial speeches were over the House of Commons adjourned. The Queen, when the day of the funeral came, telegraphed to Mrs. Gladstone from Balmoral : —

My thoughts are much with you to-day, when your dear husband is laid to rest. To-day's ceremony will be most trying and painful for you, but it will be at the same time gratifying to you to see the respect and regret evinced by the nation for the memory of one whose character and intellectual abilities marked him as one of the most distinguished statesmen of my reign. I shall ever gratefully remember his devotion and zeal in all that concerned my personal welfare and that of my family.

IV

It was not at Westminster only that his praise went forth. Famous men, in the immortal words of Pericles to his Athenians, have the whole world for their tomb; they are commemorated not only by columns and inscriptions in their own land; in foreign lands too a memorial of them is graven in the hearts of men. So it was here. No other statesman on our famous roll has touched the imagination of so wide a world.

The colonies through their officers or more directly, sent to Mrs. Gladstone their expression of trust that the world-wide admiration and esteem of her honoured and illustrious husband would help her to sustain her burden of sorrow. The ambassador of the United States reverently congratulated her and the English race everywhere, upon the glorious completion of a life filled with splendid achievements and consecrated to the noblest purposes. The President followed in the same vein, and in Congress words were found to celebrate a splendid life and character. The President of the French republic wished to be among the first to associate himself with Mrs. Gladstone's grief : ' By the high liberality of his character,' he said, ' and by the nobility of his political ideal, Mr. Gladstone had worthily served his country and humanity.' The entire French government requested the British ambassador in Paris to convey the expression of their sympathy and assurance of their appreciation, admiration, and respect for the character of the illustrious departed. The Czar of Russia telegraphed to Mrs. Gladstone : ' I have just received the painful news of Mr. Gladstone's decease, and consider it my duty to express to you my feelings of sincere sympathy on the occasion of the cruel and irreparable bereavement which has befallen you, as well as the deep regret which this sad event has given me. The whole of the civilised world will beweep the loss of a great statesman, whose political views were so widely humane and peaceable.'

In Italy the sensation was said to be as great as when Victor Emmanuel or Garibaldi died. The Italian parliament and the prime minister telegraphed to the effect that ' the cruel loss which had just struck England, was a grief sincerely shared by all who are devoted to liberty. Italy has not forgotten, and will never forget, the interest and sympathy of Mr. Gladstone in events that led to its independence.' In the same key, Greece : the King, the first minister, the university, the chamber, declared that he was entitled to the gratitude of the Greek people, and his name would be by them for ever venerated. From Roumania, Macedonia, Norway, Denmark, tributes came ' to the great memory of Gladstone, one of the glories of mankind.' Never has so wide and honourable a pomp all over the globe followed an English statesman to the grave.

IV

On May 25, the remains were brought from Hawarden, and in the middle of the night the sealed coffin was placed in Westminster Hall, watched until the funeral by the piety of relays of friends. For long hours each day great multitudes filed past the bier. It was a striking demonstration of national feeling, for the procession contained every rank, and contingents came from every part of the kingdom. On Saturday, May 28, the body was committed to the grave in Westminster Abbey. No sign of high honour was absent. The heir to the throne and his son were among those who bore the pall. So were the prime minister and the two leaders of the parties in both Houses. The other pall-bearers were Lord Rosebery who had succeeded him as prime minister, the Duke of Rutland who had half a century before been Mr. Gladstone's colleague at Newark, and Mr. Armitstead and Lord Rendel, who were his private friends. Foreign sovereigns sent their representatives, the Speaker of the House of Commons was there in state, and those were there who had done stout battle against him for long years; those also who had sat with him in council and stood by his side in frowning hours. At the head of the grave was 'the solitary and pathetic figure' of his wife. Even men most averse to all pomps and shows on the occasions and scenes that declare so audibly their nothingness, here were only conscious of a deep and moving simplicity, befitting a great citizen now laid among the kings and heroes. Two years later, the tomb was opened to receive the faithful and devoted companion of his life.

CHAPTER X

FINAL

ANYBODY can see the host of general and speculative
questions raised by a career so extraordinary. How would
his fame have stood if his political life had ended in
1854, or 1874, or 1881, or 1885? What light does it
shed upon the working of the parliamentary system;
on the weakness and strength of popular government; on
the good and bad of political party; on the superiority of
rule by cabinet or by an elected president; on the relations
of opinion to law? Here is material for a volume of
disquisition, and nobody can ever discuss such speculations
without reference to power as it was exercised by Mr. Gladstone. Those thronged halls, those vast progresses, those
strenuous orations — what did they amount to? Did they
mean a real moulding of opinion, an actual impression,
whether by argument or temper or personality or all three,
on the minds of hearers? Or was it no more than the
same kind of interest that takes men to stage-plays with
a favourite performer? This could hardly be, for his hearers
gave him long spells of power and a practical authority that
was unique and supreme. What thoughts does his career
suggest on the relations of Christianity to patriotism, or to
empire, or to what has been called neo-paganism? How
many points arise as to the dependence of ethics on dogma?
These are deep and living and perhaps burning issues, not
to be discussed at the end of what the reader may well have
found a long journey. They offer themselves for his independent consideration.

I

Mr. Gladstone's own summary of the period in which he

had been so conspicuous a figure was this, when for him the
drama was at an end : —

Of his own career, he says, it is a career certainly chargeable
with many errors of judgment, but I hope on the whole, governed
at least by uprightness of intention and by a desire to learn.
The personal aspect may now readily be dismissed as it concerns
the past. But the public aspect of the period which closes for me
with the fourteen years (so I love to reckon them) of my formal
connection with Midlothian is too important to pass without a
word. I consider it as beginning with the Reform Act of Lord
Grey's government. That great Act was for England improvement and extension, for Scotland it was political birth, the
beginning of a duty and a power, neither of which had attached
to the Scottish nation in the preceding period. I rejoice to think
how the solemnity of that duty has been recognised, and how that
power has been used. The three-score years offer us the pictures
of what the historian will recognise as a great legislative and
administrative period — perhaps, on the whole, the greatest in our
annals. It has been predominantly a history of emancipation —
that is of enabling man to do his work of emancipation, political,
economical, social, moral, intellectual. Not numerous merely, but
almost numberless, have been the causes brought to issue, and in
every one of them I rejoice to think that, so far as my knowledge
goes, Scotland has done battle for the right.

Another period has opened and is opening still — a period
possibly of yet greater moral dangers, certainly a great ordeal for
those classes which are now becoming largely conscious of power,
and never heretofore subject to its deteriorating influences. These
have been confined in their actions to the classes above them,
because they were its sole possessors. Now is the time for the
true friend of his country to remind the masses that their present
political elevation is owing to no principles less broad and noble
than these — the love of liberty, of liberty for all without distinction of class, creed or country, and the resolute preference of the
interests of the whole to any interest, be it what it may, of a
narrower scope.[1]

A year later, in bidding farewell to his constituents ' with

[1] Letter to Sir John Cowan, March 17, 1894.

sentiments of gratitude and attachment that can never be
effaced,' he proceeds : —

Though in regard to public affairs many things are disputable,
there are some which belong to history and which have passed out
of the region of contention. It is, for example as I conceive, beyond question that the century now expiring has exhibited since
the close of its first quarter a period of unexampled activity both
in legislative and administrative changes; that these changes,
taken in the mass, have been in the direction of true and most
beneficial progress; that both the conditions and the franchises of
the people have made in relation to the former state of things, an
extraordinary advance; that of these reforms an overwhelming
proportion have been effected by direct action of the liberal party,
or of statesmen such as Peel and Canning, ready to meet odium
or to forfeit power for the public good ; and that in every one of
the fifteen parliaments the people of Scotland have decisively expressed their convictions in favour of this wise, temperate, and
in every way remarkable policy.[1]

To charge him with habitually rousing popular forces into
dangerous excitement, is to ignore or misread his action in
some of the most critical of his movements. 'Here is
a man,' said Huxley, 'with the greatest intellect in Europe,
and yet he debases it by simply following majorities and
the crowd.' He was called a mere mirror of the passing
humours and intellectual confusions of the popular mind.
He had nothing, said his detractors, but a sort of clever
pilot's eye for winds and currents, and the rising of the
tide to the exact height that would float him and his
cargo over the bar. All this is the exact opposite of
the truth. What he thought was that the statesman's gift
consisted in insight into the facts of a particular era, dis-
closing the existence of material for forming public opinion
and directing public opinion to a given purpose. In every
one of his achievements of high mark — even in his last
marked failure of achievement — he expressly formed, or
endeavoured to form and create, the public opinion upon
which he knew that in the last resort he must depend.

[1] July 1, 1895.

We have seen the triumph of 1853.[1] Did he, in renewing the most hated of taxes, run about anxiously feeling the pulse of public opinion? On the contrary, he grappled with the facts with infinite labour — and half his genius was labour — he built up a great plan ; he carried it to the cabinet ; they warned him that the House of Commons would be against him ; the officials of the treasury told him the Bank would be against him ; that a strong press of commercial interests would be against him. Like the bold and sinewy athlete that he always was, he stood to his plan ; he carried the cabinet ; he persuaded the House of Commons ; he vanquished the Bank and the hostile interests ; and in the words of Sir Stafford Northcote, he changed and turned for many years to come, a current of public opinion that seemed far too powerful for any minister to resist. In the tempestuous discussions during the seventies on the policy of this country in respect of the Christian races of the Balkan Peninsula, he with his own voice created, moulded, inspired, and kindled with resistless flame the whole of the public opinion that eventually guided the policy of the nation with such admirable effect both for its own fame, and for the good of the world. Take again the Land Act of 1881, in some ways the most deep-reaching of all his legislative achievements. Here he had no flowing tide, every current was against him. He carried his scheme against the ignorance of the country, against the prejudice of the country, and against the standing prejudices of both branches of the legislature, who were steeped from the crown of the head to the sole of the foot in the strictest doctrines of contract.

Then his passion for economy, his ceaseless war against public profusion, his insistence upon rigorous keeping of the national accounts — in this great department of affairs he led and did not follow. In no sphere of his activities was he more strenuous, and in no sphere, as he must well have known, was he less likely to win popularity. For democracy is spendthrift ; if, to be sure, we may not say that most forms of government are apt to be the same.

In a survey of Mr. Gladstone's performances, some would

[1] See vol. i. p. 457.

place this of which I have last spoken, as foremost among his services to the country. Others would call him greatest in the associated service of a skilful handling and adjustment of the burden of taxation ; or the strengthening of the foundations of national prosperity and well-being by his reformation of the tariff. Yet others again choose to remember him for his share in guiding the successive extensions of popular power, and simplifying and purifying electoral machinery. Irishmen at least, and others so far as they are able to comprehend the history and vile wrongs and sharp needs of Ireland, will have no doubt what rank in legislation they will assign to the establishment of religious equality and agrarian justice in that portion of the realm. Not a few will count first the vigour with which he repaired what had been an erroneous judgment of his own and of vast hosts of his countrymen, by his courage in carrying through the submission of the Alabama claims to arbitration. Still more, looking from west to east, in this comparison among his achievements, will judge alike in its result and in the effort that produced it, nothing equal to the valour and insight with which he burst the chains of a mischievous and degrading policy as to the Ottoman empire. When we look at this exploit, how in face of an opponent of genius and authority and a tenacity not inferior to his own, in face of strongly rooted tradition on behalf of the Turk, and an easily roused antipathy against the Russian, by his own energy and strength of arm he wrested the rudder from the hand of the helmsman and put about the course of the ship, and held England back from the enormity of trying to keep several millions of men and women under the yoke of barbaric oppression and misrule, — we may say that this great feat alone was fame enough for one statesman. Let us make what choice we will of this or that particular achievement, how splendid a list it is of benefits conferred and public work effectually performed. Was he a good parliamentary tactician, they ask ? Was his eye sure, his hand firm, his measurement of forces, distances, and possibilities of change in wind and tide accurate ? Did he usually hit the proper moment for a magisterial intervention ? Experts did not

always agree on his quality as tactician. At least he was
pilot enough to bring many valuable cargoes safely home.

He was one of the three statesmen in the House of
Commons of his own generation who had the gift of large
and spacious conception of the place and power of England
in the world, and of the policies by which she could maintain
it. Cobden and Disraeli were the other two. Wide as the
poles asunder in genius, in character, and in the mark they
made upon the nation, yet each of these three was capable
of wide surveys from high eminence. But Mr. Gladstone's
performances in the sphere of active government were
beyond comparison.

Again he was often harshly judged by that tenacious class
who insist that if a general principle be sound, there can never
be a reason why it should not be applied forthwith, and that
a rule subject to exceptions is not worth calling a rule ; and
the worst of it is that these people are mostly the salt of the
earth. In their impatient moments they dismissed him as
an opportunist, but whenever there was a chance of getting
anything done, they mostly found that he was the only man
with courage and resolution enough to attempt to do it. In
thinking about him we have constantly to remember, as Sir
George Lewis said, that government is a very rough affair
at best, a huge rough machine, not the delicate springs,
wheels, and balances of a chronometer, and those concerned
in working it have to be satisfied with what is far below the
best. 'Men have no business to talk of disenchantment,'
Mr. Gladstone said ; 'ideals are never realised.' That is no
reason, he meant, why men should not persist and toil and
hope, and this is plainly the true temper for the politician.
Yet he did not feed upon illusions. 'The history of nations,'
he wrote in 1876, 'is a melancholy chapter ; that is, the
history of governments is one of the most immoral parts of
human history.'

II

It might well be said that Mr. Gladstone took too little,
rather than too much trouble to be popular. His religious
conservatism puzzled and irritated those who admired and

shared his political liberalism, just as churchmen watched
with uneasiness and suspicion his radical alliances. Neither
those who were churchmen first, nor those whose interests
were keenest in politics, could comprehend the union of what
seemed incompatibles, and because they could not comprehend they sometimes in their shallower humours doubted
his sincerity. Mr. Gladstone was never, after say 1850, really
afraid of disestablishment; on the contrary he was much
more afraid of the perils of establishment for the integrity of
the faith. Yet political disestablishers often doubted him,
because they had not logic enough to see that a man may
be a fervent believer in anglican institutions and what he
thinks catholic tradition, and yet be as ready as Cavour for
the principle of free church in free state.

It is curious that some of the things that made men
suspicious, were in fact the liveliest tokens of his sincerity
and simplicity. With all his power of political imagination,
yet his mind was an intensely literal mind. He did not
look at an act or a decision from the point of view at which
it might be regarded by other people. Ewelme, the mission
to the Ionian Islands, the royal warrant, the affair of the
judicial committee, vaticanism, and all the other things that
gave offence, and stirred misgivings even in friends, showed
that the very last question he ever asked himself was how
his action would look; what construction might be put
upon it, or even would pretty certainly be put upon it;
whom it would encourage, whom it would estrange, whom
it would perplex. Is the given end right, he seemed to ask;
what are the surest means; are the means as right as the
end, as right as they are sure? But right — on strict and
literal construction. What he sometimes forgot was that in
political action, construction is part of the act, nay, may
even be its most important part.[1]

The more you make of his errors, the more is the need to
explain his vast renown, the long reign of his authority, the
substance and reality of his powers. We call men great for
many reasons apart from service wrought or eminence of
intellect or even from force and depth of character. To

[1] See *Guardian*, Feb. 25, 1874.

have taken a leading part in transactions of decisive
moment ; to have proved himself able to meet demands
on which high issues hung ; to combine intellectual
qualities, though moderate yet adequate and sufficient, with
the moral qualities needed for the given circumstance — with
daring, circumspection, energy, intrepid initiative ; to have
fallen in with one of those occasions in the world that
impart their own greatness even to a mediocre actor, and
surround his name with a halo not radiating from within
but shed upon him from without — in all these and many
other ways men come to be counted great. Mr. Gladstone
belongs to the rarer class who acquired authority and fame
by transcendent qualities of genius within, in half independence of any occasions beyond those they create for themselves.

III

Of his attitude in respect of church parties, it is not for
me to speak. He has himself described at least one aspect
of it in a letter to an inquirer, which would be a very noble
piece by whomsoever written, and in the name of what-
soever creed or no-creed, whether Christian or Rationalist
or Nathan the Wise Jew's creed. It was addressed to a
clergyman who seems to have asked of what section Mr.
Gladstone considered himself an adherent : —

Feb. 4, 1865. — It is impossible to misinterpret either the intention or the terms of your letter ; and I thank you for it sincerely.
But I cannot answer the question which you put to me, and
I think I can even satisfy you that with my convictions I should
do wrong in replying to it in any manner. Whatever reason
I may have for being painfully and daily conscious of every kind
of unworthiness, yet I am sufficiently aware of the dignity of
religious belief to have been throughout a political life, now in its
thirty-third year, steadily resolved never by my own voluntary
act to make it the subject of any compact or assurance with a
view to a political object. You think (and pray do not suppose
I make this matter of complaint) that I have been associated with
one party in the church of England, and that I may now lean
rather towards another. . . . There is no one about whom in-

formation can be more easily had than myself. I have had and have friends of many colours, churchmen high and low, presbyterians, Greeks, Roman catholics, dissenters, who can speak abundantly, though perhaps not very well of me. And further, as member for the university, I have honestly endeavoured at all times to put my constituents in possession of all I could convey to them that could be considered as in the nature of a fact, by answering as explicitly as I was able all questions relating to the matters, and they are numerous enough, on which I have had to act or speak. Perhaps I shall surprise you by what I have yet further to say. I have never by any conscious act yielded my allegiance to any person or party in matters of religion. You and others may have called me (without the least offence) a churchman of some particular kind, and I have more than once seen announced in print my own secession from the church of England. These things I have not commonly contradicted, for the atmosphere of religious controversy and contradiction is as odious as the atmosphere of mental freedom is precious, to me; and I have feared to lose the one and be drawn into the other, by heat and bitterness creeping into the mind. If another chooses to call himself, or to call me, a member of this or that party, I am not to complain. But I respectfully claim the right not to call myself so, and on this claim, I have I believe acted throughout my life, without a single exception; and I feel that were I to waive it, I should at once put in hazard that allegiance to Truth, which is at once the supreme duty and the supreme joy of life. I have only to add the expression of my hope that in what I have said there is nothing to hurt or to offend you; and, if there be, very heartily to wish it unsaid.

Yet there was never the shadow of mistake about his own fervent faith. As he said to another correspondent: —

Feb. 5, 1876. — I am in principle a strong denominationalist. 'One fold and one shepherd' was the note of early Christendom. The shepherd is still one and knows his sheep; but the folds are many; and, without condemning any others, I am of opinion that it is best for us all that we should all of us be jealous for the honour of whatever we have and hold as positive truth, appertaining to the Divine Word and the foundation and history of

the Christian community. I admit that this question becomes
one of circumstance and degree, but I take it as I find it defined
for myself by and in my own position.

IV

Of Mr. Gladstone as orator and improvisatore, enough has
been said and seen. Besides being orator and statesman he
was scholar and critic. Perhaps scholar in his interests,
not in abiding contribution. The most copious of his pro-
ductions in this delightful but arduous field was the three
large volumes on *Homer and the Homeric Age*, given to the
world in 1858. Into what has been well called the whirlpool of Homeric controversies, the reader shall not here be
dragged. Mr. Gladstone himself gave them the go-by, with
an indifference and disdain such as might have been well
enough in the economic field if exhibited towards a protectionist farmer, or a partisan of retaliatory duties on manu-
factured goods, but that were hardly to the point in dealing
with profound and original critics. What he too con-
temptuously dismissed as Homeric 'bubble-schemes,' were
in truth centres of scientific illumination. At the end of
the eighteenth century Wolf's famous *Prolegomena* appeared,
in which he advanced the theory that Homer was no single
poet, nor a name for two poets, nor an individual at all ;
the *Iliad* and *Odyssey* were collections of independent lays,
folk-lore and folk-songs connected by a common set of
themes, and edited, redacted, or compacted about the middle
of the sixth century before Christ. A learned man of our
own day has said that F. A. Wolf ought to be counted one
of the half dozen writers that within the last three centuries
have most influenced thought. This would bring Wolf into
line with Descartes, Newton, Locke, Kant, Rousseau, or whatever other five master-spirits of thought from then to now
the judicious reader may select. The present writer has
assuredly no competence to assign Wolf's place in the
history of modern criticism, but straying aside for a season
from the green pastures of Hansard, and turning over again
the slim volume of a hundred and fifty pages in which Wolf
discusses his theme, one may easily discern a fountain of

broad streams of modern thought (apart from the particular thesis) that to Mr. Gladstone, by the force of all his education and his deepest prepossessions, were in the highest degree chimerical and dangerous.

He once wrote to Lord Acton (1889) about the Old Testament and Mosaic legislation : —

Now I think that the most important parts of the argument have in a great degree a solid standing ground apart from the destructive criticism on dates and on the text: and I am sufficiently aware of my own rawness and ignorance in the matter not to allow myself to judge definitely, or condemn. I feel also that I have a prepossession derived from the criticisms in the case of Homer. Of them I have a very bad opinion, not only in themselves, but as to the levity, precipitancy, and shallowness of mind which they display; and here I do venture to speak, because I believe myself to have done a great deal more than any of the destructives in the examination of the text, which is the true source of the materials of judgment. They are a soulless lot; but there was a time when they had possession of the public ear as much I suppose as the Old Testament destructives now have, within their own precinct. It is only the constructive part of their work on which I feel tempted to judge; and I must own that it seems to me sadly wanting in the elements of rational probability.

This unpromising method is sufficiently set out when he says : ' I find in the plot of the *Iliad* enough of beauty, order, and structure, not merely to sustain the supposition of its own unity, but to bear an independent testimony, should it be still needed, to the existence of a personal and individual Homer as its author.' [1] From such a method no permanent contribution could come.

Yet scholars allow that Mr. Gladstone in these three volumes, as well as in *Juventus Mundi* and his *Homeric Primer*, has added not a little to our scientific knowledge of the Homeric poems,[2] by his extraordinary mastery of the text, the result of unwearied and prolonged industry, aided

[1] iii. p. 396.
[2] For instance, Geddes, *Problem of the Homeric Poems*, 1878, p. 16.

by a memory both tenacious and ready. Taking his own point of view, moreover, anybody who wishes to have his feeling about the *Iliad* and *Odyssey* as delightful poetry refreshed and quickened, will find inspiring elements in the profusion, the eager array of Homer's own lines, the diligent exploration of aspects and bearings hitherto unthought of. The 'theo-mythology' is commonly judged fantastic, and has been compared by sage critics to Warburton's *Divine Legation* — the same comprehensive general reading, the same heroic industry in marshalling the particulars of proof, the same dialectical strength of arm, and all brought to prove an unsound proposition.[1] Yet the comprehensive reading and the particulars of proof are by no means without an interest of their own, whatever we may think of the proposition; and here, as in all his literary writing distinguished from polemics, he abounds in the ethical elements. Here perhaps more than anywhere else he impresses us by his love of beauty in all its aspects and relations, in the human form, in landscape, in the affections, in animals, including above all else that sense of beauty which made his Greeks take it as one of the names for nobility in conduct. Conington, one of the finest of scholars, then lecturing at Oxford on Latin poets and deep in his own Virgilian studies, which afterwards bore such admirable fruit, writes at length (Feb. 14, 1857) to say how grateful he is to Mr. Gladstone for the care with which he has pursued into details a view of Virgil that they hold substantially in common, and proceeds with care and point to analyse the quality of the Roman poet's art, as some years later he defended against Munro the questionable proposition of the superiority in poetic style of the graceful, melodious, and pathetic Virgil to Lucretius's mighty muse.

No field has been more industriously worked for the last forty years than this of the relations of paganism to the historic religion that followed it in Europe. The knowledge and the speculations into which Mr. Gladstone was thus initiated in the sixties may now seem crude enough; but he deserves some credit in English, though not in view of

[1] Pattison, ii. p. 166.

German, speculation for an early perception of an unfamiliar region of comparative science, whence many a product most unwelcome to him and alien to his own beliefs has been since extracted. When all is said, however, Mr. Gladstone's place is not in literary or critical history, but elsewhere.

His style is sometimes called Johnsonian, but surely without good ground. Johnson was not involved and he was clear, and neither of these things can always be said of Mr. Gladstone. Some critic charged him in 1840 with 'prolix clearness.' The old charge, says Mr. Gladstone upon this, was 'obscure compression. I do not doubt that both may be true, and the former may have been the result of a well-meant effort to escape from the latter.' He was fond of abstract words, or the nearer to abstract the better, and the more general the better. One effect of this was undoubtedly to give an indirect, almost a shifty, air that exasperated plain people. Why does he beat about the bush, they asked; why cannot he say what he means? A reader might have to think twice or thrice or twenty times before he could be sure that he interpreted correctly. But then people are so apt to think once, or half of once; to take the meaning that suits their own wish or purpose best, and then to treat that as the only meaning. Hence their perplexity and wrath when they found that other doors were open, and they thought a mistake due to their own hurry was the result of a juggler's trick. On the other hand a good writer takes all the pains he can to keep his reader out of such scrapes.

His critical essays on Tennyson and Macaulay are excellent. They are acute, discriminating, generous. His estimate of Macaulay, apart from a piece of polemical church history at the end, is perhaps the best we have. 'You make a very just remark,' said Acton to him, 'that Macaulay was afraid of contradicting his former self, and remembered all he had written since 1825. At that time his mind was formed, and so it remained. What literary influences acted on the formation of his political opinions, what were his religious sympathies, and what is his exact place among historians, you have rather avoided discussing. There is still some-

thing to say on these points.' To Tennyson Mr. Gladstone
believed himself to have been unjust, especially in the passages of *Maud* devoted to the war-frenzy, and when he came
to reprint the article he admitted that he had not sufficiently
remembered that he was dealing with a dramatic and imaginative composition.[1] As he frankly said of himself, he
was not strong in the faculties of the artist, but perhaps
Tennyson himself in these passages was prompted much
more by politics than by art. Of this piece of retractation
the poet truly said, 'Nobody but a noble-minded man would
have done that.'[2] Mr. Gladstone would most likely have
chosen to call his words a qualification rather than a recan-
tation. In either case, it does not affect passages that give
the finest expression to one of the very deepest convictions
of his life, — that war, whatever else we may choose to say
of it, is no antidote for Mammon-worship and can never be a
cure for moral evils : —

It is, indeed, true that peace has its moral perils and temptations for degenerate man, as has every other blessing, without
exception, that he can receive from the hand of God. It is moreover not less true that, amidst the clash of arms, the noblest forms
of character may be reared, and the highest acts of duty done ;
that these great and precious results may be due to war as their
cause ; and that one high form of sentiment in particular, the love
of country, receives a powerful and general stimulus from the
bloody strife. But this is as the furious cruelty of Pharaoh made
place for the benign virtue of his daughter; as the butchering
sentence of Herod raised without doubt many a mother's love
into heroic sublimity; as plague, as famine, as fire, as flood, as
every curse and every scourge that is wielded by an angry Providence for the chastisement of man, is an appointed instrument for
tempering human souls in the seven-times heated furnace of affliction, up to the standard of angelic and archangelic virtue.

War, indeed, has the property of exciting much generous and
noble feeling on a large scale ; but with this special recommendation it has, in its modern forms especially, peculiar and unequalled
evils. As it has a wider sweep of desolating power than the rest,

[1] *Gleanings*, ii. p. 147.   [2] *Life*, i. p. 398.

so it has the peculiar quality that it is more susceptible of being decked in gaudy trappings, and of fascinating the imagination of those whose proud and angry passions it inflames. But it is, on this very account, a perilous delusion to teach that war is a cure for moral evil, in any other sense than as the sister tribulations are. The eulogies of the frantic hero in *Maud*, however, deviate into grosser folly. It is natural that such vagaries should overlook the fixed laws of Providence. Under these laws the mass of mankind is composed of men, women, and children who can but just ward off hunger, cold, and nakedness; whose whole ideas of Mammon-worship are comprised in the search for their daily food, clothing, shelter, fuel; whom any casualty reduces to positive want; and whose already low estate is yet further lowered and ground down, when 'the blood-red blossom of war flames with its heart of fire.' . . .

Still war had, in times now gone by, ennobling elements and tendencies of the less sordid kind. But one inevitable characteristic of modern war is, that it is associated throughout, in all particulars, with a vast and most irregular formation of commercial enterprise. There is no incentive to Mammon-worship so remarkable as that which it affords. The political economy of war is now one of its most commanding aspects. Every farthing, with the smallest exceptions conceivable, of the scores or hundreds of millions which a war may cost, goes directly, and very violently, to stimulate production, though it is intended ultimately for waste or for destruction. Even apart from the fact that war suspends, *ipso facto*, every rule of public thrift, and tends to sap honesty itself in the use of the public treasure for which it makes such unbounded calls, it therefore is the greatest feeder of that lust of gold which we are told is the essence of commerce, though we had hoped it was only its occasional besetting sin. It is, however, more than this; for the regular commerce of peace is tameness itself compared with the gambling spirit which war, through the rapid shiftings and high prices which it brings, always introduces into trade. In its moral operation it more resembles, perhaps the finding of a new gold-field, than anything else.

More remarkable than either of these two is his piece on Leopardi (1850), the Italian poet, whose philosophy and frame of mind, said Mr. Gladstone, 'present more than any other that we know, more even than that of Shelley, the character of unrelieved, unredeemed desolation — the very qualities in it which attract pitying sympathy, depriving it of all seductive power.' It is curious that he should have selected one whose life lay along a course like Leopardi's for commemoration, as a man who in almost every branch of mental exertion seems to have had the capacity for attaining, and generally at a single bound, the very highest excellence. 'There are many things,' he adds, 'in which Christians would do well to follow him : in the warmth of his attachments ; in the moderation of his wants ; in his noble freedom from the love of money ; in his all-conquering assiduity.'[1] Perhaps the most remarkable sentence of all is this : '. . . what is not needful, and is commonly wrong, namely, is to pass a judgment on our fellow-creatures. Never let it be forgotten that there is scarcely a single moral action of a single man of which other men can have such a knowledge, in its ultimate grounds, its surrounding incidents, and the real determining causes of its merits, as to warrant their pronouncing a conclusive judgment upon it.'

The translation of poetry into poetry, as Coleridge said, is difficult because the translator must give brilliancy without the warmth of original conception, from which such brilliancy would follow of its own accord. But we must not judge Mr. Gladstone's translation either of Horace's odes or of detached pieces from Greek or Italian, as we should judge the professed man of letters or poet like Coleridge himself. His pieces are the diversions of the man of affairs, with educated tastes and interest in good literature. Perhaps the best single piece is his really noble rendering of Manzoni's noble ode on the death of Napoleon ; for instance : —

> From Alp to farthest Pyramid,
> From Rhine to Mansanar,
> How sure his lightning's flash foretold
> His thunderbolts of war !
> To Don from Scilla's height they roar,
> From North to Southern shore.

---

[1] *Gleanings*, ii. p. 129.

And this was glory?   After-men,
Judge the dark problem.   Low
We to the Mighty Maker bend
The while, Who planned to show
What vaster mould Creative Will
With him could fill.

.   .   .   .

As on the shipwrecked mariner
The weltering wave's descent —
The wave, o'er which, a moment since,
For distant shores he bent
And bent in vain, his eager eye;
So on that stricken head
Came whelming down the mighty Past.
How often did his pen
Essay to tell the wondrous tale
For after times and men,
And o'er the lines that could not die
His hand lay dead.

How often, as the listless day
In silence died away,
He stood with lightning eye deprest,
And arms across his breast,
And bygone years, in rushing train,
Smote on his soul amain:
The breezy tents he seemed to see,
And the battering cannon's course,
And the flashing of the infantry,
And the torrent of the horse,
And, obeyed as soon as heard,
Th' ecstatic word.

Always let us remember that his literary life was part
of the rest of his life, as literature ought to be.   He was
no mere reader of many books, used to relieve the strain
of mental anxiety or to slake the thirst of literary or intellectual curiosity.   Reading with him in the days of his
full vigour was a habitual communing with the master
spirits of mankind, as a vivifying and nourishing part of life.
As we have seen, he would not read Dante in the session,
nor unless he could have a large draught.   Here as elsewhere in the ordering of his days he was methodical,
systematic, full.

V

Though man of action, yet Mr. Gladstone too has a place by character and influences among what we may call the abstract, moral, spiritual forces that stamped the realm of Britain in his age. In a new time, marked in an incomparable degree by the progress of science and invention, by vast mechanical, industrial, and commercial development, he accepted it all, he adjusted his statesmanship to it all, nay, he revelled in it all, as tending to ameliorate the lot of the ' mass of men, women, and children who can just ward off hunger, cold, and nakedness.' He did not rail at his age, he strove to help it. Following Walpole and Cobden and Peel in the policies of peace, he knew how to augment the material resources on which our people depend. When was Britain stronger, richer, more honoured among the nations — I do not say always among the diplomatic chanceries and governments — than in the years when Mr. Gladstone was at the zenith of his authority among us ? When were her armed forces by sea and land more adequate for defence of every interest ? When was her material resource sounder ? When was her moral credit higher ? Besides all this, he upheld a golden lamp.

The unending revolutions of the world are for ever bringing old phases uppermost again. Events from season to season are taken to teach sinister lessons, that the Real is the only Rational, force is the test of right and wrong, the state has nothing to do with restraints of morals, the ruler is emancipated. Speculations in physical science were distorted for alien purposes, and survival of the fittest was taken to give brutality a more decent name. Even new conceptions and systems of history may be twisted into release of statesmen from the conscience of Bishop Butler's plain man. This gospel it was Mr. Gladstone's felicity to hold at bay. Without bringing back the cosmopolitanism of the eighteenth century, without sharing all the idealisms of the middle of the nineteenth, he resisted with his whole might the odious contention that moral progress in the relations of nations and states to one another is an illusion and a dream.

This vein perhaps brings us too near to the regions of dissertation. Let us rather leave off with thoughts and memories of one who was a vivid example of public duty and of private faithfulness; of a long career that with every circumstance of splendour, amid all the mire and all the poisons of the world, lighted up in practice even for those who have none of his genius and none of his power his own precept, 'Be inspired with the belief that life is a great and noble calling; not a mean and grovelling thing, that we are to shuffle through as we can, but an elevated and lofty destiny.'

APPENDIX

IRISH LOCAL GOVERNMENT, 1883

Page 103

Mr. Gladstone to Lord Granville

Cannes, Jan. 22, 1883. — To-day I have been a good deal distressed by a passage as reported in Hartington's very strong and able speech, for which I am at a loss to account, so far does it travel out into the open, and so awkward are the intimations it seems to convey. I felt that I could not do otherwise than telegraph to you in cipher on the subject. But I used words intended to show that, while I thought an immediate notification needful, I was far from wishing to hasten the reply, and desired to leave altogether in your hands the mode of touching a delicate matter. Pray use the widest discretion.

I console myself with thinking it is hardly possible that Hartington can have meant to say what nevertheless both *Times* and *Daily News* make him seem to say, namely, that we recede from, or throw into abeyance, the declarations we have constantly made about our desire to extend local government, properly so called, to Ireland on the first opportunity which the state of business in parliament would permit. We announced our intention to do this at the very moment when we were preparing to suspend the Habeas Corpus Act. Since that time we have seen our position in Ireland immensely strengthened, and the leader of the agitation has even thought it wise, and has dared, to pursue a somewhat conciliatory course. Many of his coadjutors are still as vicious, it may be, as ever, but how can we say (for instance) to the Ulster men, you shall remain with shortened liberties and without local government, because Biggar & Co. are hostile to British connection?

There has also come prominently into view a new and powerful set of motives which, in my deliberate judgment, require us, for the sake of the United Kingdom even more than for the sake of Ireland, to push forward this question. Under the present highly centralised system of government, every demand which can be started on behalf of a poor and ill-organised country, comes directly on the British government and treasury; if refused it becomes at once a head of grievance, if granted not only a new drain but a certain source of political complication and embarrassment. The peasant proprietary, the winter's distress, the state of the labourers, the loans to farmers, the promotion of public works, the encouragement of fisheries, the promotion of emigration, each and every one of these questions has a sting, and the sting can only be taken out of it by our treating it in correspondence with a popular and responsible Irish body, competent to act for its own portion of the country.

Every consideration which prompted our pledges, prompts the recognition of them, and their extension, rather than curtailment. The Irish government have in preparation a Local Government bill. Such a bill may even be an economy of time. By no other means that I can see shall we be able to ward off most critical and questionable discussions on questions of the class I have mentioned. The argument that we cannot yet trust Irishmen with popular local institutions is the mischievous argument by which the conservative opposition to the Melbourne government resisted, and finally crippled, the reform of municipal corporations in Ireland. By acting on principles diametrically opposite, we have broken down to thirty-five or forty what would have been a party, in this parliament, of sixty-five home rulers, and have thus arrested (or at the very least postponed) the perilous crisis, which no man has as yet looked in the face; the crisis which will arise when a large and united majority of Irish members demand some fundamental change in the legislative relations of the two countries. I can ill convey to you how clear are my thoughts, or how earnest my convictions, on this important subject. . . .

GENERAL GORDON'S INSTRUCTIONS

Page 153

The following is the text of General Gordon's Instructions (*Jan.* 18, 1884) : —

Her Majesty's government are desirous that you should proceed at once to Egypt, to report to them on the military situation in the Soudan, and on the measures it may be advisable to take for the security of the Egyptian garrisons still holding positions in that country, and for the safety of the European population in Khartoum. You are also desired to consider and report upon the best mode of effecting the evacuation of the interior of the Soudan, and upon the manner in which the safety and good administration by the Egyptian government of the ports on the sea coast can best be secured. In connection with this subject you should pay especial consideration to the question of the steps that may usefully be taken to counteract the stimulus which it is feared may possibly be given to the slave trade by the present insurrectionary movement, and by the withdrawal of the Egyptian authority from the interior. You will be under the instructions of Her Majesty's agent and consul-general at Cairo, through whom your reports to Her Majesty's government should be sent under flying seal. You will consider yourself authorised and instructed to perform such other duties as the Egyptian government may desire to entrust to you, and as may be communicated to you by Sir E. Baring. You will be accompanied by Colonel Stewart, who will assist you in the duties thus confided to you. On your arrival in Egypt you will at once communicate with Sir E. Baring, who will arrange to meet you and will settle with you whether you should proceed direct to Suakin or should go yourself or despatch Colonel Stewart *viâ* the Nile.

THE MILITARY POSITION IN THE SOUDAN, APRIL 1885

Page 179

This Memorandum, dated April 9, 1885, *was prepared by Mr. Gladstone for the cabinet :* —

The commencement of the hot season appears, with other circumstances, to mark the time for considering at large our position in the Soudan. Also a declaration of policy is now demanded from us in nearly all quarters. . . . . When the betrayal of Khartoum had been announced, the desire and intention of the cabinet were to reserve for a later decision the question of an eventual advance upon that place, should no immediate movement on it be found possible. The objects they had immediately in view were to ascertain the fate of Gordon, to make every effort on his behalf, and to prevent the extension of the area of disturbance.

But Lord Wolseley at once impressed upon the cabinet that he required, in order to determine his immediate military movements, to know whether they were to be based upon the plan of an eventual advance on Khartoum, or whether the intention of such an advance was to be abandoned altogether. If the first plan were adopted, Lord Wolseley declared his power and intention to take Berber, and even gave a possible date for it, in the middle of March. The cabinet, adopting the phrase which Lord Wolseley had used, decided upon the facts as they then stood before it: (*a*) Lord Wolseley was to calculate upon proceeding to Khartoum after the hot season, to overthrow the power of the Mahdi there; (*b*) and, consequently, on this decision, they were to commence the construction of a railway from Suakin to Berber, in aid of the contemplated expedition; (*c*) an expedition was also to be sent against Osman Digna, which would open the road to Berber; but Lord Wolseley's demand for this expedition applied alike to each of the two military alternatives which he had laid before the cabinet.

There was no absolute decision to proceed to Khartoum at any time; and the declarations of ministers in parliament have treated it as a matter to be further weighed ; but all steps have thus far been taken to prepare for it, and it has been regarded as at least probable. In approaching the question whether we are still to proceed on the same lines, it is necessary to refer to the motives which under the directions of the cabinet were stated by Lord Granville and by me, on the 19th of February, as having contributed to the decision. I copy out a part of the note from which he and I spoke : —

Objects in the Soudan which we have always deemed fit for consideration as far as circumstances might allow : —
1. The case of those to whom Gordon held himself bound in honour.
2. The possibility of establishing an orderly government at Khartoum.
3. Check to the slave trade.
4. The case of the garrisons.
A negative decision would probably have involved the abandonment at a stroke of all these objects. And also (we had to consider) whatever dangers, proximate or remote, in Egypt or in the East might follow from the triumphant position of the Mahdi ; hard to estimate, but they may be very serious.

Two months, which have passed since the decision of the government (Feb. 5), have thrown light, more or less, upon the several points brought into view on the 19th February. 1. We have now no sufficient reason to assume that any of the population of Khartoum felt themselves bound to Gordon, or to have suffered on his account; or even that any large numbers of men in arms perished in the betrayal of the town, or took his part after the enemy were admitted into it. 2. We have had no tidings of anarchy at Khartoum, and we do not know that it is governed worse, or that the population is suffering more, than it would be under a Turkish or Egyptian ruler. 3. It is not believed that the possession of Khartoum is of any great value as regards the slave trade. 4. Or, after the failure of Gordon with respect to the garrisons, that the possession of Khartoum would, without further and formidable extensions of plan, avail for the purpose of relieving them. But further, what knowledge have we that these garrisons are unable to relieve themselves ? There seems some reason to believe that the army of Hicks, when the action ceased, fraternised with the Mahdi's army, and that the same thing happened at Khartoum. Is there ground to suppose that they are hateful unless as representatives of Egyptian power ? and ought they not to be released from any obligation to present themselves in that capacity ?

With regard to the larger question of eventual consequences in Egypt or the East from the Mahdi's success at Khartoum, it is open to many views, and cannot be completely disposed of. But it may be observed — 1. That the Mahdi made a trial of marching down the Nile and speedily abandoned it, even in the first flush of his success. 2. That cessation of operations in the Soudan does not at this moment mean our military inaction in the East. 3. That the question is one of conflict, not with the arms of an enemy, but with Nature in respect of climate and supply. 4. There remains also a grave question of justice, to which I shall revert.

Should the idea of proceeding to Khartoum be abandoned, the railway from Suakin, as now projected, would fall with it, since it was adopted as a military measure, subsidiary to the advance on Khartoum. The prosecution of it as a civil or commercial enterprise would be a new proposal, to be examined on its merits.

The military situation appears in some respects favourable to the re-examination of the whole subject. The general has found himself unable to execute his intention of taking Berber, and this failure alters the basis on which the cabinet proceeded in February, and greatly increases the difficulty of the autumn enterprise. On the one hand Wolseley's and Graham's forces have had five or six considerable actions, and have been uniformly victorious. On the other hand, the Mahdi has voluntarily retired from Khartoum, and Osman Digna has been driven from the field, but cannot, as Graham says, be followed into the mountains.[1] While the present situation may thus seem opportune, the future of more extended operations is dark. In at least one of his telegrams, Wolseley has expressed a very keen desire to get the British army out of the Soudan.[2] He has now made very large demands for the autumn expedition, which, judging from previous experience and from general likelihood, are almost certain to grow larger, as he comes more closely to confront the very formidable task before him; while in his letter to Lord Hartington he describes this affair to be *the greatest* ' *since* 1815,' and expresses his hope that all the members of the cabinet clearly understand this to be the case. He also names a period of between two or three years for the completion of the railway, while he expresses an absolute confidence in the power and resources of this country with vast effort to insure success. He means without doubt military success. Political success appears much more problematical.

There remains, however, to be considered a question which I take to be of extreme importance. I mean the moral basis of the projected military operations. I have from the first regarded the rising of the Soudanese against Egypt as a justifiable and honourable revolt. The cabinet have, I think, never taken an opposite view. Mr. Power, in his letter from Khartoum before Gordon's arrival, is decided and even fervent in the same sense.

We sent Gordon on a mission of peace and liberation. From such information as alone we have possessed, we found this missionary of peace menaced and besieged, finally betrayed by some of his troops, and slaughtered by those whom he came to set free. This information, however, was fragmentary, and was also one-sided. We have now the advantage of reviewing it as a whole, of reading it in the light of events, and of some auxiliary evidence such as that of Mr. Power.

I never understood how it was that Gordon's mission of peace

---

[1] Telegram of April 4.   [2] Despatch, March 9.

became one of war. But we knew the nobleness of his philanthropy, and we trusted him to the uttermost, as it was our duty to do. He never informed us that he had himself changed the character of the mission. It seemed strange that one who bore in his hands a charter of liberation should be besieged and threatened; but we took everything for granted in his favour, and against his enemies; and we could hardly do otherwise. Our obligations in this respect were greatly enhanced by the long interruption of telegraphic communication. It was our duty to believe that, if we could only know what he was prevented from saying to us, contradictions would be reconciled, and language of excess accounted for. We now know from the letters of Mr. Power that when he was at Khartoum with Colonel de Coetlogon before Gordon's arrival, a retreat on Berber had been actually ordered; it was regarded no doubt as a serious work of time, because it involved the removal of an Egyptian population;[1] but it was deemed feasible, and Power expresses no doubt of its accomplishment.[2] As far as, amidst its inconsistencies, a construction can be put on Gordon's language, it is to the effect that there was a population and a force attached to him, which he could not remove and would not leave.[3] But De Coetlogon did not regard this removal as impracticable, and was actually setting about it. Why Gordon did not prosecute it, why we hear no more of it from Power after Gordon's arrival, is a mystery. Instructed by results we now perceive that Gordon's title as governor-general might naturally be interpreted by the tribes in the light of much of the language used by him, which did not savour of liberation and evacuation, but of powers of government over the Soudan; powers to be used benevolently, but still powers of government. Why the Mahdi did not accept him is not hard to understand, but why was he not accepted by those local sultans, whom it was the basis of his declared policy to re-invest with their ancient powers, in spite of Egypt and of the Mahdi alike? Was he not in short interpreted as associated with the work of Hicks, and did he not himself give probable colour to this interpretation? It must be borne in mind that on other matters of the gravest importance — on the use of Turkish force — on the use of British force — on the employment of Zobeir — Gordon announced within a very short time contradictory views, and never seemed to feel that there was any need of explanation, in order to account for the contradictions. There is every presumption, as well as every sign, that like fluctuation and inconsistency crept into his words and acts as to the liberation of the country; and this, if it was so, could not but produce ruinous effects. Upon the whole, it seems probable that Gordon, perhaps insensibly to himself, and certainly without our concurrence, altered the character of his mission, and worked in a considerable degree against our intentions and instructions.

There does not appear to be any question now of the security

[1] Power, p. 73 A.   [2] Ibid. 75 B.
[3] Egypt, No. 18, p. 34, 1884 (April); Egypt, No. 35, p. 122 (July 30).

of the army, but a most grave question whether we can demonstrate a necessity (nothing less will suffice) for making war on a people who are struggling against a foreign and armed yoke, not for the rescue of our own countrymen, not for the rescue *so far as we know* of an Egyptian population, but with very heavy cost of British life as well as treasure, with a serious strain on our military resources at a most critical time, and with the most serious fear that if we persist, we shall find ourselves engaged in an odious work of subjugation. The discontinuance of these military operations would, I presume, take the form of a suspension *sine die*, leaving the future open; would require attention to be paid to defence on the recognised southern frontier of Egypt, and need not involve any precipitate abandonment of Suakin.

HOME RULE BILL, 1886

Page 308

The following summary of the provisions of the Home Rule bill of 1886 supplements the description of the bill given in Chapter V. Book X. : —

One of the cardinal difficulties of all free government is to make it hard for majorities to act unjustly to minorities. You cannot make this injustice impossible but you may set up obstacles. In this case, there was no novelty in the device adopted. The legislative body was to be composed of two orders. The first order was to consist of the twenty-eight representative peers, together with seventy-five members elected by certain scheduled constituencies on an occupation franchise of twenty-five pounds and upwards. To be eligible for the first order, a person must have a property qualification, either in realty of two hundred pounds a year, or in personalty of the same amount, or a capital value of four thousand pounds. The representative peers now existing would sit for life, and, as they dropped off, the crown would nominate persons to take their place up to a certain date, and on the exhaustion of the twenty-eight existing peers, then the whole of the first order would become elective under the same conditions as the seventy-five other members.

The second order would consist of 206 members, chosen by existing counties and towns under the machinery now operative. The two orders were to sit and deliberate together, but either order could demand a separate vote. This right would enable a majority of one order to veto the proposal of the other. But the veto was only to operate until a dissolution, or for three years, whichever might be the longer interval of the two.

The executive transition was to be gradual. The office of viceroy would remain, but he would not be the minister of a party, nor quit office with an outgoing government. He would have a privy council; within that council would be formed an executive body of ministers like the British cabinet. This executive would be responsible to the Irish legislature, just as the executive government here is responsible to the legislature of this country. If any clause of a bill seemed to the viceroy to be *ultra vires*, he could refer it to the judicial committee of the privy council in London. The same reference, in respect of a section of an Irish Act, lay open either to the English secretary of state, or to a suitor, defendant, or other person concerned.

Future judges were to hold the same place in the Irish system as English judges in the English system; their office was to be during good behaviour; they were to be appointed on the advice of the Irish government, removable only on the joint address of the two orders, and their salaries charged on the Irish consolidated fund. The burning question of the royal Irish constabulary was dealt with provisionally. Until a local force was created by the new government, they were to remain at the orders of the lord lieutenant. Ultimately the Irish police were to come under the control of the legislative body. For two years from the passing of the Act, the legislative body was to fix the charge for the whole constabulary of Ireland.

In national as in domestic housekeeping, the figure of available income is the vital question. The total receipts of the Irish exchequer would be £8,350,000, from customs, excise, stamps, income-tax, and non-tax revenue. On a general comparison of the taxable revenues of Ireland and Great Britain, as tested more especially by the property passing under the death duties, the fair proportion due as Ireland's share for imperial purposes, such as interest on the debt, defence, and civil charge, was fixed at one-fifteenth. This would bring the total charge properly imperial up to £3,242,000. Civil charges in Ireland were put at £2,510,000, and the constabulary charge on Ireland was not to exceed £1,000,000, any excess over that sum being debited to England. The Irish government would be left with a surplus of £404,000. This may seem a ludicrously meagre amount, but, compared with the total revenue, it is equivalent to a surplus on our own budget of that date of something like five millions.

The true payment to imperial charges was to be £1,842,000 because of the gross revenue above stated of £1,400,000 though paid in Ireland in the first instance was really paid by British consumers of whisky, porter, and tobacco. This sum, deducted from £3,342,000, leaves the real Irish contribution, namely £1,842,000.

A further sum of uncertain, but substantial amount, would go to the Irish exchequer from another source, to which we have now to turn. With the proposals for self-government were coupled proposals for a settlement of the land question. The ground-work was an option offered to the landlords of being bought out under the terms of the Act. The purchaser was to be an Irish state authority, as the organ representing the legislative body. The occupier was to become the proprietor,

except in the congested districts, where the state authority
was to be the proprietor. The normal price was to be twenty
years' purchase of the net rental. The most important provision,
in one sense, was that which recognised the salutary principle
that the public credit should not be resorted to on such a scale
as this merely for the benefit of a limited number of existing
cultivators of the soil, without any direct advantage to the government as representing the community at large. That was effected
by making the tenant pay an annual instalment, calculated on the
gross rental, while the state authority would repay to the imperial
treasury a percentage calculated on the net rental, and the state
authority would pocket the difference, estimated to be about
18 per cent. on the sum payable to the selling landlord.   How
was all this to be secured ?   Principally, on the annuities paid by
the tenants who had purchased their holdings, and if the holdings
did not satisfy the charge, then on the revenues of Ireland.   All
public revenues whatever were to be collected by persons appointed
by the Irish government, but these collectors were to pay over all
sums that came into their hands to an imperial officer, to be styled
a receiver-general.   Through him all rents and Irish revenues
whatever were to pass, and not a shilling was to be let out for
Irish purposes until their obligations to the imperial exchequer
had been discharged.

ON THE PLACE OF ITALY

Page 415

By the provisions of nature, Italy was marked out for a conservative force in Europe.   As England is cut off by the channel,
so is Italy by the mountains, from the continental mass. . . .   If
England commits follies they are the follies of a strong man who
can afford to waste a portion of his resources without greatly
affecting the sum total. . . .   She has a huge free margin, on which
she might scrawl a long list of follies and even crimes without
damaging the letterpress.   But where and what is the free margin
in the case of Italy, a country which has contrived in less than a
quarter of a century of peace, from the date of her restored independence, to treble (or something near it) the taxation of her people, to raise the charge of her debt to a point higher than that of
England, and to arrive within one or two short paces of national
bankruptcy ? . . .
    Italy by nature stands in alliance neither with anarchy nor with
Caesarism, but with the cause and advocates of national liberty and
progress throughout Europe.   Never had a nation greater advantages from soil and climate, from the talents and dispositions of the
people, never was there a more smiling prospect (if we may fall
back upon the graceful fiction) from the Alpine tops, even down
to the Sicilian promontories, than that which for the moment has
been darkly blurred.   It is the heart's desire of those, who are

not indeed her teachers, but her friends, that she may rouse herself
to dispel once and for ever the evil dream of what is not so much
ambition as affectation, may acknowledge the true conditions under
which she lives, and it perhaps may not yet be too late for her to
disappoint the malevolent hopes of the foes of freedom, and to
fulfil every bright and glowing prediction which its votaries have
ever uttered on her behalf. — ' The Triple Alliance and Italy's Place
in it ' (Contemporary Review, Oct. 1889).

THE GLASGOW PERORATION

Page 492

*After describing the past history of Ireland as being for more than
five hundred years ' one almost unbroken succession of political storm
and swollen tempest, except when those tempests were for a time interrupted by a period of servitude and by the stillness of death,'
Mr. Gladstone went on : —*

Those storms are in strong contrast with the future, with
the present. The condition of the Irish mind justifies us in
anticipating. It recalls to my mind a beautiful legend of ancient
paganism — for that ancient paganism, amongst many legends false
and many foul, had also some that were beautiful. There were
two Lacedæmonian heroes known as Castor and Pollux, honoured
in their life and more honoured in their death, when a star was
called after them, and upon that star the fond imagination of the
people fastened lively conceptions ; for they thought that when a
ship at sea was caught in a storm, when dread began to possess
the minds of the crew, and peril thickened round them, and even
alarm was giving place to despair, that if then in the high heavens
this star appeared, gradually and gently but effectually the clouds
disappeared, the winds abated, the towering billows fell down
to the surface of the deep, calm came where there had been
uproar, safety came where there had been danger, and under the
beneficent influence of this heavenly body the terrified and despairing crew came safely to port. The proposal which the liberal party
of this country made in 1886, which they still cherish in their mind
and heart, and which we trust and believe, they are about now to
carry forward, that proposal has been to Ireland and the political
relations of the two countries what the happy star was believed to
be to the seamen of antiquity. It has produced already anticipations of love and good will, which are the first fruits of what is to
come. It has already changed the whole tone and temper of the
relations, I cannot say yet between the laws, but between the
peoples and inhabitants of these two great islands. It has filled
our hearts with hope and with joy, and it promises to give us in
lieu of the terrible disturbances of other times, with their increas-
ing, intolerable burdens and insoluble problems, the promise of a
brotherhood exhibiting harmony and strength at home, and a

brotherhood which before the world shall, instead of being as it hitherto has been for the most part, a scandal, be a model and an example, and shall show that we whose political wisdom is for so many purposes recognised by the nations of civilised Europe and America have at length found the means of meeting this oldest and worst of all our difficulties, and of substituting for disorder, for misery, for contention, the actual arrival and the yet riper promise of a reign of peace. — *Theatre Royal, Glasgow, July 2, 1892.*

THE NAVAL ESTIMATES OF 1894

The first paragraph of this memorandum will be found on p. 508: —

This might be taken for granted as to 1854, 1870, and 1884. That it was equally true in my mind of 1859 may be seen by any one who reads my budget speech of July 18, 1859. I defended the provision as required by and for the time, and for the time only. The occasion in that year was the state of the continent. It was immediately followed by the China war (No. 3) and by the French affair (1861–2), but when these had been disposed of economy began ; and, by 1863–4, the bulk of the new charge had been got rid of.

There is also the case of the fortifications in 1860, which would take me too long to state fully. But I will state briefly (1) my conduct in that matter was mainly or wholly governed by regard to peace, for I believed, and believe now, that in 1860 there were only two alternatives; one of them, the French treaty, and the other, war with France. And I also believed in July 1860 that the French treaty must break down, unless I held my office. (2) The demand was reduced from nine millions to about five (has this been done now?) (3) I acted in concert with my old friend and colleague, Sir James Graham. We were entirely agreed.

Terse figures of new estimates

The 'approximate figure' of charge involved in the new plan of the admiralty is £4,240,000, say $4\frac{1}{2}$ millions. Being an increase (subject probably to some further increase in becoming an act)

1. On the normal navy estimate 1888–9 (*i.e.* before the Naval Defence Act) of, in round numbers, . $4\frac{1}{4}$ millions
2. On the first year's total charge under the Naval Defence Act of (1, 979,000), . 2 millions
3. On the estimates of last year 1893–94 of 3 millions
4. On the total charge of 1893–4 of (1,571,000) $1\frac{1}{2}$ million
5. On the highest amount ever defrayed from the year's revenue (1892–3), . . $1\frac{1}{2}$ million
6. On the highest expenditure of any year under the Naval Defence Act which included 1,150,000 of borrowed money, . 359,000

MR. GLADSTONE'S CABINET COLLEAGUES

Page 525

The following is the list of the seventy ministers who served in cabinets of which Mr. Gladstone was a member:—

1843–45. Peel.
Wellington.
Lyndhurst.
Wharncliffe.
Haddington.
Buccleuch.
Aberdeen.
Graham.
Stanley.
Ripon.
Hardinge.
Goulburn.
Knatchbull.
1846. Ellenborough.
S. Herbert.
Granville Somerset.
Lincoln.
1852–55. Cranworth.
Granville.
Argyll.
Palmerston.
Clarendon.
C. Wood.
Molesworth.
Lansdowne.
Russell.
G. Grey.
1855. Panmure.
Carlisle.
1859–65. Campbell.
G. C. Lewis.
Duke of Somerset.
Milner Gibson.
Elgin.
C. Villiers.

1859–65. Cardwell.
Westbury.
Ripon.
Stanley of Alderley.
1865–66. Hartington.
Goschen.
1868–74. Hatherley.
Kimberley.
Bruce.
Lowe.
Childers.
Bright.
C. Fortescue.
Stansfeld.
Selborne.
Forster.
1880–85. Spencer.
Harcourt.
Northbrook.
Chamberlain.
Dodson.
Dilke.
Derby.
Trevelyan.
Lefevre.
Rosebery.
1886. Herschell.
C. Bannerman.
Mundella.
John Morley.
1892. Asquith.
Fowler.
Acland.
Bryce.
A. Morley.

CHRONOLOGY [1]

1880.

Feb. 'Free trade, railways and the growth of commerce,' in *Nineteenth Century*.

„ 27. At St. Pancras on obstruction, liberal unity and errors of government.

„ 27. On rules dealing with obstruction.

March 'Russia and England,' in *Nineteenth Century*.

„ 5. On motion in favour of local option.

„ 11. Issues address to electors of Midlothian.

„ 15. Criticises budget.

„ 17. At Music Hall, Edinburgh, on government's eastern policy.

„ 18. At Corstorphine on Anglo-Turkish convention.

„ 18. At Ratho on neglect of domestic legislation.

„ 19. At Davidson's Mains on indictment of the government. At Dalkeith on the government and class interests.

„ 20. At Juniper Green, and at Balerno, replies to tory criticism of liberal party. At Midcalder on abridgment of rights of parliament.

„ 22. At Gilmerton on church disestablishment. At Loanhead on the eastern policy of liberal and tory parties.

„ 23. At Gorebridge and at Pathhead.

„ 25. At Penicuik on Cyprus.

„ 30. At Stow on finance.

April 'Religion, Achaian and Semitic,' in *Nineteenth Century*.

„ 2. At West Calder on liberal record and shortcomings of the government.

1880.

April 5. Elected for Midlothian : Mr. Gladstone, 1579 ; Lord Dalkeith, 1368.

„ 7. Returns to Hawarden.

„ 28. Second ' administration formed.

May Anonymous article, 'The Conservative Collapse,' in *Fortnightly Review*.

„ 8. Returned unopposed for Midlothian.

„ 11. Publication of correspondence with Count Karolyi, Austrian ambassador.

„ 16. Receives deputation of farmers on agricultural reform.

„ 20. On government's Turkish policy.

„ 21. Moves reference to committee of Mr. Bradlaugh's claim to take his seat in parliament.

„ 25. On South African federation.

June 1. On government's policy regarding Cyprus.

„ 10. Introduces supplementary budget.

„ 16. On reduction of European armaments.

„ 18. On resolution in favour of local option. Moves second reading of Savings Banks bill.

„ 22. On resolution that Mr. Bradlaugh be allowed to make a declaration.

July 1. On Mr. Bradlaugh's case.

„ 5, 26. On Compensation for Disturbances (Ireland) bill.

„ 23. Explains government's policy regarding Armenia.

„ 30–Aug. 9. Confined to room by serious illness.

[1] All speeches unless otherwise stated were made in the House of Commons.

1880.

Aug. 26–Sept. 4. Makes sea trip in the *Grantully Castle* round England and Scotland.

Sept. 4. On government's Turkish policy.

Nov. 9. At lord mayor's banquet on Ireland and foreign and colonial questions.

1881.

Jan. 6. On Ireland.

,, 21. On annexation of Transvaal.

,, 28. On Irish Protection of Person and Property bill.

Feb. 3. Brings in closure resolution.

,, 23. Falls in garden at Downing Street.

March 15. Moves vote of condolence on assassination of Alexander ii.

,, 16. On grant in aid of India for expenses of Afghan war.

,, 28. On county government and local taxation.

April 4. Introduces budget.

,, 7. Brings in Land Law (Ireland) bill.

,, 26 and 27. On Mr. Bradlaugh's case.

May 2. Resigns personal trusteeship of British Museum.

,, 4. Supports Welsh Sunday Closing bill.

,, 5. Supports vote of thanks on military operations in Afghanistan.

,, 9. Tribute to Lord Beaconsfield.

,, 16. On second reading of Irish Land bill.

June 10. On the law of entail.

,, 24. On Anglo-Turkish convention.

July 25. On vote of censure on Transvaal.

,, 29. On third reading of Irish Land bill.

Aug. 6. At Mansion House on fifteen months' administration.

,, 18. On Mr. Parnell's vote of censure on the Irish executive.

Oct. 7. Presented with an address by corporation of Leeds: on land and ' fair trade.'

1881.

At banquet in Old Cloth Hall on Ireland.

Oct. 8. Presented with address by Leeds Chamber of Commerce: on free trade. Mass meeting of 25,000 persons in Old Cloth Hall on foreign and colonial policy.

,, 13. Presented with address by city corporation at Guildhall: on Ireland and arrest of Mr. Parnell.

,, 27. At Knowsley on the aims of the Irish policy.

Nov. 9. At lord mayor's banquet on government's Irish policy and parliamentary procedure.

1882.

Jan. 12. At Hawarden on agriculture.

,, 31. On local taxation to deputation from chambers of agriculture.

Feb. 7. On Mr. Bradlaugh's claim.

,, 9. On home rule amendment to address.

,, 16. On the Irish demand for home rule.

,, 20. Moves first of new procedure rules.

,, 21. On local taxation.

,, 21 and 22. On Mr. Bradlaugh's case.

,, 27. Meeting of liberal party at Downing Street. On House of Lords' committee to inquire into Irish Land Act.

,, 27. Moves resolution declaring parliamentary inquiry into Land Act injurious to interests of good government.

March 3. On persecution of Jews in Russia.

,, 6. Supports resolution for legislation on parliamentary oaths.

,, 10. On proposed state acquisition of Irish railways.

,, 17. On British North Borneo Company's charter.

,, 21. On parliamentary reform.

,, 23. On grant to Duke of Albany.

,, 30. On closure resolution.

1882.

March 31. On inquiry into ecclesiastical commission.

April 17. Opposes motion for release of Cetewayo.

,, 18. On diplomatic communications with Vatican.

,, 24. Introduces budget.

,, 26. On the Irish Land Act Amendment bill.

May 2. Statement of Irish policy, announces release of 'suspects,' and resignation of Mr. Forster.

,, 4. On Mr. Forster's resignation.

,, 8. Moves adjournment of the House on assassination of Lord F. Cavendish and Mr. Burke.

,, 15. Brings in Arrears of Rent (Ireland) bill.

,, 19. On second reading of Prevention of Crime (Ireland) bill.

,, 22. On Arrears bill.

,, 24. On Prevention of Crime bill.

,, 26–June 1. On government's Egyptian policy.

June 14. On Egyptian crisis.

,, 17. On Mr. Bright's resignation.

July 12. On bombardment of Alexandria.

,, 21. On third reading of Arrears bill.

,, 24. Asks for vote of credit for £2,300,000.

,, 27. Concludes debate on vote of credit.

,, 28. On national expenditure.

Aug. 8. On Lords' amendments to Arrears bill.

,, 9. On suspension of Irish members, July 1.

,, 16. On events leading to Egyptian war.

Oct. 25–31, and Dec. 1. On twelve new rules of procedure.

,, 26. Moves vote of thanks to forces engaged in Egyptian campaign.

Nov. 24. Opposes demand for select committee on release of Mr. Parnell.

Dec. 13. Celebrates political jubilee.

1883.

Jan. 6–16. Suffers from sleeplessness at Hawarden.

1883.

Jan. 17. Leaves England for south of France.

March 2. Returns to London.

,, 14. On Irish Land Law (1881) Amendment bill.

,, 16. On Boer invasion of Bechuanaland.

April 3. On Channel tunnel.

,, 6. On increase in national expenditure.

,, 17. On local taxation.

,, 19. On Lords Alcester and Wolseley's annuity bills.

,, 26. On Parliamentary Oaths Act (1866) Amendment bill.

May 2. At National Liberal club on conservative legacy of 1880 and work of liberal administration, 1880–1883.

,, 7. On Contagious Diseases Acts.

,, 25. On reforms in Turkey.

,, 29. Meeting of liberal party at foreign office : on state of public business.

June 2. At Stafford House : tribute to Garibaldi.

,, 12. On revision of purchase clauses of Land Act.

,, 23. On withdrawal of provisional agreement for second Suez canal.

July 27. On India and payment for Egyptian campaign.

,, 30. On future negotiations with Suez canal company.

Aug. 6. On government's Transvaal and Zululand policies.

,, 6–7. On British occupation of Egypt.

,, 18. Protests against violent speeches of Irish members.

,, 21. On work of the session.

Sept. Italian translation of Cowper's hymn : 'Hark my soul ! It is the Lord,' in *Nineteenth Century*.

,, 8–21. In *Pembroke Castle* round coast of Scotland to Norway and Copenhagen.

,, 13. At Kirkwall : on changes during half century of his political life.

1883.

Sept. 18. Entertains the Emperor and Empress of Russia, the King and Queen of Denmark, at dinner on board *Pembroke Castle* in Copenhagen harbour.

Dec. 22. At Hawarden, to deputation of liberal working men on reform of the franchise.

1884.

Jan. 5. At Hawarden on condition of agriculture.

„ 31. Receives deputations from Leeds conference, etc., on Franchise bill.

Feb. 11 and 21. On Mr. Bradlaugh's attempt to take the oath.

„ 12. On Egyptian and Soudan policy in reply to vote of censure.

„ 13. On re-establishment of grand committees.

„ 25. Moves resolution of thanks to Speaker Brand on his retirement.

„ 28. Explains provisions of Representation of the People (Franchise) bill.

March 3. In defence of retention of Suakin.

„ 6. On government's Egyptian policy.

„ 10–19. Confined to his room by a chill.

„ 19 to April 7. Recuperates at Coombe Warren.

„ 31. On death of Duke of Albany.

April 3. On General Gordon's mission in Soudan.

„ 7. On second reading of Franchise bill.

May 12. On vote of censure regarding General Gordon.

„ 27. On Egyptian financial affairs.

June 10. Opposes amendment to Franchise bill granting suffrage to women.

„ 23. On terms of agreement with France on Egypt.

„ 26. On third reading of Franchise bill.

July 8. On second reading of London Government bill.

„ 10. Meeting of the liberal party : on rejection of

1884.

Franchise bill by House of Lords.

July 11. On negotiations with Lord Cairns on Franchise bill.

„ 18. At Eighty club on relation of politics of the past to politics of the future.

Aug. 2. On failure of conference on Egyptian finance.

„ 11. On Lord ·Northbrook's mission to Egypt.

„ 30. At Corn Exchange, Edinburgh, on Lords and Franchise bill.

Sept. 1. At Corn Exchange, Edinburgh, in defence of his administration.

„ 2. In Waverley Market on demand of Lords for dissolution.

„ 26. Returns to Hawarden.

Oct. 16. Cuts first sod on Wirral railway : on railway enterprise.

„ 23. On Franchise bill.

„ 28. Defends Lord Spencer's Irish administration.

Nov. 4. Lays foundation stone of National Liberal club : on liberal administrations of past half century.

„ 6 and 10. On second reading of Franchise bill.

„ 21. On Mr. Labouchere's motion for reform of House of Lords.

Dec. 1. Brings in Redistribution bill.

„ 4. On second reading of Redistribution bill.

1885.

Feb. 23. On vote of censure on Soudan policy.

March 26. Moves ratification of Egyptian financial agreement.

April 9. Announces occupation of Penjdeh by Russians.

„ 16. In defence of Egyptian Loan bill.

„ 21. Asks for vote of credit for war preparations.

„ 27. On Soudan and Afghanistan.

May 4. Announces agreement with Russia on Afghan boundary dispute.

1885.

May 14. On Princess Beatrice's dowry.

June 8. Defends increase of duties on beer and spirits.

„ 9. Resignation of government.

„ 24. Reads correspondence on crisis.

July 6. On legislation on parliamentary oaths.

„ 7. On intentions of the new government.

Aug. 8–Sept. 1. In Norway.

Sept. 17. Issues address to Midlothian electors.

Nov. 'Dawn of Creation and of Worship,' in *Nineteenth Century.*

„ 9. At Albert Hall, Edinburgh, on proposals of Irish party.

„ 11. At Free Assembly Hall, Edinburgh, on disestablishment.

„ 17. At West Calder on Ireland, foreign policy, and free trade.

„ 21. At Dalkeith on finance and land reform.

„ 23. At inauguration of Market Cross, Edinburgh : on history of the cross.

„ 24. At Music Hall, Edinburgh, on tory tactics and Mr. Parnell's charges.

„ 27. Elected for Midlothian : Mr. Gladstone, 7879 ; Mr. Dalrymple, 3248.

1886.

Jan. 'Proem to Genesis : a Plea for a Fair Trial,' in *Nineteenth Century.*

„ 21. On government's policy in India, the Near East and Ireland.

„ 26. In support of amendment for allotments.

Feb. 3. Third administration formed.

„ 4. Issues address to electors of Midlothian.

„ 10. Returned unopposed for Midlothian.

„ 22. On comparative taxation of England and Ireland. On annexation of Burmah.

1886.

Feb. 23. On Ireland's contribution to imperial revenue.

March 4. On condition of Ireland.

„ 6–12. Confined to his room by a cold.

April 6. On death of Mr. W. E. Forster.

„ 8. Brings in Government of Ireland (Home Rule) bill.

„ 13. On first reading of Home Rule bill.

„ 16. Explains provisions of Irish Land Purchase bill.

May 1. Issues address to electors of Midlothian on Home Rule bill.

„ 10. Moves second reading of Home Rule bill.

„ 27. Meeting of liberal party at the foreign office : on the Home Rule bill.

„ 28. Explains intentions regarding the Home Rule bill.

June 7–8. Concludes debate on Home Rule bill.

„ 10. Announces dissolution of parliament.

„ 14. Issues address to electors of Midlothian.

„ 18. At Music Hall, Edinburgh, on home rule.

„ 21. At Music Hall, Edinburgh, on home rule.

„ 22. At Glasgow on home rule.

„ 25. At Free Trade Hall, Manchester, on home rule.

„ 28. At Liverpool on Ulster and home rule.

July 2. Returned unopposed for Midlothian and Leith.

„ 20. Resignation of third administration.

Aug. 19–24. On government's Irish policy.

„ 25. Leaves England for Bavaria.

„ 28. '*The Irish Question:* (1) *History of an Idea;* (2) *Lessons of the Election,*' published.

Sept. 19. Returns to London.

„ 20. On Tenants Relief (Ireland) bill.

Oct. 4. At Hawarden. Receives address signed by 400,000 women of Ireland : on home rule.

1887.

Jan.   '*Locksley Hall* and the Jubilee,' in *Nineteenth Century*.

,,   27.   Tribute to memory of Lord Iddesleigh.

,,   27.   On Lord Randolph Churchill's retirement and Ireland.

Feb.   'Notes and Queries on the Irish Demand,' in *Nineteenth Century*.

March   'The Greater Gods of Olympus: (1) Poseidon,' in *Nineteenth Century*.

,,   17.   To the liberal members for Yorkshire : on home rule.

,,   24.   On the exaction of excessive rents.

,,   29.   On Criminal Law Amendment (Ireland) bill.

April   'The History of 1852–60 and Greville's Latest Journals,' in *English Historical Review*.

,,   18.   On second reading of Criminal Law Amendment bill.

,,   19.   At Eighty club on liberal unionist grammar of dissent.

,,   25.   Criticise Mr. Goschen's budget.

May   'The Greater Gods of Olympus: (2) Apollo,' in *Nineteenth Century*.

,,   5.   Moves for select committee to inquire into the *Times* articles on 'Parnellism and Crime.'

,,   11.   At Dr. Parker's house on Ireland.

,,   31.   On Crimes bill at Hawarden.

June   Reviews Mr. Lecky's *History of England in the Eighteenth Century* in *Nineteenth Century*.

,,   'The Great Olympian Sedition,' in *Contemporary Review*.

,,   4.   At Swansea, on Welsh nationality, Welsh grievances, and the Irish Crimes bill.

,,   6.   At Singleton Abbey on home rule and retention of Irish members.

,,   7.   At Cardiff on home rule.

July   'The Greater Gods of

1887.

     Olympus : (3) Athene,' in *Nineteenth Century*.

,,   2.   To the liberal members for Durham on Lord Hartington's Irish record.

,,   7.   Moves rejection of Irish Criminal Law Amendment bill.

,,   9.   Presented at Dollis Hill with address signed by 10,689 citizens of New York.

,,   14.   On second reading of the Irish Land bill.

,,   16.   At National Liberal club : on Ireland and home rule movement in Scotland and Wales.

,,   29.   At Memorial Hall on the lessons of bye-elections.

Aug.   'Mr. Lecky and Political Morality,' in *Nineteenth Century*.

,,   16.   Lays first cylinder of railway bridge over the Dee : on railway enterprise and the Channel tunnel.

,,   25.   On proclamation of Irish land league.

,,   30.   At Hawarden on Queen Victoria's reign.

Sept.   'Electoral Facts of 1887,' in *Nineteenth Century*.

,,   12.   On riot at Mitchelstown, Ireland.

Oct.   'Ingram's History of the Irish Union,' in *Nineteenth Century*.

,,   4.   At Hawarden on the absolutist methods of government.

,,   18.   At National Liberal Federation, Nottingham, on conduct of Irish police.

,,   19.   At Skating Rink, Nottingham, on home rule.

,,   20.   At Drill Hall, Derby, on Ireland.

Nov.   'An Olive Branch from America,' in *Nineteenth Century*.

Dec.   27.   At Dover on free trade and Irish Crimes Act.

,,   28.   Leaves England for Italy.

1888.

Jan.   'A reply to Dr. Ingram,' in *Westminster Review*.

Feb.   'The Homeric Herê,' in *Contemporary Review*.

1888.

Feb. 8. Returns to London.
,, 17. On coercion in Ireland.
March 'Further Notes and Queries on the Irish Demand,' in *Contemporary Review*.
,, 23. On perpetual pensions.
April 9. On the budget.
,, 11. At National Liberal club on the budget and Local Government bill.
,, 23. Moves an amendment in favour of equalising the death duties on real and personal property.
,, 25. On second reading of County Government (Ireland) bill.
May 'Robert Elsmere, and the Battle of Belief,' in *Nineteenth Century*.
,, A reply to Colonel Ingersoll on 'Christianity,' in *North American Review*.
,, 1. On government control of railways.
,, 2. Opens Gladstone library at National Liberal club: on books.
,, 9. At Memorial Hall on Irish question.
,, 26. At Hawarden condemns licensing clauses of Local Government bill.
,, 30. Receives deputation of 1500 Lancashire liberals at Hawarden.
June 18. On death of German Emperor.
,, 26. Condemns administration of Irish criminal law.
,, 27. On Channel Tunnel bill.
,, 30. At Hampstead on Ireland and the bye-elections.
July 'The Elizabethan Settlement of Religion,' in *Nineteenth Century*.
,, 6. On payment of members.
,, 18. To liberal members for Northumberland and Cumberland on Parnell commission and retention of Irish members.
,, 23. On second reading of Parnell Commission bill.
,, 25. Mr. and Mrs. Gladstone presented with their portraits on entering on fiftieth year of married life.

1888.

July 30. On composition of Parnell commission.
Aug. 20. Receives deputation of 1500 liberals at Hawarden: on conservative government of Ireland.
,, 23. At Hawarden on spade husbandry and the cultivation of fruit.
Sept. 'Mr. Forster and Ireland,' in *Nineteenth Century*.
,, 4. At Wrexham on Irish and Welsh home rule.
,, 4. At the Eisteddfod on English feeling towards Wales.
Nov. 'Queen Elizabeth and the Church of England,' in *Nineteenth Century*.
,, 5. At Town Hall, Birmingham, on liberal unionists and one man one vote.
,, 6. To deputation at Birmingham on labour representation and payment of members.
,, 7. At Bingley Hall, Birmingham, on Irish question.
,, 8. To deputation of Birmingham Irish National club on Irish grievances.
,, 19. On Irish Land Purchase bill.
Dec. 3. On Mr. Balfour's administration of Ireland.
,, 15. At Limehouse Town Hall on necessary English reforms and the Irish question.
,, 17. On English occupation of Suakin.
,, 19. Leaves England for Naples.

1889.

Jan. 'Daniel O'Connell,' in *Nineteenth Century*.
Feb. Reviews *Divorce* by Margaret Lee in *Nineteenth Century*.
,, 20. Returns to London.
March 1. On conciliatory measures in administration of Ireland.
,, 29. On death of John Bright.
April Reviews *For the Right* in *Nineteenth Century*.
,, 4. On £21,000,000 for naval defence.
,, 9. On Scotch home rule.

1889.

May		'Italy in 1888–89,' in *Nineteenth Century.*
,,	15.	On second reading of Welsh Education bill.
,,	16.	Moves amendment to Mr. Goschen's proposed death duties on estates above £10,000.
June	5.	At Southampton on lessons of the bye-elections.
,,	7.	At Romsey on Lord Palmerston.
,,	8.	At Weymouth on shorter parliaments and Ireland.
,,	10.	At Torquay on Ireland.
,,	11.	At Falmouth and Redruth on Ireland.
,,	12.	At Truro, St. Austell, and Bodmin on Ireland, one man one vote, the death duties, etc.
,,	14.	At Launceston on dissentient liberals.
,,	14.	At Drill Hall, Plymouth, on home rule.
,,	17.	At Shaftesbury and Gillingham on the agricultural labourer.
July		'Plain Speaking on the Irish Union,' in *Nineteenth Century.*
,,	6.	Presented with freedom of Cardiff; on free trade; on foreign opinion of English rule in Ireland.
,,	25.	Golden wedding celebrated in London.
,,	25.	Speech on royal grants.
Aug.		'Phœnician Affinities of Ithaca,' in *Nineteenth Century.*
,,	22.	At Hawarden on cottage gardens and fruit culture.
,,	26.	Celebration of golden wedding at Hawarden.
Sept.	7.	Entertained in Paris by Society of Political Economy.
,,	23.	At Hawarden on dock strike and bimetallism.
,,		'The Triple Alliance and Italy's Place in it,' by Outidanos, in *Contemporary Review.*
Oct.		Reviews *Journal de Marie Bashkirtseff* in *Nineteenth Century.*
,,	23.	At Southport on Ireland.
,,	26.	Opens literary institute at Saltney, Chester.

1889.

Nov.		'The English Church under Henry the Eighth,' in *Nineteenth Century.*
,,		'The Question of Divorce,' in *North American Review.*
Dec.		Reviews *Memorials of a Southern Planter* in *Nineteenth Century.*
,,	2.	At Free Trade Hall, Manchester, on liberal unionists and foreign policy.
,,	3.	In Free Trade Hall on government of Ireland.
,,	4.	At luncheon at Town Hall on city of Manchester.

1890.

Jan.		'A Defence of Free Trade,' in *North American Review.*
,,		'The Melbourne Government: its Acts and Persons,' in *Nineteenth Century.*
,,	9.	At Hawarden on the effect of free trade on agriculture.
,,	22.	At Chester on Ireland.
Feb.	5.	At Oxford Union on vestiges of Assyrian mythology in Homer.
,,	11.	On motion declaring publication by *Times* of forged Parnell letter to be breach of privilege.
March		'On Books and the Housing of Them,' in *Nineteenth Century.*
,,	3.	On report of Parnell commission.
,,	24.	At National Liberal club on report of Parnell commission.
,,	26.	At Guy's Hospital on the medical profession.
April	24.	On second reading of Purchase of Land (Ireland) bill.
May	2.	On disestablishment of church of Scotland.
,,	12.	On free trade at Prince's Hall, Piccadilly.
,,	15.	On Local Taxation Duties bill.
,,	16.	At Norwich on Parnell commission, land purchase and licensing question.
,,	17.	At Lowestoft on Siberian

1890.

atrocities and the agricultural labourer.

April 27. Receives 10,000 liberals at Hawarden : on Mitchelstown, Irish Land bill, and Licensing bill.

June 5. On Channel Tunnel bill.

„ 13. On Local Taxation Duties bill.

„ 18. To depositors in railways' savings banks : on thrift.

July 17. At Burlington School, London, on the education of women.

„ 24. On Anglo-German Agreement bill.

„ 30. To Wesleyans at National Liberal club on Maltese marriage question, and Ireland.

Aug. 21. At Hawarden on cottage gardening and fruit farming.

„ 30. 'Dr. Döllinger's Posthumous Remains,' in the *Speaker.*

Sept. 12. At Dee iron works on industrial progress.

Oct. 21. At Corn Exchange, Edinburgh, on government's Irish administration.

„ 23. At West Calder on condition of working classes and Ireland.

„ 25. At Dalkeith on home rule for Scotland and Ireland.

„ 27. At Music Hall, Edinburgh, on retention of Irish members, procedure and obstruction.

„ 29. At Dundee on free trade and the McKinley tariff. Opens Victorian Art Gallery : on appreciation of beauty.

Nov. 'Mr. Carnegie's Gospel of Wealth,' in *Nineteenth Century.*

„ 24. Letter to Mr. Morley on Mr. Parnell and leadership of Irish party.

Dec. 1. Publishes reply to Mr. Parnell's manifesto to Irish people.

„ 2. On Purchase of Land (Ireland) bill.

„ 11. At Retford on Mr. Parnell and the home rule cause.

1890.

Publishes *The Impregnable Rock of Holy Scripture*, a reprint of articles in *Good Words. Landmarks of Homeric Study, together with an Essay on the Points of Contact between the Assyrian Tablets and the Homeric Text.*

1891.

Jan. 27. Supports motion to expunge from journals of the House the Bradlaugh resolution (1881).

Feb. 'Professor Huxley and the Swine-Miracle,' in *Nineteenth Century.*

„ 4. Moves second reading of Religious Disabilities Removal bill.

„ 13. Opens free library in St. Martin's Lane : on free libraries.

„ 16. Condemns action of Irish executive in Tipperary trials.

„ 20. On disestablishment of church in Wales.

„ 27. On taxation of land.

March 3. On registration reform.

„ 14. At Eton College on Homeric Artemis.

„ 17. At Hastings on Mr. Goschen's finance, Irish policy, and the career of Mr. Parnell.

May 'A Memoir of John Murray,' in *Murray's Magazine.*

June 19. At St. James's Hall, at jubilee of Colonial Bishoprics Fund, on development of colonial church.

July 4. Death of W. H. Gladstone.

„ 15. At Hawarden on fifty years of progress.

Sept. 'Electoral Facts, No. III.,' in *Nineteenth Century.*

Oct. 'On the Ancient Beliefs in a Future State,' in *Nineteenth Century.*

„ 1. At jubilee of Glenalmond College on study of nature and the clerical profession.

„ 2. At Newcastle on the liberal programme.

1891.

Nov. 3. At Newcastle on local self-government and freedom of trade.

,, 28. At Wirral on home rule. At Sunlight Soap works on profit-sharing and co-operation.

Dec. 11. At Holborn Restaurant to conference of labourers on rural reforms.

,, 15. Leaves London for Biarritz.

1892.

Feb.-May 'On the Olympian Religion,' in *North American Review*.

,, 29. Returns to London.

March 3. Opposes grant of £20,000 for survey of Uganda railway.

,, 16. On Welsh Land Tenure bill.

,, 24. On Small Agricultural Holdings bill.

,, 28. On Indian Councils Act (1861) Amendment bill.

April Reviews *The Platform, its Rise and Progress*, in *Nineteenth Century*.

,, 28. On Church Discipline (Immorality) bill.

May 24. On Local Government (Ireland) bill.

,, 31. At Memorial Hall on London government.

June 'Did Dante Study in Oxford?' in *Nineteenth Century*.

,, 5. At Dalkeith on Scotch home rule and disestablishment.

,, 16. Receives deputation from London trades council on Eight Hours bill.

,, 18. To nonconformists at Clapham on Ulster and home rule.

,, 24. Issues address to electors of Midlothian.

,, 25. Struck in the eye by piece of gingerbread in Chester. At Liberal club on the general election, the appeal to religious bigotry, and disestablishment.

,, 30. At Edinburgh Music Hall on Lord Salisbury's manifesto, home rule,

1892.

and retention of Irish members.

July 2. At Glasgow on Orangeism and home rule.

,, 4. At Gorebridge on labour questions.

,, 6. At Corstorphine on government's record.

,, 7. At West Calder on protection, the hours of labour and home rule.

,, 11. At Penicuik on conservative responsibility for recent wars, finance, disestablishment, and Irish question.

,, 13. Elected for Midlothian: Mr. Gladstone, 5845; Colonel Wauchope, 5155.

Aug. 9. On vote of want of confidence.

,, 15. Fourth administration formed.

,, 24. Returned unopposed for Midlothian.

,, 29. Knocked down by heifer in Hawarden Park.

Sept. 5. A paper on Archaic Greece and the East read before Congress of Orientalists.

,, 12. At Carnarvon on case of Wales.

Oct. 'A Vindication of Home Rule: a Reply to the Duke of Argyll,' in *North American Review*.

,, 22. Cuts first sod of the new Cheshire railway: on migration of population and mineral produce of Wales.

,, 24. Delivers Romanes lecture at Oxford on history of universities.

Dec. 3. Presented with freedom of Liverpool: on history of Liverpool and Manchester ship canal.

,, 21. Leaves England for Biarritz.

1893.

Jan. 10. Returns to England.

,, 31. Replies to Mr. Balfour's criticisms on the address.

Feb. 3. On Mr. Labouchere's amendment in favour of evacuation of Uganda.

1893.

Feb. 8. On amendment praying for immediate legislation for agricultural labourers.

,, 11. On motion for restriction of alien immigration.

,, 13. Brings in Government of Ireland (Home Rule) bill.

,, 28. On motion for international monetary conference.

March 3. Receives deputation from the miners' federation on Eight Hours bill.

,, 20. On Sir Gerald Portal's mission to Uganda.

,, 27. Meeting of the liberal party at foreign office: on programme for session.

,, 27. On Mr. Balfour's motion censuring action of Irish executive.

,, 28. Receives deputations from Belfast manufacturers and city of London merchants protesting against home rule.

April 6. Moves second reading of Home Rule bill.

,, 19. Receives a deputation from the miners' National Union on Eight Hours bill.

,, 21. Replies to criticisms on Home Rule bill.

May 1. On the occupation of Egypt.

,, 2. Receives a deputation of the Mining Association in opposition to Eight Hours bill.

,, 3. On second reading of Miners' Eight Hours bill.

,, 11. Replies to Mr. Chamberlain's speech on first clause of Home Rule bill.

,, 23. Opens Hawarden institute: on the working classes.

,, 29. At Chester on Home Rule bill.

June 'Some Eton Translations,' in Contemporary Review.

,, 16. On arbitration between England and United States.

,, 22. Statement regarding the financial clauses of Home Rule bill.

1893.

June 28. Moves resolution for closing debate on committee stage of Home Rule bill.

July 12. Announces government's decision regarding the retention of Irish members at Westminster.

,, 14. Moves address of congratulation on marriage of Duke of York.

,, 21. Moves a new clause to Home Rule bill regulating financial relations.

Aug. 5. At Agricultural Hall, Islington, on industry and art.

,, 30. Moves third reading of Home Rule bill.

Sept. 27. At Edinburgh on House of Lords and the Home Rule bill.

Nov. 9. On Matabeleland and the chartered company.

Dec. 19. On naval policy of the government.

1894.

Jan. 13. Leaves England for Biarritz.

Feb. 10. Returns to England.

March 1. On the Lords' amendments to Parish Councils bill.

,, 3. Resigns the premiership.

,, 7. Confined to bed by severe cold.

,, 17. At Brighton. Letter to Sir John Cowan — his farewell to parliamentary life.

May 'The Love Odes of Horace — five specimens,' in Nineteenth Century.

,, 3. At Prince's Hall on life and work of Sir Andrew Clark.

,, 24. Right eye operated on for cataract.

July 7. Announces decision not to seek re-election to parliament.

Aug. 'The Place of Heresy and Schism in the Modern Christian Church,' in Nineteenth Century.

,, 14. On cottage gardening at Hawarden.

,, 16. Receives deputation of 1500 liberals from Torquay at Hawarden.

1894.

Sept.   'The True and False Con-
             ception of the Atone-
             ment,' in *Nineteenth
             Century*.
Dec.   29.   Receives deputation from
             the Armenian national
             church at Hawarden.

1895.

Jan.   7.   Presented with an album
             by Irish-Americans : in
             favour of Irish unity.
,,   8.   Leaves England for south
             of France.
March   Publishes *The Psalter with
             a concordance*.
,,   'The Lord's Day,' in
             Church Monthly; con-
             cluded in April number.
,,   23.   Returns to England from
             France.
,,   15.   At Hawarden to a deputa-
             tion of Leeds and Hud-
             dersfield liberal clubs :
             on English people and
             political power, and on
             advantages of libraries.
June 12-24. Cruise in *Tantallon
             Castle* to Hamburg,
             Copenhagen, and Kiel.
July   1.   Farewell letter to Mid-
             lothian constituents.
Aug.   5.   At Hawarden on small
             holdings and his old
             age.
,,   6.   At Chester on Armenian
             question.
Nov.   'Bishop Butler and his
             Censors,' in *Nineteenth
             Century;* concluded in
             December number.
Dec.   28.   Leaves England for
             Biarritz and Cannes.

1896.

Feb.   Publishes *The Works of
             Bishop Butler*.
March 10.   Returns to England from
             Cannes.
,,   28.   At Liverpool on the de-
             velopment of the Eng-
             lish railway system.
April   'The Future Life and the
             Condition of Man There-
             in,' in *North American
             Review*.
,,   Contributes an article on
             'The Scriptures and

1896.

             Modern Criticism ' to
             the *People's Bible*.
May   *Soliloquium and Postscript*
             —a letter to the Arch-
             bishop of York, pub-
             lished.
June   'Sheridan,' in *Nineteenth
             Century*.
"   1.   Letter on Anglican Orders
             published.
Aug.   3.   At Hawarden horticultural
             show on rural life.
Sept.   1.   At fête in aid of Hawarden
             Institute on progress of
             music.
,,   2.   At Hawarden fête on
             Welsh music.
,,   24.   At Hengler's circus, Liver-
             pool, on Armenian
             question.
Oct.   'The Massacres in Tur-
             key,' in *Nineteenth Cen-
             tury*.
,,   16.   At Penmaenmawr in praise
             of seaside resorts.

1897.

Jan.   29.   Leaves England for
             Cannes.
March 19.   Letter to the Duke of
             Westminster on the
             Cretan question pub-
             lished.
,,   30.   Returns to England from
             Cannes.
May   4.   At Hawarden on the con-
             dition of the clergy.
June   2.   Opens Victoria jubilee
             bridge over the Dee at
             Queensferry.
Aug.   2.   At Hawarden horticultural
             show on small culture.
Nov.   26.   Leaves England for
             Cannes.

1898.

Jan.   5.   'Personal Recollections of
             Arthur H. Hallam,' in
             Daily Telegraph.
Feb.   18.   Returns to London from
             Cannes.
,,   22.   Goes to Bournemouth.
March 22.   Returns to Hawarden.
May   19.   Death of Mr. Gladstone.
,, 26, 27.   Lying in state in West-
             minster Hall.
,,   28.   Burial in Westminster
             Abbey.

INDEX

ABERDARE, Lord (Henry Austin Bruce), home secretary (1868), ii. 644 ; on Collier affair, ii. 385; on Ewelme case, ii. 387; Licensing bill of, ii. 389-390 ; on *Alabama* case, ii. 409 *note* ; on Irish University bill, ii. 439; Gladstone's appreciation of, ii. 462 ; president of the council (1873), ii. 463 *note*, 645; describes last cabinet meeting (1874), ii. 497; otherwise mentioned, ii. 421, 504; iii. 386.

—— papers, extract from, on position in 1872, ii. 389.

Aberdeen, Gladstone presented with freedom of, ii. 378.

Aberdeen, 4th Earl of : —

Chronology — on Wellington's anti-reform speech, i. 69; Gladstone's visit to (1836), i. 137; at Canada meeting, i. 641; party meetings, i. 239; on Maynooth resignation, i. 273; Gladstone's relations with, i. 280; estimate of Peel, i. 283; on Peel's eulogium of Cobden, i. 292; on freedom in official position, i. 298; home and foreign policy of, contrasted, i. 367; learns Gladstone's views of Neapolitan tyranny, i. 390, 393-395; on Don Pacifico case, i. 395; Gladstone's Letters to, i. 392, 394 *and note*, 396, 398, 399 *note* 2, 400, 401 *note* 3, 641, 642; views on papal aggression question, i. 405, 407; asked to form a government (1851), i. 405 *and note*; leader of Peelites, i. 408; Reform bill of (1852), ii. 238; attitude of, towards first Derby administration, i. 417, 419, 429; on Gladstone's attitude towards Disraeli, i. 432; on possible heads for Peelite government, i. 443; Irish attitude towards, i. 444; undertakes to form a government, i. 445; Gladstone's budget, i. 464-466; letter to Prince Albert on Gladstone's speech, i. 468; letter to Gladstone, i. 469; attitude towards Turkey in 1828, i. 480;

Crimean war, preliminary negotiations, i. 481-484, 487, 490; on Gladstone's Manchester speech, i. 483; on effect of Crimean war, i. 484; suggests retirement, i. 491-492; opposes postponement of Reform bill, i. 648; regrets of, regarding the war, i. 494, 536-537; defeat of, ii. 653; Gladstone's consultations with, in ministerial crisis (1855), i. 526, 530-535; on position of premier, ii. 416; Gladstone's projected letters to, on Sebastopol committee, i. 542 *note*; discourages Gladstone's communicating with Derby, i. 556; Lewis's budget, i. 560; Divorce bill, i. 570; Conspiracy bill, i. 575; approves Gladstone's refusals to join Derby, i. 578, 586; uneasiness regarding Gladstone's position, i. 581; Gladstone's visit to, i. 594; discourages Ionian project, i. 595; desires closer relations between Gladstone and government, i. 596; Arthur Gordon's letter to, i. 604; Bright's visit to, i. 626 *note* 2; death of, ii. 87.

Foreign influence of, i. 392, 529; foreign estimate of, ii. 351; iii. 321.

Gladstone's estimate of, i. 124, 393, 417; ii. 87, 639-644; his estimate of Gladstone, i. 613; ii. 170, 203; Gladstone's letters to, i. 425-426, 429, 463, 549; ii. 3.

Palmerston contrasted with, i. 530.

Patience of, with colleagues' quarrels, i. 520; loyalty to colleagues, ii. 639-640.

Sobriquet of, i. 177.

Trustfulness of, i. 197; ii. 113, 640, 642-643.

Otherwise mentioned, i. 139, 142 *note*, 270, 293, 294, 367, 420, 437, 458, 460, 482 *note*, 520, 539, 543, 548, 584; ii. 184, 194; iii. 228.

Aberdeen, 7th Earl of, iii. 385, 517.

Abeken, H., ii. 332-333 *and note*.

Abercromby, Sir Ralph, iii. 314.
Abolition, *see* slave-holding.
Acland, A. H. D., iii. 495 *and note*.
—— Arthur, i. 54, 59 *note*, 74.
—— Sir H. W., iii. 421.
—— Sir Thomas, member of W E G, i. 59 *note*; brotherhood formed by Gladstone and, i. 99; advice to Gladstone on Jewish disabilities question, i. 376; correspondence with Gladstone on popular discontent, ii. 172–174; on Gladstone's position (1867), ii. 227; otherwise mentioned, i. 54, 74, 148; ii. 280, 430, 431; iii. 495.
Act of Uniformity bill (1872), ii. 410.
Acton, Lord, recommended by Gladstone for a peerage, ii. 430; correspondence with Gladstone on Vaticanism, ii. 509, 511, 515, 519–521; compared with Döllinger, ii. 558; letter on Gladstone's proposed retirement, iii. 172; elected fellow of All Souls', iii. 421; Gladstone's letters to, i. 481, 628; ii. 1, 214; iii. 355–359, 413–416, 422, 456, 457, 544; criticism of Gladstone, iii. 360–361; otherwise mentioned, ii. 254, 617; iii. 103, 351, 462.
Adam, W. P., commissioner of public works, ii. 463 *note*; supports Gladstone's Midlothian candidature, ii. 584–585; otherwise mentioned, ii. 586, 602, 620.
Adams, Charles Francis (American minister), hints withdrawal, ii. 80 *and note*[2], 83; Evarts coadjutor to, ii. 189; breakfasts with Gladstone, ii. 212–213; on *Alabama* case, ii. 395–396; work on the arbitration board, ii. 411–412.
Adderley, C. B., quoted, i. 362 *note*[2].
Adullamites, ii. 205, 211, 224, 225.
Advertisements, tax on, i. 459, 462 *and note*.
Affirmation bill (1883), i. 414 *note*; iii. 14, 18–20, 107 *note*, 312.
Afghanistan:—
Cavagnari in, iii. 151.
Reversal of conservative policy in, iii. 10.
Russian action in (1885), iii. 178, 183–185, 208 *note*.
War with, ii. 583; Gladstone's references to, ii. 592, 595.
Africa South:—
Cape Colony—
Dutch sympathy in, with Transvaal, iii. 39–40 *and note*[2], 42 *note*[2], 43.

Representatives from, on South African situation, iii. 33.
Cape of Good Hope petition, ii. 545.
Confederation scheme, iii. 22–24, 31.
Frere in, iii. 2, 6.
Native affairs in, committee on, i. 358.
Orange Free State—
Advice from, iii. 32–33.
Sympathy in, with Transvaal, iii. 39–40 *and note*[2], 43.
Transvaal—
Administration of, by Great Britain, iii. 31 *and note*[1].
Annexation of (1877), iii. 25; Boer resistance to annexation, iii. 25–26, 31; Gladstone's attitude towards, iii. 27; Hartington's attitude to, iii. 27.
Cabinet abstentions on division regarding, iii. 35.
Commission suggested by Boers, iii. 35; suggestion accepted, iii. 36 *and note*[1], 40; constitution of commission, iii. 41; Boer requests regarding, refused, iii. 41; parliamentary attack on appointment, iii. 41–42; Boer attitude towards, iii. 44; Pretoria convention concluded by, iii. 44–45.
Conventions with, iii. 45 *and note*.
Forces in, iii. 31, *note*[2].
Midlothian reference to (1879), ii. 595; (1885), iii. 248.
Misrepresentations regarding Boers, iii. 31.
Native struggles with Boers in, iii. 24.
Rising of, iii. 31–32; course of hostilities, iii. 34–37; armistice, iii. 39.
Self-government promised to, iii. 25, 28 *and note*[2], 29, 30 *and note*[2]; promises evaded, iii. 30, 33.
W. H. Smith's view of proceedings in, ii. 601.
Suzerainty question, iii. 45 *and note*.
Sympathy with, from South African Dutch, iii. 39–40 *and note*[2], 42 *note*[2], 43.
Ailesbury, Lord, ii. 556.
Airey, Sir Richard, i. 651.
Alabama claims—
Arbitration accepted on, ii. 405.
Gladstone's views on, ii. 394, 396–397, 406, 409, 538.

Indirect damages claimed by Sumner, ii. 399, 406–412.
Mixed commission proposed to deal with, ii. 397; refused by United States, ii. 398; accepted, ii. 400; constitution of, ii. 400–401; work of, ii. 401–405.
Origin of, ii. 393–394.
Parliamentary anxieties regarding, ii. 390.
Soreness regarding, ii. 392.
Albania, i. 605–608.
Albert, Prince, speeches at Suppression of Slave Trade meeting, i. 227; on Peel's retirement, i. 293; presented with Gladstone's translation of *Farini*, i. 403 *note*; Gladstone's budget submitted to, i. 464; on Gladstone's budget speech, i. 469; unpopularity of, ii. 426, 652; views on Roebuck committee, i. 537; estimate of Gladstone, ii. 28; on *Trent* affair, ii. 74; on Danish question, ii. 93, 102; death of, ii. 89; Gladstone's estimate of, ii. 90–91; effect of his death on Gladstone's relations with the Queen, ii. 91; statue to, at Aberdeen, ii. 100; otherwise mentioned, i. 242, 274, 541; ii. 14, 92.
Albert Victor, Prince, iii. 322.
Alderson, Baron, i. 381.
Alfred, Prince, ii. 98, 99, 105.
Alexander II., Emperor of Russia, ii. 499.
Alexander III., Emperor of Russia, iii. 116, 117.
Alexandretta, project to seize, ii. 573.
Alexandria, English and French fleets at, iii. 79; bombardment of, iii. 81, 84, 85.
Alice, Princess, *see* Louis.
All the Talents ministry, i. 446.
Allon, Dr., ii. 134–135, 255, 458.
Alsace, annexation of, ii. 346–348.
Althorp, Viscount, Gladstone's first intercourse with, i. 101; dissuades Howick from moving for papers on Vreedenhoop, i. 105; views on Ashley's factory proposals, i. 106; Cobbett snubbed by, i. 114; contrasted with Russell, i. 118; action of, on tithe collection, i. 133; Grey opposed by, i. 430; otherwise mentioned, i. 103, 115, 649; ii. 436; iii. 503.
America: —
Canada, *see that title.*
British North, ii. 607.
United States, *see that title.*
American civil war, *see under* United States.

Annuities bill, ii. 52–53, 125.
Anonymous articles by Gladstone, ii. 345 *note* [1]; iii. 415.
Anson, Sir W. (warden of All Souls'), iii. 421.
Anstice, Prof., i. 55–56, 58, 59 *note*, 65, 74, 162, 134.
Antonelli, Cardinal, ii. 215.
Antony and Cleopatra at Drury Lane, ii. 476.
Aosta, Duke of, ii. 327.
Appointments and honours, Gladstone's care in selections for, ii. 428; iii. 97.
Arabi, iii. 73, 80, 83, 85–86.
Arbitration in *Alabama* case, ii. 405, 411–412; soreness at award, ii. 392, 413.
Arbuthnot, George, i. 519; ii. 182, 193.
Argyll, Duke of, on presbyterian view of a church, i. 158 *note*; attitude towards Gladstone's budget, i. 466; on postponement of Reform bill, i. 648; attitude towards French treaty scheme, ii. 22; on Paper Duties bill, ii. 33, 37; ecclesiastical views, ii. 37; supports Gladstone on estimates struggle, ii. 140; views on Danish question, ii. 192; advises dissolution on Reform bill, ii. 209; in Rome, ii. 217; the pope's estimate of, ii. 218; views on annexation of Alsace and Lorraine, ii. 347; on *Alabama* case, ii. 403; views on Gladstone's retirement, ii. 505; views on J. S. Mill memorial, ii. 543; on Bulgarian question, ii. 552; Hawarden, ii. 582; Indian secretary (1868), ii. 644; lord privy seal (1880), ii. 653; letter to Gladstone on outside influence, iii. 4; views on Transvaal commission, iii. 41; divergence of views from Chamberlain's, iii. 48–49; resignation, ii. 654; iii. 90; on Disturbance Compensation bill, iii. 113; on franchise disagreement (1884), iii. 127; suggested to effect conference between leaders on Franchise bill, i. 135; letter to Gladstone on election address, iii. 220–221; views on Carnarvon's interview with Parnell, iii. 229 *note* [1]; on Irish situation, iii. 280–281; refuses Gladstone's invitation to birthday dinner, iii. 322; on land question, iii. 477; Gladstone's letters to, i. 652; ii. 45, 73, 76, 288–290, 295, 462, 475, 500, 520, 524, 563, 564, 615, 636; otherwise mentioned, i. 420, 492, 495, 536, 539, 624, 635–636; ii. 47 *notes*; ii. 72, 183, 212, 459, 504, 644.

Aristotle, i. 131, 207 *note*[2].
Armellini, iii. 464.
Armenian atrocities, iii. 521, 522.
Armitstead, George, iii. 463 *and note*, 493, 525, 533.
Armstrong, E. J., ii. 195 *and note*.
Army : —
  Cardwell's work for, ii. 359.
  Commander-in-chief, position of in Parliament, ii. 362, 649.
  Estimates for (1874), ii. 483.
  Purchase abolished, ii. 361–365.
  Short service system, ii. 626, 649.
  War office, qualifications for, ii. 649.
Arnold, Matthew, views of, on *Peter Bell*, i. 220; appointment sought by, ii. 540; views on copyright, ii. 541; poem on his father, iii. 483; estimate of Wordsworth, iii. 448; on Christianity, iii. 520.
Arnold, Dr. T., sermons of, read by Gladstone, i. 100, 135; view of the church, i. 158; attitude towards Newman, i. 165; on Gladstone's first book, i. 176; on Jerusalem bishopric, i. 308; M. Arnold's poem on, iii. 483.
—— Mrs. T., iii. 358.
Ashley, Lord, on factory legislation, i. 106; on Jerusalem bishopric, i. 308, 309; votes against Gladstone at Oxford, i. 333.
—— Evelyn, ii. 51 *and note*, 153, 154, 252.
Asquith, H. H., iii. 495 *note*.
Athenæum Club, ii. 174.
Athens, i. 605; iii. 91.
Attwood, Thomas, i. 114 *note*.
Augustenburg, Duke of, ii. 116, 580.
Augustine, Saint, i. 117, 161, 207 *note*[2]; ii. 544.
d'Aumale, Duc, ii. 190.
Austin, Charles, i. 229; iii. 464.
Australia, convict transportation to, i. 359 *and note*.
Austria : —
  Alliance with, Gladstone's view of, i. 546.
  Berlin memorandum, ii. 549.
  Berlin treaty obligation, attitude towards (1880), iii. 9.
  Black Sea provisions of Treaty of Paris disapproved by, ii. 350.
  Bosnia and Herzegovina transferred to, ii. 576; iii. 82.
  Confusion in policy of, ii. 120.
  Danubian provinces, quasi-independence of, opposed by, ii. 3.
  Eastern question, attitude towards, ii. 549, 571.

Egyptian question, attitude towards, iii. 80, 82.
Excessive expenditure, effects of, ii. 53.
France, peace with, Lord Elcho's motion on, ii. 19 *note*[2]; expects aid from, ii. 337; alliance sought by (1870), ii. 323; efforts to avert Franco-Prussian war, ii. 326; neutrality during the war, ii. 344.
Ionian Islands despatch, attitude towards, i. 601.
Italy, tyranny in and war with, i. 390–402, 618, 620 *note*[3]; ii. 6 *et seq.*, 641.
Midlothian references to, iii. 8.
Prussia — attitude of, i. 489 ; war with, ii. 115, 210 *note*, 214.
Russia — policy towards, i. 488; hostility of, ii. 4.
Sadowa, defeat at, ii. 115.
Slowness of, ii. 4.
Tariff negotiations with, i. 267.
Ayrton, A. S., ii. 460–461, 463–464, 651.
d'Azeglio, ii. 17.

Bach's passion music, ii. 582.
Bacon, Lord, cited, ii. 30.
Badeley, ——, i. 380 *note*[2].
Bagehot, W., ii. 62.
Baker, Sir Samuel, iii. 145 *note*[2], 161.
Balfour, A. J., Gladstone's communications with, on Irish situation, iii. 259, 284; Irish secretary, iii. 374; on Irish rents, iii. 374; compared to Halifax, iii. 378; Irish administration of, iii. 378–379; Mitchelstown, iii. 381–382; on adverse bye-elections, iii. 427; defends Irish policy at Newcastle, i. 428; replies to Gladstone, iii. 490; moves vote of censure on Irish administration, iii. 501; tribute to Gladstone, iii. 510, 530.
Ball, Dr., ii. 264, 269.
Ballot, Gladstone's opposition to (1833), i. 99, 106; his later views (1870–71), ii. 367–368; recommended by committee, ii. 367; government bill (1870), ii. 368–369; results of, ii. 370.
Balmoral, Gladstone's visits to, ii. 97–106; Queen's fondness for, ii. 426.
Bangor, bishopric of, i. 260 *note*[1].
Bank Charter Act (1833), iii. 300.
—— of England, Gladstone in conflict with, i. 518–519, 650–651.
Bankruptcy bill (1883), iii. 112.
Banks, abolition of private notes of, desired by Gladstone, ii. 650–651.

Baptist, Chamberlain's article in, iii. 367 *and note* [2].

Baring, Bingham, ii. 534.

—— Sir E., administration of, iii. 119; advises abandonment of Soudan, iii. 147; agrees on fitness of Gordon for the work, iii. 149; warns Granville of difficulties, iii. 149, 151; telegram to, approved by Gladstone, iii. 150; procures nomination of Gordon as governor-general of Soudan for evacuation, iii. 152; gives him an executive mission, iii. 153; Gordon's request to, regarding Zobeir, iii. 155; supports request, iii. 157; forbids Gordon's advance to Equatoria, iii. 162; advises immediate preparations for relief of Gordon, iii. 163; position of, iii. 179; advises abandonment of Khartoum expedition, iii. 180.

—— Sir Francis, Macaulay and Gladstone contrasted by, i. 192–193; in whig opposition, i. 420 *and note* [1]; estimate of the coalition, i. 449–450 *and note* [1]; refuses to succeed Gladstone, i. 539.

—— T., i. 417.

Barker, Mr., i. 341, 345.

Barrow, ii. 536; iii. 467 *note*.

Bassetlaw election (1890), iii. 452.

Bath, Lord, ii. 617.

Bathurst, Lord, i. 142 *note*.

Baxter, W. E., ii. 463 *note*.

Beach, Sir M. Hicks, colonial secretary, iii. 26; negotiations with Hartington on Franchise bill, iii. 134, 136; moves amendment on budget (1885), iii. 200, 206; views on Spencer's Irish policy, iii. 213; in debate on the address, iii. 285; gives notice regarding Irish bill, iii. 287; on Collings' amendment, iii. 288; on suggestion of withdrawal of Home Rule bill after second reading, iii. 334; speech on night of the division, iii. 337–338; Irish secretary (1886), iii. 362; denounces Parnell's bill, iii. 369; repudiates policy of blackmail, iii. 369, 373; retires from secretaryship, iii. 374.

Beaconsfield, Earl of (Benjamin Disraeli) : —

Chronology — Views on slavery, i. 104–105; Gladstone's first meeting with, i. 122; on free trade, i. 265; on Gladstone's Maynooth resignation, i. 279; taunts Peel with inconsistency, i. 286; on Peel's party relations, i. 289; young England group of, i. 304–305; motion on

agricultural distress (1850), i. 354; supported by Gladstone, i. 354–356; on Cobden, i. 352; view of the colonies, i. 361; Don Pacifico debate, i. 368–369; Peel's forecast regarding, i. 374; on Ecclesiastical Titles bill, i. 414; in Derby's cabinet (1852), i. 416; on protection (1852), i. 425, 428; Aylesbury speeches, i. 428–429, 452; combination of, with Palmerston suggested, i. 431; attitude towards Peel, i. 432; on free trade, i. 432; Herbert's speech against, i. 433, 435 *and note*; budget of (1852), i. 435–440, 459; defeat of, on house duty (1852), iii. 203 *note* [2]; acceptance of defeat, i. 441–442; remark on coalition government, i. 446; correspondence with Gladstone on valuation of furniture, i. 457–458; opposes Gladstone's attempted operation on national debt, i. 472–473; on Oxford reform, i. 507–508; willing to yield leadership of Commons to Palmerston, i. 525; views on Derby's failure to form a ministry, i. 527–528; leadership of Commons by, discussed, i. 552, 555; overtures to Genl. Peel, i. 555; Derby's relations with, i. 555, 561; conversant of Derby's communications with Gladstone, i. 559; on Lewis' budget, i. 560, 561; denounces China war, i. 564; on ministerial blundering as occasion for international quarrel, i. 576; animosity against, i. 581; attitude towards Graham, i. 584, 587; Herbert's alleged attitude towards, i. 585; letter to Gladstone, i. 586; conversation with Vitzthum, i. 591 *note*; remark to Wilberforce regarding Gladstone, i. 591 *note*; schemes of, regarding government of India, i. 592; Ionian schemes attributed to, i. 613; opposes union of the Principalities, ii. 4; Gladstone's renewed conflicts with, ii. 19; on Gladstone's efforts for economy, ii. 42; on excessive expenditure, ii. 48; estimate of financial statements of, ii. 55; on Danish question, ii. 118–120; on Gladstone's franchise pronouncement, ii. 127; on franchise (1859), ii. 200; taunts Gladstone on Oxford speech, ii. 203;

Beaconsfield, Earl of — *continued*.
Chronology — continued.
on Reform bill (1866), ii. 205;
position in Derby government
(1866), ii. 211; Reform bill of 1867,
ii. 223–236; thirteen resolutions,
iii. 300 *note*[4]; cabinet divisions
of, iii. 175; proposals for Ireland,
ii. 242; becomes premier, ii. 244;
on Irish church question, ii. 247;
on the bill, ii. 264, 265 *and note*,
274, 275, 280; dissolves, ii. 248;
resigns, ii. 252; on Irish Land bill,
ii. 295; taunts Gladstone on Irish
policy, ii. 297; on Franco-Prussian
question, ii. 329, 335; on crown
prerogative, ii. 364; watchfulness
during 1872, ii. 390; speech at
Manchester, ii. 390; strikes im-
perialist note, ii. 391; on *Alabama*
case, ii. 401, 406, 407; Irish University question, ii. 435, 444; action during ministerial crisis, ii.
447–450, 452–456; Brand's view of
position of, ii. 456; letter at Bath
election, ii. 475; on Gladstone's
manifesto, ii. 488; counter manifesto, ii. 488–489; on the dissolution (1874), ii, 496; letters from,
on his wife's illness and death,
ii. 546–547; refuses adherence to
the Berlin memorandum, ii. 549;
created Earl of Beaconsfield, ii.
550; speech at Lord Mayor's feast,
ii. 558; at Berlin Congress, ii. 575,
577; attack on Gladstone's eastern policy, ii. 579; turn of popular feeling against, ii. 594;
election address (1880), ii. 605–
606; reception of defeat (1880),
ii. 612; *Daily Telegraph* inspired
by, ii. 622; on mediocrity in
cabinets, iii. 3; apprehensions
on Ireland, iii. 47; peers created
by, ii. 429 *and note*; death of
—tribute from Gladstone, iii.
89.
Deterioration in public life due to,
iii. 475.
Eminence of, iii. 89.
Estimate of, ii. 245; iii. 539.
Gladstone's estimate of, i. 356; Gladstone's antipathy to, i. 429, 432,
435, 436, 508; contrasted with
Gladstone, ii. 392, 561.
Judaism of, ii. 552–553, 558; iii.
475–476.
Novels of, i. 588.
Penetration of, ii. 122, 392; iii. 539.

Parliamentary courage of, i. 188;
debating method of, ii. 189; par-
liamentary wit of, iii. 473.
Turkish sympathies of, ii. 549, 558,
563.
Otherwise mentioned, i. 424, 433, 437,
624, 631; ii. 85 *note*[1], 100, 187, 499,
501, 620; iii. 276, 465.
Beard, C., ii. 544.
Beatrice, Princess, ii. 96.
Beaufort, Duke of, on coalition with
Peelites, i. 562.
Bedford, Duke of, ii. 229; iii. 241.
Beer duty, ii. 651; iii. 7, 187, 200.
Bekker, Dr., ii. 99.
Belgium : —
Bismarck's threat to, ii. 330.
Franco-Prussian treaty regarding,
ii. 340.
Neutrality of, guaranteed (1870), ii.
341, 580.
Severance of, from Holland, ii. 2.
Benedetti, ii. 330–331, 333 *note*, 340.
Bennett, W. J. E., i. 380 *note*[2].
Benson, Archbishop, iii. 96, 105, 131,
460.
Bentham, Jeremy, i. 82, 144, 156, 200;
ii. 60.
Bentinck, Lord George, quarrel with
Gladstone, i. 301–302; protectionist
position of, i. 352; iii. 465; on Irish
University bill, ii. 444; otherwise
mentioned, i. 294, 296, 350, 416, 430,
437 *and note*.
Berber, Gordon's arrival at, iii. 155;
Gordon shows Khedive's firman at,
iii. 160; route by, impossible for
relieving force, iii. 163; fall of, iii.
164; reconnaissance towards, iii.
165; railway from Suakin to, iii. 178.
Beresford, Lord, required to support
Roman Catholic Relief bill, ii. 649.
—— Major, relations with Disraeli, i.
369; views on the Peelites, i. 418.
Berlin congress (1878), ii. 575, 577; iii.
82.
—— memorandum (1876), ii. 549.
Berlin treaty (1878), ii. 575–576; iii.
82, 522; enforcement of, attempted
(1880), iii. 8–10.
Bernard, Mountague, i. 628; ii. 401.
Berryer, M., ii. 140 *and note*, 221.
Bessarabia, ii. 574 *and note*[2], 577.
Bessborough, Lord, presides over Irish
Land Commission, iii. 54, 56; other-
wise mentioned, ii. 274, 292, 503.
Bethell, Sir R., *see* Westbury.
Beugnot's *Chute du Paganisme*, iii.
387.

Biarritz, Gladstone's visit to, (1891–1892), iii. 463 *et seq.*; (1893), iii. 504, 508.

Biblical passages on special occasions, i. 201; biblical studies, iii. 415–416, 421, 544.

Biggar, J. G., iii. 53.

Biggar, family settlement in, i. 9 *note.*

Binney, T., ii. 134.

Birmingham: —
Bright celebration at, iii. 111.
Gladstone's visit to (1877), ii. 570; Gladstone's speech at (1888), iii. 387–389.

Biscoe, F., i. 50, 64, 80.

Bismarck, Prince, Napoleon III. in collision with, ii. 5; rise of, ii. 114; French diplomatic overtures reported by, ii. 319; views on Belgium and Holland, iii. 320; scorn for France, ii. 320; hopeful of peace, ii. 322; anxious for war with France, ii. 323–324, 329, 330–333, 335 *note* 1; complaint against England, ii. 331; condensed telegram incident, ii. 332–333; on Franco-Prussian agreement regarding Belgium, ii. 340; agrees to arrangement for neutrality of Belgium, ii. 341; understanding with Russia regarding Black Sea, ii. 350; interviews with Odo Russell, ii. 352–354; estimate of Russian diplomacy, ii. 353 *note*; on Egyptian question, iii. 79, 80, 89; French suspicion of (1882), iii. 82; Gladstone's annoyance with, iii. 121; antipathy towards England, i. 122; otherwise mentioned, ii. 356, 492; iii. 235.

Blachford, Lord (Frederick Rogers), i. 54, 59, 307; ii. 171–172.

Blackburn, Lord, ii. 383.

Blackheath, Gladstone's speech at (1871), ii. 380–381; speech on Bulgarian atrocities (1876), ii. 552, 554.

Black Sea: —
Neutralisation of (1856), i. 550.
Russian claims in (1870), ii. 349–356, 398, 400.

Blakesley, J. W., i. 135.

Blanc, Louis, cited, ii. 79.

Blantyre, Lady, ii. 95.

de Blignières, iii. 119.

Blomfield, Bishop, i. 161, 175, 274.

—— Captain, i. 607.

Board of Trade: —
Cobden offered vice-presidency of (1846), i. 244.
Functions of, formerly, i. 240 *note.*

Gladstone vice-president of, i. 240–243, 250; his views on, i. 243–245.

Boccaccio, i. 117.

Boers, *see under* Africa, South.

Bohn, H. G., ii. 476.

Bonham, F. R., i. 285.

Boniface VIII., Pope, ii. 516.

Bonn Conference, iii. 422.

Boord, T. W., ii. 490.

Booth, General, ii. 530.

Borough Franchise bill (1864), ii. 125–131.

Bosnia: —
Austrian acquisition of, ii. 576, iii. 82.
Revolt in, 548, 567.

Bossuet, i. 134, 159, 382–383; ii. 518; Gladstone compared with, i. 382–383; denounced by de Maistre, ii 518.

Bournemouth, iii. 526.

Bouverie, E. P., ii. 444 *note.*

Bowen, Lady, i. 607.

Bowen, Lord-Justice, ii. 469, 470.

Boycotting, *see under* Ireland.

Bradlaugh, opinions of, iii. 11; claims to affirm, iii. 12 *and note*; to take the oath, iii. 13; hostility to, iii. 13–14, 465; elected again (1885), iii. 20; carries an affirmation law, iii. 20–21.

Braemar, Gladstone's visit to (1892), iii. 493.

Braila, Sir Peter, i. 616.

Bramwell, Baron, ii. 383, 469.

Brancker, T., i. 61–62.

Brand, President, messages from, on South African situation, iii. 32–34, 39; on Transvaal commission, iii. 41.

—— H. B. W., *see* Hampden.

Brandreth, W. F., i. 111.

Brasseur, M., ii. 378.

Brassey, Sir Thomas and Lady, iii. 217.

Braybrooke, Lord, i. 223.

Brazil, *Alabama* case, ii. 405, 412.

Brewster, Sir D., ii. 464.

Bright, John: —
Chronology — Gladstone's first meeting with, i. 257; elected for Durham, i. 257 *note*; *Life of Cobden* submitted to, i. 282 *note*; on Disraeli's agricultural distress motion, i. 354; Palmerston's view of, i. 367; Don Pacifico debate, i. 368; estimate of Graham, i. 408; on papal aggression question, i. 408, 410; letter on the

Bright, John — *Continued.*
Chronology — Continued.
Crimean war, i. 494 *and note*[3]; on exclusion of dissenters from universities, i. 505; Peelites sit with, after resignation from Palmerston cabinet, i. 539 *and note*; unpopularity of, i. 542, 548; on Crimean war, i. 546; ii. 548, 574; view of the eastern question, i. 547; repulsed at election (1857), i. 564; return to parliament (1858), i. 574; letter to Gladstone, i. 578; on Indian government, i. 593; on the ' moral sense and honest feeling of the House,' i. 625, 632; unpopularity of, in Oxford, i. 630; suggests commercial treaty with France, ii. 20; on Paper Duties bill, ii. 34 *note*, 35; attacks fortifications scheme, ii. 47; Gladstone's protest against being classed with, ii. 49; iii. 182; letter against American war with England, ii. 75; speech on American civil war, ii. 86; Reform bill of 1858, ii. 199, 201; remarks on death of Cobden, ii. 143; Palmerston's remark on class attacks of, ii. 156; views on Reform bill of 1866, ii. 201; advises dissolution, ii. 208; Reform campaign of 1866, ii. 227; disapproved by Gladstone, ii. 223; induced to join Gladstone's cabinet (1868), ii. 254; president of board of trade, ii. 644; on Irish Church bill, ii. 264; views on Irish land question, ii. 282, 290–291, 294; iii. 55; on Education bill, ii. 305, 309–310; on civil service reform, ii. 315; on Belgian neutrality guarantee, ii. 342; on annexation of Alsace and Lorraine, ii. 347; on great thinkers, ii. 366; resignation (1870), ii. 381 *note*, 644, 650; at Hawarden (1871), ii. 381–382; succeeds Childers in the duchy, ii. 463 *note*; on the Greenwich seat question, ii. 471; chancellor of the duchy (1873), ii. 645; at Hawarden (1873), ii. 474; on Gladstone's retirement, ii. 505; radical attitude towards, ii. 630; chancellor of the duchy (1880), ii. 654; on the Bradlaugh question, iii. 12, 15; on Transvaal affairs, iii. 35, 36, *note*[1]; on suspension of Habeas Corpus Act in Ireland, iii. 50; resigns on bombardment of

Alexandria, iii. 83, 90; explanation in parliament, iii. 85; Birmingham speech on ' Irish rebels,' iii. 111–112; on Gladstone's view of Gordon's mission, iii. 177; at Spencer banquet, iii. 214; against home rule, iii. 291 *note*, 294; declines to join cabinet, iii. 303 *note*; views on exclusion of Irish members from Westminster, iii. 307, 326–327; disapproves Land bill, iii. 326–327; conversation with Gladstone on Home Rule and Land bills, iii. 326; letter to Gladstone, iii. 327; long demur regarding vote on second reading, iii. 329; letter to dissentients' meeting, iii. 336; electioneering against the bill, iii. 342.
Co-operation, faculty for, i. 189.
Forster's estimate of, ii. 123.
Gladstone's appreciation of, ii. 417, 418, 462; iii. 85, 349; his appreciation of Gladstone, ii. 177–178, 233–234, 505; Gladstone's letters to, ii. 462, 478, 599; iii. 84, 138.
Granville's estimate of, ii. 283.
Influence of, iii. 326, 336, 342.
Linguistic error of, iii. 476; otherwise mentioned, i. 423, 447, 626 *note*[2], 631, 632; ii. 128, 202, 203, 205, 224, 226, 230, 235, 260, 446, 481, 485, 495, 504, 563, 600, 617; iii. 13, 100, 288, 311.
Brodie, Sir B., i. 300, 455.
Broglie, Duc de, ii. 356.
Brontë, Charlotte, ii. 538.
Brooks, Mr., i. 441.
Brougham, Lord, loses Liverpool election, i. 20; Wetherell on, i. 71; estimates of, i. 75, 117, 133, 149; on slave-apprenticeship system, i. 146; view of social reform, i. 156; estimate of Gladstone, i. 264; on Conspiracy bill, i. 575; oratory of, i. 75, 149; ii. 589; otherwise mentioned, ii. 28, 181.
Broughton, Lord, i. 264, 288 *note*.
Brown, Baldwin, ii. 134.
Browne, Bp. Harold, iii. 95, 96 *note*.
Browning, Robert, iii. 417.
Bruce, Sir F. W. A., ii. 18 *note*.
—— Mrs., ii. 99, 103.
—— Lady Augusta, ii. 100–103.
—— Lord Ernest, i. 242.
—— F., i. 59 *note*.
—— Henry Austin, *see* Aberdare.
—— J., *see* Elgin, Earl of.
Brunnow, Baron, on war with Turkey, i. 479; in disfavour, i. 486 *and note*;

on blunders, i. 576; Gladstone desirous of an interview with, ii. 350–351.
Bryce, James, iii. 495 *note*, 497 *note* [1].
Buccleuch, Duke of, i. 374; ii. 584, 588.
Buckingham, Duke of, i. 242–243, 254.
Budgets: —
Disraeli's (1852), i. 435–440, 459.
Gladstone's — his keenness regarding, ii. 55; (1853), i. 460–472, 646–648; iii. 537; (1854), i. 514–515; (1859), ii. 19; (1860), i. 474; ii. 24 *et seq.*, 635; (1861), ii. 38–39; (1863), ii. 66, 67; (1866), ii. 68, 200; (1880), iii. 7; (1885), iii. 187, 200.
Goschen's (1887), iii. 385.
Lewis' (1857), i. 559–562.
Lowe's, ii. 373.
Whigs', i. 459.
Bulgaria: —
Atrocities in (1876), ii. 548, 553, 567.
Division of, into northern and southern, ii. 576, 577 *and note* [1].
Gladstone's first pamphlet on, ii. 552–554; second, ii. 560, 562.
Resistance of, a breakwater to Europe, i. 477.
Bulgarian Horrors and the Question of the East, The, ii. 552–554.
Buller, C., i. 65.
—— Sir Redvers, cited, iii. 372.
Bulteel, H. B., i. 58.
Bulwer, *see* Lytton.
Bunsen, Gladstone's book approved by, i. 176; Gladstone's view of book by, i. 321; otherwise mentioned, i. 309 *and note* [1].
Buol, Count, i. 602.
Burgon, J. W., i. 503, 506.
Burke, Sir B., ii. 184.
—— Edmund, Gladstone influenced by, i. 203, 208; attitude towards Turkey, i. 479 *note*; Gladstone's estimate of, iii. 280, 469; Macaulay's estimate of, iii. 280 *note*; citations from, in home rule debate, iii. 314; quoted, i. 25; ii. 51, 61, 366; otherwise mentioned, i. 265; ii. 295, 424; iii. 125.
—— T. H., murder of, iii. 67 *and note*, 68, 391 *note* [1], 392.
Burne-Jones, Sir Edward, ii. 559.
Burnett, Mr., i. 341; ii. 477.
Burton, Sir R., cited, iii. 169 *note*.
Bute, Lord, i. 293.
Butler, Bishop, Gladstone's attitude towards, i. 161, 207 *note* [2]; ii. 544; iii. 520–521; on over-great refinements, i. 210; on habit, iii. 464.
Butt, Isaac, i. 503.

Buxton, Sir T. F., i. 105, 145.
Byron, i. 159.

CABINETS: —
Angularities a cause of friction in, ii. 419.
Authority of, Gladstone's views on, ii. 396.
Committees in, Gladstone's view of, ii. 289.
Consultation of, on succession to cabinet office, not necessary, iii. 101 *note*.
Divisions in, iii. 175.
Gladstone's (1868), efficiency of, ii. 255, 414–415; his estimates of colleagues, ii. 414, 417, 419, 421; his censure of defaulters, ii. 418–419; changes in, ii. 463 *note*; cabinet of 1880, ii. 653; of 1886, iii. 296 *note* [2]; of 1892, iii. 495 *note*.
Mediocrity in, iii. 3.
Peel's view of government by, i. 300.
Responsibility of members of, Gladstone's views on, iii. 113 *note*, 114.
Caird, Dr., ii. 98.
Cairnes, J. E., cited, ii. 70 *note*.
Cairns, Lord, on Irish Church bill, ii. 270, 274–280; on Irish Land bill (1870), ii. 294.
Cambridge: —
Dissenters' disabilities at, ii. 313 *note* [1].
Famous sons of, iii. 476.
Gladstone's early visit to, i. 11; visit in 1831, i. 80; in 1887, iii. 385; his solicitude regarding, iii. 486.
—— Duke of, i. 171; ii. 455; iii. 105, 150 *note*, 524.
Cameron, Mr., i. 78.
Campbell, Lord Chancellor, ii. 33, 37, 39, 635–636.
Campbell-Bannerman, Sir H., Irish secretary (1884), ii. 654; war secretary (1886), iii. 297 *note*; war secretary (1892), iii. 495 *note*; on Home Rule bill committee of cabinet, iii. 497 *note* [1].
Canada: —
American relations with, ii. 82, 86.
Assembly in, Gladstone's speech on, i. 360 *and note* [1].
Cession of, to United States suggested, ii. 401 *and note* [2].
Commercial relations with, Gladstone's despatch on, i. 359.
Constitution suspended (1838), i. 144, 641.

Canada — *continued.*
Duty on corn from, lowered, i. 255 *note.*
Ecclesiastical position in, ii. 161.
Fishery questions of, adjusted (1871), ii. 405.
Government of Canada bill (1840), i. 360 *and note*[2].
Revolt of (1837), Molesworth's view of, i. 361 *and note*[5]; Gladstone's opposition to indemnification of rebels in, i. 353 *note.*
Irish constitution to approximate to, suggestions regarding, iii. 215, 317.
Liberal policy towards, ii. 607.
Cannes (1883), iii. 102–104; (1897), iii. 523; (1898), iii. 526.
Canning, Lady, i. 139, 149.
—— Charles John, Earl, offered lordship of the treasury, i. 126; in parliament, i. 137; Russell's disapproval of, i. 536; on Peelites' refusal to join Palmerston, i. 535; death of, ii. 88; otherwise mentioned, i. 54, 140, 420 *and note*[2], 539; ii. 193, 194, 317.
—— George, views on slavery, i. 25; Gladstone's attitude towards, i. 25, 34, 38, 89, 208, 212; call at Eton, i. 34; attitude towards reform, i. 69, 70; Peel's reference to, i. 126; Peel contrasted with, i. 248; age of, on entering cabinet, i. 261; Palmerston a follower of, i. 367; chancellor and first lord (1827), ii. 463; wit of, iii. 473; Wellington's treatment of (1827), iii. 485; Turgot praised by, iii. 491; otherwise mentioned, i. 9–10, 20, 21, 298, 372, 419, 420 *note*[2]; cited, ii. 394, 577, 589, 595; iii. 125, 465.
—— Stratford, *see* Redcliffe.
Cardwell, Lord, withdraws from Oxford election, i. 328–329; attitude of, towards liberals (1852), i. 419; Gladstone's budget submitted to, i. 464; favours dissolution, i. 467; Russell's disapproval of, i. 536; refuses to succeed Gladstone, i. 539; Gladstone's relations with, i. 551, 552, 559; on Paper Duties bill, ii. 31, 33, 37; against economy, ii. 94; estimate of Gladstone's position, ii. 171; the pope's estimate of, ii. 218; war secretary (1868), ii. 644; on Irish land question, ii. 283, 292; on civil service reform, ii. 315; on suggested Antwerp expedition, ii. 339; capacity of, ii. 359; army reforms of, ii. 359, 626–627; Gladstone's letter to, on

qualifications for war office, ii. 649; unpopularity of, ii. 389–390; Gladstone's letter to, on quarrelsome colleagues, ii. 421; objects to reduction of estimates, ii. 483–484; peerage, ii. 497; otherwise mentioned, i. 405 *note*, 420, 560; ii. 221, 243, 376, 410, 462, 478, 503, 504, 602, 636.
Carey, J., iii. 103.
Carlingford, Lord (Chichester Fortescue), views of, and correspondence with, on Irish land question (1869–70), ii. 283, 288, 290–293; electoral defeat of (1874), ii. 491; Irish secretary (1868), ii. 644; president of board of trade (1870), ii. 644; president of council (1883), ii. 654; lord privy seal (1885), ii. 654; against home rule, iii. 291 *note*; otherwise mentioned, ii. 462, 504; iii. 50.
Carlisle, Lord, i. 624.
Carlow election (1891), iii. 458.
Carlton club, Gladstone's membership of, i. 98; Gladstone insulted at, i. 441; Gladstone withdraws from, ii. 29.
Carlyle, Thomas, on Gladstone's first book, i. 176 *note*; Gladstone contrasted with, i. 195; Gladstone attracted by, i. 219; estimate of, ii. 229–230; supports Gladstone on the Bulgarian question, ii. 559; death of, iii. 98; Gladstone's estimate of, iii. 98–99, 425; otherwise mentioned, i. 329; ii. 534, 582.
Carnarvon, 2nd Earl of, i. 75.
—— 4th Earl of, suggests Gladstone for Ionian Islands, i. 594; on Irish Church bill, ii. 262 *note*[1], 268, 271; resigns, ii. 574 *note*[1]; on Transvaal annexation, iii. 25; address to House of Lords on Irish policy, iii. 211, 259; interview with Parnell, iii. 228–231; anxieties of, regarding National League, iii. 278; resigns, iii. 279, 280; otherwise mentioned, iii. 284, 287.
Carteret, i. 367; ii. 428, 542 *note.*
Castelcicala, i. 398, 399 *note*[1], 400.
Catholic emancipation, *see* Roman catholic.
Cavagnari, iii. 151.
Cavendish, i. 380 *note*[2].
—— Lord F., Gladstone's appreciation of, ii. 462; appointed lord of the treasury, ii. 463 *note*; appointed Irish secretary, ii. 654; iii. 66; murdered, i. 67, 391 *note*[1]; Gladstone's tribute to, i. 69; otherwise mentioned, ii. 195, 212, 446, 563.

Cavendish, Lady F., iii. 69-70.
—— Lord Richard, ii. 232.
Cavour, Count, interested in Gladstone's budget, i. 470; ii. 55; Gladstone's interview with (1859), i. 618; ii. 5; England a difficulty to, ii. 6; dealings with Napoleon III., ii. 7; resigns, ii. 8; Manzoni's estimate of, ii. 11; development of aims of, ii. 15; remarks on Italian free trade, ii. 17; death of, ii. 17 *and note*³; prediction of, regarding Prussia, ii. 114, 115; otherwise mentioned, i. 390, 401, 404, 480; ii. 13, 158, 356, 532; iii. 235, 475, 540.
Cecil, Lord Robert, *see* Salisbury.
Cephalonia:—
    Archbishop of, i. 603-604; ii. 532.
    Condition of (1858), i. 599-600, 603-604.
    Rising in (1848), i. 600, 603; Gladstone's despatch on, i. 620 *note*³.
Chaillé-Long, Colonel C., cited, iii. 169 *note*.
Challemel-Lacour, iii. 105.
Chalmers, Dr., Gladstone's estimate of, i. 59, 109-110, 170-171; views on church establishment, i. 169-171; otherwise mentioned, i. 137, 138.
Chamberlain, Joseph, on Education Act (1872), ii. 308; supports the resolutions on Turkey, ii. 564; with Gladstone calling on Cardinal Newman, ii. 570 *note*; president of board of trade (1880), i. 240 *note*; ii. 630, 654; popularity of, with radicals, iii. 3; on Transvaal annexation, iii. 28-29; abstains from voting in Transvaal division, iii. 35; Argyll uneasy at speeches of, iii. 49; on suspension of Habeas Corpus Act in Ireland, iii. 50; communications with Parnell, iii. 64; offers to yield Dilke his post, iii. 99; Gladstone's correspondence with the Queen regarding, iii. 100-101; views on liberty of speech for cabinet ministers, iii. 112-114; social programme of, iii. 173-174; on Crimes Act, iii. 192; suggests central board of local government for Ireland, iii. 193; opposes land purchase for Ireland, iii. 194-195; resigns, iii. 195; on conservative repudiation of Lord Spencer's policy, iii. 214-215; view of Gladstone's election address, iii. 220; Gladstone's conversation with, iii. 223-226 *and notes*; Gladstone's attitude towards (Sept. '85), iii. 222; antagonism to Hartington, iii. 233, 288; opposes home rule, iii. 233, 234;

former nationalist leanings of, iii. 233; Russian and Austrian speech of June 17th, iii. 233-234; visit to Hawarden, iii. 247; liberal losses attributed to, iii. 249; on liberal losses at the elections, iii. 251; agrarian policy of, iii. 250, 288; advises leaving Parnell to Conservatives, iii. 267; Parnell's attitude towards, iii. 275; alleged desire for Irish secretaryship, iii. 291; joins the cabinet, iii. 294-295; local government board, iii. 297 *note*; objections to proposed Home Rule bill, iii. 302; resigns, iii. 302-303; propounds federation views, iii. 316-317, 327, 339; opposed to Land bill, iii. 332; meeting of dissentients in Committee, iii. 335-337; no terrors for, in dissolution, iii. 339; Gladstone's comments on, to Acton, iii. 355; speech at Birmingham, iii. 364, 365, 367; Gladstone's comments on position of, iii. 366; at round table conference, iii. 364 *note*, 367; article in *Baptist*, iii. 367 *and note*²; gives up conference, iii. 368; Gladstone's conversation with (Ap. '87), iii. 385; Gladstone's reply to, on Home Rule bill (May '93), iii. 499-500; Gladstone's letters to, iii. 92, 133; otherwise mentioned, iii. 186, 191, 198, 264, 328.
Chancery commission, ii. 650.
Chandos, Lord, i. 628, 630.
Chantrey, Sir F., i. 112.
Chapter of Autobiography, publication of, ii. 249-250.
Charities and income-tax, ii. 65-66.
Charity, sums spent in, iii. 419-420.
Charles I., King, iii. 480-481.
Chartism, i. 276, 358.
Chatham, Lord, i. 223 *and note*¹, 367, 372; iii. 178.
Chester, speech at, on colonial policy (1855), i. 363.
Chevalier, Michel, Gladstone's letters to, ii. 336, 343.
Childers, H. C. E., on estimates (1865), ii. 140; on civil service reform, ii. 315; on Russia's Black Sea announcement, ii. 351; retirement of (1873), ii. 463 *note*; on the Greenwich seat question, ii. 472 *note*; suggested for war office, ii. 625, 627; first lord of admiralty (1868), ii. 644; resigns (1871), ii. 645; chancellor of the duchy (1872), ii. 645; retires (1873), ii. 645; war secretary (1880), ii. 654; Colley's acknowledgments to, iii. 35

Childers — *continued.*
note; efficiency of, in Egyptian campaign (1882), iii. 83 note; chancellor of exchequer (1882), iii. 99, 654; home rule views of, iii. 235, 291 note; home secretary (1886), iii. 296 note [2], 297 note; otherwise mentioned, ii. 339, 370 note [1], 376; iii. 187.
Chillingworth, i. 220.
Chiltern Hundreds, i. 288 note.
China: —
　Opium question (1840), i. 225–226; Gladstone's attitude towards, i. 226–227, 229, 239, 242, 244.
　Tai-ping rising in, suppressed by Gordon, iii. 149 note [3].
　War with (1857), i. 563–564; (1859–60), ii. 18 and note, 30, 38.
China, collection of, ii. 213, 523 and note.
Chios, Archbishop of, ii. 532.
Christianity, Acton on, iii. 360–361.
Christopher, R. A., i. 536.
Church, Dean, *Oxford Movement* by, i. 163 note [1], 168 note [2]; position of, at Oxford (1847), i. 334–335; estimate of Gladstone, ii. 155, 177; appointed to St. Paul's by Gladstone, ii. 433; otherwise mentioned, ii. 430, 560; iii. 69–70, 96, 97.
Church and State (Coleridge), i. 167.
Church Principles, i. 181, 182, 224.
Churches: —
　Anglican —
　　Antagonism of, to liberal party, ii. 307.
　　Catholic revival in, nature of, i. 159.
　　Clerical calling, Gladstone's leanings to, i. 81–82, 323–324, 382, 383, 635–641.
　　Condition of (1831–1840), i. 153.
　　Convocation, revival of, ii. 162–163.
　　Crisis in (1882), iii. 97.
　　Disestablishment — Gladstone's speech against (1873), ii. 457–458 and note; his attitude towards (1874), ii. 501–502, iii. 540; his views on (1891), iii. 471; Chamberlain's view of, iii. 225.
　　Evangelical party in, social reforms effected by, i. 156, 163; Gladstone brought up in, i. 159, 208; Tractarians in alliance with, i. 167; anti-slavery work of, i. 200 note.
　　Gladstone's position regarding, iii. 541–543.

Gorham case, i. 316, 378–381, 632.
Guizot's views on, ii. 538.
Ireland, in, *see under* Ireland.
Manning's views on outlook for (1846), i. 325.
Orders in, iii. 521.
Palmer's book on, i. 162, 167, 168 note [1].
Poetry in, iii. 484.
Preferments in, Gladstone's case with, ii. 430–433.
Rates, abolition of, ii. 161.
Ritualism in, ii. 501, 514.
Roman *versus*, Gladstone's views on, i. 317–318, 321.
State and — Gladstone's views on, (1846), i. 324–326; (1857), i. 570; (1865), ii. 159–163; growth of ideas on, i. 182–183; views modified by Lady Hewley case, i. 322; supremacy question, i. 381; Gladstone's view of concessions, ii. 159; conversation at Biarritz, iii. 470–471.
State in its Relation with the Church, The (1838), i. 172, 175.
Welsh disestablishment question, Chamberlain's article on, iii. 367 and note [2]; difficulty of, iii. 471; advance of (1892–94), iii. 495.
Distinction of, from state, in general view, i. 155.
Gladstone's interest in, i. 152; ii. 507.
Nature of, Gladstone's ideas regarding, i. 87–88, 157–159.
Roman: —
　Anglican *versus*, Gladstone's views on, i. 317–318, 321.
　Infallibility dogma of, ii. 378, 511–512, 515, 516, 520.
　Jansenists in, i. 325.
　Jesuits of, ii. 516.
　Neapolitan tyranny connected with, i. 397.
　Old Catholic dissenters from, ii. 511, 513.
　Papal aggression question (1851), i. 408; views on, i. 405–410, 414, 415 and note.
　Parnell leadership denounced by, iii. 448–449.
　Proselytising of, ii. 188, 514.
　Religion spoiling morality in, ii. 185.
　Secession to, by Newman, i. 317; by Miss Helen Gladstone, i. 318; by Hope and Manning, i. 385–387; second great tide of,

i. 378; Gladstone's views on, i. 312, 321; Manning's views on, i. 317.

Syllabus (1864) — importance of, ii. 508; influence of, on Irish legislation, ii. 511; contents of, ii. 516; Gladstone's correspondence with Acton regarding, ii. 520.

Temporal power, Gladstone's views on, i. 403, 404; ii. 512–513, 519; iii. 414; Vatican decrees in relation to, ii. 508, 517, 519.

Ultramontanes v. liberals, ii. 508–509, 511–513; basis of ultramontanism, ii. 518.

Vatican decrees (1870), ii. 502, 509 et seq.; in relation to temporal power, ii. 508, 517, 519.

Scottish, establishment question, iii. 248, 471.

Churchill, Lady, ii. 98, 102, 104.

—— Lord Randolph, party of, iii. 2, 89, 108 note; on Dutch sentiment in South Africa, iii. 42 note²; on franchise extension in Ireland, iii. 142; on Crimes Act, iii. 188–189; revolt of, against 'the old gang,' iii. 200–201; on Irish affairs, iii. 213, 278, 280; on tory prospects after the defeat, iii. 289; on Gladstone's chances of forming a government (1886), iii. 297; on 'reconstruction' of Home Rule bill, iii. 335; chancellor of exchequer, iii. 362; resignation, iii. 363, 365–366; Ulster plan of campaign encouraged by, iii. 371 note; speaks on budget (1887), iii. 385; on imprisonment of Irish members, iii. 426; on Gladstone's reply to Balfour, iii. 502.

Churton, E., i. 111.

Civil Service reform, i. 509–512, 649–650; ii. 314–315.

Clanricarde, Captain, i. 608.

Claremont, i. 242, 243.

Clarendon, Earl of, addresses House of Lords, on Irish policy (1850), iii. 211 note; attitude towards Gladstone's budget, i. 466, 467; on British policy preceding Crimean war, i. 481, 485; efforts for peace, i. 487; Aberdeen in conflict with, i. 495 and note³; attitude towards ecumenical council, ii. 510, 512; satisfies Aberdeen, i. 535; condemns Peelites' resignation, i. 542; on Garibaldi's departure, ii. 111; foreign secretary (1865), ii. 153 note; the Pope's estimate of, ii. 218; in Rome, ii. 222; foreign secretary (1868), ii.

254, 644; on civil service reform, ii. 315; foreign policy of, ii. 317–318; correspondence on reduction of armaments, ii. 321–322; Alabama case, ii. 397, 399; death of (1870), ii. 324, 644; Gladstone's appreciation of, ii. 414, 417; iii. 490; Granville's estimate of, ii. 417; otherwise mentioned, i. 481 note, 491, 493, 526, 532, 624, 648; ii. 11, 106, 189, 210, 260, 270, 352, 512.

Clark, Sir Andrew, ii. 279, 423, 446, 462, 498, 504, 563; iii. 101, 102, 159 note, 216, 387, 520.

Clarke, Mr., i. 111.

Classical education, Gladstone's view of, ii. 312, 646–649.

Clémenceau, M., iii. 103.

Clerk, Sir G., i. 420.

Clifford, W. K., ii. 524.

Closure, see under Parliament.

Clough, Arthur H., i. 329.

Clowes, Mr., ii. 552.

Clumber, i. 95, 121; ii. 144.

Clyde, Lord, ii. 359.

Coalition government (1853–59), i. 443 et seq.; cabinet harmony in, i. 495; Crimean war's effect on, i. 484, 495, 521.

Coalitions, views on, i. 533.

Cobbett, i. 114; ii. 22.

Cobden, Richard: —

  Chronology — free-trade advocacy of, i. 249, 251; Peel's eulogium on, i. 291–293, 295, 296; views on colonial government, i. 362; Don Pacifico debate, i. 368; on Crimean war, i. 548; unpopularity of, i. 542, 548, 630; view of the eastern question, i. 547; on proceedings in China, i. 563; repulsed at election (1857), i. 564; declines to join Palmerston's government, i. 626; visit to Hawarden, ii. 18, 20; French treaty negotiations, ii. 20–21, 46, 77 note³; experience on expenditure committees, ii. 46; Gladstone's protest against being classed with, ii. 49; iii. 182; writes against American war with England, ii. 75; on Danish question, ii. 118, 119; death of, ii. 143.

Co-operation, faculty for, i. 189.

Disraeli on, i. 352.

Forster's estimate of, ii. 123.

Gladstone's estimate of, i. 239, 249, 291, 292, 296 note; ii. 143, 213; Gladstone's confidence in, i. 562.

Graham's estimate of, i. 296.

Cobden, Richard — *continued.*
　Life of, cited, 282 *and note*, 291
　　note[1].
　Originality of, ii. 59, 122; iii. 539.
　Palmerston's view of, i. 367.
　Stanley's estimate of, i. 239.
　Otherwise mentioned, i. 232, 244,
　　278, 423, 447; ii. 13, 23, 37, 58, 120,
　　156, 189; iii. 431.
—— Club: —
　Chamberlain's speech at dinner of
　　(1883), iii. 112–113.
　Gladstone's eulogy of Cobden at din-
　　ner of (1886), ii. 213.
Cockburn, Chief Justice, ii. 384, 395, 412.
Coercion, *see under* Ireland.
Colborne, Capt., i. 228.
Cole, Mr., i. 59 *note*, 135.
Colenso, Bishop, i. 316; ii. 168–169, 313.
Coleridge, S. T., i. 159, 167, 176 *note.*
—— Lord Chief Justice, recommends
　Northcote to Gladstone, i. 333 *note*[1];
　uneasy regarding Gladstone's views,
　i. 628; introduces bill for removing
　tests, ii. 313; made lord chief justice,
　ii. 463 *note*, 470; on the Greenwich
　seat question, ii. 469 *and note; Times*
　libel action tried before, iii. 394.
Colley, Sir George, iii. 31 *and note*[1],
　34–38, 42.
Collier, Jeremy, cited, iii. 467.
—— Sir Robert, ii. 383–386.
Collings, Jesse, iii. 288.
Collins, i. 169.
Colonial Society, ii. 401 *note*[2].
Colonies: —
　Church in, ii. 168–169.
　Disraeli's views on, i. 361; ii. 606;
　　speech on (1872), ii. 391.
　Gladstone's views on, i. 359–361, 363–
　　364, 645.
　Home rule (Irish), attitude towards,
　　iii. 323.
　Military expenditure for, i. 362 *and
　　note*[1]; reduction of troops in
　　(1870), ii. 360 *and note*, 374.
　Protection adopted by, against Eng-
　　land, ii. 132.
Combes, M., iii. 113 *note.*
Commercial treaties — French, ii. 20–21,
　46; various (1866), ii. 200.
Companies, Gladstone's bill for regula-
　tion of, i. 268.
Concert of Europe, Gladstone's view of,
　ii. 560, 564, 573, 575; iii. 80, 82.
Condé, cited, i. 188.
Congo debate (1883), iii. 110.
'Conservative,' adoption of name of, i.
　422.

Conservative party: —
　Changes in (1870–1885), iii. 177.
　Church the rallying point of, i. 154.
　Closure by guillotine introduced by,
　　iii. 377.
　Coercion—repudiated by, iii. 212–214,
　　257; revival of, a last resort for,
　　iii. 278–279, 285; proposed by, iii.
　　287; Salisbury's 'twenty years'
　　proposal, iii. 317.
　Electoral losses of (1886–1890), iii.
　　427.
　Factions in, i. 143.
　Fourth party among, iii. 2, 89,
　　108 *note.*
　Franchise extension not inimical
　　to, iii. 129.
　Gladstone's early connection with,
　　i. 245 *note*; his views on (1885),
　　iii. 221.
　Ireland, traditional policy towards,
　　iii. 242–243.
　Irish alliance with, iii. 188–190,
　　200, 203, 258, 260, 269–271, 274,
　　276, 284.
　Liberal aid to, on important
　　measures, iii. 257–258; liberal
　　seceders' union with, iii. 350.
　Nationalist support of, at general
　　election (1885), iii. 244–245.
　O'Connell, attitude towards, i. 129,
　　138.
　Lord Spencer's policy, and, iii. 262.
　Tory democracy, iii. 173, 201, 240–
　　241.
　Whig seceders' fusion with, i. 139.
Consistency, Gladstone's view of, i.
　211–212.
Conspiracy to Murder bill, i. 574–576.
Constantinople: —
　Meeting of the Powers at (1870), ii.
　　559.
　Patriarch of, ii. 532.
Convocation, revival of, ii. 162–163.
Conway, General, iii. 181.
Copyright, Gladstone's views on, ii. 59,
　541.
Cordite vote, iii. 177 *and note.*
Corfu: —
　British retention of, advised, i. 601,
　　619–620.
　Gladstone's arrival at, i. 602; house
　　at, i. 613.
　Petition drawn up by, i. 615.
　University at, i. 605.
Corn Laws: —
　Gladstone's support of, i. 106, 114,
　　231–232, 249; modification of
　　views, i. 252–254, 260–262, 264.

Graham's defence of, i. 114.
Repeal of — Peel's policy regarding, i. 282–287, 290; results of, i. 426; liberal aid to tories for, iii. 257, 284.
Correspondence in the Octagon, ii. 526–547.
Corrie, Messrs., i. 9.
Corry, H., i. 351 note¹, 420.
Corrupt Practices bill (1883), i. 97, and note¹; iii. 110.
Court gossip, Gladstone's view of, ii. 254.
Cousin, Victor, i. 163; ii. 220–221.
Coutts, Miss Burdett, ii. 168.
Cowan, Sir J., ii. 609; iii. 517 note³, 535 note.
Cowley, Lord, ii. 28.
Cowper, Lord, iii. 65, 324, 362.
—— William (Lord Mount-Temple), i. 234; ii. 154.
Craik, Sir Henry, cited, ii. 302 note.
Cranborne, Lord, see Salisbury.
Cranmer, Archbishop, iii. 466–467.
Craven, Mrs., i. 320, 383.
Crawford, R. W., ii. 207, 210, 233.
Creighton, Bishop, ii. 535.
Crimea, Catherine's seizure of, i. 478.
Crimean war : —
  Coalition government wrecked on, i. 484, 495, 521.
  Committee on, Roebuck's motion for, i. 521, 523, 537–539, 542.
  Course of, i. 494–495, 545–548.
  End of, i. 550.
  Gladstone's view of, i. 484, 492, 544–546, 652–653; Gladstone charged with 'starving,' i. 629.
  Ignorance of facts of, among politicians, i. 547.
  Illusions of, ii. 4.
  Income-tax renewal necessitated by, i. 474.
  Kinglake's book on, i. 480–481 and note.
  Napoleon III. strengthened by, ii. 4.
  Newcastle and Herbert, charges against, i. 651–652.
  Objects of, i. 545.
  Origin of, i. 478.
  Popular British opinion on, i. 489–490.
  Responsibilities for, i. 481.
  Turkish position after, ii. 548.
Croke, Dr., iii. 449.
Cromwell, ii. 287, 555; iii. 480.
Crown : —
  Critical wave against, ii. 425–426.
  Gladstone's attitude towards, ii. 423–427.

Prerogative of, Gladstone charged with resorting to, ii. 364–365.
Crown Princess, ii. 100, 472.
Crowther, Rev. ——, i. 58–59.
—— —— ii. 217.
Cullen, Cardinal, opposes Irish University bill, ii. 434, 439–440, 443; Gladstone's meeting with (1877), ii. 571; mentioned, i. 397.
Cumberland, Duke of, i. 127, 141, 279.
Currie, Sir Donald, iii. 115, 517.
Customs, articles liable to, in various years, ii. 25 and note.
Cyprus : —
  British acquisition of, ii. 607.
  Convention regarding, ii. 576, 578; iii. 522.
  Gladstone's Midlothian reference to, ii. 592; iii. 27–28.
  Seizure of, projected, ii. 573.

Daily News, ii. 495, 625 and note.
Daily Telegraph, ii. 622; iii. 430 and note.
Dale, R. W., ii. 134–135, 304, 305, 570.
Dalhousie, Lord, i. 350; iii. 303 note.
Dalkeith, Lord, ii. 584, 612.
Dalmeny, ii. 588, 609–610; iii. 239, 491.
Dalrymple, Mr., iii. 248.
Dante : —
  Gladstone's appreciation of, i. 202, 207 note², 215, 223; iii. 423–424, 488, 550.
  Scartazzini on, iii. 387.
Darbishire, Mr., ii. 136.
Darfur, iii. 146, 149 note³, 157.
Daru, ii. 321–322.
Darwin, ii. 536–537, 562.
Davidson, Bishop, i. 498 note¹.
Davis, Jefferson, ii. 72, 79–81.
De Retz, iii. 255.
De Tabley, Lord, ii. 193.
December, important events in Gladstone's life in, ii. 256.
Delane, Mr., i. 153, 624; ii. 270, 439, 552.
Demerara, i. 22–24, 224.
Democracy : —
  Fair play a natural tendency of, iii. 308.
  Gladstone's feeling for, ii. 77; iii. 123, 125, 133, 203, 610–611; iii. 88; his efforts against besetting vice of, ii. 250–251; his faith in, i. 621, 650; iii. 173; his moulding of opinion of, iii. 537; their devotion to Gladstone, iii. 89, 90, 250, 330.
  Mazzini's work for, iii. 478.
  Oxford in relation to, ii. 35.
  Spendthrift tendency of, iii. 537.

Denison, Bishop Edward, censure of Hampden opposed by, i. 161.
—— Archdeacon, Gorham case, i. 380 note[2]; withdraws support from Gladstone, i. 451; condemnation of, for heresy, i. 557; otherwise mentioned, i. 54, 71, 79, 98 note.
—— J. E. (Speaker), ii. 198.
Denmark: —
Gladstone's cruise to (1883), iii. 115–117 (1894), iii. 517; tribute from, iii. 532.
Schleswig-Holstein question, see that title.
Deputations, i. 256.
Derby, 14th Earl of, abolition, proposals of, i. 102, 105; advocates reform, i. 143; joins conservatives, i. 144; Brougham's estimate of, i. 149; resigns on Irish church question, i. 154; Peel's annoyance with, i. 234; on tariff question, i. 263; Gladstone's relations with, i. 280; attitude towards repeal, i. 283; resigns, i. 285; on Peel's eulogium of Cobden, i. 291–292; New Zealand question, i. 298; on quarrel between Gladstone and Bentinck, i. 301–302; Graham's attitude towards, i. 368; invites Gladstone to enter the government, i. 393, 406; Gladstone declines, i. 407; views on papal aggression question, i. 406; reply to Lord Howick in sugar duties' debate, i. 644; cabinet of three men and a half (1852), i. 416; supported by the Peelites, i. 424, 428; attitude towards free trade, i. 425, 429; Oxford commission, i. 500; gratitude to Gladstone, i. 434; resigns on budget defeat, i. 441; views on Gladstone's budget, i. 472; attempts to form a ministry (1855), i. 525–526; fails, i. 527, 528; communications with Gladstone, i. 551–552, 554, 558, 561; relations with Disraeli, i. 555, 561; recommends union with Disraeli and Peelites, i. 562; vote of censure on Palmerston (1857), ii. 269; forms second administration (1858), i. 576; financial policy of, ii. 633; letter to Gladstone, i. 577; Bright's views on position of, i. 579; Reform bill (1859), i. 621; ii. 199; defeat and dissolution, i. 622; ii. 265; Gladstone in sympathy with, i. 631; Gladstone's estimate of, ii. 193; forms a government (1866), ii. 211; on Irish railways commission, ii. 243 note; on Irish church bill, ii. 268, 278; peers created

by, ii. 429; otherwise mentioned, i. 177, 432, 437 and note, 529, 530, 536, 641; ii. 156 note[1], 253, 653; iii. 289 note, 465.
Derby, 15th Earl of, on Reform bill (1866), ii. 202; on Ireland, ii. 242; on Luxemburg guarantee, ii. 320, 357 and note; declines to serve on Alabama commission, ii. 400; subscribes to Mill memorial, ii. 543; views on eastern question, ii. 551, 567, 572; resigns, ii. 574 note[1]; declines office with Gladstone, ii. 629; colonial secretary (1882), ii. 654; London convention with Transvaal (1884), iii. 45 and note; declines to join Gladstone's government (1882), iii. 99; joins as colonial secretary, iii. 100; Gladstone's letter to, on Ireland, iii. 215; declares against Home Rule, iii. 291 note, 294; otherwise mentioned, i. 103, 133, 134, 139, 177, 227, 239, 248, 296, 393, 420; ii. 499; iii. 268, 270.
Devon, Lord, i. 343–344.
Devonshire, Duke of, ii. 243 note; iii. 69, 166, 171.
Dickson, Colonel, ii. 570.
Dilke, Sir Charles, supports the resolutions on Turkey, ii. 564; declines to join Gladstone's government except with Chamberlain, ii. 630; president of local government board, ii. 654; claim of, to cabinet position, iii. 99; appointed to local government board, iii. 100; conferences on Franchise bill, iii. 138; agrees to send Gordon to Soudan, iii. 150; on Crimes Act, iii. 192; opposes land purchase for Ireland, iii. 194–195; resigns, iii. 195; speech on Irish policy, iii. 264; for home rule, iii. 291 note.
Dillon, J., iii. 448, 455.
Dillwyn, L., ii. 141.
Dingwall, Gladstone presented with freedom of, i. 476.
Disestablishment, see under Churches.
Disraeli, B., see Beaconsfield.
—— Mrs., ii. 195, 196, 546–547.
Dissenters: —
Affirmation bill opposed by, iii. 20.
Disestablishment speech by Gladstone, effect of, ii. 457–458.
Educational views of (1843 and 1847), ii. 302; (1870) ii. 303–305; estrangement of, by Education Act of 1870, ii. 307, 388; opposition to the Act, ii. 308.
Election of 1874, action in, ii. 495.

Gladstone's relations with (1864), ii. 134–135; (1868) ii. 255; (1869) ii. 272; views on Gladstone's retirement, ii. 505–506.
Home rule, attitude towards, in Wales, iii. 323.
University exclusion of, i. 505–506; ii. 313 and note [1].
Dissenters' Chapels bill, i. 208, 330, 331.
Disturbance Compensation bill, iii. 113.
Divorce: —
  French law on, i. 567 note.
  Gladstone's views on, i. 568–572 and note.
  Statistics regarding, i. 572 note.
  — bill (1857), i. 569–573.
Dodson, J. G., ii. 463 note, 654; iii. 291 note.
Döllinger, Dr., Gladstone's visit to (1845), i. 318–320 and note [2]; later visit (1874), ii. 513–515; criticisms from, on Vaticanism, ii. 521; Acton compared with, ii. 558; Gladstone's visit to (1886), iii. 351–352; Salmon's agreement with, iii. 417; death of, iii. 421; Gladstone's estimate of, iii. 422–423, 467.
Dollis Hill, iii. 385, 517.
Don Pacifico debate, i. 368–371 and note, 372, 374, 395.
Dongola, iii. 144, 163.
Donnachaidh clan, i. 16.
Douglas, Sir C., i. 419.
Dobrudscha, ii. 574 note [2].
Doyle, Francis, at Eton, i. 34, 37, 42–43; Gladstone's friendship with, i. 39, 54; Gladstone's letters to, i. 207; ii. 631; otherwise mentioned, i. 32 note, 59 note, 73, 111, 135, 581; ii. 184.
Dragonetti, the Marquis, ii. 12.
Drayton, i. 132.
Drew, Mrs. (Mary Gladstone), Gladstone's letter to, ii. 473; accompanies Gladstone to Midlothian, ii. 587; Acton's letter to, on Middlesex candidature, ii. 617; engagement of, iii. 280; Gladstone's letter to, on Robert Elsmere, iii. 356.
Drift, Gladstone's view of, ii. 352.
Dryden, iii. 484.
Duff, Grant, iii. 28 note [2].
Dufferin, Lord, urges Turkish intervention in Egypt, iii. 80; advises abandonment of Kordofan and Darfur, iii. 146; mentioned, ii. 64, 212, 294, 645; iii. 413.
Dugdale, W. S., i. 150.
Duncan, Mr., ii. 27 note.
Dundonald, Lord, iii. 180 note.

Dunfermline, Lord (Speaker), i. 150.
Dunkellin, Lord, ii. 206.
Dunrobin, i. 476.
Dupanloup, Bishop, ii. 532.
Durham, Lord, i. 144, 178.
Dyke, Sir W. Hart, iii. 279.

EASTERN QUESTION, see Turkey.
— Roumelia, ii. 576.
Eastlake, Sir C., ii. 189.
Ecce Homo, ii. 166–167, 172, 173, 533.
Ecclesiastical appointments, i. 153; ii. 122, 430–433.
— Commission (1835–36), iii. 468.
— Titles bill, i. 405, 409–415 and note; effect of Act on whigs, i. 446; repeal of (1871), ii. 517.
Economy: —
  Churchill's efforts for, iii. 365.
  Direct taxation conducive to, ii. 62.
  Gladstone's efforts for, ii. 42–45, 53, 61, 63–65, 482–484, 498; iii. 110, 507, 508, 537.
Edinburgh, Gladstone's early visit to, i. 10; reception in (June '86), iii. 343; Gladstone first lord rector of university, i. 634.
— Duke of, ii. 378, 455.
Edinburgh Review, Gladstone's anonymous article in, ii. 345.
Education, primary: —
  Board school question at Hawarden, ii. 646.
  Condition of, in 1869, ii. 302 note.
  Controversy on, nature of, ii. 306–307.
  Differences regarding, in liberal party, ii. 498.
  Dissenters' views on (1843 and 1847), ii. 302; (1870), ii. 303–305; estrangement by Act of 1870, ii. 307; opposition to the Act, ii. 308.
  Forster's bill (1870), ii. 298, 301, 303–307, 309–311, 495.
  Free, advocated by Chamberlain (1885), iii. 173, 224.
  Peel's bill (1843), ii. 299 note.
  State aid for, Gladstone's views on, i. 148; ii. 298–300, 310, 311.
  — secondary: —
  Classical course, Gladstone's view of, ii. 646–649.
  Reform of (1869), ii. 311–312.
Edwards, Jonathan, iii. 477.
Egerton, Sir P., i. 59 note.
— ii. 146–147 and note.
Egypt: —
  Alexandria — English and French fleets at, iii. 79; bombardment of, iii. 81, 84–85.

Egypt — *continued.*
　Anglo-French control in, iii. 74, 78, 118; proposal of Anglo-French occupation, i. 76–77.
　Annexation idea unfavourably viewed in England, iii. 119.
　Army, revolt of, iii. 73, 78, 83.
　British responsibilities in, ii. 631; iii. 146.
　Conference of Constantinople, iii. 81.
　Financial position of, iii. 73, 76, 120–122, 170, 192, 197; London convention, iii. 122.
　Gladstone's prognostication regarding, iii. 72.
　Northbrook's mission to, iii. 121.
　Reforms in, possible only by evacuation of Soudan, iii. 148.
　Soudan, *see that title.*
　Southern frontier of, determined (1885), iii. 180.
　Suez Canal: —
　　Construction of, i. 591–592.
　　France, attempted agreement with, regarding, iii. 122.
　　Protection of (1882), iii. 80, 82, 83.
　Tel-el-Kebir, iii. 83, 120 *note.*
　Withdrawal from, difficulties of, iii. 120; Salisbury's policy regarding, iii. 495.
d'Eichthal, Gustave, ii. 538.
Elcho, Lord, ii. 19 *note* [2].
Elections, general — (1885) iii. 249–255; (1886) iii. 345–346; (1892) iii. 492, 494; dates of Gladstone's, ii. 608.
Elgin, Lord (J. Bruce), i. 54, 59 *note*; ii. 18, 194, 636.
Eliot, Lord, i. 236.
Elizabeth, Queen, iii. 480.
Ellenborough, Lord, i. 525, 583, 641.
Ellice, E., i. 222, 237, 467, 493; ii. 194.
Elliot, Arthur, iii. 285.
Elwin, W., i. 553, 555.
Emancipation, *see* Slave-holding.
Emerson, R. W., i. 176–177 *note*, 220; ii. 458.
Employers' Liability bill (1893), iii. 504.
Endowed Schools bill (1869), ii. 312.
Epirus, ii. 576.
Errington, W. V., iii. 63.
Esher, Viscount, cited, ii. 624 *note.*
Essays and Reviews, i. 316; ii. 163–164, 431.
Estcourt, T. G. B., i. 328.
Estimates (*see also* Expenditure), (1853 and 1860), ii. 24; (1874–75) ii. 375 *note* [1], 483; (1892), iii. 507–509.
Eton, Gladstone's career at, i. 26–44; examines at (1840), i. 229.

Eton Miscellany, i. 34, 37–38.
Eugénie, Empress, ii. 458.
Evarts, W. M., ii. 189.
Eversley, Viscount (speaker), i. 266.
Ewelme appointment, ii. 386–387; iii. 540.
Exchequer and Audit Act (1866), ii. 61.
Expenditure: —
　Annual amount of (1860–65 and 1873), ii. 374.
　Army and Navy, on (1857–66), ii. 51.
　Excess in, Gladstone's efforts against, ii. 42–45, 53, 61, 63–65.
　Policy of (1853–59), i. 475.
　Spirit of, Gladstone's protest against, ii. 50, 62.
Export trade, growth of (1860–66), ii. 66–67.

Factory legislation, i. 106.
Faguet, cited, ii. 594.
Farini, i. 402–404; ii. 8.
Farquhar, Sir W., i. 162, 473; ii. 165.
Farr, W. W., i. 29.
Farrer, Lord, i. 333 *note* [1].
Fasque, family portraits at, i. 9; church at, i. 11 *note* [1]; purchase of, i. 107; Helen Gladstone buried at, ii. 604; T. Gladstone's golden wedding at, iii. 219; Gladstone's visit to (1891), iii. 462.
Favre, Jules, ii. 356.
Fawcett, H., ii. 302, 444 *note*, 455, 463 *note.*
Fechter, C. A., ii. 189 *and note*, 190.
Fénelon, i. 184, 215.
Fenians: —
　Papal rescript, attitude towards, iii. 384.
　Parnell's alleged conversation with a spy regarding, iii. 404–405.
　Plots by (1867), ii. 241–242.
　Temper of (1887), iii. 373.
Ferdinand, King, i. 392, 397, 401.
Ferguson, Dr., ii. 27.
Field, Cyrus, ii. 71, 458.
Fielden, J., i. 114.
Finance (*see also* Budgets, Expenditure, National Debt, Taxation): —
　Egyptian, iii. 170, 192, 197.
　Gladstone's masterly statements on, ii. 593; iii. 7; his principles of, ii. 26, 56–61, 63, 68.
　Home Rule bill provisions regarding, *see under* Ireland.
　Pitt's, ii. 627–638.
　Popular interest in, i. 458.
Finance bill, ii. 39–40.
Finlay, G., i. 605, 610 *note*, 614.

Fire insurance duty, ii. 373, 651.
Fish, H., ii. 82, 401–402, 406.
Fisher, Bishop, ii. 535.
Fitzgerald, Lord, i. 259.
Fitzmaurice, Lord E., ii. 463 note.
Fitzroy, Lord C., i. 419; ii. 102.
Fitzwilliam, Lord, iii. 314, 339.
Florence, ii. 8–9; iii. 387.
Follett, Sir W. W., i. 322.
Foreign affairs, British ignorance of, ii. 535–536.
Foreign Enlistment Act (1870), ii. 399 and note, 405.
— policy : —
Gladstone's views on, ii. 316–318.
Peel's influence on, i. 247.
Popular fickleness regarding, i. 480.
Forster, W. E., on American civil war, ii. 86; views on liberal party, ii. 123; vice-president of council (1870), ii. 644; Education bill of, ii. 298, 301, 303–307, 309–311, 495; Endowed Schools, bill of, ii. 312; Ballot bill, ii. 368; on *Alabama* case, ii. 403, 408; on Irish university debate, ii. 444–445; on Bulgarian question, ii. 549; Irish secretary (1880), ii. 630, 654; radical attitude towards, ii. 630: allows Coercion Act to lapse (1880), iii. 48; on Lords' rejection of Disturbance bill, iii. 409; 'village ruffian' theory, iii. 49; seeks coercive powers, iii. 49, 51; Coercion bill of, iii. 52 and notes, 296 note[1]; at Hawarden, iii. 57; Gladstone's letters to, iii. 58, 66; condition of Ireland under, iii. 379; resigns, iii. 65, 90, 654; on franchise extension in Ireland, iii. 143 note[3]; otherwise mentioned, ii. 447 note, 462, 476, 498, 504, 566, 644; iii. 64, 169, 175, 353 and note[2].
Fortescue, C., see Carlingford.
Fortnightly Review, iii. 75–76.
Fortunato, i. 398.
Fould, A., ii. 55–56, 221.
Fowler, H. H., iii. 336, 495 note.
— William, ii. 295.
Fox, General, i. 228.
— C. J., views of, on emancipation of slaves, i. 104; estimates of, by Peel and Harrowby, i. 132–133; motion of, against Lord Sandwich, i. 144; parliamentary position of, i. 445–446; protests against British interference in Crimea, i. 478.
Otherwise mentioned, i. 131, 365; ii. 230, 589.
— Henry, i. 570.

France : —
Alliance with, Gladstone's view of, i. 546; ii. 15.
Alliances sought by (1869), ii. 321, 323.
American war, joint mediation in, urged on England and Russia, ii. 85.
Austria, peace with, Lord Elcho's motion on, ii. 19 note[2].
Berlin treaty obligations, attitude towards, iii. 9.
Black Sea affair, ii. 350, 356 and note.
Commercial treaty with — suggested by Cobden, ii. 18, 20; negotiation of, ii. 21, 46; discussed in cabinet, ii. 21–22; provisions of, ii. 21 note, 23; objects of, ii. 22–23; publication of, in Belgian papers, ii. 27; results of, ii. 66, 637, 638; Gladstone's later views on, ii. 66 note.
Commune (1871), ii. 308.
Confusion in policy of, ii. 120.
Crimean war, see that title.
Danubian provinces, policy regarding, ii. 3.
Divorce illegal in (1816–84), i. 567 note.
Don Pacifico case, offer of good offices in, i. 368.
Egypt, action regarding (1881), iii. 73; understanding with Salisbury, iii. 74; the joint note, iii. 75–76; fleet at Alexandria, iii. 79; fleet withdrawn, iii. 81; agrees to British advance in Egypt, iii. 82; declines to take any action, iii. 83; Salisbury policy frustrated by, iii. 495.
German unity a menace to, ii. 319.
Gladstone's finance admired in, ii. 56; Gladstone elected foreign associate of institute of, ii. 220 and note; tribute at his death, iii. 532.
Italian unity aided by, ii. 7–8, 14, see also Napoleon.
Land question in, iii. 477.
Nice and Savoy acquired by, ii. 9, 22, 30, 108.
Orsini affair, representations regarding, i. 574.
Palmerston's attitude towards, i. 367; ii. 47, 49.
Poetry in, iii. 483.
Prussia : —
Treaty with, regarding Belgium, ii. 340.
War with (1870) — British efforts to avert, ii. 326–330, 335–336;

France — *continued.*
Prussia — *continued.*
declaration of, ii. 335 *and note*[2];
French miscalculations, ii. 337;
course of, ii. 342–343; British sympathy after Sedan, ii. 357; effect
of the war on British naval expenditure, ii. 374.
Republic — recognition of (1871), ii.
345; statesmen of, iii. 475.
Rome — occupation of, ii. 107–108, 214,
319, 323; British attitude towards
the occupation, ii. 512; evacuation
of, ii. 217, 512.
Roumania, coolness with Britain regarding, ii. 4.
Schleswig-Holstein question, ii. 116–
118.
Tariff negotiations with, i. 267.
Turkish murder of consul at Salonica, ii. 547; attitude towards
Turkey (1881), iii. 74.
Vatican decrees, attitude towards, ii.
510.
Vicissitudes of government in, i. 413.
War with (1812), iii. 471; war rumoured (1859–60), ii. 43–44, 46–47.
Zenith of the empire, ii. 5.
Franchise extension : —
Anticipations regarding (1885), iii.
172, 201.
Bill of 1860, ii. 200; bill of 1866, ii.
200–205; bill of 1867, ii. 223–236,
238, 257.
Boroughs, for, workmen's attitude
towards, ii. 125, 139, 198, 211, 227;
Palmerston's views regarding, ii.
128, 200; household suffrage strug-
gle, ii. 223–236; liberal aid to
tories for (1867), iii. 238, 257.
Counties, for, ii. 200, 475, 481; iii.
124 *et seq.*
Conservative party the gainers by,
iii. 129.
Ireland, *see under* Ireland.
Gladstone's speech on (1864), ii. 126–
130.
Manhood, Chamberlain's pronounce-
ment on, iii. 174.
Reform bill of 1866 restricted to, ii.
200.
Fraser, family of, i. 17 *note.*
—— Bishop, ii. 432.
—— Sir William, i. 8 *and note*[2], 9 *note.*
Frederick William, Crown Prince of
Prussia, i. 176.
Free trade : —
Disraeli's pronouncement on, i. 432.
Employment in relation to, ii. 57.

External agitation, production of, ii.
227.
French commercial treaty in relation
to, ii. 21 *note*, 24.
Gladstone's speech on (1881), iii. 61.
Freeman, E. A., ii. 365.
Freeman's Journal, ii. 292.
Fremantle, T. F., i. 237.
Frere, Sir Bartle, liberal disapproval of,
iii. 2, 6; responsible for Zulu war,
iii. 22; the Queen's feeling for, iii.
23–24; enquires liberal policy, iii. 28;
promises Boers self-government, iii.
30; South African Dutch exasperated
by, iii. 43 *note*; recalled, iii. 24, 32
note.
Freshfield, J. W., i. 233, 339.
Freycinet, M. de, iii. 75, 79–83.
Frohschammer, J., ii. 525.
Frost, J., i. 400.
Froude, Hurrell, i. 161, 166, 306.
—— J. A., i. 313 *note* [1]; ii. 539, 559.
Funerals, ii. 422.
Furse, C. W., ii. 433.

Gaisford, Dr., i. 49.
Gambetta, ii. 335 *note* [1]; iii. 75, 77, 78,
82, 465.
Garfield, Mrs., iii. 108.
Garibaldi — sails from Genoa, ii. 10–11;
enters Naples, ii. 17; in England, ii.
108–113; Gladstone's estimate of, ii.
109–110, 114; Italian estimate of,
ii. 113; Manning's attitude towards,
ii. 192; letters from, ii. 533; mentioned, ii. 184; iii. 532.
Gaskell, Mrs. Benjamin, i. 160.
—— James Milnes, Gladstone's friendship with, i. 39, 54; debating society
in rooms of, i. 59; speech on Reform
bill, i. 73; Gladstone's visits to, i.
95; ii. 437; otherwise mentioned, i.
34, 37, 43, 48, 49, 64, 65, 74, 75, 77, 80,
97, 131, 137, 138, 139, 229, 248.
George iii., ii. 428; iii. 181.
Gerasimus, Bishop, i. 604.
Germany (*see also* Prussia) : —
Berlin memorandum, ii. 549, 571.
—— treaty obligations, attitude to-
wards (1880), iii. 9.
Black Sea provisions of Treaty of
Paris disapproved by, ii. 350.
Colonial question in, iii. 122.
Egyptian question, attitude towards,
iii. 79, 80, 82, 89.
Italian alliance with, iii. 414.
Luxemburg affair, ii. 320, 357 *and
note.*
Poetry in, iii. 483.

Schleswig-Holstein question, ii. 114–118.

Turkish murder of consul at Salonica, ii. 547.

Unification of, ii. 358; France menaced by, ii. 319.

Vatican decrees, attitude towards, ii. 509.

Gibbon, i. 195; iii. 476.

Gibson, Milner-, Gladstone against, i. 467; efforts towards peace, i. 547; return to parliament (1858), i. 574; in Palmerston government, i. 626; unpopularity of, in Oxford, i. 630; on Paper Duties bill, ii. 33, 37–39; Gladstone supported by, ii. 36, 140, 635–636.

Gladstone, name changed from Gladstones, i. 18 and note 2.

—— Agnes (daughter), engagement of, ii. 472–473; marriage, ii. 475.

—— Anne (sister), i. 17 note 1, 160.

—— Helen Jane (sister), i. 17 note 1; Gladstone abroad with, i. 284, 318; secession to Rome, i. 318, 331; death, ii. 604.

—— Henry (son), Gladstone's message to, on learning Latin, ii. 94; at school, ii. 191; starts for India, ii. 557; Gladstone's letters to, ii. 586, 598; iii. 296.

—— Herbert (son), Gladstone's letters to, ii. 59 and note, 637; iii. 258; returned for Leeds, ii. 618; press interview of (Dec. '85), iii. 264–265; otherwise mentioned, ii. 474, 477, 614, 617; iii. 1.

—— Sir John (father), political work of, i. 9–10, 20–21, 249; churches built by, i. 11 and note 1; marriage of, i. 16; views of, on slave-holding, i. 22–24; Gladstone's defence of, in the Liverpool Courier, i. 32; loses Berwick election, i. 43; political acuteness of, i. 68–69; criticisms on W. E. Gladstone, i. 74; Howick's attack on, i. 102; Fasque bought by, i. 107; seventieth birthday of, i. 118; loses Dundee election (1837), i. 141; disapproves Jamaica journey, i. 148; transfers Demerara property to his sons, i. 224; assists Scotch training college scheme, i. 231; correspondence with Peel regarding his sons, i. 257–258; views of, on protection, i. 300, 327; baronetcy of, i. 293, 300; views on Gladstone's Oxford candidature, i. 330; on Jewish Disabilities Removal bill, i. 376; buys portion of Hawarden estates, i. 341; attitude towards Peel (1849), i. 353; death of,

i. 388; W. E. Gladstone's relations with, i. 19, 32, 43, 82–83, 98; W. E. Gladstone's letters to, i. 123, 280, 283–284, 353, 375–376, 635; letters from, on choice of profession, i. 640; W. E. Gladstone's estimate of, i. 19, 138.

Gladstone, Mrs. John (mother), W. E. Gladstone's devotion to, i. 95, 128, 131; death of, i. 131.

—— John (brother), i. 15, 17 note 1; travels of, with W. E. Gladstone, i. 86; Walsall candidature of, i. 231–232; parliamentary election of, desired by his father, i. 258; W. E. Gladstone's letter to, on family differences, i. 388; illness and death of wife of, ii. 95, 96; death of, ii. 187.

—— Mary (daughter), see Drew.

—— Robertson (brother), i. 17 note 1; appointed manager of Demerara properties, i. 224; position of, in Liverpool, i. 258; at Gladstone's Lancashire candidature (1865), ii. 146; W. E. Gladstone's letters to, i. 494, 552–553, 626; ii. 62, 130, 456.

—— Stephen (son), ii. 256, 474, 500.

—— Thomas (grandfather), i. 16.

—— —— (brother), slave-holding defended by, i. 24; attitude towards Reform bill, i. 70 note; on Gladstone's Oxford candidature, i. 330; Gladstone's letter to, on offers of a peerage, ii. 494; otherwise mentioned, i. 17 note 1, 68, 258.

—— William Ewart: —
Appearance of (1827), i. 34; (1840) i. 194; (1882) iii. 91.

Career, chronological sequence of —

1809–1831. Birth and baptism, i. 7; childhood, i. 10–14; at Eton, i. 26–44; first speech, i. 35; Oxford, i. 48–85; tries for the Ireland, i. 61, 329 note.

1832. Foreign travel, i. 86–88; impressions in Rome, i. 87; Newark candidature, i. 88–94, 96–97; election addresses, i. 90; first speech as member of parliament, i. 94; visits to Clumber, Thornes, and Leamington, i. 95; birthday, i. 97.

1833. Lincoln's Inn, i. 98; membership of Oxford and Cambridge club and Carlton club, i. 98 and note; forms brotherhood with Acland, i. 99; enters parliament, i. 100; maiden speech, i. 103; party votes (1833), i. 106; visit to Fasque, i. 107.

Gladstone, William Ewart — *continued.*
Career, chronological sequence of
(*continued*). —

1834. Visit to Seaforth and
Oxford, i. 111; at Fasque, i. 116;
treasury appointment, i. 119–120;
opposes admission of dissenters
to universities, i. 330.

1835. Returned for Newark
without contest, i. 121; meets
Disraeli at Lord Lyndhurst's, i.
122; appointed under-secretary
for the colonies, i. 123; contem-
plates resignation, i. 125; speech
on Irish church, i. 126; speech at
Newark, i. 129; committee on
native affairs at the Cape, i. 358.

1836. Death of his mother, i.
131; visit to Drayton, i. 132; visit
to Hawarden, i. 134; speech on
negro apprenticeship, i. 134 *and
note*; visit to Haddo, i. 137; committee on waste lands, i. 358.

1837. Speech at Newark on
toleration, etc., i. 138; presents
the Queen with the Oxford
address, i. 140; canvassing at
Newark, i. 140; nominated for
Manchester, i. 141; elected for
Newark, i. 141; at Dundee, Glasgow, Liverpool, Manchester, i.
141; at Fasque, i. 142; first interview with Duke of Wellington,
i. 143.

1838. Admitted to consultations on Canadian affairs, i. 144;
speaks on Molesworth's vote of
censure, i. 145; speech on slave
apprenticeship system, i. 145–147;
work on educational questions,
i. 148; influenced by Coleridge
and Palmer, i. 167–168 *note* 1; *The
State in its Relation with the
Church*, i. 172, 175; foreign
travel, i. 173.

1839. Opinions on his book,
i. 175–181; work on committees,
i. 219; marriage, i. 223.

1840. Speech on China question, i. 226; birth of eldest son,
i. 227; dines at Guizot's, i. 229;
examines at Eton, i. 229; Scotch
training college scheme, i. 230–
231, 330; committee on coloni-
sation of New Zealand, i. 358.

1841. *Church Principles*, i.
181; his brother's Walsall election, i. 231–232; visits Nuneham
and Oxford, i. 235; speaks on

sugar duties, i. 236; re-elected for
Newark, i. 238; Sir S. Glynne's
candidature — Hoylake — Hawarden, i. 239; vice-president of the
board of trade, i. 240–245, 250;
re-elected for Newark, i. 243;
correspondence with Peel on journalistic imputations, i. 245–246;
Jerusalem bishopric, i. 309; advocates increase in colonial episco-
pate, i. 330.

1842. Protection question, i.
249–254; suggests retirement, i.
253; tariff reform, i. 255–257;
shooting accident, i. 185; Glenalmond, i. 231.

1843. Enters the cabinet, i.
259; parliamentary success, i. 261;
protection question, i. 262–264;
tariff negotiations with foreign
countries, i. 267; advocates removal of prohibition on export of
machinery, i. 267–268; close relations with Manning and Hope, i.
310; anxiety regarding Newman's
position, i. 310–313; protests
against sentence on Pusey, i. 317.

1844. Bill for regulation of
companies, i. 268; Telegraph Act,
i. 268; Railway Act, i. 269; publishes Prayer-Book, i. 314 *note*;
reply to Ward's *Ideal*, i. 314–315;
Lady Hewley case, i. 322; proposes himself as Vatican envoy, i.
271–272; Maynooth, i. 271–275, 278.

1845. At Windsor Castle, i.
274–275; resigns office, i. 276–278,
279; votes for second reading of
Maynooth bill, i. 279; tariff reform, i. 279; pamphlet on results
of fiscal changes of 1842, i. 280 *and
note*; on free labour sugar proposal, i. 280; at Munich, i. 318; at
Baden-Baden, i. 320; corn law
repeal, i. 283–287; secretary for
the colonies, i. 285.

1846. Colonial clergy questions, i. 358; recall of colonial
governor, i. 359; out of parliament, i. 287–288; offended at
Peel's eulogium on Cobden, i. 291–
292; conversation with Lord Lyndhurst on conservative party, i.
293–294; with Jocelyn and Graham, i. 295; interview with Peel,
i. 297–300; quarrel with Lord G.
Bentinck, i. 301–302.

1847. Oxford candidature, i.
328–332; election, i. 333; Jewish

Disabilities Removal bill, i. 375–377; Oak farm and Hawarden estate embarrassments, i. 337, 356.
1848. Special constable against chartists, i. 358; Oxford D.C.L., i. 377; on Hampden's appointment as bishop, i. 377.
1849. Divergences from Peel, i. 353; mission for his friend, i. 364–365; Gorham case, i. 378.
1850. Supports Disraeli's agricultural distress motion, i. 354–356; Gorham case, i. 378–381 and note; death of his daughter, i. 381, 387–388; Australian Colonies bill, i. 362; Don Pacifico debate, i. 369–371 and note; death of Peel, i. 371; question of leadership, i. 373–374; opposes universities commission, i. 497; Naples, i. 389–393; on committee for exhibition medal inscriptions, ii. 539.
1851. Returns to London, i. 393; Letters to Lord Aberdeen, i. 392, 394 and note, 396–398, 400–401 and note³; invited by Stanley to take office, i. 393, 406; declines, i. 407; Ecclesiastical Titles bill, i. 409–415; secession of Manning and Hope, i. 385–386; death of his father, i. 388; letter to a Scotch bishop on religious freedom, i. 384, 426.
1852. First Derby administration, i. 417; approaches Aberdeen and Graham, i. 417–418; views on Peelite policy, i. 417–419; overtures from Russell, i. 421; supports Derby, i. 424; on Four Seats bill, i. 424 and note; re-elected for Oxford, i. 426–427; equipoise of opinions, i. 431; defends free trade, i. 433; overtures from Derby, i. 434; speech on Disraeli's budget, i. 438–440; incident at the Carlton, i. 440–441; New Zealand Government bill, i. 362 and note², 645; appointed chancellor of the exchequer, i. 448.
1853. Difficulties at Oxford, i. 450–452; re-election, i. 453; moves to house of chancellor of exchequer, i. 457; advocates reduction of force in the Pacific, i. 458; budget, i. 460–472; iii. 537; attempted operation on national debt, i. 472–473, 646–648; Latin lessons to his son, i. 464; illness at Dunrobin, i. 476; presented with freedom of Dingwall, i. 476; speech at Inverness, i. 476; Crimean war, i. 481 et seq.; speech at unveiling of Peel statue at Manchester, i. 483; case of Mr. Maurice, i. 454–456; Oxford reform, i. 500.
1854. Letter on revival of convocation, ii. 162; speeches on Oxford reform, i. 503, 509 note²; civil service reform, i. 509–512, 649; criticisms of his finance, i. 513–514; speech on budget, i. 514–515; conflict with Bank of England, i. 518–519, 650–651; Savings Bank bill, i. 519; woods and forests dismissal case, i. 520.
1855. Ministerial crisis, i. 522–543; opposes Roebuck's motion, i. 523–524; joins Palmerston, i. 536; opposes Roebuck's motion in cabinet, i. 537–538; resigns, i. 539; unpopularity, i. 542–543; efforts for peace, i. 545–548; at Penmaenmawr, i. 549; Homeric studies, i. 549–550; Chester speech on colonial policy, i. 363.
1856. Communications with Lord Derby, i. 551–552, 554; isolation, i. 553; letter to Bishop Hampden, i. 168; case of Archdeacon Denison, i. 557.
1857. Interviews with Lord Derby, i. 558–561; opposes Lewis' budget, i. 560–562; co-operation with Disraeli, i. 561; communications with Cobden, i. 562; speech on the China war, i. 563; returned for Oxford unopposed, i. 565; opposes Divorce bill, i. 570; encounters with Bethell, i. 570–571; illness and death of Lady Lyttelton, i. 572–573.
1858. Opposes Conspiracy bill, i. 575–576 and note; refuses to join Derby, i. 576–578; renewed proposal from Derby, i. 583; refused, i. 585, 590; motion on the Principalities, ii. 4; letter from Disraeli, i. 586; reply, i. 589; supports Suez Canal scheme, i. 592; letter to Graham on Indian government, i. 593; at Haddo, i. 594; commission to Ionian Islands, i. 594–618; at Athens, i. 605.
1859. At Venice, Turin, Vicenza, Verona, Milan, i. 618; interview with Cavour, i. 618;

Gladstone, William Ewart — *continued.*
*Career, chronological sequence of
(continued).* —
defends nomination boroughs, i.
621; speech on Italian question,
ii. 13; votes with Derby government, i. 625; joins Palmerston's
government, i. 626; letters on his
position, i. 627–628; trouble at
Oxford, i. 628–630; re-elected for
Oxford, i. 630; budget, ii. 19;
speaks on Italian affairs, ii. 19;
Cobden's visit, ii. 18, 20; views
on French war scare, ii. 43–44;
first lord rector of Edinburgh university, i. 634.
    1860. Budget, i. 474; ii. 24 *et
seq.*, 625; illness, ii. 26–27, 31, 34,
35; unpopularity, ii. 29, 31; defeat on Savings Bank bill, ii. 34;
speech on Paper Duty Repeal
bill, ii. 34; chief trains of cabinet
business, ii. 36, 635–636; the
fortification scheme, ii. 42, 44–47;
cabinet struggle on question of
economy, ii. 42–45; interview with
Palmerston, ii. 45–46; at Penmaenmawr, ii. 184; death of Lord
Aberdeen, ii. 87.
    1861. Budget, ii. 38–39; cabi-
net struggles, ii. 39, 93–96;
correspondence with Sir Wm.
Heathcote on finance, ii. 632–
635; attacks and abuse, ii. 48;
American civil war, ii. 70–72,
74–75; on education, ii. 312, 646;
deaths of Graham and Herbert,
ii. 87–88.
    1862. Speech on Italy, ii. 108;
correspondence with Palmerston,
ii. 49–50; panegyric on Prince
Consort, ii. 89; American civil
war, ii. 75–77, 79–82; triumphal
reception in the north, ii. 77–79;
Newcastle speech on American
war, ii. 79–82; funeral of Mrs.
John Gladstone, ii. 96; Windsor,
i. 96.
    1863. Death of his brother
John, ii. 187; budget, ii. 66, 67;
proposal to extend income tax to
charities, ii. 65–66; speech on Italy,
ii. 189; at Penmaenmawr, ii. 191;
at Balmoral, ii. 97–104.
    1864. At Balmoral, ii. 104–
106; letters on *Essays and Reviews* judgment, ii. 164; speech
on Mr. Dodson's bill, ii. 313 *and
note*[2]; Garibaldi's visit, i. 109–

113; speech on extension of franchise, ii. 126, 238; correspondence
with Palmerston, ii. 127–130; address from York workmen, ii.
130–131; Schleswig-Holstein question, i. 116–119; speeches in Lancashire, ii. 131–133; relations with
protestant dissenters, ii. 134–135;
development in ideas, ii. 121 *et
seq.*
    1865. Cabinet struggles, ii.
140; criticism of *Ecce Homo*, ii.
166–167, 172, 173; elected foreign
associate of the Institute of
France, ii. 220 *and note*; speech
on Irish church, ii. 142; death of
Cobden, ii. 143; letter to his son
on ecclesiastical affairs, ii. 159;
defeat at Oxford, ii. 145; Lancashire candidature and election, ii.
145–147; speech on conservatism,
ii. 178; letter to Russell on death
of Palmerston, ii. 151; at Glasgow, ii. 154, 155.
    1866. Leader of Commons,
ii. 156–157; tribute to Palmerston,
ii. 157; introduces Reform bill, ii.
200; disaffection of followers, ii.
202, 205–209; second reading of
Reform bill, i. 203–204; budget, ii.
68, 200; votes for abolition of
church rates, ii. 161; against vote
of confidence after debate, ii. 207–
209; audiences of the Queen, ii.
209, 211; declines to speak at
Hyde Park demonstration, ii. 212;
speech at Cobden club, ii. 213;
goes to Italy, ii. 213; in Rome, ii.
214–219; illness, ii. 217.
    1867. Dinner with the Society
of Political Economists of France,
ii. 221; household suffrage struggle, ii. 223–236; disaffection of
followers, ii. 224, 225, 227–228,
232–235; Irish church questions,
i. 243; speech at Newspaper Press
Fund dinner, ii. 235.
    1868. Correspondence with
Acland on popular discontent, ii.
172–174; bill on church rates, ii.
161; Irish church question, ii. 245–
248; election for Greenwich, ii.
251 *and note*[1]; publication of
Chapter of Autobiography, ii. 249–
250; candidature in S.-W. Lancashire, ii. 250–251 *and note*[1]; letter
from the Queen, ii. 252; forms a
cabinet, ii. 253–255; speech at
Greenwich, ii. 371.

1869. Colonial Society dinner, ii. 402 *note*; letter to General Grey on foreign policy, ii. 316; Irish church bill preliminaries, ii. 258–263; bill introduced, ii. 263–264; committee stage, ii. 266; struggle with the Lords, ii. 267–271; Lords' amendments rejected, ii. 272–275; concessions, ii. 277–278; proposes acceptance by Commons of modifications, ii. 279; illness, ii. 276, 279–280; visit to Walmer Castle, ii. 280, 422; Irish land question, ii. 287 *et seq.*; letter to Bright on principles *v.* details, ii. 290.

1870. Irish land bill withdrawn, ii. 294; *Alabama* case, ii. 399; education question, ii. 298, 303–311; on reduction of armaments, ii. 321–322; efforts to avert Franco-Prussian war, ii. 326–330; daily conferences with Granville, ii. 338; neutrality of Belgium guaranteed, ii. 341–342; views on annexation of Alsace and Lorraine, ii. 346–348; Russian claims in Black Sea, ii. 350–352, 355; difficulties with the court, ii. 360; army reform, ii. 360 *et seq.*; question of commander-in-chief's position, i. 360–361, 649; Ballot bill, ii. 368–369.

1871. Views on neutralisation of Alsace and Lorraine, i. 357; anonymous article in *Edinburgh Review*, ii. 345; instructions to *Alabama* commission, ii. 404; abolition of purchase, ii. 361–365; Ballot bill, ii. 369, 377; struggles for economy, ii. 374; visit to Tennyson, ii. 377; freedom of Aberdeen, ii. 378; at Balmoral, ii. 378; at Edinburgh, ii. 379; funeral of Sir R. Murchison, ii. 380; speech at Blackheath, ii. 380–381; conversations with Bright, ii. 381–382; Collier appointment, ii. 382–386; Ewelme appointment, ii. 386–387; licensing questions, ii. 390; repeal of law against ecclesiastical titles, ii. 517.

1872. Unpopularity, ii. 387; cleavage in party, ii. 388; attitude of radicals, ii. 388–390; *Alabama* case, ii. 409–411; indignation on American claims, ii. 406; Act of Uniformity bill, ii. 410; speech at King's College council meeting,

ii. 523; visit to Oxford, ii. 436–437; address at Liverpool on Strauss, ii. 524.

1873. Irish University bill, ii. 436–445; letters to the Queen on retirement, ii. 442–443; ministerial crisis, ii. 446–456, 652; letter to Bright, on education question, ii. 309, 646; speech against disestablishment, ii. 457–458 *and note*; the Queen's birthday, ii. 422; death of Wilberforce, ii. 459; ministerial embarrassments, ii. 460–465; becomes chancellor of exchequer, ii. 463, 645; dispute as to vacating seat thereby, ii. 465–472; at Balmoral, ii. 472; engagement of his eldest daughter, ii. 472–473; at Hawarden, ii. 473–474; cabinet embarrassments, ii. 474; marriage of his eldest daughter, ii. 475.

1874. Financial plans, ii. 478, 481–482, 487; question of dissolution, ii. 479 *et seq.*; electoral manifesto, ii. 487–489; speeches at Greenwich, etc., ii. 490 *and note*; election, ii. 490; resignation, ii. 492–493 *and note*; offers of a peerage, ii. 493–494; retirement from leadership, ii. 497–499, 503–506; death of Sir S. Glynne, ii. 500–501; Vatican decrees question, ii. 502, 509–512; visit to Munich, ii. 513–515; *Vatican Decrees* pamphlet, ii. 515–517; its reception, ii. 517–520.

1875. Meeting of Metaphysical Society, ii. 504; article in *Quarterly Review*, ii. 520; more work on Vatican question, ii. 520–521; *Vaticanism* published, ii. 521; sale of house in Carlton House Terrace, ii. 522.

1876. Letter to Herbert Gladstone on Pitt's finance, ii. 637; pamphlet on Bulgaria, ii. 551–554; speech at Blackheath, ii. 552, 554; visits in the north, ii. 555–556; work at Hawarden, ii. 557; visit to Liverpool, ii. 558; 'The Hellenic Factor in the Eastern Problem,' ii. 558; St. James's Hall meeting, ii. 559; letter on denominationalism, iii. 542.

1877. *Lessons in Massacre*, ii. 560, 562; visit to Darwin, ii. 562; the five resolutions, ii. 563–565; speech in parliament, ii. 565–568;

Gladstone, William Ewart — *continued.*
Career, chronological sequence of (continued). —

visit to Birmingham, ii. 570; views on Transvaal annexation, iii. 27, 28; visit to Ireland, ii. 571.
1878. Hostile crowds, ii. 574; declines to stand for Leeds, ii. 611; speech on treaty-making power, ii. 577 *note*[2]; speech on Anglo-Turkish convention, ii. 576–578; article on 'England's Mission,' ii. 579, 581; literary work and emoluments, ii. 581; sits to Millais, ii. 581–582; visit of Argyll and Ruskin to Hawarden, ii. 582.
1879. Invited to stand for Midlothian, ii. 584; agrees, ii. 585; the campaign, ii. 587–596; iii. 27; day at Glasgow, ii. 590–592; from Glasgow to Hawarden, ii. 596; reflections, ii. 597; correspondence on leadership, ii. 598–603.
1880. At Hawarden, ii. 603, 604; with his sister at Cologne, ii. 604; election address, ii. 606–608; Midlothian campaign in general election, ii. 608–612; letter to Rosebery, ii. 613; to Argyll, ii. 615; conversations on leadership, ii. 616–617; interview with Hartington, ii. 621–624; with Granville and Hartington, ii. 624–625; audience of the Queen, ii. 626–628; construction of cabinet, ii. 628–630; personnel of cabinet, ii. 653–654; iii. 2–3; anonymous article in *Fortnightly Review*, ii. 345 *note*; parliamentary difficulties, iii. 5–6; budget, iii. 7; illness, iii. 8; cruise in *Grantully Castle*, iii. 8; Berlin treaty obligations, iii. 8–10; Bradlaugh question, iii. 11 *et seq.*; question of Frere's recall, iii. 22–24.
1881. Colley's correspondence, iii. 34; Boer overtures, iii. 35; Majuba, iii. 37–38; letters to the Queen, iii. 40; parliamentary attack, iii. 41–42; Transvaal commission, iii. 44; Coercion bill, iii. 49–50; obstruction, iii. 52–53; Irish Land bill, iii. 53–57; letter to Granville on home rule, iii. 57; visit to Leeds, iii. 59–61; agrees to imprisonment of Parnell, iii. 61; address to common council,

iii. 61; Egyptian question, iii. 74 *et seq.*
1882. Egyptian question, iii. 78 *et seq.*; letter to Forster, on Irish local government, iii. 58; communications from Parnell, iii. 64; letter to Forster on his resignation, iii. 66; to the Queen on Irish situation, iii. 66; Phœnix Park murders, iii. 67–69; public position, iii. 89–90; political jubilee, iii. 91; appoints Benson to see of Canterbury, iii. 95–97; reconstruction of cabinet, iii. 99–101; letters to Bright on Egyptian policy, iii. 84, 85; vexed with Bismarck, iii. 121.
1883. Stay at Cannes, iii. 102–104; interview with Clémenceau, iii. 123; renewed offer of a peerage, iii. 104; at Paris, iii. 105; at Sandringham, iii. 105; objects to sending troops to Suakin, iii. 149; speech on Affirmation bill, i. 139; iii. 14, 18–20, 107, 312; letter to Bright on 'Irish rebels' speech, iii. 111; cruise to Denmark, iii. 115–117; speech at Kirkwall, iii. 117–118, 354 *note*; Congo debate, iii. 110.
1884. Agrees to send Gordon to evacuate Soudan, iii. 149, 151 *and note*[2]; advises disavowing him after his abandonment of instructions, iii. 156; opposes appointment of Zobeir, iii. 158; advises his appointment, iii. 159; illness, iii. 159 *and note*, 160, 162; views on relief expedition for Gordon, iii. 162; Franchise bill, iii. 125–126, 140; speech on House of Lords, iii. 128; memorandum on case between Lords and Commons, iii. 129; efforts at arrangement, iii. 131–133; re-introduction of Franchise bill, iii. 136; conferences with Salisbury and Northcote, iii. 137–139; cabinet divisions, iii. 175; speech at Edinburgh on Transvaal, iii. 40 *note*[2].
1885. On Chamberlain's social programme, iii. 174; Acton's letter on retirement, iii. 172; learns death of Gordon, iii. 166, 172; letter in reply to the Queen's telegram, iii. 167; memorandum on military position in the Soudan, iii. 178–179, 555–559; on Russian action in Afghanistan,

iii. 178; three cabinets on Soudan, iii. 179–180; speech on war-supply for Afghanistan, iii. 184; cabinet difficulties, iii. 185–186; budget, iii. 187, 200; cabinet disagreements on Ireland, iii. 190–195; letter to the Queen on Irish policy, iii. 192; intimation regarding Crimes Act, iii. 188; letter to Hartington on cabinet crisis, iii. 196; ministerial crisis, iii. 203–208; audience of the Queen, iii. 205; offer of an earldom, iii. 209–210; defeated on budget, iii. 200; suddenness of defeat, iii. 202; resigns, iii. 200; letters to the Queen, iii. 199, 203; letters on advance in Irish situation, iii. 215–216; throat troubles, iii. 216; cruise in the Sunbeam, iii. 217–218; election address, iii. 220; conversation with Chamberlain, iii. 224–226; consideration of Home Rule question, iii. 234–241; letter to the Queen on Crimes Act discussions, iii. 199; work on books — miscellaneous reading — reply to Réville, iii. 247; Midlothian speeches, iii. 247–248; election, iii. 248; considerations of Irish situation, iii. 256–259, 261–264, 266, 268–276; tenders support to Lord Salisbury, iii. 258–260, 284; unauthorised publication of home rule scheme, iii. 264 and note, 265; party urgency for action, iii. 267; renewal of intercourse with Manning, iii. 281; birthday, iii. 281.

1886. Political rumours, iii. 279; begins the session, iii. 281; comments on Hartington's communication, iii. 282; attitude towards home rule, iii. 283; debate on the address, iii. 284–288; supports Collings' amendment, iii. 288; accepts the Queen's commission, iii. 290; to Osborne, iii. 290; formation of government, iii. 291 and note, 296 and note 2; preparation of bills, iii. 298; difficulties in cabinet, iii. 302–304, 306; interview with Parnell, iii. 305–306; introduction of Home Rule bill, iii. 310–312; violent hostility of opponents, iii. 321–322; conversation with Bright, iii. 326; strenuous efforts for the bill, iii. 331; letter from Bright, iii. 327; Parnell's letter, iii. 333–334; party meeting at foreign office, iii. 332–333; second meeting with Parnell, iii. 334; replies to Hicks Beach, iii. 334–335; speech on night of the division, iii. 338–340; decides for dissolution, iii. 341; electioneering, iii. 342–345; elected for Midlothian and for Leith, iii. 344; letter to the Queen, iii. 344; decides for resignation, iii. 346–347; final audience of the Queen, iii. 347–348; views on Chamberlain's Baptist article, iii. 368; at Tegernsee, iii. 351–352; speaks on Tenants Relief bill, iii. 353; at Hawarden, iii. 353; article on Locksley Hall, iii. 353–354; attitude towards plan of campaign, iii. 370–372; birthday, iii. 354–355.

1887. Letters to Acton, iii. 355–359; at Sandringham, Cambridge, Hawarden, Dollis Hill, Windsor, iii. 385; speech on Criminal Law Amendment (Ireland) bill, iii. 375 and note; on introduction of closure, iii. 377; on Mitchelstown, iii. 380; Robert Elsmere article, iii. 356–360; tour in South Wales, iii. 386–387; visit to Florence, iii. 387.

1888. Attitude towards Parnell commission, iii. 398–399; sympathy with Parnell, iii. 408; speech on report of the commission, iii. 408–411; speech at Birmingham, iii. 387–389; speech on Ireland, iii. 389; visit to Naples, iii. 413.

1889. Reasons for not visiting Rome, iii. 413–415; Old Testament studies, iii. 415–416; golden wedding anniversary, iii. 417; Parnell's visit to Hawarden, iii. 420, 445–446.

1890. Letter on General Gordon, iii. 169; visit to Oxford, iii. 420–421; death of Newman and Döllinger, iii. 421; views on Parnell's position, iii. 429–433, 435–437, 440, 443–444; Parnell leadership question, iii. 450, 452–453, 455–458; memoranda on Parnell leadership question, iii. 443–445; meeting at Lord Rendel's, iii. 434; letter to Morley on Parnell leadership, iii. 436; urges publication of letter, iii. 440–441;

Gladstone, William Ewart — *continued*.
Career, chronological sequence of (continued). —
speaks at Bassetlaw, iii. 452;
Morley's visit to Hawarden, iii.
452–454; communications with
Irish party towards an understanding, iii. 455–456; speech of
condolence with the Speaker, iii.
456.
1891. Death of Granville, iii.
462; death of his eldest son,
iii. 460; Fasque — Glenalmond —
Newcastle programme, iii. 462;
Biarritz, iii. 463 *et seq.*; birthday,
iii. 477.
1892. Biarritz, iii. 480 *et seq.*;
to the Riviera, iii. 489; re-elected
for Midlothian, iii. 492; formation
of cabinet, iii. 494–495 *note*; Home
Rule bill, iii. 496.
1893. Home Rule bill, iii. 500
et seq.; reply to Chamberlain, iii.
499–500; at Biarritz, iii. 504, 508.
1894. Advocates dissolution
on Lords question, iii. 505; naval
estimates, iii. 506–508; return to
England, iii. 509; last cabinet, iii.
510–511; last speech in parliament,
iii. 511–512; at Windsor, iii. 512–
514; letter of resignation, iii. 514;
the Queen's reply, iii. 515; letter
to Sir H. Ponsonby, iii. 516.
1895-1898. Literary work,
iii. 520–521; speeches at Chester
and Liverpool, iii. 521–522; last
diary entry, iii. 523; visit to
Cannes, iii. 523; last meeting with
the Queen, iii. 524; visit to Butterstone, iii. 525; illness, iii. 525–
528; visit to Cannes, iii. 526; to
Bournemouth, iii. 526; at Hawarden, iii. 526–528; death, iii. 528 ;
parliamentary tributes, iii. 528–
531; foreign tributes, iii. 531–533;
funeral, iii. 533.
Characteristics : —
Ambition for noble ends, i. 218.
Caution — suspense of judgment,
i. 309, 376, 418, 547; iii. 343.
Concentration, i. 186, 190, 255;
iii. 88.
Considerateness, i. 195, 339, 364;
iii. 456.
Continuity, i. 190.
Conversational charm, ii. 180, 561;
iii. 482.
Co-operation, aptitude for, i. 189–
190.

Copiousness, ii. 427; iii. 502.
Courage, i. 188, 218; ii. 246; iii. 44.
Courtesy, i. 213; ii. 416, 532, 562.
Deference to colleagues, ii. 415–
416, 420, 492; iii. 4, 5, 497, 530.
Detachment — alacrity of mind —
freedom of judgment, ii. 168,562.
Disregard of appearances—regard
for things rather than persons,
i. 357; ii. 365; iii. 536–537, 540.
Duality of disposition, i. 2, 18,
189, 264.
Eloquence — oratorical power, i.
191–195, 261, 410; ii. 41, 54–55,
123, 439, 566; absence of bitterness, i. 503; battle-cry element,
ii. 592; dramatic force, ii. 589,
594; iii. 500; lofty tone, i. 5, 14;
iii. 312; persuasiveness, i. 440;
physical resources, ii. 380, 593;
iii. 60, 91, 338, 500.
Essentials, grasp of, iii. 54, 331,
371.
Excitability of temperament —
nervous sensibility, i. 83, 103,
434; ii. 40, 111, 119, 140, 381, 493,
565, 576, 631; iii. 18, 101–102,
170, 290.
Family feeling, i. 95–96, 339.
Gaiety of mind, i. 188.
Gravity of temperament, i. 212.
Growth, mental, continuance of,
i. 207–208.
Humanity, ii. 555, 561, 595, 596.
Hurry, i. 186–187, 380.
Idealism, i. 197–198, 255
Imagination, moral and political,
i. 189, 255; ii. 56, 554; iii. 244,
540.
Impulsiveness, ii. 148, 203.
Industry, i. 186, 192, 197; ii. 261,
421; iii. 88, 298, 496; in public
duties, i. 101–102; ii. 418, 422;
iii. 7–8, 110, 353, 496.
Intellectual curiosity, limits of,
i. 202, 209.
Intensity, ii. 563.
Irritability, ii. 228.
Lancashire temperament, i. 192;
ii. 41, 60.
Liberty, instinct for, *see* Liberty.
Loyalty to colleagues, ii. 599–601,
603, 619; iii. 110, 510.
Magnanimity, ii. 48.
Missionary temper, i. 231.
Modesty, ii. 561.
Musical ability, i. 98.
Nature, delight in, ii. 280; iii. 478,
479.

Opportuneness, sense of, i. 190; ii. 240–241; iii. 258, 276, 509, 539.

Optimism — confidence, i. 218, 312, 364, 611, 630; ii. 265; iii. 354.

Orderliness, i. 206; iii. 88.

Over-refining — subtlety — 'sophistry,' i. 165, 210–212, 354, 359, 453, 516; ii. 54, 396, 590; ii. 185.

Patience, iii. 185, 298, 456, 497.

Patriotism, i. 617.

Practical aptitude, i. 67, 195, 206; ii. 547, 553; iii. 88.

Personal questions, dislike of, ii. 462; iii. 455, 456.

Quietude, desire for, i. 187.

Religious temper, i. 2–4, 31, 56–57, 84, 200–201, 204; fixity of dogmatic views, i. 153, 207; religious growth, 160–162; leanings towards clerical calling, i. 323–324, 382, 383, 635–641.

Reserve, i. 196–197, 376.

Resignation, i. 215–217.

Scrupulosity, i. 261.

Self-control, i. 189, 196; iii. 195, 298.

Self-distrust, i. 190–191.

Simplicity — trustfulness, i. 194, 197, 204; ii. 570; iii. 540.

Sincerity — integrity, i. 193, 194, 261, 410, 440; ii. 531, 554; iii. 482, 540.

Slowness of mental development, i. 14, 198, 529; of judgment, i. 453.

Tact, iii. 100.

Tenacity of purpose, i. 315; ii. 38, 42, 59, 138, 207, 211, 404, 415, 569; iii. 29, 186, 209, 331.

Tolerance, i. 316–317; ii. 416, 432, 517, 535; iii. 12–13, 18.

Tradition, reverence for, i. 201–202, 209.

Unity of purpose, i. 200.

Versatility, i. 184; ii. 168; iii. 455, 467.

Vital energy, i. 185; iii. 60, 498.

Vivacity, ii. 593.

Walking, fondness for, i. 116.

Will-power, i. 185, 189, 470.

Eyesight, difficulties with, i. 111, 138, 140, 142, 143, 173, 185, 230; cataract, iii. 492, 506, 515, 517–519.

Family and genealogy of, i. 7–9 and note, 16 and note[2], 17 notes.

Horoscope of, i. 197.

Letters of, characteristics of, i. 6; ii. 180.

Residences of, i. 232–233 note; ii. 523 note.

Verses by, i. 38, 63 note, 118.

Gladstone, Mrs. W. E. (wife), on Gladstone's duality, i. 189; ancestry of, i. 223; to possess Hawarden Castle for life, i. 344; at Oxford (1848), i. 377; at Hagley, i. 572; foreign travel prescribed for, i. 596; Wood's conversations with, i. 623, 624; at Newcastle (1862), ii. 78; intimacy of, with Duchess of Sutherland, ii. 183; medical skill of, ii. 190; appears to rioters, ii. 211; accompanies Gladstone to Midlothian, ii. 587; to Cannes (1882), iii. 102; has news of Cavendish murder, iii. 67; visit to Biarritz, iii. 463; on necessity for her husband's hearing both sides, iii. 479; eightieth birthday, i. 486; Rosebery's tribute to, iii. 531; death of, iii. 533; W. E. Gladstone's letters to, i. 187, 215, 233, 272–275, 276, 285, 335–336, 339–340, 355, 383–384, 436–439, 445, 480 note, 481 and note, 519, 570–573, 575; ii. 21, 138–141, 143, 152, 154, 378–379, 500, 503, 522, 523; iii. 115, 186, 352, 420.

—— W. H. (son), birth of, i. 227; letters to, on Hawarden estate, i. 340–343, 344–349; parliamentary career of, i. 346, 348; Gladstone unwilling to bequeath a title to, i. 384; speech at his father's Lancashire candidature, ii. 147; Gladstone's letter to, on ecclesiastical affairs, ii. 159; letter on dissolution (1874), ii. 487; Worcestershire candidature of (1880), ii. 614; return to Hawarden after election, ii. 617; death of, iii. 460; otherwise mentioned, ii. 98, 139, 410, 603, 604, 617.

Glanville, cited, i. 209 and note[1].

Glasgow, Gladstone's inaugural address at (1879), ii. 590–591; public meetings, i. 591–592; iii. 562.

Gleanings, preparation of, ii. 581; later series of, iii. 521.

Gledstanes, family of, i. 8–9 and note, 16 and note[2].

Glenalmond, i. 230–231; iii. 462.

Glenelg, Lord, i. 144, 362.

Glynne, Lady, i. 274, 341.

—— Catherine (see also Gladstone, Mrs. W. E.), Gladstone's engagement to, i. 222.

Glynne, Henry, i. 342–344.

—— Sir Stephen, Gladstone's travels with, i. 173; candidature of, in Flint-

Glynne, Sir Stephen — *continued.*
shire, i. 239; financial affairs of,
i. 337 *et seq.*; repulsed at election (1857), i. 565; munificence of,
ii. 195; death of, ii. 500; otherwise mentioned, i. 223; ii. 274,
279, 373 *note* [1], 385, 410, 418, 421,
446, 476.
Goderich, Lord, i. 75, 431, 543.
Goethe, i. 159, 202; ii. 467, 534.
Gordon, Colonel, i. 228.
—— Arthur, *see* Stanmore.
—— General, advises evacuation of
Soudan, iii. 147–148, 153–154; suggested for the work, iii. 149; previous career of, iii. 149 *note* [3]; agrees
to policy of evacuation, iii. 150, 153–
155; characteristics of, iii. 151; popular feeling for, iii. 152, 156; changes
his plans, iii. 152; appointed temporarily governor-general of Soudan,
iii. 152; instructions of, iii. 153, 154,
554; views of, on the situation, iii.
153, 155; request regarding Zobeir,
iii. 155–160; shows Khedive's secret
firman, iii. 160–162 *and note* [1]; reports
himself safe, iii. 162; relief expeditions to, contemplated, iii. 162–164;
Nile expedition to, despatched, iii.
165; death of, iii. 166; Gladstone's
estimate of, iii. 169; Gladstone's
views of appointment of, iii. 177, 196.
Gorham case, i. 316, 378–381, 632.
Görres, Dr., i. 319–320 *and note* [1].
Gortchakoff, ii. 15, 343, 350, 353 *note*,
354, 355.
Goschen, G. J., included in Russell
cabinet (1865), ii. 156 *and note* [1]; on
Irish Church bill, ii. 274; bill of, for
throwing open all lay degrees, ii. 313;
on civil service reform, ii. 315; president of poor law board (1868), ii.
644; Local Rating bill of, ii. 377, 388;
first lord of admiralty (1871), ii. 645;
considered for exchequer (1873), ii.
463; opposition support of, i. 472–473;
opposes reduction of estimates (1874),
ii. 483–484; at Constantinople, iii. 9–
10; on Soudan question, iii. 175, 176;
votes with conservatives on Collings'
amendment, iii. 288; against home
rule, iii. 291 *note*, 294; defeated in
Edinburgh, iii. 343; chancellor of
exchequer (1886), iii. 364; compared
with Hartington, iii. 366; urged by
Hartington to join the government,
iii. 367; budget (1887), iii. 385; otherwise mentioned, ii. 498, 503, 504, 563,
625, 644–645; iii. 220, 268.

Goulburn, Henry, appointed chancellor
of exchequer, i. 240; attitude of,
towards repeal, i. 283; towards Lord
Derby, i. 419; otherwise mentioned,
i. 271, 420, 472.
Government Annuities bill, ii. 52–53,
125.
—— powers, i. 304.
Gower, F. Leveson, ii. 459 *note*.
—— Lord Ronald, ii. 183.
Grafton, Duke of, ii. 467.
Graham, General, iii. 176.
—— Sir James: —
Chronology — Reform advocated by,
i. 143; corn laws defended by, i.
114, 249; resigns on Irish church
question, i. 154; estimate of Peel,
i. 248, 263; attitude towards protection, i. 253, 352; bill on Irish
colleges, ii. 434; supports Peel on
repeal, i. 283; views on Peel's
eulogium of Cobden, i. 295, 296;
on Peel's changes of policy, i. 296;
on Disraeli's agricultural distress
motion, i. 354–356; Don Pacifico
debate, i. 368; papal aggression
question, i. 407; Russell's proposal to include, i. 416; decides
for Russell rather than Derby,
i. 418–421 *and note*, 423, 424;
views on Gladstone's attitude to
Disraeli, i. 432; Russell's attitude
towards, i. 444; refuses chancel-
lorship of exchequer, i. 447–448;
on Gladstone's representation of
Oxford, i. 453; on Gladstone's
budget, i. 465, 466; misgivings of,
i. 466, 467; on Napoleon III., i.
485; on Peelites' position regarding Palmerston, i. 534; opposes
Roebuck's proposal, i. 538; resigns, i. 539; reason for resigning,
i. 542; efforts for peace, i. 546;
Gladstone's relations with, i. 551,
559; position of, contrasted with
Gladstone's, i. 555; discourages
Gladstone's communicating with
Derby, i. 552, 556; views of, on
reconstructed government, i. 561;
on Divorce bill, i. 571; uneasiness
regarding Gladstone, i. 581; on
party relationships, i. 584 *and
note*; Disraeli's attitude towards,
i. 584, 587; inclines to Gladstone's
joining Derby, i. 586, 590, 591; in
sympathy with Palmerston's government, i. 628; on Russell's
despatch regarding Italy, ii. 16;
death of, ii. 87–88.

Debating, method of, i. 195.
Estimate of, i. 407–408.
Gladstone's estimate of, i. 248, 250; iii. 525; his estimate of Gladstone, i. 186; ii. 170; Gladstone contrasted with, i. 407; otherwise mentioned, i. 126, 177, 238, 248, 258, 273, 275, 293, 405 *note*, 418, 420, 445, 446, 449, 482, 490, 492, 511, 526, 535, 536, 560, 566, 576, 593, 595–596, 613; ii. 30, 37, 194, 302.

Gramont, Duc de, ii. 325–328, 330, 334, 336, 337.

Grant, General, ii. 406.

—— G., Gladstone's godfather, i. 7.

Granville, Lord: —
Chronology — On cession of Canada, i. 402 *note*; on Gladstone's budget, i. 466; on Peelites' refusal to join Palmerston, i. 535; tries to form a government, i. 625; French treaty, ii. 22; Paper Duties bill, ii. 33, 37; letter to Gladstone on his leadership, ii. 172; against vote of confidence after Reform defeat, ii. 207; on Gladstone's *Chapter of Autobiography*, ii. 249–250; colonial secretary (1868), ii. 644; Irish Church bill, ii. 261–262, 269–271, 274–279, 645; foreign secretary (1870), ii. 324, 644; efforts to avert Franco-Prussian war, ii. 325–330, 335; deprecates Gladstone's absence, ii. 422; Gladstone's daily conferences with, ii. 338; on annexation of Alsace and Lorraine, ii. 348; on Black Sea provisions of Treaty of Paris, ii. 349–351, 355; on Collier appointment, ii. 383; on *Alabama* case, ii. 403, 410, 411; opposes honours for Mill, ii. 430; consultations with, on ministerial crisis, ii. 446–447, 452; at Hawarden (1873), ii. 474; advocates resignation before assembling, ii. 492; on question of leadership, ii. 504; on Italian view of *Vatican Decrees* pamphlet, ii. 520; reports Disraeli's proposed resignation, ii. 550; on Bulgarian question, ii. 550, 552, 556, 564; views on the party vote, ii. 568; succession to power, foretold by Gladstone, ii. 582; approves Gladstone's Midlothian candidature, ii. 584, 585; views on leadership, ii. 601–602 *and note*, 620–621, 624; omission of, by the Queen,

disapproved by Gladstone, ii. 622; foreign secretary (1880), ii. 625, 626, 653; Smyrna demonstration affair, iii. 9; Egyptian question (1881–82), iii. 74, 76–80, 87; letter to Gladstone on renewed offer of peerage, iii. 104; conferences on Franchise bill, iii. 137, 138; correspondence, etc., on evacuation of Soudan, iii. 147, 149 *and note*[2], 152 *and note*, 157 *note*[2], 159, 160 *note*, 162, 164; agrees to send Gordon to Soudan, iii. 150; at his send-off, iii. 150 *note*; Gladstone's conversations with, on Ireland (May '85), iii. 191–192; favours plan of central board for Ireland, iii. 194; on Gladstone's refusal of an earldom, iii. 210; correspondence with, on relations to liberal party, iii. 232–238; at Hawarden and Chatsworth, iii. 261; Gladstone's consultations with, iii. 261, 263, 268; view of Irish situation, iii. 268; Gladstone's memorandum, iii. 270–272; declines requesting Gladstone to convene late cabinet, iii. 269; colonial secretary, iii. 297 *note*; declares for home rule, iii. 291 *and note*, 294; prefers home rule to Chamberlain's Irish scheme, iii. 291; Gladstone consults with, on birthday dinner, iii. 322; golden wedding presentation to Mr. and Mrs. Gladstone, iii. 418; meeting at Lord Rendel's on Parnell affair, iii. 434 *note*; death of, iii. 462.

Brevity of letters of, ii. 526.

Gladstone's appreciation of, ii. 414; loyalty to, ii. 599–601, 603, 619; his estimate of Gladstone, ii. 415; Gladstone's letters to, ii. 288, 289, 292, 300, 375, 381, 479, 503, 555, 556, 563, 587; iii. 57, 83, 93, 101, 103–105, 113, 131, 171, 174, 175, 210, 216, 236, 261, 268–270, 282, 413.

Temporising tendency of, ii. 602.

Otherwise mentioned, i. 415, 458, 492, 493, 495 *note*[1], 624, 635–636, 648; ii. 39, 106, 120, 189, 233, 240, 244, 283, 297, 410, 417, 459, 462, 473, 477, 484, 485, 493, 502, 519, 557, 616–617, 644; iii. 5, 102, 112, 186, 414.

Grattan, Henry, ii. 589; iii. 313–314, 339.

Gray, Sir John, ii. 292.

Greece: —
Berlin treaty's provisions regarding, iii. 8, 10.

Greece — *continued*.
  Don Pacifico case, i. 368–371, *and
    note*, 372, 374.
  Ionian Islands desirous of union with,
    i. 599, 602–605, 614; ceded to, i.
    620.
  Gladstone's budget (1860) popular in,
    ii. 29; Gladstone's political jubilee
    commemorated by, iii. 91; tribute
    at his death, iii. 532.
  Salisbury policy regarding, iii. 525.
  Thessaly and Epirus desired for, by
    Palmerston and Russell, ii. 576.
Greeks, position of, in relation to Tur-
  key, i. 477.
Green, J. H., i. 455.
—— J. R., ii. 561.
Greenwich : —
  Dockyard suppressed, ii. 374.
  Gladstone's election for (1868), ii.
    251 *and note* [1]; speech at, ii. 371;
    dispute as to vacating seat by
    becoming chancellor of exchequer
    (1873), ii. 465–472; manifesto to
    (1874), ii. 487–489; election for, ii.
    490; election address, ii. 490 *and
    note*; refusal to stand for (1879),
    ii. 584.
Greenwood, J., ii. 618 *note*.
Greg, W. R., i. 46.
Gregory VII., Pope, ii. 516.
—— XVI., Pope, iii. 62.
Grenville, Lord, i. 104, 223 *and note* [1],
  293, 445.
—— Thomas, i. 223 *note* [1].
—— George, i. 223 *and note* [1].
Greswell, Richard, i. 330, 409.
Greville, A., ii. 463 *note*.
—— C., i. 121 *note*; 243, 470; ii. 29; iii. 419.
Grévy, M., iii. 105.
Grey, General, Gladstone's letter to, on
  foreign policy, ii. 316; Gladstone's
  appreciation of, iii. 516.
    Otherwise mentioned, ii. 99, 103,
    252, 267; iii. 473.
—— Lord, dissolution by (1831), i. 69;
  resignation of (1832), ii. 653; government of, broken up (1834), i. 113, 154;
  attitude of, towards Lord J. Russell,
  i. 297; refuses office (1845), i. 367; ii.
  244; Althorp and Russell opposed to,
  i. 430; Taylor's estimate of, iii. 488;
  otherwise mentioned, i. 75, 77, 104,
  222, 241, 418, 543; ii. 238, 436, 619;
  iii. 223, 289 *note*, 535.
—— Lord de, *see* Ripon.
—— Sir George, defends slave apprenticeship law, i. 146; home secretary
  (1855), 540 *note*; leadership of Com-

mons by, desired by Gladstone, ii.
  152–153, 199; estimate of Gladstone,
  ii. 174; declines to join Gladstone's
  cabinet (1868), ii. 253; on Irish Land
  bill (1870), ii. 295; otherwise mentioned, i. 190, 297, 361 *note* [3], 576; ii.
  33, 100, 104, 105, 401, 435, 635–636.
Grillion's dining club, i. 227–228, 239.
Grosvenor, Lady, iii. 523.
—— Lord, ii. 195, 201–202, 205.
—— Lord R., iii. 269, 270.
Grote, George, i. 200; ii. 366, 370, 430.
—— Mrs., cited, iii. 4.
Guizot, F.-P.-G., on state of Italy, i.
  398; Aberdeen's letter to, i. 449;
  estimate of Cavour, ii. 6–7; letters
  from, ii. 533, 538; sends Gladstone
  his *Peel*, ii. 538; otherwise mentioned,
  i. 163, 229, 371; ii. 100, 102, 220, 240.
Gurdon, Mr., ii. 468.
Gurney, Samuel, i. 461.
Gurwood, Colonel, i. 228.

HADDO, i. 137, 594.
Halifax, Viscount (Charles Wood), on
  Gladstone's budget (1853), i. 465,
  466, 468; budgets of, criticised by
  Gladstone, i. 470; first lord of admiralty, i. 540 *note*; objects to French
  treaty project, ii. 21; on Paper
  Duties bill, ii. 31, 33, 37; estimate of
  financial statements of, ii. 55; created viscount (1866), ii. 222 *note*;
  views on condition of liberal party
  (1867), ii. 228; on Gladstone's position in the House, ii. 229; declines
  Irish vice-royalty, ii. 253; on Irish
  Church bill, ii. 278; *Alabama* case,
  ii. 401, 411; appreciation of Gladstone, ii. 414; Lord privy seal (1870),
  ii. 644; on defections of liberal party,
  ii. 436; on the Greenwich seat question, ii. 471; on election of 1874, ii.
  494; otherwise mentioned, i. 222, 297,
  420 *and note* [1], 458, 491, 492, 521, 623,
  624, 648; ii. 363, 504, 635–636.
Hall, Jane, i. 16.
—— Newman, ii. 134.
Hallam, Arthur, Gladstone's friendship
  with, i. 39–42, 66–67; *In Memoriam*
  stanzas descriptive of, i. 39 *note*;
  estimate of Gladstone, i. 95; death
  of, i. 108; Gladstone's mourning for,
  i. 108–109, 112; otherwise mentioned,
  i. 34, 37, 54.
—— Henry, i. 112, 137, 220, 230, 329; iii.
  476.
—— Henry (junr.), i. 229–230.
Hamilton, 10th Duke of, i. 102.

Hamilton, 11th Duke of, ii. 193; iii. 485.
—— E. W., ii. 493; iii. 112, 306; Gladstone's letter to, iii. 210.
—— Lord George, ii. 264.
—— Walter, Bishop of Salisbury, Gladstone's friendship with, i. 54, 161; Gladstone's letter to, on *Essays and Reviews* judgment, ii. 164; Gladstone's letter to, on state-aided education, ii. 299; otherwise mentioned, i. 78, 111, 235.
—— Sir William, i. 51.
Hammond, E., ii. 324, 411.
Hampden, Dr., Oxford estimate of (1829), i. 57; Gladstone examined by, in science, i. 78; attack on (1836), i. 161, 167, 316; Gladstone's early views regarding, i. 161, 167; Gladstone's letter to, i. 168; made a bishop, i. 377.
—— Lord (H. B. W. Brand), advice of, on Reform bill, ii. 202, 207; Gladstone's consultations with, ii. 210, 211; Gladstone's letter to, from Rome, ii. 217, 222; from Paris, ii. 221; dinner to, ii. 234–235; defines situation on Educational bill (1870), ii. 304; on Collier appointment, ii. 385; on session of 1872, ii. 390; on Irish university debate, ii. 445; on Disraeli's tactics, ii. 456; Gladstone's letter to, on the Greenwich seat question, ii. 467; reply regarding writ, ii. 470; forecast of general election (1880), ii. 605; on parliament of 1880, iii. 2; the Bradlaugh question, iii. 12–13, 16–17; action of, against obstruction, iii. 52–53; views on obstruction, iii. 57; on Bright's 'Irish rebels' speech, iii. 112; letter from, iii. 457.
—— John, i. 413–414.
Hanbury, R. W., iii. 426 *and note*[1].
Handley, W. F., i. 92–93.
Harcourt, L. V., i. 72.
—— Sir William, on Foreign Enlistment Act, ii. 399 *note*; solicitor-general, ii. 463 *note*, 470; on the Greenwich seat question, i. 470; home secretary, ii. 653; speech on Khartoum vote of censure, iii. 176; Gladstone's consultation with, iii. 288; declares for home rule, iii. 291 *note*; round table conference convened by, iii. 364, 366–368 *and note*; chancellor of exchequer (1886), iii. 296, 297 *note*; party loyalty of, iii. 296, 364; meeting at Lord Rendel's on Parnell affair, iii. 434 *note*; chancellor of

exchequer (1892), iii. 495 *note*; at last cabinet council, iii. 511; tribute to Gladstone, iii. 530; otherwise mentioned, ii. 602; iii. 67, 105, 106, 219, 268, 270, 273, 387, 429, 432, 433, 441.
Hardinge, Lord, i. 122, 351, *note*[1], 420, 432, 549, 641.
Hardwicke, 4th Earl of, i. 561.
—— 1st Earl of (1753), i. 567.
Hardy, Gathorne, opposes Gladstone at Oxford, ii. 144–145 *and note*, 149; on Irish Church bill, ii. 264; Bentinck's appeal to, ii. 444.
Harrison, B., i. 59 *note*, 78, 111.
—— F., ii. 524.
—— Archdeacon, ii. 422.
Harrowby, Lord, i. 75, 132; ii. 268, 501.
Hartington, Lord, moves vote of censure on Derby government, i. 625 *and note*; postmaster-general (1868), ii. 644; Irish secretary (1870), ii. 644; ballot bill of, ii. 368; suggested as leader, ii. 498; accepts leadership (1874), ii. 506; Gladstone's loyalty to, ii. 599–600, 603, 619; views on leadership, ii. 602 *and note*, 620–624; audience at Windsor and interview with Gladstone, ii. 621–624; suggested for India office, ii. 625, 627; Indian secretary (1880), ii. 654; war secretary (1882), ii. 654; iii. 150; compared with Palmerston, iii. 3; on local option motion, iii. 6; on evacuation of Candahar, iii. 10; opposes annexation of Transvaal, iii. 27, 28; on withdrawal from Egypt (1882), iii. 120; negotiations with conservative leaders on Franchise bill, iii. 133–134, 136, 138; against franchise extension in Ireland, iii. 141; agrees to send Gordon to Soudan, iii. 150; views on relief of garrisons, iii. 156; defence of government, iii. 163 *and note*[1]; readiness to send troops, iii. 164; Queen's telegram to, iii. 167; at Holker, iii. 166, 171; on avoidance of liberal rupture, iii. 171; defends the government against vote of censure, iii. 176; opposes plan of central board for Ireland, iii. 194; Gladstone's letter to, on cabinet crisis (May '85), iii. 196; presides at banquet to Lord Spencer, iii. 214; views on conservative repudiation of Spencer's policy, iii. 215; friction with Parnell, iii. 220, 241; friction with Chamberlain, iii. 226, 288;

Hartington, Lord, — *continued.*
opposes home rule, iii. 233, 267, 273, 291; Gladstone's letters to, on Irish policy, iii. 240, 262, 273; reproaches Chamberlain for indiscretion at the elections, iii. 251; attends banquet at Belfast, iii. 252; Granville's visit to, iii. 261; letters to Gladstone and to his chairman on Irish situation, iii. 266; letter to the *Times*, iii. 269, 270, 273; Parnell's attitude towards, iii. 275; announces possibility of counter-declaration, iii. 282; votes with conservatives on Collings' amendment, iii. 288; declines to join Gladstone's cabinet, iii. 292; explanatory letter, iii. 293; Eighty club speech, iii. 293 *note;* speech on second reading of Home Rule bill, iii. 301 *note* [1], 313; at Opera House meeting, iii. 324; decides to vote against second reading, iii. 329; declines Salisbury's offer to head government, iii. 364; Gladstone's comments on position of, iii. 365–366; declines to join round table conference, iii. 366; urges Gladstone to denounce plan of campaign, iii. 371; otherwise mentioned, ii. 447, 503, 504, 552, 564, 568, 616–617, 622, 644; iii. 99, 166, 219, 259, 322, 363, 388, 430.
Harvey, Rev. W. W., ii. 386–387.
—— i. 112 *and note*, 113.
Hastings, Warren, iii. 469.
Hatchard, J., i. 74.
Hatherley, Lord (W. Page Wood), ii. 383–385, 414, 644, 645.
Hawarden : —
Board school question at, ii. 646.
Cattle plague at, ii. 195.
Gladstone's first visit to (1836), i. 134; his marriage at, i. 223.
Oak Farm embarrassments of, i. 338 *et seq.*, 356; Gladstone's public finances influenced by, i. 474.
St. Deiniol's library, iii. 420, 521.
Tourist pilgrimages to, ii. 569.
Transference of, to W. H. Gladstone, i. 344.
Hawkins, Edward (provost of Oriel), i. 379, 627 *and note* [1]; iii. 124.
Hawtrey, E. C., i. 30, 31, 229.
Hayter, Sir W. G., i. 440, 539 *note;* ii. 29.
Hayward, A., ii. 382.
Healy, T., iii. 447, 451.
Heathcote, Sir William, Derby's intermediary, i. 551; Walpole's advances to, i. 583; Gladstone's letters to, i.

627, 630; letter to Gladstone on taxation, ii. 632; election of (1865), ii. 145 *note;* secedes from Derby government (1867), ii. 224.
Helena, Princess, ii. 98, 103.
Hellenic Factor in the Eastern Problem, The, ii. 558.
Helmholtz, ii. 536.
Henley, J. W., i. 417; ii. 31, 295.
Henry VIII., King, iii. 466.
Herbert, J. R., ii. 476.
—— George, Gladstone's estimate of, ii. 617.
—— Sidney, maiden speech of, i. 112; appointed secretary at board of control, i. 121 *note;* on Peel's eulogium of Cobden, i. 293; Russell's proposal to, i. 350; Peel's forecast regarding, i. 374; Gorham case, i. 381; attitude of, towards first Derby administration, i. 419; against Villiers' amendment, i. 433, 435 *and note;* on Gladstone's budget, i. 466, 467; favours dissolution, i. 467; invited by Derby to join government, i. 525; refuses, i. 526; inclines to join Palmerston, i. 532; wavers, i. 534; declines, i. 535; agrees to join, i. 536; resigns, i. 539; opposes joining peace party, i. 546; Gladstone's friendship with, i. 551, 559, 565–566, 577; discourages Gladstone's communicating with Derby, i. 552, 556; Derby's attitude towards, i. 577; approves Gladstone's refusal to join Herbert, i. 578; views of, on the Ionian question, i. 596; work of, during Crimean war, i. 651–652; on Paper Duties bill, ii. 33, 37; on French war rumours, ii. 43; correspondence with Gladstone on military charges, ii. 44; illness of, ii. 93; death of, ii. 88; otherwise mentioned, i. 55, 79, 351, 355, 405 *note*, 420, 423, 450, 468, 490, 492, 525, 527, 560, 576, 582–583, 585, 617, 648; ii. 47 *note* [2], 184, 238, 635–636; ii. 194; iii. 485.
Herries, J. C., i. 112, 417.
Herschell, Lord, on the Bradlaugh question, iii. 12; joins Gladstone's cabinet (1886), iii. 297 *note;* at round table conference, iii. 364 *note;* in cabinet (1892), iii. 495 *note*, 497 *note* [1].
Herzegovina : —
Austrian acquisition of, ii. 83, 576.
Revolt in, ii. 548, 567.
Hewley, Lady, case of, i. 321–323.
Heywood, J., i. 498; ii. 147 *note.*
Hicks, General, iii. 145–146 *and note*, 161.

Hignett, Mr., i. 345.
Hinds, Bishop, ii. 259.
Hobhouse, Sir John, i. 238, 266, 289, 420 and note[1].
Hodgkinson, G., ii. 225 and note, 226.
Holidays, ii. 379, 421–422.
Holker, iii. 166, 171.
Holland : —
  Belgium's severance from, ii. 2.
  Prussian attitude towards, ii. 320.
Holloway, T., ii. 459.
Holmbury, ii. 459 and note.
Holmes, Colonel, ii. 212 and note[2], 213.
Homeric studies, i. 549–550; ii. 423, 476–477, 523, 536; iii. 353, 356, 385, 415, 443–445.
Home rule, see under Ireland.
Honours and appointments, Gladstone's care in selection for, ii. 428; iii. 97.
Hook, Dean, i. 148; ii. 459.
Hooker, R., i. 160–161, 175; iii. 2.
—— Sir Joseph, ii. 536.
Hope, Admiral, ii. 18 note.
—— Beresford, A. J. B., ii. 224.
Hope-Scott, Miss, ii. 474.
—— —— J. R., Gladstone influenced by, i. 162; interest in Gladstone's book, i. 162, 172–173; offers services to Gladstone, i. 224; godfather to Gladstone's eldest son, i. 227; on Chapters bill, i. 228 and note; interest in Scotch training college scheme, i. 230–231; Gladstone's proposal to, of visiting Ireland, i. 281; on Jerusalem bishopric, i. 308, 309; Gladstone's close relations with, i. 310; acquaintance with Dr. Döllinger, i. 318; Gorham case, i. 379–380 notes; secession of, to Rome, i. 386–387; death of, ii. 458; otherwise mentioned, i. 55, 212, 260, 272, 317, 321, 393, 403; iii. 419, 485.
Horace, iii. 482, 492, 510, 512.
Horsman, E., ii. 444 note, 445.
Houghton, Lord, ii. 212, 369.
House-tax, i. 106, 436–437.
Howick, Lord, i. 102, 105, 222, 262, 420 and note[1], 644; iii. 300.
Howley, Archbishop, i. 175; ii. 271; iii. 108.
Howson, Dean, ii. 260.
Hoylake, i. 239.
Hübner, Baron, ii. 532.
Hudson, George, i. 199.
—— Sir James, ii. 5–6.
Hume, Joseph, impugns Gladstone's honesty, i. 301; views on intolerance of dissenters, i. 414; otherwise mentioned, i. 101, 106, 251 note[2], 362, 371, 423.

Hunter, John, cited, iii. 388.
Huskisson, W., John Gladstone's estimate of, i. 20; his support of, i. 249; work of, towards free trade, i. 39, 251, 255; death of, i. 66, 68, 69; otherwise mentioned, i. 89, 248, 265, 419.
Hutton, R. H., iii. 349.
Huxley, Gladstone's articles on, iii. 280–281; Manning's estimate of, ii. 308; approves Gladstone's attitude towards Vatican decrees, ii. 520; letters from, ii. 536; estimate of Gladstone, ii. 562; iii. 536; otherwise mentioned, ii. 423, 524.

IDDESLEIGH, LORD (Sir Stafford Northcote) : —
  Chronology — Works for Gladstone's Oxford candidature, i. 329, 333, 334; vindicates Gladstone (1847), i. 359 note[2]; appointed executor in Gladstone's will, i. 387; return prepared by, on civil service, i. 510, 512; Twenty Years of Finance, i. 516; refuses to serve on Gladstone's committee (1859), i. 628; article in Quarterly attributed to, ii. 94; serves on Alabama commission, ii. 401, 404; on the Bradlaugh question, iii. 12, 16–17; on measures against obstruction, iii. 53; on Land bill of 1881, iii. 53–54; on Phœnix Park murders, iii. 68; on Bright's 'Irish rebels' speech, iii. 112; on Franchise bill, iii. 135–139; moves vote of censure on Khartoum affair, iii. 175; death of, iii. 356.
  Financial ability of, ii. 637.
  Gladstone's estimate of, iii. 356, 465, 466; his estimate of Gladstone, i. 333 note[1]; Gladstone's letters to, i. 516, 517, 647; ii. 148–149, 648.
  Otherwise mentioned, i. 358, 452; iii. 6, 115, 537.
Ignatieff, General, ii. 349.
Imperialism, ii. 391–392.
Impregnable Rock of Holy Scripture, The, iii. 421 note.
Income-tax, see under Taxation.
India : —
  Burke's work for, iii. 469.
  Coolies shipped from, for West Indies, i. 24.
  Disraeli's schemes regarding government of, i. 592; procedure on bill of 1858, iii. 300.
  Gladstone's references to wrongs of, ii. 592, 595.

India — *continued.*
  Government of, contrasted with that of Ireland, ii. 284.
  Mutiny, France quiescent during, ii. 44.
  North-West frontier policy, iii. 10; difficulties (1885), iii. 177, 183–185.
  Parliamentary indifference to affairs of, i. 113.
  Troops from, for South Africa, iii. 34: refused for Soudan, iii. 147.
Indulgences, i. 319.
Inglis, Sir Robert, Oxford candidature of, i. 328, 332, 333; Gladstone proposed by, for Oxford and Cambridge club, i. 98 *note*; on China question, i. 227; Gladstone's divergence from, i. 321; political record of, i. 328; on papal aggression, i. 409; denounces Irish provincial colleges, ii. 434; otherwise mentioned, i. 120, 278, 306, 335, 336, 377, 427.
Ingogo river, iii. 35.
Ingram, Dr., ii. 437.
Innocent III., Pope, ii. 516; iii. 425.
Inshes, family of, i. 17 *note*.
Inverness, speech at, i. 476.
Ionian Islands : —
  Case of, i. 597–601.
  Gladstone's commission to, i. 594–597; his arrival at, i. 602; his scheme for, i. 610 *et seq*.
  Greece, union with, desired by, i. 599, 602–605, 614; granted, i. 620.
Ireland : —
  Act of Union —
    Gladstone's views regarding, iii. 409.
    Home rule in relation to, iii. 285.
    O'Connell's amendment for repeal of (1833), i. 106; iii. 284 *and note*.
    Resolutions preliminary to, iii. 299.
  Agitation in, relief measures due to, iii. 410.
  Ashbourne Act (1885), iii. 287.
  Assassination bill (1846), i. 430.
  Beaconsfield's reference to, in election address (1880), ii. 606; his apprehension regarding, iii. 47.
  Boycotting in, iii. 199, 243–244 *and note* [1].
  Budget of 1853, as affecting, i. 462, 465–468, 646.
  Carnarvon's statement on (1885), iii. 211.
  Central board, *see below* Local government.

Chamberlain's views on compulsory expropriation, iii. 224; his attitude towards home rule, iii. 223, 225 *note* [2], 234, 267; his speech on condition of (June '85), iii. 233–234; his federation scheme, iii. 316–317, 327, 339.
Chief secretaries for, in Gladstone's cabinets (1868–74), ii. 644; (1880–85), ii. 654; (1886), iii. 297 *note*; (1892), iii. 491, 495 *note*.
Churches —
  Presbyterian against home rule, iii. 318.
  Protestant episcopal —
    Appropriation question, i. 54.
    Disestablishment of — difficulties of, ii. 257–258; preliminaries, ii. 259–263; bill in the Commons, ii. 263–264, 266; with the Lords, ii. 266–271; back to the Commons, ii. 271–272; back to the Lords, ii. 272–279; modifications accepted by the Commons, ii. 280; debates on, iii. 57; Gladstone's letter to the Queen on, ii. 427, 645.
    Disraeli's proposals for, ii. 242.
    Gladstone speaks on, in Parliament, i. 126; at Newark, i. 129; his five resolutions on, iii. 300; his attitude towards (1865), ii. 141–143; (1865–68), ii. 239–240; his action regarding (1868), ii. 243, 245–248.
    Home rule opposed by, iii. 318.
    Reform bill, Gladstone's speech on (1833), i. 105; Inglis's opposition to, i. 328.
  Roman catholic, Parnell leadership denounced by, iii. 448–449.
Coercion : —
  Acts and bills (1833), i. 106; (1846) i. 290; (1847–85) iii. 211; (1866) ii. 200; (1870) ii. 297; (1880) iii. 56, 62; (1881) iii. 52 *and note*, 65, 71, 253, 274, 296 *note* [1]; (1882) iii. 70, 188–192, 194, 198–199; (1886) iii. 350; (1887) iii. 375 *and note*, 376 *and notes*, 377–378, 380.
  Conservative party's repudiation of, iii. 212–214 257; revival of, as a last resort, iii. 278–279; silence regarding, iii. 285; proposal of, iii. 287; Salisbury's

'twenty years' proposal, iii. 317.

English realisation of, iii. 379; English attitude towards (1890), iii. 427–428.

Liberal unionists accomplices in, iii. 368.

Parnell's view of, iii. 369; his fear of renewal of, by liberals, iii. 274–275.

Commissions and committees on (1880–86), iii. 362; (1894) i. 646.

Compensation for Disturbance bill, iii. 49, 113, 409, 410.

Conservative administration of (1886–87), iii. 369–370, 372–376, 378–383.

Consolidated annuities, i. 468 and note, 646.

Cowper commission, iii. 362, 372–374.

Crimes Acts, see Coercion under this heading.

Cromwell's insight into problem of, ii. 287.

Devon commission (1843), ii. 285.

Education grant, Gladstone's views of, i. 227.

Election results in (1880), ii. 613; (1885) iii. 252–255; (1886) iii. 346.

English traditional attitude towards, iii. 291, 307–308, 340.

Evictions in, iii. 48, 372, 379, 380, 410; compensation in cases of, see Compensation under this heading.

Famine in (1845), i. 282, 352.

Fenians in : —
Parnell's alleged conversation with a spy regarding, iii. 404.
Plots of (1867), ii. 241.
Release of prisoners (1870), ii. 297.
Secret committee on, proposed (1871), ii. 297.
Temper of (1886), iii. 373.

Financial relations commission, i. 646.

FitzGerald's stanzas on, i. 31.

Franchise extension in, iii. 139–142.

Gladstone's first cabinet concerned with, i. 261; his proposal to visit (1845), i. 281; his forecast regarding (1845), i. 383; uneasiness regarding state of, ii. 132, 174; his view of his mission regarding, ii. 252; his visit to (1877), ii. 571.

Government of Ireland bill (1886), see Home rule under this heading.

Habeas Corpus Act, suspension of, iii. 49–51, 57, 553.

Home rule for : —
Act of Union, relative to, iii. 285.
Bill of 1886 : —
Alterations of original plan of, iii. 300–301.
Amendments proposed for, iii. 332.
Cesser of Irish representation, iii. 302, 304, 307, 309, 324, 326–327; opposed, iii. 324–325, 327, 332.
Defeat of, iii. 341.
Disabilities specified in, iii. 302, 309.
Financial provisions of, iii. 305, 306, 319, 331, 560.
Introduction and first reading of, i. 363 note; iii. 310–312, 316.
Postponement of, after second reading, suggested, iii. 333–334.
Reception of, in the press, iii. 318–319; by Irish party, iii. 319–320 and notes.
Resolutions instead of, later views on, iii. 299–301.
Second reading of, iii. 313–316, 317, 330, 334–341.
Summary of, iii. 559–561.
Taxation provisions of, iii. 302, 306–307, 560.
Withdrawal of, after second reading, suggested, iii. 333–334.
Bill of 1892 — preparation, iii. 496–497 and note[1]; crux of Irish representation, iii. 497–498; second reading stage, iii. 499–500; majority, iii. 504; committee stage, iii. 498–499, 500–503; third reading, iii 504; defeat in House of Lords, iii. 504.
Cesser of Irish representation — question of (1886), see above under Bill of 1886; Gladstone's speech on, at Swansea (1887), iii. 386; question of (1892), iii. 497–498.
Chamberlain's attitude towards, iii. 325 note[2], 233, 234, 267.
Gladstone's speech on, at Aberdeen (1871), ii. 378; his letter on (1881), iii. 57; his attitude towards, before the elections (1885), iii. 215–216, 234–241; after the elections, iii. 256–257, 259, 261–264, 266, 268–276,

Ireland — *continued.*
　Home rule for — *continued.*
　　283; his pamphlet on, iii. 352
　　and note [1].
　　Hartington's opposition to, iii.
　　233, 267, 273.
　　Independence of nationalist vote
　　desirable for concession of, iii.
　　238.
　　Liberal party in relation to: —
　　Central organisation declares
　　for Gladstone, iii. 323.
　　　Cleavage in, iii. 291 *and note*,
　　　302–303, 324; Gladstone's
　　　decision to act regardless
　　　of, iii. 288–304; number of
　　　seceders on night of the
　　　division, iii. 341.
　　　Dissentients' meeting in com-
　　　mittee room 15, iii. 335–337.
　　　Meeting of, at foreign office,
　　　iii. 332–333.
　　　Vacillations of, iii. 323.
　　　Waiting attitude counselled by
　　　Gladstone, iii. 285; adopted,
　　　iii. 286.
　　National pronouncement for, iii.
　　252–255.
　　Parnell's demand for, iii. 232.
　　Popular sentiment regarding, iii.
　　330, 342.
　　Salisbury's attitude towards, iii.
　　231, 233, 239, 242–244.
　Inglis's views on, i. 279.
　Intimidation in, iii. 198, 199, 211, 283,
　287.
　Invincibles, iii. 70, 103.
　Jansenism in, iii. 384.
　Lady correspondents on turbulence
　in, ii. 531; iii. 348.
　Land League: —
　　Commission on, iii. 398, 401 *et seq*.
　　Gladstone's view of, iii. 47, 59.
　　Land Act of 1881 in relation to,
　　iii. 57, 66.
　Land tenure in: —
　　Acts and bills: —
　　　(1849) ii. 287.
　　　(1860) ii. 287 *and note*.
　　　(1870) ii. 294–296; iii. 49; pre-
　　　cautions against eviction, ii.
　　　294; debates on, iii. 57; Vat-
　　　ican decrees inimical to par-
　　　liamentary success of, ii.
　　　511; Greek congratulations
　　　on, ii. 532; effect of, iii. 257;
　　　failure of, iii. 54.
　　　(1881) iii. 53–57; debates and
　　　speeches on, iii. 56–57; Par-

nell's attitude towards the
Act, iii. 57–61; nationalist
efforts to amend the Act,
iii. 66; inadequacy of, iii.
254; effect of, iii. 257; secured by agitation, iii. 410;
unpopular, iii. 537.
　　(1885) iii. 190, 194–195, 197;
　　widespread repugnance to,
　　iii. 310, 324–327, 332.
　　(1886) pressed by Spencer and
　　Morley, iii. 301; interest in,
　　eclipsed by home rule, iii.
　　310; first reading of, iii. 313
　　note.
　　(1887) iii. 373–374.
　Dual ownership, iii. 54, 55.
　Encumbered Estates Act (1849),
　ii. 287.
　English ignorance of, ii. 281.
　Peculiarities of, ii. 285–286.
　Landed gentry, rule of, destroyed
　by liberal party, iii. 256–257.
　Local government for (other than
　home rule): —
　　Canadian scheme suggested, iii.
　　215, 317.
　　Central board scheme, iii. 193;
　　Gladstone's attitude towards,
　　iii. 191, 193–194; Parnell's ap-
　　proval of, iii. 194, 231, 291; his
　　repudiation of, iii. 215, 230;
　　his conversation with Carnar-
　　von regarding, iii. 230–231; lib-
　　eral cabinet's attitude towards,
　　iii. 194, 291.
　　County Government bill discussed
　　by Gladstone and Chamber-
　　lain, iii. 225 *and note* [2].
　　Federation views of Chamberlain,
　　iii. 316–317, 327, 339.
　　Gladstone's letter to Forster on
　　(1882), iii. 58.
　　Small holdings and allotments
　　bill, Chamberlain's views on,
　　iii. 224 *and note*.
　Maamtrasna debate, iii. 213, 279.
　Military *v.* moonlighters in, iii.
　362.
　Mitchelstown affair, iii. 380–383.
　National League: —
　　Bill to deal with, proposed by
　　Hicks Beach, iii. 287.
　　Commission upon, iii. 398, 401 *et
　　seq*.
　　Elections influenced by, iii. 255.
　　Power of, iii. 278.
　Papal intervention in, suggested, iii.
　62–63; on plan of campaign, iii.

383–385; on Parnell leadership, iii. 449.

Parnell's position in (1890), iii. 431; elections after the split, iii. 457, 458.

Peel's view of condition of (1836), i. 133; his decision against Gladstone for chief secretary, i. 241 *and note*.

Peers, Irish, called to House of Lords by Beaconsfield, ii. 429 *note*.

Phœnix Park murders, iii. 67, 90, 308, 391.

Plan of campaign : —
English and Scotch view of, iii. 373.
Gladstone's attitude towards, iii. 370–372.
Nature of, iii. 369–370, 373.
Parnell's attitude towards, iii. 370.
Pope Leo's pronouncements on, iii. 383–385.
Ulster, for, encouraged by Churchill, iii. 371 *note*.

Poerio's arrival in, i. 401.

Queen's attitude towards, ii. 425.

Railways in, Gladstone's commission on, ii. 243 *note*.

Rents in : —
Arrears bill (1882), iii. 66.
Beach on, iii. 369, 373.
Bessborough commission on, iii. 54, 56.
Buller's evidence on, iii. 372.
Conservative vacillations regarding, iii. 373–375.
Cowper commission on (1887), iii. 372–374.
Crime in relation to excess of, iii. 409, 410.
Parnell on, iii. 369, 372.
Richmond commission on, iii. 54.

Roman catholic party in, supporting English government, Gladstone's view of, i. 129.

Social condition of (1886), iii. 297 (*see also* Intimidation *under this heading*).

Tenants' Relief bill, iii. 353, 369.

Tithes bills, iii. 114.

Tractarian movement's effect on feeling towards, i. 308.

Ulster : —
Elections of 1885 in, iii. 252–253.
Gladstone's consideration of, iii. 236.
Home rule opposed by, iii. 327.
Plan of campaign for, encouraged by Churchill, iii. 371 *note*.

Separate assembly for, suggestion of, iii. 332.
Solemn League and Covenant for, iii. 318.
Variation in rents, attitude towards, iii. 374.

University education in : —
Gladstone's bill for (1873), ii. 437–445, 495.
Roman catholic attitude towards, ii. 435–436, 440–441.
Unsettled condition of, ii. 434.

Irish party : —
Aberdeen, attitude towards, i. 444.
Anti-Parnellites, Gladstone's responsibility towards (1892), iii. 493.
Bright's estimate of, iii. 328.
Cleavage of (1890), iii. 350.
Committee Room Fifteen, iii. 446 *and note* [2]–452.
Conservative understanding with, iii. 188–190, 200, 203, 258, 260, 269–271, 274–276, 284.
Criminal Law Amendment bill (1887), tactics on, iii. 377–378.
Dependence upon, undesirable for settlement of home rule question, iii. 238.
Exclusion of, from Westminster, proposed, iii. 302, 304, 307, 309, 324, 326–327 ; opposed, iii. 324–325, 327, 332; Gladstone's speech on, at Swansea (1887), iii. 386; question of (1892), iii. 497–498.
Gladstone, estrangement from, on Italian question, ii. 122; on his Vatican campaign, ii. 502; vituperation of (1882), iii. 89; general attitude towards, iii. 274; ovation to (1893), iii. 500.
Home Rule bill of '86, excitement at introduction of, iii. 311; acceptance of, iii. 319.
Irish University bill, attitude towards, 441, 444, 445.
Italian Nationality, views on, i. 618; ii. 122.
Khartoum vote of censure supported by, iii. 176.
Liberal party — attitude of (1873), ii. 441; support of (1884), iii. 143 *and note* [4]; opposition to (1885), iii. 184; dislike of, iii. 274; alliance with, apprehended by tory leaders, iii. 287; alliance accomplished, iii. 370; impossibility of uniform action with, iii. 371.
Obstructionist tactics of, iii. 48, 51–53, 57, 123, 124.

Irish party — *continued.*
　Papal rescript, attitude towards, iii. 384.
　Parnell re-elected by (Nov. 1890), iii. 438; effect on, of Gladstone's letter, iii. 442; split on leadership question, iii. 450–452; attempts at an understanding, iii. 455.
　Parnellites, iii. 458, 470.
　Revolution in parliamentary procedure effected by, iii. 377.
　Russell, attitude towards, i. 431.
　Separate parliamentary organisation of (1874), ii. 491.
　Spencer, Lord, attitude towards, iii. 108.
　Strength of (1885), iii. 253, 255.
　Violence of (1880–85), iii. 308.
Irving, Edward, i. 44, 100.
—— Sir H., ii. 604.
Ismail Pasha, iii. 145 *note* 2.
Italian language, ii. 648.
Italy : —
　Alabama tribunal, represented on, ii. 405, 412.
　Austria — tyranny of, i. 389–403; Aberdeen's views on, ii. 641–642; Gladstone's Letters on, to Lord Aberdeen, i. 392, 394 *and note*, 396; Aberdeen's view on the letters, i. 398, 399 *note* 2, 401, 641, 642; effect of the Letters, i. 396–398, 400–401 *and note* 3; Austrian war (1859), i. 618, 620 *note* 3; ii. 6 *et seq.*
　Eastern question, attitude towards, ii. 571.
　Ecclesiastical policy of, Gladstone's views on, ii. 510 *note.*
　Finance of, ii. 107.
　France — aid from, ii. 7–8, 14; alliance sought by (1870), ii. 323; neutrality during Franco-Prussian war, ii. 344.
　German alliance of, iii. 414.
　Gladstone's visit to (1850), i. 389–393; (1859) i. 618; (1866) ii. 213–219; (1889) iii. 413; Italian recognition of his services, ii. 533; iii. 532; his views on policy of (1888), iii. 413–415, 561.
　Rome occupied by government of, in Franco-Prussian war, ii. 343, 512.
　Savoy, distinct from, ii. 22.
　Smyrna demonstration favoured by, iii. 9.
　Suez canal protection, invited to help in, iii. 80.
　Unification of, ii. 17; Gladstone slow

　to advocate, i. 389, 390; ii. 12–13; effect of movement on England, ii. 123–124.
　Venetia transferred to, ii. 214.
Ithaca, i. 603.

Jackson, Dean, i. 49 *and note* 2.
Jacobson, Bp., i. 457; ii. 148.
Jamaica : —
　Apprenticeship system in, i. 145.
　Slave estates in, i. 22.
　Suspension of constitution of, proposed, i. 221.
James, Sir Henry, made attorney-general, ii. 463 *note*, 470; on the Greenwich seat question, i. 470; on the Bradlaugh question, iii. 12; Gladstone's regard for, iii. 110; Corrupt Practices bill, i. 97 *note* 1; iii. 110; Collings' amendment, iii. 288; on spies, iii. 404 *note.*
—— Sir Walter, Gladstone's letters to, i. 357, 409, 549; otherwise mentioned, ii. 557, 565.
Jansenism, iii. 384.
Jeffreys, H. A., i. 71, 72, 80.
Jelf, W. E., ii. 386.
Jenner, Dr., ii. 99, 103.
Jerusalem : —
　Bishopric question, i. 308–309, 312.
　Greek and Latin dispute regarding holy places in, i. 478.
Jessel, Sir G., ii. 463 *note*, 468–470.
—— Lady, iii. 106.
Jesuits, ii. 516.
Jeune, Dr., i. 499, 508.
Jevons, W. S., ii. 57.
Jews : —
　Admission of, to parliament, i. 375–377; opposed by Gladstone, i. 106; by Inglis, i. 328.
　Disraeli's sympathies with, ii. 552–553, 558; iii. 475–476.
　Eastern question, attitude towards, ii. 571.
　Peerage recommended for, by Gladstone, ii. 429.
　Rothschild's work for, iii. 11.
Jingoism, iii. 173.
Jocelyn, Viscount, i. 295.
Johnson, Dr., iii. 481.
—— Reverdy, ii. 401 *note* 2.
Jones, Rev. J., i. 11.
—— Ernest, i. 396, 400.
Joubert, General, iii. 25, 29, 34, 39.
Jowett, B., supports Gladstone at Oxford, i. 335; on Oxford reform, i. 501, 502; Gladstone's appreciation of, i. 508, 512; advocates civil service re-

form, i. 512; estimate of Gladstone, ii. 178; work on educational reform (1869), ii. 312.

Joy, Henry Hall, i. 29, 34.

Juxon, Archbishop, iii. 96 and note¹.

KAINADJI, treaty of, ii. 550.

Kean, Charles, ii. 528.

Keate, Dr., i. 28, 30, 32, 34, 42, 44–46.

Keble, John, i. 57, 178, 317, 380 note²; ii. 181–182.

Kempis, Thomas à, ii. 186, 187.

Kew Gardens feud, ii. 420.

Khalifa, the, iii. 144.

Khartoum, see under Soudan.

Kimberley, Earl of, lord privy seal (1868), ii. 644; on Alabama case, ii. 411; colonial secretary (1870), ii. 644; (1880), ii. 654; correspondence, etc., on Transvaal question, iii. 28, 31–36, 38, 40, 42–44; decides against a Transvaal commission, iii. 33 and note; Indian secretary (1882), ii. 654; for home rule, iii. 291 note; Indian secretary (1886), iii. 297 note; president of council and Indian secretary (1892), iii. 495 note; at last cabinet council, iii. 511; otherwise mentioned, ii. 304; iii. 50.

King, Locke, ii. 126, 653.

Kinglake, A. W., i. 480–481 and note; ii. 557 note.

Kingsley, Dr., ii. 143.

—— Rev. C., ii. 433.

Kiréeff, Colonel, ii. 557 note.

Kitchener, Major, iii. 166.

Kitson, Sir James, ii. 611; iii. 59–60.

Knapp, Rev. H. H., i. 29, 80.

Knatchbull, Sir E., i. 254, 420; ii. 156 note¹.

Knollys family, ii. 100.

Knowles, J., iii. 356, 358, 360.

Knox, Alexander, i. 161.

Knutsford, Lord, iii. 45 note.

Kordofan, iii. 146.

Kossuth, i. 402, 415.

Kruger, President, Gladstone's meeting with (1877), ii. 571; urges reversal of annexation, iii. 25, 29; correspondence with Colley, iii. 35–36, 38.

LABOUCHERE, H. L., i. 420 note¹.

Labour, war-loans as affecting, i. 517.

Lacaita, Sir James, Gladstone's acquaintance with, i. 390–391; secretary to Gladstone's Ionian commission, i. 597, 607; Gladstone's letters to, i. 399; ii. 15, 107, 219, 510, 519; otherwise mentioned, i. 396; ii. 184.

Laing's Nek, iii. 34, 36, 37, 42.

Lake, Dean, i. 335; iii. 95.

Lamartine, cited, i. 395.

Lamb, Charles, i. 215 and note¹.

Lambert, Sir John, ii. 226, 467–468.

Lamennais, i. 200, 457.

Lancashire: —
American civil war, effect of, ii. 66; Gladstone's relief works, ii. 77 note¹; fortitude under distress, ii. 124.
Gladstone's speeches in (1864), ii. 131; (1865), ii. 178; invited to stand for (1865), ii. 144; his candidature, ii. 145–147; his election, ii. 147.

Lancaster, T. W. L., i. 111.

Landed property: —
Chamberlain's pronouncements on, iii. 174.
Gladstone's views on, i. 345–349, 463; his budget proposals regarding, i. 463, 471.
Ireland, in, see under Ireland.

Langley, ——, ii. 490.

Lansdowne, 3rd Marquis of, view of, on repeal, i. 289; on reform, i. 416; retirement of, i. 445; on Gladstone's budget, i. 465, 466; attempts to form a government, i. 528; fails, i. 529; conditionally consents to join Palmerston's government, i. 533; assists Palmerston, i. 539; recommends Derby for premiership, i. 576; otherwise mentioned, i. 75, 431, 493, 530, 648.

—— 5th Marquis of, iii. 48, 90.

Lanyon, Sir O., iii. 31–32, 40, 43 note.

Laud, Archbishop, iii. 480.

Lavalette, Marquis de, ii. 324–325, 329.

Law of nations, i. 370, 371 note.

Layard, Sir A. H. L., iii. 2.

Lebœuf, Marshal, ii. 334.

Lecky, W. E. H., iii. 425.

Leeds, Gladstone elected for (1850), ii. 611 and note²; his visit to (1881), iii. 59–61; Herbert Gladstone returned for, ii. 618.

Leeds Mercury, iii. 264 note.

Lefevre, J. G. Shaw-, i. 252; ii. 654; iii. 291 note, 495 note.

Legacy duty, see Succession duty.

Legislation work, Gladstone's review of, ii. 51–52.

Legh, ——, ii. 147 note.

Leighton, F. K. (warden of All Souls'), i. 627.

—— Archbishop, i. 319.

Leith, Gladstone's election for, iii. 344.

Leo XIII., Pope, iii. 383–385.
Leopardi, essay on, iii. 548.
Leopold I., i. 449.
—— II., King of the Belgians, ii. 195, 458; iii. 162.
—— Prince, ii. 260.
—— —— (Hohenzollern), ii. 323–328, 330, 332, 333 note.
Lesseps, M. de, i. 591, 592; ii. 533.
Lessons in Massacre, ii. 560, 562.
Lewis, Sir G. Cornewall, on American civil war, ii. 69, 80, 84 *and note*; on Irish agrarian outrage, i. 281 *and note*; on Gladstone's influence in Oxford, i. 499; criticises Gladstone's budget (1859), ii. 19; succeeds Gladstone as chancellor of exchequer, i. 539–540; budget of (1855), i. 517, 559–562; Gladstone's differences with, on finance, ii. 22, 67, 623, 632; agreement with, ii. 633; objects to French treaty project, ii. 21; on Paper Duties bill, ii. 33, 37; views of, on nature of government, ii. 63; cabinet struggle with Gladstone (1862), ii. 95; Gladstone's estimate of, ii. 67; his estimate of Gladstone, i. 547; death of, ii. 67; otherwise mentioned, i. 229, 256, 374, 441, 481 note, 519, 624; ii. 31, 50, 194, 635–636; iii. 539.
Lewis, Sir Gilbert, Gladstone's letter to, ii. 67.
—— Lady Theresa, ii. 190.
Liardet, ——, ii. 490.
Liberal party:—
   Adullamites, ii. 205, 211, 224, 225.
   Apathy and disorganisation of (1879), ii. 586.
   Aristocratic element withdrawn from, iii. 293.
   Church of England, antagonistic to (1870), ii. 307.
   Cleavage in (1867), ii. 228, 232; (1872) ii. 388; (1874) ii. 499; threatened (1885), iii. 170, 185, 188, 197, 200, 265, 267, 282, 294; Gladstone's efforts to avert, iii. 220, 222, 241, 273, 282, 283; Gladstone's determination not to take part in, iii. 222; not to lead a home rule opposition, iii. 282; to act regardless of followers, iii. 288, 304; cleavage accomplished, iii. 291 *and note*, 302–303; first public mark of, iii. 324; number of seceders on night of home rule division, iii. 341; reunion desired by Gladstone, iii. 363, 366, 371 (*see also below*, Disaffection).
   Closure countenanced by, iii. 377.
   Colonial and Irish policy of, vindicated by Gladstone, ii. 606–607.
   Conservative party supported by, on important measures, iii. 257–258.
   'Construction' shibboleth of, iii. 173.
   Disaffection in (1866–67), ii. 202, 205–209, 224, 225, 227–228, 232–235; (1868) ii. 246; (1869–74) ii. 495; (1870–73) ii. 497; (1872–73) ii. 436, 442, 444 *and note*, 445; (1873) ii. 457 (*see also above*, Cleavage).
   Electoral losses of (1874), ii. 490–491; triumph (1880), ii. 609, 613–614; gains (1886–90), iii. 427.
   Foreign policy of, attacked by *Pall Mall Gazette*, ii. 579.
   Forster's view of (1863), ii. 123.
   Gladstone's junction with, i. 626; his reception by, ii. 204.
   Hartington accepts leadership of (1874), ii. 506.
   Home rule, *see under* Ireland.
   Irish party, *see under* Irish party.
   Leadership of — Hartington's acceptance of (1874), ii. 506; Gladstone's correspondence on (1885), iii. 223, 225–227.
   Majority of, in 1868, ii. 251 *and note* 2.
   Parnell's denunciations of, iii. 445, 450, 459.
   Questions tending to divide, list of, ii. 503.
   Round table conference, iii. 364, 366–368 *and note*.
   Tea-room schism, ii. 228, 232.
   Ultra-toryism in, ii. 37.
Liberal Unionist party:—
   Coercion the touchstone for, iii. 368.
   Conservatives, union with, iii. 350.
   Round table conference, iii. 364, 366–368 *and note*.
Liberalism, Acton on, iii. 361.
Liberty:—
   De Maistre on, ii. 518.
   Gladstone's feeling for, i. 60, 84, 179, 180, 384–385; ii. 518, 524, 582; iii. 18–19, 88, 144, 178, 260, 475, 535; his views regarding fitness for, iii. 58.
Licensing bills (1871), ii. 388–390.
Liddell, Dean, i. 59 note; ii. 312, 539.
Liddon, Canon, ii. 433; iii. 421.
Lieven, Madame de, i. 270, 397, 401, 469.
Life-insurance duty, i. 462.
Lightfoot, Bp., ii. 433.
Lincoln, Lord, *see* Newcastle, 5th Duke of.

Lincoln, President, ii. 75; iii. 235.
Liquor interest, influence of, on election of 1874, ii. 495.
Literary controversy, temper for, iii. 351.
Littlemore, i. 235, 310.
Littleton, E. J. L., i. 113.
Liverpool: —
  Canning's election for, i. 9–10.
  Conservatism of, ii. 605.
  Early condition of, i. 21–22.
  Electoral scandals at, i. 105.
  Gladstone, John, settles in, i. 16.
  Gladstone's debt to, i. 192; speech at (1856), i. 363 note [2]; speech at (1864), ii. 132; election speech at (1865), ii. 145–146; speech at, on reform (1866), ii. 202; address at, on Strauss (1872), ii. 524; reception at (1876), ii. 558; speech at (1895), iii. 521.
Liverpool Courier, Gladstone's letters to, i. 32.
Liverpool Standard, Gladstone's contributions to, i. 98.
—— Lord, church patronage under, i. 153; nature of government of, i. 298; policy of, i. 121; otherwise mentioned, i. 242, 419; iii. 465, 543.
Lloyd, Bishop, i. 57.
Loans for war purposes, i. 515–518.
Locke, i. 135; iii. 476–477.
Lockhart, J. G., i. 274, 314–315.
Loch-Lochy, battle at, i. 17 note.
Lochnagar, i. 116; ii. 99, 102.
Loftus, Lord A., ii. 321–322.
Lombardy, i. 248; ii. 7.
London, election results in (1880), ii. 613.
—— and N.-Western Railway, iii. 171.
—— convention (1884), iii. 45 and note.
—— protocol, ii. 562.
Londonderry, Lord, i. 419; iii. 6.
Longley, Archbishop, iii. 96 note [1].
'Lord Dundreary,' ii. 96.
Lords, House of, *see under* Parliament.
Lorraine, annexation of, ii. 346–348.
Louis, Princess of Hesse (Princess Alice), ii. 90, 97–100, 103, 187, 378.
—— xvi., iii. 480.
—— Napoleon, *see* Napoleon iii.
Louise, Princess, ii. 379, 411, 533; iii. 524.
Lowe, Robert (Lord Sherbrooke), opposes Reform, ii. 201–203, 205, 224, 228, 231, 235; iii. 300 note [4]; declines to join Derby government, ii. 211; pronouncement on franchise, ii. 155–156; on Gladstone's leadership, ii. 172; chancellor of exchequer (1868), ii.

254, 644; views on Irish land question, ii. 283, 292; urges civil service reform, i. 510; ii. 314–315; opposes transportation of convicts to Australia, i. 359; Gladstone's letter to, on treasury administration, ii. 372, 650; budgets of, ii. 373; speech at Sheffield on finance, ii. 375–376; on *Alabama* case, ii. 410, 411; attitude towards Gladstone, ii. 416; Gladstone's estimate of, ii. 417, 464–465; on Irish University bill, ii. 441; post office scandal, ii. 460–461, 463, 464; home secretary (1873), ii. 463 note, 645; on the Greenwich seat question, ii. 469; protests against Gladstone's retirement, ii. 498; viscounty desired for, by Gladstone, ii. 631; otherwise mentioned, ii. 247, 260, 504, 644, 645.
Lowther, James, ii. 295.
Lubbock, Sir John, ii. 562.
Lucas, ——, i. 258.
Lucretius, iii. 19, 481, 484.
Lushington, ——, i. 59 note.
Lyndhurst, Lord, failure to form a ministry (1832), ii. 653; attitude towards repeal, i. 283; Brougham's compliment to, i. 575 *and note*; Gladstone's estimate of, ii. 96; otherwise mentioned, i. 75, 122, 293–294; ii. 194.
Lyons, Lord, on *Trent* affair, ii. 73–75; on reduction of armaments, ii. 322; Spanish sovereign affair, ii. 325, 327–330, 336; on Black Sea affair, ii. 351; mentioned, iii. 105.
Lyttelton, Lady (Mary Glynne), Gladstone's appreciation of, i. 187; marriage of, i. 223; illness and death of, i. 572–573; mentioned, i. 274, 293; ii. 100.
—— Lord, marriage of, i. 223; examines at Eton, i. 229; attitude towards Welsh bishoprics question, i. 288; connection with Oak Farm, i. 337 *et seq.*; views on Gladstone's new policy (1865), ii. 133; endowed schools commissioner, ii. 501; Gladstone's letters to, i. 327, 381, 454; ii. 237, 299, 306, 312, 364, 646; otherwise mentioned, i. 187, 306; ii. 212, 539.
Lyttelton, Neville, on Herbert Gladstone's candidature, ii. 617.
Lytton, E. L. Bulwer, Lord, casts Gladstone's horoscope, i. 196–197; suggests to Gladstone mission to Ionian islands, i. 594; Gladstone's relations

Lytton, E. L. Bulwer, Lord —*continued.*
with, i. 609, 617; funeral of, ii. 437;
otherwise mentioned, i. 149, 561; ii.
28, 181.
—— Sir Edward, i. 609, 612.

MACAULAY, Lord, first speech of, i. 22
note[2]; Sadler defeated by, i. 99 *note*;
meets Gladstone in Rome (1838), i.
173-174; on Gladstone's first book,
i. 177-178; on *Church Principles*, i.
181; on Gladstone's political position, i. 182; Gladstone contrasted
with, i. 192-193, 195; debating
method of, i. 195; on the China question, i. 226; Gladstone's censure of,
i. 236; on Lady Hewley case, i. 322;
on Gladstone's ecclesiastical views
in 1838, i. 323; on Disraeli's budget
debate, i. 440; on Barrow, ii. 536;
iii. 467 *note; Warren Hastings*, iii.
290; Gladstone's estimate of, iii. 98,
425; linguistic purity of, iii. 476; on
Dryden, iii. 484; Gladstone's essay
on, iii. 546; otherwise mentioned, i.
220, 245 *note*, 315, 539; ii. 55, 194,
238, 249.
—— Z., i. 236.
McCarthy, J. H., on conservative overtures to Irish party, iii. 190 *and note*[2];
Gladstone's views on Parnell leadership announced to, iii. 436, 437, 444;
ignorant of Parnell's plans, iii. 439;
leads away the anti-Parnellites, iii.
451-452.
Macdonald, family of, ii. 17 *note.*
—— Sir John, ii. 401.
Macedonia, iii. 532.
Machiavelli, ii. 9 *and note*, 518, 594.
Macgregor, J., Gladstone's estimate of,
i. 250, 252.
Macmillan, Mr., i. 455.
McNeile, Rev. Hugh, ii. 545.
Magee, Bishop, ii. 258, 260-261, 265 *note*,
275 *note.*
Magyars, eastern question, attitude
towards, ii. 571, 609.
Mahdi, the, iii. 144, 149, 157, 161.
Mahon, Lord, *see* Stanhope.
Maine, ii. 405.
Maistre, Joseph de, ii. 518-519 *and note*[2];
iii. 476.
Maitland, Sir Thomas, i. 619 *note*[2].
Majuba Hill, iii. 37.
Malacca Straits, ii. 488.
Malet, Sir E., iii. 146.
Malmesbury, Lord, estimate of, i. 198;
his estimate of Gladstone, i. 431; on
co-operation with Gladstone, i. 562;

distrusted by Gladstone, i. 623, 624;
otherwise mentioned, i. 361 *note*[4],
417, 561, 595.
Maltby, Bp., i. 56.
Manchester: —
Disraeli's speech at (1872), ii. 390.
Fenian outrage in, ii. 241.
Fraser appointed bishop, ii. 432.
Gladstone nominated for (1837), i.
141; his speech at (1853), i. 483.
Nonconformist protest at, against
Education Act, ii. 308.
Manin, D., i. 402; ii. 533.
Manners, Lord J., *see* Rutland.
Manning: —
Chronology — Strongly anglican atti-
tude, i. 161; in Rome with Glad-
stone, i. 173, 174; approves *Church
Principles*, i. 182; revises MS. of
Church Principles, i. 224; godfather to Gladstone's eldest son, i.
227; with Gladstone before resignation on Maynooth, i. 273, 274;
Gladstone's close relations with,
i. 310, 313; Newman's letters to,
i. 311, 312; Guy Fawkes sermon,
i. 313 *note*[1]; on secession to Rome,
i. 317; on Gladstone's career, i.
323; on church outlook, i. 325;
Gorham case, i. 378-380 *and note*[2];
secession to Rome, i. 385-387; estrangement from Gladstone, i. 387
and note[2]; on Gladstone's Irish
church policy, ii. 143, 246, 250, 279;
letter on Oxford defeat, ii. 147, 150
note; letter to Gladstone on premiership, ii. 255; Irish Land bill
(1870), ii. 294, 296; on Education
bill, ii. 308; on Irish University
bill, ii. 439, 440; pamphlet of, replying to Gladstone's on Vatican
decrees, ii. 504, 519-521; on eastern
question, ii. 571; intercourse with
Gladstone renewed, iii. 281; on cesser of Irish representation, iii. 325;
on Parnell leadership, iii. 448-449.
Contrasted with Newman, ii. 137, 521.
Gladstone's letters to, i. 171, 230, 276,
323-325, 378; iii. 106.
Ultramontanism of, ii. 509-510; otherwise mentioned, i. 55, 141, 148, 207
note[2], 260, 321, 364, 393, 403 *note*;
ii. 192, 214-215, 474, 499, 504, 509;
iii. 191, 197.
Mansfield, Lord, i. 17, 75.
Manzoni, i. 173; ii. 11, 151 *note*[2], 533;
ode translated, iii. 549.
Marcus Aurelius, i. 207 *and note*[1].
Maria, Donna, i. 248.

Marie Antoinette, iii. 469.

Marlborough, Duke of, ii. 268, 275, 571.

Marriage — civil, legalisation of, i. 567; deceased wife's sister question, i. 569; Gladstone's views on, i. 568–572.

Marriott, C., i. 59 *note*, 334.

Marsham, Dr., i. 336, 426–427.

Martin, Sir J., ii. 383.

—— Sir Theodore, ii. 47 *note* [1].

Martineau, Miss, ii. 541.

—— James, ii. 136; iii. 525.

Maskell, Rev. W., i. 380 *note* [2].

Match tax, ii. 373 *and notes*.

Mathew, Father, ii. 192.

Maurice, F. D., influence of, i. 54; Newman compared with, i. 165; proceedings against, i. 168, 316, 454–455; on Gladstone's Oxford candidature, i. 331–332; King's College attack on, i. 454–455; appointed to Vere St., i. 456; otherwise mentioned, i. 54, 59 *note*, 60, 64, 79, 149, 376; ii. 534.

May, Sir T. E., on the Greenwich seat question, ii. 467, 469; assists Speaker against obstruction, iii. 53; memo. by, iii. 285 *note*; mentioned, iii. 306.

Maynooth : —
  Conservative advantage regarding Act, iii. 238.
  Gladstone's retirement on question of, i. 632; ii. 238, 240.
  Inglis opposes grant to, i. 328.
  Irish Church bill (1869) concerned with, ii. 263, 266.
  Peel's policy regarding, i. 270; Gladstone's attitude towards Peel's policy, i. 271–273, 278.
  Russell's speech on, i. 411–412.

Mazzini, i. 390, 396, 402; ii. 150, 184; iii. 464, 478.

Melbourne, Lord, dismissal of (1834), i. 118 *and note* [2]; Hampden appointment, i. 166–167; on Peel's position (1843), i. 266; nature of government of, i. 298; Gladstone's estimate of, iii. 472; long administration of, iii. 493; otherwise mentioned, i. 143, 543; iii. 471, 490.

Melvill, H., i. 100.

Menschikoff, i. 486, 494.

Mérimée, Prosper, ii. 533.

Merivale, Charles, ii. 539.

Metaphysical Society, ii. 524.

Metaphysics, Gladstone's attitude towards, i. 209.

Metastasio, i. 108.

Metternich, i. 366; ii. 319.

Mexico, French embarrassments in, ii. 84–85.

Miall, E., ii. 305, 444.

Middlesborough, ii. 78 *and note*.

Midlothian, Gladstone's invitation to stand for, ii. 584; agrees, ii. 585; general outlook, ii. 586–587; the campaign, ii. 587–596; iii. 27; the Queen's disapproval, ii. 628; iii. 102; his return for (1880), ii. 611–612; (1886) iii. 344; (1892) iii. 492; his farewell to, iii. 535–536.

Mignet, F.-A.-A., ii. 220.

Miguel, Don, i. 248.

Miles, ——, i. 264.

Mill, James, i. 144, 200; ii. 366–367.

—— J. S., views on the Tractarians, i. 163–164; on civil service reform, i. 509; estimate of Gladstone, ii. 123; on government of India, ii. 284; on Irish land question, ii. 293; on education, ii. 302; against the ballot, ii. 366–367; memorial to, ii. 543–544; Gladstone's estimate of, ii. 544; otherwise mentioned, i. 187, 189, 229, 314; ii. 220, 282, 430, 534; iii. 491.

—— Dr. W. H., i. 319, 380 *note* [2].

Millais, Sir J., ii. 581–582.

Milman, Dean, i. 56, 166; ii. 166, 539.

Milnes, R. Monckton, i. 135, 149, 177, 229, 234.

Milton, Gladstone's estimate of, i. 96; views on the church, i. 155; on marriage, i. 568, 572; Gladstone compared with, ii. 555.

Minghetti, ii. 533.

Mold, speech at (1856), i. 363 *note* [2].

Moldavia, ii. 3.

Molesworth, Sir William, views on toleration, i. 138; on Canadian revolt, i. 361 *and note* [5]; in coalition cabinet, i. 447, 450; Denison's attitude towards, i. 451; supports Gladstone's budget, i. 466; attitude towards Crimean war, i. 482 *note*; on colonial policy, i. 645; otherwise mentioned, i. 144, 358, 361, 362, 458, 492, 648; iii. 13.

Moltke, ii. 321, 324, 332–333.

Moncreiff, Rev. Sir H. W., i. 59, 73.

Money dealings, i. 206; iii. 419–420.

Monsell, W., postmaster-general (1870), ii. 460–461, 463 *note*, 479, 644.

Montalembert, De, i. 178; ii. 185, 476, 481; letter from, ii. 544.

Monte Cassino, ii. 218–219.

Montenegro : —
  Berlin Treaty's provisions regarding, iii. 8–10.

Montenegro — *continued*.
  Revolt in, ii. 549, 553, 561, 566–567.
  Sympathy in Gladstone's illness, iii. 527.
More, Hannah, i. 12.
Moriarty, Bishop, ii. 512.
Morier, Sir Robert, ii. 525.
Morpeth, Lord, i. 222.
Morley, Arnold, iii. 429, 433, 434 *note*.
—— John, appointment of, as Irish secretary, iii. 295, 297 *note*; previous utterances of, on Irish question, 296 *note*[1]; presses Irish land bill, iii. 301; in communication with Parnell, iii. 304–306, 320 *note*[1]; letter from Parnell against withdrawal of bill after second reading, iii. 333; letter on Parnell's view of resignation, iii. 347; at round table conference, iii. 364 *note*; Gladstone's letter to, on Churchill's retirement, iii. 364; interviews with Parnell, iii, 369, 370; Gladstone's letters to, on plan of campaign, iii. 371–372; Bingley Hall meeting, iii. 388; Parnell consults with, on *Times* letters, iii. 394; Gladstone's letter to, on Italian policy, iii. 414; Gladstone's letter to, on Parnell, iii. 429–431; meeting at Lord Rendel's on Parnell affair, iii. 434 *note*; Gladstone's letter to, on Parnell's leadership, iii. 436; interviews with Parnell, iii. 439–441, 444; visit to Hawarden (1890), iii. 452–454; Gladstone's letters to, on Kilkenny election, iii. 457; on his birthday, iii. 458; on death of eldest son, iii. 461; at Biarritz, iii. 463 *et seq.*; at Dalmeny, iii. 491–492; Gladstone's letter to, on election, iii. 494; Irish secretary (1892), iii. 495 *note*; at Butterstone with Gladstone, iii. 525; farewell visit, iii. 528; otherwise mentioned, iii. 387, 423, 497 *note*[1], 499 *note*, 500.
Mortgage of land, Gladstone's views regarding, i. 347, 349.
Mozley, J. B., i. 334.
—— T., ii. 260.
Mulgrave, Lord, iii. 211 *note*.
Mundella, A. J., iii. 297 *note*, 495 *note*.
Münster, Count, iii. 247.
Murray, Archbishop, i. 178.
—— Sir G., i. 112; ii. 156 *note*[1].
—— John, i. 274; ii. 382.
Murchison, Sir R., ii. 380.
Myrianthes, Archimandrite, ii. 532.

NAPIER, SIR CHARLES, on Ionian islanders, i. 598–599.

Naples : —
  Gladstone's visit to (1850), i. 389–393; later visit (1888), iii. 413.
  Misgovernment of, i. 390–393; ii. 12, 16–17.
  Victor Emmanuel's entry into, ii. 17.
Napoleon I., i. 320 *and note*[1]; iii. 482, 485, 549.
—— III., plot to slay, i. 574; aids Italy, ii. 7–8, 14; estimate of, by a papal official, ii. 10 *note*; difficulties of, with French ultramontanes, ii. 15; Cobden's negotiations with, ii. 20; estimate of Gladstone's budget speech, ii. 28; friendliness towards England, ii. 46; Palmerston's mistrust of, ii. 49; urges plan of representations to America, ii. 84–85; on Garibaldi, ii. 111; on Danish question, ii. 117, 118, 580; Gladstone dines with (1867), ii. 221; uneasiness regarding Prussia, ii. 321; deposition of, ii. 343; letter from, ii. 546; otherwise mentioned, i. 485–486, 489, 490; ii. 3–7, 325, 328 *note*[1], 329, 334.
National Debt : —
  Conversion scheme (1853), i. 472, 513, 647.
  Proposals regarding (1866), ii. 57, 200.
  Reduction of (1868–73), ii. 375.
  Terminable annuities for paying off, ii. 651.
—— Press Agency, iii. 264 *note*, 265.
Nationalist party, *see* Irish party.
Nationality : —
  Emergence of principle of, ii. 2–3.
  Gladstone's attitude towards (1851), i. 389, 390; (1854) ii. 12–13; (1859) i. 618; (1885) iii. 260; (1888) iii. 361.
  Napoleon III.'s views on, ii. 7.
Negro apprenticeship, Gladstone's speech on, i. 134 *and note*.
Neilson of Springfield, i. 16.
Nelson, Thomas, i. 110.
Neruda, Mme. Norman, ii. 459.
Nettleship, Mr., iii. 519.
Neville, Father, iii. 388.
Newark, Gladstone's candidature and election for (1832), i. 88–94, 96–97, 181; returned for, without contest (1834), i. 121; speech at (1835), i. 129; speech at (1837), i. 138; returned for (1837), i. 141; (1841) i. 238; end of his connection with, i. 287.
Newcastle, Gladstone's visit to (1862), ii. 76–78; his speeches at (1891), iii. 462.

Newcastle, 4th Duke of, offers Gladstone influence in Newark, i. 88–89; views of, i. 91–92; Gladstone's relations with, i. 94; Gladstone's visit to, i. 95; Sadler a nominee of, i. 99; Gladstone's first book approved by, i. 176; mentioned, i. 286.

—— 5th Duke of, informs Gladstone of parliamentary opening at Newark, i. 88; re-elected (1846), i. 288; on Gladstone's quarrel with Bentinck, i. 302; Russell's proposal to, i. 350; advises Gladstone to decline office, i. 406; desires leadership of Peelites, i. 408; attitude towards Derby, i. 418; ideas of a third party, i. 419, 423; supports Gladstone's budget, i. 466; war minister during Crimean war, i. 651–652; suggests substitution of Palmerston for himself, i. 522; on Peelites' refusal to join Palmerston, i. 535; favours Ionian project, i. 595; attitude towards French treaty scheme, ii. 22; on Paper Duties bill, ii. 33, 37; supports Finance bill proposal, ii. 39; death of, ii. 143; Gladstone trustee for, ii. 151; Gladstone's estimate of, ii. 193, 256; otherwise mentioned, i. 54, 74, 113, 119, 242, 285, 287, 355, 420, 443, 480 note, 490, 491, 493 *and note*, 528, 536, 584, 648; ii. 237, 238, 635–636.

Newdegate, C. N., iii. 15.

Newman, Francis, i. 329; letter from, ii. 177, 539.

—— Cardinal, J. H., Gladstone's early contact with, i. 57–58 *and note*[1]; sermons by, i. 58, 79, 86; Gladstone's estimate of, i. 163 *note*[1]; on *Church Principles*, i. 181; on J. R. Hope, i. 228 *note*; Gladstone's correspondence with, i. 272; Tract Ninety, i. 306–307, 311; view on Jerusalem bishopric, i. 308, 309, 312; on system of Roman church, i. 310; position of (1843), i. 310–313; Gladstone on treatment of, i. 316; secession of, i. 317; letter of, describing Gladstone's position, i. 632; contrasted with Manning, ii. 137, 521; on Gladstone's criticism of *Ecce Homo*, ii. 167; on Gladstone's *Chapter of Autobiography*, ii. 250; reply to Gladstone's *Vatican Decrees* pamphlet, ii. 520; to *Vaticanism*, ii. 521; last letter from, ii. 547; Gladstone's call on, with Chamberlain, ii. 570 *and note*; Gladstone's letter to, on papal responsibility for disloyal priests in

Ireland, iii. 62; reply, iii. 63; death of, iii. 421; otherwise mentioned, i. 159, 165, 168, 235, 319; ii. 192, 504; iii. 388.

Newnham College, iii. 385.

New Zealand, i. 297–298, 358, 645.

Nice, French acquisition of, ii. 9, 22, 30, 108.

Nineteenth Century, iii. 356–360, 519.

Nomination boroughs, i. 621.

Nonconformists, *see* Dissenters.

Normanby, Lord, i. 407.

Norreys, Lord, i. 72.

North, Lord, i. 133; ii. 467; iii. 181.

North Notts, i. 287.

Northbrook, Earl of, Gladstone's letter to, on Egyptian mission, iii. 121; agrees to send Gordon to Soudan, iii. 150; against home rule, iii. 291 *note*, 294; otherwise mentioned, i. 450 *note*; ii. 654; iii. 268.

Northcote, Sir S., *see* Iddesleigh.

Norway, Gladstone's cruises to (1883), iii. 115–117; (1885) iii. 217–218.

Novalis, cited, iii. 466.

Novikoff, Mme., ii. 557, 574, 582.

Nubar, iii. 149, 153, 157.

Oakeley, F., i. 310.

Oak Farm, financial embarrassments of, i. 337 *et seq.*; Gladstone's preoccupation with, i. 272, 340, 342; his public finance influenced by experiences with, i. 474.

O'Brien, W. Smith, i. 400.

—— W., iii. 448.

Obstruction, *see under* Parliament.

O'Connell, Daniel, repeal amendment of (1833), i. 106; iii. 285 *note*; on Harvey committee, i. 112 *note*, 113; influence of, on Gladstone, i. 113; tory attitude towards, i. 129, 138; visits Newark, i. 130; on Gladstone's first book, i. 178; Peel's attitude towards (1844), i. 270; Gladstone contrasted with, ii. 593; crime denounced by, iii. 50; otherwise mentioned, i. 101, 266, 372; ii. 227; iii. 11, 62, 493.

Octagon, the, ii. 526–548.

Office, Gladstone's view of desire for, i. 554.

O'Hagan, Lord, ii. 292.

Okes, Provost, i. 11.

Oliver, Mrs., i. 9 *note*.

Opium question, i. 259–260.

Oratory, political, i. 191–195, 411, 470; ii. 589; iii. 312 (*see also* Gladstone, W. E.—characteristics—eloquence).

Orsini affair, ii. 24, 44.
Osman Digna, iii. 178.
Ossory, Archdeacon of, ii. 265.
Oswald, Alex., i. 419.
Otho, King, i. 479, 605.
Ottomans, *see* Turkey.
Owen, Professor, ii. 537.
Oxenham, ——, i. 59, *note.*
Oxford : —
    Bias of, i. 60, 70, 84.
    Chandos opposes Gladstone at, i. 628.
    Christ Church, enthusiasm at, after Gladstone's election (1847), i. 336.
    Democracy, attitude towards, ii. 35.
    Dissenters' disabilities at, ii. 313 *and note.*
    Ewelme appointment, ii. 386-387.
    Famous sons of, iii. 476.
    Gladstone's career at, i. 48-85; his feeling for, i. 80, 84-85; ii. 148; iii. 486, 528; his combination of Lancashire and, i. 192; ii. 41; his visits to (1834), i. 111; (1847) i. 235, 377; (1853) i. 457; (1872) ii. 436-437; his reception of D. C. L. degree at, i. 377; his advice to his son at, i. 205; sympathy from, iii. 527.
    Gladstone's candidature for (1847), i. 328-333; election, i. 333-335; his return for (1852), i. 426-427; return for (1853), i. 452; return for (1857), i. 565; return for (1859), i. 614 *note*, 630; defeat at (1865), ii. 145-148.
    Gladstone's membership for, effect of, on his career, i. 327, 429, 453; on the university, i. 499; as it appeared to himself, i. 630.
    Influence of, i. 501.
    Method of study at, i. 50-51 *and note.*
    Reform — commission proposed by Lord J. Russell (1850), i. 497; opposed by Gladstone, i. 426, 497; Oxford resistance to, i. 498; conduct and report of, i. 499 *and note*[4]; Gladstone's scheme, i. 500, 501, 506-507; its reception, i. 502-503; results of, i. 508-509; Tractarian movement's effect on, i. 57.
    Tests, i. 506-507; abolition of, ii. 313 *and note*; i. 314.
    Tractarian movement, *see* Oxford movement.
    W E G Essay Club at, i. 59-60.
Oxford and Cambridge Club, Gladstone's membership of, i. 98 *and note.*

Oxford movement : —
    Gladstone unaffected by, i. 161; his election affected by, i. 328.
    Ireland affected by, i. 308.
    Nature of, i. 163-165.
    Oxford, influence on, i. 496.
    Second phase of, i. 305.
    Tracts for the Times, i. 329; Tracts Eighty and Eighty-seven, i. 307 *note*; Tract Ninety, i. 235, 306, 310, 311; iii. 422.

PACIFIC, Gladstone advocates reduction of force in, i. 458.
Paget, Miss, iii. 524.
—— Lord Clarence, ii. 112, 140.
Paine, Thomas, ii. 127.
Pakington, Sir J., i. 561.
Palgrave, F. T., ii. 474.
Pall Mall Gazette, ii. 579-580, 618.
Paley, cited, i. 422.
Palmer, Kelly and, i. 518.
—— Roundell, *see* Selborne.
—— William, Gladstone influenced by, i. 162, 167; Gladstone's estimate of, i. 235; on Maynooth grant, i. 279.
Palmerston, Lord : —
    Chronology — On sugar duties, i. 236; on free trade, i. 265; on Spanish treaties, i. 280; on repeal, i. 289; Don Pacifico debate, i. 368-371; on Neapolitan tyranny, i. 394, 400; ii. 13; relations with Kossuth, i. 415, dismissal by Russell, i. 415; amendment on Militia bill, i. 416; in opposition to Peel, i. 420 *and note*[1]; section represented by, i. 431; moves amendment against Villiers, i. 433; joins coalition government, i. 446-447; on Gladstone's budget (1853), i. 465-467; different views of, on eastern question, i. 480; communications with preceding Crimean war, i. 481-482; approves Lord Stratford, i. 488; desired as war minister during Crimean war, i. 651; on Black Sea affair, ii. 349; Derby's vote of censure on (1857), i. 561-562; ii. 269; defeat of, on Cobden's motion, i. 564; ii. 265; urges postponement of Reform bill, i. 490, 648; Gladstone's letter to, on Crimean operations, i. 494; Aberdeen in conflict with, i. 495 *and note*[3]; foreign office reconstructed by, i. 510; suggested by Newcastle as substitute for himself, i. 522; invited by Derby to join govern-

ment, i. 525; refuses, i. 526; approves Gladstone's refusal, i. 527; Peelites' attitude towards, i. 531–535; satisfies Aberdeen, i. 535; intention of, to oppose Roebuck's committee, i. 538, 542; advises acceptance of Roebuck's committee, i. 539; on Crimean war, i. 548; triumph of, at election (1857), i. 564; defeated on Conspiracy bill, i. 574–576; suggested as leader of Commons by Disraeli, i. 587; views on Suez Canal scheme, i. 591; on Corfu, i. 619; hands over Ionian Islands to Greece, i. 620 *and note* ²; communications with Russell, i. 624; forms a government (1859), i. 626; views of, identical with Derby's, i. 631; the Principalities, ii. 4; French treaty scheme, ii. 20, 22; Paper Duties bill, ii. 31–33, 37, 39; Finance bill, ii. 39; franchise proposals of, ii. 200; supports Herbert, ii. 44; fortifications scheme, ii. 47; makes a peace speech (1859), ii. 48; correspondence with Gladstone, ii. 49–50; on *Trent* affair, ii. 74; favours suggestion of representations to America, ii. 75–77, 85; advises Gladstone regarding Newcastle speech, ii. 76; on American separation, ii. 82; on reduction in naval estimates, ii. 94; receives Garibaldi, ii. 110, views on Garibaldi's departure, ii. 112; on Danish question, ii. 115–118, 120; on Gladstone's franchise pronouncement, ii. 127–130; on cabinet government, ii. 142; death of, ii. 151; Gladstone's action regarding funeral of, ii. 153; Gladstone's speech on, ii. 157.

Career and abilities of, i. 543.

Characteristics of, i. 366–368.

Compared with Lansdowne, i. 530; with Aberdeen, i. 530; with Gladstone, ii. 172; with Disraeli, ii. 551; with Hartington, iii. 3.

Ecclesiastical appointments of, ii. 122, 430.

Foreign estimates of, i. 366, 367, 392.

Foreign policy, principles of, i. 367; Granville's view of, ii. 348.

Frankness of, i. 554.

Gladstone's relations with, from 1850, i. 371; his opposition to, i. 553, 558, 566, 585; ii. 43; his harmony of sentiment with, i. 628;

Gladstone's estimate of, i. 567; ii. 35; his estimate of Gladstone, ii. 171; Gladstone's conflicts with, on expenditure, ii. 43, 138–139.

Leadership of, ii. 172.

Life-objects of, ii. 45.

Peers created by, ii. 429.

Popularity of, i. 400, 493, 543, 564; ii. 633; cooling of, ii. 50, 176.

Queen's attitude towards, ii. 98.

Selection of work by, ii. 465.

Otherwise mentioned, i. 120 *note*, 226, 402, 431, 444, 450, 526, 528, 579, 622; ii. 3, 19, 63, 80, 100, 104, 106, 111, 131, 171, 189, 194, 256, 423, 435, 494, 576, 577, 595, 619, 635–636; iii. 96 *note* ¹, 178, 228, 300, 419, 443, 475.

Panizzi, Sir A., influence of, on Gladstone, i. 389–390; interview of, with king of Naples, i. 401; Gladstone's letters to, i. 402; ii. 107, 151; illness of (1868), ii. 196; otherwise mentioned, ii. 110, 184, 552.

Papal States, ii. 108, 185.

Paper duty, ii. 24–25, 30–41, 238–239, 636.

Paris, Comte de, ii. 189; iii. 103, 470.

—— Treaty of (1856), i. 550; ii. 349–356, 607; iii. 522.

Parish Councils bill (1893), iii. 504, 505, 511.

Parliament:—

House of Commons:—

Attendance in — Gladstone's diligence regarding, i. 102; ii. 418, 422; iii. 7–8; Peel's view of, i. 299.

Balance of parties in (1850), i. 373; (1852) i. 428; (1853) i. 446, 448–449.

Burning of, in 1834, i. 114.

Closure, introduction of, iii. 377; Gladstone's distaste for, iii. 124; drastic form of, on Parnell commission bill, iii. 401.

Colonial affairs, indifference to, i. 362.

Committee Room Fifteen, Irish party proceedings in, iii. 446 *and note* ², 454.

Composition of first reformed, i. 101.

Ecclesiastical discussions in, ii. 502.

Excitement in, manifestations of, iii. 441; on introduction of Home Rule bill (1886), iii. 310–311.

Parliament — *continued.*
House of Commons — *continued.*
Executive sphere invaded by, iii. 6.
Expenditure controlled by, under Exchequer and Audit Act (1866), ii. 61.
Gladstone's diligence for duties of, *see above,* Attendance; his feeling of powerlessness in, i. 221; his care for rights and traditions of, ii. 492–493; iii. 7, 206, 208, 510, 530; his mastery of, i. 193, 410–411, 470; iii. 312; his place in (1847–52), ii. 211 *note*; his position in (1858), i. 581; his isolation in (1867), ii. 229.
Grote's estimate of, ii. 370.
Indian discussion, indifference to, i. 113.
Intolerance of, in the Bradlaugh matter, iii. 13–20; resolution of 1881 struck off records of, iii. 21.
Irish members of, *see* Irish party.
Irish representation in, cesser of, contemplated, iii. 302, 304, 307, 309, 324, 326–327; opposed, iii. 324–325, 327, 332; Gladstone's speech on, at Swansea (1887), iii. 386; question of (1892), iii. 497–498.
Lords, conflict with, *see below* under House of Lords.
Majorities, large, dating from Gladstone's premiership, ii. 264–265.
Obstruction in, Irish, iii. 48, 51–53, 57, 123–124; unionist, iii. 499.
Party obligations in, i. 292, 295, 299.
Payment of members, Gladstone's views regarding (1861), i. 611 *note*; his scheme for (1891), iii. 478–479; Chamberlain's pronouncement, iii. 174.
Popular influence on, i. 150; iii. 4.
Position of seats in, significance of, i. 422–423, 539; iii. 363; Gladstone's place (1853–1866), i. 631 *note.*
Procedure of, violated by Disraeli, ii. 189; altered by Gladstone, ii. 631; Gladstone's advocacy of reform in, iii. 123.
Reform, *see that title.*
Reversal of previous vote ruled not out of order, i. 462 *note.*

Shah's interest in, ii. 459.
Supply, rights regarding, ii. 38, 40, 61.
Tactics in, Stephen on, i. 147; Russell's skill in, i. 467; Gladstone's, iii. 538–539.
Temper, school of, i. 199.
Temporary retirements from, Gladstone's views of, i. 357–358.
Uncertainties in, i. 650.
Variety of style desirable for stating a case in, i. 192.
House of Lords : —
Ballot bill rejected by, ii. 369.
Chamberlain's attitude towards, iii. 173, 225.
Commons' feeling against premier from (1894), iii. 513.
Compensation for Disturbance bill rejected by, iii. 49, 409, 410.
Conservative influence in, iii. 258; occasions of defeats, ii. 269.
Employers' Liability bill mutilated by, iii. 504.
Franchise bill struggle (1884), iii. 126–139.
Gladstone's first hearing of debate in, i. 75–76; his first conflict with, i. 471; his refusal of position in, iii. 104, 209; his attitude towards (1884), iii. 127–128, 130; his later attitude towards (1894), iii. 504–505; his speech against (Mar. 1), iii. 511–512.
Home Rule bill (1892) thrown out by, iii. 504.
Irish church question, attitude towards, ii. 246, 258, 267–279.
Opposition by, a stimulus to popular causes, ii. 248.
Paper duty struggle with Commons, ii. 25, 31–40, 238–239, 636.
Parish Councils bill maimed by, iii. 504, 505, 511.
Parnell's apprehensions regarding, iii. 240.
Peel's view of, ii. 133.
Permanent opinion represented by, Gladstone's exposure of the theory, iii. 128.
Preponderance of cabinet in (1865), ii. 153–154.
Reform bill of 1867 amended by, ii. 226.

Jews, admission of, i. 375–377.

Premiership, labours entailed by, i. 297–299.

Parnell, C. S. (*see also* Irish party), number of followers of (1880), ii. 613; party of, iii. 2; obstructionist tactics, iii. 48, 53, 57, 123–124; attitude of, towards Compensation for Disturbance bill, iii. 49; indicted for seditious conspiracy, iii. 50 *note*[1]; attitude towards Land Act of 1881, iii. 57, 61; Gladstone's warning to, at Leeds, iii. 61; imprisonment of, iii. 61–62, 228, 233; Chamberlain's communications with, iii. 64; offers to resign his seat, iii. 70; on franchise extension in Ireland, iii. 143; supports government (May 1885), iii. 184; conservative understanding with, iii. 188–190, 200; not counted on by Gladstone, iii. 191, 197; favours plan of central board for Ireland, iii. 194, 231, 291; repudiates it, iii. 215, 230; on Maamtrasna case, iii. 213; friction with Hartington, iii. 220, 241; speech of (Aug. 1885), iii. 220, 228, 233; public estimate of, iii. 228; Carnarvon's interview with, iii. 228–231; home rule demanded by, iii. 232; victory of adherents of, at the elections, iii. 253, 255; Salisbury's reference to, at Newport, iii. 243; gives Irish vote to conservatives at the election, iii. 244–245; speculations regarding, iii. 267, 268; attitude towards Gladstone, iii. 274; tactics after elections (1885), iii. 274–275; in communication with Morley, iii. 304–306; characteristics of, iii. 304, 311; interview with Gladstone, iii. 305–306; objections to financial provisions of Home Rule bill, iii. 305, 306, 319, 331; consultations with colleagues, iii. 319–320 *and notes*; on introduction of Home Rule bill, iii. 311; on continued Irish representation at Westminster, iii. 324; opposed to withdrawal of the bill, iii. 333; second meeting with Gladstone, iii. 334; speech on night of the division, iii. 337, 340; deprecates ministerial resignation, iii. 347; systematic disagreement with, iii. 369; illness of, iii. 370, 376; disapproves plan of campaign, iii. 370; tactics on Crimes bill (1887), iii. 376–377; produces Tenants Relief bill, iii. 369; on papal rescript, iii. 38; forged letter in *Times*, iii. 391 *and note*[1];

denial in the House, iii. 392; further letters, iii. 394; personal statement in the House, iii. 395; asks for select committee, iii. 395; special commission, iii. 396–399; alleged interview of, with spy from America, iii. 404; Gladstone's sympathy with, iii. 408; visit to Hawarden, iii. 420, 445–446; speech at Liverpool, iii. 446 *note*[1]; divorce suit, iii. 428–430; public opinion regarding the verdict, iii. 430–434, 448–449; question of leadership of, iii. 435 *et seq.*; Gladstone's letter to Morley regarding, iii. 436, 444; attitude of, iii. 438, 442–443; re-elected by Irish party, iii. 438; interviews with Morley, iii. 439–441; manifesto to the Irish people, iii. 445; committee room fifteen, iii. 446 *and note*[2]–448, 449–452; denounces liberal party, iii. 450–459; elections adverse to, iii. 458; last speech of, in England, iii. 459; death of, iii. 459; otherwise mentioned, ii. 492; iii. 56, 225 *and note*[2], 240, 286, 367, 369, 372, 493.

Parnell, Sir Henry, i. 251.

Parnellism Unmasked, iii. 406.

Parnellites, *see under* Irish party.

Party: —
   Elements deciding relations of, i. 422, 435.
   Gladstone's views on, i. 304, 405.
   Tenacity of system, i. 448 *note*[1].

Pascal, i. 153.

Patronage, i. 649; ii. 428.

Patten, Wilson, i. 351 *note*[1], 438.

Patteson, Bishop, ii. 581; iii. 419.

—— Sir T., i. 455.

Pattison, Sister Dora, ii. 604.

—— Mark, iii. 482.

Paxo, i. 601.

Pearson, C. B., i. 77.

Pedro, Don, i. 248.

Peel, General, i. 351 *note*[1], 355.

—— Arthur, ii. 492; ii. 463 *note*; iii. 455.

—— Mrs., iii. 455.

—— Sir Robert (2nd Bart.): —
   Chronology — Oxford University representation resigned by, i. 53; Oxford honours of, i. 79–80; praises Gladstone's maiden speech, i. 103; views on emancipation, i. 104; on Irish Church Reform bill, i. 105; Cobbett's attack on, i. 114; Gladstone encouraged by, i. 114; election promises of, ii. 489; summoned

Peel, Sir Robert — *continued.*
Chronology — (*continued*).
    to form a government (1834), i.
118; Gladstone offered treasury
post by, i. 119; Gladstone appointed under-secretary of the
colonies by, i. 123; cabinet of
(1835), i. 420; composition of
whig opposition to, i. 419–420
and note[1]; resigns, i. 127; views
on Ireland (1836), i. 135; speaks
at Glasgow (1837), i. 138; Stanley dines with, i. 139; on Canada
question, i. 641; on Molesworth's
vote of censure, i. 145; on slave-
apprenticeship law, i. 146; on
Wilberforce, i. 150; defeated on
Irish church question, i. 154;
views on Gladstone's first book,
i. 177; Jamaica case, i. 221–222;
misunderstanding with the
Queen, i. 222; China question,
i. 225, 242; annoyance with
Stanley, i. 234; views on sugar
duties, i. 236, 280, 644; turns
out whigs by majority of 1 (1841),
i. 237; ii. 203 *note*[2], 264; party
meetings, i. 239; forms a government (1841), i. 240; Gladstone's
inclusion in cabinet, i. 240, 305;
privy council, i. 243; position
of, regarding protection, i. 250–
253, 258, 262–263, 282–287; lays
duty on Irish spirits, i. 646;
miscalculation of, regarding income-tax (1842), i. 474 *and note*;
letter to Sir John Gladstone, i.
257; appeal to Pope Gregory, iii.
62; Lady Hewley case, i. 321, 322;
Irish Land bill introduced by
government of (1845), ii. 285;
Maynooth, i. 270–274; precarious
position of, i. 264–266; resigns, i.
283; agrees to resume office, i.
283, 285; iii. 207 *note*[1]; repeal of
corn laws, i. 208, 282–287, 290,
459; hostility towards (1846),
iii. 322; resigns (1846), i. 290–
291; eulogium on Cobden, i. 291–
293, 295, 296; party relations of,
i. 289–290, 292, 293, 295; Gladstone's farewell interview with,
i. 297–300; Russell's overtures to
(1846), i. 350; votes for Gladstone at Oxford, i. 333; advocates
keeping protectionists out of
office, i. 352, 373; Gladstone's
divergencies from, i. 353, 354; letter on Gladstone's mission for his

friend, i. 365; Don Pacifico de-
bate, i. 368–369, 372; death of, i.
371; statue of, inaugurated at
Manchester, i. 483.
Administration of (1842–44), im-
portance of, i. 247; character of,
i. 298, 642–643; ministerial discipline of, iii. 114.
Age of, on entering cabinet, i. 261.
Changes of policy of, i. 266, 425.
Compared with Grey, i. 248; with
Gladstone, i. 269; with Palmerston, i. 367; with Russell, i. 373;
with Aberdeen, ii. 640–641.
Courage of, i. 188, 289.
Debating method of, i. 195.
Disraeli's attitude towards, i. 432.
Estimate of, i. 372; estimate of
financial statements of, ii. 55.
Gladstone — relations with, i. 112;
280, 286; confidence in, and ap-
preciation of, i. 139, 221, 241, 243,
246, 252, 257, 259, 261, 277, 354;
estimate by, i. 254; iii. 465; influ-
ence upon, i. 269; forecast regard-
ing Disraeli and, i. 374.
Graham's estimate of, i. 248, 263.
Guizot's book on, ii. 538.
Influence of, in the House, i. 373.
Justice of, ii. 640.
Liberalism of, i. 418, 419.
Oxford training of, i. 497; convoca-
tion mob at election, i. 629.
Parliamentary tactics of, i. 254.
Peers, views on, ii. 133.
Premiership of, length of, ii. 61.
Otherwise mentioned, i. 49, 98, 126,
128, 149, 192, 212, 227, 236, 238,
245–6, 258, 263–4, 293, 300, 356,
416, 419; ii. 147, 154, 156 *note*[1],
178, 229 *note*, 277 *and note*, 288,
328, 423, 433–435, 463, 498, 619,
623, 627, 628; iii. 238, 277, 486.
—— Sir Robert (3rd Bart.), ii. 444 *note.*
—— Lady, i. 469.
Peelites: —
The tory whip's attitude towards,
i. 418.
Derby's first administration supported by, i. 424; Derby's second
administration supported by, i.
428; Derby's questions regarding
(1856), i. 551.
Dissolution of, as a party, i. 591.
Disturbing effect of, i. 551–552, 558,
567.
Divergencies of, i. 351, 353, 417–420.
Gladstone's view on best policy for,
i. 417–419.

Leadership of — discussed (1850), i. 373-374; accepted by Aberdeen, i. 408.
Palmerston, designs of, i. 447; attitude towards (1855), i. 531-535; in cabinet of, i. 536; resignation, i. 539; public outcry, i. 541.
Papal aggression question, attitude towards, i. 410.
Position of seats of (1852), i. 422-423.
Protectionists, attitude towards, i. 407.
Russell's proposal to include (1852), i. 416.
Third party, position as, i. 417.
Whigs, coalition with (1853), i. 443 et seq.
Peerage : —
Additions to, during various premierships, ii. 428-429 and note.
Offer of, to Gladstone, iii. 104, 209.
Pembroke, Lady, i. 293.
Pembroke Castle, Gladstone's cruise in, iii. 115-117.
Penjdeh, iii. 183.
Pensions, political, iii. 107-108 note.
Penzance, Lord, ii. 383.
People, the, see Democracy.
Perceval, Spencer, i. 298, 543; ii. 467 and note.
—— Mr., i. 452.
Persico, Monsignor, iii. 383.
Persigny, ii. 20.
Petty, Lord Henry, ii. 156 note [1].
Phillimore, Sir Robert, on Hawarden settlement, i. 343-344; assists in Oxford reform scheme, i. 501, 502; on Gladstone's China war speech, i. 563; on Ionian Islands mission, i. 594; interview with Gladstone, i. 623; Gladstone assisted by, at Oxford, i. 628-629; on paper duties debate, ii. 33; on Gladstone's franchise pronouncement, ii. 130; on Irish church, ii. 141, 279-280; on disaffection of liberals, ii. 232, 234-235; on Gladstone's Chapter of Autobiography, ii. 250; on Gladstone's intention of retiring, ii. 388; on Gladstone's Irish University bill, ii. 437; on resignation of ministers (1874), ii. 493; Gladstone's letters to, i. 325-326, 388, 409, 616; iii. 94; otherwise mentioned, i. 54, 65, 75, 79, 80, 393, 623 note; ii. 26, 29, 31, 34, 35, 47 note [2], 48, 73, 88, 92, 127, 214, 295-296, 422, 432, 461-462, 475.
Phillpotts, Bishop, ii. 530.
Phipps, Sir C., ii. 98.

Pickering, ——, i. 75.
Piedmont, growth of, ii. 7-9, 17.
Pierrepont, Hon. H. E. (American minister), ii. 552.
Pitt, William (the younger), finance of, ii. 58-59, 637-638; views of, on emancipation of slaves, i. 104; Glynnes related to, i. 223 and note [1]; income tax imposed by, i. 255; free trade theories promulgated by, i. 265; habits of, i. 298; Palmerston contrasted with, i. 367; Scott's lines to memory of, i. 371; Gladstone compared with, i. 469, 472; warlike preparations of (1791), i. 478; censured for French war, iii. 471; length of premiership of, ii. 61; resolutions of, preliminary to Act of Union, iii. 299; on the Union, iii. 313, 314; otherwise mentioned, i. 372, 419; ii. 230, 264, 343, 428, 435, 589, 619; iii. 256.
Pius IX., Pope, syllabus of 1864, issued by, see under Churches — Roman; Italian federation under, suggested, ii. 7; French ambassador's estimate of, ii. 10; invasion of territories of, ii. 11, 15; annexation to Piedmont of states of, ii. 17; misgovernment in states of, ii. 108; Gladstone's intercourse with, ii. 215-216, 218; attitude towards eastern question, ii. 571.
Playfair, Lord, ii. 444, 463 note, 562; iii. 53.
Plimsoll, S., ii. 620 and note.
Plumptre, ——, i. 146.
Plunket, Lord, ii. 589; iii. 139-140.
Poerio, imprisonment of, i. 391, 396, 401; views of, i. 392-393; exile of, i. 401; Gladstone's efforts on behalf of, ii. 11; Gladstone's letter to, ii. 13; speech at Gladstone dinner (1867), ii. 218; compared with Mazzini, iii. 478.
Poland : —
French feeling in regard to, ii. 118.
Gladstone's interest in, i. 248.
Peel's forecast regarding, i. 133.
Russian dismemberment of, i. 477.
Warsaw, meeting of monarchs at, ii. 5, 16, 184.
Pollok, Robert, i. 132.
Ponsonby, Sir Henry, messages during ministerial crisis (1873), ii. 447-450, 452; in Lords and Commons controversy, iii. 131; on North's American policy, iii. 181; interview with, on ministerial crisis, iii. 205, 207 and note [1]; brings Gladstone the Queen's commission, iii. 290; states the

Ponsonby, Sir Henry—*continued*.
   Queen's message, iii. 291; on feeling
   against peer premier, iii. 513; Glad-
   stone's letters to, iii. 112, 179, 516.
Poor Law Act (1834), i. 115, 121, 140.
Porter, ——, i. 55, 64.
Portland, Duke of, i. 543.
Portugal : —
   British preoccupation with affairs of,
   i. 248.
   Tariff negotiations with, i. 267; ii.
   641.
Positivists, iii. 358.
Post office : —
   Gladstone's admiration for, ii. 182.
   Scandal regarding, ii. 460–463.
   —— —— Savings Banks, i. 651; ii. 52,
   125.
Postage, cheap, ii. 57, 60.
Preaching, English and Italian, i. 174.
Premiership : —
   Age for quitting, Gladstone's view
   on, ii. 423, 443.
   Foreign secretary, Gladstone's view
   of relations with, ii. 399.
   Limitations of, ii. 416, 420.
   Parliamentary labours entailed by,
   i. 297–299.
   Responsibilities of, ii. 416.
Prerogative of the crown, Gladstone
   charged with resorting to, ii. 364–365.
Press : —
   Excitement fomented by, ii. 650.
   Gladstone popular with, ii. 41, 184;
   his views on, ii. 41, 557.
Pretoria convention, iii. 44–45 *and note*.
Prevost, Sir G., ii. 382.
Prince Imperial, iii. 6.
Princess Royal, i. 275.
Privy council appointment, ii. 382–386.
Protection : —
   Colonial, against England, ii. 132.
   Gladstone's position regarding, i.
   249–254, 260, 262, 264, 283–285.
   Peel's position regarding, i. 250–253,
   258, 262–263, 282–289; his appre-
   hensions regarding, i. 352; iii. 465.
   Peelites' views regarding, i. 351–352,
   373, 407.
   Rout of, i. 425, 428, 441–442.
Proudhon, i. 157.
Prussia (*see also* Germany) : —
   Army of, ii. 359.
   Austria—attitude towards (1853), i.
   489; war with (1866), ii. 210 *note*,
   214.
   France : —
      Treaty with, regarding Belgium,
      ii. 340.

War with (1870)—British efforts
   to avert, ii. 326–330, 335–336;
   declaration of, ii. 335 *and note* [2];
   French miscalculations, ii. 337 ;
   course of the war, ii. 342–343;
   effect of, on British naval expenditure, ii. 374.
Schleswig-Holstein question, ii. 114–
   118.
Tariff negotiations with, i. 267.
Public Worship Regulation Act, Gladstone's suggested substitute for, ii.
   514 *note* [3].
Purcell, cited, i. 58 *note* [1], 379–381 *and
   note*.
Pusey, Dr. E. B., on Jerusalem bishopric,
   i. 308; on Newman's letters, i. 311;
   intolerance towards, i. 316, 317 ; supports Gladstone's Oxford candidature, i. 335; on Jewish Disabilities
   Removal bill, i. 375; Gorham case,
   i. 380 *note* [2]; on Gladstone's reform
   scheme, i. 504; Gladstone's relations
   with, ii. 135; Manning's letters to,
   ii. 137; on *Ecce Homo*, ii. 166–167;
   on Temple's appointment, ii. 432;
   Gladstone's meeting with (1872), ii.
   437; death of, iii. 94; Gladstone's
   letters to, i. 316; ii. 181; otherwise
   mentioned, i. 57, 163 *note* [2], 179, 235,
   317; ii. 144, 236.
—— Philip, on Irish agrarian outrages,
   i. 281.
Pym, John, i. 413–414.

Quarterly Review, i. 315; ii. 520.

RADICAL PARTY : —
   Beer duty opposed by, iii. 187, 200.
   Chamberlain's popularity with, iii. 3.
   Characteristics of, Gladstone's views
   on causes of, iii. 240–241.
   Coercion for Ireland opposed by, iii.
   190–191.
   Eastern question (1877), attitude
   towards, ii. 564, 568.
   Educational views of, ii. 303.
   Gladstone not popular with (1867),
   ii. 229; Gladstone criticised by,
   for resorting to crown prerogative,
   ii. 364; his attitude towards (1872),
   ii. 388–390; (1880), ii. 630; iii. 5.
   Irish land purchase opposed by, iii.
   190, 194–195.
   Social programme of (1885), iii. 173–
   174.
   Suffrage, attitude towards, ii. 227.
   Utilitarian reforms effected by, 156.
Raikes, H. C., iii. 96.

Railways, i. 269, 353.
Rampolla, Cardinal, iii. 521.
Ramsay, Dean, ii. 379–380.
Rangabé, i. 605.
Rawson, ——, i. 333 note.
Reading aloud, ii. 558.
Reclamation work, iii. 419.
Redcliffe, Lord Stratford de (Stratford Canning), views on Neapolitan question, i. 407; on eastern question, i. 486–488; ii. 555; otherwise mentioned, i. 406, 417, 420 note, 523.
Redistribution of Seats bill, iii. 137–139, 176–177, 203, 205, 246.
Redmond, J., introduces Arrears bill, iii. 66 note; on Parnell leadership, iii. 447; otherwise mentioned, iii. 66, 494.
Reform, i. 490; ii. 370.
—— bills: —
    (1832), i. 69–70, 75–76; ii. 227; iii. 125, 535.
    (1851), i. 415.
    (1852), ii. 238.
    (1854), i. 648.
    (1860), ii. 26, 29–30.
    (1866), ii. 200 et seq.
    (1867), ii. 223–236; iii. 57, 125, 175, 300 note 4.
    (1884), iii. 125 et seq.
    Various, ii. 199.
Reid, J. J., ii. 612.
Religion: —
    Gladstone's prepossession by, see under Gladstone, W. E. — characteristics.
    Ecclesiasticism versus, ii. 306.
    Peerages independent of, ii. 430.
Religious controversy, temper for, iii. 351.
—— Disabilities Removal bill (1891), i. 414 note.
Renan, ii. 476.
Rendel, Lord, iii. 386, 413, 434, 523, 526, 533.
Retz, De, iii. 480.
Reynolds, Henry, ii. 134.
Ricasoli, Baron, ii. 8, 218–220, 533; iii. 475.
Richards, Dr., 332 and note.
Richmond, Duke of, i. 262; iii. 130, 131.
—— George, i. 233.
Rio, i. 319.
Ripon, Earl of (F. J. Robinson), at board of trade, i. 240, 243, 257; Gladstone's estimate of, i. 250; at board of control, i. 259; otherwise mentioned, i. 252, 253, 254, 255, 641–642.

Ripon, Marquis of (Lord de Grey), war secretary (1865), ii. 153 note; education bill (1870), ii. 300–301, 303; on civil service reform, ii. 315; president of Alabama commission, ii. 400–401, 404, 408, 411; created marquis after treaty of Washington, ii. 408 note; president of council (1868), ii. 644; retires (1873), ii. 463 note, 465; on Transvaal suzerainty question, iii. 45 note; Gladstone's letter to, iii. 69; for home rule, iii. 291 note; first lord of the admiralty, iii. 296 note; colonial secretary (1892), iii. 495 note.
Robert Elsmere, iii. 356–360.
Roberts, General, iii. 41.
Robertson, Provost, i. 7–8, 17 note.
—— Anne, i. 16.
—— Colin, i. 12.
Robinson, see Ripon, Earl of.
—— Sir Hercules, iii. 32 note, 34, 41, 43.
Roebuck, J. A., i. 239, 521, 523, 537–539, 542; ii. 173.
Rogers, Frederick, see Blachford.
Rogers, S., i. 137, 149, 176, 320; ii. 540.
Roman catholic church, see under Churches.
Roman catholics: —
    Affirmation bill opposed by, iii. 20.
    Cesser of Irish representation opposed by, iii. 325.
    Election of 1874, action in, ii. 495.
    Emancipation of, i. 52–53, 277 note, 328, 506; ii. 227; iii. 257, 284.
    Irish university education, attitude towards, ii. 435–436, 440–441.
    Peerages recommended for, by Gladstone, ii. 429–430.
Rome: —
    Church of, see under Churches.
    Ecumenical council at (1869), ii. 508, 510–512.
    French — occupation by, ii. 214, 319, 323, 512; evacuation by, ii. 217, 512.
    Gladstone's visit to (1832), i. 86–87; his feeling for, i. 174; his reasons against visiting (1888), iii. 413–415.
    Italian occupation of, ii. 343, 512.
    Misgovernment in, ii. 12.
Romilly, Lord, ii. 168.
Roon, Albrecht, Count von, ii. 332–333.
Roscoe, W., i. 117.
Rose, Sir John, ii. 400.
Rosebery, Lord, invites Gladstone to stand for Midlothian, ii. 584; Gladstone the guest of, ii. 588, 609; speech after Gladstone's election, ii. 612;

Rosebery, Lord — *continued.*
first commissioner of works, ii. 654;
lord privy seal, ii. 654; at Hawarden,
iii. 261; Gladstone's consultations
with, iii. 261, 263, 268; for home rule,
iii. 291 *note*; foreign secretary (1886),
iii. 297 *note*; foreign secretary (1892),
iii. 495 *note*; Gladstone's letters to,
ii. 613; iii. 4, 239; farewell visit to
Gladstone, iii. 528; tribute in parliament, iii. 531; otherwise mentioned,
iii. 270, 414, 533.

Rothschild, Baron, ii. 325, 328 *note*; iii.
11.

Rouher, M., ii. 221.

Roumania, ii. 4; iii. 532.

Roumelia, iii. 91.

Round, Mr., i. 329, 330, 332, 333.

Round table conference, iii. 364, 366,
368 *and note.*

Rousseau, i. 128, 203.

Routh, Dr., i. 330, 384.

Ruskin, John, i. 329; ii. 559, 582.

Russell, Hastings, ii. 232.

—— Lord John (Earl Russell): —
Chronology — on Irish Church funds,
i. 127; on Ireland (1835), i. 130;
proposes 8s. corn duty, i. 254;
Edinburgh letter, i. 282, 289, 444;
Jewish Disabilities Removal bill,
i. 376; defeat of (1851), ii. 653;
Grey's refusal to join (1845), i.
367; ii. 244; fails to form a government, i. 283; takes office (1846),
290; overtures to Peel (1846), i.
350; on colonial government, i.
363; Palmerston dismissed by, i.
367, 415; on Neapolitan tyranny,
i. 400; Ecclesiastical Titles bill, i.
405, 409; Durham letter, i. 408,
444; defeated (1852), ii. 264; resigns, i. 406; overtures to Gladstone, i. 421; on Four Seats bill, i.
424; views on leadership of coalition government, i. 444; joins
Aberdeen's government, i. 445;
budget of, i. 459; Gladstone's budget, i. 465–467, 469; negotiations
preceding Crimean war, i. 481–482;
approves Lord Stratford, i. 488;
postpones Reform bill, i. 648; on
Crimean war, i. 493; Aberdeen in
conflict with, i. 495, *and* note[3];
Oxford reform, i. 497, 503; on exclusion of dissenters from universities, i. 505; on civil service
reform, i. 511; on woods and forests dismissal case, i. 520; resigns
on Roebuck's notice of motion, i.

521; his explanation, i. 523; Gladstone unwilling to join, i. 528; attempts to form a government, i.
530; fails, i. 531; complains of
Peelites, i. 536; colonial secretary,
i. 540 *note*; resigns, i. 548; opposes
Lewis' budget, i. 560; Graham's
relations with, i. 584 *note*; on
Gladstone's Ionian commissioner-
ship, i. 613; on Italian nationality,
i. 618–619; ii. 13; declines Palmerston dinner, i. 624; states conditions of joining Granville's government, i. 626; on economy, ii.
48; on the Principalities, ii. 4;
despatch of, on Italian question
(1860), ii. 15–16; supports French
treaty scheme, ii. 22; on Nice and
Savoy, ii. 23; Reform bill of
(1860), ii. 26, 29–30; on Paper
Duties bill, ii. 32–33, 37; supports
Gladstone in finance debate, ii.
40; Trent affair, ii. 74; on American war, ii. 76–77, 83, 85; on Gladstone's Newcastle speech, ii. 80;
interview with Mr. Adams, ii. 83;
statement on Morocco loan, ii. 92–
93; opposes reduction in naval
estimates, ii. 94; on Danish question, ii. 117–118; Gladstone's letter
to, on Palmerston's death, ii. 151;
commissioned to form a government, ii. 152; offers Gladstone
leadership of Commons, ii. 154;
Reform bill of 1866, ii. 199, *et seq.*;
the supplemental charter, ii. 435;
resigns, ii. 208; audience with the
Queen, i. 209–210; disaffection
against, ii. 228; on Irish church
question, ii. 239; retires, ii. 243;
asked by Gladstone to enter his
cabinet, ii. 253; education proposals of, opposed by dissenters,
ii. 302; on *Alabama* case, ii. 394–
397, 409 *and note*; on Thessaly
and Epirus, ii. 576; Gladstone's
visit to (1878), ii. 582.

Compared with Althorp, i. 118; with
Peel, i. 373.

Gladstone's estimate of, i. 237; ii.
244; his attitude towards, i. 429;
ii. 122.

Impatience during recess, i. 235.

Irish attitude towards, i. 430.

Leadership of, i. 300.

Palmerston's views regarding, i. 622.

Parliamentary courage of, i. 188.

Queen's mistrust of, ii. 98.

Otherwise mentioned, i. 143, 146, 208,

266, 277, 280, 289, 420, 422, 430, 446, 450, 500, 526, 527, 543; ii. 12, 14, 20, 106, 116, 120, 144, 196, 229, 251, 295, 476, 577, 595, 623, 635–636; iii. 125, 238, 300, 476.

Russell, Odo, ii. 352–354, 509, 510; iii. 179 note.

Russia: —
Accusations against, applicable to, i. 652.
Afghanistan, action in (1885), iii. 178, 183–185, 208 note.
American war, mediation in, declined by, ii. 85.
Austria, attitude of, i. 488; hostility to, ii. 4.
Berlin memorandum, ii. 549.
Bessarabia claimed by, ii. 574 and note 2, 577.
Bismarck's estimate of policy pursued by, ii. 353 note.
Black Sea claims of, ii. 349–356, 398, 400.
British secret agreement with, ii. 575, 577.
Confusion in policy of, ii. 120.
Crimean war, see that title.
Don Pacifico case, offer of good offices in, i. 368.
Egyptian question, attitude towards, iii. 82, 178.
France, estrangement of, from England the aim of, ii. 4; neutrality in Franco-Prussian war, ii. 344.
Germany, attitude towards, ii. 343, 348.
Gladstone's attitude towards, i. 545; ii. 3, 499; tribute at his death, iii. 532.
Ionian Islands despatch, attitude towards, i. 601.
Rise of, i. 477.
San Stefano, treaty of, ii. 572, 575.
Smyrna demonstration favoured by, iii. 9.
Turkey, war with (1771), i. 477; (1828) i. 480; (1853) see Crimean war; (1877) ii. 562, 569, 572.
Rutland, Duke of (Lord John Manners), i. 238, 303–305; iii. 533.
Ryder, see Harrowby.

Sadler, Michael T., i. 99 and note.
Sadowa, ii. 115, 214, 302, 319, 359.
St. Asaph, bishopric of, i. 260 note 1.
St. Deiniol's, iii. 420, 521.
St. Germans, Lord, i. 420.
St. Leonards, Lord, i. 416, 448 and note 1.
St. Paul's Cathedral, i. 12, 233–234.

Salisbury, Marquis of: —
Chronology — Views on the Principalities, ii. 4; on Gladstone's American war speech, ii. 86; on Danish question, ii. 120; retires from Derby government (1867), ii. 223, 231, 235; Disraeli's sarcasms against, ii. 247; on Irish Church bill, ii. 268, 270–271; on religious tests, ii. 314; subscribes to Mill memorial, ii. 543; at Constantinople, ii. 559–560; at Berlin congress, ii. 575, 577; Egyptian policy, iii. 74, 180 and note, 495; on Franchise bill (1884), iii. 132, 135–139; overtures to Irish party, iii. 188–190; unwilling to take office (1885), iii. 204–207; takes office, 208; countenances repudiation of coercion, iii. 212–213; Carnarvon's interview with Parnell unauthorised by, iii. 229 note 1; but known to, iii. 230–231; speeches on Irish policy (Oct. 7), iii. 233, 242–244, 260; (Nov. 9) 239; nationalist support of, at the elections, iii. 244–245; on destruction of government system in Ireland, iii. 256–257 and note 1; Gladstone's tender of support to, iii. 258–260, 284; resigns, iii. 289; Hottentot speech, iii. 317–318; at Opera House meeting, iii. 324; offers Hartington premiership, iii. 364; on rents in Ireland, iii. 374–375; on Times forgeries, iii. 392; on report of special commission, iii. 402; Gladstone's estimate of, ii. 560; his estimate of Gladstone, i. 3; iii. 529; hesitation of, iii. 277; otherwise mentioned, i. 127; ii. 203, 587; iii. 90, 131, 203, 344, 365, 525.
—— Lady, iii. 526.
Salmon, Dr., iii. 417.
San Juan boundary question, ii. 405.
San Stefano, treaty of, ii. 572, 575.
Sand River convention, iii. 45.
Sandon, Lord, i. 103.
Sandwich, Lord, i. 144.
Sandwith, Humphry, ii. 561.
Sanquhar, i. 11.
Sarpi, Father Paul, i. 598.
Saunders, Dean, i. 52, 80.
Saunderson, E., ii. 410.
Savings banks, i. 519; ii. 34.
Savoy, French acquisition of, ii. 9, 22, 30.
Say, Léon, iii. 486.

Scartazzini, iii. 387.
Science, Gladstone's attitude towards, i. 209; iii. 359.
Schiller, i. 108.
Schleswig-Holstein question, ii. 114–120, 265, 580; Prince Consort's view of, ii. 93, 102.
Schleiermacher, i. 166.
Schouvaloff memorandum, ii. 575.
Schwarzenberg, Prince, i. 395–396, 398, 399, 600.
Scott, Hon. F., i. 356.
—— Sir Claude, i. 18.
—— James Hope, see Hope-Scott.
—— Dr., Dean of Rochester, i. 61, 329 and note; ii. 433, 536.
—— Sir Walter, i. 159, 337, 371, 387 note 1; iii. 424, 491.
Scotland : —
    Disestablishment question in, iii. 471.
    Election results in (1880), ii. 613–614.
    Enthusiasm of, ii. 588, 599, 608–609.
    Home Rule (Irish), attitude towards (1886), iii. 323, 324, 346.
    Liberalism of, iii. 536; liberal losses (1874), ii. 490.
    Local government suggested for, iii. 198.
    Peers, Scotch, called to House of Lords by Beaconsfield, ii. 429 note.
    Reform Act's effect on, iii. 535.
    Religious freedom in, Gladstone's views on, i. 384.
    Scotch Patronage bill, ii. 501.
Seaforth, i. 107.
Seaton, Lord, i. 228.
Seats bill, see Redistribution.
Seely, C., ii. 113 note 2.
Selborne, Lord (Sir R. Palmer), ignorant of Irish land tenure, ii. 281; on Irish Land bill, ii. 295, 296; on Education bill, ii. 306; on abolition of army purchase, ii. 363, 364; on Collier appointment, ii. 385; on Alabama case, ii. 403; on the Greenwich seat question, ii. 469–472; on leadership discussion, ii. 602 note; lord chancellor (1872), ii. 645; on Irish Church bill, ii. 646; otherwise mentioned, ii. 99, 165, 232 note, 239, 243, 436, 504, 627, 653; iii. 13, 53.
Selden on contracts, iii. 45–46.
Selwyn, Bishop, i. 38, 39, 43; iii. 419.
Semon, Dr., iii. 216.
Servia, i. 477; ii. 549, 553.
Settembrini, i. 396, 401; ii. 11.
Seward, W. H., ii. 75.
Sexton, Thomas, iii. 69, 447, 451, 452 note.
Seymer, H. K., i. 49, 59 note.

Seymour, ——, i. 230.
Shaftesbury, Lord, i. 163; ii. 111, 113, 122, 171, 367, 369.
Shah, the, ii. 459.
Shaw, Sir F., iii. 114.
—— W., ii. 613.
—— Lefevre, see Lefevre.
Sheil, R. L., i. 135, 195, 208, 221, 263–264, 322–323.
Shelburne, Lord, i. 265; ii. 401 note 2.
Sheldon, Archbishop, iii. 95.
Shelley, i. 96, 159; iii. 484, 549.
Shepstone, Sir T., iii. 43 note, 45.
Sheridan, i. 265; ii. 589.
Shurey, Mrs., i. 27.
Sibthorp, Col., i. 288 note.
Sidmouth, Lord, i. 431.
Simeon, Charles, i. 11 and note 2.
Simon, Jules, ii. 221.
Sinclair, Sir G., i. 113, 178.
Sinking Fund, ii. 68.
Sinope, i. 490.
Skingley, ——, i. 113.
Slavery : —
    American war, ii. 70 et seq.
    Apprenticeship system, i. 134 and note, 145–147, 221.
    Demerara estates question, i. 22–24.
    Education scheme for slaves, i. 125.
    Emancipation question, i. 102–105; iii. 300.
    Evangelical party against, i. 200 note.
    Gladstone's reply to Poulett Thomson on, i. 142 note.
    Gordon's decree sanctioning, iii. 156; his observations on, iii. 158–159.
    Suakin retained to check slave trade, iii. 180 note.
Slave Power, The, cited, ii. 70 note.
Smith, Adam, i. 251; ii. 58.
—— Goldwin, i. 499, 508, 630; ii. 312, 561.
—— John, i. 22 and note.
—— Sydney, i. 56, 135.
—— W. H., view of, on South African affairs, ii. 601; against franchise extension in Ireland, iii. 141; Irish secretary, iii. 279; rapid visit of, to Dublin, iii. 296; on introduction of closure, iii. 377; on Times letters, iii. 395; on bill for special commission, iii. 397.
Smyrna, iii. 9.
Smyth, Sir J. C., i. 24 note 1.
Soap duty, i. 462, 465, 466.
Social question, Gladstone's attitude towards, ii. 56, 60; his disapproval of socialism, iii. 221.
Socrates, ii. 538.

Solferino, ii. 7.
'Some of my Errors,' quoted, i. 179.
Somerset, Duke of, ii. 33, 153 *note*, 635, 636; iii. 358.
Soudan : —
  Egyptian misrule of, iii. 144–145; loss of, iii. 146.
  Evacuation of, advised, iii. 145–148; difficulties of, iii. 147, 149; determined, iii. 180; agreed to, by Gordon, iii. 150, 153–155; intention of, divulged by Gordon, iii. 160–161 *and note* [1].
  Foreign attitude towards embarrassments in, iii. 177–178, 183.
  Garrisons in, to be extricated, iii. 148, 151; Mahdi's treatment of, iii. 149 *note* [1]; Gordon's opinion regarding abandonment of, iii. 156; Zobeir's appointment urged for extrication of, iii. 159.
  Khartoum, garrison of, to be relieved, iii. 150, 151; Gordon's arrival at, iii. 155; disaffection of tribes round, iii. 160; fall of, iii. 166; expedition to, urged by Goschen, iii. 176; deprecated by Baring, iii. 180.
  Mahdi's rise in, iii. 144.
  Nile campaign, iii. 165–166.
South Sea stock, i. 472, 513, 647.
Southey, i. 140; ii. 538.
Spain : —
  Hohenzollern candidate for throne of, ii. 323–328, 330, 332, 333 *note*.
  Land question in, iii. 477.
  Palmerston on treaties with, i. 280.
  Tariff negotiations with, i. 267.
Special commission, the, unconstitutional character of, iii. 390, 400, 401; offer of, by government, iii. 396; bill for, iii. 397–401; sittings of, iii. 401–407; scope of, iii. 402; report of, iii. 402, 408–411; effect of, on public opinion, iii. 411–412.
Spectator, ii. 175–177.
Spedding, James, i. 509; ii. 534.
Spencer, 3rd Earl, i. 235, 292.
—— 4th Earl, i. 341.
—— 5th Earl, interview of, with Cardinal Cullen, ii. 439–440; president of the council (1880), ii. 653; Irish viceroy (1882), iii. 65, 654; magnitude of task in Ireland, iii. 70–71; Irish party, attitude towards, iii. 108; on renewal of Crimes Act, iii. 190, 192; views on Land Purchase bill, iii. 194–195; conservative attack on, iii. 213–214, 262; banquet to, 214, 233; at

Chatsworth and Hawarden, iii. 261; Irish administration of, 261, 379; Gladstone's consultations with, iii. 261, 263, 268; Gladstone's letter to (Dec. 30), i. 272; for home rule, iii. 291 *note*; views on Chamberlain's Irish scheme, iii. 291; president of council (1886), iii. 297 *note*; first lord of admiralty (1892), iii. 495 *note*; Gladstone's intention to recommend, as his successor, iii. 512; otherwise mentioned, ii. 260, 265; iii. 50 *note*, 67, 69, 105, 186, 195, 198, 301, 306, 429, 497 *note*.
Spencer, Lady Sarah, iii. 518.
Sport, Gladstone's view of, i. 116.
Spring-Rice, T., Lord Monteagle, i. 420 *and note*.
Spurgeon, Rev. Charles, ii. 135, 272, 530, 531.
Stafford, Augustus, i. 356.
Standard, iii. 264 *note*.
Stanhope, Lord (Lord Mahon), i. 351 *note*, 438, 569; ii. 536.
Stanley, Dean, position of, at Oxford (1847), i. 335; on Oxford reform, i. 498, 503; serves on Oxford commission, i. 499; on religious tests, i. 506; visits to Monte Cassino, ii. 219; in Rome, ii. 222; death of, iii. 98; otherwise mentioned, i. 15, 46–47; iii. 98.
—— Edward, Bishop of Norwich, i. 46.
—— Lady Augusta, ii. 216 *and note*; ii. 222.
—— of Alderley, Lord, ii. 39–40, 118.
——, Lord, *see* Derby.
Stanmore, Lord (Arthur Gordon), private secretary to Gladstone, i. 597, 604–608; Gladstone's letters to, i. 573; ii. 225, 550, 639; iii. 139; otherwise mentioned, i. 399 *note* [2]; 490; ii. 88.
Stansfeld, Sir James, ii. 113 *note* [2], 415, 504, 645; iii. 297 *note*.
State in its Relation with the Church, The, Hope's interest in, i. 162, 172–173; Gladstone's purpose in, i. 172; his later estimate of, i. 179–180; opinions on, i. 175–177; German translation of, i. 181 *note*.
Stead, W., ii. 550 *note*.
Stephen, Sir James, i. 127, 142 *note*, 146, 147, 359.
Sterling, John, i. 177; ii. 534.
Stewart, Colonel Sir Herbert, iii. 145–147, 155, 160, 165.
Stocker, C. W., i. 78.
Stockmar, Baron, ii. 244.

Stopford, Archdeacon, ii. 258–259.
Storks, Sir Henry, i. 614, 616, 617; ii. 649–650.
Stowe, Mrs. Beecher, ii. 72.
Strahan, Sir George, iii. 32 *note.*
Stratford, Lord, *see* Redcliffe.
Strauss, ii. 524 *and note*[2], 525.
Strossmayer, Bishop, iii. 352–353.
Stuart, R., i. 237.
Stubbs, Bishop, ii. 535, 561.
Suakin, iii. 178, 180 *note.*
Succession duty, i. 463, 465, 474, 513.
Success, Gladstone's view of, i. 213–214.
Suffrage, *see* Franchise.
Sugar duties, i. 236, 643–644; ii. 632–634.
Sullivan, Sir Edward, ii. 264, 279, 283.
Sumner, Bishop, iii. 96 *note.*
—— Charles, i. 441; ii. 70, 75, 398, 401, 402.
Sunbeam, Gladstone's cruise in, iii. 217–218.
Sussex, Duke of, i. 178.
Sutherland, Duchess of, Gladstone's letters to, ii. 71, 88, 89, 146, 182–197, 215–217, 218, 246; friendship for Gladstone, ii. 183, 197; death of, ii. 197.
Sutherland, Duke of, ii. 111, 112, 185–186.
Sutton, Manners- (Speaker), i. 100.
Sydenham, Lord (Poulett Thomson), i. 142 *note.*

Tait, Archbishop, on Oxford commission, i. 499; Gladstone's letter to, on *Essays and Reviews* judgment, ii. 164; consultations with, on Irish Church bill, ii. 261–262, 267–270, 274, 278, 624; conversation with Disraeli, ii. 265 *and note;* on Gladstone's concern at outbreak of Franco-Prussian war, ii. 335; Gladstone's relations with, iii. 94; erastianism of, iii. 471.
Talbot, ——, i. 380 *note*[2].
—— Bp. of Rochester, ii. 436.
Talfourd, Sir T. N., i. 135, 136; iii. 467.
Talleyrand, i. 515 *note;* ii. 343; iii. 485.
Tariff revision (1842), i. 255–257; (1845) i. 279.
—— treaties, attempts at, i. 267; ii. 21.
Taste, i. 190.
Taunton, Lady, ii. 183.
Taxation: —
    Chamberlain's views on (1885), iii. 174, 224.
    Collection of taxes, ii. 650.
    Conveyance duties, ii. 373, 651.
    Customs, articles liable to, in various years, ii. 25 *and note.*
    Direct, ii. 62, 63, 634.

Fire insurance duty, ii. 373, 651.
    Gladstone's policy regarding (1857), ii. 632–635.
Home Rule bill's provisions regarding, iii. 302, 306–307.
House tax, i. 106, 436–437.
Income tax: —
    Assessments for, in 1842 and 1862, ii. 67.
    Chamberlain's pronouncement on, iii. 174.
    Charities, proposed extension to, ii. 65–66.
    Committee on (1851), i. 459.
    Crimean war, effect of, i. 474.
    Disraeli's proposals regarding (1852), i. 436.
    Expenditure, spirit of, fostered by, ii. 62.
    Gladstone's policy regarding (1853), i. 460, 462, 465, 466, 468, 471, 472; iii. 537; (1857) ii. 632–634; (1869) ii. 651; (1874) ii. 478, 483.
    Ireland, proposals regarding, i. 465, 646.
    Peel's policy regarding, i. 251; his miscalculation, i. 474 *and note.*
    Rate of, in 1866, ii. 58.
    Repeal of, possible only in 1874, ii. 496.
    Rise of, in 1859, ii. 19.
    Unpopularity of, i. 254–255.
Indirect, ii. 21, 63, 634.
Local — Goschen's Local Rating bill, ii. 337, 388; question of (1874), ii. 479, 481, 482.
Malt duty, i. 436; ii. 651; iii. 7.
Match tax, ii. 373 *and notes.*
Powers regarding, ii. 40.
Probate duty, ii. 650.
Soap duty, i. 462, 465.
Sugar duties, i. 236, 643–644; ii. 632–634.
Tea duty, Disraeli's operation on (1852), i. 436; Gladstone's operation on (1853), i. 462; Lewis' additions to, ii. 633; Gladstone's policy regarding, ii. 632–635.
Tea licences, ii. 650.
War, for, i. 515–518.
Arthur Young's view of, i. 559.
Taylor, Colonel, ii. 448.
—— Sir Henry, remark of, on Gladstone, i. 27; on money-dealings, iii. 420; otherwise mentioned, i. 135, 205 *and note;* ii. 55, 195 *note,* 358; iii. 488.

Tea duties, *see under* Taxation.

Tegernsee, iii. 351–352.

Telegraph Act (1844), i. 268.

Tel-el-Kebir, iii. 83, 120 *note*.

Temple, Archbishop, position of, at Oxford (1847), i. 335; advocates civil service reform, i. 512; views on Gladstone's Irish Church bill, ii. 264 *note*[1]; work on educational reform (1869), ii. 312; appointment to Exeter, ii. 431–432.

—— William, i. 392, 400.

Temporal power, *see* Churches—Roman.

Tenants Relief (Ireland) bill, iii. 353.

Tennyson, Alfred, Lord, Essay Club's vote on, i. 59; lines on Prince Consort, ii. 95; Gladstone's estimate of *Maud*, ii. 184; iii. 547–548; later estimate, ii. 581; given Gladstone's translation of *Iliad*, Bk. I. ii. 190; Gladstone's visit to (1871), ii. 377; on Irish self-government, ii. 540; pension of, ii. 540 *note*; reads *Harold*, ii. 557; conversation with, on theology, ii. 558; with Gladstone on *Pembroke Castle*, iii. 115, 116; at Kirkwall, iii. 117–118; views on Franchise bill, iii. 132; *Locksley Hall*, Gladstone's article on, iii. 353–354; early work of, iii. 484; Gladstone's essay on, iii. 546–547; otherwise mentioned, ii. 183, 187, 192, 193.

Tenterden, Lord, ii. 405, 410, 412.

Terrible, Gladstone's voyages in, i. 602, 605–606, 618; cost of constructing deck cabins on, ii. 64–65.

Tests, religious : —
Abolition of, i. 328; ii. 313 *and note*[1], 314; iii. 257.
Gladstone's early attitude towards (1833), i. 106; later (1863), ii. 313.

Tewfik, Khedive, constitutional position of, iii. 73; embarrassments of, iii. 78, 118; claims of, on England, iii. 119.

Thackeray, W. M., ii. 189, 538.

Theological studies as mental training, i. 514–515 *and note*.

Thessaly, Palmerston's and Russell's views regarding, ii. 576.

Thiers, M., opposes war with Prussia, ii. 335 *note*[1], 336; mission to courts of Europe, ii. 345; anecdote of, ii. 486; otherwise mentioned, ii. 5, 221.

Thirlwall, Bishop, Gladstone's estimate of, ii. 248; on Irish Church bill, ii. 269; on Gladstone's disestablishment speech (1874), ii. 502; letters from,

ii. 536; memorial to, i. 209 *note*[2]; otherwise mentioned, i. 229; ii. 228.

Tholuck, F. A., i. 181 *note*.

Thompson, ——, ii. 147 *note*.

—— Dr. W. H., ii. 228.

Thomson, Dr. Andrew, i. 110.

—— Poulett (Lord Sydenham), i. 142 *note*.

Thornton, ——, i. 59 *note*.

—— Sir Edward, ii. 401.

Thring, Lord, i. 501.

Times —
Chamberlain's *Baptist* article in, iii. 367 *note*[2].
Forged letters published by, iii. 391 *and note*[1], 405; libel action, iii. 393–394.
Franco-Prussian treaty divulged by, ii. 340.
Gladstone's retirement, article on (1875), ii. 504; on his position (1882), iii. 90.
Hartington's letter to, iii. 269, 270, 273.
Irish land question, letters on (1870), ii. 293.
Parnellism and Crime article, iii. 391, 393.

Tocqueville, de, i. 415 *note*; iii. 470.

Toleration : —
Bradlaugh's question, iii. 12–13, 18.
Gladstone's growth towards, i. 138–139, 316; ii. 137.
Papal aggression question in relation to, i. 410.

Torquay, i. 89.

Tory democracy, iii. 173, 201.

—— party, *see* Conservative.

Tosti, Padre, ii. 219.

Total abstinence, Gladstone's view on, ii. 192.

Townsend, M., ii. 175–177.

Tractarians, *see* Oxford Movement.

Traill's *New Lucian*, iii. 91 *and note*.

Treaties : —
Berlin convention (1878), ii. 575–576; iii. 82; enforcement of, attempted (1880), iii. 8–10.
—— memorandum (1876), ii. 549.
Kainardji, ii. 550.
London convention (1885), iii. 122.
Paris (1856), i. 550; ii. 349–356, 607; iii. 522.
San Stefano, ii. 572, 575.
Transvaal, with, iii. 45 *and note*.
Washington, ii. 390, 405, 410.

Trench, Archbishop, views on Irish church question, ii. 248, 258, 262 *note*; Gladstone's letter to, offering help in

Trench, Archbishop — *continued.*
organising Irish voluntary church,
ii. 280.
Trent affair, ii. 73–75, 580.
Trevelyan, Sir Charles, i. 510, 512.
—— Sir G. O., views on abolition of
army purchase, ii. 361; county franchise extension pressed by, ii. 475;
iii. 124; views on Bulgarian question,
ii. 559; question by, on Turkey, ii.
566; Irish secretary (1882), ii. 654;
iii. 71; chancellor of the duchy (1884),
ii. 654; Scotch secretary, iii. 294, 297
note; at round table conference, iii.
364 *note*; against home rule, iii. 291
note; resigns, iii. 302–303; Scotch
secretary (1892), iii. 495 *note*; otherwise mentioned, ii. 463 *note.*
Truro, Lord, i. 92, 93, 121.
Tupper, M. F., i. 53 *and note*, 65.
Turgot, iii. 4, 91.
Turkey : —
Armenian atrocities, iii. 521–522.
Berlin treaty obligations repudiated
by, iii. 9; effect of pressure, i. 10.
Britain — support from (1771), i. 477;
secret convention with, ii. 575,
579, 592; antipathy of (1881), iii.
74.
Bulgarian atrocities (1876), ii. 548 *et
seq.*
Crimean war, *see that title.*
Egypt, pretensions in, iii. 73; irritation at the joint note, i. 76;
declines to join European con-
ference, i. 79; complications of
the conference, i. 81; unfitness of
the Sultan to be protector of the
Khedive, i. 118; interference in,
suggested, iii. 147; frustration of
Salisbury policy in, iii. 495.
Foreign consuls murdered in, ii. 548–
549.
French hostility towards (1881), iii.
74.
Gladstone's distinction regarding
government of, towards Christians and orientals, iii. 74 *note*;
his achievements against, iii. 538.
Lebanon government, ii. 580.
Problem of, i. 477, 544.
Roumania and Servia partially re-
leased from, ii. 2.
Russia, war with (1828), i. 480; (1853)
see Crimean war; (1877) ii. 562,
569, 572.
Salisbury policy regarding, iii. 525.
San Stefano, treaty of. ii. 572, 575.
Secret convention with, ii. 607.

Suez canal scheme as affecting, i.
591–592.
Turkey, Asiatic, British protectorate
over, ii. 577.
Turner, ——, ii. 146–147 *and note.*
—— Dr., i. 46.
Tyler, J. E., i. 78.
Tyndale memorial, i. 209.
Tyndall, John, ii. 524.

ULTRAMONTANISM, i. 404.
Unitarian chapels, i. 321–323.
Unitarianism, i. 160; ii. 136.
United States : —
Alabama claims, *see that title.*
Church in, ii. 169.
Civil war : —
Books on, cited, ii. 70 *note.*
Course of, ii. 75, 81.
Forster's attitude towards, ii. 301.
France and Russia, attitude of, ii.
85.
Gladstone's view of, ii. 70–72, 74–
77, 79–82; later view, ii. 124;
his speeches on, ii. 79–82, 85
and note[2], 86.
Lancashire, effect on, ii. 66, 77
note[1], 124.
Lewis' estimate of, ii. 69.
Principles of, ii. 70.
Rams built at Birkenhead for
confederates, ii. 395–396.
Gladstone — popularity of, ii. 82–83;
tribute to, iii. 532.
Irish — on Home Rule bill, iii. 318,
323; on papal rescript, iii. 384;
spy from among, at Parnell com-
mission, iii. 404; Parnell repudi-
ated by, iii. 459.
Materialism of, iii. 475.
Palmerston's attitude towards
(1845), i. 367.
Roman catholic prelates in, chances
of, ii. 511.
Senate of, ii. 407.
War with (1782), iii. 181–182.
Universities, Gladstone's view of (1833),
i. 106 (*see also* Cambridge *and*
Oxford).
Utilitarians, i. 156.

VATICAN DECREES, Döllinger's attitude
towards, iii. 422.
*Vatican Decrees in their Bearing on
Civil Allegiance*, ii. 515–517; recep-
tion of, ii. 517–520.
Vaticanism, ii. 521; iii. 281.
Vattel, cited, ii. 16.
Vaudois valley, i. 87.

Vaughan, Mr., ii. 79.
—— Rev. ——, i. 59 *note*.
—— Dean, ii. 433.
Vauvenargues cited, iii. 482.
Veitch, Prof. John, i. 9 *note*.
Vestiges of Creation, ii. 165, 166 *and note*.
Victor Emmanuel, King, ability of, ii. 8; Gladstone's appreciation of, ii. 107, 114; Gladstone's audience of, ii. 218; otherwise mentioned, ii. 17, 356, 532.
Victoria, Princess, ii. 103.
—— Queen: —
Chronology : — Gladstone's first presentation to, i. 140; misunderstanding with Peel, i. 222; at swearing in of Privy Council (1841), i. 242–243; Gladstone's audience of, on Maynooth resignation, i. 276; on Peel's retirement, i. 293; premier's correspondence with, i. 297, 299; on Palmerston's relations with Kossuth, i. 415; on Gladstone's budget speech, (1853), i. 469; consults Aberdeen on Crimean question, i. 482; views on Stratford's policy, i. 487; Gladstone dines with, i. 490; Newcastle recommended to, i. 493; refuses resignation of coalition ministry, i. 522; sends for Derby, i. 525; for Lansdowne, i. 528; for Russell, i. 530; desires continuance of Palmerston government, i. 537; on Peelites' resignation, i. 540–541; commends Gladstone's offer regarding Ionian position, i. 612; reply of, to Corfiote petition, i. 615; sends for Lord Granville, i. 625; for Palmerston, i. 626; draft of letter to, on Peel's government, i. 642; grief at Prince Albert's death, ii. 89–90, 99; references to Prince Albert, ii. 96, 98, 104, 105; at Balmoral, ii. 97–106; on Danish question, ii. 102, 104, 117, 192; on Garibaldi, ii. 113 *note*[3]; action on Palmerston's death, ii. 152, 155; commends Gladstone's leadership, ii. 157; Russell and Gladstone in audience, ii. 209–211; sends for Lord Derby, ii. 211; advised by Disraeli to dissolve, ii. 248; difficulty regarding Lord Clarendon, ii. 254; Irish church disestablishment, ii. 259–262, 267–271, 273, 278, 427; urged by Gladstone to open

parliament (1870), ii. 293; suggested action of, to avert Franco-Prussian war, ii. 327; army reform, ii. 360, 363, 649; at Balmoral (1871), ii. 378–379; seclusion of, criticised, ii. 425–427; Gladstone's report to, on Irish University bill, ii. 439, 441; ministerial crisis, ii. 446–455, 480; Gladstone's communications to, on dissolution, ii. 484–487; offers peerage to Gladstone, ii. 493; receives ministers' resignations, ii. 493 *note*; remarks on Gladstone's retirement, ii. 504–505; averse to meddling with ecumenical council, ii. 510; on Disraeli's proposed resignation, ii. 550; Hartington's audiences of, ii. 621–624; views on Lowe's viscounty, ii. 631; friendship for Dean Wellesley, iii. 93; desirous of Harold Browne's appointment to Canterbury, iii. 95–96; on cabinet reconstruction (1882), iii. 100; urges Gladstone's acceptance of a peerage, iii. 104; Gladstone's memorandum to, on case between Lords and Commons, iii. 129; her efforts towards settlement, iii. 130–139; on Egyptian question, iii. 80, 159, 162, 167, 179; Gladstone's letters to, on ministerial defeat, i. 199, 202; suggests continuance, i. 203; summons Lord Salisbury, i. 204; Gladstone's audience of, i. 205; negotiations through Sir H. Ponsonby, i. 205–208; offers Gladstone an earldom, i. 209; Gladstone's audience of (Feb. 1, '86), iii. 290, 291; views on Gladstone's electioneering, iii. 344; Gladstone's final audience of (1886), iii. 347–348; Gladstone's last cabinet report to, iii. 511; Gladstone's last audience of, iii. 513–514; last meeting with Gladstone, iii. 524.
Enthusiasm, dislike of, ii. 425.
Gladstone, letters to, ii. 89–90, 185, 252, 459, 526, 527, 649; iii. 15–16, 40, 115–117, 167, 180, 192, 199, 202, 209, 515; appreciation of, ii. 267, 426; friction with, ii. 427–428, 599; his estimate of, ii. 424, 626, 628.
Gladstone, Mrs., letter to, ii. 472–473; telegram to, iii. 531.
Home Rule, attitude towards, iii. 291.

Victoria, Queen — *continued.*
Otherwise mentioned, i. 199, 274, 276, 448; ii. 31, 67, 74, 104–141, 182, 186, 189, 191, 208–209, 418, 472, 499, 617; iii. 6, 23–24, 385.
Villafranca, ii. 7, 13.
Villiers, de, chief justice, iii. 33, 41.
—— C., i. 249, 433; ii. 33, 37, 45, 635–636.
Virgil, iii. 481.
Vitzthum, i. 576 *note*, 591 *note*.
Vivian, third Lord, iii. 116.
—— Sir Hussey, iii. 386.
Vivian Grey, ii. 499.
Votes of confidence, Gladstone's dislike of, ii. 209, 442.

WAKEFIELD, E. G., i. 358, 361 *note*[3].
Wales: —
Bishoprics question, i. 260 *and note*, 288.
Church disestablishment question in, iii. 367 *and note*[2], 471, 495.
Election results in (1874), ii. 490; (1880) ii. 613, 614.
Gladstone's tour in (1887),iii. 386,387.
Home rule (Irish), attitude towards (1886), iii. 323, 346.
—— Prince of (King Edward VII.), on Danish question, ii. 120; on Phœnix Park murders, iii. 68; friendliness to Gladstone, iii. 103, 105; Gladstone's letter to, iii. 108; gift to Gladstone on golden wedding anniversary, iii. 417; letter from, on Gladstone's impending resignation, iii. 510; Gladstone's estimate of, ii. 294, 378; iii. 200; otherwise mentioned, i. 275; ii. 92, 141; iii. 322, 385, 524, 533.
—— Princess of (Queen Alexandra), ii. 99, 189, 499; iii. 117, 417, 510.
Walewski, i. 491; ii. 21.
Wallace, D. Mackenzie, ii. 561.
Wallachia, ii. 3.
Wallenstein, ii. 101.
Walpole, Sir R., i. 37; ii. 59, 61, 91, 638.
—— Spencer H., i. 561, 583, 631; ii. 31, 39.
—— Spencer, i. 467 *note*.
Walsh, Dr., iii. 449.
—— Father, ii. 535.
War: —
Gladstone's opinion of, iii. 182–183 *and note*; 547–548.
Manchester school's view of, iii. 182.
Popular fevers for, ii. 221, 574, 575.
Preparations for, effect of, ii. 44.
Taxation and loans for, i. 515–518.
Ward, Mrs. Humphry, iii. 357–359.
—— W. G., i. 274, 313–316, 331; ii. 165.
Waste lands, committee on, i. 358.

Waterford, Lord, iii. 143 *and note.*
Watson, Colonel, iii. 149.
Watts, George, ii. 541–543.
Webster, Daniel, ii. 369.
—— Sir Richard, iii. 394, 398, 409.
Welby, Lord, iii. 306, 526.
Wellesley, Dean, i. 39; ii. 89, 273–275; iii. 92–94.
Wellington, Duchess of, iii. 93.
—— Duke of, retrenchments by, i. 121; unpopularity of, i. 122; at Drayton, i. 133; methodical ways of, i. 134; Gladstone's first interview with, i. 143; view of, on church question, i. 155; on China question, i. 225; Gurwood on, i. 228; on boundary question, i. 260; on 'the Queen's government,' i. 283; advises dissolution, i. 290; on Peel's view of party, i. 290; as premier, i. 300; on Ionian Islands, i. 598; leadership of Lords by, ii. 369; brevity of, ii. 532, 545; letters from, ii. 545; cabinet fight over statue of, iii. 5; Gladstone's estimate of, iii. 481; position of, iii. 485–486; otherwise mentioned, i. 68–69, 75, 110, 120, 149, 376, 543, 641–642; ii. 641, 649, 653; iii. 277, 473.
Wells, David Ames, ii. 373.
Wesley, John, i. 319.
West, Sir Algernon, ii. 279.
Westbury, Lord (Sir Richard Bethell), Gladstone assisted by, i. 472 *note*[1], 501; views on Divorce bill, i. 570–571; on Ionian Islands, i. 620 *note*[2]; on stamp duties, ii. 64; on Danish question, ii. 118; *Essays and Reviews* judgment, ii. 164; otherwise mentioned, i. 502, 518.
Westminster, Duke of, iii. 523 *note.*
—— Lord, i. 239.
—— Abbey, ii. 460; iii. 6, 533.
Wharncliffe, Lord, i. 75, 242.
Whately, Archbishop, i. 51, 57, 158.
Whigs: —
Characteristics of (1853), i. 446.
Coalition of Peelites with (1853), i. 443 *et seq.*
Defeat of (1841), i. 237; ii. 203 *note*[2], 264.
Finance of, i. 458, 459.
Fusion of seceders with tory party, i. 139.
Influence of, till 1868, iii. 293.
Name of, discussed, 422.
Opposition of, to Peel (1835), composition of, i. 419–420 *and note.*
Protectionist combination with, i. 290.

Whitbread, S., iii. 12, 303 *note*.
White, Blanco, i. 57, 74, 217.
—— Edward, ii. 134.
Whiteside, Chief Justice, ii. 128.
Wigan, i. 287.
Wilberforce, Samuel, Bishop (of Winchester), advice to Gladstone, i. 150–151; on marriage question, i. 569; advocates revival of convocation, ii. 162; on rise of Disraeli, ii. 230; archbishopric of York desired for, by Gladstone, ii. 430; death of, ii. 459; Gladstone's estimate of, 460; *Life* of, ii. 597; Gladstone's estimate of, i. 227; ii. 460; his estimate of Gladstone's position, ii. 134, 171; Gladstone's letters to, i. 387; ii. 149, 159, 162; otherwise mentioned, i. 568; ii. 183, 423, 534; iii. 96 *note*.
—— William, Gladstone's meeting with, i. 12; emancipation views of, i. 104; Gladstone's estimate of, i. 106–107; Peel's view of, i. 150; otherwise mentioned, i. 23, 213, 236.
Wilbraham, Mrs., i. 234.
Willes, Sir James Shaw, ii. 383.
William I., Emperor, on Russell's despatch, ii. 16; interviews with Benedetti, ii. 330–331, 333 *note*; San Juan boundary question referred to, ii. 405.
—— III., King, iii. 284 *note*.
—— IV., King, Melbourne government dismissed by, i. 118 *and note*; death of, i. 140; perversity of, i. 144; otherwise mentioned, i. 103; iii. 653.
William George Ward and the Oxford Movement, i. 313 *note* [2].
Williams, Isaac, i. 111, 307 *note*.
—— R., i. 309–310.
Wilmslow, ——, i. 46.
Wilson, Sir Charles, iii. 165.
Winchelsea, Lord, i. 279.
Window duty, i. 106, 459.
Wiseman, Cardinal, i. 173, 174, 318, 408.
Wolf, F. A., iii. 543.
Wolowski, Count, ii. 220.
Wolseley, Lord, in South Africa (1879),

iii. 25–26, 31 *note* [2]; defeats Arabi at Tel-el-Kebir, iii. 83; at Gordon's send-off, iii. 150 *and note*; advises preparations for relief expedition, iii. 163; appointed to command, iii. 164–165; asks reinforcement, iii. 178; position of, 179; cited, ii. 360.
Wolverton, Lord, at Hawarden, ii. 474; letter on leadership, ii. 601–602; Gladstone's reply, ii. 602; discusses leadership with Gladstone, ii. 616–617; at Hawarden (June 1885), iii. 196; otherwise mentioned, ii. 462, 463, 485, 493, 563, 564, 584; iii. 102.
Wood, Sir Charles, *see* Halifax, Lord.
—— General Sir E., on South Africa, iii. 37–41; on General Gordon, iii. 149.
Woods and forests dismissal case, i. 520.
Woolner, Thomas, ii. 191, 192.
Wordsworth, Charles, Bishop of St. Andrews, i. 50, 74, 329.
—— Dr. Christopher, i. 80, 213.
—— William, Gladstone's estimate of, i. 96, 135, 220; intimacy with, i. 136–137; on Gladstone's first book, i. 176; on Kendal railway scheme, i. 269 *note*; ii. 540; pension of, ii. 540 *note*; Gladstone's reminiscences of, iii. 483–484, 488; otherwise mentioned, i. 159, 204 *and note*.
Wortleys, the, i. 123, 468.
Wyndham, Sir W., i. 223 *note* [1].
Wynford, first Baron, i. 75.

YORK, address from, ii. 130–131.
Young, Arthur, cited, i. 559.
—— Sir John, i. 420, 595, 601, 611.
—— Lord, ii. 469.
Young England group with Disraeli, i. 304–305.

ZAMBELLI, Napoleon, i. 616.
Zante, i. 599, 604.
Zetland, Lord, ii. 78.
Zobeir, iii. 155–160.
Zulu war, ii. 583, 592, 595; iii. 6, 22.